Dorothy Deran

SOFTWARE ENGINEERING

SOFTWARE ENGINEERING

RANDALL W. JENSEN

Senior Scientist

and

CHARLES C. TONIES

Manager
Data Processing Systems Laboratory
Hughes Aircraft Company

PRENTICE-HALL, INC., Englewood Cliffs, New Jersey 07632

Library of Congress Cataloging in Publication Data

JENSEN, RANDALL W.
    Software engineering.

    Bibliography: p.
    Includes index.
    1. Electronic digital computers—Programming.
I. Tonies, Charles C. II. Title.
QA76.6.J46   001.6'42   78-15659
ISBN 0-13-822130-8

Printed in the United States of America

10   9   8   7   6   5   4   3   2

PRENTICE-HALL INTERNATIONAL, INC., *London*
PRENTICE-HALL OF AUSTRALIA PTY. LIMITED, *Sydney*
PRENTICE-HALL OF CANADA, LTD., *Toronto*
PRENTICE-HALL OF INDIA PRIVATE LIMITED, *New Delhi*
PRENTICE-HALL OF JAPAN, INC., *Tokyo*
PRENTICE-HALL OF SOUTHEAST ASIA PTE. LTD., *Singapore*
WHITEHALL BOOKS LIMITED, *Wellington, New Zealand*

CONTENTS

PREFACE

*The past is but the beginning of
a beginning, and all that is and
has been is but the twilight of
the dawn.*

H. G. Wells
The Discovery of the Future (1901)

The need for a radically different approach to the development of large data processing systems became apparent in the late 1960s and early 1970s. With this need
came an evaluation of existing design practices and the realization that those practices
were inadequate. Several new software design methodologies were introduced with
some methods indirectly suggesting an engineering design approach. Other methods
claimed to be engineering approaches, but were so in name only. One paper referred
to software engineering as a branch of mathematics. After a considerable amount of
research and careful evaluation of the material related to software development
methodologies in general, and software engineering in particular, we concluded that
there was no published, uniform treatment of this subject. In the frantic scramble to
find ways to improve the production of reliable and cost-effective software, industry had
essentially approached software engineering much like the proverbial group of blind
men and their various interpretations of the physical characteristics of an elephant.

Now that the dust from that initial scramble to solve the world's software problems has cleared, it is possible to look objectively at the sources of the problems
plaguing software developers and formulate an organized methodology for a solution
of those problems.

This textbook represents the culmination of many studies delving into the nature
and methods of software development. This text presents software engineering, not as
an isolated software design methodology or as a simple set of development tools and
techniques, but as a comprehensive, broad, problem-solving discipline very similar
to other branches of engineering. Our coverage includes the management, legal, and
security aspects as well as the technical aspects of the subject (structural design, structured programming, and verification and validation techniques), since we feel it is
also necessary for software engineers to be conversant in all aspects of software
engineering to be effective in their tasks. We suggest that you examine the proposed curricula topics listed in the Appendix to obtain a picture of the educational
requirements for software engineers. This book is intended to be used as a textbook
either in a comprehensive software engineering course or in a sequence of courses

covering this broad range of software engineering topics, or as a single, software engineering reference source. Each of the chapters in this text is intended to serve as an introduction to the topic covered by that chapter, as well as a reference source for those already familiar with the subject material. Each chapter is essentially self-contained and can be presented as an individual unit, independent of the other chapters. The units of information (chapters) can be presented in any order.

The primary purpose of Chapter 1 is to institute a viable definition of software engineering. This is accomplished by discussing first the conditions that created the need for a more organized approach to software development and describing the environment in which software is developed. The use of the term software engineering is then established based upon the definition of an engineer and the engineering approach to the solution of problems. The role and qualifications of a software engineer are discussed within the framework afforded by this definition.

Chapter 2 discusses the fundamentals of software project management. It provides a thorough insight into those basic environmental elements that the manager and his staff must control for smooth, effective project operation. The unique concept of entropy in the software life cycle process is introduced as a fundamental parameter of the development cycle; this concept serves as a basis for direct and striking comparisons between software management and the pure physical processes in nature. Management tools and techniques are discussed in the context of entropy control. Although the illustrative material is oriented toward a large, formal project environment, the methods and concepts presented are primary ones that apply equally well to all software development tasks.

Chapter 3 introduces techniques for software development. It discusses the overall problems to be solved and relates the definition of software requirements to the general engineering approach to problem solving. The importance of clearly understanding a user's problem and matching the quality of the software product to the user's desires is emphasized. Illustrative material is oriented toward large-scale systems design and the more difficult case wherein hardware and software are developed in parallel. The relationship among the systems engineer, the hardware engineer, and the software engineer, as seen from the software engineering point of view, is introduced at this point. Software design is then explained as a development of the software architecture that bridges the total system design requirements and the detailed module design, which is presented in Chapter 4. Structured design methodology is presented as a technique that has proven effective in real-time programming wherein a total system is being developed. Each major design phase of requirements analysis, system design, and software design is approached with an example for a real-life program.

Chapter 4 presents a comprehensive, modern approach to structured programming in a production environment. The chapter opens with an analysis of the objectives and history of structured programming and proceeds to define a structured program. A broad, powerful set of program control structures are introduced and described; these controls are compatible with the definition and primary objectives of structured programming. Design notations for structured program development and stepwise-refinement structuring are described as tools for creating well-structured programs. Implementations of the structure set introduced here are described for the FORTRAN, COBOL and PL/I programming languages.

Verification and validation (Chapter 5) are the primary means of providing software quality assurance. The importance of V&V is likely to amplify as software takes on increasingly crucial roles where failures could have a catastrophic effect on life or property. In this chapter, software testing as a primary V&V tool is extensively treated, including the topic of automatic test tools where an example application is presented. A summary of verification and validation considerations over the software life cycle, including testing and other activities, is provided. A concluding section covers future trends in this area.

Chapter 6 focuses on the serious problem of computer security. Tools for generating secure software are presented, and the discussion exposes the inadequacy of some currently used tools, such as the operating system. The question of personal privacy in a society of computers is addressed, and some methods for preventing the compromise of an individual's privacy are provided. Finally, some ideas on measuring system security are outlined. And while perfect security is probably unattainable, it is shown here that the cost of penetrating a system can be raised to a level that would make penetration unprofitable.

Chapter 7 provides the basic legal considerations that a software developer needs to survive in business and to protect the products of his labor. Basic business forms are discussed plus specific procedures associated with conducting a business, including software program protections (patents, copyrights, and trade secrets), contract law, negotiations, tax considerations, and labor law. Liability for software performance, a major concern of most software developers, is addressed both as to present liabilities and as to possible trends (that is, more protection for an innocent purchaser or victim). The chapter stresses legal awareness, both as a guide for proper business conduct and as an aid in knowing when to obtain professional assistance.

For the fine support and the excellent review they supplied to critique and improve our manuscript, we wish to express our appreciation to Hank Kennedy and Paul Becker of Prentice-Hall. In addition we wish to thank the contributing authors for their efforts in writing this book, and to express our appreciation especially to Sally Patt for her outstanding work in editing and assistance in putting the manuscript together.

To the management of Hughes Aircraft Company and in particular to T. J. Burns thanks are also due for the general support and encouragement provided to the editors and contributing authors.

RANDALL W. JENSEN

CHARLES C. TONIES

1 INTRODUCTION

RANDALL W. JENSEN
CHARLES C. TONIES

Editors

> *"When I use a word," Humpty Dumpty said,*
> *in a rather scornful tone, "it means just*
> *what I choose it to mean—neither more nor*
> *less."*
> *"The question is," said Alice, "whether*
> *you can make words mean so many different things."*
> *"The question is," said Humpty Dumpty,*
> *"which is to be master—that's all."*
>
> LEWIS CARROLL
> *Through the Looking-Glass*

Software engineering is a subject that has been cloaked in mystery since the introduction of the term in the late 1960s. Papers and books have been written (many of them excellent), conferences have been presented, multitudes of courses have been taught, extolling the virtues of software engineering as a panacea for the problems that have been associated with software development over the last two decades. However, careful study of the definitions proposed and of the many generally vague descriptions has made it apparent that the needs of the software community must be more thoroughly analyzed and a formal definition of software engineering must be established.

The purpose of this chapter is to present a formal definition and detailed description of software engineering and to describe the qualifications of software engineers. The definition established here results from many detailed studies of software development practices, methodologies, and problems, and of the people involved at all levels of the software development activity. Software engineers, as we describe them in this chapter, are the essential elements of any software engineering activity of significant magnitude.

We begin this chapter by describing the growing data processing problem known as the "software crisis" that led to the recognition of a need for a new approach to software development. With the necessity for a new approach to software established, we proceed by describing the environment in which software engineers must function. The environmental factors are seldom discussed or even mentioned in most treatises on the subject of software engineering, but they are an important facet in the consideration of the qualities essential to the engineer.

With an obvious need and an environmental framework described, we pose and justify a definition for software engineering which satisifies both the present and future requirements of the industry. We then describe the essential characteristics of the "new" individual we refer to as a software engineer. We conclude the chapter with a discussion of the engineering approach to design problems which is common to all fields of engineering, including software engineering.

1.1
The Software Crisis

Crisis is a strong word. It suggests a situation that demands resolution. The conditions that represent the crisis will be altered, either toward favorable relief or toward a potential disaster. Webster's various definitions of crisis are:

> The change of a disease which indicates recovery or death; the decisive state of things or the point of time when an affair has reached its height, and must soon terminate or suffer a material change; a time of great danger or trouble, whose outcome decides whether possible bad consequences will follow; turning point; conjuncture.

Then how is it that the data processing community can talk about a software "crisis" existing for years? Should not the crisis have been resolved one way or another by now? Yes, if it were a true crisis according to Webster's definitions; we would be able to look back into the history of the software problem and identify some peak or turning point after which conditions changed discernibly for the better or worse. We cannot presently identify this point in time. So we may ask: "Has there really been a crisis related to software, and what is the current situation?" It is true that we have had neither relief nor complete disaster in terms of schedule and cost performance associated with the industry's software problems, but it is also true that we have experienced many near disasters, that is, very unpleasant experiences and very few conspicuous successes. There is also a growing lag between computer hardware development and software technology. The cost of raw computing power has been reduced by several orders of magnitude in the last 25 years, and the unit cost of memory and storage has been reduced at a compound annual rate of 40% over this same period. On the other hand, the cost of producing the software necessary to exploit the growing computing capacity has risen steadily, and the increasing complexity of systems and application software has nearly overwhelmed us. The record shows few software projects which have been completed within the constraints of their original cost, schedule, and performance specifications. We can say, then, that we have had at best a continuing serious problematical situation in the area of software, and resolution of the problems has been slow.

It is not clear which author first used the "software crisis" term, and it is not important in our discussion. B. W. Boehm, without using it directly, described the situation in an impressive way in his well-known *Datamation* article in 1973.[1] Boehm's hardware/software cost trends diagram, shown in Figure 1-1, has probably been reproduced and referenced more often than any other graphic in all of the data processing-related literature. The cost trends diagram pointed out the high and rising

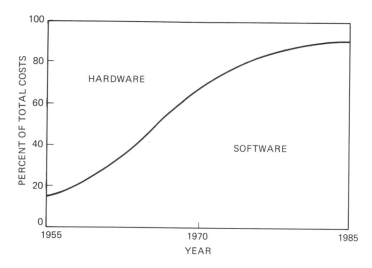

Fig. 1-1 Hardware/software cost trends

relative cost of software at a time when most people within or close to the data processing industry were still thinking of data processing investment as mainframes, peripherals, an operating system that came with the equipment, and a "few applications programmers." The concept of spending more on software than hardware was difficult to perceive for most managers and buyers. If a decision maker was relatively new to large-scale data processing, he was probably working with a procurement or project management plan that called for the bulk of his data processing funds to be allocated to hardware purchase, installation, operation and maintenance. Software was a relatively minor part of his budget. One can see that a manager in this situation, if he were to be confronted with data supporting the Boehm cost trends diagram, was suddenly presented with something of a "crisis" associated with software. He had the dilemma of either rebudgeting his project or ignoring the software cost data, hoping it was not true. Either course was difficult and caused many an executive to develop a sour taste for software—in some cases temporary, in others permanent. The first part of the "software crisis," then, is the dramatic rise in the relative cost of software versus hardware.

As software development projects are implemented, customers and managers typically encounter another facet of the problem—the talent shortage. There have

[1]B. W. Boehm, "Software and Its Impact: A Quantitative Assessment," *Datamation*, 19, No. 5, May, 1973, pp. 48–59. Reprinted with permission of *Datamation*® magazine, Copyright 1977 by Technical Publishing Co., Greenwich, CT 06830.

never been enough competent software designers, developers, and managers to meet industry's needs. Because of this skilled manpower shortage, software development projects have often been carried out by a mix of people with various levels and types of data processing and engineering skills. The schedule and cost pressure created by the lack of qualified manpower have led project managers to abandon the good programming practices known at the time in attempts to find shortcuts and meet the project constraints. It is no wonder the record shows so many overruns and marginal products.

In retrospect, we can characterize the software experience of the last 10 to 15 years as one of being overtaken by events. Computer hardware technology advanced so rapidly, and the requirements for sophisticated software systems became so demanding, that a significant lag in technology, management methodology, and availability of properly educated engineers was created. In some particular situations such as the predicament described above, legitimate crises developed; but looking at the picture over the entire industry, we think the word *exigence* describes the situation more accurately. Again, according to Webster:

> Exigence. ek' si-jens. n. The state of being urgent or pressing; urgent demand; urgency; a pressing necessity; emergency.

We can best describe the exigence involved in the development of computer software with the illustration shown in Figure 1-2. The software complexity has steadily increased over the last two decades as the computing power of the hardware and the sophistication of the customer/user have evolved. During the first part of the same twenty-year period, the software technology, including both managerial and development methodologies, was able to satisfy customer needs because the software requirements were relatively simple due to hardware limitations and the level of user sophistication at that time. As the hardware became more powerful and more imagi-

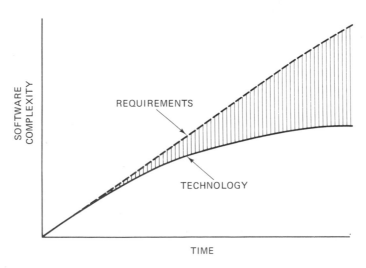

Fig. 1-2 The growth of exigence in the software industry

native requirements were defined, the degree of software complexity required reached a point at which the technology necessary to satisfy them was inadequate. This gap between the requirements and the ability of the software development technology to meet those requirements (indicated by the shaded area in the figure) produces the exigence that has been continually increasing since the 1960s. The software technology progressed during this time, but not at a rate adequate to decrease the exigence.

The situation today has not shown any significant improvement. The need for more capacity to develop and maintain software is more widely recognized, and budgets are more realistic, but the gap between software technology and requirements still exists. The hardware side of the data processing industry is charging ahead with refinements that continue to provide more computing power and storage capacity; the minicomputer population continues to proliferate, and the semiconductor people have made such enormous strides in technology that the era of the microprocessor is upon us. Society, industry, and our country's national defense are all highly dependent on computing systems. The demand for new and upgraded systems is greater than ever. National expenditures for data processing software are estimated at more than $20 billion per year.[2]

Meanwhile, progress in the advancement of software technology and tools, our management techniques, and our educational curricula has been slow by comparison. The efficiency we are able to achieve in producing $20 billion worth of software products is improving but still leaves much to be desired. There *is* progress, but if we are to relieve the state of continuing exigence, the progress must be accelerated. Speaking for one of the major sponsors of software development, J. S. Gansler recently stated:

> Within the Department of Defense, we are presently spending over three billion dollars per year on Defense Systems Software (excluding Automatic Data Processing). In my opinion, we have been doing a poor job managing this necessary important resource, and further we have been doing little research and development on the ways and means to improve it. Both these shortcomings must change![3]

We need more software professionals, as well as more effective tools and methods. Effectiveness of the software professional is also an issue of importance. The greatest single need in the industry is for effective software *engineering*. In the following sections we discuss the elements of effective engineering performance in the industrial environment.

1.2

The Industrial Environment

Specific conditions and roles that software engineers encounter in industry vary widely as a function of the particular type of company, agency, or institution of which they are a part. The conditions even vary from company to company in the same type of industry, or from agency to agency within the government service. But there

---

[2]B. W. Boehm, "Software Engineering," *IEEE Transactions on Computers*, C-25, No. 12, December, 1976, pp. 1226–41.

[3]J. S. Gansler, "Keynote: Software Management," *Proceedings of the Symposium on Computer Software Engineering* (New York, N.Y.: Polytechnic Press, 1976), p. 1.

are some common characteristics that can be found in nearly any job situation that software engineers are likely to encounter today. These characteristics of nearly all industrial operations represent the essence of the environment in which software-oriented employees must function. The environmental aspects include more than the elements related to the physical environment (lighting, temperature, office size and decoration, etc.). The environment also includes the company organization structure, policies governing employee-supervisor and employee-employee interactions, product development methodologies, and the unquantifiable environmental elements that contribute to the general esprit de corps and affect the quality and productivity of an organization. We are saying that it is essential that the individuals recognize and accommodate these environmental characteristics in order to enjoy comfortable, challenging, and productive careers. The individuals need not approve of all aspects of industrial modes of operation in order to succeed, still it is in their best interests that they understand the system if they are to be immersed in it.

Experience has shown us that there are an amazing number of individuals employed by industry who do not seem to understand, or perhaps refuse to consciously acknowledge, the raw facts of their employment situation. Software engineers are no exception; in fact, there is much evidence that software people, perhaps because they are engaged in a relatively new and dynamically changing discipline, are among the most disoriented professionals in industry. The summary given in this section is intended to provide an awareness of the most important factors that affect the modern software engineer's existence.

1.2.1 BASICS

There are two fundamental points we must emphasize that will affect the careers of all software engineers. First, when an individual takes a position with a company,[4] he or she establishes a business arrangement. The company agrees to pay a salary and provide certain other benefits such as vacations, life and health insurance, etc., in return for the individual's contribution toward advancing the company's objectives. The last part of this agreement is often incompletely understood. All individuals have their own objectives, which is natural and usually healthy, but unless the individuals are aware of their part of the bargain and find ways to reconcile their goals and the company's goals, the relationship is in for trouble. Over an extended period of time the arrangement between the employer and the employee must be adjudged mutually beneficial if the arrangement is to be stable. The adjudication of the relationship is performed by both parties with the individual on one side and supervision and higher management on the other, and they must both find this relationship beneficial. Strictly speaking, the judgments are all that count, not the facts; but, realistically, it is unusual that one party deceives the other for any appreciable length of time.

This brings us to the second important point. When we enter industry, we are taking on long-term relationships foreign to most of our previous orientation. Throughout our early lives, we are primarily subject to short-duration situations. Family

---

[4]We use the word *company* for convenience. The employing organization may be any product-oriented entity.

relationships are one exception, but other than relationships of this type, most environments and interactions last for periods of only a few months to a few years. We pass through various schools; friends and romances come and go; temporary employment situations usually last but months; military service is relatively brief unless it becomes a career. In general, our activities, our physical location, our relationships, our objectives and commitments, and our responsibilities all change frequently during the first 20 years of our lives. Furthermore, we pass through all of these experiences leaving, for the most part, only a temporary and volatile record of our performance and behavior. Except for criminal records and grades at the time of transitions from one school to another, the world takes little note nor remembers what we say or do.

An industrial career is different. It is a long-duration proposition during which our work performance is rather carefully recorded. This record follows us from job to job, and organization to organization. It is available to those members of present and potential employing organizations whose evaluations may have significant effects on our careers and general welfare. The professional career is a long, continuous recorded experience. In these respects it is in direct contrast to most of our experience leading up to it. Transition to a permanent career represents a discontinuity that is more significant than most of us realize at the time. There is a need for changes in plans, in our approach to individual work assignments, and in our work environment values in general. The discontinuity in our lives and the need for adjustments typically go unrecognized, and several years (or more) pass before some of us fully realize the extent to which we are being affected by our "new" environment.

There is no fundamental reason why this awareness process should take place entirely after the fact. Anticipation of the real demands of the industrial environment will enhance the education process, smooth the discontinuity, and contribute to comfortable early professional years.

Let us continue to identify the basic aspects of the industrial environment. So far we have introduced the fundamental requirement to establish a sustained, mutually beneficial business arrangement between the engineer, the employer, and his or her fellow employees. The key to this equitable arrangement is an effective employee. If we make the reasonable assumption that the supervisors will recognize and reward valuable performance, then the individual's and the company's fortunes will benefit in direct proportion to the effectiveness of his or her performance.

Effectiveness is realistically defined as the relative amount of contribution to advancing the company's goals or to developing the company's products. At first, this may seem to be an overly restrictive criterion for evaluating the effectiveness of an employee. It suggests the question: "How can one evaluate the individuals involved in administrative support jobs in the accounting, finance, publications, personnel, and contracts organizations? These are necessary functions and yet they do not contribute directly to products. Are the people in these positions considered to be ineffective?" The realistic answer is that they are, in most industrial firms, considered to be less effective in contributing to the company's goals than people at equivalent levels in the mainline product-related organizational elements of the company. However, the product-oriented concept also applies to organizational support elements. The support organization products are usually consumed internally, e.g., accounting reports, financial projections, personnel services (we are including services in our definition of "product"), property inventory reports, etc. Staff members in such an organization will also fare better if they take the time and trouble to carefully identify their organization's "internal" products and to analyze their roles and responsibilities in producing them. The industrial environment is a product-oriented environment. The more the individuals can contribute to the products, the more valuable their services are, and the more the mutual benefits will grow.

1.2.2 THE EFFECTIVENESS FORMULA

There are some software-related positions in industry that do not require frequent interaction with other people. They are rare. Pure research assignments and one-person development tasks represent a very small fraction of the total activity within the data processing sector of industry. The typical software engineering position is highly interactive because the typical software development environment is highly interactive. The user, the customer, the project management, the analyst/designers, the programmers, the test engineers, and others are all involved as a loosely knit team during one or more phases of every project life cycle. Software engineers may appear in any of these roles, but no matter which assignment they have, they will interact with all of the other members of the team. Literally, every day the engineers will find it necessary to stay aware of the activities of those around them and to understand the significance of each of those activities. They will find it necessary to understand and to act in concert with the project management plan, communicating coherently with a variety of individuals.

If software engineers are not capable or are not motivated to participate in the inevitable ebb and flow of management decisions and if they are not capable or not motivated to receive from and transmit information to the members of the team daily, their technical contribution, no matter how brilliant in itself, will be diminished because it will, in all probability, not match the real product requirement. Software system development is a dynamic activity. No matter how effective our baseline and configuration control methods and no matter how stable the project staff, some degree of rethinking, replanning, redefining, and redirection is necessary as the project proceeds. Furthermore, communications among the team members are not always perfect, just as the best football teams lose yardage due to missed plays. Incomplete and incorrect understanding of requirements, designs, and specific interfaces is inevitable. In fact, it is quite common. Frequent communication among all participants on a software development project is the only way that misunderstandings can be corrected. The process of achieving coherent communication along all the required paths is an iterative one.

For these reasons the software engineer's value to an organization operating in the industrial environment is dependent on three attributes. These are technical talent, the ability to understand management concepts, and the ability to communicate. All three are so intimately involved in the software engineering process that the net effect of an individual's effort is best represented by their product:

$$E = C[M(CS)]$$

where $E =$ net effectiveness

$C =$ communication skills (0—1)

$M =$ management concept awareness (0—1)

$CS =$ computer science technical ability (0—1)

This relationship defines the *effectiveness* formula. Our experience in the software industry, and especially in product-oriented environments, has shown it to be a realistic model of software engineering performance. While it is true that we are still in an age of technical specialization, it is also true that software development work is by its very nature a complex interactive process. It requires careful, intense management, and even the most specialized of the contributors must act in concert with his colleagues and the management plan if the development process is to be efficient.

Now that we have described the software engineering environment and the factors that determine the engineer's effectiveness within that environment, let us investigate in more detail the definition of software engineering.

1.3

Software Engineering

There have been several definitions of software engineering posed since the early 1970s. These diverse definitions have placed the software engineer in vaguely specified roles such as applied mathematician and well-trained programmer as well as roles approaching those normally associated with engineering. In this section we delineate software engineering and the software engineer.

The first step in the delineation is to establish a definition of software engineering—based upon the premise that software engineering is engineering—that will serve as a framework upon which we can describe the software engineer. Once the definition is established, we will proceed with an analysis of the characteristics, methods, and functions of engineers, in general, and software engineers, in particular, to present the clearest picture possible to this unique individual and, hopefully, eradicate some of the fuzzy and erroneous impressions of the software engineer.

Among the many definitions of software engineering proposed since 1970, the most accurate and descriptive was by F. L. Bauer of the Technical University, Munich, Germany, in 1972. His definition[5] can be stated:

> The establishment and use of sound engineering principles (methods) in order to obtain economically software that is reliable and works on real machines.

This definition of software engineering encompasses the keywords that are the heart of all engineering discipline definitions: sound engineering principles, economical, reliable, and functional (works on real machines). For example, we can replace

[5] F. L. Bauer, "Software Engineering," *Information Processing 71* (Amsterdam: North Holland Publishing Co., 1972), p. 530.

the word software with automobiles and have a reasonable definition of automotive engineering.

Jeffery and Linden of the National Bureau of Standards reinforce the Bauer definition with their observation:[6]

> Software engineering is not just a collection of tools and techniques, it is engineering . . . software engineering has more in common with other kinds of engineering than is usually appreciated. Software engineers can learn from other engineering disciplines; and, conversely, recent methods developed for software engineering may be useful to engineers in other areas. It is time that software engineering is recognized as a full-fledged engineering discipline. . . .

The observation is certainly valid. Our discussion of the "Software Crisis" in Sec. 1.1 highlighted numerous symptoms such as: software is unreliable and needs permanent maintenance; software is always delivered late, exceeds costs, and does not satisfy the original specifications; software is impossible to maintain, lacks transparency, and cannot be modified or improved. These problems exist because the software builders (we hesitate to call them designers or engineers) fail to apply the basic design procedures[7] that are common to all engineering disciplines to their product. The resulting product is almost always poorly planned, poorly designed, and inadequate.

There is one outstanding difference between software engineering and all other branches of engineering. Engineers usually deal with *material* (visible and tangible) objects. From the beginning of time, engineers have designed wheels, bridges, chariots, steam engines, airplanes, and electronic hardware. Even the French term *ingénieur*, used to describe the 17th century builders of fortresses, implied material construction. Electrical engineering is the most abstract of the classical engineering fields since electricity is not a material, but, through the use of appropriate tools, electricity exhibits characteristics that are both visible and tangible. Electricity can thus be dealt with as if it were a physical object. Software, however, is nonmaterial in every sense. Software is better visualized as a process.

The entities involved in nonsoftware engineering can be sensed—observed, touched, etc. Using the sensed information, the nature of a solution can be analyzed and a judgment made concerning its merit or validity. The abstract nature of software limits this evaluation of a solution. However, tools are becoming available to allow some insight into the performance of software by making some of its attributes visible.

The abstract nature of software is one of the problems it poses with respect to patent law. Is software patentable? Can instructions to the human mind be patented? Is a process spelled out in computer instructions, even if ingenuity is definitely involved in the process design, patentable? Obviously, there are legal problems to be resolved.

---

[6]S. Jeffery and T. A. Linden, "Software Engineering is Engineering," *Proceedings of the Computer Science and Engineering Curricula Workshop.* Reprinted with permission. The Institute of Electrical and Electronic Engineers, June 6–7, 1977, p. 112.

[7]Details of the engineering design process will be discussed in Sec. 1.4.

Performance verification is one of the most severe problems faced in software engineering. This problem is amplified by the abstract nature of the software itself. The performance of most engineering products is relatively simple to verify. For example, even the performance of the most complex physical systems and structures can be verified by a finite number of tests, and the performance of the product can be monitored, either visually or with instrumentation, to observe the performance characteristics. The performance of some systems can be extremely difficult to verify under some conditions. For example, the test to validate the performance of a communication system in the presence of electromagnetic interference or the problem of verifying the performance of a digital computer arithmetic processor near ground zero of a nuclear weapon test can be arduous tasks, but such problems are surmountable because they are finite. A computer program is both intangible and complex. Even a modest-sized program (< 5000 executable statements) can contain enough executable paths (i.e., ways to get from the beginning of the program to the end) that the processes of testing each path through the program are prohibitively expensive. Creating test conditions to force execution of any paths other than the principal program paths is often so difficult that the testing of non-primary paths must be ignored. One of the software engineer's primary tasks is to configure and design software such that the limited testing possible can provide a reasonable degree of reliability.

Software engineering, in spite of the abstract nature and complexity of the product, is obviously a major branch of engineering. With the definition of software engineering established and some of the functions of the field described, we can now move ahead and consider the individual who does the work: the software engineer. It is best to approach the subject by first examining the basic engineer independent of any particular discipline. After establishing the characteristics of the basic engineer, we will concentrate on the unique features associated with the software engineer.

Engineers are basically problem solvers. They are practical people, pragmatists who tackle mundane problems and solve them efficiently and economically. Their solution to a problem may appear complex or seem to be a trivial bit of inventiveness; however, the solution's simplicity often masks a true work of inspiration and perseverance.

This practical person, who approaches problems from several different paths, may be trying to find a better way to do a job, develop a totally new system, or apply an old concept in a new and imaginative way. It is difficult to form a sharp picture of an engineer. He or she is a person of many talents. Some engineers are specialists in diverse fields such as TV antenna installation or medical instrumentation. Many of today's modern engineers are executives and managers working with teams of other engineers skilled in several technologies and able to coordinate the efforts of these teams to solve a problem.

One reason for the hazy impression of an engineer is his or her close association with scientists. Both of these professionals communicate in the same language, use mathematics as a fundamental tool, and frequently work side by side on a given task. It is often difficult to tell where the scientist's work is finished and where the engineer's work begins.

The basic difference between the scientist and the engineer lies in their goals. A scientist strives to gain new knowledge about the workings of our universe while the engineer puts that knowledge to work for the needs of mankind. Engineers may not have or need to have total knowledge of the concept they are applying to solve a problem. Universities, recognizing the difference between engineers and scientists, have established both colleges of science and colleges of engineering.

It is also important to note that the scientist's training concentrates on the application of the *scientific method*[8] while the engineer's training concentrates on the use of the engineering design process described in Sec. 1.4.

Engineers and scientists depend on each other to provide knowledge and tools with which to pursue their individual goals. We should not overlook the fact that engineers existed long before there was any significant body of scientific knowledge. At that time engineering was mostly art since the scientific knowledge available to support their designs was nonexistent. Today, with the tremendous improvement in man's understanding of the universe, engineering is addressing the same types of problems but with a broader scientific basis. The inventiveness, expert judgment, and empirical knowledge used in the past are still heavily relied upon in the solution of engineering problems. Engineers do not solely apply science; rather, they solve problems by using scientific knowledge when it is available.

Perhaps our drawing a close parallel between the evolution of medicine and engineering will shed additional light on the modern engineer. Physicians existed long before the fields of bacteriology, physiology, and other biological sciences developed. Medicine was originally an art with no significant body of knowledge from which to draw information. As the body of scientific knowledge developed, physicians began to apply the knowledge in the treatment of medical problems.

Both physicians and engineers are problem-solvers who have assumed the responsibility for applying the available knowledge in their respective fields. They are both problem-oriented fields of endeavor. If either the physician or the engineer is faced with a problem for which scientific knowledge does not supply a solution, he or she will still attempt to solve the problem. A surgeon will not walk away from an operation if a situation is discovered for which science has not prescribed a solution. Both the physician and the engineer have jobs to do, and they will arrive at solutions to their problems through ingenuity, common sense, and experimentation, and any other means if the current scientific knowledge is inadequate.

We have established that the basic engineer is a problem-solving individual. Next we will delve into the make-up of this engineer to describe the qualities that make him or her a good problem solver. The engineering qualities can be divided into three main categories: basic knowledge, skills, and attitudes. The basic knowledge consists of (1) fundamentals of physical sciences, such as physics, that provide the foundation upon which all additional knowledge is assembled; (2) applied physical sciences, such as electrical network theory and thermodynamics, which bridge the gap between the fundamental sciences and the engineering design; and (3) other empirical knowledge

---

[8] The scientific method is the systematic attempt to construct theories that correlate wide groups of observed facts and are capable of predicting the results of future observations. Such theories are tested by controlled experimentation and are accepted only as long as they are consistent with all observed facts.

gained from experience. All three of these facets of basic knowledge are necessary engineering tools. In order to solve problems, a fundamental understanding of the physical laws that govern our universe is necessary. At the same time the engineer must be equipped with a body of knowledge that supplies the means of applying the principles of science to practical problems. Referring to the similarities between engineering and medicine again for a moment, we know that when a person is sick, we would never call in a physician trained in chemistry and basic physiology for a treatment recommendation. Rather, we would refer the problem to a physician trained in diagnostic medicine. Similarly, there is a big gap between a training in fundamental physical sciences and applied engineering. We seldom approach a physicist to design electronic circuits. The engineering training in applied sciences must bridge that gap.

The third segment of basic knowledge consists of empirical knowledge gained from experience. As the engineer matures, many ideas, observations, and practices that are not based on established scientific fact, but which have been demonstrated to be sound, are collected and stored for future reference. Some of these pieces of information are recorded and passed on in engineering design courses, journals, and conferences. Other information is mentally stored and augments the engineer's inventiveness.

Engineering skills, the second quality catagory, are a little harder to quantify. Since proficiency in design is an important attribute, and inventiveness is a key element of design proficiency, we must accept inventiveness as an important skill. In addition to inventiveness, there are a number of equally important but less obvious skills. For example, we can immediately list good judgment and the ability to reach reasonable, intelligent conclusions, mathematical or computational dexterity, and the ability to effectively use information resources.

We must also stress the "ability to think" as one of the primary skills of the engineer. One of the major goals of engineering education is to develop the reasoning, or analytical ability, of the student. This emphasis is seldom explicit, but reasoning is an important tool in any design process.

One of the most misleading portraits of the typical engineer is that of a "loner," a person who wears a white laboratory coat, carries a slide rule or calculator, and works alone in creating revolutionary devices to improve the quality of life on our planet. Engineering involves innumerable contacts with many people throughout almost every problem-solving task. Maintaining a cooperative working relationship with all of these people as either a manager or a member of a development team is an important element in the successful completion of a task.

We cannot stress enough the importance of communication skills in an engineering career. Engineers must be able to express themselves clearly and concisely if they aspire to be successful. Academic training tends to emphasize training in the applied sciences (or the basic engineering tools) at the expense of communications, but that is not indicative of the true value of good oral and written expression in engineering. We are constantly bombarded with pleas voiced by many employers and graduates to place more emphasis on communication skills in college. Many of the chapters in this text emphasize the need for effective communications in the development of software and the disasterous effects of communication failures in the design process.

The third basic category of engineering qualities includes those attributes related to attitude or point of view. Probably the best representative of the ideal engineering attitude is Mr. Spock, the Science Officer aboard the starship USS Enterprise from the TV series Star Trek. Spock approached problems objectively and made decisions based on logical reasoning without influence from tradition, outside pressure, or biases. He was open-minded to new and different approaches to a problem. His attitude toward his work and his colleagues was entirely professional. There was never any doubt that his decisions could be trusted or that his services or responsibilities would be performed ethically.

Spock also exhibited an intense curiosity, or questioning attitude, that is a necessary engineering attribute. There are many good ideas and profitable information that result from curiosity and from the questioning skepticism that drives us to challenge the validity of some fact, the necessity of certain procedures or components, or the feasibility of some solution. Questioning ourselves and others in engineering decisions usually leads to more cost-effective and reliable products.

We have isolated and discussed the qualities and characteristics of the being known as an "engineer." The knowledge, skills, and attitudes of the complete engineer have been described in this section. We have emphasized that engineers are basically problem solvers. They are responsible for the creation, design, and construction of devices, structures, and processes that represent solutions to these problems.

Each branch of engineering has its own class of problems to solve. Electrical engineering concerns itself with the solution of problems related to things electrical in nature. These problems all exist within the scope of the basic and applied sciences associated with the engineering branch. Mechanical engineering is usually associated with the design of systems by which energy is converted to useful mechanical forms, and also with the design of mechanical structures. Software engineering is related to the design of software or data processing products as stated in Bauer's definition already given. The problem-solving domain of the software engineer encompasses the class of problems related to software and data processing. The software engineer must then be able to determine the actual needs of a user; select a general approach to the system development; analyze requirements to determine and resolve conflicts; establish a design to achieve the desired performance within constraints imposed by cost, schedule, and operating environment; develop new technical solutions; and, finally, manage a group of individuals with a wide range of personalities, disciplines, and goals.

The software engineer is not a theoretician as is the computer scientist. As a problem solver, we are more likely to recognize him or her as the "general practitioner" in the computing world. Much like the general practitioner in the medical or other engineering fields, the software engineer confronts a vast array of problems and must possess skills and knowledge in a wide range of areas to solve these problems.

The training of a software engineer parallels that of other engineering disciplines. That is, the training includes both basic and applied sciences as well as design courses and, hopefully, an emphasis on communication and management skills. The engineer must also be trained in the engineering approach to problems and in design methodologies. Recommendations for a meaningful software curriculum are outlined in Appendix I.

1.4

The Engineering Design Process

There is a general procedure used by engineers to obtain solutions to problems. This procedure, or problem solving process, is common to all branches of engineering. The six steps in the process, illustrated in Figure 1-3, are briefly:

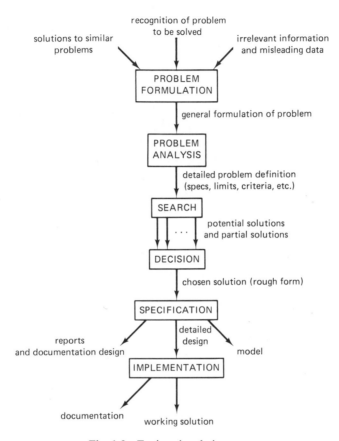

Fig. 1-3 Engineering design process

Problem formulation—the problem is defined or described in broad terms without detail.

Problem analysis—the problem definition is refined to supply essential detail.

Search—a set of potential solutions to the problem is gathered.

Decision—each of the potential solutions is evaluated and compared to the alternates until the best solution is obtained.

Specification—the chosen solution is described in detail.

Implementation—the finished product is constructed from the design.

The design process encompasses activities from the recognition of the problem through the implementation of an economical, functional solution to that problem. It is this methodology by which engineers apply their knowledge, skills, and creative ability in the development of new devices and processes.

Although it will not be explicitly stated in the descriptions of the various phases of the design process, it is important that we realize that the process is not conducted in a vacuum, i.e., with no outside communication. Each of the phases involves a myriad of written and oral communications with managers, users, customers, and colleagues. The effectiveness of the engineers in the design cycle is directly proportional not only to their technical skills but also to their ability to communicate with others and to their understanding of basic management sciences. This concept will be discussed further in Chapter 2.

PROBLEM FORMULATION

The first and most important step in the design process is the formulation or definition of the problem. The problem formulation is primarily a point of view, i.e., the manner in which the engineer perceives the problem. Thus it is important for the engineer to gain as broad a perspective of the problem as possible at the outset. Breadth of perspective becomes virtually impossible to achieve once he or she becomes immersed in a problem detail.

Only in rare instances is the true problem presented to the engineer. An accurate picture of the problem must be developed because the original problem statement is usually obscured by considerable irrelevant information and distorted by misleading opinions, current solutions, and standard ways of viewing the problem.

One of the most disastrous ways of formulating a problem is by immediately trying to adapt it to an existing solution or by adapting a current solution to a poor understanding of the problem. This tendency forces one into a sea of detail and prevents a broad, objective view of the problem.

There is no single verbal or graphical method for formulating a problem. There are almost as many formulation methods as there are engineers. One of the most effective ways for studying a problem is through the use of a conceptual "black-box." This method, shown in Figure 1-4, is a graphical means of formulating a problem,

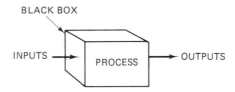

Fig. 1-4 Black box description of process

allowing the engineer to gather information about the problem inputs and outputs without having to be concerned with the details of the process representing the problem solution. The details of the process are hidden within the black box and are normally not known at this stage. All the engineer must recognize is that some function must be performed on the inputs to provide the desired outputs. The simplicity of this approach actually belies its effectiveness as a problem formulation tool.

PROBLEM ANALYSIS

The second step of the engineering design process is the analysis of the problem. In the first step it was sufficient to identify the input and output quantities. However, to solve the problem the engineer must obtain detailed qualitative and quantitative characteristics of these inputs and outputs. Since the characteristics are seldom constant, the inputs and outputs are usually treated as variables subject to constraints. For example, in the design of a wristwatch, the input variable w (weight) is constrained such that $0 < w \leq 0.25$ lb; the output variable t_d (accuracy in sec/day) must be within $-5 \leq t_d \leq +5$. Before the design can proceed, adequate information on the input and output variables, their constraints, and the relative importance of the constraints must be available. If an absolute upper price limit of $10.00 is also specified, for the wristwatch, the accuracy tolerance of ± 5 sec/day may have to be relaxed because it may not be possible to satisfy the cost, weight, and accuracy constraints simultaneously. However, it may be possible to meet the cost constraint with an accuracy of ± 10 sec/day.

The analysis of the problem will also provide a set of solution variables and an accompanying set of restrictions on the solution fixed by management or customer guidelines, or by Mother Nature herself. The solution variables and restrictions govern the means by which the problem can be solved. Some restrictions are subject to negotiation when conflicts with other restrictions or constraints occur. If it is apparent that the various imposed restrictions are incompatible, one or both of the restrictions must be relaxed if a feasible solution is to be found. Many restrictions are irrevocable. A digital wristwatch cannot have a 64-minute hour just because it simplifies the binary counting mechanism.

Most decisions regarding restrictions or courses of action are suboptimum for one reason or another. It is difficult to make truly objective decisions because of personal bias, relatively short time spans for making decisions, the amount of judgment necessary because of inadequate or erroneous data, the element of chance in the search for alternate solutions, and unforeseen elements—or interaction between elements—of the problem. Thus the restrictions imposed on the solution cannot be automatically assumed fixed but must be weighed in the analysis of the problem.

The solution variables include the possible ways in which solutions to a problem can differ. For example, one of the solution variables in the wristwatch problem is the method of displaying time; another variable is the method of determining time; a third is the type of power source. Selecting an LED time display influences the other solution variables. The final solution to the problem will consist of a final value for each of the solution variables.

During the problem analysis, the criteria for selecting the best solution should be specified. The criteria usually include parameters of cost, reliability, ease of maintenance, accuracy, and efficiency. The relative weights of the individual parameters determine the order of importance of these criteria in any project.

Other criteria that enter into the problem analysis are the skills and needs of the end user and the anticipated usage of the product.

The most effective way to analyze a problem of any significant size is through a process of decomposition, or "stepwise-refinement." This stepwise refinement process is one of successively increasing the level of detail (lowering the level of conceptualization) of the problem in a series of distinct steps. It is a process in which the problem is treated as a collection of intellectually manageable pieces with interfaces between the pieces that are as simple and functional as possible. In considering, for example, the problem of designing a computer, the task is begun by defining a unit called "computer," as shown in Figure 1-5. Using the black-box concept mentioned earlier,

Fig. 1-5 Computer function block

the inputs, processes, and outputs associated with the general-function computer are described at the first (highest) level of conceptualization. There is no need to worry about memory size or access speed or the power dissipation of the basic adder. Next, in order to reach the second level of conceptualization, the computer is decomposed into a set of subunits. This decomposition (used in reaching each level of conceptualization) can be performed by using one of two basic methods: random and functional partitioning. The first method, based upon the random partitioning of the computer into smaller pieces as shown in Figure 1-6, is the "quick and dirty" approach that requires little

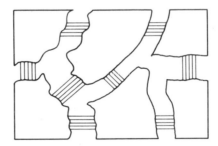

Fig. 1-6 Random partitioning of computer function to block

thought and produces an extremely complex interface between the elements of the set. The second method of decomposition, based on the functional partitioning of the problem, is much more effective in breaking the problem into mentally manageable pieces. Since the partitioning, or decomposition, between each level of conceptualization is along functional lines, the interface between each of the subunits is as simple as possible. Also, the level of detail is such that the specifications for each functional subunit can be specified independently and the interfaces between each subunit specified. As at the first level, the inputs, processes, and outputs for each of the subunits are defined at the appropriate detail level. The functional decomposition method is obviously more desirable. The second level of conceptualization of the computer, derived by functional decomposition, is shown in Figure 1-7.

At the third and succeeding levels of conceptualization, each subunit is subdivided and specifications prepared for the entities at that level until a level is reached at which subdivision is no longer meaningful. The lowest level of conceptualization for the computer arithmetic processor involves specification at the gate level, that is, the logic type, signals, power dissipation, timing, etc. It can be noted that the spe-

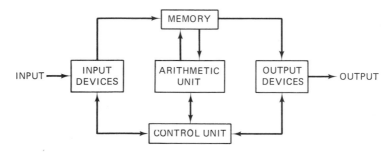

Fig. 1-7 Functional partitioning of computer function block

cifications at each lower decomposition level must conform to the specifications at the higher levels. Gate delays of 100 nanoseconds cannot be allowed if memory cycle times of 50 nanoseconds are to be achieved.

By approaching the problem analysis through stepwise-refinement of the problem, the problem is never allowed to become mentally unmanageable or to exceed the engineer's ability to comprehend. This method also allows the engineer to avoid (or hide) the details of the problem until he or she is in a position to deal with them reasonably.

SEARCH

After the analysis of the problem is completed, the third step of the engineering design process is entered: the search for alternate solutions to the problem. Generally, solutions appear during the analysis of the problem as byproducts of the analysis. These solutions should be collected and saved for this third step during which an active search for alternate problem solutions is conducted. By concentrating on a solution during the analysis, the engineer can inadvertently bias the analysis data to fit the possible solution, or worse yet, not approach the problem analysis objectively. The search is a straight-forward process of exploring all possible avenues for a solution to the problem. The avenues include individual experience, textbooks, technical journals, existing practices, and the important element—creativity. This creativity, or ingenuity, is a vital tool in the solution of many aspects of technical problems not covered by published books and papers. Ingenuity, one of the most difficult of the avenues to pursue in searching for a solution, is an avenue that is developed primarily through problem-solving experience. Fortunately, ingenuity is not solely an inherited gift. Rather, it is a combination of several characteristics: aptitude (inherited), attitude, knowledge, perseverance, and an effective search methodology. Since all but one of the characteristics of creativity are under each individual's control, the individual can control his own level of creativity to a great extent.

The objective of the search phase of the design process is to maximize the number and variety of solutions from which a final selection can be made. The search for potential solutions should not be centered about the present solutions to similar problems (conservative approach), but should sample all areas of possible solutions that satisfy the real constraints and restrictions imposed in the previous step. The tendency to allow the search to be confined by artificial restrictions imposed by erroneous information, opinion, or past approaches should be avoided.

The search for prospective solutions should not be terminated early due to premature involvement with the details of any proposed solution. Solution details hinder the search in two ways: first, preoccupation with details of one solution tends to hamper the ability to search for alternate solutions and biases the final selection (the old forest-and-tree problem); and second, the time that should be spent searching for alternates is wasted in the mire of unimportant detail. At this stage of the design process, all potential solutions—independent of their apparent merit—are gathered for the following decision phase.

DECISION

In the previous phase the number and variety of alternate solutions were expanded to provide the broadest solution space possible from which to select a preferred solution. The potential solutions have been specified in both general and frequently imprecise terms. Some of the alternates may appear ridiculous or unworkable, but some of the features or characteristics of these awkward solutions may contain elements that will improve or benefit one or several of the more reasonable solutions.

As this phase of the design is entered, it is important that the list of potential solutions be reduced and, finally, the preferred solution be selected in an objective manner. If the engineer begins by glancing through the list of alternates and casting out the most "absurd" of the lot, he or she will have fallen into the ageless trap of subjective thinking. Many worthwhile solutions to engineering problems have been lost because, at first glance, the solution was unworkable or unprofitable. An organized, objective selection process must be established. This decision process will vary somewhat from problem to problem, but will generally follow a series of four steps:

1. The selection criteria must be defined, and the relative weight of the individual elements of the criteria assigned;
2. The performance of the alternate solutions with respect to these criteria must be predicted as accurately as possible;
3. The performance of the alternate solutions must be compared on the basis of their predicted performance;
4. The selection of the preferred solution must be made.

The selection criteria can be based upon many factors, including cost of production, functional performance, efficiency, reliability, maintenance, ease of use, etc. Other less technically pure factors, such as political environment, must also be considered in most decisions. The proper establishment of the selection criteria for a solution is almost as difficult a task as the formulation of the problem itself. Data used in determining the selection criteria are usually gathered at the same time as the data for the problem formulation.

The second step in the decision process is the most demanding part of this phase. Each of the proposed solutions must be evaluated objectively to predict its performance with respect to the individual elements of the criteria. Many of the judgments involved in determining predicted performance are value judgments based on vague, limited, or nonexistent data. Some elements of the selection criteria are also unquantifiable. Remaining totally objective under these circumstances is difficult.

If two or more alternate solutions are of nearly equal merit in the evaluation, additional study may be required to predict more accurately its performance, or the elements of the selection criteria may have to be expanded or weighted differently, or the solutions may be of equal merit, and the final choice can be made on aesthetic value (subjectively).

SOLUTION SPECIFICATION

At this point in the design process, the engineer has arrived at an approach that best satisfies the chosen selection criteria. Most of the solution is in rough form (notes, sketches, computations, etc.) and very incomplete. The solution is probably disorganized and still partly a mental image. In other words, it is not yet implementable.

This nontrivial task refines the rough solution to a level from which the end product can be built. The physical and performance characteristics of the design (or solution) must be specified in sufficient detail so that the design can be reviewed, analyzed, and its feasibility verified. The level of detail must also be adequate to allow production of the product. The fact that the design may be implemented, operated, and maintained by another person makes it essential that the design be carefully and effectively documented.

This phase of the design cycle is the most visible of the entire process. Outsiders often conjure up a vision of the earlier steps of the cycle as a mysterious, or at least strange, ritual in which an engineer, dressed in a white smock, spends long days and sleepless nights creating a brilliant solution to an unsolvable problem. In the specification phase, the engineer is usually pictured with sleeves rolled up and slide-rule in hand, working over a cluttered drafting table to complete the design. In reality, the specification phase is an orderly and straightforward process that is seldom understood completely by the outsider.

The specification step usually involves considerable detail. Some of the work may be transferred to technical assistants, but the majority of the specification, such as dimensions, tolerances, power consumption and cooling, human interfaces, etc., can be supplied only by the designer and remains his responsibility.

The output of the specification step usually consists of two items. First, a set of detailed specifications must be prepared. The specifications include a report and a set of working drawings. The report—the most important output from the cycle—is a formal document that completely describes the solution, using both words and diagrams. The report also describes the performance of the design and presents a thorough evaluation of it. It is primarily through this report that the solution is transmitted to the outside world, and much of the value of the report relies on an ability to communicate effectively. The size of the report varies dramatically from project to project, depending on system complexity and contractual requirements.

The second item frequently produced as output in the specification phase is a model of the end product. The model may appear as a scale model of a bridge, a working electronic prototype, a computer algorithm represented by a program listing and sample output, or a myriad of other ways. The model provides an effective means of illustrating and describing the final solution.

IMPLEMENTATION

The final step in the design process is the implementation and delivery of the end product. The responsibility of the engineer seldom ends with the specification of the solution but extends into producing the product, gaining acceptance of the design, training the user in the operation of the product, observing and evaluating the design in its operational environment, maintaining the design in the field, and participating in design improvements.

The design process as we have described it is an idealistic view of the cycle. We have allowed for the design process to move only forward. Ideally, the search phase has ended; the decision phase proceeds with no need to return to the search phase. Unfortunately, the design cycle is not so simple. The design cycle is realistically more like the representation in Figure 1-8. At each step in the cycle, new information or

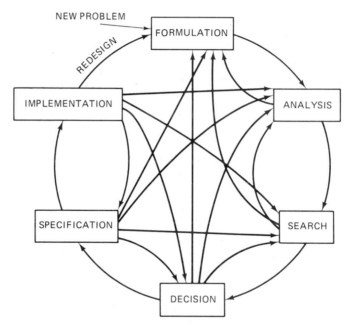

Fig. 1-8 Realistic engineering design process

insights into earlier decisions become available. This information may modify or invalidate the decisions that have led us to our present understanding of the problem and force an iteration of one or more preceding cycle steps. Each of these iterations costs both time and resources. The increase in cost is directly proportional to the number of design cycle steps spanned by the iteration, which leads us to our version of an old adage: "There is always enough time to do it right the first time." The more thoroughly that each of the design steps is performed, the more cost-effective the design cycle will be. Of course, that does not imply that we can stay on step one forever. There will occur a time in each phase in the design cycle when the solution is adequate and, even though minor improvements are possible, the cost of the improvements outweighs the advantage gained; the process must move forward to the next phase. One quality of most good engineers is that they are never totally satisfied with a design and are constantly trying to improve it. Economics usually does not allow this luxury.

The engineering design process may vary slightly from problem to problem because of schedule, constraints and restrictions, or economics, but the design cycle we have outlined in this section is basic to all branches of engineering. Software engineering is one of those branches.

2 PROJECT MANAGEMENT FUNDAMENTALS

CHARLES C. TONIES

Manager, Data Processing Systems Laboratory
Hughes Aircraft Company

> *"The question, O me! so sad,*
> *recurring—What good amid these,*
> *O me, O life?*
>
> *Answer*
>
> *That you are here—that life*
> *exists and identity,*
> *That the powerful play goes on, and*
> *You may contribute a verse."*
>
> WALT WHITMAN
> *O Me! O Life!*

2.1
Introduction

Software management in this country has been, and still is, problematical. Management science in general is still in an adolescent stage, and there are relatively few managers in any field who make effective use of it. Peter Drucker characterizes the state of affairs:

> But there has been little work, little organized thought, little emphasis on managing an enterprise on the risk-making, risk-taking, decision-making job. Throughout management science—in the literature as well as in the work in progress—the emphasis is on techniques rather than principles, on mechanics rather than on decisions, on tools rather than on results, and, above all, on efficiency of the part rather than on performance of the whole.[1]

If management science is immature, then we can expect software management science to be especially immature, since the software industry is itself so new and is

[1]P. F. Drucker, *Management: Tasks, Responsibilities, Practices.* New York: Harper and Row, Publishers, 1974.

expanding so quickly. The probability, then, of finding effective software management would seem to be small. It is.

The rapid expansion of software related activity combined with its brief history are enough to cause a definite shortage of management talent. There are not enough people with adequate experience to go around. Software management ability, like any other kind, requires a degree of experience in the field. The degree is different for different people and different conditions, to be sure, but an "average time to management competence" is necessary (not sufficient), and across the industry this time requirement has generally not been satisfied.

The shortage of experience is not the only problem. The shortcoming Drucker attributes to management science in general—that of emphasizing efficiency of the part rather than performance of the whole—permeates the software management state of affairs today. There is much attention on individual phases and functions of the software development sequence, but little on the whole life cycle as an integral, continuous process—a process that can and should be optimized.

There have been a number of impressive advances related to specific development functions and these do contribute positively to the management cause; we do not mean to minimize their importance. Most of these are treated in later chapters of this volume (e.g., design decomposition and recomposition techniques, structured programming, systematic verification and validation).

But this chapter is devoted to the total management problem, and the solution to the problem involves more than just finding better tools and local optimization methods; it calls for an integrated approach to the entire scope of the development and maintenance cycle. A systems treatment of the whole process from conceptual stage through product installation and operation is needed. Some movement toward such an integrated management methodology has occurred. The most notable items are structured design and test methods, the Chief Programmer Team concept forwarded by Mills and Baker of IBM,[2] recent U.S. Military Standards that emphasize end-to-end configuration control,[3,4] and Fred Brooks' compendium of valuable insights in *The Mythical Man-Month*.[5] Much more of this type of thought is required. In this chapter we therefore present a concept that we feel will play an important part in software project planning and management in the future. This concept—modeling of the software life cycle process in terms of entropy effects—is unique in the management realm. We feel that it represents a contribution to software management science, and it also serves as a basis for a deeper understanding and appreciation of the material in later chapters of this book. The concept is presented in the last part of this chapter.

Since we are treating the general subject of software management in an introductory manner, the first part of the chapter is devoted to a straightforward description

[2]F. T. Baker, "Chief Programmer Team Management of Production Programming," *IBM Systems Journal*, Vol. II, Spring, 1972, pp. 56–73.

[3]Department of Defense Directive 5000.29, "Management of Computer Resources in Major Defense Systems," Apr. 26, 1976.

[4]Air Force Regulation 800-14, Vol. I, "Management of Computer Resources in Systems," 12 Sept., 1975, and Vol. II: "Acquisition and Support Procedures for Computer Resources in Systems", Sept. 26, 1975.

[5]F. P. Brooks, Jr., *The Mythical Man-Month*. Reading, Mass.: Addison-Wesley, 1975.

of a typical large software project. The nature and the importance of sound preparations and comprehensive project planning are stressed.

2.2
Overview of a Software Project

Each software project has its own character. Its size, duration, technical content, working conditions, and delivery requirements significantly affect the nature of the project structure and the resources required to carry the job through to a successful conclusion. Brooks,[5] points out, for example, that the total effort required to complete a project depends strongly on the anticipated utilization of its output. If the objective is to create computer programs for internal use, that is, for use by the individuals who developed them, the effort required to complete the task will be considerably less than if that software is to be released externally as a "product." A product must be more thoroughly and more formally tested, documented, and maintained than an in-house, personalized computer program.

Likewise, the effort required to produce several programs that function interactively as a system is greater than the effort needed to produce the same set of programs that are only required to function independently. For example, five programs that are each required to perform certain functions, plus exchange data and in other ways automatically affect the operation of the other four programs in the system, are more difficult and costly to produce than are five independent programs that perform the same general functions but do not exchange data with each other.

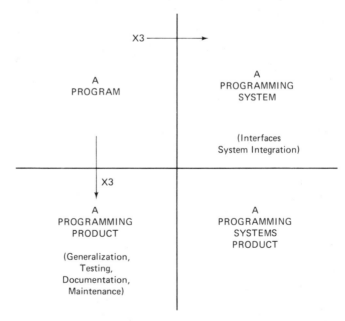

Fig. 2-1 Evolution of the programming systems product. From F. P. Brooks, *The Mythical Man-Month*, 1975, Addison-Wesley, Reading, MA

Brooks summarizes both the "product" and the "system" effects in a single diagram presented in Figure 2-1. This provides us with a very useful picture to recall when establishing the size of a project or performing productivity analyses.[6] The figure shows that effort increases by a factor of three as we move from a program to a programming product *or* from a program to a programming system. To produce a programming system product requires nine times the effort that would be necessary to create a corresponding set of individual in-house programs. As Brooks points out, much confusion and misinterpretation currently associated with software productivity comparisions may be due to a lack of realistic understanding of these factors. Most of the extra effort expended in order to transform programs into products and systems is not reflected in additional operational code; therefore, the productivity rate that can be expected in developing an individual program (upper left quadrant) is higher than for any of the other quadrants in the diagram, assuming that all project costs are included in the productivity computation.

The role of productivity analysis in software project planning is discussed in a later section. It is sufficient to note now that the profile of a software project, its duration, manpower requirements, cost demands, and management problems depend on the nature of the item to be produced. Throughout the remainder of this chapter and, for the most part, throughout this book, we will be addressing the problems associated with development of programming systems products, represented by the lower right quadrant of Figure 2-1. Although Brooks was referring primarily to computer operating system products, especially the IBM OS/360, his analysis applies equally well to applications software systems.

We have elected to use the most complex and demanding type of project (a large, interactive, deliverable system of programs) as background for our discussion for two reasons:

1. The fundamental software management principles that we will present are best illustrated in the context of a large project with a deliverable product, and
2. A software engineer is more likely to be involved in a system/product project than in any other type.

The first point may seem to be a paradox. If we are dealing with fundamental principles in this chapter, why shouldn't small, simple examples suffice? To some extent they do, but the effects and consequences of nonadherence to sound principles are much more pronounced in large, product-oriented project situations. A small software development can be handled by a few people working closely together, perhaps informally. The need for explicit management methods is greatly reduced in such a situation because the various roles and responsibilities are easily defined and followed; configuration control is simple; and—most importantly—communication is easily accomplished. On the other hand, even a medium-sized project necessitates the formalization and systematic management of these functions.

---

[6]Productivity is the rate of production of the product, e.g., lines of code produced per unit time, pages of documentation produced per unit time, etc. Productivity analysis is the study and derivation of these rates. It is discussed in detail in Sec. 2.4.

We are saying here that the members of a small project team may be able to keep most of the information necessary for interfacing and integrating the system in their heads; they may be able to accomplish all necessary communication verbally, thereby obviating the need for sophisticated management methods. But this simplicity works *only* for very small teams. As the size of the job and the size of the staff grow, the control and communication requirements increase geometrically, and can no longer be satisfied by verbal and informal procedures.

In this context a small project team is 5 or fewer persons; a medium-sized team is 6 to 15 workers, while more than 15 people is considered "large." Management techniques become more and more important as staff size rises beyond 15; at the 50–100 level, for example, effective management techniques are critical to the success of a project.

Therefore our descriptive overview is of a large project. The principles and methods presented later are applicable to both medium and large efforts. In presenting the overview, we will first discuss the "front end," that is, the early procurement-related activities. This adds perspective to the total picture and highlights the proposal phase. The software engineer who enters industry, whether it be with a selling contractor or a buying agency, will certainly be engaged in proposal work of some kind at more than one point in his or her career.

After the mechanics of procurement are described, the software life cycle is defined and reviewed in detail. Then the elements of a project plan are presented together with an brief description of each of its contents.

2.2.1 PROCUREMENT MECHANICS

In practice, the project objectives and constraints are defined by a combination of written official agreements between buyer and seller and the subsequent interpretation of those agreements by participating parties on both sides. The subtle political and business maneuvering associated with this subsequent interpretation is beyond the scope of this book. In this section, we concentrate therefore on the macroscopic aspects of procurement, namely, the formal agreements and documents that pass from buyer to seller and seller to buyer. These represent the first-order definition of the task to be performed; they define the essential characteristics of the project.

In one form or another, the sequence of steps leading to a software development "buy/sell" agreement is:

1. Seller learns of buyer's need.
2. Seller describes his offering to buyer. (The Proposal)
3. Buyer expresses interest but may suggest changes in Seller's offering.
4. Seller counters with adjusted offering, which may or may not be the same as in 3.
5. Buyer counters Seller's latest offering, if necessary.
6. The 4, 5, 4, . . . iteration continues until real or apparent agreement is reached.
7. Formal statements of work, product description, and price are documented and signed by both parties (The Contract).

Specific mechanisms and documentation vehicles that are employed to carry out this sequence vary significantly, depending on the buying agency and the size and type of software system being procured, but the essence of the sequence is the same for all. Here we use examples taken from the Department of Defense (DOD) procedures that are oriented toward large, complex systems; the procedures are, therefore, quite highly structured and formalized and are a study in themselves. For our purposes now, we will treat only the major elements that are common to almost all procurements in one form or another.[7]

To establish a context, consider Figure 2-2. This diagram represents activities that the government carries out before a contract is awarded. The bidding contractors take part in this process by preparing and submitting proposals. Referring to the seven-step pattern just listed, we now correlate the first few of them with the figure.

Step 1 (Seller learns of buyer's need) is accomplished by the government's distribution of a Request for Proposal (RFP). The RFP describes a product or service that the government is prepared to buy, and it states conditions of procurement such as type of contract, government-furnished equipment provisions, security requirements, etc. It contains a preliminary contract Statement of Work (SOW), a preliminary Procurement Specification (SPEC), and a Contract Data Requirements List (CDRL). These represent three of the five principal "official agreements" with which the project manager and his staff are concerned. The fourth will be the schedule; the fifth is the price. All five eventually appear in a single, signed contract; however, it is convenient for us to consider them separately now.

Nothing in the RFP is official or binding yet; steps 2 through 7 must be carried out before that happens. Yet some project activity is typically under way even *before* an RFP is received. In a competitive environment, headstarts are highly desirable and are often possible by means of anticipating the buyer's specific needs before an RFP is released. This pre- and post-RFP receipt activity is the proposal phase, a period of intense action, during which a definitive project plan is developed. A complete plan must be prepared for the proposal (Step 2), usually in a short period of time.

This first version of the project plan, though not binding and subject to change, is extremely important for two reasons: 1) it will influence the buyer in his contract award decision, and 2) the contractor is expected to be able to implement it! Reason 2 should be obvious, but experience in the industry to date gives clear indication that it has either not been obvious, or it has been at least partially ignored.

In the early years of the software industry, the RFPs or their equivalent were not always sophisticated. Typically they called for relatively grandiose products on unrealistic cost and schedule bases. In some instances, bidding companies—realizing that adjustments or overruns were inevitable no matter who did the job—submitted proposals to do the work more or less as called for in the RFP. The logic was "let's win the contract first; then we'll show the customer where his requirements are unreasonable, and together we'll draft a new plan."

Sometimes this worked out well; more often it did not. The customer refused to make major changes, or the revised plan was also unrealistic, or the contractor decided

---

[7]For the reader interested in pursuing DOD software procurement methods in detail, footnote 8 is highly recommended.

Sec. 2.2 Overview of a Software Project

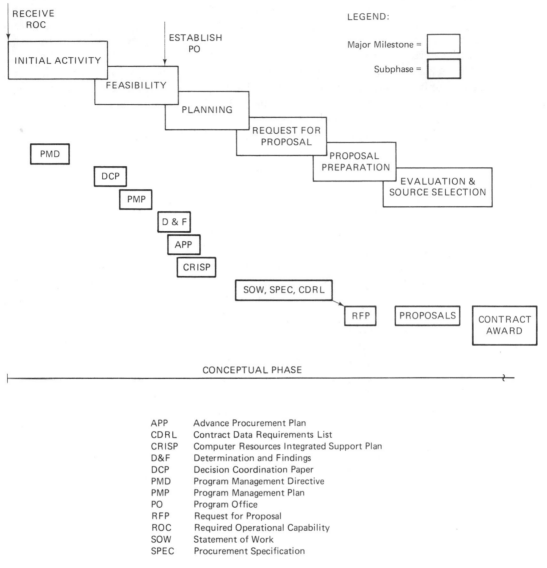

RECEIVE
ROC

ESTABLISH
PO

LEGEND:

Major Milestone =

Subphase =

INITIAL ACTIVITY

FEASIBILITY

PLANNING

REQUEST FOR
PROPOSAL

PROPOSAL
PREPARATION

EVALUATION &
SOURCE SELECTION

PMD

DCP

PMP

D & F

APP

CRISP

SOW, SPEC, CDRL

RFP

PROPOSALS

CONTRACT
AWARD

CONCEPTUAL PHASE

APP	Advance Procurement Plan
CDRL	Contract Data Requirements List
CRISP	Computer Resources Integrated Support Plan
D&F	Determination and Findings
DCP	Decision Coordination Paper
PMD	Program Management Directive
PMP	Program Management Plan
PO	Program Office
RFP	Request for Proposal
ROC	Required Operational Capability
SOW	Statement of Work
SPEC	Procurement Specification

Fig. 2-2 Pre-contract award activity

to go ahead and overrun both cost and schedule because it was becoming apparent that most software contracts were overrun. In other instances, the winning contractor himself did not know that his plan was not viable until very late in the project.

In all cases where projects got off to a start with such marginal plans, the results were essentially the same. Cost and schedule overruns became apparent to both buyer and seller, and disagreement on the product definition usually developed. Salvaging these projects was painful, expensive, and embarrassing to all parties.

There are too many of these overrun situations yet today but, by percentage, far less than a few years ago. Both suppliers and consumers are rapidly becoming more systematic and competent in dealing with software procurements. Today the typical RFP is basically a sound proposition. A credible and sincere proposal should be submitted in response. Anything less leads to remorse both for buyer and seller.

PROPOSAL PHASE

Presentation of the actual proposal—Step 2 in our buy/sell agreement sequence—is a contractor's tentative commitment to perform the task outlined and to deliver products.

It is tentative in the sense that binding commitment is made only after selection and formal negotiation take place. The proposal contains the contractor's Statement of Work, the System Specification, CDRL items, a complete program plan (schedule of events), and the bid price.

An abstract description of a system specification is given next. An example of a Statement of Work is shown in Table 2-1, CDRL list contents are shown in Figure 2-3, and a summary of Program Plan items (milestones) is shown in Figure 2-4. All four are taken from the very useful *Management Guide to Avionics Software Acquisition, Volume II: Software Acquisition Process*, which is available from the Department of Commerce. The figures will not be discussed at this time.

> The system specification gives the technical and mission requirements for the system as an entity, allocates requirements to functional areas by defining the Computer Program Configuration Items (CPCIs) and segments (such as subsystems within the system), and defines the interfaces between the functional areas. Programming language requirements, program design standards, and coding standards are examples of the requirements contained in the system specification. When the system is sufficiently large to be divided into segments, the system specification is used to generate segment specifications that identify each of the CPCIs that comprise the particular segment, to specify all functional interfaces between member CPCIs and other system segments, and to identify the quality assurance requirements to be used in formal test and evaluation of the segment. The final version of the system specification establishes the functional baseline for the system.[8]

The proposal also contains complete technical and financial management plans and as much detailed technical design information as is deemed necessary to win the competitive award. It is this specific expository content that the buyer uses to gain insight and confidence into the contractor's offering. If the information provided in the detailed management plans, and the technical design approach is coherent and competent, and if the contractor actually has the intention and capacity to carry them out, then the proposal is sound; and the project will be on a firm footing if awarded.

This is not always easy to achieve. A proposal is also a sales proposition, and the temptation to tell the buyer what he wants to hear is strong. But in the long-term scheme of things, a contracting company's fortunes depend on performance and credibility more than on glowing promises. The proposal writer must walk the line, therefore, between good salesmanship and realistic project planning.

[8]*Management Guide to Avionics Software Acquisition, Volume II: Software Acquisition Process.* Technical Rept. No. ASD-TR-76-11. Logicon, Inc., Dayton, Ohio, June 1976. Available from U.S. Dept. of Commerce, National Technical Information Service.

Table 2.1 Statement of Work Outline

Number	Section Title

1. SCOPE
2. APPLICABLE DOCUMENTS
3. REQUIREMENTS DEFINITION
    - 3.1 Functional requirements
    - 3.2 Interface requirements
    - 3.3 Other requirements
    - 3.4 System design review
    - 3.5 CPCI requirements review
    - 3.6 Part I specification
    - 3.7 Scientific simulation
4. DESIGN
    - 4.1 Top Level Design
    - 4.2 Preliminary design review
    - 4.3 Detail design
    - 4.4 Critical design review
    - 4.5 Preliminary part II specification
    - 4.6 Engineering simulation
    - 4.7 DT&E test plan
5. CODING AND CHECKOUT
    - 5.1 Coding
    - 5.2 Checkout
    - 5.3 DT&E Test Procedures
    - 5.4 Deliveries
6. TESTING
    - 6.1 Prequalification tests
    - 6.2 CPCI Test review
    - 6.3 Qualification tests
    - 6.4 DT&E test report
    - 6.5 Other documentation
    - 6.6 Deliveries
    - 6.7 Configuration audits
    - 6.8 Support for integration testing
7. MANAGEMENT
    - 7.1 Planning
        - 7.1.1 Computer program development plan
        - 7.1.2 System engineering management plan
        - 7.1.3 Configuration management plan
        - 7.1.4 Data management plan
    - 7.2 Periodic status review
    - 7.3 System engineering management
    - 7.4 Configuration management
    - 7.5 Data management
    - 7.6 Schedules
    - 7.7 Maintenance and support
    - 7.8 Cost reporting
    - 7.9 Periodic progress reports

ATCH NR _____ TO EXHIBIT _____
TO CONTRACT/PR _____

CONTRACT DATA REQUIREMENTS LIST
CATEGORY _____

SYSTEM/ITEM _____
CONTRACTOR _____

1. SEQUENCE NUMBER	2. TITLE OR DESCRIPTION OF DATA / 3. SUBTITLE	4. AUTHORITY (Data from Number) / 5. CONTRACT REFERENCE	6. TECHNICAL OFFICE	7. 00250 REQ	8. E.P 600K (A)	9. INPUT 101AC (B)	10. FREQUENCY / 11. AS OF DATE	12. DATE OF 1ST SUBMISSION / 13. DATE OF SUBSEQUENT SUBM/EVENT ID	14. DISTRIBUTION AND ADDRESSEES (Addresses—Regular Copice/Repro Copies)	15. TOTAL
1.	2. Computer Program Development / 3. Specification	4. DI-E-3119 / 5.	6.	7. DD	8. AN	9.	10. 2 TIME / 11.	12. 30DSDR / 13. PREL: 30DCPRR FINAL: 30DPDR REVISED: PCA	14. DRAFT / PREL: / FINAL: / REVISED:	
	16. REMARKS — Specification to be form 1a. Update copy to be identical to final copy except for the incorporation of AF approved changes.									
1.	2. Computer Program Development / 3. Specification	4. DI-E-3120A / 5.	6.	7. DD	8. AN	9.	10. 1 TIME / 11.	12. 30DCDR / 13. PREL: 30DCPTR FINAL: PCA	14. DRAFT: / PREL: / FINAL:	
	16. REMARKS Specification to be form 1a. Draft copy of top level design flowcharts to be delivered 30DPDR. Final copy to be identical to preliminary copy except for the incorporation of AF approved changes.									
1.	2. / 3. (Title from DID)	4. (appropriate DID number) / 5.	6.	7. DD	8. AN	9.	10. 0 TIME / 11.	12. (selected date) / 13. FINAL: (selected date)	14. DRAFT: / FINAL:	
	16. REMARKS									
1.	2. / 3.	4. / 5.	6.	7.	8.	9.	10. / 11.	12. / 13.	14.	
	16. REMARKS									

PREPARED BY | DATE
APPROVED BY | DATE
PAGE _____ OF _____ PAGES

DD FORM 1423
1 JUN

REPLACES EDITION OF 1 APR 68, WHICH IS OBSOLETE'

Fig. 2-3 CDRL form and entries

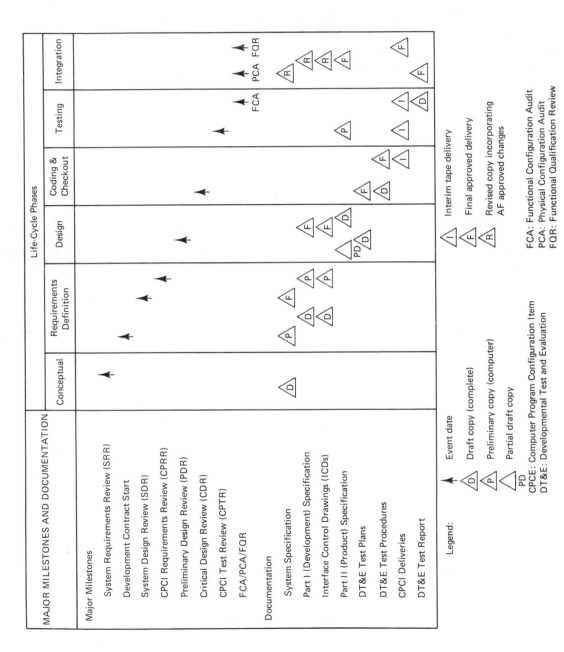

Fig. 2-4 Typical milestone schedule for software development

SELECTION AND NEGOTIATION

Returning to our basic sequence of events in the "buy/sell" pattern, steps 3 through 6 represent the selection and negotiation process. The buyer (the Government in this example) may enter into a dialogue with more than one contractor as part of the selection process and may, in fact, award multiple contracts. A final version of the contents of the contract, derived from the proposal, will be negotiated and agreed upon. This process usually proceeds in parallel with final price negotiations. Primary responsibility for contract negotiation rests with designated members of the contracts offices of both buyer's and seller's organizations. Members of the technical staff are nearly always involved in the process, however, in the roll of supporting "fact finding." This is the process of explaining and justifying the contents of the proposal to the buyer's representatives. Final negotiation results are always influenced by these information exchange sessions. They cover both the technical and management-related items in the proposal. Here again, we see a need for the software engineer, whether he be on the buyer's or seller's side, to possess a working knowledge of management and basic business affairs if he is to participate intelligently in the fact-finding activities. The negotiations are, in effect then, the process of arriving at a final contract statement of work with its associated CDRL, system specification, schedule, and price (step 7). These, not the proposal, are now the official agreements that the contractor must honor. They are the legal basis for the software manager's plans and management actions.

Official agreements, if well conceived, are an asset to both buyer and seller. They represent a first, big step toward eliminating communication problems and misunderstandings; they are the foundation for an effective sequence of product definition and configuration control.

Consider now the development period itself.

2.2.2 THE SOFTWARE LIFE CYCLE

The phrase "software life cycle" became popular in 1975–76. It caught on and has remained in use because it conveys an impression of multiple phases and extended life, for there was a great need to characterize software systems in such a manner. The previously popular conception of computer programs as items that are developed out of someone's head, *coded*, and used for a day or 10 years without change has frustrated most of the people in the industry at one time or another. The facts are, and have been for some time, that coding represents a small percentage of the money and effort spent on a typical software system. One classic model is 40%–20%–40% for analysis/design, coding, and test and integration, respectively. Even the 20% is probably high for most large systems. If the maintenance phase is included, the relative percentage for coding drops to a very low value. So the concept of a life cycle is welcome and realistic because it calls attention to phases other than coding and emphasizes the fact that software systems live a long time.

There are many representations of the life cycle. Each subculture of the software industry has its own (or several) representations, and each of these tends to be modified somewhat for specific projects. We hope that some degree of standardization can be

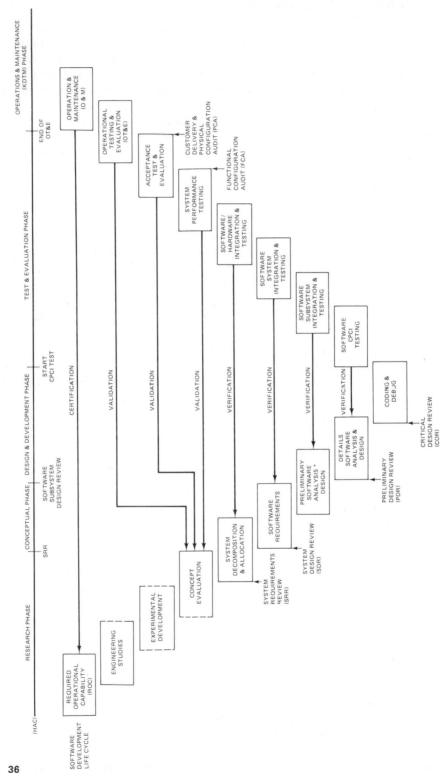

Fig. 2-5 Software life-cycle plan

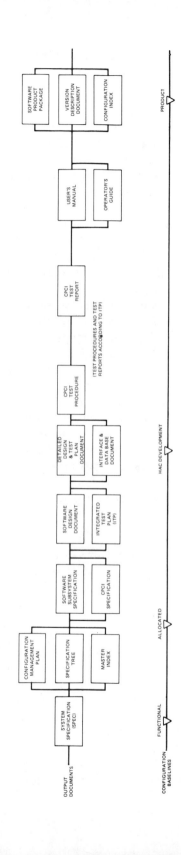

Fig. 2-5 (*cont'd.*) Software life-cycle plan

arrived at before long, at least for purposes of productivity comparisons. In the following subsection, we present an overview of one of the most highly structured life-cycle plans in use in industry today.

PHASES

The basic elements are the same for all life-cycle representations, the differences being in detailed terminology for the most part. Figure 2-4, which we presented as an example of a program plan, shows the phases that are most often referred to; however, for detailed planning it is necessary to break these down into more specific functional activities. Figure 2-5 depicts the basic software life-cycle plan used by Hughes Aircraft Company. It is designed to match Department of Defense procurement practices; however, its generic content is applicable to any large-scale data processing system development. We shall describe only the highlights of this plan, since the remainder of the chapter and several other parts of the book elaborate on the techniques applied in each phase of the plan.

The top line of the plan names the phase that seems most natural for the subphases shown beneath it. The subphases are the real key to this project management scheme. Note that the subphases are arranged in a "V" shape with "Coding & Debug" at the vertex. This format is intended to depict the complementary processes of problem decomposition on the left and system recomposition on the right. Chapters 3, 4, and 5 of this book provide extensive descriptions of both processes. Note also the emphasis on verification and validation (V&V) of the system. As the product is synthesized (recomposed), each step accomplishes either a verification of implementation against a design baseline or, in the later phases, a validation of performance against requirements. Chapter 5 contains a comprehensive discussion of V&V philosophy and techniques. Annotations with small vertical arrows [e.g., System Requirements Review (SSR)] indicate requirements and design review events plus the audits conducted just before delivery. Reviews and audits are discussed in this chapter and in Chapter 5.

OUTPUT DOCUMENTS

The line near the bottom of Figure 2-5 marked "Output Documents" displays the primary CDRL items required for most developments. The System Specification (SPEC) is the same document as the Procurement Specification listed in Figure 2-2. Its contents are proposed and negotiated as part of the "buy/sell" sequence, and it is the product definition to which the contractor adheres. Here we can now pick up where we left off in the previous section (2.2.1 Procurement Mechanics).

Looking to the top left subphase block of Figure 2-5, we see that some boxes are shown that precede the SPEC in time (ROC, Engineering Studies, Experimental Development). These represent contractor activities that sometimes takes place prior to award of a development contract. They are funded studies that are oriented toward establishing product feasibility or toward specific contract definition.

In our full development contract example, the contract award takes place sometimes during the Concept Evaluation; then the first significant technical event in the contractor's performance is the Systems Requirements Review (SRR). Contents of System Specification (SPEC) are the subject of this review. Changes to the SPEC may or may not result. The primary purpose of this and all reviews is to sustain buyer/seller understanding and agreement.

Moving along the Output Documents line of Figure 2-5, we can see that design documents provide the material for the Software System Design Review (SDR), Preliminary Design Reviews (PDRs) and Critical Design Reviews (CDRs) shown above. Near the end of the development cycle, the various test results and essentially all other documentation are the subject of the Functional Configuration Audit (FCA). The Physical Configuration Audit (PCA) is merely an accounting for all physical deliverable materials: that is, the tapes, cards, documents, etc., that are the physical product. Other documents indicated on the output documents line of the chart are described briefly below and are explained in more detail in Section 2.2.3.

Configuration Management Plan—a description of the methods the contractor will use to control requirements definitions, designs, the computer programs themselves, test results, and documentation within his own house.

Specification Tree—lower level specifications that result from decomposing the System Specification into requirements and design information for the major system components, including hardware. These are the basis for the SDR.

Master Index—an equipment list for the system.

Software Subsystem Specification—design specifications for the software components of the system. A further decomposition of the system design problem.

CPCI Specification—Computer Program Configuration Item (CPCI) identification. CPCIs are the entities that will be tracked by configuration control. They may be routines, programs, groups of programs, or the entire software subsystem (if it is small). The purpose of identifying CPCIs is to provide a convenient way to control and account for the software components by aggregating the many parts into a relatively small number of packages. The aggregate of CPCIs is the software system.

Software Design Document—design specification for an individual software program, module, or routine. It is the basis for the PDR for that component.

Integrated Test Plan (ITP)—the master plan for all software tests.

Detailed Design and Test Plan Document—further decomposition of the Software Design Document. This is the "build-to" and "test-to" description of the individual component. It is the basis for the CDR.

Interface and Data Base Document—a detailed description of all controlled interfaces within the software system and between the system and its platform environment. It is usually a computer output listing, since interface control is usually mechanized. All data base definitions are handled in the same manner.

CPCI Test Procedures—detailed instructions for carrying out the acceptance test of each CPCI.

CPCI Test Report—detailed description of the results of testing each CPCI.

User's Manual and Operator's Guide—detailed instructions for use of the system in the operational environment. The User and the Operator are generally different people than any who have been directly engaged in developing the product.

Software Product Package—the physical product.

Version Description Documents—the "as built" description of each CPCI and individual software component. These are very detailed and typically voluminous.

Configuration Index—an accounting of the individual items that constitute the product.

BASELINES

If we look now at the bottom line in Figure 2-5, we see "Configuration Baselines." The general definition of a baseline is a reference. The triangles on this line represent points at which the software system definition is formally reviewed, agreed upon, and published as the new reference. It serves as the basis of understanding across the entire population of interested parties: that is, the developers, analysts, customers, and the eventual users. Changes to baselines are accomplished only through a formal change control process or a formal transition to a new baseline level.

Configuration baseline levels shown on this chart represent the minimum number that would be expected on a project of any substantial size. Others can be and are added on specific projects, depending on particular conditions. The number of configuration levels to be baselined is established by considering the tradeoff between the control and visibility gained versus the time and cost expended to conduct formal reviews and update baseline documents.

2.2.3 THE PROJECT PLAN

We have seen that it is necessary to draft project planning material for the proposal and fact-finding phases of a typical software procurement. When the time comes to actually implement the project, these plans must be solidified and made consistent with the final negotiated form of the contract, and they must be augmented with internal coordination agreements and procedures. We have touched upon some planning documents in overviewing the software life cycle; we now present a more comprehensive rundown of the components of a complete project plan. A brief synopsis of the contents of each part of the project plan is given. This overview represents a summary of the basic subjects with which the project planner must come to grips.

Not all elements of the plans indicated are necessary for all projects; in fact, it is one of the tasks of management to select which aspects of the activity will be formally planned and controlled and which will be informal or ad hoc. The selection criteria are simply the necessity versus the cost. In general, formality costs effort, time, and money; if it is not necessary, it should not be exercised. On the other hand, lack of formal planning and/or controls carries the risk of anarchy and chaos. These can easily lead to problems that are far more expensive than the controls that would have prevented them. The judgments are, in principle, the management's to make, although in most procurements of any magnitude, at least some elements of the plan are dictated by the buyer/customer.

PURPOSE OF THE PLAN

The project plan serves primarily as a coordination document. It is the project manager's message to all concerned that he intends to organize and manage as described in the plan, and it is an appeal (or a directive) for cooperation. The plan is the most effective way he can provide to all those who must work in concert with him a reference document that can serve as a guide for their own decisions and actions. For this reason it is quite important that the plan be clear and complete, and changes to it should be controlled and distributed with care. The project plan for a medium- or large-scale software development is like the written score for a symphony orchestra. It is necessary that all players understand their parts if the performance is to be a success.

ELEMENTS OF THE PLAN

Two notes on terminology are in order here before proceeding to the material that follows. Our term "project plan" is generic. A typical procurement calls for a *set* of plans related to specific aspects of the project, and we shall refer to them separately in the material below. The set, however, taken all together represents the total project plan as we refer to it. Secondly, the context of "procurement" should be put in perspective. Our examples and general theme of project characteristics are indeed drawn from the government-procured and contractor-produced arena, but this fact does not limit any of the concepts or techniques presented. Any software project that is required to produce a usable product and to account for the time, money, and resources spent in doing so will have the same characteristics as we describe. Direct analogies between formal, contractual procurements and other forms of agreements can usually be found by inspection. The plan outlined below, then, applies to all software development projects. It covers all aspects of the life cycle described above.

Scope and Applicable Documents—a brief statement of the purpose of the plan and identification of all documents that either serve as authority for the plan or are incorporated by reference.

Technical Description of the System—an overview of the system to be built and a description of its capabilities. This is not a specification or a complete design. It is a description complete enough to provide a basis for understanding the remainder of the plan.

Configuration Items and Deliverables—descriptions of the programs, subsystems, etc., that have been specified as configuration items: that is, entities to be placed under configuration control. The place and function of each within the system are explained. A list of specific deliverable items is given.

Organization Plan—one of the larger and more important components of the plan. It shows the project organization chart and explains the charter, roles, and responsibilities of each organizational element. It also details arrangements and agreements with other organizations within the company or agency. It details subcontracting plans and arrangements.

Methodology—a summary of the practices, standards, and techniques to be employed in developing the product. These are essentially technical items such as programming language and allowable logical control structures. Program development methods include structuring techniques and the like, documentation conventions, internal design review procedures (e.g., walk throughs), interface specification standards, etc. This section is also used as a catch-all for quality assurance items that do not fit in other parts of the plan.

Configuration Management Plan—also a substantial part of the overall plan. It describes in detail how the requirements, specifications, design, source code, test plans, and test procedures for each configuration item will be controlled. The point in the schedule where each document or program goes under control is specified. Procedures for changing configured items are described, including the paperwork, approval authority, and approval rationale. Responsibilities for all aspects of the Configuration Management operation are delineated.

Documentation Plan—all documents that will be produced are identified and their contents described. A schedule for release and delivery is shown. Internal review and coordination control procedures are described.

Data Management Plan—in this context "data" refers to information supplied by the contractor to the customer. It includes the technical documents identified in the Documentation Plan, but it also includes much more, namely, everything in the CDRL list previously mentioned. The CDRL calls for financial, status, and logistical information, as well as the technical plans and reports. The Data Management Plan describes how all of this information will be collected, formatted, and transmitted.

Resources Management Plan—identification of the resources that will be required and the manner in which they will be utilized. The manpower plan is included, as are those resources needed for computer utilization, test equipment, and other facilities. This is obviously one of the most critical of the plans and requires considerable, careful effort to prepare. These are the resources that will be characterized as energy in the energy/entropy concepts presented in Sec. 2.3.

Integrated Test Plan—the master plan for all testing and integration. It contains a test versus system requirements traceability matrix, subsystem and system integration sequences, test problem reporting procedures, error correction procedures, and acceptance criteria.

Training Plan—the means and the schedule by which users of the system will be trained in its operation and maintenance.

Security Plan—a very important matter for today's systems. Two kinds of security are involved here: national security matters and secure system features.

Requirements for safeguarding information related to our national defense are imposed by the Government where appropriate. The contractor's security plan is a description of the methods that will be employed to comply with those requirements.

The second security consideration is related to the characteristics of the system itself. If the system is required to protect data during its operation (e.g., credit data, personnel information, classified technical data), then the design information should probably be protected because an individual who is intimately familiar with the design may learn how to defeat its secure operating mode features. The Security Plan should include a discussion of measures designed to prevent such leaks. Chapter 6 of this volume is devoted to the subject of security and computers.

Schedule—or "program plan," should not be confused with "project plan" as we are using it here. The schedule or "program plan" is a set of diagrams showing where in time all important project events take place. Milestones, reviews, key meetings, audits, documentation releases, product deliveries are all indicated on a series of calendarized charts. This is one of the most used of all the planning documents—by all parties involved—and it represents the project's commitment to perform at a specified pace. The schedule must obviously be tightly coordinated with all other plans.

This completes our descriptive overview of a software project. We have shown where various activities fit into the procurement and life cycle phases, and we have identified the planning items that the proposal writer and software manager must address. We move now into a discussion of the planning and management philosophy that is the basis for our integrated management approach.

2.3
Project Planning and Management Philosophy

One of the most effective software development managers we have ever encountered once revealed part of the reason for his success with this statement:

> It's knowing ahead of time where the trouble is going to come from that makes the difference. When I take on a development job, I analyze the task and the situation until I'm convinced I have identified the likely problem areas and have established their relative severity; then I feel comfortable about organizing the resources and planning my management approach.[9]

It is not an unusual statement for a successful manager in any line of endeavor to make. Why is the experienced manager, or planner, or proposal writer more effective than an inexperienced colleague—no matter how brilliant? The first-order answer is: "Because he knows what it takes to do the job." Correct as far as it goes. But the inexperienced estimator can specify the resources that *should* be required to carry out a task if he uses the recorded experience of others and some generalized estimating guidelines. Yet, we all have the feeling that these estimates and plans will very likely be much less reliable than those of the person who has been through it all before. What is the real difference? The answer is implied in the quote above. It is the ability of the successful manager to structure the task realistically, and to structure the project activities such that applied resources *match* the task requirements at all levels. The concept is illustrated below with the aid of a simple analogy.

We arbitrarily define three levels of awareness in project planning and management for purposes of the following discussion. They are most easily explained in terms of ability to assess the type, amount, and structure of resources that will be required to complete a project successfully. A first-level planner would define the resources needed to accomplish a task of the general nature of that presented to him under near-ideal conditions. This corresponds to a success-oriented view that assumes highly efficient application of all resources, no downstream changes in assumed task definitions, and no mistakes. A second-level analysis would take some account of the uncertainties and inefficiencies that are unavoidable facts of life in all project environments. These include effects as obvious as lunch hours, vacations, sick leaves, terminations, training time, etc.; they include some not so obvious factors such as suspect system specifications, physical logistics, computer time limitations, long lead constraints on equipment, or manpower acquisition, etc.; and finally a "pad" would

[9]Norman Alperin, Hughes Aircraft Company. Private communication.

be included in cost and schedule estimates as a contingency against "all those things that might go wrong." This is second-level planning.

Third-level planning encompasses the first two and also includes an *analysis* of "all those things that might go wrong." The analysis is based on experience with similar situations. The third level of awareness makes it possible to recognize potential risk areas and trouble spots as the task and resource characteristics are defined. This, in turn, makes it possible to apply resources and management methods that are explicitly matched to the total task as it will actually manifest itself.

The experienced manager, then, operates at level three while the inexperienced person uses level one or two techniques and tries to guess at (and sell) the contingency fund pad that will be required to accommodate unexpected developments and problems. The first- or second-level planner is actually pushing part of his management task ahead of him, counting on his ability to recognize, manage, and pay for solutions to problems and new developments as they arise. There are two fundamental disadvantages with this approach: (1) some problems will be partially or completely insoluble by the time they are recognized, and (2) the contingency fund is seldom adequate.

Most software development planning today is done at level two as described here. This is an improvement over the typical first-level approach of just a few years ago, but it still leaves much to be desired. We should be drafting more comprehensive, better coordinated, more intelligent plans if the efficiency of development efforts is to keep pace with the growing size and complexity of the systems that are required.

To illustrate the concept of structuring both task and resources, the level three approach, let us examine a simple analogy involving a clerical filing system. Figure 2-6 shows how three clerical filing systems A, B, and C would appear if they were set up with methods analogous to our first-, second-, and third-level planning approaches, respectively. Note that the miscellaneous files in systems A and B expand beyond planned size.

With first-level planning, there will almost certainly be a large unplanned expansion in effort required (the miscellaneous file), and the contingency resource "pad" will be grossly inadequate. At the second level the effect is still present, but not so disastrous. With third-level planning, the miscellaneous file is present, but it is small and remains small, just as it would be in a well-conceived filing system. Just as the businessman and secretary who know their business can establish an effective filing system, so the software project manager who knows his business can thoroughly and precisely define his task. In each case they categorize and structure the material to be handled in such a way that a human can interact with it in an efficient manner. In a clerical file the material is simply filed papers; in software development it is the detailed set of tasks and activities to be performed.

To carry the analogy further, let us assume that numerous people are required to use the clerical file every day. The process of accessing the file and handling its contents will go smoother and remain more stable generally if the task assignments of each individual and the file structure are matched so that an individual works primarily with one small part of the file, rather than across its entire extent. In this way the individual becomes familiar with the contents of that part of the file, acquires a feeling for its accuracy, and develops some responsibility for its integrity. The efficiency of the human/file operation and the condition of the file contents are both improved by

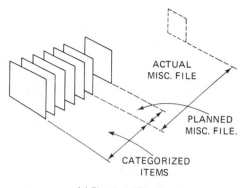

(a) First Level Planning

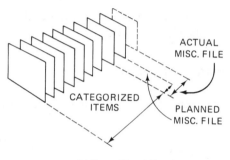

(b) Second Level Planning

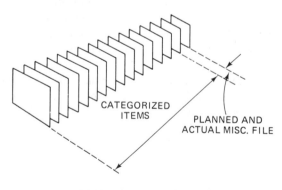

(c) Third Level Planning

Fig. 2-6 Clerical file analogy

matching file structure to individual task assignments. In more general terms, the concept is to structure both components of the interactive process in such a way that the operation can proceed with maximum efficiency.

Now the problems associated with a large miscellaneous part of a file are even clearer. All parties must access it to search for pertinent information and, as it grows (as in the Figure 2-6 A and B systems), human task assignments and responsibilities must be modified and added. This is a disruptive and expensive process because it induces confusion, wasted motion, and mistakes.

Carrying the analogy one step further, we can imagine up to 100 people trying to use the clerical file each day. The A system with its growing, unstructured miscellaneous mess would soon induce chaos, while the C system would be conducive to an efficient operation. The B system falls somewhere in between.

We will later refer to situations such as that induced by first-level planning (the A system example) as "high entropy processes," while third-level planning (the well-structured C system) will be associated with "low entropy." Obviously the third-level approach is the desirable one; we feel it is today feasible and appropriate. Third-level management consists of structuring the task and the resources to the maximum extent possible, and at the earliest time possible, and then controlling the interaction of resources and task so as to minimize the dissipation of resources,—to minimize the entropy.

The remainder of this chapter is devoted to further description of this "entropy control" approach and to its implementation.

2.3.1 ENTROPY IN THE SOFTWARE LIFE CYCLE

We now define *entropy* and describe how it plays a central role in the software development process.

ENERGY AND ENTROPY DEFINED

The entropy parameter, due to nineteenth-century thermodynamicists, is one of the most elegant contributions to science and engineering. Entropy is one of the most profound and yet, outside the field of thermodynamics, one of our least understood engineering concepts. Its broad and fundamental significance is elegantly stated in a quotation by Robert Emden that has stood the test of time:

> As a student, I read with advantage a small book by F. Wald entitled "The Mistress of the World and Her Shadow." These meant energy and entropy. In the course of advancing knowledge, the two seem to me to have exchanged places. In the huge manufactory of natural processes, the principle of entropy occupies the position of managing, for it dictates the manner and method of the whole business, whilst the principle of energy merely does the bookkeeping, balancing credits and debits.[10]

In other words, the entropy effect is present in *all* natural processes and, in a fundamental sense, dominates them.

Entropy is a concept just as energy is a concept. We feel comfortable with the word energy because we can relate it to physical processes that we feel we understand. The swinging pendulum of a grandfather clock provides a convenient vehicle for illustrating potential and kinetic energy, for example; and the gyroscope's motion, though more difficult to characterize, is an observable example of the principle of conservation

[10]R. Emden, "Why Do We Have Winter Heating," *Nature*, **141**, May 1938, p. 908.

of angular momentum, which is easily related to energy. Even Professor Einstein's equation for the total energy represented by a physical mass:

$$e = mc^2$$

is comprehensible because we feel we know what energy is.

To get to know what *entropy* is, let us first adopt a simplistic definition:

Entropy is associated with a process; it is the measure of difference between the value of energy input to a process and the value of the products that issue from it,

$$e_i = w + s$$

where e_i = input energy

w = external work performed (products)

s = entropy

Figure 2-7 is a schematic representation.

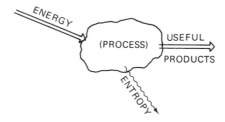

Fig. 2-7 Simplified definition of entropy

For many engineering applications, this definition is adequate. What it fails to convey, however, is the inevitability of the entropy effect and the nature of the measures required to control it. It will be necessary for us to have some feeling for this inevitability and to be familiar with the mechanisms of entropy generation if the relationship of the principle to software project management is to be clear. To this end, we present in the next few paragraphs a brief overview of the entropy principle in the context where it was developed: that is, physical science and, in particular, thermodynamics. With this foundation, it will be possible to find direct analogies in the software life-cycle process.

The word *entropy* is not used much outside a few physical engineering disciplines. Why is it such an unfamiliar concept to most of us? There are two generic reasons. The first, and most important for the purposes of this discussion, is that it represents the unavailable energy in a physical system; and since most of engineering is concerned with managing the available energy, the entropy function gets much less attention. Second, we give special names to particular forms of entropy. Let us consider the grandfather clock example again. The weights are elevated early one morning, adding a given amount of energy to the system, which we will take to be the clock and its immediate surroundings. At the same time the next morning (or the next week), the weights have descended to the point where they were initially, and more energy must be added if the operation of the clock is to be sustained. Our model of conservation of energy (the pendulum) has not conserved it at all. The total energy of the physical clock is the same as it was 24 hours before, and the energy added by raising the weights has disappeared. The engineering explanation is quite simple and familiar to all of us. We say that the energy has dissipated through friction; it heats up the clock mechanism slightly, and the heat in turn disappears into the surrounding atmosphere. For purposes of understanding the energy aspects of grandfather clocks, this explanation is usually adequate. If we are going to build one, we concentrate on minimizing the friction of the bearings and gear interactions, and that is the extent of our concern with the entropy function. However, if we are dealing with processes more complex than the clock, it is useful to delve into the more general concept because the entropy function takes on many forms, some of which are much more subtle than a simple friction mechanism.

There is one more important point that the clock can contribute before we leave it. The energy added each day by raising the weights is in turn converted to entropy, and the clock itself returns in 24 hours to its previous energy state. The sequence is repeated daily. Because we are energy oriented, we are inclined to say the system requires a daily addition of energy. But the net effect of the cycle is not an addition of energy to the clock; if it were, the clock would grow warmer and warmer, or larger and larger, or somehow manifest its monotonically increasing energy state. This doesn't happen, of course, and the explanation is that over one or more complete cycles of the sequence, the net effect of our interaction with the clock system is the addition of entropy. All of the energy added is converted to an unavailable state. The only useful products of the process are the information given by the position of the hands on the face of the clock, and the slow, pleasant tick, tock. When the clock stops, there is no residual useful product.

The point is this: as we apply the entropy concept to software engineering functions we will do well to maintain a certain perspective; though we will be associating entropy with negative effects (losses, inefficiencies, etc.), we should also be aware that some necessary processes must be sustained by the continuous, deliberate addition of entropy.

Now let us provide more insight into the general nature of the entropy principle. Given below is a mix of physical laws, definitions, and equivalences that, in concert with the examples already given, should make the reader more comfortable with the notion of entropy in physical systems.

Paraphasing the laws of thermodynamics:

1. The first law:

> Every thermodynamic system possesses a characteristic property (parameter of state) —its energy. The energy of the system is increased by the quantity of heat, dQ, absorbed by it, and decreased by the external work, dW, performed. In an isolated system the total amount of energy is preserved.

In effect this says there is a certain amount of energy in a system, and some, or in principle all, of it can be converted to external work. In other words, for an ideal system and process, the useful work out can be *equal to* the energy in, it can never be greater. In real systems the useful work output is always less than the energy input per the Second Law below.

2. The second law:

All thermodynamic systems possess a property that is called entropy. It is calculated by imagining that the state of the system is changed from an arbitrarily selected reference state to the actual state through a sequence of states of equilibrium and by summing up the quotients of the quantities of heat dQ introduced at each step and the "absolute temperature" T; the latter is defined simultaneously in this connection. During real (nonideal) processes, the entropy of an isolated system increases.

We needn't go deep into the significance of the equilibrium states and the dQ and T ratios. It will suffice for our purposes to imagine an interactive process taking place within a system, which results in a series of changes of the states of that system; e.g., the clock running down or the human/file interaction. As the system passes from one state to another, not all of the energy introduced (dQ) is retained in a recoverable form (T). Some of the energy is transformed into a nonrecoverable form. This "unavailable energy" is the entropy of the system. It always increases as any real interactive process takes place. The second law says, in effect, that the useful work out is always *less than* the energy in. (See Figure 2-7.)

3. The second law has many ramifications. One of the most quoted is:

It is impossible to design a perpetual motion engine of the second kind, i.e., one that would work periodically and would cause no other changes except the lifting of a weight and the cooling of a heat reservoir.

The key to understanding this is the phrase "no other changes." For any real system, "other changes" such as frictional effects or heat loss would indeed take place.

4. The microscopic point of view of entropy brings us closer to a direct analogy with the problems of organizing and managing a software development effort (or any team effort):

Random motion of individual molecules against intermolecular forces does not constitute work. Work (i.e., output work) requires order or orderly motion. When input energy is dissipated into internal energy, the disorderly motion of molecules is increased. This is the natural direction of a *spontaneous* interactive process. The system proceeds toward a state of maximum entropy. It is possible to regard all physical processes as taking part in this trend and, therefore, to conclude that there is a tendency on the part of nature to proceed toward a condition of greater disorder.

5. Entropy in nature, then, is directly related to such things as:

Friction and resistance
Heat loss
Turbulence
Random motion and disorder

Corresponding effects in the human realm are:

>Uncooperativeness
>Incoherence
>Confusion
>Undirected or misdirected action

We shall discuss these human-related effects extensively as we apply the entropy concept to software management.

To summarize, then, the energy input to an interactive process in a system is converted to work output plus entropy. *Entropy is the energy that is dissipated during a process and is not available to contribute to the work.* Every real interactive process generates some amount of entropy. The amount of entropy generated by a system is proportional to the amount of random motion or disorder in that system.

THE SOFTWARE DEVELOPMENT INTERACTIVE PROCESS

The software life cycle represents a process. It includes transforming concepts and desires into a real, operable software system and then operating it. We separate development and operational phases for purposes of this discussion because the planning and management problems, though definitely related, are somewhat different in detail. This discussion deals primarily with development.

The development process is actually a *series* of transformations or changes of state. The original entities (concepts and desires) are changed into a state we call system requirements; these are further transformed into a design that is then implemented in the form of computer programs. A test and integration process then qualifies the code as an operational entity. Documentation follows a parallel sequence of changes of state and becomes part of the final product. The similarity between this language and that of the second law of thermodynamics, quoted earlier, should be apparent. To carry the analogy further, consider Figure 2-8, which represents the software life cycle as a system in which an interactive process takes place. Five "changes of state" are shown for purposes of this discussion; however, this system represents the full life cycle, no matter how many subphases are defined. (This discussion can be applied equally well to the life-cycle chart shown in Figure 2-5).

Consider the design phase as an example. The requirements developed in the definition phase are brought forward to the design process. Resources[11] are applied to the requirements statements for the purpose of transforming them into a design. (In Figure 2-8 we have not shown the requirements-to-design-specification step; it is a subprocess included in the process shown.) The interaction of resources with the subject material—the requirements in this case—is the process of interest. There are many specific interactions taking place, of course. The resources simultaneously interact among themselves, with the project staff and management, the customer, the user, and support facilities, etc., all taking part. In our analogy with a physical process, the resources represent the input energy, but it is important to realize that in the case of

---

[11]"Resources" as used in this chapter, is defined to mean the totality of expendables that are used to carry out the software development process. They include facilities, manpower, computer time, calendar time, and money.

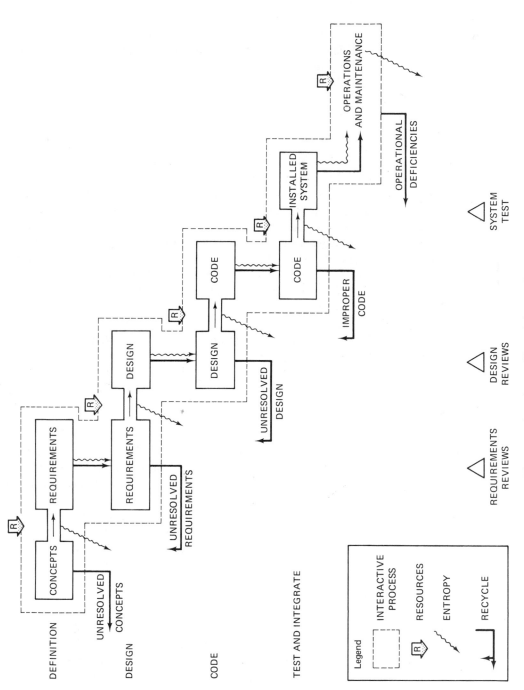

Fig. 2-8 The software life-cycle interactive process

DEFINITION

DESIGN

CODE

TEST AND INTEGRATE

CONCEPTS

UNRESOLVED
CONCEPTS

REQUIREMENTS

REQUIREMENTS

UNRESOLVED
REQUIREMENTS

DESIGN

DESIGN

UNRESOLVED
DESIGN

CODE

CODE

IMPROPER
CODE

INSTALLED
SYSTEM

OPERATIONS
AND MAINTENANCE

OPERATIONAL
DEFICIENCIES

REQUIREMENTS
REVIEWS

DESIGN
REVIEWS

SYSTEM
TEST

Legend

INTERACTIVE
PROCESS

RESOURCES

ENTROPY

RECYCLE

a software project there are multiple sources of energy, each of which interacts with all others.

What are the products of the process? Four lines are shown emerging. In a traditional concept of the software development activity, only one would be shown: the straight line connecting the two DESIGN boxes. This would represent a straight feed-forward action with no accounting for redesigns, errors, omission, inefficiencies, or causes of entropy. The other lines shown are associated with entropy effects that we will describe below.

Effective planning and management require that we account for the fact that we are dealing with real people who are not perfectly efficient. Because the activity is a real interactive physical process, we can be certain that feedbacks and entropy will be among the products of the activity, just as surely as they are in physical systems, as stated by the second law of thermodynamics.

The feedback arrows represent that part of the requirements statement that is not transformable into design. The failure to transform may be due to inconsistencies among the requirements; it may be caused by requirements that do not lend themselves to design or are deemed too expensive to meet, or it may be due to a gap in requirements that is identified in the design process. Feedback—or recycling to earlier phases—is not at all uncommon in software development; in the case of large or complex systems, some of it is inevitable. But it is an expensive, high-entropy effect, and project planners and managers strive to minimize it.

The slanted wavy lines and the feedback arrows all represent the forms of the energy lost to entropy, energy that does not contribute to the product of this phase. The feedback problem mentioned just above is one source of entropy for the following reason. The design phase, for example, is planned and organized for the design effort. The individuals assigned to tasks are there because they are design oriented; they are on a schedule to produce design documents, and they assume, at least to a first approximation, that the requirements presented to them are valid. When this operation encounters incoherence in the requirements set, some degree of turbulence is introduced. All aspects of the design already worked out must be verified and perhaps changed; confidence in the requirements work is lowered, and, in general, the efficiency and momentum of the design phase is reduced. Wasted time and effort result. Disorder has been induced.

Each phase of development suffers from this same general effect. The product of the previous phase is not perfectly complete and accurate, and the imperfections introduce a degree of disorder, or entropy, as they are discovered and addressed. This aspect of the development process, incomplete changes of state, is indicated by the vertical wavy line parallel to each output product line. We can think of this phenomenon as "carrying entropy forward" or perhaps "entropy on its way to happen" in some later phase.

The amount of entropy that is eventually generated is a function of the phase or phases in which it surfaces and of the length of the associated feedback loop. The later the phase where an error or omission is discovered, the more expensive it is to correct; also the greater the number of phase processes that must be recycled, the greater the total entropy generated. Therefore, a coding error discovered in the coding phase is relatively easy to fix. A requirements problem uncovered in the coding phase is significantly more expensive because it introduces considerable entropy in the coding activity itself, and because the definition and design processes must be repeated to patch up the unresolved requirement area.

Several investigations have been conducted into the actual cost of correcting problems as a function of the phase in which they are corrected. Two very useful papers on the subject are by Fagan of IBM[12] and Boehm of TRW.[13] The cost figures they show represent a direct measure of the amount of entropy induced by each type of error. Recognition of the cost of entropy effects, and especially the "entropy forward" problem, is now causing increased emphasis on validation and verification activities for each phase of development. (See Chapter 5, this volume.)

Our model of the software life cycle is now established. We shall think of it as a system in which a highly complex, highly interactive process takes place. This "system" consists of the total environment in which the software project exists, including the facilities, computers, the buying customer, ultimate product user, managers, analysts, designers, programmers, test engineers, administrative support people, and all other people and things that have a significant involvement in the project. And it includes the task.

The process that takes place in this system is the interaction of the active constituents (the resources) with the task *and* with each other. This interactive process results in the transformation of the initial task statement, through a series of states, into an operational software system. By direct analogy to physical system processes and the second law of thermodynamics, we conclude that the software development interactive process does induce entropy. The primary objectives of software management are to identify the causes of entropy in the system and to control them effectively.

2.3.2 SUMMARY OF THE ENTROPY MANAGEMENT APPROACH

We have now characterized the objectives of software development management in terms of one parameter, entropy. It is the goal of management to minimize the total integral of entropy in the system depicted in Figure 2-8. This requires that each phase be planned and managed with all interactions within that phase *and with all other phases* in mind. Finding the best management solution is analogous to solving a system of simultaneous differential equations; the answer is found by addressing the total intradependent system, not the individual parts. Local optimization of a software development subprocess may not (in fact, usually does not) contribute to a reduction of the total entropy integral. A simple example familiar to all of us will serve to illustrate this point.

Assume we are in the coding phase and that one staff member has a strong preference for coding in assembly language versus any higher-order language. He is an excellent designer and coder in his preferred mode, and we know that he can complete

---

[12]M. E. Fagan, "Design and Code Inspections and Process Control in the Development of Programs," *IBM Report IBM-500 TR-21.572*, December 1974.

[13]B. W. Boehm, "Software Engineering," *IEEE Transactions on Computers*, **C-25**, 12, December 1976.

his programming tasks more quickly and more accurately if he is allowed to operate in that mode. But the remainder of the system is being written with a higher-order, structured language approach; furthermore, the system is deliverable to an outside organization (it is a product), so maintainability is a significant consideration. Permitting the use of assembly language in this situation would amount to local optimization of a subprocess with the net effect of *increasing* the total entropy of the system. Specifically, we would be reducing the entropy associated with the interactions between this particular programmer and his task, and between him and his management; but we would be inducing entropy into many other interactions that take place during coding and subsequent phases.

During the coding phase, for example, we may wish to apply "walk throughs" or "peer group reviews" as part of our quality assurance method. These are practices that call for programmers to critique each other's work for accuracy and consistency with other parts of the system. It will probably be difficult for others to understand the assembly language code because they are oriented toward the higher-order language, and it is likely that our assembly language coder has incorporated some "neat tricks" that save a few compute cycles. The explanation of these short cuts and the verification that they do indeed work as desired will also require extra time and effort by other members of the staff.

In subsequent phases, this code is likely to cause entropy. If there are bugs in it, or even if bugs are suspected, we will have the same problem of spending extra effort to dig into the code and verify its integrity. This must be done manually, whereas automated tools are available to assist in analyzing higher-order language code. We have therefore introduced entropy into the test phase by something we did in the coding phase. This is a specific example of the "entropy forward" effect. Carrying this example one step further, visualize what happens when the product system is in operation or in the maintenance phase. If changes are required in the assembly language part of the code, the same problems arise, and we have induced more entropy. Documentation for this part of the system will also differ in some ways and will require special attention both when it is written and when it is used.

The entropy management question is simply: "Which is greater, the entropy avoided by using this coding or the entropy induced thereby in other processes?" Or: "Which course of action will cause minimum entropy throughout the total system and over the complete life of the system?" This is the essence of entropy management. In this particular example the entropy induced in the long run by the assembly language code would far exceed that avoided by indulging the individual coder's desires at the time of coding.[14]

Entropy management then implies the ability to anticipate high entropy interactions in order to avoid them. We proceed now to a discussion of specific causes of entropy in a software life-cycle system and the use of modern tools and methods for managing and controlling entropy.

[14]It has been typical experience in the aerospace industry that assembly language code is four times as expensive to maintain as are higher-order languages.

2.4
Causes and Control of Entropy

This section surveys the most prevalent causes of entropy in the software cycle, groups them according to characteristics that are meaningful to a project manager, and outlines the important methods available for dealing with each group. The discussion of sources covers all phases of software development; however, the methods discussion emphasizes project planning and structuring only. Chapters 3, 4, and 5 deal with design, programming, and validation/verification functions, and these chapters present fully detailed descriptions of effective and efficient methods for carrying out those phases of the software cycle.

As we attempt to identify the causes of entropy in the software life-cycle system, it is convenient to consider two distinct classes. The first includes causes that must be accepted because they are directly related to inalienable values. Vacations, sick leave, normal lunch hours, morale functions, personal telephone calls, and restroom visits are examples. Some level of control over the time and expense associated with these causes must be exercised to prevent their abuse, but basically these forms of entropy are expected and accepted. If we recall the grandfather clock example, we can see the direct analogy. We willingly add to the system energy that we know will be transformed to entropy, and we do not try to prevent it. Just as with the clock, we have concluded *a priori* that this type of entropy is required to sustain operation of the system. We call this type 1 entropy and analyze it no further, because it is not a problem in software management per se.

Type 2 entropy *is* a problem for software management; in fact, it is convenient to think of *all* software management problems in terms of *its* causes and control. Type 2 entropy is that which is induced by causes that need not be accepted.

The generic causes of type 2 entropy were introduced in a very brief fashion in the section on Energy and Entropy Defined, where we said:

Entropy in nature, then, is directly related to such things as:

> Friction and resistance
> Heat loss
> Turbulence
> Random motion

The corresponding effects in the human realm are:

> Uncooperativeness
> Incoherence
> Confusion
> Undirected or misdirected action

When these "human realm" effects manifest themselves we experience entropy in the software system. Every condition, situation, and activity that causes these effects is a source of type 2 entropy, and should be the object of management attention.

To attempt to identify *all* such sources in detail would be palpably foolish. There is an infinite number. But we can list specific causes and look for common characteristics among them. If we are able to find a few common characteristics, they will serve as warning flags to the software manager as he or she plans and manages the project.

Perhaps the most meaningful way to do this is to approach it from a quality-assurance point of view. Imagine for a moment that we are responsible for conducting quality-assurance audits of software development projects. Our job is to review and evaluate the approach, the methods, the status, and the prognosis for success of each of a large number of real software projects. We record what we find in each case, and then we summarize and classify the results. If we did perform such a survey in the role of quality-assurance auditors, we would generate, among other things, a list of "common problem areas." These are symptoms and conditions that recur with conspicuous frequency in nearly all project environments and that seem to affect the quality of the software product and/or the cost and schedule performance of the project team adversely.

In fact, such surveys have been conducted, in one form or another, and some results are available, although few are published. A digest of the available information is given in Table 2-2.

The individual items in Table 2-2 show up as specific problems and failings. It is an imposing list. In our model we can think of them as specific causes of entropy. They induce confusion and disorder. We may well ask: "Are these all present in a typical project, or is this an aggregation of all problems found on all projects?" The answer is more the former than the latter. Most of these failings plus others can be found, to one degree or another, on all software projects. The degree of severity varies, to be sure, with the type of project and with the competence of the management and staff, but the point is that there are many individual causes of entropy—type 2 entropy— and they all contribute, even in the best managed projects.

Assessing the seriousness of an individual cause is a formidable task. How, then, does a manager identify the significant causes of entropy in his particular project, and how does he select the mechanisms he will use to control the level of entropy induced by each? Further examination and interpretation of Table 2-2 leads to workable answers.

Looking at the items in group A in Table 2-2, we see that these represent the problem of matching the amount of resources to the size of the task. Failure to provide an adequate level of resource energy will clearly result in an incomplete or unacceptable product. We recall the *first* law of thermodynamics here: the useful products (work) out of a system (process) are equal to no more than the energy input. In fact, as we have seen, the input energy must be equivalent to the sum of output products plus entropy. An underfunded or poorly scheduled project inevitably requires replanning and reorganizing at some point late in the schedule. Work that has already been done will be partially wasted; roles and responsibilities must be altered; morale is affected, and, in general, the rate of entropy generation increases dramatically. It is seldom possible to salvage a poorly funded or poorly scheduled project by adding extra resources after such a project is in trouble. Assimilation of the new resources is a high entropy process; hence, the net effect of adding them may be *negative*, at least

Table 2-2 Common Causes of Entropy

Group	Characteristic Causes
A. Undersized task	1. Schedule too short 2. Budget too small 3. Contingencies and inefficiencies not considered
B. Project resources not matched to task	1. Types and amounts of talent 2. Roles and responsibilities 3. Scheduling and phasing of activities
C. Poor requirements baselines	1. Fuzzy understanding of requirements among user, customer, and project 2. Requirements documents incomplete 3. Requirements changes not tightly controlled 4. Incomplete or untimely distribution of change information 5. Lack of appreciation for impact of requirements changes during later phases of project
D. Weak design and programming methods	1. High-risk areas not identified 2. Lack of structured methods 3. Lack of automated development tools 4. Standards and practices not published 5. Uneven application of discipline in enforcing use of methods
E. Poor test discipline	1. Poor trace to requirements 2. Short cuts in incremental testing 3. Unreliable test input data 4. Compromises in evaluating test results
F. Spotty configuration controls	1. Source code library system inadequate 2. Specification and design baselines not tightly controlled 3. Change control boards and mechanics not optimized
G. Poor communication	1. Between user and customer 2. Between customer and project 3. Among parallel project design groups 4. Between design and programming groups 5. Between requirements and test groups
H. Ineffective project management controls	1. Poor visibility of product status 2. Absence of timely cost information 3. Weak authority over commitment/decommitment of resources 4. Uneven support of management by staff

for a certain period of time after they are introduced. Brooks[15] states the matter in definite terms.

> Oversimplifying outrageously, we state Brooks' law:
>
> "Adding manpower to a late software project makes it later."
>
> This then is the demythologizing of the man-month. The number of months of a project depends upon its sequential constraints. The maximum number of men depends upon the number of independent subtasks. From these two quantities one can derive

[15] F. P. Brooks, Jr., "*The Mythical Man-Month*," Reading, Mass.: Addison-Wesley, 1975.

schedules using fewer men and more months. (The only risk is product obsolescence.) One cannot, however, get workable schedules using more men and fewer months. More software projects have gone awry for lack of calendar time than for all other causes combined.

Schedules and subschedules that do not conform to the reality of sequential operations create problems that cannot be solved in any way except, ultimately, a schedule extension. Projects on such schedules are destined to have high entropy processes in their later stages, and adding more manpower is simply adding entropy or, to use Brooks' term, "mythical man-months." It is critical, therefore, that a viable schedule and budget be established at the beginning of a project. The principal mechanism for achieving this is called *productivity analysis*. Reduced to its essentials, productivity analysis is an exercise in arithmetic. It consists of performing these five steps:

1. Establish quantitative levels of the products to be generated: that is, the number of lines of code, number of pages of documentation, etc.
2. Establish productivity rates that a project staff can achieve: that is, the number of lines of code per man-month, number of pages of documentation per man-month, etc.
3. Divide product size quantities by productivity rates to obtain the number of man-months required.
4. Distribute the man-months so as to satisfy any imposed staffing and schedule constraints.
5. Derive the corresponding cost.

The key to carrying out this analysis successfully is to estimate the product size and staff productivity numbers accurately. These are not easy to arrive at, since all of the entropy effects must be considered. The ratio of real to mythical man-months must be estimated. Personal experience with similar situations is the most reliable guide in making this estimate. However, a body of knowledge on the subject is building, and reliable data is being published. An excellent case report on the results of a productivity survey is given in an article by Walston and Felix in the January 1977, *IBM Systems Journal*.[16] Table 2-3 is taken from this reference. This table is a study in itself, not only because of the raw productivity experience data contained there, but also because we can easily relate the variations in productivities to entropy effects. Note, for example, the first entry: "Customer interface complexity." Productivity rates [that is, delivered source lines/man-months (DSL/MM)] found in this survey range from 500 down to 124. The drop here is due to time and effort lost because it was necessary to communicate and coordinate with the customer through complex entropy-producing mechanisms. Sources of entropy can likewise be associated with every entry in the table. Some are essentially unavoidable, as in the case of security restrictions; others, such as using no design and code inspection, are certainly avoidable. In the middle ground are factors such as staff experience and computer access, which may or

[16]C. E. Walston and C. P. Felix, "A Method of Programming Measurement and Estimation," *IBM Systems Journal*, **16**, 1, 1977, 64–5.

Table 2-3 Variables that Correlate Significantly with Programming Productivity

Question or Variable	Response Group Mean Productivity (DSL/MM)			Productivity Change (DSL/MM)
Customer interface complexity	< Normal 500	Normal 295	> Normal 124	376
User participation in the definition of requirements	None 491	Some 267	Much 205	286
Customer originated program design changes	Few 297		Many 196	101
Customer experience with the application area of the project	None 318	Some 340	Much 206	112
Overall personnel experience and qualifications	Low 132	Average 257	High 410	278
Percentage of programmers doing development who participated in design of functional specifications	< 25% 153	25–50% 242	> 50% 391	238
Previous experience with operational computer	Minimal 146	Average 270	Extensive 312	166
Previous experience with programming languages	Minimal 122	Average 225	Extensive 385	263
Previous experience with application of similar or greater size and complexity	Minimal 146	Average 221	Extensive 410	264
Ratio of average staff size to duration (people/month)	< 0.5 305	0.5–0.9 310	> 0.9 173	132
Hardware under concurrent development	No 297		Yes 177	120
Development computer access, open under special request	0% 226	1–25% 274	> 25% 357	131
Development computer access, closed	0–10% 303	11–85% 251	> 85% 170	133
Classified security environment for computer and 25% of programs and data	No 289		Yes 156	133
Structured programming	0–33% 169	34–66% —	66% 301	132
Design and code inspections	0–33% 220	34–66% 300	> 66% 339	119
Top-down development	0–33% 196	34–66% 237	> 66% 321	125
Chief programmer team usage	0–33% 219	34–66% —	> 66% 408	189
Overall complexity of code developed	< Average 314		> Average 185	129
Complexity of application processing	< Average 349	Average 345	> Average 168	181

Table 2-3 cont.

Question or Variable	Response Group Mean Productivity (DSL/MM)			Productivity Change (DSL/MM)
Complexity of program flow	< Average	Average	> Average	
	289	299	209	80
Overall constraints on program design	Minimal	Average	Severe	
	293	286	166	107
Program design constraints on main storage	Minimal	Average	Severe	
	391	277	193	198
Program design constraints on timing	Minimal	Average	Severe	
	303	317	171	132
Code for real-time or interactive operation, or executing under severe timing constraint	< 10%	10–40%	> 40%	
	279	337	203	76
Percentage of code for delivery	0–90%	91–99%	100%	
	159	327	265	106
Code classified as nonmathematical application and I/O formatting programs	0–33%	33–66%	67–100%	
	188	311	267	79
Number of classes of items in the data base per 1000 lines of code	0–15	16–80	> 80	
	334	243	193	141
Number of pages of delivered documentation per 1000 lines of delivered code	0–32	33–88	> 88	
	320	252	195	125

may not be subject to influence by the project manager. The Walston-Felix article is highly recommended as a pseudo-work-shop for the study of entropy effects in software development.

When performing productivity analysis, a project manager takes into account as many of these influences as he or she can identify, estimates their effect on productivity, and derives the best net estimate. In effect he or she is performing an energy/ entropy analysis. The manager estimates the resources (energy) needed under ideal conditions, then estimates the potential entropy effects, and then discounts the predicted productivity accordingly. The objective here is to derive a cost figure and a schedule that assume the minimum total integral *that can be actually realized.* If one assumes too little entropy, he or she will create a nonviable plan that leads to overruns. Assuming more entropy than necessary will result in default on the basic management responsibility, which is to carry out the project with as much efficiency as is practicable.

Continuing our discussion of Table 2-2, we briefly summarize the other specific items and draw some conclusions related to their common characteristics. Groups B and C are related to the definition of the project task and the corresponding structure of project resources. "Corresponding structure" is the key here. When B task definitions—product requirements statements—are incomplete or unclear, confusion and misdirected actions result. Likewise, poor structuring of resources—personnel roles and responsibilities, or even unrealistic computer scheduling—leads to inefficient interactions. It is useful to recall the clerical file example in an earlier section. There the interaction of users with the file could be smooth or rough, depending on the structuring of the file contents *and* the using group. The direct analogy in software development is a clear and comprehensive statement of technical and administrative tasks *and* a resource structure that assures that each resource component interacts with its given tasks in an efficient and timely manner.

Groups D and E contain items related to design, programming, and test methods. Since we devote a full chapter to each of these activities, we shall not discuss them in detail here. The entropy-related aspects can be summarized easily: the entropy control objective is met by use of the most coherent methods of implementing design, program structure, code, test requirements and procedures, and test results. The greater the coherence, the less the confusion, and the lower the entropy.

Group F refers to configuration control. This is the practice of maintaining strict change control over requirements, design, code, and test activities. It is the means by which the project staff, management, and customer remain coordinated as to the current definition of the task and the product. It is an extremely important group. Configuration control is an essential mechanism for avoiding very high entropy situations.

Group G identifies the general communication problem. This group of items often relates to all others. Most of the shortcomings found in a software project can be traced in part to communication failures and resultant misunderstandings. No other single phenomenon contributes as much entropy to the life-cycle process as poor communication does. Conversely, no other area of management attention has greater potential for reducing entropy. There are two essential ways to avoid communication failures. The first is to reduce the member of communications required as much as possible by partitioning tasks so that interfaces and interchanges are as simple as possible. The second way is to provide coherent, readily available communication channels and mechanisms wherever they are needed.

Finally we come to Group H. It should be apparent by now why project management must maintain a high degree of awareness of the status of all project matters. The project is a highly interactive, continuously operating system. No matter how complete and competent a project plan may be, there is a need for adjustments and explicit decisions every day. The absence of such decisions is tantamount to allowing the process to drift toward a state of higher entropy.

Take special note of item H4. It states that lack of support by the staff in management-related matters is a cause of entropy. This single point cannot be overemphasized. In software development the management process, like all others, is interactive. The results of that interaction depend on the awareness and cooperation of all parties involved.

Now let us review in positive terms what our brief look at the causes of entropy has revealed. Tables 2-2 and 2-3 present a substantial number of representative examples. We have discussed some common characteristics of the principal causes of entropy and have indicated some specific management methods that are effective in their control. These methods are summarized briefly

Provide adequate resources
Match task and resource structures
Use structured design, programming, and test practices

Establish comprehensive configuration control
Maintain coherent communication among all project participants
Sustain effective management visibility and control

These are the basic elements of sound software project management. Much more can be written about each of these elements, of course, but this chapter must be limited to fundamentals because further elaboration would require a volume by itself.

Bibliography

DRUCKER, P. F., *Management: Tasks, Responsibilities, Practices.* New York: Harper and Row, Publishers, 1974.

BROOKS, F. P., *The Mythical Man-Month.* Reading, Mass.: Addison-Wesley, 1975.

Management Guide to Avionics Software Acquisition, Volume II: Software Acquisition Process. Technical Rept. No. ASD-TR-76-11. Logicon, Inc. Dayton, Ohio, June 1976. Available from U.S. Dept. of Commerce, National Technical Information Service.

EMDEN, R., "Why Do We Have Winter Heating," *Nature,* **141**, May 1938, 908.

FAGAN, M. E., "Design and Code Inspections and Process Control in the Development of Programs," *IBM Report IBM-500 TR-21.572,* December 1974.

BOEHM, B. W., "Software Engineering," *IEEE Transactions on Computers,* **C-25**, 12, December 1976.

WALSTON, C. E., and C. P. FELIX, "A Method of Programming Measurement and Estimation," *IBM Systems Journal,* **15**, 1, 1977, 64–5.

ROYCE, W. W., "Software requirements analysis, sizing, and costing," *Practical Strategies for the Development of Large Scale Software.* Reading, Mass.: Addison-Wesley, 1975.

BELL, T. E., and T. A. THAYER, "Software requirements: Are they a problem?" *Proc. IEEE/ACM 2nd Int. Conf. Software Eng.,* Oct. 1976.

COUGER, J. D., and R. W. KNAPP, eds:, *System Analysis Techniques.* New York: Wiley, 1974.

DAVIS, C. G., and C. R. VICK, "The software development system," *Proc. IEEE/ACM 2nd Int. Conf. Software Eng.,* Oct. 1976.

ALFORD, M., "A requirements engineering methodology for real-time processing requirements," *Proc. IEEE/ACM 2nd Int. Conf. Software Eng.,* Oct. 1976.

BOEHM, B. W., "Some steps toward formal and automated aids to software requirements analysis and design," *Proc. IFIP Cong.,* 1974, 192–197.

THAYER, T. A., "Understanding software through analysis of empirical data," *Proc. Nat. Comput. Conf.* 1975, 335–341.

MORTISON, J., "Tools and techniques for software development process visibility and control," *Proc. ACM Comput. Sci. Conf.* Feb. 1976.

WILLIAMS, R. D., "Managing the development of reliable software," *Proc. 1975 Int. Conf. Reliable Software,* April 1975, 3–8, available from IEEE.

WHITAKER, W. A., et al., "Department of Defense requirements for high order computer programming languages: 'Tinman,' " Defense Advanced Research Projects Agency, April 1976.

THAYER, T. A., M. LIPOW, and E. C. NELSON, "Software reliability study," TRW Systems, Redondo Beach, Calif., rep. to RADC, Contract F30602-74-C-0036, March 1976.

Defense Management J. (*Special Issue on Software Management*), Vol. II, Oct. 1975.

HOROWITZ, E., ed., *Practical Strategies for Developing Large-Scale Software*, Reading, Mass.: Addison-Wesley, 1975.

METZGER, P. J., *Managing a Programming Project*. Englewood Cliffs, N.J.: Prentice-Hall, 1973.

WEINBERG, G. F., *The Psychology of Computer Programming*. New York: Van Nostrand Reinhold, 1971.

WOLVERTON, R. W., "The cost of developing large-scale software," *IEEE Trans. Comput.,* **6,** 4 (June, 1974), pp. 615-36.

BARRY, B. S., and J. J. NAUGHTON, "Chief programmer team operations description," U.S. Air Force, rep. RADC-TR-74-300, Vol. X (of 15-volume series), pp. 1-2–1-3.

"Management of computer resources in major defense systems," Department of Defense, Directive 6000.29, Apr. 1976.

3 SOFTWARE·DESIGN

Judith C. Enos

R. L. Van Tilburg

Software Engineering Division
Hughes Aircraft Company

> *All engineering is characterized*
> *by the engineer's dissatisfaction*
> *with the achievement of just a*
> *solution. Engineering seeks the*
> *best solution in established terms,*
> *within recognized limitations, and*
> *making compromises required by*
> *working in the real world.*
>
> E. Yourdon and L. Constantine
> Structured Design

In this chapter we discuss the principles of software engineering as they apply to the three phases of software design: the *definition phase* or requirements analysis; the *systems design phase* as it is developed in conjunction with the overall data processing system design; and the *software design phase*, which involves picking up the functions allocated to software in the system design and developing the overall architecture of the computer programs. Throughout the discussion of these phases we will emphasize five basic themes that are of critical importance. Our software design themes are: (1) software design is a human problem-solving process; (2) software design results in a product designed for someone's use other than the creator of the design; (3) software design is very closely tied to system engineering; (4) all design is structured; and (5) verification of design is a continuous process, starting with identification of the problem and a statement of requirements.

This chapter is organized in five major sections paralleling these five themes. The first section deals with the dynamics of software design as a human, creative process, stressing the active relationship between the tools and techniques used for design and the performance characteristics associated with the user's requirements. In this section we emphasize the theme that software design is essentially a human problem-solving process. While trends in software engineering point toward a higher degree of automation to aid the design process, the creative aspect of synthesizing solutions to complex problems is, and will continue to be, a function allocated to the human. The processes that we will discuss focus on techniques that reduce the complexity of a design problem and its solution to levels that can be easily comprehended and resolved by individuals.

The next three sections reflect the three phases of the design process and are organized in the format of a discussion of the concepts and techniques of each phase followed by a sample problem. The three phases discussed are:

1. *Requirements definition phase* or formalizing the statement of user's requirements. Here we examine the theme of software as a product and the discipline required by the software engineer in the development of such a product. Designing a software product imposes requirements and constraints not normally observed in many other kinds of data processing activities. Formalization of user's requirements is difficult and often ignored for the easier job of developing solutions to what the programmer thinks the problem is.

In this section we emphasize that software can and should be designed for use by people other than a designer/programmer. Many of the software design disciplines discussed in this chapter would be of less importance if we were writing a program solely to solve a problem uniquely our own. A group of three or four programmers, working closely together to produce a program of limited applicability, may likewise find many of the software design disciplines of limited use. However, the software engineering principles presented here evolved out of the experience of many programmers who organized themselves to build complex programs in order to solve complex problems with which they often had no direct experience. In many cases, the solution actually advances the state of the art. The programmer faces further difficulty in that users, more often than not, do not know how to state their wants in a manner that software designers can clearly understand. Some users become familiar with software and state reasonable goals at the beginning in the requirements phase, whereas others, who are not so knowledgeable, rely on technically qualified consultants (or consultant organizations) to assist them in translating their needs into statements of data processing requirements. Still other users rely on the software engineer to analyze the needs and formalize the requirements for the software product. Here we assume the latter case when discussing techniques used to formulate a definition of requirements. The software design phase is constrained in the beginning by the complexity of the problem and the sophistication of the user in stating the requirements. This situation places a premium on developing methods of interpreting someone else's problem and developing a viable, satisfactory solution. A premium also applies to developing forms and techniques of communication in order to inform the users as to exactly what they will be provided.

2. *System design phase* or translating requirements into a system design. Here we are discussing software engineering as it relates to system engineering. This task is less difficult when the hardware configuration is off-the-shelf or already in existence. It is more difficult when hardware is designed and developed concurrently with software. This phase highlights the problem of communication of concepts between the design and implementation teams so they can accomplish the development of a usable system.

Here we emphasize the theme that the software design process is very closely tied to the system engineering process. The systems that we are referencing here are made up of a combination of hardware, software, people interfaces, operating procedures, and communication interfaces, all brought together to solve a specific problem or set of problems. This theme of software design relating to system design is often overlooked by developers of information systems, since they work mostly within the envelope of a systems software package that is transparent to the hardware. These information systems tend to be isolated from concurrent hardware development, thus limiting involvement of hardware trade studies and of hardware/software trade-offs. The isolation of system design from software design is not feasible within the context of the design effort we are addressing here. Again, this theme highlights the need for communicating the software design to nonsoftware engineers who are working on the same problem. Furthermore, the software engineer must communicate with other engineers in the formalization of design requirements, since designers and developers are sometimes different people due to organizational charter and staff turnover.

3. *Software design phase* or developing the overall architecture of the software. All designs have a structure, but some are better than others. Our theme here is that the structure chosen should reflect the nature of the problem the software is expected to solve. Implementation strategies are discussed, and the design is developed to the point at which a module is functionally identified along with its input and output interfaces. Structuring starts with analysis of activities, during which a conceptual model of the system that will satisfy the user's requirements is formulated and the performance characteristics the user expects to see in the software end product are identified. Structuring of software continues in the system design process where it is closely akin to design methodologies in general use by systems engineers. However, software engineering is introducing tools and techniques to enhance the software engineer's portion of the system activity. The structuring process presented in this chapter features a synthesis of contemporary structuring techniques that have been found to be effective in the design of large, complex, real-time software systems.

The final section covers the subject of continuous verification and validation in the design phases. Our basic theme is that each step in the design process is verified and validated. However the discussion is left to the summary section to make the process more easily understood. The process of verifying and validating the design of the software begins with the validation of requirements and continues with the verification and validation of design at each step. Verification emphasizes checking the consistency of the design at each metamorphosis, starting from the initial formalized requirements and proceeding to the design of a working module. Validation techniques emphasize checking the design for consistency with the user's requirements prior to implementation. Verification alone at each step does not assure compliance with the formalized requirements. Techniques in simulation/modeling for validating the resulting design are emphasized.

In the chapter, we have made basic assumptions. The phases of the software design process (requirements analysis, system design, and software design) are discussed as they apply to the more complex case of concurrent hardware and software product development. Since the first two phases deal with the data processing system as an entity that includes software as an element of the system, many of the principles discussed are stated in terms of the overall data processing system, or simply, the system. When we use the word "system" in this context, the reader should understand that we are referring only to those principles of engineering that apply to the software engineer's view of the system. The design activities discussed in this chapter are limited to providing the architecture of a solution to a problem. The discussion stops when the design solution is defined in terms of a structure of entities that we will call modules. Each module describes a single function within the context of the overall structure. We believe that the techniques and methods used in the architectural design, particularly those of large, complex systems, differ significantly from those used in the detailed design of the processing steps within a module. The techniques of the former type of design activities are very dependent on the type of product being developed and on the type of user's problem being solved. The techniques of good design within the module, on the other hand, are fairly standard and can be prescribed for any software being developed. The detailed design techniques and implementation of modules are given in Chapter 4—Structured Programming.

3.1

The Human Problem-Solving Process

The popularity of general purpose computers and the spectacular growth of data processing over the last 25 years can be attributed to the fact that we can solve problems with software (and, of course, data processing hardware) faster than by any other means. Using computers, we can even undertake data processing tasks that were impossible to conceive of a generation ago. Being a young and optimistic industry, we still tend, at times, to undertake tasks that are beyond our capability to accomplish. However, the essential ingredient to the successes that have been accomplished in data processing is in the solutions incorporated into the software. Software provides the cohesiveness and control of data flow that enables systems to solve problems. The solution of the problem is accomplished within the design framework of the software.

In the engineering of the software design, the dynamics of the engineering process are essentially the same as the dynamics of any problem-solving activity. Software design is not a mechanical process but a basic human activity, requiring much clear thinking, work, and rework to be successful. We invest this human-oriented problem-solving activity with the constraints of formal engineering disciplines and call it software engineering.

In this section various aspects of the software design process are reviewed to illustrate the dynamic actions that take place during all phases of the design activity. First, we will discuss the software design process as a human creative process. Only humans can solve problems, not tools or techniques, however cleverly automated. We will discuss how to keep the design within limits of human understanding. In conjunction with this theme, we will present several methods for conceptualizing a system.

Next, we will discuss some techniques for recognizing good design in order to set goals for evaluating the relative worth of the design and the resulting end product. These goals for good design are stated in terms of characteristics and attributes of an effective software product. Then we will review in summary fashion some of the techniques and aids used in the various phases of the design process, including analytic aids, system design aids, and software design aids. Finally, we will summarize the software design process as the interaction of humans using tools and techniques to produce a design that has the desired characteristics and attributes.

3.1.1 DESIGN IS A CREATIVE PROCESS

In data processing, human beings solve problems while machines (computers) implement the solutions. In between the user's problem statement and the object program that runs on the computer, there are many steps during which techniques and tools of design and programming can assist in developing a software product that is reliable and useful. However, there are many points where the programmer's decision-making process is critical. This is particularly true in the definition and design phases because the product to be designed is always unique to the user's problem but must be reduced to a common level of design for effective implementation. With the variety of problems to be solved, there can be no cookbook technique or mechanization of the design synthesis that will act as a universal panacea. The techniques of analysis may be augmented with automated tools directed toward improving precision of communication and consistency checking, but the development of designs (the synthesis of solution) still requires the touch of human creativity. We hope that software engineering methodology, as described herein, will enhance the creativity of those designers who are experienced and effective and will assist in uncovering the errors of the less effective designers.

The basic steps in the problem solving process are simple and have been described in numerous ways for many years. First, we define the problem, collect as much information as we can about the problem, and analyze it to gain a thorough understanding of the problem. Second, we hypothesize solutions to the problem. Third, we analyze, evaluate, iterate, and select the best solution to the problem.

Philosophers and logicians have been pointing out for years that problem analysis is the first step in determining the solution, but it is surprising how many people do not recognize this basic premise. Perhaps it is because we are culturally conditioned by sales and advertising techniques that emphasize solutions (products) looking for problems (those who need the products), and sales pitches made to convince customers that they have a problem that only this salesman's product can solve. Perhaps it is because we programmers are prone to jump into programming too quickly. We are engrossed in and fascinated by the game-like process of coding—where our personal ego rewards come. In either case, these ways of thinking do not enhance our analytic ability to identify problems. Therefore, we must learn to concentrate upon and recognize the user's needs rather than merely to sell a product that we have already designed if we are to provide usable solutions to our customers.

Having defined the problem, the next step is to conceptualize alternative solutions to the problem. There can be many solutions to a problem, some of which can work to an acceptable degree, and others that are patently poor or impossible. The trick is to find the best solution to the problem. Unfortunately, most of the time the way we tell if one solution is better than another is by the "eureka" phenomenon— the design is good because the designer thinks it is good. The designer is often satisfied with the solution if it can handle all possible variations that he can conceive and the design is aesthetically pleasing—simplistically elegant in concept and probably somewhat similar to a design that he, the designer, used with success on a past project.

Sometimes the test of the design solution has been only whether or not it will solve the problem. Previously, the issue of how well it solves the problem, for the most part, has been trial-and-error type thinking—the designer tries to think of all possible conditions and designs for their occurrence. However, the state of design has improved to the point at which design constructs now lead to prediction of reliability, and simulation modeling has evolved as a tool for testing the performance of a design.

In software engineering terms, analyzing the problem to be solved is generally referred to as requirements definition. Theoretically, this implies stating the user's problem in functional terms. We are defining "WHAT" is to be accomplished by the system. Generally, this has been interpreted as stating the overall functional performance requirements, design constraints, and standards for development. It mostly includes detailed textual and mathematical descriptions for each of the desired data processing functions. For each detailed functional description, input data processing and output data are defined. Input data is stated as source, method of insertion, and desired validity checks. The approach to processing includes accuracies, sequence, and timing as well as an algorithm. All output data is described as control parameters, reports, and displays. Obviously for all but the most trivial problem, this kind of stating of "WHAT" presumes extensive analysis and understanding of the user's requirements before such a description can be given.

The proposed solution is stated as conceptual design. That is, after the statement of "WHAT" the solution to the problem traditionally has been given in terms of "HOW" the requirements are to be met by the data processing system. This step in the process is generally described in terms of data processing entities—programs interfacing with programs and hardware, hardware configurations, and human interface procedures. Interfaces and control sequences of the data processing entities are described along with descriptions of data that flows between processing entities (which are also covered in interface descriptions) and memory allocation estimates.

With respect to testing the solution against the problem, the traditional method has been for a panel of informed experts to review the design against the requirements and to determine if they can spot any inconsistencies or omissions. Real testing as in hardware development, whereby a conceptual design is checked with a hardware breadboard model or prototype hardware to see if the solution will work, has not been a prevalent practice in software development. Recently, some aspects of design have been evaluated in a more formal manner. Simulation/modeling has been used to evaluate a proposed design's ability to handle the processing load, assuming an allocation of resources in terms of software architecture and hardware configuration. Although the idea of using simulations/modeling as a method of evaluating requirements and proposed solutions is relatively new, the trend is growing. This is similar but in addition to the practice of building prototype software using higher order languages.

These three steps, requirements definition, conceptual design, and design reviews or testing, reflect very closely the three steps of problem definition, hypothetical solution, and test of hypothesis used in any type of problem solving. The chief difference here is that when we describe the problem-solving steps in programming terminology, the description falls into the formal phased steps of software development, illustrating the mixing of the design process with the management of the process. From the above description there now appears an inconsistency in the software design process as compared to the problem-solving process because the human creative process is essentially an individual act performed by an individual using his experience and knowledge of a problem to formulate a solution. Committees and design teams cannot conceive overall solutions; only individuals can. The issue that has evolved is: we tend to confuse the microsteps of individuals solving problems in the data processing world with the macrosteps of managing people on a project. The design methodologies and formalized procedures of design and programming allow committees and design teams to effectively integrate individual creativity in problem solving. This provides for solutions of problems beyond the ability of a single individual. We often increase individual creativity with teams by using formal methodology.

The source of this confusion in thinking is easily understood if we look into the history of programming. Initially, programmers solved their problems on an individual basis. The jargon of the software design process matched the real process of problem solving—and still does when applied to problems on the scale where an individual can master the process. It is only when we try to expand the scale of the problem-solving process to the point at which the creativity in analysis, design, and evaluation is spread over a number of people that the results are at best not very satisfactory. The major software engineering problems to be solved now are how to apply the individual creative steps of problem identification, conceptual solution, and test of solution to the problem of the complex, large scale, real-time data processing installations we are now developing.

The answer to the problem of scaling up individual creativity to contemporary data processing problems lies in the systematic decomposition of user's problems and design solutions to a point at which individual creativity can be effective, and communication between individuals can be established, thus allowing them to work together in achieving a solution. This process of formalizing creativity in a team environment is what we call dynamics of software design. The process requires a dynamic interaction of the human creative side of problem solving with the formal design methodologies to achieve the stated attributes of design that give some measure of quality to the resulting effort. All must be applied in a team effort to solve the problem.

Since we have defined the process of design as a human problem-solving process, similar to the general process used by people to solve scientific and engineering problems, let us review some techniques employed by the engineering community to keep the problem within the scope of human understanding.

3.1.2 KEEPING THE DESIGN WITHIN LIMITS OF HUMAN UNDERSTANDING

Part of the answer is to be found in the organization of a project. As discussed in the previous chapter, the various forms of organization—functional organizations, chief programmer teams, Weinberg's[1] egoless programming team concept—all are forms of organization that emphasize certain strong points in organizing people for communicating and performing complementary work on one project. These are concerns addressed by management. In this chapter on design, we are more concerned with the techniques of intellectually breaking the problem into components that can be effectively handled by individual designers. Essentially, this means providing techniques for viewing the requirements definition and design solution phases as a series of discrete "levels of refinement" that move from a high-level statement of the user's problem to a solution that can be implemented within the constraints imposed. Each level of refinement can take on the human-oriented steps of problem analysis, conceptualization of solution, and test of solution against the requirements of the problem. Iterated, this then provides the human dynamics of the design process that allow for the best engineering solutions to be developed.

Our basic thesis is that design has to be broken down into chunks that are amenable to human comprehension. This is generally accomplished by attacking the problem at an abstract level and then proceeding to more detailed levels of design. This way of looking at the problem as a decomposition or refinement from a high level to a detailed level provides the methodology that, in one way or another, has been successfully used on many large-scale programs to date. It provides for unfolding the successive levels of design while retaining the necessary iteration of the three steps of the human thinking process in the design. As problems grow larger and more complex, the more imperative the decomposition process becomes because it is this process of design refinement that maintains the design solution activities within the bounds of human comprehension.

The whole process of development of programs can be viewed as moving from an abstract statement of the problem to a concrete representation of the solution in code that can be executed on the target machine. The process can be viewed as leading to a series of models. By model, we mean an abstract representation of the real system to be developed. Initially we build this model at a very high level so that we can deal with the interpretation of the user's world in a conceptual manner. Later, as we develop more specific ideas of the kind of requirements the user has, the conceptual model becomes more detailed. Thus, we can state that the first model represents the user's statement of the problem and his expectation of how he wants the solutions presented to him. The second model presents an overall system solution to his problem, including a description of the problem in terms of the objects to be manipulated along with their characteristics or attributes, the events that are expected to occur, and the relationships between events and attributes. A third model includes a presentation of a system in terms of a high-level design representation of the structure of the data processing

[1] Weinberg, G. M., *Psychology of Computer Programming*, Van Nostrand Reinhold, 1971.

elements (program modules, and data) within a configuration of hardware (computer(s) and peripheral devices) on which the software is to run.

Since we are concerned here primarily with software development, the next model presents the control structure of the software modules, the function naming, and the data flow between modules. Depending on size and complexity, there may be several levels of detailing of the software architecture that depict the flow of data through a structured hierarchy of modules and data design. Ultimately, we arrive at the level of design whereby we describe in our model individual modules that perform a single function along with the inputs and outputs to each of the modules. The next model reflects the reality of data processing more closely by taking the design to the point at which the model is translatable into machine-executable code, using a programming language. Thus, the total development design process can be viewed as a series of conceptual models, beginning with an abstract model of the user's problem and ending with a concrete model—the solution of the problem that can be executed in the machine and tested against the real world of the user. The beauty of this concept is that it recognizes the abstract nature of the design process. Even in the concrete representation of the model solution in executable code, the process is still an abstraction of the real world and has to be tested in the real world to ascertain if the model is a true representation of the user's needs. It also emphasizes the movement from a high level of conceptualization to a low level of detail in the building of successive models. The work of Dijkstra[2] and Wirth[3] support this method of conceptualizing the design process.

In addition to moving through levels of conceptualization in decomposition of the problem, we find that we must iterate the steps in the process. Most often our initial approach to solution is not the best. As we move from one level of conceptualization to another, we gain more insight into the ramifications of the problem. We, therefore, must go back and redo the steps in decomposition to include the new aspects of understanding of the problems. This process of iteration is the key to good design of reliable and cost effective systems.

This practice of using levels of refinement to keep the design within human limits of comprehension has prevailed for a long time. Beginning with a high-level design and proceeding to lower and lower levels of detail is only a natural way of intellectually tackling a large, complex problem. The generic term "top-down design" has been applied to this process, and all followers of design methodologies profess to follow this general approach—with a minor difference or two that makes their approach better. Similarly, it is generally recognized that there is a constant iteration between levels as analysis and synthesis at one level uncover deficiencies in the design at a higher level. Hence, we see an iteration loop feeding back details to a higher level, thus forcing a more complete definition of requirements at the higher level.

In this sense, the process of designing by levels of refinement and iterating a design as deficiencies are uncovered would appear to be a self correcting mechanism that, if left to its own devices, would insure that the end product of this process would be perfect. Obviously, it doesn't work that simply. We have identified at least two

[2]Dahl, O. J.; Dijkstra, E. W.; Hoare, C. A., *Structured Programming*, Academic Press, 1972.
[3]Wirth, N., *Systematic Programming*, Prentice-Hall, 1973.

factors that present problems to the smooth transitioning between levels. There are little human quirks in the process that cause difficulty, and management's need for insight necessitates some degree of boundary definition between phases.

The human-orientation problem appears to stem from the fact that the career path for software people has been from code implementors to detail software designers to software system designers to software engineers. In progressing up this scale, it is only natural for programmers to regress to detailing designs that are familiar to them and to perform the same level of job that they have done before rather than operating within their current position. This results in implementation details being shoved up into higher level design—where they not only distract, but sometimes cause the whole design to be slanted toward the wrong objective.

One of the most significant lessons to be learned in software engineering is the discipline of maintaining the design at the proper level of refinement based on the design phase, and not introducing irrelevant detail. Each level of refinement being developed has its boundaries, and these boundaries must be respected. The original analysis activity, during which the "WHAT" is explored in detail so that all implications are understood, is distinct from the synthesis activity in the top-down method where possible architectural schemes of implementation in the "HOW" are pursued. Furthermore, detailing the "HOW" of implementation is distinct from defining design architecture. As we will see later in the section on structuring of software design (Sec. 3.4 of this chapter), the cycling of "WHAT," "HOW," and "STRUCTURE" is iterated to refine the design to a point where it meets the requirements. Software engineers must remain cognizant of the aspect of the design cycle in which they are operating. When the designer *cannot* keep the distinctions in mind as to what aspect or level of activity is being pursued, the result is chaotic.

The problem is even more complicated on large, complex efforts where many individuals with differing backgrounds in analysis, design, and programming interact and the cycling of the creative design process is accompanied by management's requirements for documented milestones. For example, it is typical that three levels of design are defined: (1) analysis, which produces a system design and a set of requirements to be allocated to software; (2) software design wherein the concept of the solution to software requirements is set forth in a possible scheme for implementation; and (3) implementation where detail design is turned into a functioning system. These phases are often thought to proceed in rigid order, and each phase is assigned to people specializing in the activities of one and only one phase. Since the natural approach to problem solving is by microphases (implementation is the "test" activity for higher levels of refinement), there has always been an iterative crossing and recrossing of the phase boundaries. This results in confusion that is blamed as the cause of much software failure. Since the crossing of the activities is a natural function of the problem-solving process, it is important that the software engineering design process provide for discrimination between activities so multi-man projects can be organized and managed in a reasonable fashion.

The formalization of the macrophases within a project is not without a realistic basis. When software products represent large-scale implementations, there is a requirement for specialization. Not all programmers are versatile enough to communicate with users in terms of the problem that they see and yet retain the skills necessary for design and implementation. If a person is skilled in analysis and design, the talent is usually so rare that few managers are willing to expend the talent's time in generating code, which could be adequately generated by newly trained programmers entering the field of data processing.

A different view of the decomposition process that is worthy of consideration has been put forth by Ross and Schoman[4] in their presentation of Structured Analysis and Design Technique (SADT[R]). This concept sets forth a methodology for controlled functional decomposition with the objective of ensuring that system objectives and interfaces are maintained while defining chunks of design within well-defined boundaries. Again the concept of levels of refinement is maintained. The principal addition to the levels concept is the methodology of diagramming the levels to preserve identity of relationships between parts of design. This allows the designers to exercise their creative design talents within the bounds of a particular level. It also illustrates breaking up a level into manageable chunks for analysis and design. The different levels show that functional decomposition proceeds in detail without letting implementation decisions intrude until they are called for. This idea is in consonance with Parnas's[5] concept of information hiding where information that is not needed for that level of design (or by that particular element of design—program, subprogram, or module) is not made available. The concept in this case is that keeping designers at the appropriate level of detail is as critical as keeping data inviolate.

In addition to this consideration of diverse human capacities, there appear to be some real discontinuities in the analysis, synthesis, and test cycle of problem-solving activities at different levels of conceptualization that seem to result from differences in techniques and methodologies that have been developed. The techniques used to elicit a formal statement of software requirements from a user's view and understanding of this problem are more heavily oriented to the expression of the dynamics of the system than toward structure. They tend to explicitly describe operations of the system to be developed—as they should. On the other hand, formalization of the tools and techniques of conceptualizing the design architecture of an acceptable solution to the user's requirements appears to be more oriented to hierarchial structures and representations. Implementation techniques are more dynamic in consideration of limited segments of the solution, but static with respect to the overall system until integration is attempted. These natural discontinuities in technology, along with diversity of human capacities, tend to keep some semblence of the traditional separation of the phases into requirements analysis, system design, software design, implementation, and test as a reality to be dealt with. Good software engineering practices must provide for maintaining the correct balance in the interfaces between phases and allow for parallelism and overlap of phases that naturally occur.

A final, and perhaps critical, consideration for keeping the boundaries distinct in the development of a software system is the very practical problem of knowing when to stop designing and begin implementation. This habit appears to be one of those human weaknesses illustrating that when designers get seriously involved in designing a

---

[4]Ross, D. T., and K. E. Schoman, Jr., "*Structured Analysis for Requirements Definition.*" Proceedings of the Second International Conference on Software Engineering, 1976.

[5]Parnas, D. L., "On the Criteria to be Used in Decomposing Systems into Modules," *Comm. of the ACM* No. 12, December 1972, pp. 1053–1058.

portion of the software system, it is most tempting for them to continue the design down to the lowest level of detail. After all, isn't that the only way we can be positive that the design is implementable? Of equal, but more serious, consideration is the tendency to rework and design again and again. We have shown that the natural problem-solving process is one of iteration at each level of refinement and between levels of refinement. The management considerations of time and money set bounds to the phases of requirements definition and architectural design. Left to themselves, designers appear willing to work forever to obtain the perfect design. Indeed, recent practice has been to extend the portion of a project schedule devoted to design phases, since experience has shown that a longer design phase makes for a shortened integration and test phase as well as a better product. However, there is an optimum finite length for each project, and the software engineer should work within that context.

The bounds that we have set for software design begin with formulating user's requirements and end with a detail design of the architecture of the system as it is to be implemented in the software. Limiting the detailing of design to the architecture of the solution rather than proceeding to detail design is important. It is a management and technical requirement to assess the overall design approach in validation of the design prior to beginning of implementation. The architectural design must describe the arrangement (or structure) of the component parts (called modules) that communicate (through interfaces) in proper sequence (control structure) to solve the user's problem. The design cannot be developed and reviewed in parts, but must be completed as an entity, complete within itself, and in consonance with the goals set by the user of the end product. For this evaluation to be complete, the design must be taken down to the working level module that names and describes a single function to be performed, and to the description of the logical data entities that are passed to and from the module. A design at this level can be evaluated against the requirements definition by using verification and validation tools such as simulation/modeling and design reviews. Design at lower levels (detail design of modules) can proceed independently according to the strategy of integration, which will set priorities for scheduled completion of modules.

Since a specific problem of the design phase is that of determining when the architectural design has been iterated or recycled enough so that the design will meet all requirements efficiently and effectively, it is one of the responsibilities of management to see that the attributes of good design that are appropriate to the user's problem and resources are prioritized and made explicit prior to start of the design. Most of these attributes of good design are qualitative in nature. As an example, a design is expected to be maintainable. This has a bearing on module size and interface between modules. If the concept of maintainability is made explicit (if the program is expected to change at a rate of 5% or 10% a year or less), and if the maintenance is to be performed by programmers experienced with the system design and operation, we as designers will know how much emphasis to place on this attribute of design. Since engineering of design is a compromise, we will be better able to decide in advance the compromise solution we will accept for the design and be more willing to stop when we feel we have reached that point. Otherwise, the termination of design may be dictated by when the alloted time and/or money runs out, resulting in a very haphazard design.

At this point we have noted that the definition and design in an individualistic human creative process consist of the basic steps of problem analysis, conceptualization of a solution to the problem identified, and a test or review of the solution against the requirements, iterated over and over again until the problem is completely defined and architecture of an acceptable solution is obtained. Since the problems subjected to software engineering are generally large and complex enough to require the specialized efforts of many individuals, there must be some technique of breaking the overall problem into chunks that can be comprehended by an individual and organized so they can be coordinated. This is usually accomplished by defining the problem at levels of refinement that proceed from an abstract level through various expansions of the solution, level by level, until the basic working module is defined.

The methods used in thinking about the software system are dependent on the conceptual view we have of the system (or software system) we are designing.

3.1.3 CONCEPTUAL VIEWS OF A SYSTEM

The way we design a system (or software system since the terms are interchangeable in the early design stages) is very much influenced by how we conceive or think about the system at the very highest level of conceptualization. In the initial stages of requirements definition, we tend to think about a system, not as a hardware system or software system, but as a systematic way of performing functions to solve a user's problem. The allocation of these functions to hardware and software occurs later in the design process. In turn, the methodologies and tools that we develop and use are influenced by what we define as a system and how we think about those aspects of a system that influence the software we develop. Concepts determine methodology, which in turn determines the tools developed to support the methodology. Therefore, it is important that we establish the concept of what is meant by a system. After establishing the concept of the system, we can then talk about the methodologies and tools that support the system development process.

In recent years, some effort has been made toward establishing theoretical models of systems that identify the characteristics of the design in its general sense so as to provide the guidelines for developing a methodology. The goal of these theoretical models is to identify the elements of a software system in a general sense, and to identify how these elements relate to each other. These theoretical models possess a number of common characteristics that will be summarized in terms of a logical construct consisting of a hierarchical structure of modules, and a physical model consisting of a physical network of components. Subsequent to this general presentation of the empirical models we discuss in this chapter, alternative theoretical models, with which the reader may wish to be familiar, are presented. A key issue to be noted in all of the theoretical models is that consistencies can be identified between the approaches. A system is viewed as a set of elements (we will call them modules). The modules will be described in terms of their input/output and processing performed to accomplish a transformation from input to output. The modules will have relationships to each other that will be described both as to the static way the modules relate to each other, through a logical structure, and as to the dynamic way they relate to each other, through communication as members in a network. A control mechanism (also defined as a modular structure) will be assumed, which assures the correct operational sequence of execution. Characteristics can be assigned for the modules that aid the evaluation of the system's performance. Finally, a graphical representation will be employed to show the relationships between the modules.

A HIERARCHICAL STRUCTURE OF MODULES (A LOGICAL VIEW OF THE SYSTEM)

The major premise of this way of looking at a software system is that the design of the system should be expressed as a structure. During the early days of programming, software was considered as a single monolithic entity. A program was generated to perform the processing required of software. Subprograms and subroutines were introduced into the coding purely as convenience factors to avoid duplicating blocks of code. As the size of programs grew, some partitioning was necessary for comprehension's sake. Large-scale systems, such as we are dealing with here, exceed the ability of the human mind to grasp in toto if they are viewed as single entities. It is in the nature of human logic to subdivide a mass of information into separate parts so that each separate part can be understood in itself. In addition, the subdivision must be performed according to some logical rules so that the interrelations between the parts can be understood. In this manner if the parts are understood and the relationships between the parts are understood, the total should be understandable. Thus, the system as we conceive it will be separated into parts that are classed as data (information acted upon) and modules (the action entities). The interrelationships between the data and modules in any combination are defined as interfaces. Interfaces are described in terms of data flowing between the modules and between the modules and the data. The modules and the data are represented as a structure. The nodes of the structure constitute both the modules and the data. The connectors of the structure constitute the interfaces.

The second premise is that the structure is hierarchical; i.e., it is depicted as a layering of nodes. Each layer represents a level of abstraction concerning the system. Each successive layer appears to be a decomposition of a previous level into its constituent parts. In actuality, the layers emerge as a result of the successive iterations and analysis. The act of decomposition is the trial and error process of problem solving discussed previously, but the final result looks like a simple decomposition. Thus, the top level of the structure is the system. The second level is a decomposition of the system into its major parts. Each successive level is a decomposition of a node in the structure into its major parts. Thus, the structure of the system takes on a tree structure appearance as shown in Figure 3-1. A true tree structure, however, would preclude the possibility of a single module common to multiple branches of the structure. This is a restriction we do not wish to impose. Therefore, the hierarchical structure of the system is represented as a directed graph rather than a tree structure. However, since a tree structure is inherently easier to understand than a directed graph, a tree structure is used to establish the characteristics of the structure during the design phases. Independency of the branches is a design attribute that is viewed as leading to simpler, less complex, and, hence, more reliable software. During the design phases, the structure will be developed as a tree structure. As the design is prepared for implementation (packaged), common usage of modules and data will be recognized, and the

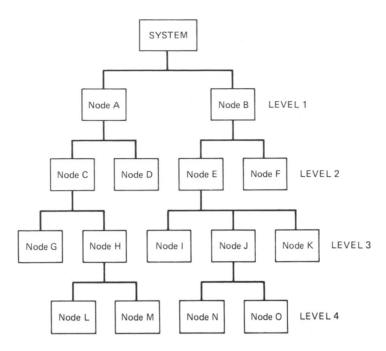

Fig. 3-1 Tree-like structure of nodes in a system

structure will take on characteristics of a directed graph. Every deviation from a pure tree structure should be analyzed to assure that inefficient restrictions are not being placed on the modules to meet performance requirements of the multiple branches.

The third premise is that the decomposition of the modules conforms to standard forms of structural constructs. We can identify these types and establish basic characteristics of the modules and data tables. Because of this, we can establish a methodology for decomposing the system into modules and data tables so that it will meet the characteristics desired. It is precisely this metholology and the characteristics of the modules resulting from this methodology that are presented in the section on techniques of structuring.

The fourth premise is that the structure will decompose to some logical point of termination. The point of design termination is closely related to the implementation criteria that we will establish for a module. That is, a module must describe a logically distinct function as opposed to a disjoint operation. The function performed by the module will be within the realm of human understanding to deal with as a single unit in its implementable state. We cannot comprehend all the processing performed by a system in its implementable state if it is viewed as a single unit. That is why we must decompose it. Likewise, it is highly unlikely (unless we are dealing with an extremely simple system) that the first, second, or even the third decomposition will yield a module that is completely understandable as a single unit with respect to all its processing implication. The number of levels in any one branch of the system is dependent on the complexity of the system. At some point, however, we will reach a point at which further decomposition no longer yields increased understanding, but in actuality may add superfluous detail that distracts from an understanding of the overall design. It is generally not logical to think of a sine function, for instance, as anything other than a sine function within a design structure. We would generally not want to think in terms of determining the quadrant, performing the calculations (or table search if that is the mode of implementation), and scaling the results for output. These are all parts of the detail design of the sine function. However, they do not particularly aid our understanding of the system. Thus, they represent a point of decomposition to which we do not wish to proceed in designing the system. We recognize that at this point the determination of when to stop is a gray area in the art of software design. It is still a value judgment. In the real world, the designer will learn through experience when it is best to cease decomposition and to transition to detail design of modules. There are a number of characteristics of the modules that will aid us in determining this terminus, which will be discussed in detail in the section on structuring. At this point, we contend that we can recognize a place to stop the decomposition process, and that system understandability is the major criterion determining the termination point.

The final premise we will make about structures regards the manner in which they are constructed. A structure can be constructed from the top down through essentially a discovery process by which the logical components of the system are determined. It can be constructed from the bottom up through a forced combination of known, possibly existing parts, i.e., reusable modules; or it can be constructed from what is termed "both ends in." Known parts exist and are used to weight the thinking process, but the structure is derived basically from a top-down approach until the point of the known module is reached. The argument is propounded that known modules constitute a cost savings, since they can be constructed as reusable modules. The counter argument proposes that if the use of a reusable module results in added complexity in the system design, the saving is only illusory. If reusable modules increase complexity, they are not truly reusable. The design should proceed, based on system requirements, not on the desire to use existing code. A more sophisticated version of information hiding can be considered here. For example, the design of a system can be simplified with the design of modules that hide awkward characteristics of the machine with which we are working. Modules that handle interrupt processing can be designed from the bottom up, so to speak. This is not changing the overall top-down design, but rather simplifying the problem solution by defining primitive elements as an aside process.

We have established a view of the system as a hierarchical structure of modules and data, with the module and data having identifiable characteristics with respect to the structure. The decomposition of the system into its structure proceeds to identifiable limits through a top-down design approach. It is important at this point that the reader understand that we are using the term top-down design in a generic sense. We design from a high-level abstract conceptualization through a decomposition process to a low level of detail conceptualization. The term *top-down design* has also been applied to a specific design and implementation methodology that has as its theme "design a little—code a little." We are distinctly *not* recommending this specific approach to design.

A NETWORK OF COMPONENTS
(A PHYSICAL VIEW OF THE SYSTEM)

Superimposed on the logical structure of the system is the actual physical configuration that will perform the transformations on the data that are indicated in the structure. Thus, we have a model of the system in its physical form described as some configuration of physical components. The components may be humans who execute prescribed procedures to interface with the equipment; they may be hardware devices such as computers, card reading devices, sensor devices; or they may be software contained within the computers and executing as programs. The allocation of the system to physical resources determines the performance characteristics of the system. That is, humans have certain characteristic response times, fatigue levels and conceptual synthesis capabilities. Hardware also has certain characteristics: size, speed, processing repertoires. Software characteristics are more flexible, based on the type of design employed, but these characteristics, too, are constrained by the equipment in which they execute.

This physical view of the system is presented as a network of components in Figure 3-2. The components of the network are the modules and data tables of the structure allocated in some combination to the physical resources of the system. The

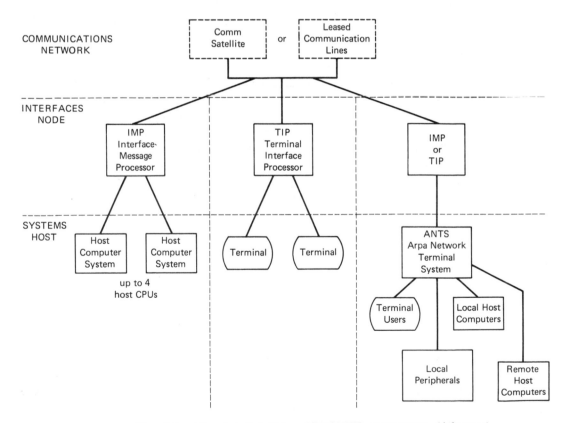

Fig. 3-2 Allocated functions: ARPANET components (Advanced Research Projects Agency Network)

interface between components is described in communication protocols that establish the exact form and content of the communication. The structure of the network can take on a number of forms that constitute the system configuration. Various options of ring structure, hierarchical structures, etc., will be discussed in the section on system design factors impacting software design.

The system configuration determines the physical characteristics of the system. Hence, it presents the dynamic nature of the system in terms of how long does it take actions to occur, whether there are capacity restrictions, etc. Whereas the static nature of the system can often be evaluated through a visual analysis of the logical structure, the dynamic view of the system often becomes so complex as to its operation that it requires automated aids to assist in collecting and evaluating information relative to the projected system's execution. Tools such as simulation/modeling have been devised for this purpose. Any methodology for software design must recognize the impact of the dynamic nature of the system on the static nature. Therefore, the methodology for discovering and evaluating the dynamic nature of the system will be discussed further in the sections on system design and simulation/modeling.

ALTERNATE VIEWS OF A SYSTEM (THEORETICAL MODELS)

Three theoretical models are worth review and further study: finite state machines, directed graphs, and Petri-nets.

Finite State Machines—The concept of finite state automata or finite state machines has been reviewed and discussed in computer science literature. As a conceptual device, it is very useful in decomposition or systematically breaking a design into small, easily understood pieces. To begin with, the system is thought of as a simple machine processing inputs to outputs. In the processing, the machine can assume only a limited number of states, and the relationships among inputs, machine states, and outputs can be explicitly stated. To be comprehensible to the human mind, the system must be describable as a fixed number of states with a fixed number of transformations that cause the system to change from one state to another.

The elements of the model for such a system are the fixed set of transformations described as functions, data, functional flows, and control. The functions of the system constitute the processing performed to accomplish a specified state change. The functions require input (data), do processing, and produce output (data). The functional flow describes the dynamic relationship between functions via the data output from a function as it relates to data input to another function. The system control assures that the functions of the system are performed in the desired sequence. Control is itself a finite state machine in that it is described as functions operating on data in a fixed sequence. Therefore, levels of finite state machines exist within the system. This approach has been well described by Salter[6] and also used in the Aeronutronic report on system decomposition performed for BMDATC entitled "Data Processing System Requirements."[7]

[6]Salter, K., "A Methodology for Decomposing System Requirements into Data Processing Requirements." Proceedings Second International Conference on Software Engineering, October 1976.
[7]Data Processing System Requirements—Final Report by Aeuronutronic Ford Corporation—CDRL A0007, 30 June 1976.

Directed Graphs—For a long time, analysts have been analyzing systems by noting the procedure flow and relating the changes of data from input to output by means of data flow charts. More formally, by noting the cause-effect relationship between the transformations in the system, the methodology closely follows the systems data flow developed in analysis of requirements. Again, the terminology is input data, transformation, and output data, all referenced as elements in the system. The key differences in this approach are in the manner in which the system is visually represented. Whereas finite state machine design is represented as a hierarchy of machines, each setting forth in more detail the processing hidden in the more abstract machine, the directed graph attempts to set forth all the elements of the system in forms of nodes connected by directed arcs that represent the input/output pairs between the elements. This methodology is well described by Belford.[8] It emphasizes information content and flow, or procedural steps. Since each of the nodes can be systematically expanded, the methodology can be used in the step-wise refinement of the design of a system.

Petri-Nets—Petri-nets are a refinement of directed graphs. The chief difference is that in the directed graph the node represents a transformation, but the Petri-net recognizes two kinds of nodes: conditions and events. The notation used indicates condition (or places) with circles and events in transformations with vertical bars. The Petri-nets have the advantages of showing procedural relationships as well as directed graphs, but also provide a closer approximation of a simulation model of the system. This is possible because the conditions for initiating transformations can be described by using logical condition statements. The methodology is described in detail by Balkovich and Engleberg.[9]

3.1.4 RECOGNIZING A GOOD DESIGN

In our discussion of dynamics of the design process, to this point, we have covered the concept that the software design process is essentially a human problem-solving process, common to other scientific and engineering problem-solving processes. We have covered the concept of breaking the problem into sizes that we can understand and ordering them into levels of refinement. We have also described a set of concepts that are useful in thinking about a data processing system in terms of structures that help us to maintain perspective on the overall problem the conceptual system is to solve. Now that we have considered these human aspects of design, it is time to consider the criteria by which we can recognize a good design, the desired product of these disciplined ways of thinking.

There are many definitions of good design, ranging from "it is one that can be understood and implemented within cost and schedule" to "it has advanced features that the user will really appreciate once he is familiar with the program." Actually, the attributes of good design are predictive in nature; they are the characteristics that,

[8]Belford, P., et al., "Specifications—A Key to Effective Software Development." Proceedings Second International Software Engineering Conference. October 1976.

[9]Balkovich, E., and G. Engleberg, "Research Towards a Technology to Support the Specification of Data Processing System Performance Requirements," Proceedings Second International Software Engineering Conference, October 1976.

when implemented, will result in a product that has the qualities that the user requires in his product. The term "attribute" is used in the design phase to describe the characteristics of performance that we call "qualities" in the end product. When describing the performance of the end product, it is tedious and time consuming for the user to distinguish the difference between the hardware system and the software system, so we generally refer to the generic term *system* in talking of performance qualities. When attributes specifically relate to software, we will use the term *software system*.

It is very difficult to establish a comprehensive and universally acceptable list of attributes that determine good software system performance. There are quantitative measurements for which a fixed value can be determined, i.e., cost, schedule, manpower to produce, manpower to operate, manpower to maintain, response time by function, resource utilization, et al. There are judgment factors that are associated with a qualitative evaluation for which more precise evaluation metrics are only now being developed, i.e., usability, maintainability, system security, and legal implications. Reliability currently falls in a gray area between the two. It is defined in somewhat hardware-oriented terms as mean time between failure (MTBF), but failure is a function of the current options being exercised. Softwere exercised under identical conditions at all times should presumably never fail. However, since software does fail, a pertinent question for the software engineer to ask is: "Should a system exercised within a very small range of its total capabilities with few failures be termed more reliable than a system exercised over a wider range with more failures?"

Selection of a particular attribute to identify good software design is based on required overall system performance characteristics or qualities. Therefore, we need to examine some of the factors or measures of system quality before we can define the attributes of a good software system design. For example, maintainability is most often cited as a desirable quality of software, yet the cost of the initial design for maintainable software may not be justified, due to the limited life cycle or time the software will be used as a part of a system. A small program that will be used only in the testing of the software end product is not worth the cost of designing for maintenance. The selection of specific attributes to be included in the design is a part of the systems trade studies performed during the design phase. With multiple attributes, ranking schemes are indicated in the trade studies to select the more important attributes.

It must be recognized that the individual quality of the end product is interrelated with overall cost and performance of the product. For example, reliability of the software product is important, and, in general, we know that some designs are inherently more reliable than others though we have pointed out there is considerable difference of opinion as to the definition of software reliability, much less to the set of metrics for measurement of reliability. The cost associated with achieving a relative degree of reliability may or may not, however, be warranted. An obvious example is that a real-time patient monitoring program, used in a hospital for monitoring patients in an intensive care ward, cannot have any logic paths in the design structure that will allow the program to terminate because of a transient input of data that is out of normal range of acceptability. Similarly, we would expect a check processing program to have error checking procedures that permit printing of dollar amounts only within a set range of acceptable values (and certainly not to print negative numbers). However, in the case of the patient monitoring program, procedures to recover from transient out-of-bounds data, though necessary, are expensive to design, implement, and test. Such a level of reliability may not be required, for example, in a program designed to process cards used to maintain inventory control. In this case, termination of the program on receipt of data out of bounds may be an acceptable characteristic, though inconvenient to the operator as he would have to review an input deck to change any erroneous card and rerun the program. The point is, reliability, like any other quality of design, has an impact on the cost of the product.

It is important that the qualitative statement of the expected attribute (in this case, the degree of reliability) be included in the definition of requirements prior to design so the designer has some measure of knowing when his design will yield the desired qualities that the user understands and demands in the end product. For example, reliability is a popular buzz word, yet different people have varying interpretations of what the word means. For one user it means that the system will give identical answers each time the same problem is presented. Other users have a broader view and think of reliability as meaning that the system will continue to perform basic functions in a usable manner (i.e., within acceptable levels of tolerance) even if the problems presented or the total environment in which the system is operating is quite different from that assumed in the design.

Usability or utility of a program is often considered the single most important expression of overall quality of the product. The pertinent questions regarding usability are: "Does the software design perform the functions in a manner that meets the user's intended needs, and are the human interfaces adequately defined so use is not limited by jargon difficult to understand or is computer oriented?" The product must be convenient to use and practical. There should be enough flexibility in design so that the product can be useful in more than the restricted requirements imposed in initial development.

A checklist of qualitites desired in the end product is provided below to give some indication of the considerations involved in the process of software design:

Reliability—The product will perform the intended user's functions accurately under normal conditions and will do so consistently and completely. Abnormal conditions may cause degraded performance, but will not result in erroneous performance masked as correct performance.

Testability—The end product possesses the characteristic of testability when it is so structured and defined that its performance can be evaluated against the user's statement of requirements in a quantitative manner.

Maintainability—A product is maintainable when it is easily understood by the maintenance programmers and is easy to modify and test when updating to meet new requirements, rectifying a deficiency, correcting errors, or moving to a different but similar computer system.

Efficiency—A product is efficient to the extent to which it performs useful tasks for the user without excessive waste of resources. Efficiency is not measured in terms of computer processor utilization, but in terms of the useful work it performs for the resources available where the term resources is defined in terms of computer processor utilization and peripheral cost of operation per task performed or report generated.

Understandability—The product package is understandable to the extent that the user can easily grasp the functioning of the product and the relationship between the product and other products and system components. There should be no hidden meanings or operating characteristics that come to light only after months or years of use.

Adaptability—A product is adaptable if the characteristics of design include legibility, device independence, structuredness, and self-containment so the product can stand by itself and be easily moved to a different but similar computer.

Obviously, the list of qualities for software can be extended, but the listing above should give the reader some understanding of the different qualities that can be found in software products. Not all qualities would be emphasized in each product in the same way. It is management's task to see that the specification of the desired software design attributes is made during the definition process and that management plans are made to ensure that the design includes provision to include the specified qualities in the end product.

The software engineer must consider the inclusion of the attributes that yield quality software in his design. These attributes of good design are somewhat different from the qualities desired in the end product, yet are necessary if the end product is to meet the desired user's requirements. The desirable attributes of a good software design are:

Necessity—Only those performance requirements and design features necessary to meet the requirements of usability are included in the design. Extra features that might be nice to have, but are not really needed, are deleted. All those favorite design features the designer has always wanted to develop, but are of no utility to the user of the product, are excluded. This calls for some strong measures of self-discipline on the part of the software engineers who may have evolved from relatively unrestrained design environments. A basic engineering criterion of a good design is simplicity.

Completeness—All of the modules in the structure are identified; all interfaces are specified, and all environments are specified. TBDs (To Be Determined at a later date) are not acceptable as part of a design. Completeness does not mean low level of detail, but rather that all functions and tasks to be performed by the software to meet user's requirements are identified and defined in the appropriate levels of design.

Consistency—Design philosophy incompatibilities have been identified and resolved.

Traceability—This characteristic refers to the fact that there must be an audit trail that can relate user stated requirements to the elements of design much in the manner that we construct a specification tree. The end functions performed by the product must be relatable to a requirement of the user.

Visibility—The elements of design must be relatable or traceable to the design decisions made in trade-off studies. This type of backup to design decisions provides for flexibility in changing design to meet requirements that are "discovered" or evolve in the process of developing the design.

Feasibility—The critical elements in the design must have been demonstrated—by implementation of a feasibility demonstration program if necessary—to be attainable in the current state of the art. The design must be evaluated to be implementable within the constraints of cost and schedule. If constraints of a specific computer con-figuration have been placed on the design, then it must be shown that the proposed design is implementable within the defined constraints of time and core.

If we software engineers design our software with an understanding that the design attributes must meet the specified quality in the end product and have the character-istics in the software design described above, we have a high probability of producing a good design. We must remember the old, but most useful, criteria of good design that have been used by engineers for decades—economy and simplicity are the marks of a good design.

Having reviewed the creative aspects of problem solving and some of the criteria that we can use to identify good design, we can now proceed to examine at a high level the techniques of the design process.

3.1.5 TECHNIQUES OF THE DESIGN PROCESS

Since the design of software is a creative process, most of the software design methodologies focus on techniques for organizing information in a format that is easily understandable. The goal is to coordinate the creative efforts of individuals by organizing the enormous amounts of conceptual and design data generated in the pro-cess of design into a form that enhances communication between designers and with the users of the system to be designed. The actual tools that have been created to assist in the design process are few. The most effective tool that has proven itself through use is simulation/modeling. Several language capabilities have been developed to quickly and effectively create a model to simulate the design. These models are used in evalu-ating the completeness of a formalized requirements statement and for measuring resource utilization of a proposed system design. Other tools being developed include specification languages for capturing precise statements of requirements in machine-readable form for consistency checking and analysis. The trend is toward the develop-ment of a higher level of automated tools that will enable the software/systems engineering organization to enter into a dialogue with a computer-based, integrated design-support system. The dialogue would allow the creative abilities of the engineer to be directly supported by the deductive logical capabilities and the bookkeeping capabilities of a computer system. At present, however, the design process is primarily manual with techniques or methods designed to assist the software engineer's thinking process. Figure 3-3 summarizes various techniques that will be discussed as they relate to the measures of software quality identified in the previous section.

We software engineers should be familiar with the range of methodologies avail-able to us and pick and choose the techniques most appropriate to our task. We are presenting, for instance, in this chapter a methodology termed structured design for use in the system/software design process. This methodology is most appropriate for the larger-scale computer programs (50,000 to 500,000 lines of code) that require multi-man efforts. It also supports the more difficult design process wherein hardware is being designed concurrently with the software. Smaller systems and problems that are particularly oriented toward data handling may find variations in the methodology to be effective. This methodology is constantly being refined, based on constructs and

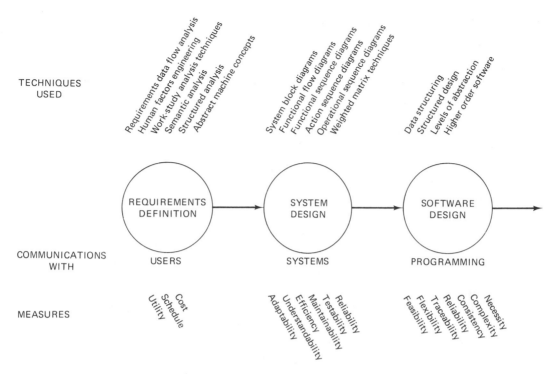

TECHNIQUES USED

Requirements data flow analysis
Human factors engineering
Work-study analysis techniques
Semantic analysis
Structured analysis
Abstract machine concepts

System block diagrams
Functional flow diagrams
Functional sequence diagrams
Action sequence diagrams
Operational sequence diagrams
Weighted matrix techniques

Data structuring
Structured design
Levels of abstraction
Higher order software

REQUIREMENTS DEFINITION → SYSTEM DESIGN → SOFTWARE DESIGN →

COMMUNICATIONS WITH

USERS   SYSTEMS   PROGRAMMING

MEASURES

Cost
Schedule
Utility

Reliability
Testability
Maintainability
Efficiency
Understandability
Adaptability

Necessity
Complexity
Consistency
Reliability
Traceability
Flexibility
Feasibility

Fig. 3-3 Techniques and measures by phase of design

technology evolved in other areas, illustrating a continual evolution of techniques toward the eventual development of a set of fully automated tools. Systems engineers have been designing complex hardware systems for some time and have developed other techniques with which the software engineer should be familiar.

The definition of the requirements for a data processing system in large-scale embedded computer systems has classically been the responsibility of the system engineer with support from the software engineer. System engineers have evolved a number of tools and techniques whereby they deal with the man-machine interaction, establish performance constraints for the system, and allocate the design to hardware, software, or, in recent years, firmware. Thus, they establish the software requirements, based on their understanding of the system design. They describe these requirements in a set of documents called by many titles but which can be summarized as a software requirements specification that tells the software engineers what they are to design in the way of software. These documents are intended to describe to the software engineer the basic structure of the system, the software, and the specific performance constraints that the software elements must meet. The deficiencies in this division of documentation are many. The software engineers apply their understanding to the software design specifications. Errors in interpretation are introduced, which propagate through the implementation and testing phases until they are discovered only during final system testing and sell-off to the customer.

With the awareness of this problem has come the trend toward involving the software engineer in the analysis and system definition phases. The software engineer is becoming an integral member of the system design team. They can contribute in making the trade-off decisions that will impact software and can gain the in-depth understanding possible only through direct involvement. The software engineers bring to the analysis efforts their own set of tools and techniques that promise to enhance their ability to express the design in a manner suitable for subsequent software development.

The methodologies associated with the design effort may be categorized as to traditional systems design methodologies counterbalanced by the evolving software engineering methodologies. It is important that software engineers be familiar with both the software design tools and methods and the tools of systems and hardware engineers with whom they are working. With this knowledge, they are best able to judge the most suitable tool for the job at hand and plan the development effort more judiciously. The description of these design methodologies can be categorized as requirements analysis aids, system design aids, and software design aids. We will also introduce the concepts of design validation and verification aids and general communication aids used to organize, coordinate, and test designs.

REQUIREMENTS ANALYSIS AIDS

The aids or techniques used in requirements analysis are, generally speaking, the least developed of the design tools. However, one basic feature emerges for all of the techniques referenced below—that of information flow. The users, in describing their requirements for a system, generally talk of the functions they want to do better. The analyst is left with the task of identifying the users' requirements in terms of paths or flows of information. The users are not concerned with the structure of software, nor with the flow of data from module to module, but rather with what the system will do for them (the users) in terms of desired output for a given input. Thus, the users are concerned with the flow of information both into and out of the system, and the overall performance of the system as it is associated with that data flow.

The dynamics of the system must be understood in order to identify the functions to be performed. The functions performed by the system are identified in terms of transformations that the data undergoes. The performance characteristics of the system are identified as quantifiable measures applied to the transformations of the system. The data flow developed with the user becomes the basis for relating the user's requirements to the system design.

The traditional techniques of user's requirements analysis are those associated with human factors engineering and work-study analysis.

Human Factors Engineering—Human factors engineering addresses the problems of human interaction with the system. It has as its goal aiding the design effort in producing systems that respond to human characteristics in a well-organized manner.

Work Study Analysis Techniques—Work-study analysis monitors the existing interaction of humans within a system with the goal of determining improved procedures and efficiency of movement. It uses layout diagrams to capture movement patterns. It also utilizes the operational sequence diagrams to define operator interactions.

There is considerable interest in the development of analytic aids to assist in defining the user's true requirements as a prerequisite to the system and software design phases. Three of these bear mentioning—semantic analysis, structured analysis, and abstract machines. The first two are considered emerging technologies. The last is commonly recognized by the system engineering community. Precise methodologies for their use have yet to be defined and refined through use on large scale projects. All have similarities in that they recognize the system as a structured hierarchy of modules. The major differences are found in the emphasis placed on the characteristics of these modules.

Semantic Analysis—Semantic analysis is based on the premise that our thought or conceptualization of a system is based on our ability to express those concepts in language. It adheres to the philosophy of Whorf[10] that language determines thought. The approach in this methodology is to identify the terms used to talk about a system, to classify these terms properly, and then to use the classifications as guides to steer the design. That is, the "objects" of a system are identified and classes of objects established based on similar criteria. This technique establishes a data structure for the system. The object classes are then used to derive a processing structure. This approach, as seen in initial descriptions, appears to feed directly into the data structuring approach to system/software design espoused by Jackson,[11] which is discussed in the section on structuring methodology.

Structured Analysis—This term has been coined by Yourdon[12] in his work on requirements analysis. Similar to semantic analysis, it is based on adapting a software design approach to the process of requirements analysis. This type of analysis, however, is based on a software design technique called structured design. Because of the relationship between structured analysis and structured design, this analysis aid has an inherent appeal for us and so will be alluded to in the following section. Its major thrust lies in identifying processing requirements, based on the total system state at any point in time rather than on data structure. The methodology is emerging and requires refinement through use on several large-scale projects before it can be expected to receive general industry-wide acceptance.

Abstract Machines—Abstract machine concepts closely relate to the concepts of "information hiding" and "levels of abstraction." When viewing a system, major branches in the structure or major components can be designed as "black boxes." Requirements are stated, not in terms of the working details of a concept, but in terms of a "black box" that will take the information given it and transform that information to the desired results. The manner in which the "black box" accomplishes this transformation is not identified until it becomes necessary to design the inner workings of that "black box."

Software engineers have taken this concept of "black boxes" and extended it to the concept of "abstract machines." Thus, the analyst can identify a "processing machine" that has the capabilities of performing any assigned number of transformations on given inputs and producing the desired outputs without reference to any

[10]Whorf, Benjamin Lee, *Language, Thought and Reality*, MIT Press, Cambridge, Mass.
[11]Jackson, M., *Principles of Program Design*, Academic Press, 1975.
[12]Yourdan, E., and L. Constantine, *Structured Design*, Yourdan and Company, Inc., 1976.

specific hardware device(s) or software architecture. This technique does have the implied connotation that the design can be developed independent of the actual hardware on which it will be implemented. It provides a useful conceptualization of independency of major branches in the structure with processing identified strictly in terms of function performed on identifiable interfaces.

SYSTEM DESIGN AIDS

A trend in system design aids is noted in which the decisions concerning allocating tasks to implementable modules is postponed until the scope of the design is known from the structure of the system. Interleaved with the structuring process are configuring decisions such as what modules will reside in common processors if a multi-processor system is involved or what modules will reside in common overlays if a single processor with memory overlays is involved. Indeed, an entire range of hardware/software trade-off decisions are made, based on the structure. Allocation to an implementation medium (hardware, software, firmware) can be made by using such techniques as weighted matrices and simulation/modeling techniques. The recognition that hardware decisions can impact design, often to the detriment of good design, has been recognized. The packaging of the system is a synthesis process wherein the components of the system are identified as to their actual physical attributes and the system is recognized as an aggregate of components. Attempting to build a system from the bottom up with known components, or placing too stringent constraints on the system through too early identification of hardware, can introduce unnecessary complexities or inefficiencies into the design.

The design techniques traditionally used by the systems engineering community are: (1) functional flow diagrams (used in initial design of systems); (2) functional sequence diagrams; (3) action sequence diagrams, used in detailing interactions among the elements of the system; (4) operational sequence diagrams that detail human interfaces with the system; and (5) weighted matrices that are useful for minimizing subjectivity in selecting options and alternatives. These are surveyed below with examples being given later.

Functional Flow Diagrams (FFDs)—These diagrams are used to depict the top-level functional processes in a system. They are based on the concept of layered levels of abstract machines. The system is broken down conceptually into major functions or processes that are thought to be necessary, and the processes are related by pointers showing the kind of relations that will exist between the processes.

The functional flow diagrams are a useful technique for blocking out a first approximation of how a system can be configured; i.e., how a series of black boxes representing finite state machines can be related structurally to provide a base for further analysis. Functional flow diagrams are very useful in laying out a general approach for coordination between several analysts.

Function Sequence Diagrams (FSDs)—These diagrams are similar to functional flow diagrams, but are more general in that they describe the functions of the system as pertaining to sequences on a timeline rather than just the static relationship of processes.

Action Sequence Diagrams (*ASDs*)—The ASD technique developed by Hughes Aircraft Company provides an analysis tool employed to define and allocate actions, decisions, and processes necessary to translate system requirements into software requirements. The analyst develops detailed sequences of actions that define the operator, subsystem, equipment, and software interfaces required during any particular operation.

An ASD is constructed for each function allocated to the software subsystem. ASD construction is an iterative process. All operators, equipment, and other subsystems expected to interface with the software subsystem are listed. The actions and data flow necessary to implement the system as derived in functional and operational analyses are diagramed on the form along with decision points. Therefore, the ASD becomes an important tool in identifying the complete interface of the software system with its environment.

Operational Sequence Diagrams (*OSDs*)—Operational sequence diagrams are used to depict the data flow from data acquisition through its processing and eventual output. The data is related to its source, either men or equipment. Each type of information flowing in the integrated system is completely traced as it flows through and interacts with the system and other types of information in the system.

OSDs can be thought of as specialized action sequence diagrams used primarily to analyze the interaction of humans with the system. Operator work stations are identified, and the actions taken by the operator are defined. The processing that handles the operator actions is described in graphic terms (similar to flow charts). System files are identified. Paths of events are traced generally with conditions identified that determine the choice of paths.

Weighted Matrices—Weighted matrices are aids that assist in evaluating alternative choices. Specific measurements are applied to various criteria under evaluation. That is, the number of choices to be considered is listed. The criteria to be evaluated in making the choice are enumerated. A measurement scale is established and a weighting value is assigned for each criterion. The criteria are evaluated individually, and a relative measurement value fixed. The individual measurements, multiplied by the weighting scale, are totaled to give an overall ranking. This value then indicates the preferable overall choice with individual factors "smoothed out" over the total set of criteria. The validity of the selection can be determined by a sensitivity analysis that identifies how much any one factor affects the total outcome.

This approach is a tremendous aid in communicating relative judgments instead of the usual method that uses subjective terms; for example, better, significantly better, excellent, good, poor, inferior, acceptable, etc. The weighted-rating approach also facilitates reevaluation of the decision after the trade study has focused attention on critical items where more detailed study will be most effective in reducing uncertainties and insuring proper decisions.

We note that the more powerful techniques of design analysis center around the use of data flow depictions of one type or another (OSDs, ASDs, FFDs, etc.), and that these techniques bear a striking similarity to the data flow depictions used in structured design methodologies. Transform analysis, resulting in data flow diagrams, is an integral part of the structuring process. However, it is evolving as an integral tool to the system design effort because it provides a tool for evaluating the dynamic data flow of the system that leads to the structuring process. Thus, there is the beginning of convergence of the system design techniques with the software design techniques.

SOFTWARE DESIGN AIDS

In the area of software design methodology we are now seeing a number of different methods of system decomposition emerge. We will identify four of the leading methods here and describe a general composite approach to structured decomposition in Sec.3.4.

Data Structuring—A design approach that is attracting much attention is that of Michael Jackson.[11] The approach recognizes the necessity for the design of the program to reflect the structure of the problem. To do this job Jackson has, in a way, brought together the standard computer science notations such as context-free grammars, co-routines, and backtracking into a unified design methodology.

He starts by defining the input and output data structures, using context-free grammars. Next, he creates a general program structure to match both the input and output data structures. This is the creative step in the design, but there are no guidelines for performance. Finally, elementary operations are listed and each is allocated to program components.

Jackson defines a structure clash as occurring when a single program cannot handle both input data structures and output data structures. Such clashes are resolved by the formation of two or more programs rather than a single program. The several programs will communicate during their separate processing phases by using an intermediate sequential file of records. The records are so chosen that the data structure does not clash with either the input or the output data structures.

This method rigorously defines both input and output data structures. Modifications can be systematically treated so the program structure continues to represent the problem structure.

The methodology starts with the generalized concept of a loop invariant for the program. A loop invariant is a predicate that is true. Jackson generalizes the loop to the entire program and the predicate to a general program structure. By using the co-routine concept and backtracking notions, he has focused on an excellent separation of concerns. The aim is to produce programs that have a simple structure which does not conflict with either the input data structure or output data structure.

Structured Design—This methodology is based on Constantine and Myers'[13] design technique of structured design. In this approach the data transformations are analyzed through a process called transform analysis. The structure is derived by applying design rules and guidelines to create the structure from the data flow diagram resulting from the transform analysis. The emphasis is on deriving the processing requirements, based on a knowledge of the total system state at any point in time. Figure 3-4 is a classical example of a data flow diagram that depicts the requirements from a systems point of view. Figure 3-5 is an example of a classical structure chart based on the data flow that shows the structure of the program in terms of control, functional modules, and data flow.

[13]Myers, G. J., "Composite Design: The Design and Modular Programs," Technical Report TR 002406, IBM, Poughkeepsie, N.Y., January 29, 1973.

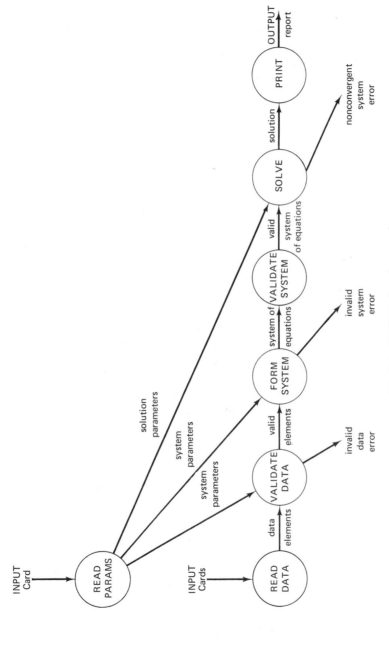

Fig. 3-4 SEIDEL data flow graph

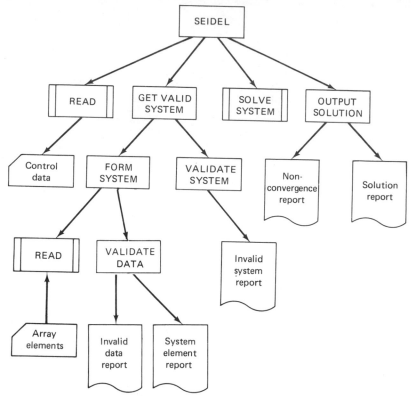

Fig. 3-5 SEIDEL program structure chart

Levels of Abstraction—The relationship of this technique to the abstract machine methodology has already been noted. Its primary value is in its emphasis on the characteristics of a module. Nodes in the structure should present a completely self-contained abstraction to the viewer so that he does not need to look further down in the structure to understand the processing performed by that node and all nodes subservient to it. Indeed, a prime purpose in generating a structure is so we can deal with an understanding of the system at comprehensible levels. Thus, the levels of abstraction technique supports a basic concept of the system design effort.

Higher-Order Software (*HOS*)—Efforts are in progress to define the design constructs along more rigorous lines. Hamilton and Zeldin[14] were instrumental in the development of HOS, which has as its basis the axiomatic definition of design constructs. Their work originated out of an analysis of the most common errors detected in the design of a large-scale, real-time project. The errors were found to lie primarily within six basic categories that are related to the way modules interfaced with each other. As a result, six basic axioms were defined, restricting the manner in which modules can control other modules, pass data to other modules, and use data within a

[14]Hamilton, M., and S. Zeldin, "Higher Order Software—A Methodology for Defining Software," *IEEE Transactions on Software Engineering*, March 1976.

————, "Integrated Software Development System/Higher Order Software Conceptual Description, Research and Development Technical Report", ECOM-76-0329-F, U. S. Army Electronics Command, Fort Monmouth, N.J., 1976.

module. Their work assumes a basic premise that encompasses the completely functional description of a system. It enhances the structured design methodology by providing additional criteria for evaluating design constructs that are presented in detail in the section on structuring.

There are strong indications at present that the methodologies of data structuring and structured design are merging into a hybrid technology further advanced by the concepts of levels of abstractions and the mathematical discipline of HOS. The technique of structuring presented later in this text is an evolution of structured design derived by E. Jensen,[15] which reflects this hybrid trend and emphasizes the iterative nature of transform analysis and structuring. This approach is most consistent with the dynamics of the design process and, therefore, will be presented in this context. The section on structuring will deal with the process in depth.

Basically, transform analysis applies to analyzing the changes or transformations the data undergoes as it passes through the system. A high-level structure diagram is then generated from the transform analysis that incorporates the control and implementation scheme into the design. The process is applied iteratively in that the transform analysis is used to analyze the structure diagrams to further decompose the transformations. The process draws a distinction between design modules and implementation modules. The methodology includes criteria for "packaging" modules together for implementation.

DESIGN VERIFICATION AND VALIDATION AIDS

Design verification and validation tools fall into two general categories: (1) those techniques that seek to verify that the design is in accordance with the attributes stated as desirable features of the design, and (2) those techniques that seek to validate that the design conforms to user's requirements.

The general goal of validation techniques is to determine if the design satisfies the performance requirements of the user.

The general goal of verification techniques is to evaluate the quality of design as it conforms to some measurable attribute for "good" design. No specific measurements for design attribute and characteristics exist yet within the industry. Some effort is underway to identify the factors that lead to "reliable software" that can then lead to criteria for evaluating design. Since no universally recognized measurements exist for measuring quality, this section can do little more than enumerate the trends.

Design Reviews—Design reviews are a general methodology applied to both verify and validate the design. They consist of a manual analysis of the design conducted in a group discussion by qualified reviewers. The design reviews are structured in that they have formal goals established, based on the type of review being conducted. Formal procedures exist as guidelines for the review process as discussed in the final section on verification and validation.

Simulation/Modeling—Simulation/modeling is the technique applied in evaluating the dynamic nature of the system prior to its implementation. A model of the

---

[15] Jensen, E., "1975 IR&D Structured Design Methodology," Formal Report 75-17-691, Hughes Aircraft Company, 1975.

system is built, using a simulation language that describes the basic configuration of the system. Performance characteristics are then determined from the characteristics of the allocated components. The simulation model is run as a computer program that collects information on the resource utilization (time, core, percent of CPU utilization, percent of device utilization, etc.). The results are used to validate the design feasibility as it relates to the ability to meet performance criteria. Methods of building and using simulation/modeling as well as applicable modeling languages are discussed later.

Software Physics—Kolence[16] addresses the problem of measurements for software in his work by utilizing what he labels "software physics." He provides computer processing definitions for such physical elements as work and power; e.g., work is defined in terms of changes to bytes within a computer. He provides methods of actually measuring work. His techniques to date have particular applicability to data processing service centers in which existing configurations are evaluated for potential growth. Software physics has the potential for developing as a requirements analysis aid since its goal is to aid in evaluating projected system improvements.

COMMUNICATIONS AIDS

The product must be described not only in terms that enable the user to understand how to use the system, but also in terms that enable other designers to evaluate the design and the implementor to implement the design accurately. Communication is an important aspect of the design process, second perhaps only to clear thinking. A design that cannot be communicated is worthless as a design. We software engineers must communicate our design decisions as well as produce the design documentation.

Graphics—Many of the design tools that we have surveyed show, as a major benefit, clear and concise description of the design in graphic terms. Functional flow diagrams, data flow diagrams, structured hierarchical charts, etc., all have as a common feature the presentation of data in graphic terms. These graphic tools are an aid to human understanding through a visual medium.

Languages—Humans communicate abstract concepts with other humans through language. Humans have also developed a communication medium with computers through languages. Two types of languages exist: programming languages and design languages.

Programming languages (such as FORTRAN, COBOL, PASCAL) have as their primary purpose the expression of the design in a form that can be converted for execution by the computer. The language statements are processed (by computer programs) for the primary purpose of generating machine-executable zeros and ones. The assemblers/compilers (those programs that process the language statements) do incidentally produce diagnostic messages of a form that aids the coder in detecting statements that do not conform to the syntax of the language. The point can also

---

[16]Kolence, K., *The Meaning of Computer Measurement: An Introduction to Software Physics*, Institute for Software Engineering, 1976.

be made that languages vary greatly in their aids to design reliability from the standpoint of the features that they provide. A good example is data type and data-type checking. In a language such as FORTRAN, for example, it is very easy to mistype things, to call a subroutine with a floating point value when the subroutine is expecting an integer. In languages such as SNOBOL, data typing doesn't exist at all which is even worse. A variable can, at one moment, contain an integer and at another moment, contain a string. From a design standpoint, this means that data structures tend to be very sloppy if we are not cautious. On the other hand, a language like PASCAL is very specific; a variable is of a specific type, and a routine expects variables of an explicit type. Thus we tend to be much more careful with the types of variables used in the program. From this discussion, we can see that languages not only vary greatly in providing programming aids and locating errors, but also affect the design. Ultimately variables and data must be defined explicitly in the programming language. The language we select for use can force us to define them much earlier in a more methodical way.

Design languages, on the other hand, encompass those languages with the primary purpose of describing the design in a clear, precise communication medium. The purpose of the design languages is two-fold: to aid the communication between designers by identifying a set of terms clearly understandable among all parties involved in the design process, and to capture the design decisions in a machine-processable form (as opposed to a machine-executable form). The basic goal is to provide a mechanism for capturing the design in a data base. Expressed in machine-processable form, any number of programs can be derived to provide information about the design. A number of such languages are emerging. The kinds of automated aids provided with such languages can include: (1) automated documentation generation to prescribed formats, (2) automated analysis for conformance to specific design constructs, (3) automated testing and evaluation of the design through simulation interface, and (4) automated configuration management and requirements tracing.

One of the promising developments in specification of information processing systems has been in the development of languages to provide tools for describing the information flow of a system, the tasks to be performed, and the data to be processed. Specifying a system in these terms primarily means using a formal language with a precise syntactical structure to define the semantics of the system and to establish the relationships. Among the most promising representatives of this approach to specification of requirements is the Problem Statement Language (PSL) of the ISDOS Project under D. Teichroew[17] at the University of Michigan. His work has been used as an approach to increase the amount of design automation in the definition phase. A precise syntax is used to provide for entry of the specification into a machine-processable form. This then allows for the automation of consistency checking and the production of a variety of forms of documentation to aid the analyst and designer in the development of a design. In addition, formal documentation to a standard format can be produced. The PSL concept has been picked up and augmented by other

[17]Teichroew, D., and E. Hershey, III, "PSL/PSA: A Computer-aided Technique for Structured Documentation and Analysis of Information Processing Systems," Proceedings of Second International Software Engineering Conference, October 1976.

workers in the field. Another development of the concept (called Requirements State-ment Language) and the best extension into the arena of system design (as opposed to data-base oriented information systems) has been by the group of contractors at Ballistic Missile Division Advanced Technology Center, working for C. Davis.[18] They have undertaken the task of augmenting the specification language concept that supports static analysis of the requirements. They have introduced extensions for handling the dynamic concepts of design performance characteristics and task per-formance.

In general, the problem statement languages are in their early stages of devel-opment and are just beginning to be used in working environments. Evaluations of their effectiveness are beginning to appear in the literature, and results have been mixed. There is a consensus that such a development is the next important tool that must be developed for use in software engineering. This trend in development of speci-fication languages will eventually provide a capability for a general and informal dialogue among the software engineer, systems engineer, and the computer whereby the computer system acquires deductive reasoning capabilities in the sense of being able to perform all of the routine design work for the analyst, leaving to the analyst the creative portions of design.

3.1.6 SUMMARY OF THE DESIGN DYNAMICS

In the foregoing section, we have discussed the basic elements that interact in the dynamics of the design process. The elements, in summary, are:

- Design is an individual, creative act. Designs are created by individuals who use the basic creative problem-solving techniques common to science and engi-neering, namely, problem definition, proposal of a solution, and test of the solution against the problem definition.
- Problem solutions have to be brought within the scale of human understanding. Since the problems being addressed are of a large scale, there must be methods for breaking the problems and proposed solutions into chunks that can be understood by the designer. The statement of the problem is iterated through different levels of refinement to keep the problem within the scope of human comprehension.
- Solutions follow human concepts of the system. Since the designs represent a view of the world, a model of how a designer conceives a system is described.
- Design quality is measured by nonquantitative metrics. The attributes of good design are described in qualitative measures and applied by using trade-off techniques that make the evaluations more objective.
- Techniques are primarily human-based methods. The tools, techniques, and methods used in the design process are surveyed for later discussion. We noted that most of the techniques were manual methodologies and that automated tools for system/software design are only now evolving.

[18]Davis, C., and C. Vick, "The Software Development System," Proceedings of Second Inter-national Software Engineering Conference, October, 1976.

Throughout the discussion, it should be apparent that the design process is human oriented and that there are no cookbook methods that can be used to design good software at this time. We have indicated that further automation of design tools will provide better support to the designer; but the acts of problem identification, solution design, and evaluation of solutions will remain the province of human endeavor.

The dynamic action of any process is the function of combined forces of varying strengths and vectors. The software design process is no different. We have described in outline the basic forces that converge on the software engineer during the technical process of design. These forces include the performance requirements and attributes desired in the design by the user of the product, the techniques and tools used by the designer in the process of design, and the steps in creative problem solving that are iterated through levels of refinement in arriving at the basic design. Added to these forces are the management controls on the designer, the pressures of staff coordination, milestones to be met and costs to be controlled, as well as interfaces to be maintained with user/customers and other design activities. Thus we can see the dynamics under which software designs are created.

The result in all cases is a compromise of conceptualizations, objectives, and goals with a resultant design that will, when implemented, meet with the user's satisfaction. The idea of compromise is acceptable. After all, the discipline of engineering is one of arriving at a compromise that best meets the user's requirements.

3.2

Software Design to Produce a Product

In analyzing requirements, we, as software engineers, must be concerned with obtaining a complete and precise description of the product desired by the user of the software system. To do this, we must first find out who the real user of the system is. Then we must discern the user's particular problems in terms of the environment in which the user works. At this point, we can introduce some special techniques that have been found useful in analyzing the user's problem relative to the environment. Finally, we will present some ideas on formalizing the statement of the user's requirements, including a discussion of evolving trends in problem-statement languages. To illustrate the techniques we have been discussing, we will describe a sample problem taken from a study of an embedded computer system.

3.2.1 WHO IS THE REAL USER?

The software engineer, concerned with defining requirements for a software product, must get these requirements from potential users of the product—the people who are going to pay hard money for a computer program. In talking about the user, it is important to understand who is the real user. It is convenient to identify two kinds of users in the system—the ultimate user, who sees the necessity of creating or purchasing a software product to solve a problem, and the operators of a system, who will use the software product in their day-to-day work. We can view the ultimate users as people in management positions who are faced with the day-to-day responsibility for operations of a business, an industry, a bureaucracy, or a military organization. The ultimate users live and work in a world of decision making based on data often insufficient, supplied by a number of sources, automated, manual, word of mouth, etc. Their view of the system is that of a product that will assist them by providing information in one or more areas of problem solving. For example, the captain of a ship has many responsibilities relating to the safety of the ship and crew and the accomplishment of the ship's charter, whether it is transportation of oil from one port to another or a destroyer's mission of protecting a carrier. Among the captain's duties is seeing that navigation of the ship is performed accurately. The navigation system aboard is only one of many systems—propulsion, cargo handling, crew support, communications, survival systems, etc. The captain may be interested in incorporating a system for determining location based on satellite data inputs because, along with established systems' radio direction finders, it gives increased accuracy of position location. The requirement for such a system is that it perform its functions accurately, reliably, and efficiently. It must be maintainable aboard the ship with the resources at the captain's disposal. The operator of the system, the navigator, is also a user of the system but differs from the ultimate user. The navigator's interest in the system is in the day-to-day use of the system, a somewhat narrower view than that of the captain's, and one that is directed more toward the ease of use and understandability of the operations of the system in addition to its overall accuracy and reliability. The user/operator is interested in how easy the system operates and how well it performs. The ultimate user of the system in this illustration, the captain, determines the overall relationship of the proposed system to the other systems aboard. The captain also determines overall policy for the use of the system, assumes responsibility for its performance in operation, and has the authority to reject or order changes made to the system. As the operator, the navigator uses the system in performing everyday tasks and, in doing so, becomes a part of the system. The operator is the "man" in the system, the "man" in the man/machine interface, the person considered as operator in human factors studies. The navigator's ability to handle the man/machine interface is an important aspect of the performance of the overall system that makes it acceptable to the ultimate user, the captain of the ship.

In addition to the ultimate user and operators of the system, there are many others who make their appearance on the user's side of the fence. They come under labels of legal counsels and purchasing agents (in preparing statements of work and conditions under which the system will be delivered and placed under warranty); technical consultants to the user who can help the user/buyer understand what he is getting in the software package; and other miscellaneous personnel such as training people, documentation experts, auditors, the user's software maintenance people, etc. All have an input to stating requirements.

When dealing directly with the user, the software engineer or analyst needs to be very careful in reacting to the real users of the system, i.e., the ones that actually use the system, as opposed to those in the user's group who have some understanding of the user's problem but are not the final users. Harlan Mills[19] very vividly describes the dangers of talking to the wrong group of users in his paper presented at the second Software Engineering Conference:

> In illustration, consider a software system needed for inventory control in an enterprise, say to be developed over a three-year period. Right off, there is a conflict. The people who know what inventory control is really required in the enterprise are too busy doing it to spend much time on requirements analysis, so surrogate experts with more time available (guess why!) are found. After some time (but not much help from the key people) a software specification is developed, probably incomplete, probably inconsistent, and almost certainly based on a set of amateur opinions about how to do inventory control. And at this point the software specification begins a life of its own—frozen except for strict change control. The specification is a marvelous shield for programmers during implementation. They can hide behind it, while the users-to-be wonder what is going on. In the meantime, the inventory control department has to operate as best it can, with all the new ideas and procedures it can think up. But left alone for three years, the programmers finally complete the implementation and testing, and the system is ready for initial operation. However, there remain a few difficulties. The people doing inventory control are suspicious and skeptical of the new system, especially when it produces idiotic results now and then, and requires idiotic instructions to operate. Furthermore, few of the new ideas of the past three years have been incorporated in the new system, so that these new ideas must be abandoned if the system is to be used. But most critically of all, the software project has been conceived and managed as a terminal three-year project, with all the tradeoffs and compromises that implies, while the inventory control operation goes on indefinitely.

Special organizations are sometimes developed to manage the procurement of large, complex data processing systems. These organizations bring together experts who are knowledgeable in system development, software development, and management of large programs, and represent the user in the procurement by interpreting his needs, reviewing proposed designs, and handling the day-to-day management of the system development. Military organizations that have had much experience in the procurement of complex systems have developed special program offices (SPOs), each dedicated to the procurement of a system, to represent the military organization in the development of the system. Sometimes the SPO proceeds through the requirements definition phase prior to commitment to system development. This results in the requirements being defined in detail before the software engineer or analyst ever has an opportunity to become exposed to the user's problem. Isolated from the ultimate user and operator of the system, the analysts' problem in design lies in understanding the user's real requirements as interpreted in the formalized specifications set forth by the SPO. In this case, we, as software engineers, are faced with the problem of reconstructing the user's problem and environment and reanalyzing the requirements in order to reconstruct the necessary logic of the requirements development. The techniques used are the same as those used in originally recognizing and defining the user's problem.

[19]Mills, H., "Software Development," Proceedings of the Second International Software Engineering Conference, 1976.

3.2.2 RECOGNIZING THE USER'S PROBLEM

In analyzing a user's problem, it is often the tendency of the analyst to listen to a statement of the problem and then to compare that problem immediately to a similar one that has been solved previously. We suggest that the analyst approach the problem more circumspectly. We, as analysts, can accomplish this in three steps. First, we must carefully draw a distinction between the specific problem a user is trying to solve and the multitude of other actions with which the user is dealing in the total environment. We must recognize that we may not be able to build a system to solve all the processing requirements of the user. Second, we must determine if the overall problem can be solved within the current state of the art, and within the resources and tolerance of the ultimate user. Third, we must categorize or size the problems in terms that can be brought to a conclusion within a reasonable length of time. Some problems can be bounded with ease. Others are open-ended and defy simple solutions. We must recognize this situation and deal with it accordingly.

In analyzing the user's problem, it is important to recognize the difference between the user/operator's environment and the ultimate user's environment. The user/operator's area is only a portion of the system environment for which the ultimate user is responsible. Our analysis must recognize all the aspects of the environment in which the ultimate user operates. In the example of the satellite navigation system on board the ship, the navigation system was just another system to the captain that could contribute to the goals of safe and efficient movement of the ship from one port to another. To the navigator, this is one of several systems and manual procedures that help to perform the job of knowing where the ship is at all times. Further, the position-measuring system on board the ship is only a part of the larger system of launching and maintaining satellites in orbit. Conceptually, the software engineer handles the relationships between these systems as interfaces between abstract machines when conceiving and analyzing requirements.

The basic approach to assessing the system within the operator's and ultimate user's total environment is to set bounds to the user's problem in order to determine the feasibility of the solution that will be attempted. It is only too easy in our enthusiasm of working on a complex problem to overstate the capabilities to solve problems as well as to underestimate the resources required. In setting the bounds to the problem, we start by listening to users state the problem in their own terms. A determination is then made as to the kind of problem to be solved, such as whether it will be a closed- or open-ended design. Part of the answer comes in looking at the complexity of the problem. Relatively uncomplicated problems that admit to complete solutions can be designed within the context of a turnkey system. A system package that completely solves the stated problem can be turned over to the user, along with a demonstration of performance and a training program to insure understanding of and full utilization of the product capabilities. An example of such a system is an inventory control system that can be tailored to the ultimate user's needs and turned over to them as a complete system. Inventory control systems are not new; we can estimate that about as many inventory control systems have been developed as payroll systems. The problems of developing such a system have been solved in several different ways by numerous individuals in the data processing profession. Off-the-shelf packages are advertised in software trade journals.

On the other hand, there are user's problems that do not admit ready solution. This state can exist either because the user is unable to define the true nature of the problem to be solved or because the problem does not admit to a single, simple solution in the sense that a program can be written that immediately solves the problem. In other words, the problem is heuristic in the sense that the answer is recognized by the user as being the best that can be obtained at that time with the available information. This is in contrast to programs, such as commercial banking systems, whereby it is possible to verify that the end result of calculations are correct by using checks and balances. The heuristic problems profit by extended exposure of the user (both the ultimate user and operators of the system) to the data processing capabilities and their use in a real-time environment. In heuristic type systems, as the user's experience grows, the demands on the system grow and the requirements change. We must design a way of handling these changing requirements without continually reprogramming. We can handle the problem definition by additional effort and expenditure of resources. However, we must conduct extended studies (a research phase) or build test beds and prototype software to provide for the definition of the problem. Prototype systems, in which attributes of reliability, maintainability, efficiency, and testability are minimized (e.g., self-test of hardware operability during system operation is ignored) and only those functions related to the basic tasks desired by the user, can be implemented on a trial basis. This gives the ultimate user and the user/operator an opportunity to evaluate the functioning of the system in order to properly define requirements that will meet their needs.

For those systems that are inherently undefinable in the normal mode of definition, design, and implementation of a product package, a possible strategy for analysis is to view the solution as an extensible system. In this case, the users are given a basic capability to control processing information and a capability to formulate the relationships between processing and data, using basic functions that reflect their own way of viewing a problem. These basic functions constitute primitive operations or tasks that reflect the processing elements in terms with which the user is familiar. This concept has been used successfully in problem-oriented languages and has been applied to a limited number of user applications. It is particularly useful for those information processing systems of a heuristic nature where there is no way to predetermine the correct solution to the problem. In addition, the user will need a capability for extending the primitives or processing tasks that are available for use in the system. The example we will be using in this chapter to illustrate the application of the technologies of design falls into this category of extensible or evolutionary program development.

Another important consideration in analyzing the user's problem is that of selecting attributes of quality that are called for by the problem. As we have said earlier, usability is a composite attribute that we strive to design into the product. Usability is generally composed of those qualities known as reliability, testability, maintainability, efficiency, understandability, and adaptability. In order to formulate the discipline of software engineering, the definition of the user's problem must include not only the required functions and their performance characteristics, but also the quality of the product that is required if the software is to fulfill the user's needs. Each of the attributes must be defined in terms of the user's needs. For example, the reliability desired in the end product must be stated as a design goal if the product is to have the necessary degree of reliability for the amount of resources available. Trade-offs must be made as to the relative importance of these attributes. Reliability and maintainability may be high on the priority list, but if efficiency of operations with limits of time and core resources is of primary importance, the overhead associated with maintainability may have to be redefined.

Along with the definition of the user's problem, there must be some understanding of the degree of system engineering involvement with respect to design of new hardware. We can postulate a continuum in system/software product development that shows one extreme where no new hardware is being developed and the prime focus is on the development of information processing capabilities, utilizing a hardware configuration currently existing in the user's installation. The other extreme illustrates that the processor(s) and peripherals (including displays and sensors) are not specified and are to be designed and developed concurrently with the software. An example of the first extreme of the continuum, which we will call information processor systems, is, again, the inventory control problem. An example of the second extreme, which we will call the embedded computer system, is a missile with an on-board processor capable of threat evaluation, target identification, and flight profile reprogramming within set bounds. In between these extremes, we can find a wide spectrum of software product development with the difference being the amount of specialized hardware being concurrently developed. Taking the example of the inventory control program, many forms of this type of system can be run on a general-purpose computer operated as a service center if the input is designed for card format. The system can be run in batch mode with printer output. However, at the next level of development, we can develop special terminals for input to a general-purpose machine that has a time-sharing mode. Status reports can be obtained via terminal queries. At a still higher level of hardware involvement, whereby we are moving closer to an embedded system, the system for inventory control can be related to storage and movement control of parts (including automated conveyor and distribution systems) wherein standard commercial processors are dedicated to standard display consoles for control of the system, and feedback from the operations of the conveyor or distribution system is provided by off-the-shelf monitors. Entry of data relating to parts availability and use can be implemented by any one of several remote data entry devices available off-the-shelf. A final step toward the embedded computer system would be the tailoring of sensor or display peripherals as a part of the overall system. This is similar to the development of a typical command/control communication system where dedicated processor networks process sensor data and convert that data into a data base for support of command decisions, which are then transmitted as controls to weapons.

We should note that the design and implementation complexity increases as we embark on concurrent hardware and software design. The reason is the number of paths of communication between designers and implementers that develop when one attempts to design a hardware and software system at the same time. Generally, this joint venture involves the services of an arbitrator—the systems engineer—who understands both the roles and technologies of the software engineer and hardware engineer. His function is that of performing the overall analysis, synthesis, and allocation that allow for the development of a system that provides a satisfactory solution to the user's problem. It is our intent to point out the interfaces of the software engineer with the hardware and systems engineer, but not to describe the techniques and methodologies of the systems engineer. We will be examining methodologies of definition as they generally apply to software systems where the hardware is not a particularly large element of concurrent development.

3.2.3 TECHNIQUES IN REQUIREMENTS DEFINITION

The techniques we use in defining a system in the software requirements definition phase are the same as those generally used in the systems analysis phase. Since the general methods and techniques of systems analysis have been covered in excellent texts elsewhere (J. Weinberg[20]), there is no need for us to cover the subject in detail here. We will direct our attention to the software engineering problems by addressing the specific techniques found useful in development of requirements for larger embedded computer systems. Most of the techniques are oriented toward gaining an understanding of the ultimate user's view of the world and the set of expectations he has about what a system should do for him. The techniques we will review are: (1) structuring techniques as a means of identifying the nature of the problem relative to its environment, (2) the need to derive a concept of operation based on human factors considerations, (3) techniques for validating the operational concept through scenario definition and simulation/modeling, and (4) sizing the user's problem based on desired attributes of the system.

IDENTIFYING THE ENVIRONMENT

Two very useful methodologies for analysis that are evolving as a single concept are semantic analysis and structured analysis. The work of Yourdon on structured analysis and the general work on semantic analysis are pointing the way for this approach. Since we see them merging as a common concept, we will discuss them as a single entity and present them as a composite view of how to analyze the user's environment.

The goal is to state the user's requirements by utilizing a very rigorously defined syntax—paying particular care to the definitions of the elements in the user's statement of his requirements. Once the elements of the user's environment have been precisely defined, they can be constructed into a logically sound model of the user's operational environment. The syntax used to describe the environment is limited to defining the user's world in terms of objects (names of things), events (things that happen), relationships (how objects relate one to another and to events), and attributes (the modifiers of objects and events). This provides the basis for capturing a precise statement of the requirements, using the concepts of specification languages being evolved at this time. If requirements are stated in such a way as to be clear,

---

[20]Weinberg, J., *An Introduction to General Systems Thinking*, John Wiley & Sons, Inc., 1975.

concise, complete, and easily understood by the designer, then the likelihood of achieving clear, concise, and complete design that satisfies the requirements is much enhanced.

Describing the user's world forces an identification of the environment of the system as distinct from the desired system. The system's environment can be conceived of as the "super" system of the user. That is, the requirements will be stated in terms of the system's environment as a level of abstraction above the desired system. This concept of stating requirements in terms of a super system is not universally recognized within the engineering community. However, it has been found to constitute a reasonable conceptualization of the requirement definition phase, and so it will be employed here. It forces the analyst to look at the world through the eyes of the user.

Therefore, the requirements definition phase proceeds as follows:

Identify the objects surrounding the system—It is important at this point to distinguish between two types of objects, i.e., objects can be categorized as data that exists in the environmental system or agents that cause events to happen, accomplishing actions within the environmental system. Let us disregard the agents for the time being because this concept implies an assignment/allocation to a person or a piece of equipment, something that we are not prepared to designate at this time. We identify only the data existing in the environment that will interface with the system. We list the data and give them names stated in conceptual terms.

Identify things that happen in the environment—These are action items, things that occur, which we call predicates. We list them and give them names. In listing the objects and predicates, rules of semantics are continually applied to arrive at as clear and precise a term as possible to describe the data or the action. At this point our goal is to identify all known data and all known actions occurring within the environment. We will not be complete with our first attempt, and additional requirements may be identified as the design process proceeds.

Given the list of data (objects) and the list of actions (predicates), it should now be obvious that we have the beginnings of a data flow. We describe the data flow of the environment as an operational flow by using the steps outlined in the structured design process. That is, we create a top-level data flow diagram that depicts the operation of the environment that contains the system to be developed. It may not be entirely clear at this point exactly how the system reacts to its environment. Iterations may be necessary to flush out the complete understanding of the existing system. However, the next step of system design will proceed more efficiently if it is based on stated user's operational requirements.

The technique described here is intended as an aid in identifying the requirements of the system, assuming they are unknown. The object is to identify the most optimum functions to be performed by the system in response to the user's needs within the context of the desired environment. This can be done only by analyzing the environment itself as a subsystem of the total real-world environment. The operational flow identifies the relationships existing within the system environment. The required system can now be identified, i.e., the system solution trade-offs at the conceptual level can now be evaluated. Given the general structure, the functions can be tentatively allocated to resources, the operators that will interface with the model system, other systems that interface with the model system, and the model system itself. We now should be able to draw a circle around a portion of the environment and say, "This is my system." (See Figure 3-6) If these statements cannot be made and there

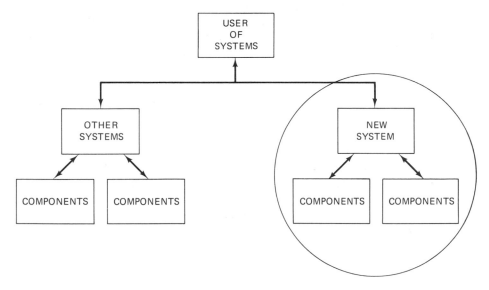

Fig. 3-6 System within environment

are disjointed areas, then multiple systems are being identified, or functions are being allocated to the system that are not logically a part of that system. The other elements of the environment define the interface of the environment with the system. Their allocation will determine performance characteristics. A function allocated to an operator predetermines that the interfaces for that function are limited by the human capabilities of the man. Once all the characteristics of all known interfaces to the system have been identified, the system has been completely constrained. We now have a complete statement of the requirements imposed on the system in terms of interfaces, the exact performance characteristics of the interfaces, and the functions performed by the system in order to perform its required role within the environment. We can also determine that the system solution is a feasible solution, not some arbitrary statement of need.

HUMAN FACTORING THE REQUIREMENTS

The human factors engineering discipline addresses the problems of man/machine interaction with the system. It aids the design of systems that seek to merge human characteristics with a usable system. This discipline is directed toward matching human capabilities and limitations to the specifics of the designed man/machine interface. It addresses such problems as human reaction to given stimuli, psychological factors determining user acceptance, and physical factors determining user's comfort, endurance, etc., all of which contribute to the usability of the system.

Many system development efforts, however, do not employ or provide for specific activities in human factors engineering. Since the software engineer is responsible for the ultimate usability of the product and the acceptance by the user of the product as a feasible method of solving the problem, the software engineer must consider human factors engineering.

Human factors engineering and the related area of work study analysis had its beginning in the late 1940s when the complexity of man/machine interface was given higher reliability and response time goals. Since then it has reached a degree of maturity in certain restrictive areas related primarily to the manned space flight projects. At present there is a fairly substantial amount of information available about some areas of operators' performance and at least partial information about certain others. In some areas information is quite limited, and in still others there are virtual information voids.

The human factors directly concerning software engineering will be categorized as user/operator capabilities and user psychology as the user interfaces with the system. The subject of user/operator capabilities addresses such factors as: (1) overall physical response times, (2) level of mentality, (3) level of training, and (4) orientation or type of training. The engineer must understand the user/operator enough to identify the level at which the user can be expected to and wants to react with the system, i.e., the category of user must be established and the user's characteristics determined. The user is one element of a system. The user's "properties" must be established, just as equipment and software properties are established.

Two psychological factors can be identified and significantly impact how a user views a system—the system's response time to user's requests and the system's handling of error conditions. The desired system response time is a quantitative measure, based on the type of user interaction with the system. A job submitted to a service center for generation of fixed reports requires a significantly different response time than a query typed in an interactive mode from teletype for a specific answer to a question. Both require a different response time than an operator seated in front of an air traffic control console. A feasible response time for the first may be measured in hours, for the second in minutes, and for the third in seconds. Any desire to reduce the reaction time will require more automation. However, a response time of days instead of hours for the first case may well result in the reports losing their relevancy. If a system's response exceeds a few minutes for a teletype operator, the train of thought may be lost. A response time exceeding a few seconds at an air traffic control console may result in an operator's inability to take appropriate action. The system must be engineered to respond to the user in a timely manner, based on the function being performed.

Humans are not perfect; they do make errors. The key question we must ask is, "How can the system be expected to handle the error?" Obviously, errors that are catastrophic to the entire system should be avoided. However, extensive, involved error checks may increase the programming size past reasonable limits for the job at hand. From the user's point of view, the key element in error detection is relevancy. How well does the error indication isolate the problem for the user? The error indication must appear within close proximity in time and space to where the error occurs, and it must be sufficiently descriptive to indicate the true nature of the problem.

Work study analysis monitors the existing interaction of man within a system and includes employee evaluation techniques to project efficiency improvements via automated methods or modified human procedures. Work study analysis has devised methods for capturing data on operator response times in order to support its analysis. It employs layout diagrams to depict movement patterns from which it derives recommended improvements. It uses as a basis for its analysis some form of operational sequence diagrams (OSDs). OSDs identify human actions, required data to perform the actions, approximate delay time ("think" times) as the action is performed, and resultant data generated by the human. These are related to the system counterpart as it receives the data, performs its processing with its delay times, and returns new data to the user. In the process of generating OSDs, data files are identified, properties are identified for both human processing and system processing, and appropriate trade offs, such as automated versus nonautomated functions, are performed. Operational sequence diagrams will be presented in a more detailed form in the section on system design.

MODELING THE USER'S PROBLEM

Obviously the system environment as we have defined it is not a "whole-world" environment, but a very definitized, constrained environment, and the exact nature of those constraints must be defined. The system we conceive will be expected to fulfill certain capabilities relating to its environment. During the requirements definition phase, the specific manner in which the system must operate in order to fulfill its desired capabilities, based on its interfaces, must be identified. Conceptually, it is convenient for us to think of the system defined as a model system operating within the world of the user environment (Figure 3-7).

A general concept used by the analyst in developing the model system is the use

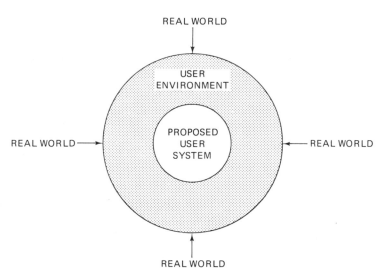

Fig. 3-7 System as a part of user systems

of a scenario. The scenario is a verbal and sometimes graphical description of all the events a user would experience in performance of the tasks that constitute the problem to be solved. The scenario is a sequence of events and actions connected by statements of significant relationships and data exchanged. The scenario can be a representation of existing action sequences that occur, or it can be hypothetical, depending on the type of requirement being examined. It is particularly useful if it is prepared by using the language and concepts with which the user is familiar. The user can say it is a true representation of the problem. It is a method of obtaining agreement between the analyst and the user as to the exact nature of the problem with which they are dealing. Further, the scenario can be used to evolve quantitative data as to occurrences of events and can be used as a basis for setting performance criteria. The techniques of modeling vary from general functional models to discrete event simulations. The development of simulation languages has made discrete event simulation of system models very efficient and effective.

Hughes Aircraft has incorporated techniques for evaluating man/machine interfaces into its modeling technology in the form of an automated man/machine model. Man/machine modeling (also referred to as work-load modeling or environment simulation) seeks to project human interaction within a planned system and make the simulation of the work load more realistic. This modeling/simulation technique has proven a valuable design tool for use during the requirements definition phase of system development, and it also serves as an operational feasibility validation tool for validating system requirements. System analysts describe human/system interaction via operational sequence diagrams. The actual execution of the operational sequence diagrams is simulated via a computer program. Output includes operator loading analysis diagrams that aid the analyst in determining the feasibility of the procedures, the completeness of data provided, operator and system loading, and potential bottlenecks. Used in an iterative manner during the design stages, this methodology provides invaluable insight into planned system execution.

SIZING THE USER'S PROBLEMS

Using the techniques of structured analysis, human factors engineering, and modeling, we should have by this time a good concept of what the user wants in the system. Now is the time for us to consider the attributes that contribute to the quality of the system and make it usable to the user. Each item on the qualities check list should be reviewed to determine the extent and desirable features the user requires in the end product.

Reliability—How much reliability does the user really need in the system? Is operation of the system critical in the sense that errors in the system can cause a major crisis? Will the malfunctions in the system cause loss of human life or simply an inconvenience to the operator?

Testability—How much testing of the system does the user want to prove reliability? For a system that requires high reliability, this will be important.

Maintainability—Who will be maintaining the system, and what will be the skill level of the people maintaining the system? Will one group be kept to correct errors in the system and another group used to make improvements in the system and rectify design deficiencies?

Efficiency—What are the measures of efficiency the user considers important? Is cost of operating single jobs more important than overall efficient use of physical resources? Is response time to input the most important consideration?

Understandability—Can the user readily understand how to use the system? Does he comprehend the variations in use and how to operate the system in varying relationships with other systems in his environment?

Adaptability—Can the system be readily moved to a similar computer?

Using this checklist, we should be able to begin making a gross estimate of the cost of the system. Cost in the system can be estimated by roughly computing the overall size of the software programs involved, the necessary through or response time, and the computer resources (main frame and peripherals as well as any special hardware devices that are needed). This estimate is a planning purpose estimate and is used to keep the detailing of the system within the constraints of the user's budget.

3.2.4 FORMALIZATION OF USER REQUIREMENTS

The technology discussed in the preceding section enables a user to state the problem, to determine the environment in which the user operates as well as resources available, and to identify the several qualities desired in the final product. We now need to formalize these statements into a logical definition of requirements. This formalization of requirements takes on the aspect of procedural-like statements such as how the user would like to see events take place as the result of actions on the part of other people or other events, the kinds of results the user would like to see, the desired qualities of the system, and resources available for the product. The process of formulating a logical statement of requirements in the past has been somewhat informal, with the designer being willing to accept whatever information obtainable as to the kind of system that would satisfy the user. At that time, this was not considered a handicap by the analyst because it allowed the designer to maximize creativity in the design of a system that, obviously, the designer knew more about than the user. After all, the user came to the designer as the expert in systems design, so the user had reason to have confidence in the designer's ability. Unfortunately today the user's problems are becoming more complex and the users more educated in their expectations for software—sometimes through the bitter experience of being promised systems that did not live up to expectations. Now the wise software engineer formalizes an understanding of the user's requirements and gains approval of the requirements to insure an understanding of what the user is saying.

This formalization of requirements is not only fed back to the user for approval, but it also serves as the basic input to the system design effort. The statement of requirements must be precise and complete so the system designer will have sufficient understanding of the user's operations and the user's preferences or biases so as to make intelligent trade-offs. The designer should not be constrained in the physical design unless the constraints constitute a limitation of resources committed by the user to the system. The requirements statement should not allocate processing to physical resources, nor should the architecture dictate the software details of program design or specific data file structures. The requirements must be able to specify what functions and performance attributes the user requires and yet not commit to any particular physical solution.

The format for formalizing requirements varies as much as users vary. More sophisticated users present their requirements in terms of: (1) a description of the environment in which the system is to operate (the physical environment); (2) the other systems with which there will be an interface; (3) the people who will work with the system; (4) the functions that the system is to perform; (5) the data in forms of messages, sensor readings, or other forms that will enter the system (including format, frequency, accuracy, and precision); and (6) the desired data or control to be output (again in terms of format, frequency, accuracy, and precision). The resources that the user is committing are given in terms of human resources (people and skills), physical space, power, schedule time for development, and dollar amounts. Other users will be less specific in stating their requirements, and the software engineer, or the systems engineering team, must extract this information from the user and formally state the requirements in a statement of work.

Of course, if we are designing a general software product for a broad market, there will be no specific user or user community to talk to in developing the software requirements. However, if the product is to be successful, there will have to be some form of market survey and analysis to determine the characteristics of the user's operations and requirements before embarking on a design. A high degree of failure of small software houses in recent years can be attributed partly to the fact that they started with a solution looking for a problem. The nature of the data processing industry—providing solutions to problems that are unmanageable in a manual information processing system—implies some dependency on a user statement of the problem to be solved. Software engineers do not invent problems; they are supposed to solve them!

The formalized requirements are documented according to the standards established by the procuring organization. These may take the forms of high-level information flows (data flow diagrams), control structure diagrams, and conceptual data definitions. Design documentation format is not a subject covered in this chapter.

Determining the validity of the requirements has always been a problem. The usual method is to have the requirements reviewed by competent people who represent the actual users. This review can be assisted by using a simulation/model to demonstrate feasibility of requirements against a conceptual design by running the simulation/model against environment data generated from the scenario.

The logical consistency of the requirements may be checked against the constraints imposed by structured design. Checking is generally a manual process with a single designer or several designers involved. Automation of this verification process is only now being attempted. (See the discussion on languages for the survey of promising systems.) At this point, however, a basis for system design has been established.

3.2.5 THE ETAPS EXAMPLE (REQUIREMENTS DEFINITION PHASE)

To illustrate the concepts and techniques of requirements analysis, we have taken an actual design of a medium-sized data processing system that is midway on the scale between a simple information processing system and an embedded computer system. The design has elements of concurrent hardware development so that the relationship of the software engineer participating as part of a team with hardware and systems engineering personnel can be observed.

The example is a typical user's problem that calls for a medium-sized data processing system with a very large data base. The problem is one that requires a decision between use of a large general-purpose machine (which the user has on hand) or dedicated processors, or a mix of the two. The problem also includes consideration of development of specialized display consoles, so we show concurrent hardware design in development of the overall system. We think it aptly illustrates the software engineering process as it is a case from real life and treats a contemporary complex data processing problem. The overall problem is too extensive and complex to treat in detail, but we feel that we can illustrate the key points of software engineering by summaries from the overall study.

The ultimate user in this case is a government organization charged with the responsibility of monitoring the economic activities of the United States. This organization determines economic trends through observing patterns in the day-to-day activities of selected elements of the business community and isolates new factors in economic behavior as they arise. The results of the trend analysis will be used in generating economic policy with respect to trade agreements, fiscal policy, and government spending activities.

USER'S STATEMENT OF THE PROBLEM

A group of economic analysts is responsible for evaluating large amounts of data in order to establish characteristics and trends of economic data. Their existing system for doing so has become outmoded. The current system uses paper and analog devices for information collection and display. The data is extracted manually from source documents and prepared as input to computer programs that analyze the data and provide summary reports for the analysts' review. Computer processing is performed in batch mode. The volume of data has increased so much that it can no longer be handled efficiently by the current system. Moreover, the current methods discourage heuristic analysis, and excessive errors are introduced into the data.

Since the analysts are faced with an increasing work load and potential new sources of data, a new system is needed to enhance system throughput. At the same time it is desired to upgrade the system to enable the analysts to evaluate the data more accurately and efficiently. A new system has been conceived to provide interactive retrieval, display, and computation capabilities to the analysts as operators of the system. The data is to be collected automatically from the new data sources and maintained in a centralized data base. The analysts are to work at interactive consoles to process the data. At least "x" consoles are projected in use at any one time. For convenience, the proposed system is to be called Economic Trend and Analysis Processing System (ETAPS).

ETAPS STUDY PLAN

A plan is established to design a system suitable for implementation by the user's supporting programming organization. The plan is three-fold:

1. identify the projected system environment in order to establish a concept of operations for the analysts' use of the system (requirements definition),
2. establish a generic configuration of the system that will achieve the desired capabilities at a minimum cost commensurate with performance (system design), and
3. establish design specifications to the level of detail necessary to begin programming implementation (software design).

The user's statement of requirements, as can be seen, is not particularly extensive or illuminating. It is necessary to expand the requirements by using the general system analysis techniques of:

- Observing current operations
- Reading problem reports and reviewing previous operations
- Noting deficiencies and complaints about current operations
- Conducting interviews
- Using questionnaires to focus on specific problems
- Documenting study findings for review

The findings are used to define operational objectives and methods of evaluation of requirements.

The techniques used in the ETAPS requirements definition phase are described in this section, while the system design portion of this problem example is shown in Sec. 3.3.6, and the software design portion of this example appears at the end of Sec. 3.4.7.

IDENTIFYING THE OPERATIONAL ENVIRONMENT

The data with which the analysts deal is converted to machine-readable form and introduced by data entry devices periodically during the day or month as appropriate to the data. Therefore, it includes all the information collected about events interleaved, but in time order. It is the analysts' job to collect and enter the data in some meaningful fashion, analyze the data to arrive at conclusions concerning the economic events as they occur, and thereby project hypotheses concerning future economic trends.

The analysts need a system to view the data in a graphical form so that they can recognize patterns of occurrences. They need the data displayed as charts and graphs rather than as lists of numbers or statistics. They also require graphic display manipulation capabilities to process the data interactively. The analysts' interactive manipulation of the data results in processed graphs and charts used by other analysts in their work of interpreting trends. Thus we can see multi-levels of analyst activity: data preparation for entry, conversion to processible graphic data, and summary of trend data.

Personal interviews are conducted with the analysts to refine the understanding of the functions performed by them as they process the different levels of data. The primary system function is technical data analysis, but three secondary system functions are identified: (1) the preparation of specialized job-dependent programs (system extension), (2) data base management, and (3) management reporting. In addition, if the analyst is to interface interactively with the system, tertiary functions are necessary to control the analysis session at the terminal. All functions other than the primary function are fairly well understood by the analyst. The secondary functions, however, have significant impact on the system design, as will be seen. The primary analysts' functions had to be further analyzed and are identified as: (1) selecting critical events, (2) editing the point data over the critical event periods, (3) automated curve smoothing for graphs (curve fitting), (4) data analyzing and fitting to heuristic patterns recognized by the analysts, (5) several specific types of trend analysis and report construction, (6) hypothesis evaluation through modeling, and (7) trend display and report generation. The concept of the analysts' operation is defined as a terminal session involving any of the above interactive functions with possible retention of resulting data in the data base, i.e., the manipulator of data has capability to reject data. Table 3-1 summarizes the required analysts' functions as presented above.

Table 3-1 Analysts' Functions

1. Primary analyst functions	Data preparation
	  Select critical event
	  Edit point data
	  Curve fit
	  Data analysis
	Trend analysis
	  Economic activity analysis—Type 1
	                                                  Type 2
	                                                  Type 3
	    Trend data construction
	Hypothesis evaluation
	  Modeling
	Printout
	  Report preparation

2. Secondary analyst functions	Construct user programs (system extension) Data base maintenance Management reporting
3. Tertiary analyst functions	Terminal session set-up Terminal session terminate

The detailed steps performed in the accomplishment of the above functions are then identified. Table 3-2 shows the basic steps identified for a single analyst's function (select critical event). This analysis is conducted for all the analysts' functions and

**Table 3-2 Sample Expansion of an Analyst's Function
to Primitive Functions**

Select Critical Event

1. Select Event
2. Scroll—to determine critical events
3. Scale display—to enhance examination of critical time periods
4. Select (critical) points
5. Display value—measure (critical) points
6. Annotate (critical) points
7. Enter data to user file—for subsequent cataloguing as processed data.

commonalities are identified. These steps are at the lowest level of conceptualization that the analysts wish to consider in the evaluation of their work. Therefore, these steps are defined as "primitive" functions to the analysts and so identified. A summary of the primitive steps constituting the analysts' functions is presented in Table 3-3. A matrix

Table 3-3 Primitive Functions

Display functions	Select display format
	Select event
	Select time subset
	Scroll
	Scale
	Offset
	Select point
	Select tabular alphanumeric display item
Point selection/measurement	Display value
	Compute differences
	Annotate point
	Build list of points
	Add point to event file
Hard copy	Display screen snapshot
	Off-line report
Execute program	
Math functions	Arithmetic
	Trigonometric
	.
	.
	.
Generate special display formats	Histogram
	.
	.
	.
File manipulation functions	List file names
	Select file
	Copy data to file
	.
	.
	.
Digitizer tablet	

Table 3-4 Primitive Functions/Analyst Functions

Primitive Functions	Select Critical Event	Edit Point Data	Curve Fit	Data Analysis	Trend Analysis Type 1	Trend Analysis Type 2	Trend Analysis Type 3	Trend Data Construction	Modeling	Report Preparation
Display functions	X	X	X	X	X	X	X	OX	X	
Point selection/ measurement	XX			XX	X	XX	OX	OX		
Hardcopy	X	OX	X	XX	XX	X	X	OX	X	X
Execute program		X	X	XX	XX	XX	X	XX	X	
Math functions		OX	OX	XX	XX	OX	OX	OX		
Generate special display formats				X	XX	OX	OX	OX	OX	OX
File manipulation functions	OX	X	X	X	OX	OX	X	OX	OX	
Digitizer tablet		X	X	X	X	X	X	X		

OX Low Usage   X Average Usage   XX High Usage   XXX Very High Usage

of requirements is also presented in Table 3-4, identifying the range of applicability of the primitives to the functions.

The primitives are ranked as to required, desired, and potential growth to aid the system designers in identifying priorities for design and implementation of the system. Operator sequence diagrams are prepared, graphically portraying the steps required to accomplish the various functions with primitives. Response times that could be tolerated are identified for each primitive, such as instantaneous (less than x seconds), moderate (x seconds to y seconds), and slow (greater than y seconds). The operator sequence diagrams with the assigned rates are used to validate system loading in the simulation/modeling of the conceptual design.

DISPLAY SYSTEM STUDY
HUMAN FACTORING THE REQUIREMENTS

The display capabilities available to analysts are seen as a factor significantly impacting the operational concept. This impact is verified by using the man/machine modeling effort. Therefore, a human factors study is conducted to establish a method of analyst/machine communication that will support rapid and convenient interaction. Also, from this study specific display procurement specifications will be identified.

It is known that the operator will be viewing charts and graphs on a display screen and will be taking actions to process the data. The exact methodology for doing so has to be identified. Based on such factors as speed, accuracy, and fatigue levels, a menu-driven scheme rather than a free-form command entry scheme is decided upon. Tabular alphanumeric lists are presented to the analysts from which they can determine the action alternatives and information available at any point in the work session. They, in turn, can indicate the desired action through various interactive entry techniques, such as variable or fixed function keys, alphanumeric keyboard entry, light pen or joystick, and graphic tablet entry. This implies the need to identify: (1) the types of display formats (alphanumeric versus graphic), (2) the quantity of data to be displayed, (3) recommended formats for displaying the data, and (4) the resolution (size and brightness) necessary to accommodate these formats. Therefore, these factors are evaluated for each of the analyst's functions. The ability to display alphanumeric data is required as well as graphic information consisting of lines and points. The quantity of data is estimated for each analyst's function. The quantity and data in turn, determines resolution requirements to retain readability (Table 3-5). A reasonable solution is to split the screen into two sections—a primary area that presents the standard menutype action options available to the analyst, and a working area

Table 3-5 Summary of Estimated Data Display Requirements

| | | Primary Area | | | | | |
| | Tabular Alphanumeric Data | | Alphanumerics | | No. of Dots | | No. of Lines | |
Analyst Function	Required	Desired	Required	Desired	Required	Desired	Required	Desired
Data Preparation								
Select critical event								
Type #1	1,300	1,800	630	1,100	3,200	6,400	160	290
Type #2	1,300	1,800	450	450	—	—	300	300
Edit point data	250	750	500	500	2,200	4,200	90	90
Curve fit	250	1,100	500	500	1,600	1,600	90	90
Data analysis								
Trend type 1	350	850	450	650	1,600	3,200	90	90
Trend type 2	900	1,600	650	850	3,200	4,800	160	225
Trend Analysis								
Economic activity analysis								
Type 1	500	1,300	550	550	2,000	8,000	320	320
Type 2	500	1,300	600	600	1,300	2,400	210	210
Type 3	350	1,300	600	600	1,500	1,500	120	120
Trend data construction	350	1,100	550	850	3,000	6,000	120	225

Table 3-6 Tabulation of Preferred Interactive Techniques

	Fixed Function Key	Variable Function Key (VFK)	Light Pen	Trackball/ Joystick	Numeric Keyboard	Alphanumeric Keyboard	Graphic Tablet
Selection techniques							
Select display format	X	X	XX	—	—	—	X
Display manipulation	XX	X	X	X[1]	X	—	X
Data item selection	X	X	X	—	X	—	X
Entry techniques							
Edited points	XX	X	—	XX	X	—	X
Curve fit data	X	X	—	XX	—	—	X
A/N entry	—	—	X	—	XX	XX	?
Graphic data	—	—	—	—	—	—	XX
Analysis techniques	X	XX	XX	X	X	X	X

[1]Dials may also be used.

Key: X—Applicable   XX—Very well suited for function

Chap. 3 Software Design

that contains the graphic data with which the analyst is working. General formats for each area are prepared.

The interactive techniques are then evaluated through a matrix evaluation scheme (Table 3-6). The various options are listed and then designated as applicable/not applicable, according to the analyst's functional requirements. Based on this analysis, a combination of techniques is projected where the technique for interactive interface is dependent on the general functions being performed.

The display hardware requirements are then projected according to the standard display specification criteria—screen size, aspect ratio, resolution, character data, line data, size, etc.

OPERATIONAL CONCEPT VALIDATION
MODELING THE USER'S FUNCTION

A scenario is developed to evaluate the feasibility of the established operational concept. The purpose is to evaluate typical storage and processing loads to determine if the desired response times can be achieved within the user's general system concept, given the expected work load imposed by the analysts. Production-oriented tasks rather than analysis tasks are selected in order to achieve a high rate of interaction with the system. A man/machine model is used to drive the simulation model of the system. The operational sequence diagrams (OSDs) provide the scenario script for simulating the man/machine interface with the system. Loading figures are estimated according to the individual actions for: (1) the number of auxiliary memory I/Os, (2) the number of display I/Os, (3) the amount of auxiliary data transferred per I/O, (4) the amount of display data transferred per display I/O, and (5) the number of instructions executed per logical path in the OSDs. The scenario drives the generalized simulation model in order to evaluate the ability of the system to meet the required loading figures. No major problems are detected in the operational concept at this point in the investigation.

SYSTEM PROCUREMENT CONSTRAINTS (SIZING)

Guidelines or attributes to constrain the system design effort are established. Existing hardware and software are to be procured whenever feasible. In-house development of application software is to be kept to a minimum to reduce maintenance costs. Costs are to be minimized, but if a trade-off is necessary between costs and performance, the performance characteristic is to take precedence. System extensibility is stated as a prime requirement.

3.3

Software Design and System Engineering

In this section, we are describing the process whereby the operational requirements identified in Sec. 3.2 are translated into formal design entities that represent basic elements of a system—the hardware of the system, the software, the people in the system, and the communications that exist among these entities of the system (including the man-machine interface). To repeat, these four basic entities or subsystems exist in all information processing systems and embedded computer systems. Sometimes their presence is not obvious, particularly if we are developing an application program that will run on an existing data processing installation. However, at some time or other, someone or some group had to put together the original hardware configuration and systems software. Even when we are developing an embedded computer system, there is usually an antecedent system (manual or semi-automated) for handling the type of problems under analysis. This means there is available to the analyst an accumulation of data concerning the environment in which the system will operate, the kind of people who will be operating the system, and the characteristics and desires of the ultimate user of the system.

When we are developing the requirements of a system that builds onto existing hardware and software, we are tied to the technology of the predecessor system. On the other hand, there are opportunities that do arise where the problem and the requirements analysis indicate the undertaking of a system design that will involve an advance in the state of the art. Frequently this involves the development of new peripherals, such as sensors or data storage and retrieval devices. It could be an upgrading of an existing system to new processing concepts, such as a distributed processing system using a network of mini-computers to replace an overburdened central processor. It could also be that the requirements stipulate a processing load that must be distributed throughout the system in a federated network of microprocessors with the functions, allocated to mini-computers for preprocessing data at nodes in the system, and large processors netted to control the system and data bases and to perform the large data processing tasks. When the requirements (and user's resources) allow for an advance in the state of the art, we move into a phase of design that focuses on the total system design considerations, including a fresh appraisal of the four entities of the system enumerated above. For large, complex systems or complex embedded computer systems featuring new processor and/or peripheral developments, this part of the design process is formally recognized as the system design phase, having as its inputs the formal documentation of the user's requirements and ending with a system design specification.

In the preceding section on definition of user's requirements, we developed an operational concept. The necessity for understanding the user's operational requirements forced consideration of broad system issues such as overall size of system, possible configurations of hardware and software architectures, and the role of the human in the system. Overall sizing of the system at that time also brought into consideration the level of technology to be applied to the system and the kinds of attributes the system should have.

In generating the system design specification, the four steps of (1) structuring the primary functions reflecting the user's requirements; (2) allocating these functions to the hardware, software, firmware, and human elements; (3) iterating the design to include the secondary functions, and (4) validating the overall system design against the requirements are accomplished as illustrated in Figure 3-8. After the allocation of functions, there is usually a synthesis of the system. In this synthesis, the designer steps back and looks at the overall design to see if it meets the user's requirements, if it has adequately provided for possible variation in operations that could cause unreliable

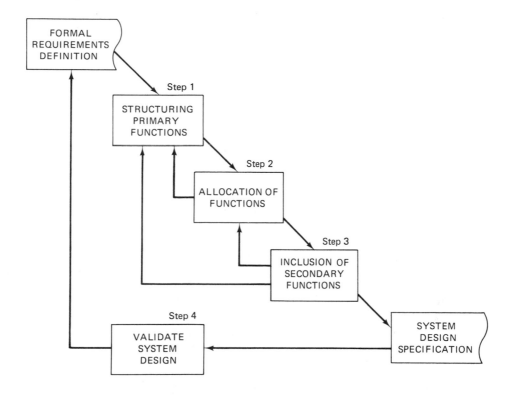

Fig. 3-8 Steps in the system design process

performance, and if the overall design meets the engineering requirements of simplicity and economy of design.

Prior to discussing the four steps of the system design process, we will describe who is who on the system design team—or the role of the software engineer in the design process. Then we will begin by discussing the starting of the system design process in terms of structuring the primary functions identified in the user's requirements definition phase. Second, we will go into detail in describing the allocation of functions to the different elements of the system. In this discussion, we will examine the system structures, including consideration of the control structures of the system, data structures, data flow control, and application structures. We will also spend some time defining and listing key hardware considerations in system design as seen from the software engineering point of view. The third step of the system design process, the iteration of the design to include secondary requirements, will be discussed next. Finally, we will review the techniques of design validation. After a brief note on formalizing system design as per formalizing requirements, we will again illustrate the techniques with the ETAPS portion of the system design study.

It is important at this point that the software engineer understand that we are concentrating in this section on the system design aspects of the development phase. The concepts and techniques that we are discussing here are systems engineering and hardware engineering techniques and concepts with which the software engineer will need to be familiar in order to communicate properly as a member of the system design team. It is not the intent to give readers the necessary insight into the system design techniques so they may be able to employ them in analysis. We are including them in the discussion in order that software engineers will have some understanding of the techniques used so they can properly do their job—the preparation of the software design. However, understanding the system functional descriptions is important because they form the basis for initiating the structured design process for the software. The structured design methodology that we will present in the section on software design, while it is applicable to the system design phase, is a software engineering tool that is gaining recognition as having a wider applicability than that of strictly software design.

3.3.1 WHO'S WHO ON THE SYSTEM DESIGN TEAM

The system design phase involves the coordinated efforts of representatives of the three disciplines of systems engineering, hardware engineering, and software engineering. To be productive, the team cannot be very large (2 to 6 people), but size and complexity of the task require a variety of skills that cannot be found in one individual to the extent necessary for the detailed work involved in a complex system. Also, although the creative process is a uniquely individualistic skill, the mutual stimulation of several capable people working closely together on the same task is very productive. It allows for exchange of ideas, the "trying out" of new thoughts, and the informal checks and balances of mutual review that keep the design evolving along the right path.

The systems engineer is usually the one responsible for this phase of the design. Their skills are those oriented toward the analysis of the user's requirements and the synthesis of the details in the system design to provide a good solution to the requirements. They are knowledgeable of the techniques and methods of both the software engineer and the hardware engineer. Perforce they will not go into the detail of these disciplines, but will maintain a perspective of the total system design. Their ability to abstract and generalize, and then return to the detailed analysis of both the requirements and overall design, is most important. The discipline of system engineering also includes the understanding of human factors engineering necessary to design a man/machine interface that is understandable both to the ultimate user and to the operators of a system. The system engineering discipline also includes an understanding of the attributes of reliability, testability, maintainability, etc., which are a necessary part of the design process and must be skillfully incorporated into the design if it is to be successful as a product. Above all, the systems engineer is aware of the virtues of simplicity and economy in design and sees that the end product reflects these attributes.

The hardware engineer must understand the systems engineering process and also be able to work with software engineers in the context of the total system. The skills of the hardware engineer are more directly related to the techniques of hardware configuration and implementation. In these days of modular packaging and standardization, they have a broad familiarity with the applicable processors and peripheral devices that are available and becoming available. They are skilled in the specification and performance analysis of those elements that must be developed for the system. They know how to design new hardware that supports the software implementation (i.e., interfaces are designed so that data crossing an interface can be easily handled and checked by the software).

Software engineers must also be knowledgeable of the systems engineering process and the techniques of analysis used in systems design. They must be able to communicate with the systems engineer and hardware engineer in their own languages. They must have an understanding of the software capabilities of many processors and standard peripheral devices in order to work with the hardware engineers. They must be knowledgeable of the general state of the art in data processing systems in order to correctly assess the impact on software of the proposed hardware that will be developed for the system. As team members, they are expected to be particularly aware of the software aspects of the system. As the team considers first one function and then another, and how these can fit into the overall system, the software engineers are expected to supply detailed estimates on design aspects of the software and explain how software will perform its functions. Typical inputs to the design process that the software engineers provide are:

1. Size—how much space the program occupies in terms of memory locations and/or file space.
2. Time to execute—generally figured as an average execution time over a characteristic sampling, but may be figured under worst-case conditions—often estimated during design as a number of instructions per execution. (A standard execution time per instruction is calculated from a characteristic mix of instructions.)
3. Residency requirements of the program and its data—must it be core resident, or can it be loaded on demand and subsequently overlayed by other programs that also are loaded on demand? This predetermines a delay time to execution.
4. Program scheduling priority and method.
5. Data base accessing priority and method.
6. Resource utilization and method of gaining control—the input/output device utilization—calls or tasking of other system functions.

Software engineers participate in the analysis of requirements and in the structuring of design along with other members of the design team. Therefore, they must understand the system design process, the use of various techniques in trade studies, and the impact of human factors on design in order to correctly design the software. Although they do not play a lead role in systems design, the software engineers are instrumental in bringing all the elements of the system together in the final system product and making them operate correctly. Therefore, the software engineers play a major synthesis role in the design process.

In the case of producing software to run on an existing data processing configuration, the formal system design phase is often bypassed, and the analyst moves directly from the definition of requirements to the design of the software. The role of the software engineers in this case is that of analyzing a user's requirements, coming up with a conceptual design for the software system, and then proceeding directly to the software design phase and the implementation. However, in this chapter we want to illustrate the more complicated design case, so we are digressing to the overall system design phase and including hardware design considerations. The example design of ETAPS also includes hardware and software trade-offs in the design phase.

The system design team, as shown in Figure 3-9, works together in the develop-

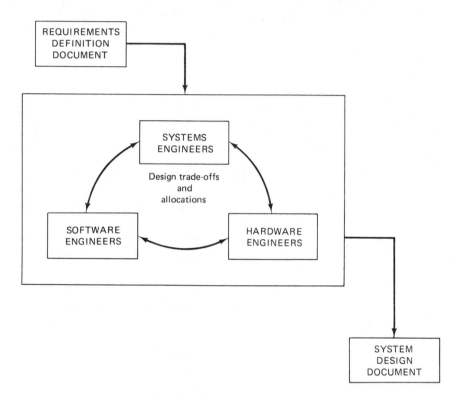

Fig. 3-9 The system design team

ment of a set of documents known as a system design specification. The portion of the system design that is of most interest to the software engineer is the software functional design or those functions in the system design allocated to software and the software architecture conceived to support the system design. These software functions and architectures as described in the system design are sometimes written as a software requirements document, but more often they are just an intermediate step to the software design documentation. The hardware engineer is primarily interested in the hardware performance specification and in overall hardware design. The systems engineer maintains cognizance of the system design specification. Even if the members of the team have different end uses of the system design, they all are equally interested in the development of the system design. They are members of a team, working together to develop a system that will be responsive to the user in an economical way.

3.3.2 STARTING THE SYSTEM DESIGN PROCESS

The first step in the system design process is that of generating an initial structure of the system to reflect the primary functions the user expects in the system. These primary functions reflect the necessary operations or tasks to be performed to accomplish useful work. For example, the ETAPS system has as its primary function the analysis of data to accurately determine economic trends. It is of secondary interest that the analysis is performed quickly and that the system is secure from tampering by unauthorized outside sources. In other words, the primary functions represent the basic functions that are of most importance to the ultimate user of the system.

Of course, this presumes that requirements have been stated in a structured manner. In the existing world of systems development, this is not always the case. Sometimes, in fact, the requirements are specified by outside organizations and "turned over" to the systems/software designers as contractual items to be designed and implemented. Recognizing this fact, designers must be prepared to reconstruct the conclusions of the requirements definition phase. Reviewing the requirements that are submitted the designers should be able to reconstruct the environment, define the operational flow, identify the systems interface and its required performance characteristics, and verify that the system is operationally feasible. Inconsistencies or impossible logic conditions in the requirements may be found during the system design, based on the analysis of the system solution in the trade studies.

FUNCTIONAL FLOW DIAGRAMS/FUNCTIONAL SEQUENCE DIAGRAMS. With the formalized requirements and a conceptual design of the system, the designers begin the structuring of the primary functions. The operational concept is extended by using functional flow diagrams that show the flow of data from inputs to the function (or process) being performed and outputs from the functions. This naming of functions and the data that passes into, out of, and between is essentially the same as the development of data flow diagrams used in structured design of software except that it is performed by the system engineers at a high level and includes functions that will be performed by people and hardware as well as software. At this time, it is best to concentrate on the development of an accurate flow of data that identifies what is to be done rather than how the functions are to be performed. Thus, in developing the functional flow diagram, the emphasis is on blocking out the relationships between functions rather than the accuracy of processing algorithms. Figure 3-10 shows a typical functional flow diagram. As we can see, it is very high level. The sequence of functions is noted by numbers in the block, and relationships are shown by lines and the use of "and/or" gates. Functional flow diagrams have been in use by systems designers for years, in one form or another, and their ease of understanding and development make them readily understood and used by all members of the systems design team.

A variation on the form of the functional flow diagram is the functional sequence diagram (FSD), another old standby of the systems designer. The functional sequence diagram more closely approaches the data flow diagram of structured design practice except that a timeline is placed at the bottom of the diagram. Also in the data flow diagram used in structured design, inputs to the system are depicted as occurring on

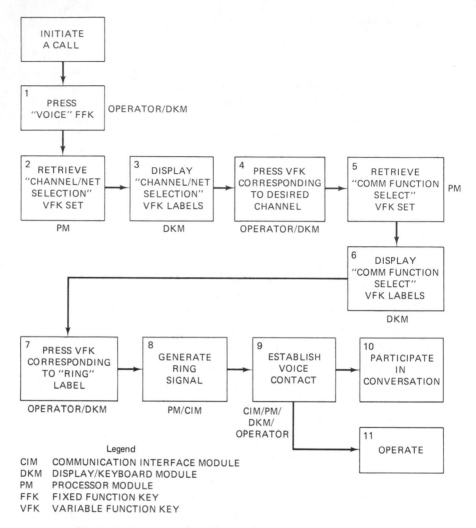

Fig. 3-10 Functional flow diagram for a message switching system

the left while system outputs are shown as resulting on the right. In both, the functions are shown by sequence in time as they occur. By adding the data that flows between the functions and the data that is maintained as data structures to the FSD, one arrives at the data flow diagram used in structured design. We must remember that functional flow and functional sequence diagrams are general techniques for converting requirements to a system, and are not techniques specialized for software design. They do provide a valuable input into the design of the software system.

FUNCTIONAL BLOCK DIAGRAMS/SYSTEM BLOCK DIAGRAMS. These two diagrams are the traditional means used by systems designers in pulling the system together after the analysis/allocation process. The system block diagram depicts the hardware elements of the system and the flow of data among the elements. It is most useful in synthesizing an approach to a solution and as a point of departure or baseline for subsequent analysis and redesign during the engineering process. In the block diagram, the blocks are named and given the standard nomenclature for the product, if it is an off-the-shelf item such as an AN/UYK-20 computer. If the block is to be developed, it is treated as a black box, given a name, and described in terms of its inputs, the functions it performs, and outputs. This black box concept is very much the same as the Parnas'[5] concept of information hiding. The data flowing between the functions or blocks are named and expanded into data format lists that define the format and content of messages passing between the blocks.

OPERATIONAL SEQUENCE DIAGRAMS/SCENARIOS. The next level in design of data processing systems that has proven very useful in large-scale systems is the development of operational sequence diagrams. The operational sequence diagrams (OSDs) are used in conjunction with a scenario to analyze in detail the interrelationships between actions and processing tasks in a data processing system. The scenario is a narrative description of a typical chain of events that will occur with the proposed system in its operating environment. The scenario is used to set the stage for operating the system. Sometimes several scenarios are developed in order to exercise the system in different ways. This provides for adaptability of the system. With a detailed scenario, this method of analysis can be particularly useful in decomposition of a system that has a heavy man/machine interface load.

Operational sequence diagrams are used to depict the data flow from data acquisition through its processing and eventual output. This technique relates information types with operational functions, their sequences, and the performing men and equipment. In this manner, each type of information flowing in the integrated system can be completely traced as it flows through and interacts with the system and other types of information in the system.

OSDs can be used as specialized flow diagrams to analyze the interaction of humans with the system. The actions taken by the operator are defined, and the processing to handle the operator actions is described in graphic terms (similar to flow charts). Paths of events are traced, generally, with identified conditions that determine the choice of paths. Performance criteria are assigned to the various paths. Figure 3-11 shows a typical OSD with the emphasis on human interaction.

In the case of real-time processing activities, the OSDs can depict sequences and reaction times as well as the uniqueness of processing that exists within that subsystem; however, here again an advantage of integration will be revealed as the OSD shows usage of the combined data bases. Each type of information and each source of information can be graphically identified and related to other sources and types in a readily interpreted manner.

The level of automation versus manual performance of system functions is also clearly documented on the OSDs, thus providing insight to areas where future automation can be efficiently implemented or pointing out where functional relationships can be adjusted to advantage.

It should be noted that the OSDs imply an allocation to a system configuration. This configuration can be the operational concept carried over from the requirements analysis or it can be the functional block diagram of the system. The systems analysts iterate between FSDs, FBDs, and OSDs. Thus, the iteration process that results in

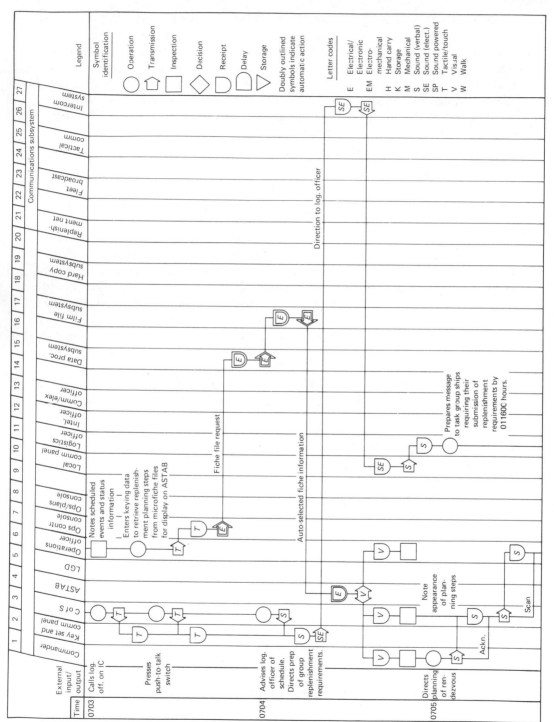

Fig. 3-11 An example of an operational sequence diagram

design decomposition through levels of refinement occurs between data flow and structure in both systems engineering and software engineering.

Action Sequence Diagrams. Another useful methodology for working with data processing systems is the action sequence diagram (ASD). The ASDs are particularly useful in identifying specific software requirements as a unique subsystem of the system. An ASD is constructed for each function that is allocated to the software subsystem. ASD construction is an iterative process, beginning with preliminary lists of data base requirements, display requirements, operators, equipments, and software processes, and continuing until the software function and all of its interfaces are completely defined.

The ASD is structured from the outputs of requirements studies and earlier analysis as illustrated in the attached partial example (Figure 3-12). We note that this example is preliminary and illustrative in nature rather than a finished product. All operators, equipment, and other subsystems expected to interface with the software subsystem are listed as columnar headings. The actions and data flow necessary to implement the system as derived in functional and operational analyses are diagramed on the form, along with decision points.

A simple symbology, with cryptic notation, is used on the ASD. An "X" indicates the input source commencing a sequence, with an "asterisk" representing an alternate source. A "circle" identifies a termination or intermediate step in the data flow, and the line connecting an "X" and a "circle" represents the requirement for a transfer of data by the computer. The cryptic notation identifies the entry or action. The alphanumeric inside the circle is a reference to the ASD key, such as a list that can be expanded in a separate table. Each sequence begins with an entry and continues, with connecting lines, through all automatic steps until the processing and data flow ends. Such decision points, which are entries of data to start another sequence of automatic processing, are represented by a "diamond" shape.

With each iteration of the ASD and its key, the preliminary conceptual description is refined, and the lists of software processes, data base requirements, and display requirements are expanded.

Supplementary to the ASD and keyed to the sequences thereon, a form is prepared to assist in identifying subfunctions and functional interfaces. The analyst who constructs the ASD indicates on this supplemental form, at each step, the software function(s) (other than the function being diagramed) that implements the step. For instance, in constructing an ASD for the defense assignment function (as illustrated), it is convenient to indicate that tracks are entered into the system and identified. These steps and others, though implemented by other functions, help to illustrate more clearly the context within which the defense assignment function operates. The end result of the application of the ASD methodology is a functional description of the software requirements which forms the basis for initiating structured design of the software.

The ASD is useful in these additional ways:

- Provides a detailed input into the simulation model of the system for validation of design.

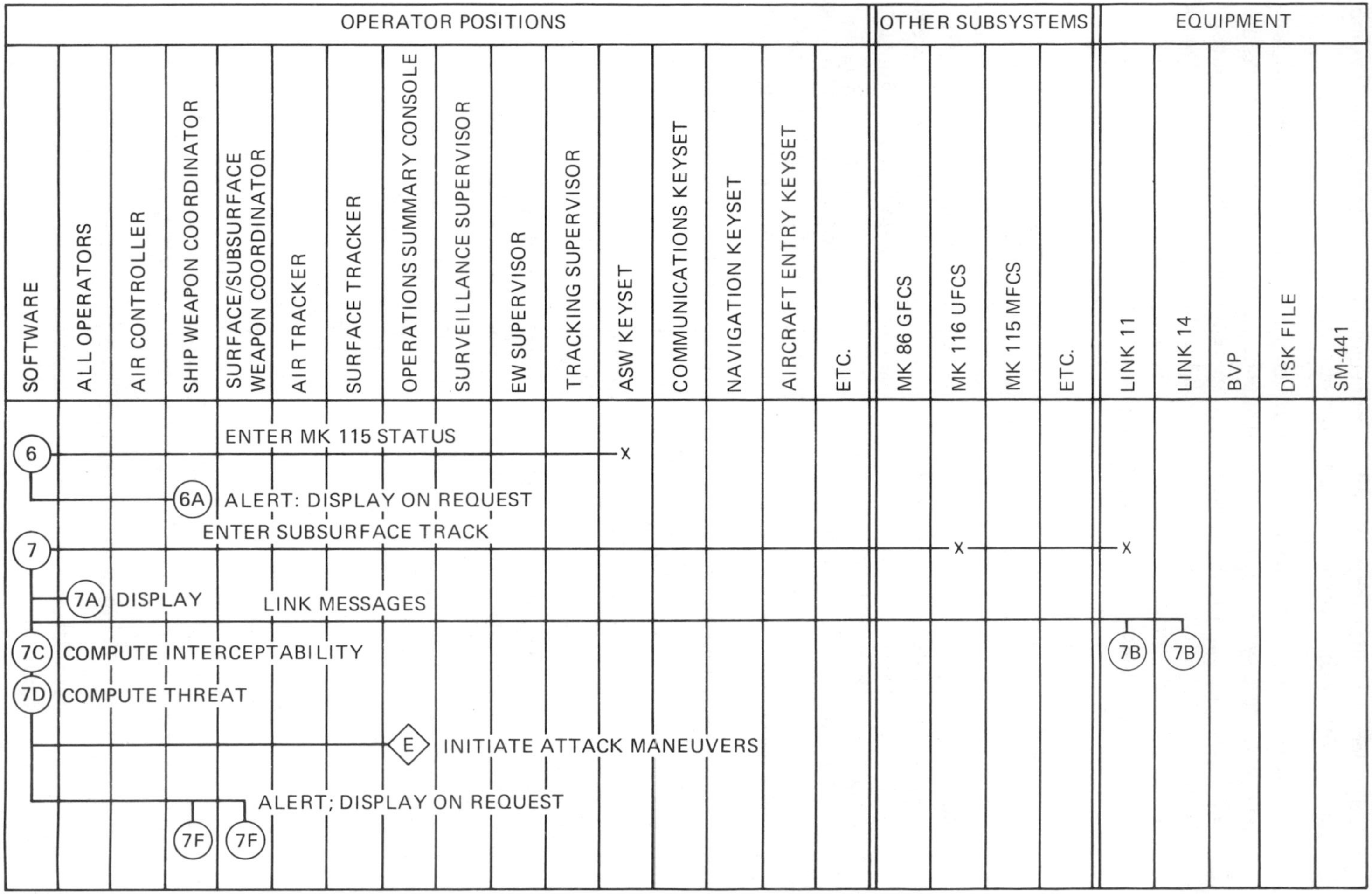

Action sequence diagram with columns grouped under three headings.

EQUIPMENT: SM-441, DISK FILE, BVP, LINK 14, LINK 11

OTHER SUBSYSTEMS: ETC., MK 115 MFCS, MK 116 UFCS, MK 86 GFCS

OPERATOR POSITIONS: ETC., AIRCRAFT ENTRY KEYSET, NAVIGATION KEYSET, COMMUNICATIONS KEYSET, ASW KEYSET, TRACKING SUPERVISOR, EW SUPERVISOR, SURVEILLANCE SUPERVISOR, OPERATIONS SUMMARY CONSOLE, SURFACE TRACKER, AIR TRACKER, SURFACE/SUBSURFACE WEAPON COORDINATOR, SHIP WEAPON COORDINATOR, AIR CONTROLLER, ALL OPERATORS, SOFTWARE

Action steps:
- 6 — ENTER MK 115 STATUS
- 6A — ALERT: DISPLAY ON REQUEST
- 7 — ENTER SUBSURFACE TRACK
- 7A — DISPLAY
- 7B — (LINK 11 / LINK 14)
- 7C — LINK MESSAGES
- 7D — COMPUTE INTERCEPTABILITY
- COMPUTE THREAT
- E — INITIATE ATTACK MANEUVERS
- 7F — ALERT; DISPLAY ON REQUEST

Fig. 3-12 Example of an action sequence diagram

- Assists in studies of loading of operators at individual stations, showing too many or too few requirements.
- Assists in studies of timing of operator actions by showing dependencies on other actions and data.
- Assists in confirming that necessary data is provided to all operators while eliminating excessive data readouts; integration of data flow is thus enhanced.
- Points out the need for special processing, such as specialized alert schemes for individual operating stations.
- Assists flexibility of implementation by allowing designation of alternative sources/terminations of data.

BASELINES.   The system design iterates through different levels and combinations of options. These iterations are called baselines. When a level is described to the detail that is felt to be necessarily complete, it is "frozen," i.e., established as a controlled document that identifies a level of design detail. Then, the designers go back to the requirements specification, and the iteration begins all over again until a new baseline is established. This successive baselining continues until functions have been allocated to their respective subsystems. Thereafter, the specialists in subsystem design begin their individual design efforts, coordinated by the system engineering organization which sees that they do not go astray.

3.3.3 ALLOCATION OF FUNCTIONS IN THE SYSTEM

The primary functions, as structured, are then allocated to entities of the system, using as a starting point the conceptual design generated in the requirements definition phase. The allocation of functions is a trial and error type of process that proceeds according to the skill of the analysts. In the allocation process, a human might be assigned to one task; a machine is assigned to another; an executive is appointed to control the program; a data management function is defined; programs/data are assigned to be maintained on disc. In other words, system trade-off studies are conducted. The system is allocated to resources, and the resources are identified as to their specific performance characteristics. The impact of such decisions results in specific interfaces between subsystems that occur due to the specific characteristics of the allocation. These interfaces are noted in the overall structure, and the design is adjusted to reflect the allocation. If an allocation perturbs the entire system design, alternate solutions are sought. The trade-off studies seek to discover the optimum solution, given the constraints of the system design requirements as determined from the original definition of the system requirements.

The allocation process assigns functions and tasks to subsystems that generally reflect techniques of implementation or operation. Obviously, at the highest level of choice the possible alternatives are: (1) hardware, (2) firmware, (3) software, or (4) manual (human). Time was when this decision was easy—software did everything the hardware couldn't do and the human didn't want to. Software was touted as the flexible medium that could compensate for all the inadequacies of hardware or the inefficiencies of the human being. Similar to Archimedes' "Give me a vantage point on which to stand and I can move the world," was the attitude of the programmer:

"Give me enough time and enough core and I can do anything." Unfortunately, there was never enough time or enough core, so a more reasonable approach had to be analyzed, selected, and adopted.

The human mind is still the only tool known to be capable of logical analytical thinking—of abstracting conclusions when given a basis of information on which to work. The tendency in some systems has been to try to over automate—to do for the human what he is more capable of doing for himself. Human factors engineering, which we discussed previously, addresses the problems of system designing for human usability. The goal of any system, in its ultimate use by and for humans, is to present the information required for human judgment in a manner that best aids decisions. Therefore, the goal is to allocate to the data processing systems those functions which the human cannot (because of time constraints) or will not (because of tedium) do for himself, and allocate to the human those functions that involve value judgments.

The cost of data processing hardware has been decreasing rapidly in proportion to software. The relative cost of data processing hardware versus software is expected to switch from 82% of total system cost for hardware versus 18% for software in 1955 to an estimated 80%+ for software versus 20% for hardware in 1985. Attendant with this switch has been a change in emphasis on hardware/software trade-offs. Software is no longer a sop to hardware. The concept of "software first" is reaching acceptance. Thus, the software is designed through at least an intermediate design stage prior to determining hardware requirements, and software requirements are driving hardware selection rather than vice versa. Therefore, in the allocation to the system, the cost of developing software makes it attractive to allocate certain functions to hardware, particularly those functions that are simple, independent of other software functions, and can be expected to remain the same over a long span of the system life cycle. This trend has caused the emergence of a new discipline—firmware engineering.

Sometimes the choice is between hardware (analogue) and microprocessors (firmware). Functions having low bandwidth and high precision requirements can best be handled by microprocessors, whereas high bandwidth and low accuracy functions can be handled by analogue devices.

Software allocations are made in situations whereby the control concept is not stable nor well defined and whereby data handling tasks predominate. Functions are allocated to software where change is anticipated over the life of the system. Also, and more important, we allocate to software those functions that integrate all the elements of a system into one smooth operation. Thus, we can see software as the means of bringing all elements of the system together for successful operation.

There are also some periphery system design activities required to support the trade-off studies. We must establish hardware configurations and design facilities to contain the equipment. We may also have to consider initiating hardware/software procurement activities. We may have to consider site building activities. Manning requirements to support the system will be identified, and personnel classification (in terms of training required, skill levels, and cost) for performing operators' tasks will be established in the human factors studies. While these activities may not directly impact the system structuring process itself, we find they affect overall costs and schedules. Hence, the trade-off studies will, in turn, impact the structuring process.

There is one important methodology we apply in the process of allocating functions or tasks to system entities—the use of the weighted matrix. It provides a measure of objectivity to the evaluation of different alternatives in the trade studies.

Weighted Matrices—This approach involves assignment of numerical weights and ratings to subjective factors. There are differences in scale factors and linearity of ratings between persons. However, the approach is an aid in communicating relative judgments instead of the usual method that uses subjective terms (e.g., better, significantly better, excellent, good, poor, inferior, acceptable, etc.). The weighted rating approach also facilitates reevaluation of the decision after the trade study has focused attention on critical items where more detailed study will be most effective in reducing uncertainties and insuring proper decisions.

An attractive feature of the weighted rating approach is that it permits the user to easily modify the criteria weightings originally assigned by the designer, thereby making judgments more responsive to potential changes in user's requirements.

This method of evaluation consists of four steps:

- Weighting of the criteria
- Rating of the alternatives
- Developing weighted ratings
- Validating selection

Weighting of the criteria—After the criteria for the trade-off study have been selected, the importance of each criterion must be established relative to all the others. A convenient way of doing this is to assign a weight of 100 to the total. For the example shown in Table 3-7, there are five criteria typical of those that would be used in an actual study. In the example, cost is considered most important and judged to be almost as important as all the others combined. Manning is next important. Schedule, availability, and space are given the remaining weights. This process obviously depends heavily on judgment, which is influenced by the requirements of the system and the desires of the user.

Rating of the alternatives—Starting with one criterion, each alternative in the trade-off study is given a rating. Cost, for example, is rated by determining the esti-

Table 3-7 Example of Weighted Rating Chart

Example Criteria or Characteristics	Weight*	Alternative 1		Alternative 2	
		Rating**	Weighted Rating***	Rating**	Weighted Rating***
Cost	40	1	40	0.7	28
Schedule	10	1	10	0.5	5
Manning	30	0.7	21	1	30
Availability	5	1	5	0.6	3
Space	15	0.6	9	1	15
	100		85		81

*Weight: Represents relative importance of the criterion or characteristic
**Rating: Represents relative merit of each alternative for each criterion or characteristic
***Weighted Rating: The sum of the products of the weights times the ratings provides an overall measure of effectiveness of the alternatives with respect to the criteria.

mated dollar value of each alternative, normalizing the lowest to unity (since low cost is better), and using an appropriate fraction for the remaining alternatives. The other criteria may not be as easily rated due to the difficulty of assigning specific numbers. Mathematical analysis and computer simulations may be required to obtain performance measurements. One by one, each criterion is exercised, and each alternative is rated.

Developing weighted ratings—After the matrix is completed, the next step is to develop the weighted ratings. The method used is to multiply the weights by the rating for each criterion. To determine the combined merits of each alternative, these products are added. The alternative with the highest total is the one selected as superior.

Validating selection—After the first pass through the weighted rating approach, sensitivity and consistency analyses can be performed. A sensitivity analysis examines how much the weightings and ratings would have to be changed in certain areas in order to change the decision. The consistency analysis examines the relative point differences in various areas for consistency in significance. In evaluations showing cost as one of the factors, the entire evaluation becomes calibrated in dollars per rated point. This can be useful in the consistency analysis by bringing cost-effectiveness considerations into sharp focus.

Just because a function or task is allocated to hardware does not mean that the software engineers can forget about it and continue designing software. As a member of the system design team, we must maintain constant dialogue with the hardware engineer who is designing the various hardware subsystems. The same goes for understanding the characteristics of communications interfaces and subsystems. The following paragraphs discuss the factors to be considered in the software subsystem and data base as these factors interface with the hardware and with the overall system structures.

SYSTEM STRUCTURES

During the design analysis and allocation of functions to the hardware and software, the software engineer develops the software architecture or high-level structure of the software that will perform the primary user's functions. The high-level structure of the software will look very much like the system structure, but software characteristics begin to emerge with an identity of their own. The generic system structures that are introduced at this time and are later extended into the software are: (1) control structures, (2) data structures, (3) data flow control, and (4) application structures.

A control structure permits multiple users to share system resources in such a way as to avoid conflicts of usage. A data structure provides capabilities for interfacing with a data base, which minimizes user's involvement with physical data structures and also resolves multiple-usage conflicts. The data flow controls provide the definition of interfaces that integrate multi-processor systems. The application structures are those programs designed to perform the system functions of primary interest to the user. These structures are discussed in terms of primary and secondary functions throughout the system.

CONTROL STRUCTURES. Control structures can be divided into operating systems and executives. The purpose of an operating system is to permit multiple users to share system resources in an optimum manner. An executive is a subset of an operating system; the "users" are functions of a real-time system generally dedicated to a specific task (command/control, air traffic management, etc.). Thus, an operating system enables general purpose multiple users to execute "simultaneously" by managing the systems resources in such a manner as to avoid conflicts of usage, whereas executives manage the resources for dedicated users.

The users communicate resource utilization requirements to the operating system via a job control language in which the resources to be used and the various options associated with their use are identified. Thus, the user can request input/output services to be performed, define auxiliary storage requirements, and control the execution/scheduling of other tasks or functions. These requests are honored by the operating system and scheduled for execution in such a manner as to enable these operations to operate efficiently in concert with other operations requested by other users on a noninterference basis.

The characteristics of the operating system are determined by the user's service requirements for the system. Operations of a computer checkout facility may require only that a user load a program into a computer and initiate execution with some capability for capturing data to be used in checking the validity of the program's execution. Batch processing systems provide a strictly sequential execution of user's jobs according to the steps for job execution specified by a sequence of job control statements. Multi-program execution within a single computer is possible since I/O operations can be carried out by an I/O controller, independent and concurrent with central processor execution. Thus, programs can request I/O services and suspend operation until the I/O operation has been completed. The operating system executes other jobs awaiting processing while the I/O proceeds under control of the I/O controller. On completion of I/O, the operating system initiates appropriate action toward resuming the execution (resurrecting) the suspended program. The processing of jobs in a real-time multi-programming configuration is controlled via some scheme that is termed its scheduling algorithm.

Program execution in a multi-processor environment is possible under an operating system that controls the interaction of the processors and the execution of jobs within these processors. Several operating system configurations are possible within multi-processor configurations as appropriate to various hardware configurations. For example, a master/slave configuration consists of a system level controller that exists in one processor and controls the execution of the operating systems in the other processors. These processors in turn control local program execution and resources. A distributed software operating system has a system control function in each processor that coordinates with the system control function in the other processors in order to schedule the local tasks and resources. Control functions may be allocated to hardware or firmware in addition to software. A hardware network operating system has local software operating systems to control local scheduling and execution, but system scheduling is provided by hardware or firmware.

From this discussion we can see that regardless of the operating system configuration, there are certain basic functions that must be provided by the operating system. An in-depth discussion of these is provided by P. B. Hansen.[21] Briefly they are:

[21]Hansen, P. B., *Operating System Principles*, Prentice-Hall, Inc., 1973.

Request Handling/Interrupt Control—The operating system must recognize when a request is being made and take appropriate action dictated by that request. Thus, the operating system will respond to interrupts, maintain a record of the action required, and initiate action based on the type of interrupt.

Task Control (*Scheduling and Dispatching*)—The primary purpose of the operating system is to permit multiple users to share the resources of the system. Thus, the operating system recognizes requests for job execution and schedules these requests for execution based on some scheme termed its scheduling algorithm. The primary difference between scheduling algorithms is the manner in which users are selected for preferential treatment. Thus, in general, the algorithm is determined by the arrival pattern of the requests (scheduling), the priority in which they must be executed (dispatched), and the performance requirements associated with the request. Generally, separate lists or queues are created, based on the type of servicing that must be provided by the operating system. Requests are entered onto the queues and worked off the queues according to some fixed priority. Thus, jobs are processed according to some scheme; first come—first served, round robin, do the shortest job next, or do the next job based on some calculated basis. The system performance is dependent to a heavy extent on the algorithm selected.

Resource Allocation—The operating system must handle assignment of resources to jobs in such a manner as to avoid conflicts in usage. Thus, the operating system manages the peripherals attached plus the system internal memory and auxiliary storage (random access devices). It will handle input/output requests. It will load programs from auxiliary storage devices as needed and restore them to auxiliary storage devices when not needed.

Fault Monitoring—The operating system monitors program execution for a number of reasons. The system must continue operating regardless of erroneous execution on the part of any particular user program. Many of the provisions for inhibiting user interference to other programs is provided with hardware—such as limit registers that determine the range over which a program can access information and privileged instruction sets that can be executed only in the executive state. On recognizing error conditions (such as excessive execution time, excessive data output, illegal computation, out-of-range accessing of data), the operating system generally makes some provisions for providing the user with status information. This takes the form of abort dumps of the program or a printout of error conditions if or when the program cannot be aborted.

A final word on operating systems is in order. Manufacturers generally provide a standardized operating system with their equipment. The operating system through its job control language can make the machine a much more attractive tool by eliminating problems of error handling and multiple user resource contention problems from the concern of the designers of application programs. But in the effort to be all things to all people, and given the obvious necessity for standardizing for configuration control, operating systems can be inefficient, unreliable, and difficult to use. In a real-time environment, the processing time overhead to system execution that can result from a standard executive may be a problem. This can be solved in several ways: (1) develop a specialized executive for the particular system application, (2) use a standard executive but modify it, i.e., tailor it for the given application, and (3) use a standard executive and solve any problems by designing the system application programs around the constraints known to exist for the given executive. All three approaches have their advantages and disadvantages. The first two obviously present cost and configuration control problems. The latter may or may not present a cost problem, depending on whether additional computers and resources are required or system complexity is compounded to overcome a standard executive's shortcomings.

The problem is not easily solved. The structured design methodology suggests that the executive control structure be "discovered" as the system is designed and that as a part of the final design stages the applicability of any existing executive be determined. This is perhaps a bit idealistic. A better approach is to know and understand existing options available, to evaluate these options as an integral part of the system design process, to assume the use of a standardized executive, and only under extreme circumstances where the evidence points overwhelmingly toward modification, consider adapting an existing executive or generating a new executive. Total life-cycle costs must be considered, not just immediate developmental problems. Standard executives can be cost effective from the standpoint of overall software costs. They can lower the risk in developing application programs. They can also be just the reverse when they are not applicable to the problem. Engineering judgment is required.

Although we have said that the technique of structured design tends to delay the formalization of a specific operating system, the basic functions of control which are provided by operating systems (and executives) are of prime concern in the development of data flow throughout the system and in allocation of functions. The software engineer is expected to be knowledgeable in all the software techniques used in operating systems and to provide the technical expertise to the design team when the team is considering those aspects of the design.

DATA STRUCTURES. One of the more critical system design tasks is the building of the data base. The task begins with the analyst's naming the objects and their attributes that will be transformed by events in the requirements definition phase. It continues in the system design phase with the detailing of data that will be flowing through the system via data flow diagrams, and in the definition of the data base in static presentations of the system via system block diagrams and hierarchial structure charts.

A data base is generally viewed as a collection of information that is accessed and maintained by the users in some integrated manner. The users of the data base may be either the users of the system or programs of the system. While "data base" may be used in some instances categorically to refer to *all* data defined for a system, the term generally refers to operational data only accessible over the entire system and does not include such "local" data as input/output, work queues, buffers, and data used only by particular functions.

There are a number of distinct advantages in maintaining a centralized data base for a system:

1. Centralized control is possible through some agency specifically designated for maintenance of the operational appropriateness of the data.

2. Redundancy of information can be avoided.
3. Inconsistency of the data can be avoided (hopefully).
4. The validity of the data can be maintained.
5. Security restrictions can be enforced.
6. Standards for definition and control can be enforced.
7. Optimum design of the data base can be determined from overall system requirements rather than the specific users.

The primary disadvantage is that a centralized data base can increase program complexity through pathological connections. This is described in the upcoming section on structuring.

Data bases can be considered from two distinct points of view—a physical view and a logical view. The physical view is concerned with the physical characteristics of the data as it exists on some physical data storage medium—a disc, tapes, or primary storage. The logical view is concerned with the characteristics of the data as it is viewed by the user. A mapping function defines how the logical view relates to the physical view and determines such aspects as the efficiency of accessing and maintaining the data base.

The physical view of the data base is described in terms of actual (stored) fields, stored records, and stored files. A stored field is the smallest unit of data in a data base. A specific value is associated with each occurrence of a field. A stored record is some identifiable collection of stored data fields. A number of types of stored fields are collected into a stored record. An occurrence of a stored record is associated with an occurrence of each field that constitutes the record. A file is the collection of all occurrences of one type of record. The records within a file are organized in some manner—sequentially, for instance, or logically by some value in one or more fields (a primary key plus associated indexes)—and they may or may not be blocked within the file.

Logical fields, records, and files may or may not be equivalent to stored fields, records, and files. Data independence is possible and desirable. That is, we can design a system such that any knowledge of the physical characteristics of the data is avoided in the application programs. They deal solely with the logical structure of the data. All interface with the data base is performed through a data base management language that presents the logical view of the data base to the programmer referencing the data and determines the physical nature of the data base from its defined structure. Thus, we can change the stored structure of the data base and/or the access methods without impacting the logic of the application programs. Inherent in this, of course, is an added overhead to the system of the data base management functions that translate a request for storage and retrieval of logical data into the actual storage and retrieval of physical data.

Implied, of course, is a means of providing this information to the data base management system. The mapping of the logical data to the physical data is provided via data definition capabilities in the data management system. The efficiency of accessing physical structures from logical structures is reflected in the performance of the data base management system. There are a number of strategies designed to improve the performance of the data management systems—associated indexes, pointers, chaining, hash-addressing, binary trees, balanced trees. A good discussion of these issues can be found in C. J. Date.[22] These *should* impact the performance, but not the logical interface with application programs, based, of course, on the degree of data independence achieved by the data management system.

A data base, both as it is viewed logically and stored physically, possesses a structure. There are three distinct approaches to defining the structure of a data base: hierarchical, network, and relational.

A hierarchical data base structure is similar to a hierarchical system structure. There is an ordered level of relationship where any subset of data is contained within its superset, and any given set of data is identified uniquely only within the context of all higher levels of the data structure. A high-level data set may have many subsets, but for any given subset, only one superset exists. IBM's Information Management System (IMS) is an example of a data base system that was developed as a hierarchical data structure.

A network data base structure is also similar in concept to a network system structure. Any given node in the structure may have any given number of superior nodes as well as any given number of subordinates. Thus, a many-to-many relationship may exist, which links any one set of data to any other set of data. The data base task group of CODASYL has identified a network data base structure.[23]

The relational view of the data base is founded on the mathematical theory of relations. The data base is viewed by C. J. Date as a collection of (time-varying) normalized relations of assorted degrees. It is necessary to view the data base as time-varying to account for the maintenance operations of adding, deleting, and modifying. A relation is defined as follows: "given sets $D_1, D_2, \ldots, D_n$ (not necessarily distinct), R is a relation of these n sets if it is a set of ordered n-tuples $\langle d_1, d_2, \ldots, d_n \rangle$ such that d_1 belongs to D_1, d_2 belongs to $D_2 \ldots, d_n$ belongs to D_n."[23] Sets $D_1, D_2, \ldots, D_n$ are called the domains of the relation R. The value n is called the degree of the relation. The relation is "normalized" if every value with a relation is an automatic nondecomposable data item. Given these definitions, the mathematical theory of relations can be applied to describe the attributes of the data base explicitly in exactly the same manner in which they are represented.

Within a multi-processor configuration, the data base and data base management system can take on a number of configurations. The data base and data management system (DMS) can be fully distributed to local processors. The data base elements can be associated with local processors while the DMS is associated with a central processor. The data required at local processors can be associated with that local processor and accessed through a local DMS, and the global data required by the system can reside in and be controlled by the DMS associated with the central processor. For a centralized configuration there is no distributed data base or DMS. It is obvious that certain of the configurations are more compatible with certain system and operating systems configuration. The message traffic between processors is significantly different for different configurations.

The software engineer works closely with the systems engineer in the design of data structures. The team develops the data structure as a critical design element at

[22]Date, C. J., *Introduction to Data Base Systems.* Addison-Wesley Publishing Co., Inc. 1975.
[23]CODASYL Systems Committee, *Data Base Task Group Report*, ACM, New York, April 1971.

the same level of importance as the consideration of the prime functions. Data structure is identified at each level of design and iteratively modified as the structure is evolved to the point at which the logical structures of data are laid out. During the allocation, the physical device allocations are made for data just as for program elements. The development of communication networks for controlling data flow is also a function of this system engineering/software engineering team.

DATA FLOW CONTROL. With the breakthrough in processor costs and the increased use of microprocessors in systems, the design and allocation of functions in a system to actual hardware entities have stimulated interest and understanding of the importance of formalizing the communication among entities in the system. This is particularly true in the case of distributed processing systems where we are concerned with the netting of several processors in a system. It is also true in the design of systems where functions are allocated to microprocessors (as implemented in firmware) and to general-purpose processors, but which are integrated into a physical system. To facilitate the design of these distributed processing systems, a distinction has been made between information processing functions (in the application programs) and the network processing functions. A good reference in this area is Becker.[24] The network processing functions provide the control of the data flow and encompass the functions that make it possible for the exchange of information within the network. Within a network, operating systems, data, and application programs are configured among the various nodes of the network. The data flow mechanism establishes the protocol that permits the data to flow between the nodes.

A primary goal in conducting system trade-off studies on the data flow control is to define the data flow control functions so that they are as transparent as possible to the application functions. The hardware, operating system, data structure, and data flow control functions ideally should be completely benign to the application functions.

It must be remembered that the system functions that we are describing can be allocated to hardware, firmware, or software. Thus, the network processing functions are seen to consist of both the hardware and the software functions that are required to control the data flow through the network as a whole. The information flow through the system can be viewed at various levels. In essence, the information flow is in and out of the system. To accomplish the required transformations, the information flows basically between application programs. Within a network, however, to accomplish this information flow, the data flows from application program to the operating system along logical communication paths and across actual physical communication paths.

When we view system design in terms of data flow, the problem is one of defining an optimum system for collecting, processing, and distributing the information. We view data initially as that information entered by the user. A variety of additional information is usually required for use by the network in determining how to route the message to its proper destination. Thus, header information is appended to the user information to form a data packet. The form and the content of this header information vary as the information traverses the various levels. The data is routed through the system from its source to its destination. The software engineer must be

[24]Becker, H. B., *Functional Analysis of Information Networks—A Structured Approach to the Data Communications Environment.* Wiley-Interscience, John Wiley & Sons, Inc., 1973.

prepared to deal with both the physical communication paths and logical communication paths.

The factors we consider in dealing with the physical communication paths are:

1. the characteristics of the information source—the point at which the data originates,
2. the distribution network—the path that the data must take to get to its target, and
3. the characteristics of the information destination—the target point to which the output or results must be delivered.

At the information source and destination, the primary concern is the interface that accomplishes the input/output of source information to the system. As the information flows through the system, the primary concern is control of the message flow.

Thus, the factors that we must consider in analyzing the physical communication paths are:

1. Data concentration (multiplexing)—the collection/distribution of information flow from a number of source/destination nodes for transmission to another network node over a smaller number of lines or trunks. This includes consideration of such factors as the number and speed of terminals, the way they are clustered, the distance of the cluster from the center, and the desired level of service or availability to be provided.
2. Data source/destination interface—the operating characteristics or disciplines of the source or destination devices that must be evaluated to determine their effects on the information network's hardware and/or software elements.
3. Device coupling (synchronization)—the hardware technique used to connect source/destination devices and other network elements to the trunks and/or lines of the distribution network.
4. Data distribution net—the network of lines and trunks that provides the medium or path over which information flows between nodes in the information network.
5. Line switching—the means of physically establishing or altering the path of information flowing through a node in the network. For example, circuit switching involves the establishment of physical connection between sender and receiver. Message and/or packet switching is concerned with maintenance of logical paths between sender and receiver at the hardware level.

We have been placing a great deal of emphasis on the structuring of a hierarchical representation of the system. In translating the concept of the system into discrete, comprehensible designs that can express the correct emphasis on communications, we need to preserve the concept of hierarchy. This will keep our design understandable by maintaining levels of refinement. At the higher level of refinement, the concern is with maintenance of logical communication paths. The factors we must consider in analyzing logical communication paths are:

1. Information routing—how the information will be directed to its appropriate destination, including queuing disciplines.
2. Network integrity—the controls necessary to guarantee the accuracy of the data and the accuracy of the flow.
3. Journaling—the controls necessary to provide historical data recovery.
4. Statistical information recording (performance monitoring).
5. Utility—overhead functions such as format control, code translation, and interface routines necessary to maintain transparency of data.
6. Supervisory control (error control)—exception condition or manual intervention conditions that require human intervention.

The reader may note that we started out describing a way of configuring the operating system, data, and data management systems within a single processor. We then expanded the discussion to include considerations that hold true when we design a distributed processing system. The software engineer must be familiar with the concepts of communication processing in order to participate with the system engineer in the trade studies that support allocation of the primary functions.

APPLICATION STRUCTURES.   The application structures are the functions that do useful data processing of interest and value to the ultimate user. The applications functions operate in the context of the operating system structure, the data structures, and the data flow established for netting elements of the system together. Specifically, the application functions reflect the unique user's data processing tasks identified in the user's requirements definition phase, whereas the control structures and data flow control structures represent system approaches to supporting the data structures and application functions.

The application functions are designed to perform specific user's tasks. The approach adopted to solve the tasks is represented by the algorithm used, which determines the functional characteristics of that program. Thus, questions such as accuracy requirements on the output, constraints imposed on the function in performing its task, and quantities of input it must handle within given time constraints will determine one or more algorithmic approaches for consideration. Often extensive analysis must be conducted to determine which of multiple approaches will yield the optimum performance, given the resources available.

The application functions or structures selected for primary functions are a result of analysis of user's requirements by the system engineer and the software engineer. The software engineers must understand the full implication of the requirements in order to correctly interpret the function into an algorithm for processing. This is why they perform the design activity better when they are included as members of the requirements analysis team.

HARDWARE CONSIDERATIONS

There are two basic aspects of hardware with which the software engineer is concerned, the properties of the individual hardware elements as they impact software, and the hardware elements as they are configured into a system. We recognize that there are numerous factors of hardware design that are of significant concern to the hardware engineer and to the system engineer, but which are not important factors to the software engineer. These include such features as size, weight, dimensions, resistance to humidity, radioactivity, power demands, temperature, shock resistance, etc. In general, the hardware interfaces to the computer are of special concern to the software engineer in two ways. We are concerned with the overall content of the data as it flows through the system since, in the end, it is the software that integrates the system operations. We share this concern equally with the system engineer and the hardware engineer during the design of the system. We are also concerned with the interfaces between hardware elements as they affect the design of the software. In this concern, we are working primarily with the hardware engineer in developing interfaces that make for good design. The different kinds of interfaces will be described below. In preparing these interface descriptions, we have taken the approach of listing the critical elements that are of immediate concern to the software engineer.

HARDWARE ELEMENTS. The basic hardware elements to be considered in the allocation/trade studies are listed as:

Processors—In general, the processor consists of these elements:

1. A central processing unit (CPU) that contains the control logic of the computer for executing the instructions, which in total constitute the system software.
2. The memory banks in which both data and instructions are stored and retrieved by the CPU in the process of executing its instructions.
3. The input/output controller that controls the input/output to the processor through input/output channels. Generally, the I/O controller operates in an asynchronous manner to the CPU, once processing has been initiated. The I/O controller and the CPU contend for access rights to the data banks.
4. Data buses by which data communication is accomplished between the elements of the processors.

The attributes of the processor of concern to the software engineer are:

1. The instruction repertoire (i.e., the number of instructions and their capabilities) provides the programmer with the necessary capabilities to build a program that causes the computer to perform the necessary tasks of the system. Formerly, the instruction repertoire significantly impacted the ease of programming the computer. Programmers prided themselves on the clever way they could accomplish tasks with "tricky" use of the instructions (i.e., shifting left to accomplish a multiple by powers of 2). With the advent of higher order languages, the concern with exotic manipulation of the instruction repertoire is rapidly diminishing.
2. The memory size (amount of core) is a factor because it contributes to determining the number of processors required in the system and/or capabilities required of the operating system.
3. The instruction execution time determines the amount of time necessary to accomplish the tasks, which, in turn, contributes to system effectiveness. In general, core utilization can be reduced by increasing program execution time, or program execution time can be reduced by increasing core utilization. Both

Sec. 3.3 Software Design and System Engineering

core and execution time can be reduced, to a limit, only at the expense of programmer time. It is generally cheaper to procure additional processors.

4. The word size (number of bits/bytes that constitute the basic unit of information in the computer) impacts the method and accuracy within which data can be represented.

5. The I/O controller capabilities determine the manner in which the I/O units interact with the processors. Input/output is enabled across channels between the processor and the devices. A priority for data input/output is established, based on a priority of channel assignment to the I/O controller. Channel and memory contention can occur as the I/O controller and CPU contend for use of common data banks. Attendant slow-down of both the CPU and I/O controller results. The integrity of the system can be jeopardized if data is lost due to the priority scheme or the memory contention conflicts.

6. Communication between input/output devices and the central processor is based on an "interrupt scheme." On completion of input/output, an interrupt is generated within the CPU, forcing the CPU into interrupt processing routines that respond to the action designated by the interrupt. The number and type of interrupts determine the attendant operating system overhead to handle these interrupts.

Lines—Lines or channels are the generic terms used to apply to connecting links between computers or between computers and devices. Lines imply a data transfer medium. Of concern is the rate of transfer and the type of line. A simplex line transmits data in one direction only. Duplex lines transmit data in two directions at the same time. Multiplex lines have modems at each end of the lines that allow for several channels of communication to be transmitted almost at the same time.

Random Access Devices (*Discs, Drums*)—The random access device (RAD), also called Direct Access Storage Device (DASD), is divided into partitions (tracks and sectors) of stored data. The number and size of the partitions determine, of course, the storage capacity of the device. The data is input/output to the devices through movable read/write "heads" that are positioned by track and sector at the spot where they are to read or write data to the RAD. The time to position the read/write heads (a rotational latency factor or seek time) as well as the I/O transfer rate determines the physical access time. In systems requiring heavy utilization of RAD devices, the scheduling algorithm (i.e., the manner in which read/write requests are prioritized) more significantly impacts the access time. Requests may be honored on a first come, first served basis. Other algorithms attempt to minimize the total seek time by enqueuing the read/write requests on a priority basis. The time in queue (average and worst-case conditions) determines the algorithm selected in order to meet system requirements.

Tapes—Tapes like RADs are classified as mass storage devices. We distinguish tapes from RADs in terms of the access method. Data is stored on tapes as a series of "files" composed of "records" containing data. To locate specific data, the tape is searched sequentially, either on some search key that must be read and tested or on a position basis by spacing over some number of files and/or records. Performance characteristics of concern include: (1) storage capacity, (2) seek rates, (3) storage transfer rates, and (4) the data organization as it impacts system performance.

Archival Storage Devices—These are storage devices, such as film and chip storage elements, that, once data is written on them, can only be read again. They differ from read-only memories (ROMs), which are used to store microcode, in that archival devices are utilized to store reference data in permanent files. The data need not be retrieved rapidly. The archival devices provide low-cost permanent data banks for retaining reference material.

Unit Record Equipment—Included in this category are card readers, punches, and printers. The equipment is characterized by start or "clutch" times, line transmission delays, and character transmission rates. The character encoding may be dependent on the particular device. Code conversion, since data is transferred from device to device, may be required.

Terminals—The characteristic feature of terminal devices (teletype, etc.) is their slow speed in relation to CPU processing speed. Therefore, multiple terminal devices are generally connected to a single I/O line/channel to the computer.

Display Devices—Display devices come in a variety of forms and formats. Stock quotation devices and ticket counter consoles are examples with which the reader may be familiar. A few of the factors requiring analysis are:

1. the data transfer rate
2. the data encoding
3. the buffering factor
4. the interrupt scheme
5. the control interface between computer and device
6. data accuracy as it supports required system accuracy
7. human implications in man/machine involvement.

The development of minicomputers and microcomputers that can easily be embedded in the display device has led to what is known as "smart" terminals. Some of the smart terminals have display functions like automatic refresh capability, character and line formatting, etc., built into the microprocessors. Others may have general capabilities to perform common display functions. A general knowledge of the display device capability is required for the analyst to properly perform allocation of functions to various elements of the system. The recent development of smart terminals is representative of the trend we see in dispersing functions throughout the system network made possible by the development of microprocessors.

Sensor devices—This category of devices comes in the greatest variety of forms, particularly in the development of embedded computer systems. Sensor devices include radars, sonars, electronic eyes, counting devices, tension gages, noise detectors, all of which pick up data for entry into the system with little or no intervention from humans.

A special category of sensor devices of interest to information processing is source data automation. Sensor devices translate the physical word into digital formats that can be processed by the computer(s). Examples are voice recorders, optical character readers, supermarket price readers, etc. Source data automation devices and readers also can translate the symbolic world of words and numbers into a format for direct input into the system rather than the indirect route of keypunching cards or entering data via key to disc devices. Features of interest to the software engineer are essentially the same as those of the display devices, except for the human factors implications.

Again, the development of microprocessors has allowed many functions to be allocated to digital hardware in the sensors that formerly were incorporated in software.

Control devices—Systems are built not only to print out data and reports or display information on a scope, but also to directly control machines or processes in the real world. Processes controlled by embedded computer systems range from military defense and weapons systems to integrated processing facilities such as oil refineries, traffic control systems, factory production lines, automated test equipment, etc. Again, from the software engineering point of view, the characteristics of the interfaces with these devices are the same as those of sensor devices.

HARDWARE CONFIGURATIONS. Hardware structure is derived from the system structure. The hardware structure is defined by the hardware elements and the manner in which they are interconnected. As the system functions are identified, trade-off studies are conducted to determine the optimum method of performing the various hardware functions. Generic devices are identified that provide the general capabilities required—i.e., a processor, a random access device, a radar, a display, a printer. The real problem, of course, is how best to determine the number, the specific type, and the way the devices are interconnected within the system. The selection of hardware presupposes fixed performance characteristics that, in turn, determine the characteristics of the system. All are structured into the physical model of the system.

We view the hardware configuration of an information processing system as a network, consisting of one or more processors connected via data communication lines to other processors, imput/output devices or interim storage devices. Networks are defined as any system requiring one or more information processors that are to be interfaced with one or more remote information sources and/or destinations on a full- or part-time basis. Some of the various network configuration options are: (1) centralized computer—consists of a single computer with peripherals connected to the computer via lines; (2) front-end, back-end computer network—consists of a "host" as central computer augmented with a front-end communications type processor and a back-end support-type processor(s) for functions such as display processing, data management, tracking; (3) top-down hierarchical network—all external I/O to the system is handled by a processor at the top of the hierarchy. Information and control flow is down the hierarchy through a number of levels of processors. The processors at the bottom of the hierarchy form a pool of resources that are used to perform the system processing functions. Other examples could be cited, but are unnecessary for this discussion.

When configuring hardware elements into a network, such problems must be addressed as: (1) the types of nodes in a network (source, relay, destination), (2) the way in which they are coupled (connected), (3) the method of routing data within the network, and (4) the network integrity. These considerations were addressed under data flow control structures.

3.3.4 INTEGRATING SECONDARY FUNCTIONS

The secondary functions are incorporated into the design subsequent to the clear identification of the primary purpose and structure of the system. By secondary functions we mean those functions that are not necessary to accomplish the primary user's

Chap. 3   Software Design

functions of the system, but are necessary to meet constraints of reliability, testability, etc. Presumably these functions will be benign to the system and, hence, their incorporation into the system design structure should be possible without modification to the basic design. Hopefully, secondary functions can be laid on top of the existing structure with minimal disturbance to the initial structure and its defined interfaces. If they impact the design in major areas, then serious consideration should be given to redefining the secondary functions as primary functions. If we do this, a complete reiteration through the requirements definition and initial system design stages could be necessary. The question comes up as to why secondary functions were not simply included in the initial structuring of the overall design. Experience has shown that too early incorporation of secondary functions into the design process tends to obscure the thinking on the primary functions of the system, and poor design will result.

Included in our definition of secondary functions are: (1) the design structures necessary to meet the attributes of good design defined in the requirements definition phase, and (2) support software.

SECONDARY ATTRIBUTES OF PERFORMANCE

We must provide capabilities within the design to satisfy those attributes that we defined as desirable by the user during the definition phase. That is, the design must be reliable, testable, adaptable, maintainable, etc. Many of these characteristics are implicit results of the design process itself as we have defined it. It is our contention that software reliability is a function of complexity. If we produce software that is less complex because of careful design, it will necessarily be more reliable.

Traditionally, we have implemented these attributes as software design functions such as performance monitoring, fault location, fault isolation (or hardware diagnostics), reconfiguration, security, simulation, error handling, and error recovery. Several of these types of functions are described below. The user's requirements will dictate the relative importance placed upon them.

Performance Monitoring—The purpose of performance monitoring is to determine the operational status of selected components of the system—be it hardware or software.

The information required is, of course, dependent on the component being monitored and the purpose for which the data is being collected. As an example, we may monitor hardware elements for malfunction, and use the information gained on the malfunction characteristics to aid the engineer responsible for the fault location and correction. Software components may be monitored for loading and the information gained on the various component utilization applied toward identifying bottlenecks and guiding potential optimization of the scheduling algorithm. Information gathered on system hardware component status is used to guide either manual or automated reconfiguration of the system to compensate for malfunctions during operation.

As an added note, performance monitoring functions can be allocated to either hardware or software for execution. Software performance monitoring is dependent on the insertion of the proper "hooks" at the proper paths in the program so that the information can be collected. Although we normally think of using software to monitor software performance, a number of hardware devices on the market are designed to monitor the status of software execution by builiding profiles on processor memory utilization. An example of such a device is the hardware device produced by Boole and Babbage. It monitors the software operation by sampling specified instructions as they are passed through registers. If the monitoring is performed by sampling data at test points in the hardware, there is no time penalty attached to the monitoring as there would be in the case of software monitors. Thus, the true throughput of the system is measured. These devices are proving quite beneficial during all phases of software and system checkout.

Fault Location/Maintenance Software—Special purpose software is developed to aid the operator or maintenance engineer in the task of isolating and correcting malfunctions in the hardware. In many systems two measurements—mean time between failure (MTBF) and mean time to repair (MTTR)—are critical factors affecting user's acceptance of the system. The first factor (MTBF) is a statistical measure of the failure rate as applied at a component level and reflects the technology used in component production as well as overall system architecture. The mean time to repair is, of course, significantly affected by the tools available to isolate the cause of a problem. Presuming hardware malfunctions, the fault isolation diagnostic software can be used to accelerate the fault location process and speed up the repair time. The system may be stopped completely, or the system can be configured to operate in either a reconfigured or degraded mode while repairs are made. Special software (fault detection) is loaded and used to methodically exercise each aspect of the equipment. Pass or fail indications are passed to the maintenance engineer to guide him in his search for what needs to be repaired. The development of software such as this is particularly suited to software engineers interested in the detailed workings of the equipment. They often are as familiar with the logic diagram of the hardware as the hardware designers themselves.

Presuming software malfunctions, a similar mode of operation is necessary. Special software is used either in an on-line or off-line mode to aid the software engineer in his search for the cause. This category of software, of course, encompasses the debug tools used to check out software, which will be discussed in a subsequent chapter. The concept of MTBF is just now being developed for software, but there is no body of statistical data to back up MTBF figures for software as there is in hardware. However, MTBF goals have been allocated to software in some systems in order to meet system reliability performance goals. In these instances, we recognize that software does not fail in the same manner as hardware, i.e., a software bit does not deteriorate. What is being measured is the mean time between detection of latent errors in the software.

Configure/Reconfigure—System configuring/reconfiguring may either be a manual operation involving a procedure as simple as wheeling in a tape drive and plugging it into the computer in place of a malfunctioning tape drive, or it may be an automated process such as the system's recognizing the failure in a network path (identified by the fault detection software) and initiating a search for an alternative path in the network by which to reach the target node. An important aspect of the design that facilitates automated system configuration is the concept of logical devices, logical equipment, logical paths, etc. If the system is designed to deal with the logical aspects of the components at a level of abstraction removed from the physical aspects of the hardware components, then the system configuring/reconfiguring functions can deal with the physical reassignment of components completely transparent to the systems operation. Therefore, the concept of levels of abstract machines is particularly applicable in the design of systems for which automated configuring requirements are expected.

Security—Security is a special topic being addressed as a separate chapter. Controlling the authorization for access to data from outside sources is of more concern to some systems than others. However, a key problem of concern to all systems is maintaining the integrity of the data. This aspect of security, data integrity, is discussed here.

Modules interface through their use of data. The interface may be obvious and direct through data passed from one module to another. The interface may be through multiple use of common data. When we design a system to interface modules by passing data from one module to another, no data integrity problem exists if a few common constraints are followed. Modules may be re-entrant as opposed to serially reusable. Serially reusable modules are designed to process to completion each call to execute. Re-entrant modules can be entered for multiple calls to execute prior to completion of previous calls. The impact, of course, is that re-entrant modules are designed to maintain data integrity by call while serially reusable modules maintain data integrity by execution. The decision to design modules as serially reusable or as re-entrant depends to a large degree on the programming language available. It is rather awkward to program a re-entrant module in a language that does not support re-entrant code generation.

Practically speaking, data integrity problems in the design of large-scale embedded computer systems that assume a common data base cannot be easily resolved. The operating system presumably provides capabilities for controlling resource utilization (including the data base) between multiple users. In summary, any multiple use of a data base is subject to integrity problems.

On-Line Simulation—There are military defense systems that, hopefully, will never execute in a real environment. It is critical to national defense, however, to assure that such systems will operate as expected, if the situation warrants. More practically, there are many systems that are not feasibly tested in a real environment prior to acceptance for installation and use. We do not find it always practical, for example, to send an airplane up to fly just to provide input to allow a programmer to check out a tracking program. We find it much more practical to simulate the environment in a way that gives to the programs the appearance of the actual interface without the actual existence of the real interface. On-line simulation programs serve this precise purpose. They provide the input to the system in the form provided by the interfacing device being simulated. They receive the output and presumably respond as the interfacing device would respond. The degree of sophistication in simulating actual devices is a design decision dictated by costs, schedules, availability of the simulated element, etc. The on-line simulation does provide for system exercising, determining readiness of the system, and for individual and team training.

Error Handling/Error Recovery—We have a very basic system philosophy in question here that will determine the method applied to handling errors. The choice is based on design requirements and cost. The question is whether a fault-tolerant system is required or not. There are two basic approaches—either the input will be screened to filter out all errors so that the system proper can assume valid data exists, or the error handling is dispersed throughout the system with many modules responsible for determining the validity of the data.

In the first case, heavy emphasis is placed on screening the data to meet all possible constraints imposed on the data internal to the system. The error handling is more centralized but is more extensive, since it presumably must handle all possible constraints. The error handling within the system proper is relegated to handling intermittent hardware failures that presumably are handled in the equipment or the operating system and, hence, are transparent to the application programs. The problem in this approach is that heavy emphasis must be placed on identifying all possible ranges of conditions tolerated by the system. Error conditions that are not recognized and inadvertently creep into the system can cause serious inconsistencies that may not be readily identifiable or traceable to their cause.

In the second case, fault-tolerant software implies that individual modules are responsible for determining the validity of the data. Error handling is dispersed throughout the system. There may be higher overhead in the amount of code required. However, the error conditions are more readily isolated. Identification of the source of the error condition may still be difficult.

Another basic question of philosophy is how the system will react to errors. Will it discard the data categorically, or will it attempt to correct it? Error recovery techniques imply preserving a base of known correct data on which to fall back. When error conditions are detected, the system can recover, either with manual intervention or by automatically restoring the data base to the last known correct data. Historical file maintenance is thus a key feature in this approach to system design.

We mentioned earlier that sometimes the functions described above are secondary, and sometimes they are not. Let's discuss this with an example of the configure reconfigure function. If the use of the system, as determined by the ultimate user, is that of turning out reports summarizing the number of changes made to parts used in production of X brand automobiles, the operation is not time critical. The final use of information could be updating the parts reference catalogue distributed to repair shops every six months. The cost of extra hardware and software development for on-line reconfiguration can hardly be justified in this case. If the application was that of controlling an oil refinery and a breakdown or loss of automated control could cause the entire plant to shut down or possibly blow up, then the system reliability provided by on-line reconfiguration is worth the investment. Another example is the data processing system in a satellite. Here it is not so much the immediate response time as it is the inaccessibility for repair and reconfiguration. It is not very practical to call the maintenance operator to change tape drives on a satellite 300 miles up in orbit!

SUPPORT SOFTWARE

We are discussing support software here since the impact of these programs on the primary function should be of a secondary nature—i.e., not of critical importance to the user even though they are of prime importance to the implementer of software. We define support software as:

- The languages used to describe systems and to convert problem statements into machine-readable format.
- The software used as programming aids in the coding, debugging and testing of software.
- The software used in integration and maintenance of user's programs.

Languages—Our concern with languages is based on whether they support the user's problem. A first consideration is the requirement for maintenance of the system after it is developed. Here we are concerned with who is performing maintenance, the anticipated rate of change to the software once it is developed, and the capabilities of the group that performs the maintenance. If the maintenance is to be performed by the group developing the system, then the choice of languages is open; but if the maintenance is to be performed in the user's environment, then a strong factor in selection of language is the user's knowledge and experience with language. If the user's community of maintenance programmers is working only with FORTRAN and COBOL, then it is not wise to introduce APL in the development, as the cost of introducing APL in the user's maintenance shop would be excessive. On the other hand, if the software being written will not be changed very often, then there is less emphasis on maintenance in the life-cycle cost to the system. For example, a process control program is changed rather infrequently, as contrasted to a command-control system that is continually being modified to incorporate new doctrine and tactics. Also, the capabilities of the people maintaining the system need to be considered. It is easier to train new people in the effective use of a high-level language than in assembly language. If we are to train new programming personnel in maintenance, then certainly we will choose to work with a high-level language.

Another element in the choice of languages is the capability to support the problem. Obviously, the use of assembly language provides a very flexible means for programming almost all problems. Higher order languages, on the other hand, are more problem-oriented, and selection is based on the compatibility of the language to the problem under consideration. We certainly would not consider COBOL for calculation of a satellite trajectory. Considerations here are:

1. Overall compatibility to the problem—The growth of Higher Order Languages (HOL) offers selection from a number of languages that are tailored for such diverse problems as text processing (SNOBOL), business report generation (COBOL), general scientific processing (FORTRAN), hardware testing (ATLAS), sensor processing (SPL), command control processing (JOVIAL, CMS-2, TACPOL), as well as the more general languages like APL and PASCAL, which offer specific advantages for handling information.
2. The structuring of the problem in terms of data handling—Some languages (JOVIAL for example) have an excellent capability for handling a common data base. JOVIAL is suited to systems that have large common data bases and is easier to use on those systems than FORTRAN. JOVIAL has capabilities for bit and byte handling, which is also useful in the large data bases.
3. The efficiency of the language—Efficiency of the language is to be evaluated in terms of its ability to express clearly and concisely the problem statements of the user (semantics are close to the user's problems, and syntax is simple);

the expansion of the language when source statements are converted to machine language (this is a function of the code generation phase of the compiler constructed for a particular machine); and the efficiency of the compiler itself (how many resources and how much time are used to compile a program).

4. The diagnostic capability of a compiling system—Selection of a compiler with good software diagnostics improves productivity.

5. The implementation technique planned for the project—If structured programming is to be used in coding, then it is more efficient to select a language that supports the constructs that are selected for use in implementation.

Programming Aids—There is a variety of software that is useful in implementation. Many of these aids have no impact on the design as they are primarily of interest to the code and debug phase, such as the debugging (trace, dump, snapshot, breakpoint) capabilities. Other aids, such as system generation programs that allow assembly of load programs from a master file and configuration management programs that provide for status control, are necessary for large-scale programs that break into small units for compiling and later assembly into an operational program. These are important from the design consideration point of view because they impact the structure of the implemented programs. Software testing tools are also important. We need to determine if such aids are available at the start of the project, or if they have to be developed during the project. Here we are talking about module test tools, simulation programs that replace hardware in the configuration for testing, message generation programs that generate test data, and data reduction programs used in evaluation of data. These kinds of programs are necessary for development of large systems, particularly where hardware is being developed concurrently with software.

Test and Maintenance Software—This type of software is used in integration and testing, and includes test tools like Code Auditor, RXVP, and others. Since they are more extensively covered in later chapters, we want to mention only that the test tools (in the sense of test drivers, etc.) must be considered as a part of the overall planning of the production effort. Selection of a CPU and language that supports these tools is a design consideration.

3.3.5 FORMALIZING THE SYSTEM DESIGN

In the system design phase, we started with a formalized statement of requirements for the system and proceeded to partition the functions into building blocks and to allocate the functions to hardware, firmware, and software elements within the system. We used the weighted matrix methodology to assist in performing the trade studies in order to bring some objectivity into our judgments. Now, we bring the overall design back into focus as a system and evaluate our design against the formal requirements and performance characteristics stated originally during the requirements definition phase.

The development of the design is an iterative process In the preliminary design phase, we take as input data the requirements definition in the form of a description of operations, scenarios, and environments of the user, and analyze those requirements by using the techniques of Functional Flow diagrams, OSDs, ASDs and other techniques of the systems engineering community. We fabricate a concept of the system (sometimes the same as the conceptual design used in evaluation of the requirements) and form the first structure of the system (called Baseline 0). This baseline, documented as a system block diagram, is, in a sense, a hierarchical structure of the system in that it depicts the hardware elements of the system and the flow of data between the elements. Studies and analysis are performed to identify alternate designs or ways of accomplishing the system requirements. As new trade-off studies are made to determine effectiveness of alternatives, a new baseline design (Baseline 1) is created to stand as a basis for further design analysis. Now, the secondary functions are taken into consideration, along with the supporting system design studies in the area of:

- Reliability, Maintainability, Availability (RMA)
- Hardware Support Logistics
- Manning studies
- Electromagnetic Compatability studies (EMC/EMI)
- Quality Assurance studies
- Test and Evaluation plans.

This again gives rise to additional analysis and trade studies and revisions of Baseline 1. Figure 3-13 shows the sequential relationships of successive baselines.

Finally, the design is at a point whereby simulation modeling, using discrete event simulation techniques, can be applied to evaluate the design against the performance requirements stated in the requirements definition phase. The design should also be reviewed to see if it meets all of the requirements identified in the definition phase. The use of simulation techniques in addition to design reviews is a powerful way of validating the design.

Generally, the design is iterated one or two times more, going through the analysis and trade-off phases to create another baseline before the system design is formalized in a performance or development specification. This specification describes the system, the subsystems that go to make up the system, the subsystem interfaces, and the software and software interfaces. The software system description and the software interface specifications are the basic input to the software design activities which we will describe in the following section. During this final synthesis of the system, the experience of the design team is brought into play to evaluate the overall design in terms of its goodness. The evaluation is in terms of design simplicity and economy of use of resources. From the software engineer's point of view, the focus of attention is on how well the software supports the overall design in meeting operational requirements and the practicability of the resulting software requirements.

3.3.6 CONTINUATION OF ETAPS EXAMPLE (SYSTEM DESIGN PHASE)

At the conclusion of the requirements definition phase, the analysts have formalized a description of the requirements for the ETAPS system as described in Sec. 3.2.5. A fairly accurate view of the interface between the economic analysts and the system has been established. Also, a fairly complete description of the display requirements for man/machine interaction has been established. A system configuration to support the work environment is yet to be defined. The basic concept of a system that will support the analyst functions can now be postulated. The structure postulated is

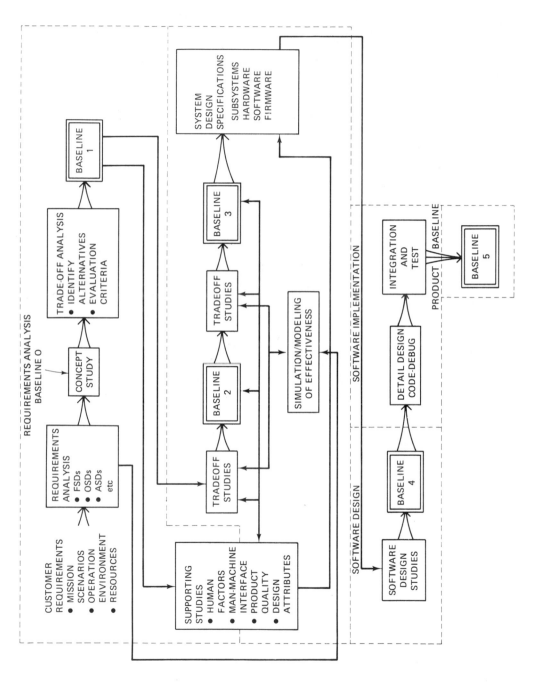

Fig. 3-13 System baselining as it relates to the overall system design process

that of a transaction center. That is, an input branch of the system structure will handle analyst-to-machine communication. An output branch of the structure will handle machine-to-analyst displays. The transaction center itself will provide computational, information management, storage, and language processing capabilities in one-to-one correspondence with the primitives used by the operators. An operating system is assumed that controls the resource utilization of each work station (analyst) independent of concurrent users. The functional concept of the system was visualized as four basic functions of Data Base Maintenance, System Extension, Analysis, and Management Reporting. The concept of the system is shown in Figure 3-14.

SYSTEM ANALYSIS

The raw data of the operational environment is input into the system as a set of files organized by event. For any given named economic event, a set of files exists that contains all the information about that event. A catalogue of events is maintained that identifies all events for which information exists in the system. The catalogue identifies the named event and the location and identification of the files of information on that event.

Generally, an analyst is concerned with the entire set of data collected about an economic event. However, a limited number of types of data are used by the analyst for particular kinds of investigation associated with the specific trend functions in which he is interested. Thus, the data is grouped by type before entering the system and retained that way for ease of access. The time-ordered relationship is retained so that the data files consist of a series of time-tagged data points. All data within a particular data file describes a particular functional time line of an event. The data files are catalogued by event and indexed by data type within the event. The data files can thus be analyzed by event and across events as required by the analysts.

The processed data is also organized by files and catalogued according to the type of analytic processing that has to be performed. Separate analysts are responsible for separate types of analytic processing. The relationship to the events is also retained in the event description as a dictionary of reference files associated with each type of analytic processing. The event catalogue structure is conceived as a substructure to the system file structure described in a system catalogue. At this point, the data structure is viewed as shown in Figure 3-15. The catalogues can be searched by event or by data type within an event.

Having analyzed the flow of data in the system and the general functions of the system, we are now ready for allocating functions to configurations—establishing our first design baseline.

ALLOCATION OF FUNCTIONS

Many of the functions associated with ETAPS displays and display formatting must be assigned to either hardware, firmware, or software. A number of capabilities are viewed as candidates for off-the-shelf procurement rather than development, but the efficiency and throughput of the system would be affected by the actual system configuration. The cost of procuring a new system and then transferring processing from the old system to the new system would also be significantly impacted by the

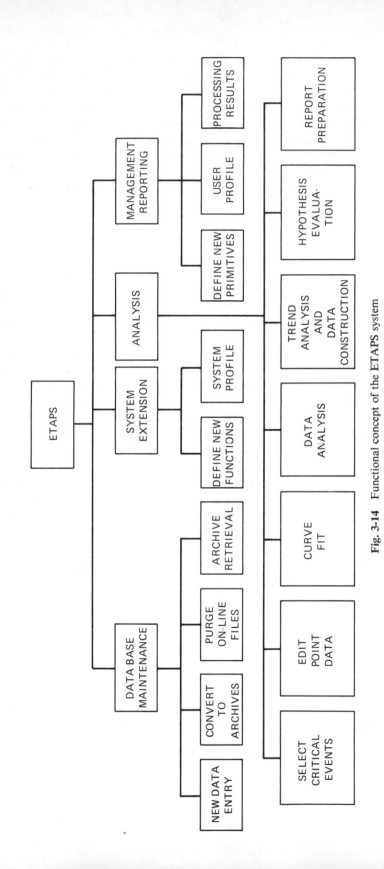

Fig. 3-14 Functional concept of the ETAPS system

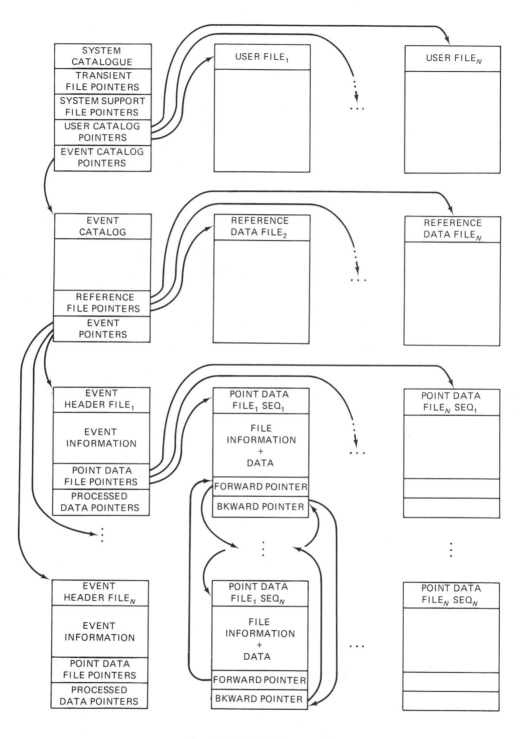

Fig. 3-15 ETAPS data structure

interface between the two. Hence, the problem of allocation of functions and component configuration was addressed in a series of trade studies in the system design phase of the ETAPS problem.

The existing system consists of an IBM 360/195 running as a remote batch processor under ASP/OS, and an IBM 360/67 running under CP/CMS. The system is being upgraded, however, because of increased work loads independent of the analysts problem. Therefore, by the time the new ETAPS system is developed, the facility will be upgraded by replacing the 360/67 with a 370/158 running under VM/370. A centralized system configuration is hypothesized, consisting of the 370/158 with on-line mass storage, archival storage capabilities, and "x" on-line interactive terminals. The question to be asked is whether this new centralized configuration can handle both the expected increase in general work load plus the increased ETAPS analysts' usage in an interactive mode. As an alternative, an autonomous configuration is hypothesized that consists of a satellite computer handling the ETAPS analysts' data base problems through its own on-line mass storage, archival storage, and interactive graphics terminals. Figure 3-16 depicts the two computer configurations selected for trade-off study.

Variations in the display subsystem architecture are also considered, ranging from "smart" terminals to "dumb" terminals. A dumb terminal consists of one or

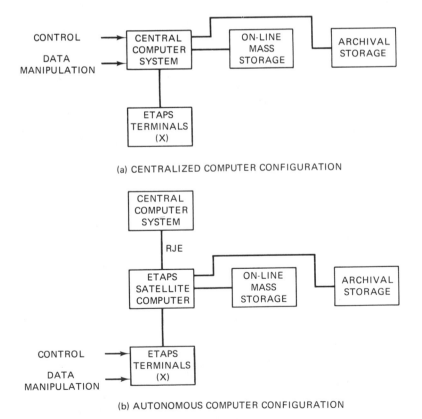

(a) CENTRALIZED COMPUTER CONFIGURATION

(b) AUTONOMOUS COMPUTER CONFIGURATION

Fig. 3-16 Two computer configurations used in trade stuides

more CRTs, including the associated display generators and operator entry devices with all controls being performed by software from the main processor. A smart terminal consists of the same dumb terminal with its display generators and entry devices, but adds a programmable processor to each terminal to perform display and graphics functions, thereby off-loading graphics and analysts' interface processing from the central processor. Figure 3-17 shows the two display subsystem configura-

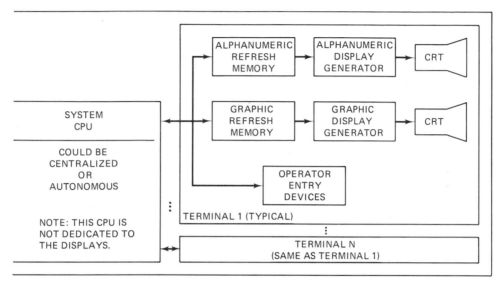

(a) Dumb Display Terminal Architecture

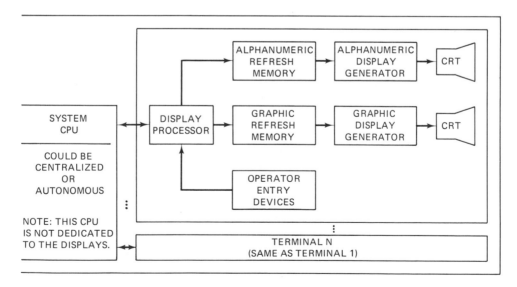

(b) Smart Display Terminal Configuration

Fig. 3-17 Two display subsystem configurations used in the trade studies

tions selected for trade-off study. Thus, the hardware configurations to be considered consist of any combination of the two display subsystem configurations and the two computer configurations with any range of variations in software allocation among the processors in the configurations.

The technique of weighted matrix evaluation is applied in conducting the trade-off studies. The criteria for evaluation along with the weighting factor to be applied to each criteria are established. One obvious hardware cost impact area is the amount of core required. Cost to develop the software for handling interprocessor communications, while not as obvious, potentially can offset any cost savings of the cheaper hardware. In addition, cost benefits have to be weighed against the projected performance improvements to obtain the highest performance at the best price. In all, seven major criteria are identified for evaluation. These seven criteria will be applied to evaluate the alternatives in the areas of: (1) system configuration (Table 3-8); (2) display subsystem configuration (Table 3-9); (3) data processing hardware configuration

Table 3-8 ETAPS System Level Performance Evaluation Criteria

Criterion	Weight
Response time	(15)
Immediate response functions	10
Moderate response functions	5
Growth	(5)
More terminals	1
More functions	2
More data capacity	2
Flexibility	(15)
Adapt to new data formats	5
Adapt to new applications	10
Impact on analyst performance	(30)
Functional requirements satisfied	10
Human factors	10
Throughput	10
Impact on central processor	(10)
Processor resources	3
Peripheral resources	3
Archival storage	1
Development impact	3
Implementation	(20)
Hardware availability	3
Hardware reliability	5
Hardware maintainability	2
Software availability	5
Software reliability	3
Software maintainability	2
Operation	(5)
Physical environment required	2
Support personnel required	3

Table 3-9 ETAPS Display Subsystem Performance Evaluation Criteria

Criterion	Weight
Response time (Picture update)	(18)
Growth	(10)
More functions	5
More terminals	2
More data	3
Flexibility	(10)
Formatting	3
Data manipulation	4
Existing graphic packages	2
Interface	1
Impact on analyst performance	(40)
Functional requirements satisfied	10
Ease of use	10
Visual quality	10
Data capacity	10
Impact on central processor (Processor resources for display control)	(10)
Implementation	(10)
Availability	5
Reliability	3
Maintainability	2
Operation	(2)

(Table 3-10); and (4) software configuration (Table 3-11). This gives a composite picture that can then be used to select the optimum configuration.

The methodology to be used to derive the measurements is determined next. Certain measurements are established through fairly subjective evaluation. This is particularly true of such areas as growth, flexibility, software reliability, and maintainability, for which no real specific measures have been established or standardized within the industry.

Cost statistics are accumulated for both system procurement and system operation and maintenance. An interesting result from this analysis is that the centralized system configuration, while much cheaper to procure, is much more expensive to operate. Estimates are that, within five years, reduced operating costs for the autonomous configuration will more than offset the increased procurement costs.

Performance with respect to response times, analyst throughput, and impact on the main processor are evaluated through simulation/modeling. A representative model of each configuration is run against the scenario established in the requirements definition phase to evaluate the relative performance ranking. The simulation model provides profile diagrams on the response time characteristics for each configuration under various loads. During this evaluation, the most time-critical operation is found to be the graphic "scrolling" operation. The analysts need to display a time-ordered graph of data points (trace) for an event and have the display continuously updated to

Table 3-10 ETAPS Data Processing Hardware
Performance Evaluation Criteria

Criterion	Weight
Response time	(15)
Data acquisition from archival files	5
Memory cycle time	10
Growth	(15)
Memory expansion capability	6
Multi-processing capability	4
Upward software compatibility	3
Interface expansion	2
Flexibility	(15)
Microprogramming capability	3
Interface	4
Instruction set	4
Word sizes	4
Impact on analyst (Data capacity)	(10)
Impact on central processor	(20)
Display control	10
Execution of applications programs	10
Implementation	(15)
Availability	10
Reliability	3
Maintainability	2
Operations	(10)
Physical environment required	5
Support personnel required	5

provide a continuous time-scan of the event. In this manner, the analyst will be able to recognize trends and patterns that will require more detailed analysis. The conclusions from this simulation investigation are two-fold.

First, the centralized computer configuration cannot handle the projected loading and still meet response time requirements, even assuming the most optimum conditions in which the smart display processor unburdens all the servicing of the operator entry devices and the display refresh memory content modification. Adding this fact to the life-cycle cost conclusions, the autonomous computer configuration becomes the logical choice. However, it is noted by the analyst that there are large-scale jobs, not requiring analyst interaction, that can still be performed in a batch mode. The simple addition of a high-speed data link between the autonomous computer and the central computer will enable the autonomous computer to serve as a remote job entry medium to the central computer. Thus, the core size of the autonomous processor can be minimized with no apparent impact to the analyst in his interactive use of the total system.

The second conclusion is that the console configuration best suited to performing the scrolling operation is a compromise between a smart and a dumb terminal. The dumb terminal cannot be refreshed rapidly enough to meet the time requirements. However, it is not feasible to have all display and graphics operations performed in the terminal. Because of hardware limitations of display requirements, large data

Chap. 3 Software Design

Table 3-11 ETAPS Software Performance Evaluation Criteria

Criterion	Weight
Response time	(10)
Applications programs	3
Graphics routines	4
Operating system	3
Growth	(15)
More functions/applications	4
Service more terminals	4
Service bigger data base	4
Program production facility	3
Flexibility	(15)
New data formats	4
Interactive language	5
Program production facility	6
Impact on analyst performance	(25)
Interactive language	10
Functional requirements satisfied	15
Impact on central processor	(10)
Interfaces	3
Display control	3
Application program execution	2
Data retrieval	2
Implementation	(20)
Availability	10
Reliability	5
Maintainability	5
Operations	(5)

buffers are required in the terminal to maintain the desired display image. Therefore, the programs in the terminal have to be kept to a minimum to make room for the buffers. It was determined from the simulation that the operator interface can logically be handled in the central processor and still meet response time requirements. Based on these decisions, the choice is made to go with the compromise display configuration. The graphics operations will be performed in the terminal processor. The analysts' interaction will be performed in the central processor. The impact on software design is as follows. The graphics processing performed in the terminal processor can be satisfied in main with a number of graphics packages provided as standard software by the vendor of the display consoles. Minor modifications may be required, but they can be kept to a minimum. Packages of these types also provide a set of graphics commands that can be used to control the graphic software in the terminal processor. Therefore, the software residing in the central processor can interface completely with the graphics package through a discrete set of graphic commands. This design results in a significant reduction in the complexity of the software.

The peripheral devices are also evaluated through the simulation. Response time requirements dictate that discs are required for currently active data storage. As much as possible, inactive data files can be archived to tape to reduce costs.

Thus, the autonomous system configuration is selected, consisting of a central processor, a modified concept of smart terminals, on-line discs for working files, and off-line tapes for archives. The central processor will be used to handle large-scale simulation jobs only through remote job entry from the autonomous computer. The simulation indicates the response time requirements can be met with this configuration. While the cost of procurement is higher than the centralized configuration, it is still within acceptable limits set by the customer. Furthermore, the cost of acquisition will be recovered in less than five years through decreased operating costs.

The structure at this point incorporates all primary functions for interactive response, data handling, and computational capabilities. Next, secondary functions must be identified and incorporated into the system structure. These include such features identified by the user as: system accounting, performance monitoring, security protection for data set protection, and an ANSI FORTRAN compiler for analysts' program generation. As they are incorporated into the structure, these functions are found to be benign to the system structure, providing an added degree of confidence in the basic design.

Two additional features of the system have yet to be established, the accessing method for the data base and the job control interfaces. Both are viewed as potential impact factors to system performance and usability, based on previous experience. The operating system and the data base management system are considered potential candidates for procurement rather than development. Existing software packages are evaluated for their ability to meet the primary performance requirements.

To summarize the design decisions at this point, all applications software functions required of the system are performed in the autonomous computer—with the exception of large-scale simulations, which will be performed in the centralized IBM system. The generic graphics functions will be performed in the terminal. The existence of the separate computers is transparent to the analyst.

An overall software configuration is established as shown in Figure 3-18. The operating system, graphics package, language processors for system extension, and a number of utility packages (disc off-load for archiving, etc.) can be procured as standard software. A time-sharing monitoring capability will have to be added to the selected operating system to meet performance requirements, and the graphics package will have to be modified to a minor degree to enhance its capabilities.

No general-purpose data management system exists to meet the data accessing requirements that will permit the data files to be accessed and moved to the display rapidly enough to meet the continuous scrolling constraints. Therefore, the data accessing requirements are investigated in more detail to determine if a special purpose data management system is feasible. As mentioned, the data analyst is concerned solely with data as it relates to an event. Therefore, all data will be retrieved by data type and by event. Once the selected data file is located, however, the scrolling operation requires purely sequential accessing. Special purpose data management routines are hypothesized to interface with the file management routines of the operating system for performing this specialized type of data accessing. Simulation runs are made to determine if the time constraints can be met. The simulation verifies the design performance goals. Therefore, the notion of a general purpose data management system is scrapped in exchange for a special purpose data management system. The

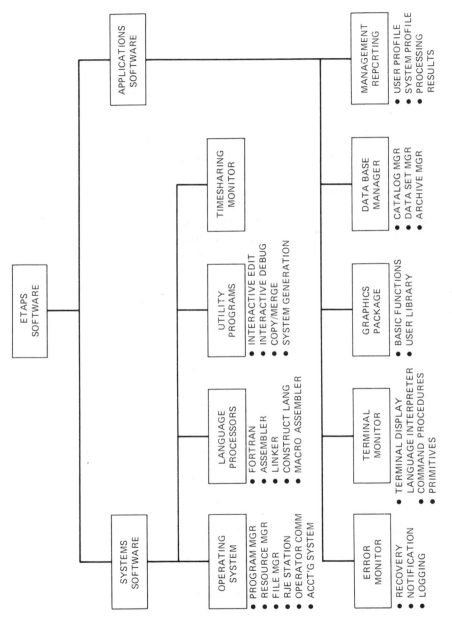

Fig. 3-18 ETAPS software structure

data structure is refined to include forward and backward links to sequential data sub-files to further increase performance. The special purpose data base management system and all other application software, including the terminal monitor, error monitor, and all application-dependent software, remain to be developed.

3.4
The Structuring Process

So far in this chapter we have reviewed techniques and methods used to define the user's requirements for the data processing system and the process by which the software engineer can work with the system design team in developing an optimized data processing system to meet the user's requirements. We ended the section on system design with a very high-level structure of the software as needed for a data processing system. In this section, we pick up this high-level structure of the software and discuss the techniques and methods whereby the software design is detailed to the point of describing the overall architecture of the software design in terms of software modules as transformations with required inputs and outputs.

Within this section, we will be describing the reasons for using the structured approach to software design and the tools and techniques that are available for use in structured design. We will include some ideas on how to identify modules by discussing how to keep naming conventions useful in the design process. We have included a section on guidelines for structuring and standard constructs that are applicable to structured design. We will go into the iterative process of design, the dynamics of achieving a good structure, and the packaging of modules into clusters that can be easily managed. Finally, we will illustrate the structuring process with a design of the software for our ETAPS example.

3.4.1 USING STRUCTURED DESIGN TECHNIQUES

The basic purpose of the design process is to arrive at an architecture for the software system. The structured design methodology is based on the premise that the design proceeds from a high-level conceptualization represented by a top-level structure to a fine level of detail represented by what we will call a "fully factored and packaged" structure suitable for implementation. It leads the designers through a logical analysis of the system in which they progressively define and refine their knowledge about the system. This permits them to build the system progressively to a finer and finer level of detail, each level based on a solid understanding of the level that precedes it. It is precisely this technique of refinement as it supports the defining of the software system architecture that we wish to demonstrate.

In any methodology, the key element is the intelligence and capabilities of the software engineer. It is the common experience of managers of software projects that differences among the programmers' performance on the same task swamp any differences that might have been found due to production methods. Presuming this to be true for the production effort, it is safe to conclude that the intelligence and capabilities of the designer are the most important elements in the successful design of a system. Hence, the intent is to describe the kind of reasoning, the logical progression of analysis, that must be followed in order to arrive at a reasonably sound design that is capable of being implemented and maintained in an optimum manner. Our goal is to demonstrate a reasoning process in such a manner as to enable the reader to *think* through his problem to a reasonably sound and efficient solution.

Before proceeding with the description of the design process, it may be wise to reiterate the list of attributes we are striving to achieve. The attributes desired for the system are reliability, testability, maintainability, efficiency, understandability, and adaptability. The qualities of the software design deemed necessary to achieve these goals are necessity, completeness, consistency, traceability, visibility, and feasibility. In all cases, economy and simplicity are the marks of a good design.

The concept of structured design is selected for this demonstration because it has many attributes that make it an effective methodology for use by the software engineer in achieving these goals. It is comprehensive in that it covers the total system design process. It is probably the best defined process in that its interaction within the system development process has been described in some detail. It can be understood by nonprogramming personnel and, hence, serves as an efficient communication device between personnel of varied disciplines. Rules and guidelines are being developed for evaluating the merit of a design as it is developed by using structured techniques. Because of the graphic nature, the design is presented in visual terms that can be easily error checked. It provides a clear, concise description of the system design as it emerges. The concepts of the system are clearly identified so that they aid as tools in understanding the system. Problems in the design are evident from poor or incorrect structures. The structure of the design also reflects the conceptualizations about the system. Complex problems or unclear thinking will result in complex or unclear structures, but the problems will be pinpointed, and the structuring process will help concentrate our attention on these problem areas. Required modifications can be determined by examination, and changes can be incorporated. As with any tool, experience and practice are required for effective utilization. Insight and understanding are developed through application.

The methodology presented constitutes a synthesis of approaches with predominate emphasis on the structured design methodology espoused by Constantine and Meyers.[13] The approach presented has been used with considerable success on several large real-time systems by a large aerospace company, due primarily to the work of E. Jensen of Hughes Aircraft Company in adapting the methodology to real-time command and control systems.

3.4.2 THE TOOLS OF STRUCTURED DESIGN

There is the conjecture that any one-man project, assuming a reasonably capable one man, cannot possibly fail. There is also the conjecture that the success of the team approach is due to the limited number of closely knit people working directly together. Realistically, all projects cannot be covered by a single team of only a few people. Therefore, not only must the software engineer be capable of analyzing the problem through to its completion, the engineer must be capable of communicating this work within the structure of a large organization and contributing to the final end solution. The structured design methodology provides a technique for communication across many disciplines. The methodology does this through the graphic aids it supplies and through the forms it uses to present the software architecture.

COMMUNICATING DESIGN WITH GRAPHIC AIDS

The graphic tools of the structured design methodology serve the same general purpose as the familiar flow charts and flow diagrams employed in traditional methods. Their purpose is to portray the design in graphic terms for increased understandability. Charting standards have been established in order to aid understanding by associating fixed symbols with fixed aspects of the design (i.e., a rectangle implies a process: data communicates along directed lines, etc.). The charting standards can be found in Constantine and Meyers[13] or in the publications of E. Jensen.[15]

Basically, three types of graphic tools are used in the structured design process, the data flow (or bubble) chart, structure diagrams, and table definitions. Each has its specific role to play in aiding the engineer to conceptualize and define the design. The data flow chart is the tool used to analyze and discover the information flow through the software system. The structure diagram is used to determine the organization of the software, i.e., the architecture. The data table is used to summarize data definitions and to show relationships between pieces of data, i.e., control relationships and information relationships. In designing a system, the software engineers will use these tools interactively as they proceed with the task of identifying exactly how and what the software must do. They must continually ask, "What is the data; how does it flow; what must the system do to best process that data; and, above all, what terms must I use to best describe what must be done?"

The Data Flow Chart—The purpose of the data flow chart is to define the transformations the data undergoes as it flows through the system. It contains no control information nor does it purport to define time sequence of actions. Its purpose is to aid in analyzing the changes that occur to the data input to the system in order to achieve the desired output. However, it is procedural in that it shows a sequence of steps as data is transformed from input to output, even though it does not show the time sequence of events as they are performed by the system. Because the data flow chart is procedural, it can be used to assign performance constraints. A data flow presents, in essence, paths of information flow. It is against these paths that performance constraints can be assigned.

The data flow chart describes data along directed lines and shows transformations proceeding left to right. Data entering a transformation (circle) must undergo some change to result in data output from the transformation. A "good" data flow chart will possess certain characteristics. It is the fact that a data flow chart possesses characteristic features that will aid us in evaluating the state of the design. Inadequacies in the data flow chart will aid us in discovering and rectifying inadequacies in the thinking process. Therefore, we will analyze the description of the data flow for certain basic features. All input to the system is identified, beginning at the left. All output is identified, ending on the right. The data must be clearly named in order to identify its precise contents as opposed to other data within the system. A series of transforms represented by circles will convert the input to the output. The transformation the data undergoes must be in as clear and precise terms as possible in order to understand exactly what is happening to the data. Each transform will receive a set of data to produce a set of output. The transform will either break out the data in some manner or it will combine the data in some manner. It is illogical for a transform with a single input to produce a single output since this implies some change was achieved with no catalyst to achieve change. Likewise, it is illogical for multiple input to produce multiple output since this implies more than a single change is being described.

Data flow charts provide the first attempt at defining the data used within the system. Data flow charts are used to define structure diagrams and vice versa. Figure 3-19 provides an example of a data flow chart.

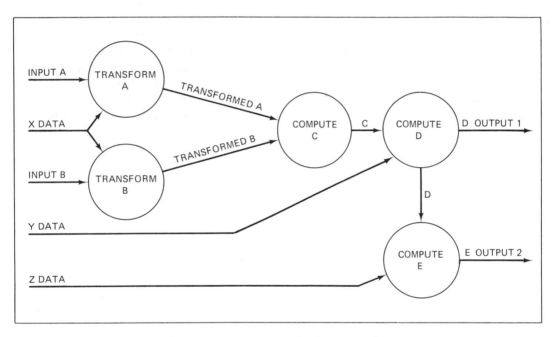

Fig 3-19   Example of data flow chart

Structure Diagrams—The purpose of the structure diagram is to define the organization of the system in hierarchical terms. The relationships of the modules to each other are defined, and the interfaces between modules are identified along with the method of control. The modules identified within the structure diagram will eventually relate directly to actual modules implemented within the system. Data is first identified in conceptual terms in the structure diagram. Thus, the structure diagram includes a complete description of the system with respect to modules, data, their interrelationship, and control.

The structure diagram is generated from the data flow chart. The transformations of the data flow chart become the modules (rectangles) or nodes of the structure diagram. The decomposition (partitioning) of modules is identified according to various options of decomposition that will be discussed subsequently. Submodules to a module are identified at a level below the module with the data sent from the module to the submodule, and from the submodule back to the module identified along the connecting line. Arrows indicate the direction of flow. The data passed between modules may be used as either information to modules or as a control flag to the module. The terminals of the arrow indicate the type of flow, whether data or control. Additional graphics exist to portray iteration, decision factors, data, etc.

A "good" structure diagram will possess certain features. Again, it is this fact that will aid us in evaluating the state of the design. Structure that does not conform to prescribed patterns has been found to yield incomplete, complex, or incorrect design. Therefore, we will analyze the structure diagram for conformance to basic design constructs. Terminal nodes will do the processing while all higher-level nodes will perform a control function. Only terminal nodes will interface with data tables. A node will not interface with a table and another node as this would imply a dual function performed by the node. Decomposition will conform to basic types of decomposition. All data communicated between nodes will be identified. The control constructs will be identified. Figure 3-20 provides an example of a structure diagram.

Table Descriptions—Data is described within the system in tabular form. The name of the table identifies the grouping or collection of data that is organized as an entity within the system. The contents of the table identify the items that will be contained within the table. Data is designed to preserve the functionality and independence of the structure diagram. Data is initially identified in conceptual terms as data

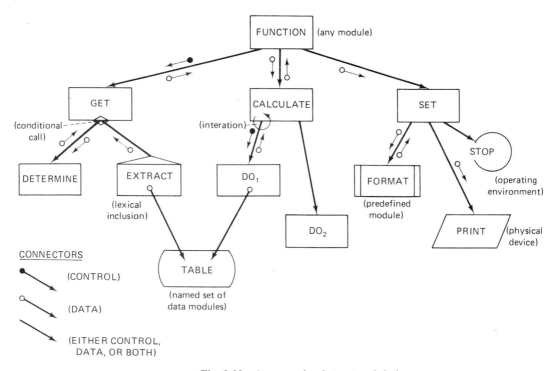

Fig. 3-20 An example of structured design

tables in the structure diagram. As the decomposition of the system processing occurs, the contents of the data table are identified from the data flowing into and out of the table. During detail design, as described in the next chapter, the data base is defined in terms of exact bit configurations, size, range of variance, etc. Our experience has been that it is possible to go from a high-level description of the data tables obtained from the structure diagram directly to implementation of the data base, especially if a higher-order language (HOL) is available. At this point in structuring the high-level design, table descriptions, and their logical content are listed for reference from the structure diagram, simply as a directory of table names and their contents.

HOW TO IDENTIFY MODULES (SEMANTICS)

There is a theory in semantics that states that our thought processes are controlled by our language. To apply that concept to design, we theorize that we cannot understand the system unless we can find the proper words to describe the system. Arriving at the terms used to describe the system is no easy task. Finding appropriate terminology is the heart of the design process itself.

Graphics aid the communication of design and are the tools used to guide the thinking process, but it is the semantics (the way we name things) that is the heart of the design process. We must strive to identify each node in as precise and concrete a manner as possible. In this manner we identify precisely what the system does. As an example, refer to Table 3-12. This table presents the results of an analysis of the semantics used for designing a real-time radar system as the design progressed through several phases. The terms became progressively more definitive and concrete as the understanding of the system became increasingly more defined and concrete.

Table 3-12   Refinement of Semantics at Different Stages of Design

		Version I		
Data Flow Chart			Structure Chart (Node Names)	
Transform	Data	Verb	Noun	Adjective
Validate	Radar data	Get	Transaction	Valid
Build transaction	Simulation data	Build	Item	
Active track smooth	Safe data	Read	Radar	
Track identification	Manual inputs	Validate	Manual input	
Passive track smooth	Flight plans	Compute	Safe data	
Build outputs	Weather	Put	Flight plan	
Update internal tables	Valid track transaction		Long-range radar	
Put flight plan	Valid nontrack transaction		Height radar	
Put weather conditions			Simulation tape	
Put displays			Channel	
Put record			Display	
Put safe data			Disc	
Put height request			Manual entry	
Put height radar			Tracks	
Put disc			Active smooth	
Put tape			Passive smooth	
Put channel			Outputs	
Put manual entry			Record	
			Manual	
			Tape	

Table 3-12 (Cont'd.)

Data Flow Chart		Structure Chart (Node Names)		
Transform	*Data*	*Verb*	*Noun*	*Adjective*
Validate	Radar	Get	Cycle schedule	Valid
Build execution tables	Simulation	Read	Cycle data	
Scheduling	Manual inputs	Validate	Manual inputs	
Build result tables	Track	Supplement	Schedule	
	Item	Build	Master schedule table	
	Control	Load	Safe data	
	Commands		Radar data	
	Options		Disc	
	Raw tracks		Channel	
	Correlated tracks		Radar inputs	
	Flight plans		Simulation	
	Equipment status		Long-range radar	
	Safe data		Height	
	Display		Tape	
	Recording			
	Console assignments			
	Height request			

Data Flow Chart		Structure Chart (Node Names)		
Transform	*Data*	*Verb*	*Noun*	*Adjective*
Validate	Radar in	Initialize	Plots	Valid
Convert to X, Y	Manual in	Get	Input tables	
Type	Safe data	Predict	Actions	
Save	Start-up Request	Update	Information	
Smooth	Geography table	Add	Radar	
Predict/update	Flight plan table	Change	Strobes	
Build request	Height	Drop	Nonplot item	
Load table	Information	Compute	Track	
Select flight plan	Search + Beacon	Put	Output tables	
Analyze	Height reply		Mode tables	
Add a track	Strobe		Display	
Change a track	Simulation table		Record	
Drop a track	Impossible Indication		Height	
Determine phase	Track		Cross	
Pair with target			Safe	
Predict performance			Switch-over	
Analyze performance			Restart Request	
Display			Simulate Request	
Calculate heading			Stop Request	
Compute lost tracks				
Compute display edge				
Update track store				
Compute automatic requests				

The semantics approach to system design seeks to identify the language constructs most appropriate for stating design. Processing is represented by predicates since they specify action. The implied subject is, of course, the system. The object identifies the result of the action. The predicates represent the conceptualization of what the system does. The objects become the conceptualization of what information is used and produced by the system. Semantic models of a system will address the use of prepositional phrases to describe conditions for iteration, logical decision, etc. Therefore, the semantic approach to design seeks to subset the English language by establishing the subset of constructs available.

Naming restrictuons are imposed solely by the application. Thus, we are restricted to action items (predicates), but the entire set of verbs is available to us in naming the action. We can define objects, but the entire set of nouns is available to use in naming the objects. The naming process is the key. It represents our conceptualization, our understanding, of the system.

The structured design approach recognizes the importance of semantics in the design process. However, it uses a combination of semantics and graphics tools to accomplish the design. Graphics establish a nonambiguous symbology. The terminology used within the symbology is subject to rigid semantic patterns. The structure design methodology deals entirely with predicates and objects. Prepositions are represented graphically in the structured design methodology with looped arrows depicting iteration, and diamonds depicting logical decision. The objects of the prepositions become the control items of structured design.

Since semantics are of such paramount importance to the design process, some guidelines are in order to aid the designer in choosing properly the words that he will use in describing his system.

The terms must be descriptive. The terms must convey meaning, preferably to the entire set of people involved in the design process. Terms that can be misunderstood should be defined in a dictionary, as should abbreviations. Eventually, during implementation, conventions will have to be established for naming data and modules that will conform to the language conventions in which the programs are to be written. This is an implementation problem that should not intrude upon the design process. Predicates and object names should be as descriptive as possible of the real processing during the design phase.

The terms must be precise. Their meaning must be unambiguous. They must describe exactly what is done by a module and exactly what is produced by that module. For this reason, certain terms will be found to be much more appropriate than others. For instance, the term "update" is a popular term in describing a process, but what does it really mean? How is the information to be updated; what transformation actually occurs; what is really done to the data? Is a new item within an entry being created, or is a currently existing item merely being modified? Terms such as "add new track," "calculate velocity," "drop out-of-range track," would be more appropriate. Therefore, generalized terms must be avoided. Specific action words must be employed for predicates; specific names must be used for objects. The processing performed by the system, i.e., the conceptualization of the system, is discovered by the process of continually searching for the most precise and accurate descriptive words.

The terms must be complete. If a piece of data (say, a track) has been verified, it is not just a track; it is a verified track. If it is correlated, it is a verified correlated track. As the data transformations are identified, the data descriptions should become increasingly more definitive until the name contains a complete description of the state of the data. The names of modules must describe the complete processing done in that module. It is only by analyzing the completeness of a name that we can determine the accuracy of the naming.

The terms should be grammatically simple. There should be no compound predicates or objects. These would indicate that multiple functions are being described. This is contrary to basic rules of good design that dictate a decomposition into modules performing single, discrete functions. If, in describing a process, compound verbs are found to be necessary, then a generalization of the process is in order with subfunctions identifying the multiple actions or multiple objects.

3.4.3 GUIDELINES FOR STRUCTURING

Our purpose here is to provide general guidelines for evaluating the design structure (following in general Constantine's rules) and then to show how they apply during the design process. All of the following criteria are intended as specific evaluation guidelines that can be used to evaluate the structure to determine its quality.

COUPLING. Coupling is a measure of the relationships that exist between modules. We measure coupling, not only by the number of connections, but by the type of connection and the type of information communicated in that connection. The simpler and fewer the interrelationships between modules, the more likely it is that the system will possess the desired attributes. Thus, a low measure of coupling is desirable.

Modules must at least communicate data, or no useful work can be done by the system. Thus, data coupling between modules is a necessity. However, the amount and complexity of data passed constitute a measure of coupling. A low amount of simple, obvious data yields a low measure of coupling. A large amount of complicated, obscure data yields a high measure of coupling. A measure of coupling is thus obtained from analyzing the data for information content. Coupling increases directly in proportion to the information content passed between modules, i.e., 20 bytes of data are less complex if they contain one piece of information than 1 byte of data if it contains 4 control flags.

Likewise, as has been shown, structures of modules are a necessary part of the conceptualization process. However, the system is simpler and easier to understand if a module controls the execution of its subservient modules in as clear and simple a manner as possible. The simplest type of communication between modules is through a call for execution with parameters passed as input data. Modules that interface directly with each other through parameters are said to be "normally connected." References from one module to internal elements within another module yield a significantly higher measure of coupling than connections that reference the module as a whole. Modules that reference internal elements within another module are said to be "pathologically connected directly." A special case in point is when two or more modules interface with a common environment, as, for example, modules that reference common track store tables. They are coupled whether or not they have any direct relationship to each other. Modules that interface indirectly through a common environment are said to be "pathologically connected indirectly." Pathological connections constitute a higher measure of coupling than normal connections. Pathologically indirect connections via a common data base are a necessity in large embedded computer systems. These types of systems maintain several large data bases—such as track store tables, weapons tables, area geography, etc. These types of systems are pathological in nature and inherently more complex because of these interfaces. An important aspect is that every module coupled to a common environment is pathologically connected. The complexity of the problem, however, is reflected in the complexity of the solution. Since all designs that have modules referencing a common data base will have pathological connections, this type of design should be used sparingly and with caution.

The third factor determining the measure of coupling is the type of information passed between modules. The sending of control flags between modules that are then used to modify the execution paths performed by a module is an undesirable form of coupling. The control should be inherent in the module, not external to it. The difference between control and data information is subtle. The important distinction is how the information that is passed from one module to another is viewed by the sending module. Information generated by one module that is used as control information by the target module is not control coupling unless the sending module expects to control the target module. That is, the sending module is using the information to control or alter the execution of the target module. Control coupling constitutes a higher measure of coupling than data coupling. Also, control flags should never be passed more than one level in the structure. If control flags are being passed through multiple levels, an alternative structure that eliminates the need for control coupling should be investigated. This will become clearer when the sample problem is discussed.

Thus, the three factors that determine the measure of coupling are: information content, type of connection, and type of communication. A matrix of relationships between the measure of coupling and the contributing factor is provided in Table 3-13. To repeat, a low measure of coupling is desired.

Table 3-13 Relationships Between Measure of Coupling and Type of Relationship

	Information Content	Type of Connection	Type of Communication
Low coupling	Simple, obvious	Normal	Data
↑		Pathological, direct	
↓			
High coupling	Complicated, obscure	Pathological, indirect	Control

COHESIVENESS. Cohesiveness is a measure of the type of relationships that exist between elements in the same module, i.e., the binding between statements. The stronger the relationship, the more likely the module can and should be viewed as a single unit. Thus, high cohesiveness is desired. The scale of cohesiveness from low to high is: (1) coincidental, (2) logical, (3) temporal, (4) communicational, (5) sequential, and (6) functional. The scale is not linear. Functional is by far the strongest form. Coincidental and logical are by far the weakest. The measure of cohesion is determined by the highest category applicable to the module since, for instance, a functional module may have minor aspects of temporal or communicational cohesion within it. For each type, a brief definition and explanation of its merits and/or deficiencies will be presented.

Coincidental—Coincidental binding implies that there is no meaningful relationship existing between the elements of the module. Coincidental binding can occur if modules are combined for packaging purposes when no meaningful relationship exists, or if modules are split for packaging purposes when no meaningful rationale for splitting exists.

Logical—Logical binding implies that the elements of the module are related by some class relationship, i.e., they are all interrupt processors, they are all input handlers, etc. Presumably they are included together to take advantage of some characteristic processing of the common class. What normally results is tricky or shared code that defeats the purpose of "good" design.

Temporal—Temporal binding implies that the elements are related in time. That is, the elements constitute a set of elements that are executed sequentially at a fixed point in time. These are generally routines such as startup, start over, terminate. Temporal modules tend to take on the characteristics of logical binding. However, it ranks higher on the scale because these types of modules are generally simpler, and they are all executed at a common point in time with no intervention of other applications.

Communicational—Communicational binding implies that the elements of the module reference the same set of data. A module that controls the referencing of various elements in track store would be communicational. Communicational binding begins to present a fair level of cohesion.

Sequential—Sequential binding implies that the output of one element is the input to the next element. Thus, sequential binding results from a highly procedural orientation—"do this, then do this" type of thinking. Sequential binding has a close relationship with how we view the problem. As will be noted, we conceptualize the system in procedural terms. Therefore, a tendency exists to structure modules sequentially. It is not the highest level of binding because sequential modules usually will contain either multiple functions or partial functions. It is not the best type of decomposition for the solution.

Functional—The definition for functional binding is circuitous. Functional binding implies that all elements of the module perform a single function. A better description might be that it is none of the other types of binding. So the question really is, "What is a function?" A number of definitions have been propounded. A function is a transformation of input into output. A functionally bound module performs a single goal. Constantine suggests that a useful technique in determining if a module is functionally bound is to write a statement describing the module and then determine:

1. Does the statement contain a compound verb? If so, it is probably sequential or communicational.
2. Does the statement contain time descriptions? If so, it is probably sequential or temporal.
3. Does the statement contain compound objects? If so, it is probably logically bound.
4. Does the statement contain terms such as initialize, terminate, and so on? If so, it is probably temporal.

If none of the above is true and if the module can be named according to the rules of semantics presented in the previous section, then it is probably functional.

PARSIMONY. The principle of parsimony states, "Never do more than you have to." The simplest design is the best design although the tendency of many engineers is quite the reverse. Note that the implication of this principle is: "We will never design generalized modules." If at some point we determine to use a module to satisfy multiple branches in the structure, it is because the structure shows us that a single module satisfies the single function required at those multiple points. To try to design generalized modules into the system initially only adds complexity. Conformance to this principle requires a significant reorientation in many people's thinking. The problem is, however, that we are "poor prophets" concerning the future requirements of a module. The best step is to design what is needed, *and only what is needed*. This does not preclude us from using modules that have been designed as "black box" type modules where the operation of the module is known from its interfaces. It does imply that we use such modules only if they fit the problem.

SCOPE OF EFFECT/SCOPE OF CONTROL. The scope of control of a module consists of that module plus all the modules ultimately subordinate to it. That is, the scope of control encompasses all nodes in all branches emanating from the module. The scope of effect of a module consists of all modules affected by a decision of that module. The system is simpler if the scope of effect is contained *within* the scope of control. The failure to conform to this principle results in an increased number of control flags that must be passed between modules. This has been shown to result in high coupling and increased complexity.

PREDICTABILITY. A module is predictable if, given identical inputs, it will produce identical outputs. The question might naturally be asked, "What would cause a module not to be predictable, presuming it has been checked out and is operating properly?" A random number generator is one example of such a module. The results it returns are dependent on the number of times it has been called. At any point in time, the number returned is unpredictable.

A predictable module is independent of its environment. It does not maintain knowledge of its own state. This precludes the incorporation of initialization and termination procedures into the body of the module. To do so would introduce temporal qualities into the module and reduce its cohesion.

The operation of a module is predictable only if all interfaces with that module are identified. Thus, predictability is a function of completeness of interface definition. This characteristic of modules is what has been referred to as the black box concept. It is also related to module independence. The function of the "black box" module is known and understood from its interfaces. It is not necessary to know anything about its internal workings to assure that the results are as expected.

SIZE. No hard and fast rule can be made on the size of a module that leads to "good" design. However, a figure of 50 statements, in whatever coding language will be used, is generally accepted as a design goal. Actually, the figure 30 seems to constitute an upper limitation of understandability, based on general human factors considerations. Too detailed a decomposition, however, increases complexity and decreases understanding by increasing the number of modules of which the engineer must be cognizant. Therefore, size is closely related to human comprehension. Modules significantly larger than 30 to 50 statements probably should be decomposed further. Modules significantly smaller may have been decomposed past a logical limit. It must be noted that judgment must be applied to restricting size. A module consisting of a type check and then a series of calls to other modules, based on the outcome of the type check (i.e., a transfer vector), may exceed the size limitation if the options are excessive. However, it would not be logical to decompose this module solely because of its size.

ERROR HANDLING. A closely related characteristic to predictability is how error conditions are treated within the design of the module. Error flags are a form of control coupling and, hence, increase coupling. The system will be simpler if modules can be designed to eliminate the need for error flags. This implies that the modules, if possible, should handle their own error detections and correction. As will be shown in the ETAPS example, it is possible to do this. In the example, an illegal operator action is reformatted into a "legal" command to the system. The command happens to result in an "illegal" response to the operator, but as far as the internal system is concerned, the command is treated the same as any other command until the final module is reached in a transaction center that actually executes the output.

ABSTRACTION. During initial stages of design, the structure will have a very important characteristic—it will be independent of actual implementation constraints. It will be expressed in abstract form. Abstract items are uncommitted to any hardware or data configuration. This is a decided shift in philosophy from earlier days of system design and even from a number of current applications. The system design must be discovered as a basic solution to the problem. It must not be force-fed into preconceived ideas of how the system should appear. Undue constraints for using existing software that may not serve the need of the problem can introduce undesired complexity into the system. Hardware decisions made before the requirements are known can introduce complexity again and may be extremely costly. The trend has already been noted in what has been termed "software first" engineering. In essence, this reflects the trend toward decreased equipment costs and increased software costs.

It is better to design the system first to the point that its processing is known before imposing the constraints of actual allocation of hardware onto software.

3.4.4 STANDARD STRUCTURES

One of our basic assumptions is that the structure of the problem solution reflects the structure of the problem itself. The extent to which this is not so reflects the extent to which we do not understand the problem. The extent to which this is true reflects the extent to which certain basic structures can be recognized for certain basic problems. Thus, certain common patterns to the structure emerge. We can, through experience, recognize good patterns of structure independent of the actual descriptions of the system operation contained within the graphics. Therefore, the graphics of the structure itself become an aid to evaluating the quality of the design. Recognition of "good" design structures is a matter of experience and continual application of the evaluation criteria provided above. However, we can provide some guidelines to recognizing common structures.

A basic structure is recognized for the types of systems with which we are dealing. The system receives input, processes it, and outputs results. Thus, the basic decomposition of a system will have three major branches: (1) an afferent branch that will receive the input and format it for processing, (2) the central transform that will do the processing, and (3) an efferent branch that will format the data for output. Multiple branches exist within each category. The number of levels will vary. In general, however, the basic structure diagram of the system will look like Figure 3-21.

The modules of structured design decomposition will take on certain characteristics based on the level at which they exist. Nodes at the top or intermediate level of the structure serve solely as control functions to their subordinates. The actual pro-

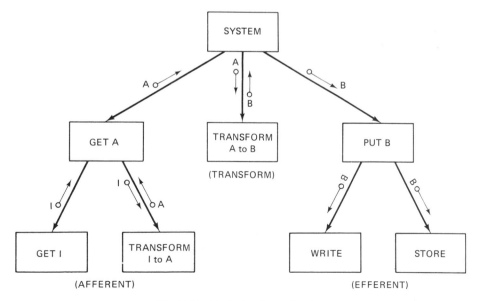

Fig. 3-21 Basic structure of system

cessing of the system will be described in the terminal nodes of a branch. The terminal modules are where all the work is done. We can understand all the processing performed by the system by understanding all the terminal modules; we will call them processing modules. However, we cannot understand the system itself without the intermediate modules. The intermediate modules control the execution of the processing modules and are used to understand the operation of the system. The intermediate modules define why the terminal nodes are required. They provide the continuity that describes the system as a system rather than as disjoint processing. Therefore, all intermediate modules will perform control functions, and only the terminal modules will do the processing. This explains another characteristic of the

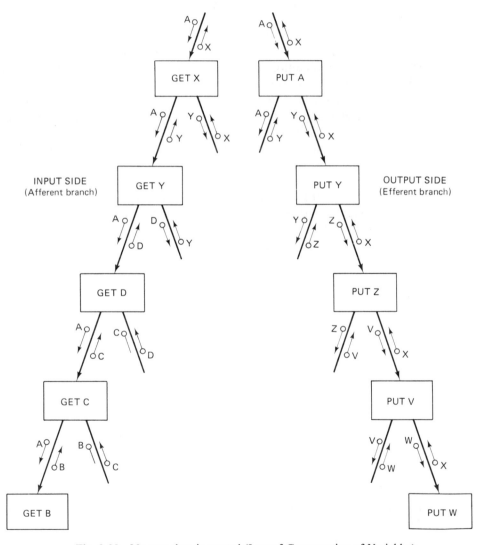

Fig. 3-22 No new data is created (Law of Conservation of Variables)

processing modules. Only the terminal modules will interface with the data tables. The control modules will receive and pass data, but only the processing modules will transform the data.

Likewise, a basic pattern emerges relative to the interfaces between modules. The pattern has been labeled the "law of conservation of variables." It is based on the premise that data is only *created* external to the software system. Within the software system, data is transformed until it is of the form required for output. The software system itself, however, never creates new information; it creates only changed information. Therefore, the data to be used by a branch is passed down the branch until it reaches a terminus node—the processing module where the transformation is performed. (See Figure 3-22.) The output parameter is transferred up the structure from the point where it was created to the point where it is used.

Structured design states that decomposition must proceed according to the prescribed rules identified above, but it identifies no specific forms other than the transaction center. Transaction centers are simply alternative constructs. (See Figure 3-23). Some parameter (the transaction code) determines the function to be executed

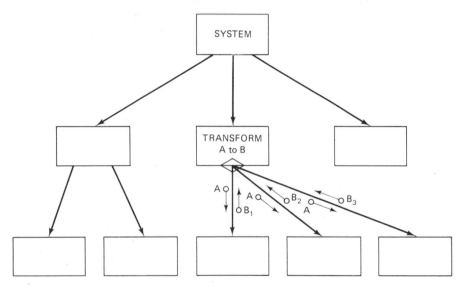

Fig. 3-23 Alternation construct

from the total set of options (the transaction center). There has been some effort to define the permissible constructs for decomposition in more concrete terms, based primarily on the part of Hamilton and Zeldin[14] in their work on Higher Order Software (HOS). Their work is characterized as a mathematical function decomposition of the system. That is, all data transformations are expressed in mathematical terms as: $y = f(x)$, where x is the input data, y is the output data, and f is the transformation. Three types of decompositions have been identified: (1) sequencer (functional composition), (2) selector (set partition), and (3) coordinator (class partition).

The rules for functional decomposition are:[14]

- Make the structure chart a hierarchical tree structure (note currently this is imposed by structured design as well) with each node being a function and a controller to all functions subordinate to it.
- Every function must influence its subfunctions in some way.
- Every subfunction must be influenced by its parent in some way.
- The priority of a function must be greater than any of its subordinate functions.
- Insure that the decomposition of a function is complete, i.e., the immediate lower-level subfunctions express the entire parent function.
- Use at least two functions at every level.
- Make each functional node of the tree unique.
- Decompose a system by one of the following decomposition types, examples of which follow:

Functional Composition

Set Partition

Class Partition

1. Sequencer (functional composition)—A module is decomposed into a series of modules, all of which are executed in sequence to accomplish the function. Consider Figure 3-24:
   a) One and only one function (f_2) controlled by f_1 receives the input data, x, from the module f_1.
   b) One and only one function controlled by f_1 produces the output data, y, for the module f_1. In the example of Figure 3-24, f_3 produces the output data.
   c) All other input and output data produced by functions controlled by f_1 reside in local variables. In the example of Figure 3-24, z is a local variable.
   d) All functions controlled by f_1 execute for each execution of the controller.
   e) Every local variable must exist as both an input variable for one and only one subfunction and as an output variable for one and only one different subfunction on the same level.

2. Selector (set partition)—A module is decomposed into a series of modules, only one of which will be executed. Once a subfunction is selected on a given level, other subfunctions on that level are no longer required. Consider Figure 3-25:
   a) Each function controlled by f_1 produces output data, y.
   b) All functions controlled by f_1 receive input data from the same variable, x.

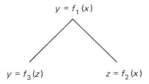

Fig. 3-24 An example of composition

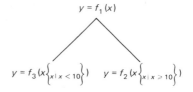

Fig. 3-25 An example of set partition

c) Only one function controlled by f_1 executes, based on an execution of the controller.

d) The values represented by the input variables of a subfunction represent a subset of values represented by the input variables of the controller.

e) There is no communication between subfunctions.

Note: In structured design terms, the set partition takes the form of a transaction center and would have the counterpart structure that includes the getting and typing of the data into a transaction code as part of the decomposition, as well as the selection of the option based on the transaction code. This points up a major difference in the two types of descriptions. The HOS approach carries the data communication within its function description. Structured design identifies the getting of the data as a module.

3. Coordinator (class partition)—A module is decomposed into a series of functions; each subfunction acts upon a subset of the input variables to produce a subset of the output variables. In mathematical terms, the input and output can be considered coordinates of a vector. Consider Figure 3-26:

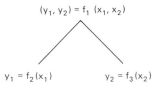

$$(y_1, y_2) = f_1 (x_1, x_2)$$

$$y_1 = f_2 (x_1)$$ $$y_2 = f_3 (x_2)$$

Fig. 3-26 An example of class partition

a) The inputs for each function controlled by f_1 are received directly from f_1.

b) The outputs of all functions controlled by f_1 are produced directly for f_1.

c) For execution (i.e., each new input/output value of a function) of a controller, all functions controlled by f_1 are executed.

d) Each input of f_1 can only be accessed by one function controlled by f_1.

e) No two subfunctions access the same variable.

f) There is no communication between subfunctions.

Note: The class partition represents in essence an asynchronous processing condition. That is, the calculation of y_1 can proceed independent of the calculation of y_2. Both must be completed, however, for f_1 to complete. If the decompositions of f_2 and f_3 continue as separate branches in the tree structure, then a true asynchronous processing condition exists. This can be valuable to recognize during the packaging stages when it may be necessary to assign various functions to different processors. If, instead, the functions f_2 and f_3 *essentially* rejoin at a lower level through use of common modules, this fact will be obvious from the structure diagram. In the latter case, the structure will be found to be weak because of a high degree of coupling in the lower modules.

We have found the constructs of HOS to be more precise, but the criteria of structured design are more qualitative. In addition, the structured design methodology provides guidelines for deriving the decomposition in a dynamic mode. There-fore, the methodology for deriving the structure is explained in the following section in terms of structured design. The criteria and constructs of good design should be applied to deriving the system/software structure, and especially to reviewing the structures.

3.4.5 THE DYNAMICS OF THE SOFTWARE DESIGN PROCESS

There are two basic forces that come into play to provide the dynamics of the software design process, using structured design principles. The first dynamic force relates to the manner in which we iterate between the data flow charts and the hierarchical structure charts. This process will be described in some detail. The second force relates to the manner in which we move from a very high level of design (the software architecture) to the detailed module definition through successive levels of refinement.

We have discussed the general concept of levels of refinement in Section 3.1 but here we will cover the process in more detail relative to the iteration between data flow charts and the structure diagrams. The software design trade-offs considered while iterating through these levels of design will be presented as well as the techniques for verifying software design.

DATA FLOW CHART-STRUCTURE DIAGRAM ITERATION

An important aspect of the iterative nature of the design process is that each step in the process can and may impact any and all previous steps in the design process. As we analyze a function for decomposition, the impact of that decomposition must be evaluated against the previous conclusion reached about the software system. The purpose of the design process is to continually refine and define the knowledge about the software system so, as each new detail is added and as knowledge of the system is acquired, it can be evaluated against the previous statement of design. We must be prepared to go back, to reorganize, to consolidate, and to add new functions to the structure as design considerations are discovered that were previously not recognized. During the initial stages of design, the repercussions can be rather far-ranging, impacting virtually all previous design. The structure may fluctuate radically. We must be prepared to throw out—to restart, if need be. As the design progresses, however, the area of impact will become progressively less universal and more local-ized. During the final stages of design, decisions should impact a very localized area of consideration. The point we are emphasizing is that changes will occur, and we must be attuned to evaluating design decisions within the context of all previous design. The structured design methodology attempts to aid us in accomplishing that specific goal.

The major purpose of the design process is to establish the structure of the system. The data flow charts, structure diagrams, and table of descriptions are used interactively to accomplish this purpose. During each phase of design, the tools are employed for their specific purpose and the results evaluated against the established criteria for design. Each tool serves its purpose and must be used properly, or inbreed-ing of design occurs and progress is slow.

The interaction of use proceeds in a fixed manner as design proceeds from initial stages, to intermediate, to final detailed structuring. The data flow chart is used initially to discover the overall information flow of the system. From this initial overview, the structure diagram is used to discover the top-level structure and functional relationships of the system. The data tables are used to define the conceptual data relationships. We are continually saying, "I know the information flows in this manner; therefore, I know the system must be structured in this manner to best accomplish that flow." Finally, as knowledge of the system becomes definite, the data flow chart ceases to fluctuate. The structure diagram is decomposed to its logical conclusion and packaged for implementation. Figure 3-27 exemplifies the desired iteration.

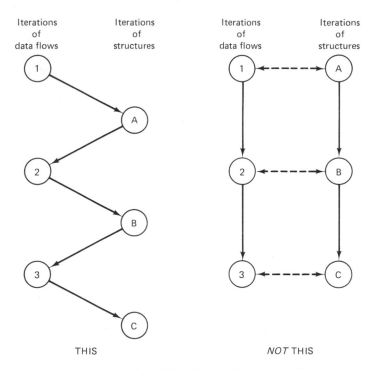

Fig. 3-27 Iterations of data flows with structure charts

CREATING THE INITIAL DATA FLOW CHART. We will initiate the dynamic process with an initial system description established by using transform analysis. A data flow chart will be developed from which the initial structure can be generated. The data of the system is related to the actions that occur within the environment. If the data is utilized by the action, it becomes input to the action. If it results from an action, it becomes output from the action. Any two in any combination should determine the third. If input plus action determines output, input plus output determines the action, and action plus output determines the input. Therefore, we first create a data flow chart of the system. We list all the objects used as input along the left of the chart and all the objects received as output along the right. We connect the input to the output via actions. We now have identified the transformations and named the transformations with predicates and objects. It should be obvious that significant design work is necessary to accomplish even this first tentative description of the information flow. There will be holes, undefined data, and transformations that must be determined. Research may be necessary to satisfy these discrepancies. There will be a number of iterations of the data flow. However, our goal is a data flow chart that satisfies all the constraints listed for a good data flow chart. The information flow is thus identified for the system.

We have also taken a preliminary step toward identifying the system data in conceptual terms. It has been named. We can begin to identify properties/attributes of this data. The data structuring process has begun.

CREATING A STRUCTURE DIAGRAM FROM A DATA FLOW CHART.   Our next step is to create a structure diagram of the system from the data flow chart. The top-level structure is identified as the three basic types of branches: (1) the afferent (input) branch that collects and formats the input data in a form ready for processing, (2) the transform that performs the basic function of the system, and (3) the efferent (output) branch that formats and disperses the output. This top-level structure is determined by dividing the data flow chart into its afferent, transform, and efferent elements. The afferent element of the data flow chart is the point at which the input data stream is most processed but still considered input. All processing to the left is the afferent branch of the structure. The efferent element is that point at which the output stream is least processed but still able to be called output. All processing to the right is the efferent branch of the structure. All processing in the middle is the

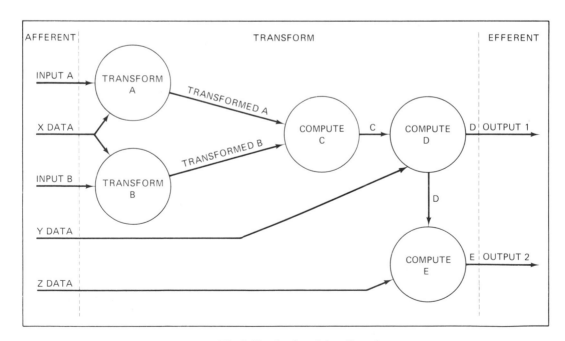

Fig. 3-28   Sectioned data flow chart

transform branch. Figures 3-28 through 3-35 depict various divisions of a data flow chart and the resultant structures. As a rule, the "best" structure chart results when the sum of the conceptual data streams cut by the afferent/transform and transform/efferent lines is at a minimum. Figure 3-35 represents such a structure. At this point we

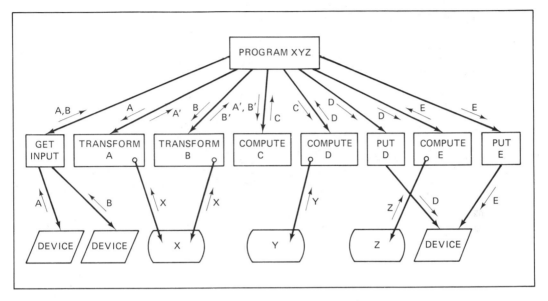

Fig. 3-29   Resulting structure chart

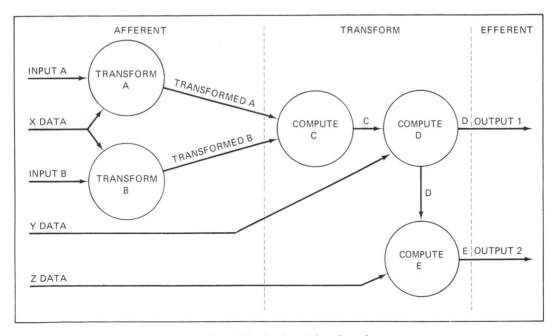

Fig. 3-30   Sectioned data flow chart

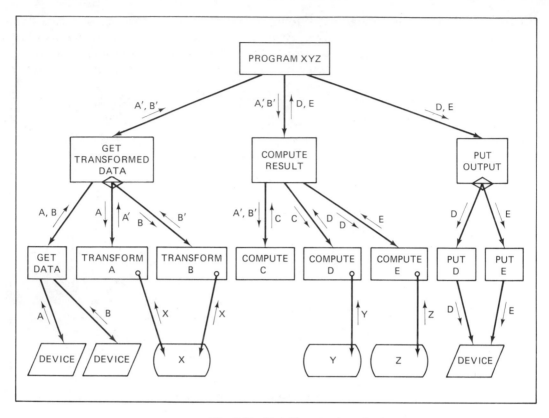

Fig. 3-31 Resulting structure chart

have identified the basic tasks along with the basic input and output. We have established an initial structure and identified control elements. This will constitute a top-level statement of the software system.

GENERATING DATA FLOW CHARTS FROM STRUCTURE DIAGRAMS. Our next step is to analyze the data flow for each independent section of the structure and in this way to expand the knowledge about the system so that the next step in detail refinement of the design can be developed. The structure diagram is analyzed to determine "data streams." There are four distinct types of data streams: (1) input to table, (2) table to table, (3) table to output, and (4) input to output. The structure diagram is used to discover the different data streams. Independent data streams are identified as any logical combination of separate data streams: multiple input to a single table, multiple tables to a single output, multiple tables to a single table, etc. For each independent data stream identified from the structure diagram, a separate data flow chart is drawn. In essence, we are asking again, "How does the data flow, what changes does it undergo, what are the transformations?" The data input to the data flow chart is identified on the left, the data output on the right. The transformations that convert the input to the output are described. The principles of semantics are applied as we are in the process of conceptualizing the design. We must struggle with the terms, the descriptions, and the exact words that describe the processes. The construction of

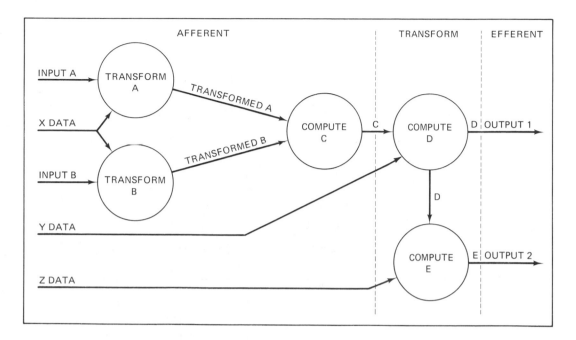

Fig. 3-32 Sectioned data flow chart

the data flow chart assists us by leading us to ask the questions we do not know and must discover. We have found that experimenting with data flow specification forces an understanding as to what is going on in the system. Again we review the data flow chart to insure that it conforms to the constructs of a good data flow chart. Common sections of the data flow will be recognized and combined into chunks. These chunks are renamed to present accurate conceptualizations of the processing. This process is performed for each independent data stream in the structure diagram.

Our next task is to combine the independent data flow charts into a single data flow chart. The single chart will again list the system input data streams on the left side and the system output data streams on the right. Major data tables have now been identified. One class of programs will create and maintain information, and another class of programs will use the data in the information file. Other types of tables (minor tables) should not appear on the data flow chart. These tables are "information collectors" or buffers.

We will serially connect the charts by analyzing all data streams. We will connect all data streams that terminate at the same major table. Likewise, we will connect all data streams that initiate at the same major table. We will continue connecting the data streams until we have a single data flow chart with conceptual system inputs on the left and conceptual system outputs on the right, and all transformations identified between data tables. We will analyze the types of data communication in the data tables. All minor tables will be removed. This is strictly a matter of abstraction. It will aid in our understanding of the data structure and requirements.

We now have a single data flow chart constructed from a structure diagram. It should be reviewed to insure that it accurately describes the system and conforms to

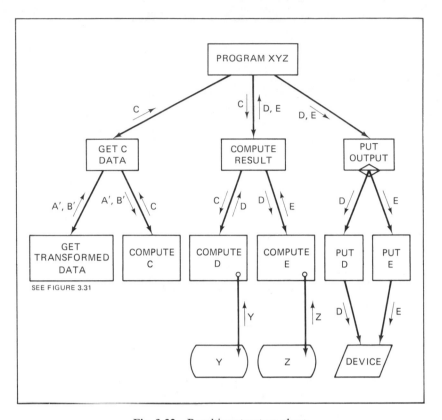

Fig. 3-33 Resulting structure chart

the constructs of a good data flow chart. It will be used to generate a new structure diagram. This process will continue until no new knowledge is derived from data flow diagramming. The resultant structure diagram should now show the system decomposed to a number of independent branches of a tree structure.

COMPLETING THE STRUCTURE. Finally, we will complete the structuring process by decomposing all branches of the structure to their logical conclusion. The technique varies somewhat, based on whether the branch is an afferent branch, a transform, or an efferent branch. We use as our guidelines for decomposition the standard structures previously described. We continually apply these patterns until we arrive at a level of decomposition that experience tells us is terminal in the design. It is not necessary to fully decompose one branch down to the lowest level of detail before working on another branch, but it is important to identify all of the immediate subordinate modules of any given module before turning to any other module. Thus, an afferent branch is decomposed by identifying an immediate subordinate transformation module whose purpose is to generate the data element defined as the input data element. A second immediate subordinate module is defined as an input module producing the data necessary for the new transform module, i.e., an afferent branch is decomposed into an input module and a transform to that input. This process is repeated for the newly defined input module until the input branch is fully factored,

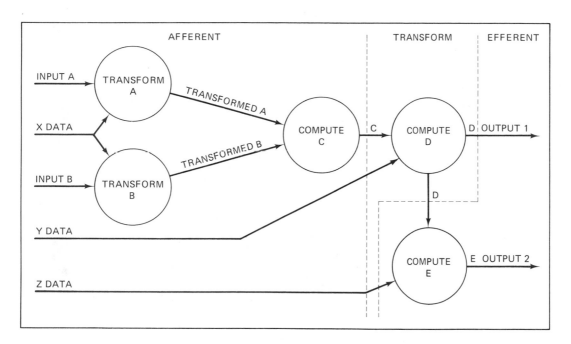

Fig. 3-34 Sectioned data flow chart

i.e., the physical input or logical I/O module is reached. Review Figure 3-22 for an example of this pattern.

An efferent branch is decomposed in a manner similar to that of afferent branches. An immediate subordinate transform module is defined; its purpose is to transform the output data element to the next format closer to the ultimate output. A new output subordinate module is defined to output this new data format. The new output module is again factored as above until the physical output or operating system I/O module is reached.

The central transform modules are decomposed by using the important considerations of coupling and cohesiveness. The basic pattern is identified (transforms versus transaction centers in structured design terminology—functional composition, set partition, class partition in HOS terminology). Decomposition proceeds according to the basic pattern selected as appropriate. For example, the steps in decomposing a transaction-centered design are:

1. Identify the source of the transaction.
2. Identify an analyze module—A new subordinate analyze module is drawn to accept the transaction as an input, determine the type of transaction, and then supply an indicator to the superordinate module, providing for the dispatch to the appropriate transformation. Quite often this module is trivial, and it is absorbed by the superordinate module.
3. Identify all the transactions and their defining actions.
4. For each transaction, define a transaction module to completely process it.
5. Decompose each transaction module as appropriate.

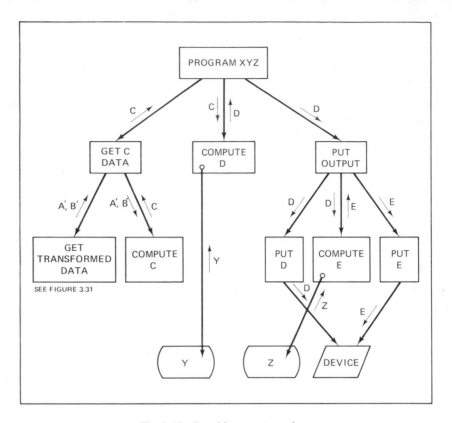

Fig. 3-35   Resulting structure chart

See Figure 3-23 for an example of a decomposed transaction center. When the system is fully decomposed, we have a system structure suitable for packaging.

DATA BASE DESIGN.   Data is designed to preserve the functionality and independence of the modules. The data requirements are discovered through the analysis of the functions required by the system. Therefore, data design is established only after the data requirements have been identified through the interactive use of the data flow charts and structure diagrams. As the design begins to stabilize, the data base design and its structure can be identified. This identification of the data may modify the design somewhat, but the impact should be minimal. Thus, the data and logical relationships have been identified, but the exact definition of the data tables is left to the detail design phase.

LEVELS OF REFINEMENT

As we have seen in the sections on requirements analysis and system design, the design iteration is further affected by the manner in which we progress through the different levels of design refinement. The software design proceeds from a high level of abstraction associated with the top-level system design to a high level of detail associated with a final, fully structured software design. Data design is interwoven throughout the process and proceeds also from a general level of understanding (naming the tables) to identifying their contents. The tools and concepts are continually applied as the engineer works his way through levels of refinement down to a precise definition of the system. System design trade-offs will be continually applied as design decisions are made and reflected into the structure.

As the design undergoes the series of refinements within each phase—which we have already identified as requirements definition phase, system design phase, and software design phase—the thinking of the designer gradually changes. Table 3-14 describes this changing emphasis in terms of design considerations. Applying a weighting scale to the various factors associated with design where 1 implies heavy emphasis and 5 implies mere consideration, we can see the shift in the emphasis and orientation as design proceeds. The reason for this variation in importance of the design considerations is to reduce the scope of the problem to be solved at each step—thereby simplifying the design effort. This variation in importance forces us to do "first things first."

Table 3-14   Relative Importance of Design Principles in Phases of Design

Design Consideration	First Cut	Intermediate			Final	
		Early	Mid	Late	Early	Late
Levels of abstraction	1	1	1	1	1	2
Binding	3	1	1	1	1	2
Control/effect	4	3	2	2	1	2
Predictability	4	3	2	1	1	1
Parsimony	4	2	1	1	1	2
Simplicity	2	2	1	1	1	1
Conceptual data flow	1	1	2	3	1	2
Specification interpretation	1	2	3	1	2	2
Data base	5	5	4	3	2	1
Structure chart	2	1	1	1	1	1
Data flow chart	1	1	1	2	1	3
System control	5	5	4	2	3	1
Module internals	5	5	4	3	2	1

1 is most important
5 is least important

During initial design, we must think conceptually in order to identify the problem the system is intended to solve. We cannot possibly develop the data base, the system control, etc., until we know what the problem is. Therefore, abstract concepts, data flow and accurate interpretation of the requirements are of prime importance. Characteristic here is that everything is conceptual. When we have defined the problem the system is intended to solve, we are ready to move to the intermediate design phases.

There is a gradual change in the intermediate phases from *what* the system is supposed to do to *how* the system is supposed to do it. This is characterized by a change from conceptual description to concrete description. The attributes of the structure become increasingly important. We are defining a solution to the system problem. The intermediate phases blend together. Part of the design may be in one subphase and part in another simultaneously.

At this point in the design, during which the system is factored into very small modules, the data base and system control logic are finalized, and the hardware/software packaging is performed. Only during final stages of design does the system control and actual physical layout of the data design become of primary concern.

DESIGN TRADE-OFFS

Software engineering has been discussed within the context of systems engineering in Sec. 3.3. The theme stated there was that software is an integral part of the total system. Software is concerned with system architecture, the hardware configuration, the operators and users of the system, and the communication between all elements of the system. Design trade-offs relating to the total system structure were discussed at that time. Now we will discuss the several design trade-off decisions of particular concern to software.

IMPLEMENTING CHUNKS AS APPROACH TO MEETING REQUIREMENTS. It is important to note that the implementation phase is not a part of the design phase. Any reasonable implementation strategy can be used, once the structure of the system has been established. A key point of the structured design methodology, however, is that the design is completed to a fully factored stage before implementation is initiated. Those who choose the "design a little, build a little" approach must recognize that the design phase is not complete until the fully factored stage is reached. Interspersing the overall design effort with implementation introduces the aura of inflexibility onto existing design that may have been coded already. This may work to the detriment of the design process. It is much easier to change a structure diagram than to recode. If the change works to the benefit of design simplicity and clarity, then the restriction of premature implementation is unwarranted. It is our contention that those who "design a little, build a little" must work either with very small systems (where all important aspects of the design are complete in their heads) or with systems that they have designed before; otherwise they would surely change their approach. Failure is almost certain.

An implementation strategy that has been found of value, particularly if related back to system requirements, is implementation by "chunks." Harlan Mills[19] states that 20% of the code supports 80% of the system requirements. The key, then, is to identify that critical portion of the design that satisfies the major share of the requirements. Thus, branches or chunks of the design should be related to the system requirements. A clear relationship between requirements and design can be established from structure diagrams. Critical chunks can then be identified, and major effort can be expended to complete and develop those critical chunks. Development then proceeds with a knowledge of how the system will be melded during implementation to meet the customer's needs.

STANDARDIZED SOFTWARE (OR REUSABLE MODULES). The topic of standardized software or reusable modules has already been addressed indirectly. Software developed as standardized programs for generalized use will have inefficiencies introduced in order to presumably satisfy multiple users under multiple conditions. The problem is that we are often poor prophets, and standardized software results in "tailored" software as changes become necessary to force-fit the program to meet the system requirements.

The method of designing the "standardized" software is, of course, key to its usability. If it has been designed to reduce coupling with increased cohesion, and if it has been designed as a "black box" concept, then the likelihood of its applicability is significantly enhanced. In this case, the applicability is dependent on only one factor, the standardization of the application, rather than on many factors—the standardization of interfaces.

Design is more likely to be transferable than code. Implementation is heavily weighted by the machine and language characteristics. Design, because of its independence from implementation, is a more likely candidate for standardization. The actual coding requires less time and is easier to accomplish than design. Therefore, it would appear to be more cost effective to attempt design transferability than code transferability. Design that follows the constructs identified above can be easily tailored, if necessary, to particular needs.

Like problems may have like solutions. Therefore, if a common need is identified, we can attempt to transfer the design elements in module chunks developed as "black box" constructs.

OPTIMIZATION TO MEET PERFORMANCE REQUIREMENTS. At some point in time, we will have to analyze the design structure to find out to how it will execute on the selected hardware. The problem is insuring that performance constraints can be met, given the system configuration proposed. Simulation is often required to provide information on the impact to system throughput, potential queuing problems, and possible overloads of the proposed system configuration. For example, queues may be building up faster than they can be processed, causing overload conditions to occur. Alternate configurations may be necessary to handle these types of problems. As a result, modifications to the structure may be necessary due to such factors as overlay structuring, multiprocessor operation, hardware problems, core utilization, time utilization, etc. For instance, if modifications are necessary due to the requirements to use overlay or multi-processors, then we must split the design into pieces and allocate them to specific locations. The communication between pieces is generally via tables. These communication tables must be identified so as to minimize the interface required.

A special word should be said about the time versus core controversy. The decision to limit core is based on the desire to limit hardware costs. The decision may be a false economy if it introduces complexity and excessive software costs. Presuming, however, that reduction in core utilization is desired, the data base is generally the greatest user of core. A different overlay scheme may be possible, or a different partitioning of the tables. The amount of savings accrued from combining modules is based on the language conventions for module communication. However, combining modules increases complexity. If a reasonable structure has been built, combining modules is not generally a reliable alternative.

Time utilization can best be reduced by modifying the implementation strategy. A search mechanism (table look-up) can take a lot of time, especially if the table being searched is long. A keyed index search can save time, for example, but generally at the expense of core. The major users of time can generally be isolated to a small percentage of code. On one large embedded computer system, for instance, we found that 55% of the time was spent in 5% of the program. Logically, then, we would address that area of the program in trying to save time. Time utilization can be improved by recoding higher-order language routines in assembly language. Simulation can aid in identifying the problem prior to implementation. Areas of extensive looping are also candidates for optimization to improve time.

If both core and time utilization are problems, the system design is most likely the source of design problems rather than software design. Multi-processors, additional core, front-end processors, etc., are alternatives that should be considered.

DESIGN VERIFICATION

A continual evaluation effort accompanies the design effort. Design reviews are conducted incrementally over the life of the project. The design criteria are continually applied toward evaluating the validity of design decisions.

There is considerable effort in progress within the industry toward developing requirements statement languages and design languages to aid the design process. Such languages are used to transcribe the design into a machine-processible syntax. Automated tools, working off this syntax, can analyze the design for conformance to specified design criteria.

A key issue is to determine the performance of the system prior to its implementation. Performance evaluation seeks to determine: (1) performance characteristics due to algorithmic design, (2) performance characteristics due to system allocation and configuring, and (3) performance characteristics due to structure interfaces. As has been mentioned, simulation/modeling constitutes a valuable tool for evaluating system and software performance. Simulation/modeling is viewed as a design tool that is used interactively within the design process to provide necessary feedback to the designers as to the impact of their design decisions. Because of its applicability across all areas of the effort, simulation/modeling is included in the verification/validation summary section.

3.4.6 PACKAGING THE SOFTWARE DESIGN

At last we are ready to design modules that will actually be coded. The fully factored design has created many small modules. These modules should be entirely functional because decomposition was functional. Likewise, they should be fully decomposed because we continued until no further logical decomposition was possible. Now the problem is to combine these modules in some manner that will optimize their performance within the context of the system allocation without increasing the complexity of the design.

Module Compression—The design process has created many modules (especially control modules) that aid the understanding of the design, but which are not necessarily efficient with respect to the total system. Interface between modules costs code. It may be possible to compress a number of modules into a single module for the sake of efficiency.

Guidelines for compressing are provided by the guidelines for modules, i.e., they will not be larger than about 50 lines and they will be highly cohesive and low in coupling. If there are modules with only one subservient module, a poor structure, then the subservient module should be compressed into its parent. If a module calls another module within a loop, this is also a likely candidate for compression. Modules that use the same data may be compressed. The guideline for compression is system complexity. If the compression increases complexity—do not compress. Compressed modules are indicated on the structure diagram, using the charting convention of "lexical includes." Their identity is retained to aid comprehension. Their packaging characteristics are indicated via the graphics.

Module Design—At this point the design structuring is complete. It remains to specify the internal operation of the modules so that they perform as indicated on the structure diagram. Hierarchical Input Processing Output (HIPOs) is a technique for documenting internal modules. Schematic Logic is another method for presenting the internal design of a module. These and other module design techniques will be discussed in the subsequent chapter on programming.

3.4.7 CONTINUATION OF ETAPS EXAMPLE (SOFTWARE DESIGN PHASE)

In Sec. 3.3.6, we finished the example ETAPS system design with an overview of the ETAPS Software Structure (Figure 3-18). In this section we will illustrate the process of converting the overall architecture of the software to a software design. However, the process of structuring the entire software design will be too lengthy for this text, so we will select a portion of the ETAPS software for our example. The portion we are illustrating is the Terminal Monitor program in the Applications Software. The system structure diagram shows the Terminal Monitor program as being composed of the functions of: (1) Terminal Display Language (TDL) Interpreter, (2) the Command Processor, and (3) the Primitives themselves. As the first step in structuring the design, we draw an overview diagram (Figure 3-36) that shows the program as processing requests from the analysts, using both raw data and processed data maintained in

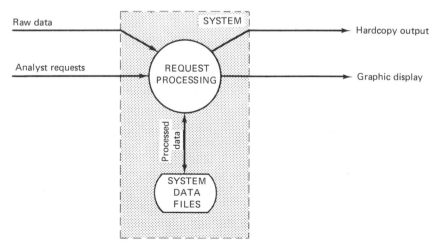

Fig. 3-36 Overview diagram of the terminal monitoring function

system data files to produce both graphics displays and hardcopy output for the analysts' review and evaluation. We have already established that the software consists of an operating system to handle the sharing of resources and the application programs that handle the individual analyst's requests. The operating system contains time-sharing capabilities that enable analysts to work concurrently with the appearance of a dedicated computer. We have identified the availability of a standardized graphics package to handle the interface with the displays and standardized utility programs and language processors to fulfill those unique functions of the system. We have hypothesized a special purpose data management system that will have to be designed, but for which we assume certain generic capabilities to support the building and maintenance of the system data base. We have identified a basic structure for the system data files. We are now ready to expand the structure of the software system.

The first step is to expand the request processing function. To do this, we will generate a top-level data flow chart (Figure 3-37). We recognize the need to validate

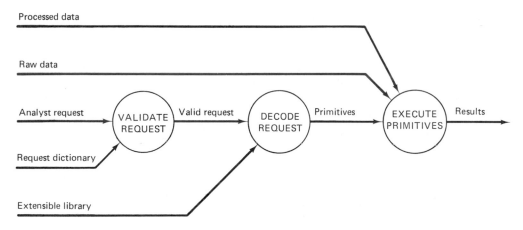

Fig. 3-37 Top-level data flow chart for terminal monitor

a request from the analyst before execution, and we stipulate a tabular-driven validation process to meet system extensibility requirements. All recognizable requests will be identified as to the criteria that must be met via tabular entries in a request dictionary. The request may or may not be a primitive operation. All functions performed by the analyst in Sec. 3.2 were decomposed into a series of primitives so that an operator's request could expect to be synonymous with a primitive. But we also stipulated in the system design an extensible system so that the analyst could combine the primitives into meaningful sequences and request that these sequences be performed via a single statement or "request" as we have called it. Therefore, the request must be decoded into its primitives because the primitives can be executed via special routines. We stipulate in the system design an extensible library of analysts' requests identified in terms of primitives. Once we have identified the primitives to be executed, we can initiate their execution through a transaction center. Each primitive function is now responsible for performing its unique function and outputting its unique results. Note that the data flow chart may have had to be iterated but at this point it is a fairly simple extension of the initial description and it does contain all elements of the input and all elements of the output.

The structure diagram that reflects this data flow chart is shown in Figure 3-38. The structure is basically a transaction center, and the process and efferent branches are buried in the transaction center. Each primitive, however, has a process and efferent branch. The afferent branch is cut at the most processed point at which the data can still be identified as input. The major breakout of language interpreter and language executor seems reasonable, based on the original system structure. Three problems can be recognized. First, we have let a predilection toward language processors creep into the naming of the modules, and it is going to slant our thinking in a way we may not wish. The modules should be renamed to reflect exactly what is done. Second, an iteration is shown between the language interpreter and the language executor that is incorrect. Decoding the request results in a multiple-to-one expansion of primitives versus requests. Every entry into the language interpreter results in a primitive list—not a single primitive. Figure 3-39 presents a corrected version of the structured diagram for this point in the design. Rather than passing one primitive at a time, the entire set is passed as a primitive list. The primitive executor becomes a simple list processor with branches to the individual primitive routines. Third, we are assuming an error message handler that prompts and escapes if an invalid request is processed. As a simple case, this doesn't seem to perturb the design drastically. As a general rule, it is dangerous and should signal a possible problem area.

At this point, the "execute request" branch seems fairly straightforward. It remains to further expand the individual primitive execution routines, but that should have minimal impact on the structure. Therefore, we address our attention to expanding the "interpret request" branch. We generate a data flow chart (Figure 3-40) to analyze in more detail the flow from the point of getting a request to generating a primitive list. At this point, we introduce the concept of exactly what constitutes a request. We view a request as composed of a verb and any number of arguments. To get and validate a request, it is necessary to get the verb and validate it. Then, based on that verb, we will know how many arguments we need. We can then get the arguments and validate them. When we have all the arguments required by the verb, we presumably have a complete and valid request that we can now decode into the primitive list. Perhaps additional validating checks can be applied to a complete request over and above the validity checks of the individual arguments that validate the consistency of the arguments across the bounds of the request. Such checks are not immediately apparent, but since they may exist and we may wish to use them, we incorporate those checks into the data flow.

The expanded structure diagram for the interpret request branch would look something like that shown in Figure 3-41. We won't discuss this structure diagram further other than to indicate that it does reflect the data flow chart as it exists. It is invalid and incomplete. However, further effort in arriving at an accurate structure diagram to reflect the data flow diagram of Figure 3-40 would be a waste of time.

Our analysis of the information flow through the data structuring technique has made us aware of a design aspect established during the operational concept definition phase. The data flow diagram of Figure 3-40 is significantly different from previous data flows. It indicates two operator inputs (possibly at different times). The

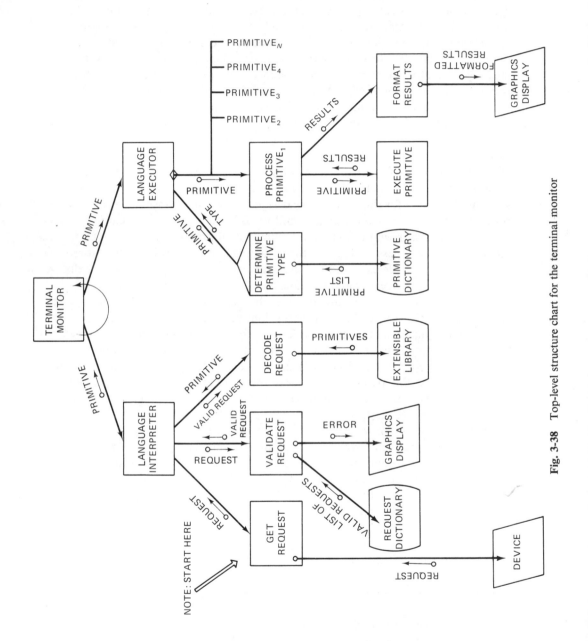

Fig. 3-38 Top-level structure chart for the terminal monitor

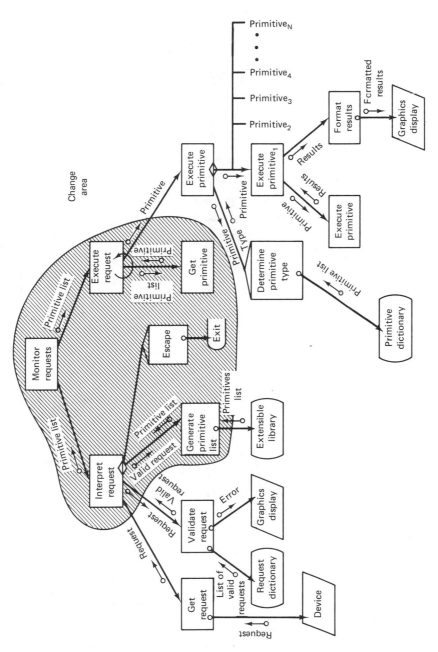

Fig. 3-39 Revised top-level structure chart

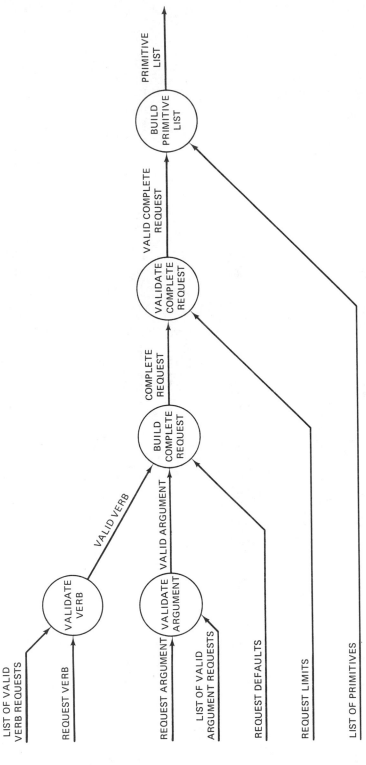

Fig. 3-40 Data flow chart of interpret request structure

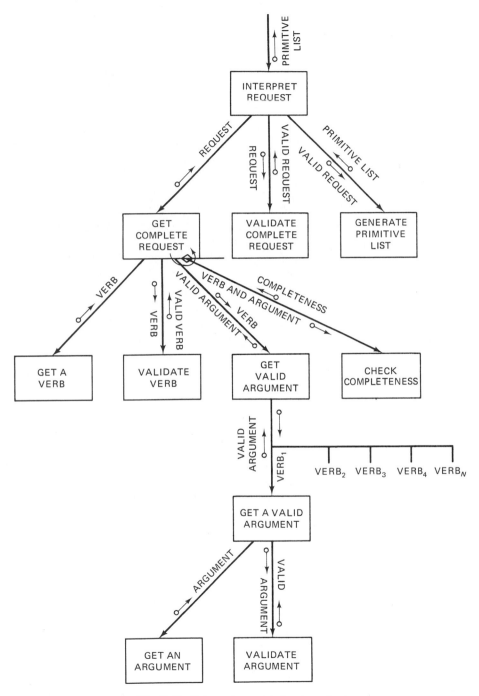

Fig. 3-41 Interpret request structure chart

problem was that our previous design had failed to recognize the methodology for interactive display input established during the operational concept definition phase. We may think of a request as a logical entity consisting of a verb and its arguments, and indeed the analyst thinks in terms of a request as a logical entity that he inputs as a verb and its arguments. In all likelihood, all training material and presentations will deal with requests as verbs with their arguments. However, the methodology selected for the analyst to interactively interface with the display console does not support the handling of the request in this manner. Let's review how the analysts will be working at the console. They know and understand how they must use the primitives and extended primitives, i.e., the options available to do the job. They have a standard menu of options available to them, i.e., the verbs of their request. They light-pen the selected verb. They expect then to see an indication that the verb was accepted and recognized—generally as a prompt for additional information in the entry work area of the display console. They then light-pen their selected options or, if keyboard entry is required, enter the data. The point is that the human factors engineering establishes light-penning of selected options from menus as an approach to interactive entry of data rather than a single free-form keyboard-entered statement or a fill-in-the-blanks to a fixed-format prompting message. Thus, speed, accuracy, and fatigue level are trade-offs against the logical continuity of a total request presentation. The analysts are expected to supply the logical continuity between verb and argument in their own minds through a speedy prompting/response interaction. The impact on the data flow chart is reflected in Figure 3-42. This flow is exactly like the one in Figure 3-40 except that the prompting has been factored in. The discontinuity in the processing becomes immediately apparent.

Furthermore, the impact of the hardware should be obvious by this time. The light-pen action, or the keyboard action, or function key action, or any action of the analysts is recognized by the display microprocessor. The display microprocessor can be designed to collect all information until an end-of-request indicator of some sort is detected. But again, the decision was made that the microprocessor can handle primarily the buffers for scrolling with minimum processing contained within the microprocessor. The microprocessor provides the buffers but minimum programming. Therefore, the display processor will perform no processing on the analyst actions, but will simply format each action individually and route it to the central processor for processing. The operating system can be expected to perform message routing functions, but no individual processing of messages. The collection of actions into a meaningful request and all error checking is obviously a function of the request monitor. Therefore, the primary input to the request monitor is not a request at all, but rather an analyst action. The request monitor is not a request monitor at all. It is an action monitor. The action monitor must determine the type of action and build the request from a discontinuous sequence of actions. Figure 3-43 reflects the reorientation from analyst's request to analyst's action as it impacts the data flow chart. This now represents a realistic view of the processing performed by the system which the previous approach did not. The action is accepted and typed. Valid verbs will be used to initiate the building of a request.

The case of a verb being entered prior to the completion of a previous verb needs to be addressed. One of two options exists—any valid verb can be recognized and used

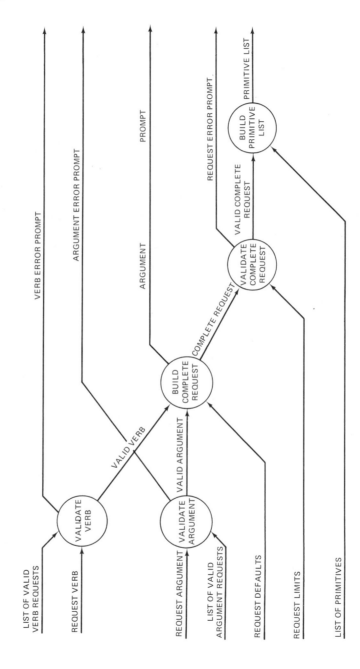

Fig. 3-42 Revised data flow chart of interrupt request structure

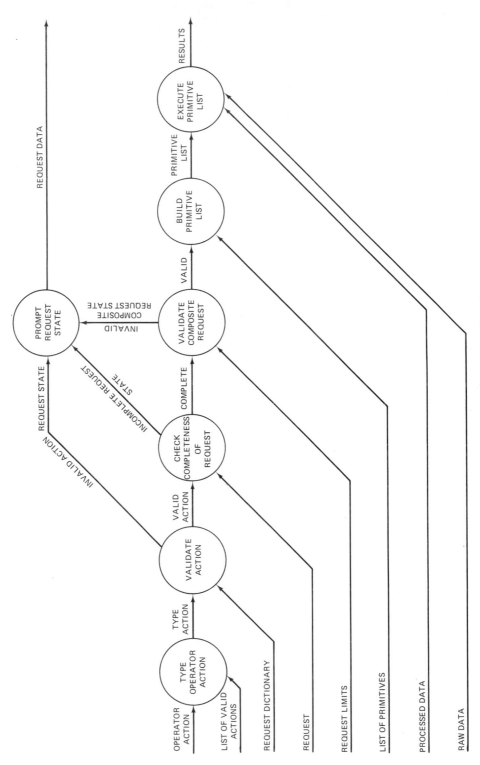

Fig. 3-43 Second revision of data flow chart

to override any previous entry; or if another verb is entered prior to completion of the verb in progress, then an error condition exists. In the latter case a specific cancel operation is necessary to terminate an incomplete request. The latter case is selected as a desired precaution against operator entry of an inadvertent verb during argument entry. A special cancel operation is identified, which would override any request in progress. We note that the "type entry" can recognize the cancel operation as a verb for any operator action, and the verb processing automatically handles the situation so that no special processing is necessary other than to provide a primitive cancel operation routine in the transaction center.

The structure diagram that reflects this reorientation in thinking is shown in Figure 3-44. The impact on the structure diagram is considerable. The whole afferent

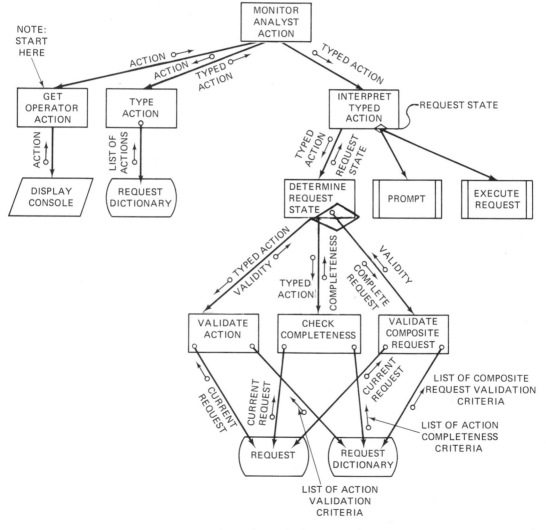

Fig. 3-44 Revised structure chart

branch shifts forward. The action is the most processed data that can still be identified as input. Therefore, "get action" becomes the afferent branch. The typing of the action is the central transform, and the interpreting of the action is the efferent branch. The action is used to build a request. The request state is used to determine the reponse to the action. The execution of the action is performed after (1) the action has been tested for validity, (2) the action has been tested for terminating a request (the request is now complete), and (3) the composite request has been tested for validity. All other conditions cause a prompt to the analyst. The prompt is a function of the request state. The temporal nature of the entire program is apparent. The validity of any action is dependent on previous actions taken by the analyst. However, that is a stated condition of the analyst interface. Thus, the nature of the solution reflects the nature of the problem. Figure 3-45 shows a completed structure chart of the request execution portion of the problem.

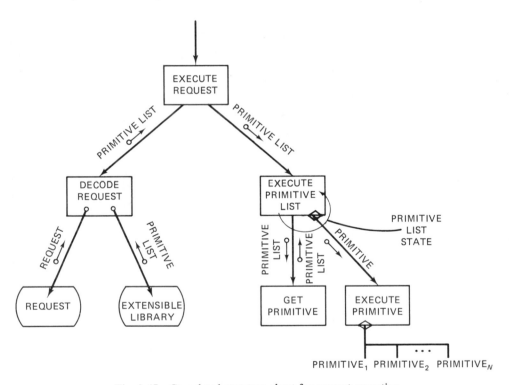

Fig. 3-45 Completed structure chart for request execution

At this point, the design appears fairly solid, at least to the conceptual level to which it is extended. The processing has been decomposed to a level that is logical, given the knowledge of *how* the system is structured. That is, we know that the display processor will pass an analyst's entry that it will have formatted as a message to the action monitor (terminal monitor). We do not need to know exactly how this is done. There are other designers working on the system. We will have established the interface through message formats and contents. Likewise, the other modules seem to have been decomposed to a logical limit below which it is unnecessary to go. The primitive execution routines will have to be expanded. But the logical structure of the terminal monitor appears to be fairly complete.

Any secondary characteristics that have been identified as desired will be incorporated into the design at this point. In this case, performance monitoring is expected to collect the execution time on both a primitive basis and on a request basis so as to provide historical data on the ability of the system to comply with the stated requirements for response time. The time for primitive execution must be collected from the point that the primitive is first recognized until it has completed execution. The time for request execution must be collected from the point that a valid request has been accepted until the complete primitive list for that request has been processed. Also at this point, the need to provide for noncore resident primitive routines is recognized, and the use of the operating system to provide overlay loading is stipulated. This function is also benign to the structure diagram. Figure 3-46 reflects the incorporation of both the performance monitoring and the load monitor. The collection points are inserted and appear to have little impact on the basic structure.

Data tables have been identified as:

1. message communication between the displays and the terminal monitor,
2. a dictionary of recognized actions,
3. a request that is temporal in nature and maintained as an on going status of operator action, and
4. a request procedure library that defines a request in terms of primitives, thereby enhancing system extensibility.

As can be seen, the data is still described in conceptual terms. The information content is increasingly defined as the system design proceeds as an iterative process. As information needs are discovered in the design process, their structure is reflected in the data description. The record structure of the files is identified and the method of linking data files further refined. This expansion of data definition proceeds in concert with the increased refinement of the system/software design.

EPILOGUE. This concludes the description of the ETAPS software design process. For the reader who has become interested in the ETAPS project, we would like to add that Hierarchical Input Processing and Output Diagrams were generated for each of the primitives. Each primitive was designed as a discrete action that the analyst could take in any sequence meaningful to him. Therefore, interfaces between primitives were nonexistent. The working files maintained the continuity of data usage from operation to operation. Data sharing between the analysts was possible, but was transparent to the user because of the design of the data management system. Standards were established for primitive protocol. Attributes were established for each primitive and were appended to it as a prologue to enable system-level semantic error checking to be done for all calls to primitives. Any errors occurring were detected by the primitive; the user was prompted, and the primitive terminated. If the constraints for primitive execution were met, then the main body of the primitive would perform the required processing, using the graphics and data management subroutines as necessary. On completion, the primitive would exit to the terminal monitor for performance monitoring which, in turn, would exit to the operating system.

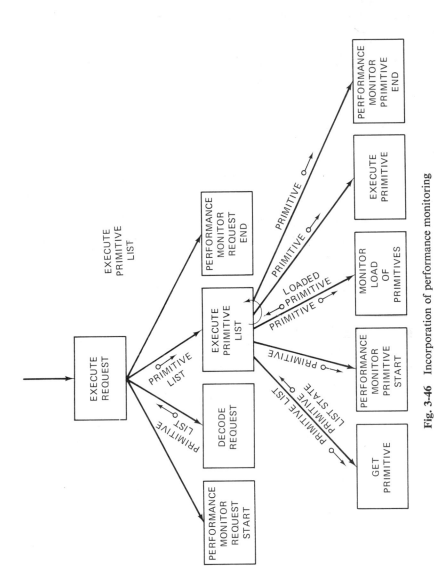

Fig. 3-46 Incorporation of performance monitoring

As a final step the procurement effort was scheduled. Manpower projections were submitted. A management plan was produced, which identified testing and acceptance criterion. A phased procurement plan was developed. Due to the structure of the system, the requirements could be traced directly to discrete primitive modules, graphic capabilities, and data management handling routines that would satisfy those requirements. Therefore, a basic system could be identified which would present, in essence, a separate virtual machine to each user. The users had available to them a fixed subset of commands and could operate on a fixed subset of data. A fixed subset of graphic displays was presented to them. This basic system was gradually expanded by the addition of primitives, graphics capabilities, and data management capabilities on a phased implementation basis. As a final step, the monitor system was extended to handle the full loading of consoles. As an added benefit of the design, the only expansion necessary to increase the capabilities of the system was tabular redefinition for new devices and new users.

3.5

Continuous Verification and Validation

Throughout the description of the requirements definition phase, the system design phase, and the software design phase, we have alluded to the verification and validation activities that are continuously taking place. It is our theme that this continuous evaluation is a necessary part of the design process. Since the verification and validation techniques that apply to the design process are primarily those of design review and simulation modeling, we reserved our discussion of these techniques to this section as a summary of how they are used in all three phases.

In the discussion of these techniques, we use the traditional definitions of the terms. Verification techniques determine the logical consistency of the design as it evolves from the previous step in the design process. Validation techniques determine the ability of the design to function according to stated user's requirements. Design errors can lead to two basic types of problems in the resultant product: incorrect functioning of the software itself and incorrect performance of the system relative to the user's requirements. Incorrect functioning results from incomplete, inconsistent, or inaccurate design. A program does not handle all ranges of possible conditions; it assumes data scaled at a value other than its actual scaling; it does not return the values expected of it. Incorrect performance implies the system does not supply the user with the expected capabilities; it cannot respond in the desired time frame, or it cannot be produced under specified time and cost restrictions. Therefore, the problem in evaluating design is two-fold: we evaluate the internal consistency of the design, and we evaluate its external performance characteristics. Moreover, performance characteristics must be expanded to include cost considerations. In the current competitive market place, we find it necessary, but not sufficient, for the design to be simply consistent and functional. We must also produce a product that is cost effective to develop and maintain. Therefore, an additional requirement has been imposed on the design verification and validation process. We must demonstrate that the resultant product will be a quality product in terms of cost, reliability, maintainability, flexibility, etc. This need gives rise to studies in reliability and life-cycle costs, which are now factored into the design process during trade-off studies.

The cost of correcting design errors increases significantly as the development effort progresses. Figure 3-47 depicts the cost of correcting errors relative to the phase of development. Testing applied to an implemented system follows a different pattern of error detection than verification/validation applied during design:

1. errors in implementation are detected first during module testing;
2. module interface errors are detected next during module assembly and program testing;
3. design functional errors are detected during system integration; and
4. performance errors—errors in compliance with user's requirements—are not detected until the final stages of system acceptance testing.

It is not our intent to discuss all the aspects of software testing because this subject is covered in Chapter 5. Our discussion here applies only to the interrelationship of validation and verification in the design process as a means of reducing error costs. The thrust is toward verification and validation at the completion of each phase in the design process. At the end of the requirements definition phase, we verify user's requirements for operational feasibility. During the system design phase, we verify design for logical consistency, feasibility of resource utilization, and conformance to accuracy constraints. In addition, the design is validated for conformance to stated

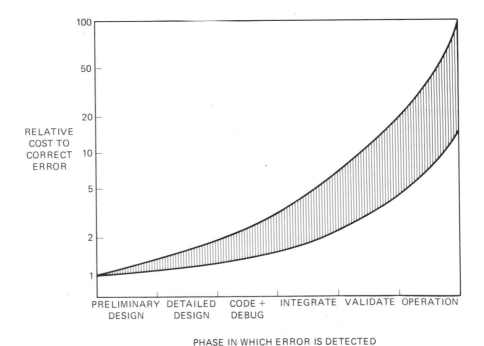

Fig. 3-47 Cost of error correction in design phase versus test phase

performance requirements. In the software design phase, we verify the design's completeness and its ability to meet performance goals.

Offsetting the savings accrued in early detection and resolution of the problem is, of course, the added expense of conducting the check via some other means than testing the actual implementation. If simulation/modeling is used, for instance, to verify the system design, the cost of developing and running the simulation must be offset by an increased reliability of the resultant product and an attendent reduction in final testing costs. In other words, a set of checks and balances is desired, which can be continually applied to the design process in order to produce a more reliable, better quality product. The cost-effective nature of these checks and balances applied to verifying and validating design must be shown to constitute an optimum method of finding and resolving the errors.

The techniques discussed herein for design verification and validation have been demonstrated as cost-effective approaches for use within the framework of current system development procedures. Design reviews are used as a management technique to retain visibility and to assure conformance with directed standards. Imposing standards on design constructs yields structures significantly reduced in complexity. Simulation/modeling can demonstrate operational feasibility, system resource utilization feasibility, program design feasibility, and the adequacy of the algorithm prior to implementation.

3.5.1 TECHNIQUES FOR DESIGN REVIEWS

The evaluation of any design is difficult. The actual designers have been close to the design, but so intimately involved that they may have developed "blind spots" —any number of preconceived biases, erroneous or not. However, any other reviewer is not as knowledgeable about the design. Our goal is to use the designers' intimate knowledge of the system, but to break down the established biases and raise them to a level of objectivity so that they and others can review their perspective of the problem solution for accuracy.

These goals obviously cannot be achieved in a haphazard manner. The design reviews must be planned, organized, and conducted with specific goals in mind.

Establishing the Goals—There are three major aspects to any design review: (1) to analyze the internal workings of the design for accuracy and conformance to prescribed standards, (2) to evaluate the individual design area relative to the total system, and (3) to evaluate the individual design relative to the specified requirements. Naturally, we find it unfeasible to assume that all three types of reviews will be conducted at a single review. Therefore, the initial step is to clearly identify the purpose of the review. If the purpose of the review is unknown, then we will save time and money by not having it. Therefore, a specific plan should be established for design reviews based on the phase of design.

Formal Design Reviews—Generally, formal design reviews are established as a part of the overall management plan, either in conjunction with established company practices or with dictated customer procedures. The Department of Defense dictates formal design reviews as part of an overall software development management plan.

Since documentation requirements, design reviews, and configuration control are integrally related, they will be discussed as a unit here in order to define formal design review procedures.

The specific names applied to documentation to be reviewed vary widely from company to company and between customers, be they government or commercial. The documentation requirements for computer programs fall into four general categories: (1) the system functional requirements, (2) a computer program development specification (system design), (3) the computer program design document, and (4) final delivery documentation. We assume that specific formats for each of these documents will be available prior to initiation of the attendent development phase if we expect a good product. Format definitions should take the form of specific guidelines plus concrete examples of contents. Considerable manpower can be saved if the engineers know exactly what they must produce in the way of documentation and exactly how and when. In addition, documentation requires a coordinated approach that must be reviewed and planned. It cannot be expected to occur naturally.

1. System Functional Requirements contain as a minimum:
   a) interface characteristics of the system with its environment
   b) functional requirements of the system to react to its environment
   c) allocation of functions to hardware, software, firmware, and operators of the system
2. Computer Program Development Specifications contain as a minimum:
   a) structure of the system
   b) interface characteristics of all elements within the system
   c) functional requirements of all elements within the system
   d) performance characteristics of all elements within the system
   e) logical data design
3. Computer Program Design Documents contain as a minimum:
   a) a structure of the modules and data structure
   b) a functional description of the modules
4. Final Delivery Documentation will contain the above documentation plus module internal designs, listings, tapes, card decks, etc.

Associated with each of the documentation phases identified above is an associated design review. Thus major design reviews are identified as:

1. System Analysis Design Review—will seek to discover errors due to:
   a) misunderstanding customers requirements
   b) excess over-design
   c) incorrect trade-off criteria
2. System Mechanization Design Reviews—will review such areas as:
   a) software/hardware trade-offs and functional allocations
   b) errors due to lack of understanding of critical design areas
   c) top-level software partitioning
3. Detailed Software Design Requirements Review—will examine:
   a) detailed module descriptions

    b) interface descriptions
    c) data base decomposition
4. Detailed Configuration Audits—will be conducted as official audits to evaluate conformance of prepared documentation to contractual requirements.

Subsequent to review, design documentation is released into the configuration control cycle and is established as a baseline document. Baseline documentation is defined as contractually required documentation. Its purpose is to fix a point of reference from which subsequent efforts can proceed. Baseline documentation serves as an "accepted" base against which any future changes (proposed or requested) can be evaluated for cost and schedule impact. Design is like "walking on water; it is much easier if it is frozen." Baseline documentation is categorized as (1) functional, (2) allocated, (3) development, and (4) product baseline.

INFORMAL DESIGN REVIEWS (STRUCTURED WALK THROUGHS). In addition, the software engineer should be prepared to participate in or request informal design reviews on an as-needed basis. In other words, we should look on design reviews as an integral part of our day-to-day work since they contribute to our increased knowledge of the design requirements.

Participants—The participants in the design review are a key factor in the relative worth of the review in terms of detecting and successfully resolving problems. The participants of the design review should be specifically selected, based on the goal to be achieved and their ability to contribute to achieving that goal. Both a technical and a management perspective are required regardless of the level of the design to be reviewed.

Responsibility for conducting the review rests with the individual responsible for the activity. A review panel is designated. Responsibility rests with the reviewer to acquire the review material, read it, identify any areas of concern, and be prepared to discuss and resolve these concerns.

A primary difficulty in the design review process is getting engineers from the various disciplines interested and involved in the review process. The structured design methodology has been found particularly effective in this area. It serves as a common base of communication between the various engineering disciplines. The structured design presents the information flow and design structure in a form that is easy to follow. It leads the engineer directly into an understanding of the structure of the system and the software; thus, it enhances considerably the total effectiveness of the design review process.

Design Review Packages—The material to be reviewed must be organized and available for analysis prior to the review. Design review packages are prepared and submitted to the participants with the review schedule identified. The design review package should contain the specific documentation required by the review phase. In addition, any supportive material that was used to arrive at various design decisions should be readily available and, hence, will serve to corroborate the decisions made. The history file of design trande-offs is imperative to eliminate work redundancy. All software engineers should be responsible for maintaining a record of decisions, information available on which they based their decisions, and the conclusions reached.

These should be in a form readily understandable by the reviewers so that the validity of the engineers' conclusions can be ascertained. Generally, we maintain all the data relative to the module unit in the design packge. This also provides back-up in case of employee transfers, termination, etc. It is costly in time and money to have to reconstruct or duplicate various analysis efforts.

The Review—During the review, the reviewers are expected to comment, first, on the completeness, accuracy, and general quality of the work product. Major concerns are expressed and identified as areas for potential follow-up. The designers present a brief overview of the product. They then "walk" the reviewers through the design in a step-by-step fashion that simulates the function under investigation. They attempt to review the material in enough detail so that the concerns expressed at the beginning are either explained away or identified as action items. Significant factors that require further action are recorded as they are identified.

Action Item Resolution—It is the responsibility of the reviewee to insure that all items on the action list are successfully resolved. The reviewers are notified of the actions and/or corrections. Follow-up design reviews may be necessary.

Documentation Release—Subsequent to action item resolution, the resultant design is released into the control cycle, according to prescribed configuration control methods.

3.5.2 SIMULATION/MODELING AS A DESIGN EVALUATION TOOL

Throughout this chapter, we have made reference to the use of simulation/modeling. First, we referred to its use, along with the man/machine simulation modeling, as a technique to be utilized in validating requirements during the requirements definition phase. Next, we referred to its use in the system design phase as a means of evaluating various design alternatives during the trade studies that result in allocation of functions to system elements. Finally, we referred to the use of simulation/modeling as a method of verifying that the software design can meet the allocated performance parameters. Now we will examine in more detail the technique of simulation/modeling.

THE TECHNIQUE OF SIMULATION/MODELING. Modeling is by definition a representation in abstract form, generally simplified, of some part of the real thing. We recognize degrees of representativeness of the end product in the model that we produce. Some models are more realistic than others. Indeed, in our illustration of the levels of representation, which we used to illustrate the concept of successive models, we move from a very abstract conceptualization of the user's view of the system to the detailed design of the software, each model being more comprehensive and more representative of the real product than the preceding one. A model, then, must represent the desired characteristics of the products being evaluated, and it must do so to the detail necessary to give valid answers that predict performance of the product.

We must, at all times, remember that the model is not an end in itself, but a tool for predicting the performance of the end product, the thing being modeled. If we are concerned with high-level design decisions, the model need not be overly detailed. However, if we are concerned with predicting throughput for a particular design, then the model must represent the end product in a detail that represents the design architecture, the configuration, and hardware performance characteristics. It must include a detailed scenario of the environment in which the system will operate.

Simulation is a versatile software tool that has many uses in the development of a product. During software development, the hardware may be simulated prior to its actual procurement so that software checkout and integration can proceed independent of hardware development and procurement schedules.

There is distinct advantage in testing software on proven equipment prior to integration with hardware that is still in the process of being developed. During system evaluation and maintenance, there are often overriding considerations for testing a system against a simulated environment rather than a live environment. This type of simulation is termed on-line simulation because it is used to drive the implemented system. The kind of simulation we are talking about in the design process is the building of a model of the design to simulate the system being developed. It would probably be more precise to call this activity modeling, but we began using simulation techniques to model systems, and so the name has remained simulation/modeling. The practice of modeling a system has evolved from laboriously simulating a model in a procedural language like FORTRAN to the development of several specialized languages that provide for ease of implementation. Examples of simulation languages are IBM's General Purpose System Simulation (GPSS), RAND's Extendable Computer System Simulation (ECSS), SIMSCRIPT, and System Analysis Machine (SAM). These languages have the common objective of making modeling easier, faster, and more cost effective than simulation with a procedural language.

WHEN TO USE MODELING.   Modeling has been found to be appropriate for the type of problem that: (a) cannot be solved by manual analysis efforts, (b) cannot be solved by experimentation because of the excess costs, and (c) for which intuition or past experience does not provide the proper insight. Modeling is useful in: (1) conducting configuration trade-offs and/or optimization, (2) determining conformance to performance expectations, (3) evaluating design options, and (4) optimizing new design. Simulation/modeling has applicability throughout the entire system development process. During the requirements definition phase, problems of operational feasibility are addressed. The environment may be simulated and interaction of various system approaches evaluated within that environment. During the system design phase, problems encompass both total overall system feasibility and the practicality of specific techniques and algorithms. A model of the entire system may be generated to evaluate component interfaces, resource utilization, information flow through the system, etc. In addition, individual algorithms or techniques may be investigated via such efforts as a tracking model or an intercept effectiveness model. During the software design phase, problems encompass such areas as the relative feasibility of potential executive systems, delay attendant with various disc access algorithms, etc. Potential processing bottlenecks may be identified. Proposed changes to a system can be evaluated via a system model prior to implementation and incorporation into a system.

APPROACHES TO SIMULATION. In one approach, simulation is run concurrent with the design process. The modelers use design information, as it is derived by the analysts and systems engineers, to develop their model. They run the model to derive information on the performance of the design for feedback to the engineers who, in turn, use the results to impact the design. There are a number of problems with this approach, primarily relating to ease and timeliness of obtaining results. Simulation efforts that cannot keep pace with the design effort tend to diverge away from representing the real system. Therefore, they lose their value as design aids. Also, a modeling effort that is sufficiently large and costly tends to be shunted aside as the pressures of real-system development increase. The simulation/modeling languages seek to reduce these problems and have met with considerable success. R. Willis[26] reports on the evolution of simulation as a design aid in the development of embedded computer systems. His work in this area is well worth review. He also addresses the problem of quickly representing the operational environment as a load against the model, particularly where man/machine interfaces play a large role in system response time. Environmental simulators that preprocess operator interactions with the system have been developed. Used as a preprocessor, they can take data from the Operator Sequence Diagrams developed in the system design phase as direct inputs for developing the systems load scenario.[27]

Another approach to simulation tries to guarantee the validity of the simulation by requiring it to gradually become the system. In this method, a separate simulation language is not used. The implementation language provides capabilities for running with both real and simulated modules. However, the real hardware and real environment loading conditions are required. Larger portions of the design must be programmed (implemented) before any significant results can be obtained from this method.

For each approach to be successful, sufficient management understanding and support must exist. Tools are satisfactory only if used in the manner and for the purpose for which they were intended. Again, the engineers must know and understand their tools and apply them wisely.

THE MODELING EFFORT. In order to generate a system model, the modelers need to know: (a) the hardware characteristics of the system, (b) the system interrelationships, (c) the software characteristics, and (d) the environment characteristics. Obviously, in other words, they need to know the design. Therefore, the modelers are an integral part of the design team. They serve not only as recorders of design decisions, but also, in many cases, as catalysts for design decisions; They are the pacers through which design needs are identified and resolution efforts instigated.

Modelers use the language available to them to transcribe the design into a simulation program. Obviously, the capabilities of language significantly impact the ease of performing this step. Features of ECSS, for instance, significantly facilitate this effort because ECSS contains syntax elements in one-to-one correspondence with elements of the system. Terms exist for describing: (1) processors, discs, and display

[26]Willis, R. R., "Computer Simulation Modeling—A Test Bed for New Software Technologies," *Proceedings 1974 Winter Simulation Conference*, p. 426.

[27]Willis, R. R., "A Man Machine Workload Model," *Proceeding European Computing Conference on Computing Performance Evaluation*, Eurocomp, London, September 1976.

devices in terms of their data generating rates etc., (2) software in terms of execution rates, and (3) interfaces in terms of messages, etc.

The modeler determines the statistics needed as output in order to demonstrate that the model is operating properly and that the design represented by the model provides the proper solution to the problem being investigated. ECSS provides, as standard output, utilization figures for resources defined within the system. It also provides capabilities to support the modeler in extracting and presenting data in suitable form for evaluation.

The initial responsibility of the modeler is to demonstrate the validity of the model. That is, he must show that the model is indeed an accurate representation of the system. He does this by: (1) checking the reasonableness of his results, (2) setting up test-case conditions for comparison to known results, and (3) reviewing the output with the users.

Once the validity of the model has been established, it can be used as an investigative tool to evaluate alternatives by modifying various parameters to the model. Options are identified for investigation. Required statistics are determined. The model is run under varying conditions and the results used to support design decisions.

3.6

Summary

In conclusion, we have addressed the topic of software design from five aspects:

1. Software design as a human-thinking process.
2. Software design as it satisfies the user's requirements for a product.
3. Software design as an integral part of a system design effort.
4. Software design as a structuring process.
5. Verification and validation of software design as a continuing process.

It should be evident at this point that we consider software engineering an integral part of all aspects of the system development process. The software engineer who expects to deal solely with software structures—operating systems, languages, data management systems—is losing sight of his overall responsibilities as a contributing member of the system development team. Likewise, the system development team must recognize the unique contribution made by the software engineer. The software engineer brings to the design process a set of tools and techniques that are of proven value in the total design process. Structured design is a case in point. The techniques have demonstrated value in the requirements analysis and system design phases as well as the software design phase. System engineering and hardware engineering acceptance of this design tool is dependent on the capabilities of software engineers to demonstrate it as a viable adjunct to the design process.

A natural question might be, what constitutes a good designer? We hope we have answered that question, indirectly, through demonstration in this chapter. A good designer is one who can apply the general techniques of problem solving to think through a problem to its conclusion. A good software engineer can recognize a problem, hypothesize its solution, and test that solution against the known constraints and do so, not just from one point of view, but within the context of a team of engineers addressing a user's problem. One needs to lift one's hand from the coding sheet and look to the world around—to think and to communicate.

Bibliography

ALEXANDER, CHRISTOPHER, *Notes on the Synthesis of Form.* Yourdon & Co. 1976.

ALFORD, M., "A Requirements Engineering Methodology for Real-Time Processing Requirements," Proceedings for Second International Conference in Software Engineering, San Francisco, 1976.

BELL, T. E., and T. A. THAYER, "Software Requirements: Are They Really a Problem?" Proceedings of Second International Conference on Software Engineering, San Francisco, 1976.

BENNETT, E. M., J. DEGAN, and J. SPIEGEL, *Human Factors in Technology*, McGraw-Hill, 1963.

BOEHM, B. W., "Software and Its Impact: A Quantitive Assessment." *Datamation*, May 1973, 48–49.

CARLSON, W. E., "Software Research in the Department of Defense," Proceedings of the Second International Conference on Software Engineering, San Francisco, 1976.

CHAPANIS, A. R. E., *Research Techniques in Human Engineering*, Johns Hopkins Press, 1959.

DAVIS, C. G., and C. R. VICK, "Ballistic Missile Defense Advanced Technology Center—The Software Development System," Proceedings of Second International Conference on Software Engineering, San Francisco, 1976.

FREEMAN, P., R. WASSERMAN, and R. E. FAIRLEY, "Essential Elements of Software Engineering Education," Proceedings of the Second International Conference on Software Engineering, San Francisco, 1976.

HAMILTON, M., and S. ZELDIN, *The Foundations for AXES: A Specification Language Based on Completeness of Control*, Charles Start Draper Laboratories, Inc., Cambridge, Mass., 1976.

KRUTZER, W., "Evaluation of Computer System Simulation Tools," Proceedings European Computing Conference on Computer Performance Evaluation, Eurocomp, London, September 1976.

MCCORMICK, E. J., *Human Factors Engineering*, McGraw-Hill, 1964.

SHANKAVARD, K. S., and C. S. CHARDERSEKAVAN, "Data Flow, Abstraction Levels and Specifications for Communications Switching Systems," Proceedings Second International Conference on Computer Performance Evaluation Eurocomp, London, September 1976.

SCHNEIDEWIND, N. F., and T. F. GREEN, "Simulation of Error Detection in Computer Programs," Naval Post Graduate School, Monterey, Calif.

4 STRUCTURED PROGRAMMING

RANDALL W. JENSEN

Senior Scientist
Data Processing Laboratory
Hughes Aircraft Company

> *The whole of science is nothing more than a refinement of everyday thinking.*
>
> ALBERT EINSTEIN
> Physics and Reality

4.1

Introduction

This chapter deals with the last stages of the software development process; that is, the process of converting module specifications into executable source code in a specified programming language. The earlier steps of the development process, dealing with the transformation of the problem definition into module specifications, are contained in Chapter 3.

We base our development of structured programming on the definition of the term and on the lessons we glean from the historical development of program design from the mid-1960s to the present and on the objectives of good design.

We approach the techniques of structured programming in a rather bottom-up fashion. We begin by establishing a set of primitive control structures necessary for the construction of structured code. In this way we raise the level of the target machine[1] to facilitate implementation of the new methodologies. Having armed ourselves with the appropriate tools, we describe the structured programming process and implementation techniques.

We conclude the chapter by discussing implementation of the structured programming tools in three major high-order programming languages (FORTRAN, COBOL, and PL/I), and finally introduce the use of a precompiler.

---

[1] Target machine is the computing system in which the software will be executed.

The term "structured programming" has appeared innumerable times in the software literature during the past few years with nearly as many associated meanings. The term has been cryptically defined as everything from a "return to common sense" to "the way our leading programmers program." As examples of typical definitions, we find:

1. Structured programming theory deals with converting arbitrarily large and complex flowcharts into standard forms so that they can be represented by iterating and nesting a small number of basic and standard control logic structures.[2]
2. Structured programming is a manner of organizing and coding programs that makes the programs easily understood and modified.[3]
3. The fundamental concept [of structured programming] is a proof of correctness: . . .[4]
4. Structured programming is no panacea—it really consists of a formal notation for orderly thinking—an attribute not commonly inherent in programmers or any other type. It is a discipline which must be acquired and continuously enforced through conscious effort. It is worth the trouble.[5]

Many of the definitions we find also include a more than casual reference to the absence of any **go to** statements in a "proper" structured program. Definitions of this latter type were influenced by the famous letter by Dijkstra "**Go To** Statement Considered Harmful."[6] Other definitions place a more realistic perspective. For example, Mills[7] states:

Structured programs should be characterized not simply by the absence of **go to**'s, but by the presence of structure.

The definition we find most accurate was given by Wirth[8]:

'*Structured programming*' is the formulation of programs as hierarchical, nested structures of statements and objects of computation.

Wirth's statement, by itself, does not define the tools or logical control constructs that can be used to achieve a program structure, nor does it limit the structure formulation

[2]H. D. Mills, "Chief Programmer Teams: Principles and Procedures," *IBM Technical Report FSC 71-5108*, (Gaithersburg, MD, International Business Machines Corp., June 1972).

[3]J. R. Donaldson, "Structured Programming," *Datamation*, **19**, 12, December, 1973, 52–54.

[4]R. A. Karp, *Datamation*, **20**, 3, March, 1974, 158.

[5]D. Butterworth, *Datamation*, **20**, 3, March, 1974, 158.

[6]E. W. Dijkstra, "Go To Statement Considered Harmful," *Communications of the ACM*, **11**, 3, March, 1968, 147–48. Reprinted with permission of the Association for Computing Machinery.

[7]H. D. Mills, "Mathematical Foundations for Structured Programming," *IBM Technical Report FSC 72-6012*, (Gaithersburg, MD.: International Business Machines Corp., February 1972).

[8]N. Wirth, "On the Composition of Well-Structured Programs," *Computing Surveys*, **6**, 4, December, 1974, 247–259. Reprinted with permission of the Association for Computing Machinery, Copyright 1974.

techniques available to the program designer. Some of these tools and techniques are developed in later sections of this chapter.

Structured programming is considered by many programmers as a synonym for modular or top-down programming. In an inverted way of reasoning they are correct. Actually, modular programming is a subclass of design methodologies within a general class of problem decomposition methods known as structured programming. Structured programming can be visualized as the application of basic problem decomposition methods to establish a manageable, hierarchical problem structure. These problem decomposition methods are common to all engineering disciplines as well as the physical, chemical, and biological sciences.

The preceding chapter was devoted to the process of decomposing a given problem into successive layers of more manageable or comprehensible pieces that result in a hierarchical structure describing the problem and/or a solution in levels of increasing detail. This process was referred to as "levels of conceptualization." The highest conceptual level represents the general description of the problem with each lower level providing a greater magnification or additional detail about the problem. This process of conceptualization is carried out in a series of steps. Each step brings into focus greater problem detail or refines the knowledge available in the preceding step. Hence, the expression "stepwise refinement" as suggested by Wirth[9] is often used to describe the abstracting or decomposition process that is fundamental to the definition of structured programming.

To gain a greater understanding of the differences between the various methodology subclasses contained within structured programming, we must first consider the goal of the refinement process. We are given a problem, usually poorly specified in our native language, and are required to provide a solution to the problem in a high-order programming language. Unless the problem is more complex than "compute the sum of A and B," which can be mentally translated directly into RESULT = A + B, we are forced into obtaining the solution through a series of refinements. If the problem is large or complex, the system defined to solve the problem must be decomposed into subsystems which, after a number of refinements, appear in the hierarchy (structure chart) as modules. After additional refinement, the results are lines of instructions in the specified programming language. This entire process, often referred to by software designers as "chunking," is a means of reducing the complexity of the chunks to a level where the goal (a statement in a programming language) can be reached in a single, mentally comprehensible transformation. The stepwise refinement of the problem must be performed in a systematic manner to minimize the coupling between chunks and their components and between components on the same level in order to isolate the component for the next level of abstraction. Failure to do this is akin to cutting diamonds with a sledgehammer. The result is just as worthless.

Each methodology subclass can be described by: (1) the refinement process range over which the methodology is effective, (2) its approach to the refinement process, and (3) the applications for which it is useful. Three of the major subclasses are described briefly in Table 4-1. The descriptions are intentionally fuzzy, since our

[9]N. Wirth, "Program Development by Stepwise Refinement," *Communications of the ACM*, **14**, 4, April, 1971, 221–27.

Table 4-1 Structured Programming Methodologies

Name	Approach	Range	Applications
Top-down design[10, 11]	Based upon decomposition by trial and error	Full range	Data processing and algorithmic*
Structured design[12] (Constantine)	Based upon decomposition determined by data flow or data transformations	From system to module specification	Data processing and algorithmic*
Jackson method[13]	Based upon decomposition determined by data structure	Full range, limited capability for decomposing large, complex systems	Data processing

*Implementation determined primarily by algorithm that defined function (e.g., Gauss-Seidel iterative method for solving system of linear equations)

objective is to illustrate that the major program structuring techniques are variations of the stepwise refinement philosophy with variations in the decomposition guidelines. Complete descriptions of the individual approaches can be found in the references. In this chapter, we use the top-down approach exclusively because it is the most straightforward and the easiest to master. The top-down approach is also the most widely used method at the module level.

The methodologies can be used together to complement the capabilities of each. For example, the structured design method can be applied to a problem to obtain an overall program structure and individual module specifications. The detailed module decomposition or design can then be performed by using either the top-down or Jackson methodologies, or both. Figure 4-1 coarsely illustrates a combination of all three techniques applied to a problem containing both data processing and algorithmic (scientific computation) elements. No single methodology is ideal for all applications, of course.

We can conclude that structured programming is a basic scientific methodology for obtaining, in an orderly manner, solutions to complex problems. This methodology provides rigorous techniques for subdividing a problem into its constituents, each of which is totally contained in the aggregate from which it was divided. There are several approaches to the decomposition or subdivision process, each of which has value in producing effective problem solutions.

4.1.2 OBJECTIVES OF STRUCTURED PROGRAMMING

The search for new programming methodologies can be attributed to a "software crisis" that is characterized by the increasing costs of producing software systems and the relatively poor quality/cost ratio of the completed systems. The increasing life-

[10] H. D. Mills, "Top-Down Programming in Large Systems," *Debugging Techniques in Large Systems* (Englewood Cliffs, N.J.: Prentice-Hall, Inc., 1971), pp. 41–55.

[11] J. Maynard, *Modular Programming* (Princeton, N.J.: Auerbach Publishers, 1972).

[12] W. P. Stevens, G. J. Myers, and L. L. Constantine, "Structured Design," *IBM Systems Journal*, **13**, 2, May, 1974, 115–39.

[13] M. A. Jackson, *Principles of Program Design* (London: Academic Press, Inc., 1975).

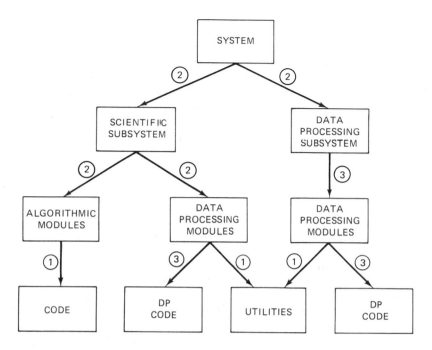

1 STEPWISE-REFINEMENT METHODOLOGY
2 STRUCTURED DESIGN METHODOLOGY
3 JACKSON METHODOLOGY

Fig. 4-1 Typical application of multiple methodologies to solve a complex problem

cycle cost of the software product is experienced in terms of a low productivity rate for the average programmer (sometimes as low as two or three lines of finished code per man day) and in terms of the high proportion of the total data processing system costs that can be attributed to the software subsystem.

Low productivity rates are certainly related to the high cost of software. When an outsider sees production rates as low as 10 lines of code in a high-order language per day and a finished product still loaded with errors[14] ("bugs"), he wonders how a programmer spends most of his day. We know that programmers spend more of their time repairing code than they do writing it. They spend a significant amount of their time reworking faulty code attributable to faulty logic and communications.

Most of us have had to correct errors or modify a program exhibiting behavior that resembles Brownian motion[15] more than any kind of orderly flow. All attempts to read and understand the listing were frustrated by the continued skipping between segments of the program that were sometimes separated by several pages. When incor-

[14]Each new release of the IBM operating system OS/360 contains approximately 1000 new software errors. Also, after a *thorough* checkout, there were 18 errors, or discrepancies, found in the ten-day flight of Apollo 14. (B. W. Boehm, "Software and Its Impact: a Quantitative Assessment," *Datamation*, **19**, 5, May, 1973, 48–59.)

[15]A constant, random movement of small particles in a fluid, caused by the collisions with molecules of the fluid.

porating a change, there was always the deep fear that the modification would create a disaster in a remote part of the program.

We also know that errors in thinking, not coding, are the primary programming productivity limitations, and that the poor quality of the completed software product is simply another aspect of the thinking problem. The large number of errors that continue to exist in a system after delivery is related to the complexity of the system, which is sometimes artificial due to poor logical construction in the original design and the difficulty of isolating software faults by testing in an environment with a finite schedule and funds.

From our knowledge of the causes of the software crisis, we conclude our primary goals must be:

1. To minimize the number of errors that occur during the development process.
2. To minimize the effort required to correct errors in sections of code found to be deficient, and to replace sections when more reliable, functional, or efficient techniques are discovered.
3. To minimize the life-cycle costs of the software.

In other words, we must reduce the software complexity if we are going to attack the problems that characterize the crisis.

Some of the benefits that accompany the program complexity reduction are:

- Fewer testing problems
- Increased programmer productivity
- Improved program clarity
- Improved program maintainability
- Improved program modifiability

Structured programming, through its logical approach to program design and implementation, provides us with an ideal tool for application in the reduction of software complexity.

Structured programming, however, is not a remedy for all of software's difficulties. Any assessment of its role in the development of software must consider the particular problem areas where its virtues can offer little or no improvement. There are two major problems for which structured programming cannot provide hope. First, many of the errors present in software arise from failures in the software specification. Low programmer productivity is due in part to time wasted in solving the wrong problem. In other words, structured programming cannot resolve communication failures due to deficient specifications. Second, the disciplines and rigors of structured programming are beyond the abilities of a certain class of programmers. Structured programming, improperly applied, is no better than traditional methods of program design.

Indirectly related to the second problem is a human tendency to reject any new technology that involves significant change in standard practices. This attitude toward the basic principles of structured programming has contributed much toward the misapplication and misunderstanding of the subject. Some of the familiar negative reactions to structured programming are: "All of the stifling new rules and regulations imposed by structured programming in addition to the standards I presently have to follow are ridiculous . . . .The unstructured programs I write without the new standards are at least as good as can be written by using top-down techniques . . . . Structured programming removes the creativity from the programming process."

The first two reactions are difficult to argue in a logical manner. First, some programmers balk at any change in their design methods independent of the value of the change. Discipline or formality is abhorred. Second, structured programs may require more execution time and/or more storage space than an optimized, unstructured, equivalent version of the program. A well-designed, unstructured program might satisfy the goals of structured programming. However, unstructured programs are less likely to satisfy these goals than structured programs are.

The creativity argument is particularly poor. The framework of the design process is changed by the new technology, but designing programs within that framework is at least as challenging as the design process is outside the framework. Identical negative statements about restrictions of human freedom were made when FORTRAN and other high-order programming languages were introduced and programmers were isolated from the machine by the language processor. As an example, Backus and Heising stated:[16]

> At that time, most programmers wrote symbolic machine instructions exclusively (some even used absolute octal or decimal machine instructions). Almost to a man, they firmly believed that any mechanical coding method would fail to apply that versatile ingenuity which each programmer felt he possessed and constantly needed in his work. Therefore, it was agreed, compilers could only turn out code which would be intolerably less efficient than human coding (intolerable, that is, unless that inefficiency could be buried under larger, but desirable, inefficiencies such as the programmed floating-point arithmetic usually required then). . . .
>
> . . . The [development] group had one primary fear. After working long and hard to produce a good translator program, an important application might promptly turn up which would confirm the views of the sceptics: this application would be of the sort Fortran was designed to handle, and even though well programmed in Fortran, its object program would run at half the speed of a hand-coded version. It was felt that such an occurrence, or several of them, would almost completely block acceptance of the system. . . .

Structured programming is now defending itself against accusations almost identical to those faced by the creators of FORTRAN. When programmers find their structured programs are sometimes running at slower speeds and using more resources than their unstructured programs, many will retreat from structured programming and return to the old methods without considering the positive benefits produced by their structured code. The zealots' emphasis on the elimination of the **go to** statement as the first principle of structured programming could add to the rejection of the new programming methodology because of the increased program complexity caused by total **go to** elimination in nontrivial applications.

[16]J. W. Backus and W. P. Heising, "FORTRAN," *IEEE Transactions on Electronic Computers*, EC-13, 4, August, 1964, 382–85.

4.2

History and Background

It is difficult to ascertain the earliest applications of an approach to programming that we now refer to as "structured programming." This style of programming, called a "return to common sense" by at least one author, had been unknowingly approached, but not achieved, by many over the years in efforts to produce cost-effective programs.

Professor Edsger W. Dijkstra, of the University of Eindhoven, Netherlands, was one of the first to formally recognize the value of structured programming. In 1965, Dijkstra published a paper[17] advocating the construction of programs in a structured manner. In the same paper he also suggested that the **go to** statement be eliminated from programming language. As he pointed out:

> ... two programming department managers from different countries and different backgrounds—the one mainly scientific, the other mainly commercial—have communicated to me, independently of each other and on their own initiative, their observations that the quality of their programmers was inversely proportional to the density of goto statements in their programs.
>
> ... I have done various programming experiments and compared the Algol text with the text I got in modified versions of Algol 60 in which the goto statement was abolished. ... The latter versions were more difficult to make: we are so familiar with the jump order that it requires some effort to forget it! In all cases tried, however, the program without the goto statement turned out to be shorter and more lucid.

These comments, and other similar comments published about the same time,[18,19] had little impact on the programming community for two reasons. First, the majority of the industry was struggling with early versions of FORTRAN and COBOL. Second, no positive approach to solving the problems alluded to by Dijkstra and others had been proposed.

The first major step toward structured programming was made in a paper published by C. Böhm and G. Jacopini[20] in May 1966. They demonstrated that three basic control structures, or constructs, were sufficient for expressing any flowchartable program logic. The basic constructs, shown in Figure 4-2, include: (1) a sequence mechanism, (2) a selection mechanism, and (3) an iteration mechanism.

As we will see later, the three basic constructs do indeed form a sufficient, but not necessarily optimum, set of blocks to express any program flowchart. Thus, it is theoretically possible to write programs in languages like PL/I and ALGOL without ever using an explicit **go to** statement. When writing programs in FORTRAN, the use of the

[17]E. W. Dijkstra, "Programming Considered as a Human Activity," *Proceedings of the IFIP Congress*, 1965, pp. 213–17.

[18]P. J. Landin, "The Next 700 Programming Languages," *Communications of the ACM*, **9**, 3, March, 1966, 157–66.

[19]P. Naur, "Program Translation Viewed as a General Data Processing Problem," *Communications of the ACM*, **9**, 3, March, 1966, 176–79.

[20]C. Böhm and G. Jacopini, "Flow Diagrams, Turing Machines and Languages with Only Two Formation Rules," *Communications of the ACM*, **9**, 5, May, 1966, 366–71.

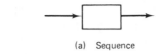

(a)   Sequence

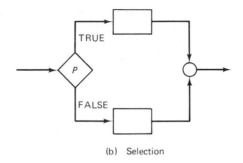

(b)   Selection

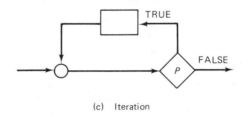

(c)   Iteration

Fig. 4-2   Basic control structures

go to statement could be restricted theoretically to those instances necessary to emulate the three basic constructs. For example:

```
  if(le)              IF (.NOT.le) GO TO 10
     A = B               A = B
                         GO TO 20
  else             10 CONTINUE
     X = C               X = C
  end if           20 CONTINUE
```

is an acceptable way to represent a selection construct in FORTRAN.

Dijkstra forcefully repeated his ideas about program structure and the **go to** statement in a March 1968 *Communications of the ACM letter*[6] under the title "Go To Statement Considered Harmful." He opened the letter with:

> For a number of years I have been familiar with the observation that the quality of programmers is a decreasing function of the density of **go to** statements in the programs they produce. More recently I discovered why the use of the **go to** statement has such disastrous effects, and I became convinced that the **go to** statement should be abolished from all "higher level" programming languages (i.e., everything except, perhaps, plain machine code). . . .

Because of the sentiment that had been built up against the **go to** statement in some circles, the reaction to the Dijkstra letter was rapid and strong. Hordes of programmers rushed to support Dijkstra's proposal with an enthusiasm akin to religious zeal. Structured- and **go to**-less programming became synonymous in their eyes, and the objectives of structured programming (readability, reliability, and programmer efficiency) were ignored in their wild effort to eliminate the **go to**. There probably hasn't been as much religious zeal shown since the seventeenth century witch hunts in Salem. As an example of the present impact of this letter, I quote from a published interview with a prominent nameless computer science professor:

> . . . In the earlier days we used to take off a full letter grade for each **go to** in the program. Now I simply state that an unstructured program is unacceptable.

The 25th ACM National Conference included an entire session entitled "The **go to** Controversy" because of this controversial aspect of structured programming. Although W. A. Wulf advocated the elimination of the **go to** statement in his paper[21] entitled "A Case Against the **go to**," his primary attack was upon the misuse of the **go to** in creating programs with obscure logical structures. Similarly, M. E. Hopkins pointed out in his paper[22] "A Case for the Go To" that the **go to** statement was misused in many programs, but still was valuable in creating readable, maintainable programs.

Niklaus Wirth's 1971 paper[9] presented some of the basic principles of structured programming. The paper "Program Development by Stepwise Refinement" established the basic structured programming procedure. He suggested that program construction consists of a sequence of refinement steps. Each step of the construction consists of breaking a given task into a number of subtasks. This refinement in the program description should be accompanied by a parallel refinement in the data description, which constitutes the communication means between subtasks.

Later in 1971, Dr. Harlan Mills and F. Terry Baker first demonstrated that there was considerable value in applying structured programming techniques in a production programming environment. The qualified success of the classic *New York Times* online information retrieval system project,[23] in spite of the short delivery schedule (22 months) and the magnitude of the effort (over 83,000 lines of code), proved that structured programming was more than an academic exercise. A significant improvement in programmer productivity was achieved during this project due largely to the use of structured programming techniques.

The first significant textbooks on structured programming[24,25] were produced by Weinberg, and Dahl, Dijkstra and Hoare in 1972.

The December 1973 issue of DATAMATION proclaimed structured program-

[21]W. A. Wulf, "A Case Against the GOTO," *Proceedings of the ACM Conference*, August, 1972, 791–97.

[22]M. E. Hopkins, "A Case For the GOTO," *Proceedings of the ACM Conference*, August, 1972, 787–90.

[23]F. T. Baker, "Chief Programmer Team Management of Production Programming," *IBM Systems Journal*, **11**, 1, January, 1972, 56–73.

[24]G. Weinberg, *Structured Programming in PL/C* (New York: John Wiley and Sons, Inc., 1973).

[25]O. J. Dahl, E. W. Dijkstra, and C.A.R. Hoare, *Structured Programming* (New York: Academic Press, 1972).

ming to be a "programming revolution" and devoted five articles[26,3,27,28,29] to the subject.

The next major driving force toward the acceptance of structured programming techniques was the largest consumer of software products—the United States government. Their increased awareness of the value of this new methodology in combatting skyrocketing software costs led to a series of directives that "encouraged" the use of structured programming in all software procurements.

Since the end of 1973 the acceptance of the new technology has grown at an ever-increasing rate. Software developers and universities alike are striving to gain practical experience with structured programming as a continuing stream of positive results is obtained. We can expect that future software development projects will continue to demonstrate the greater programmer efficiency and reliability of programs written by using these concepts, and we may expect to see considerably wider acceptance of structured programming in the software community.

4.3
Theory and Techniques

The heart of structured programming is the process we introduced in the previous section as "stepwise refinement." In addition to stepwise refinement there are other subordinate concepts that are important to the proper utilization of the program development methodology. We find ourselves in a quandry at this point due to the difficulty of discussing these ideas in their order of importance. We cannot illustrate the refinement process without introducing the subordinate logical control structures, nor can we describe the necessary logical control structures without establishing some fundamental terminology. The obvious solution is to present these topics in the reverse order (i.e., foundations, control structures, and, finally, the structuring process). The problem with this solution is that the student may tend to fall into the same mire that many others have and lose sight of the fundamentals of structured programming. By introducing the individual control structures before we introduce the process, we are artificially and unwillingly emphasizing the importance of the structures instead of the thinking or design approach. This artificial emphasis on individual structures is amplified by the general outward appearance or visible characteristics of a structured program. Two prominent characteristics attract our attention when we inspect a well-structured program: (1) the presence of rather unique control structures and the nested indentation of program segments, and (2) the rare occurrence of **go to** statements. These two characteristics, which are frequently misconstrued as structured programming, are merely symptoms of methodology; they are not structured programming.

[26]D. D. McCracken, "Revolution in Programming: An Overview," *Datamation*, **19**, 12, December, 1973, 50–52.

[27]E. F. Miller and G. E. Lindamood, "Structured Programming: Top-Down Approach," *Datamation*, **19**, 12, December, 1973, 55–57.

[28]F. T. Baker and H. D. Mills, "Chief Programmer Teams," *Datamation*, **19**, 12, December, 1973, 58–61.

[29]R. L. Clark, "A Linguistic Contribution to GOTO-less Programming," *Datamation*, **19**, 12, December, 1973, 62–68.

With this forceful note of caution, we will introduce the theory and techniques of structured programming as we proposed. We will provide some definitions that are fundamental to our endeavor, followed by the introduction of a broad, but powerful set of control structures, and a notation for describing the design process. Finally, a systematic approach to the formulation of programs (at the module level), which is the key to structured programming, will be discussed.

Since the intent of this section is to present the basic concepts of the methodology and not the restrictions of any implementing language, we will avoid the language details by using a pseudo-language throughout the section. Our pseudo-language is a combination of a hierarchical English dialect and the most convenient features of the existing high-order programming languages. Prior to the discussion of a systematic approach to program formulation, we will describe the use of this pseudo-language (after referred to as pseudocode) as one of the more important program design tools.

4.3.1 FOUNDATIONS

Before embarking on a discussion of the tools and techniques of structured programming, there are many key definitions and concepts that must be introduced as a foundation for our further work. It is essential that these definitions be understood before proceeding further. We have already formulated a fundamental definition for structured programming that we will rephrase here for emphasis: *Structured programming* is the formulation of programs by stepwise refinement, resulting in hierarchical, nested structures of statements and objects of computation.

We can represent a program in several ways. Among the most common of these representations are: (1) a source code listing, (2) A HIPO diagram,[30] (3) a schematic logic diagram, (4) a pseudocode listing, and (5) a flowchart. The first two representations are primarily documentation methods, which are not available until after the program is complete, and thus provide little assistance during the program development. It is inappropriate to discuss these methods here. The last three representations, which serve both as documentation methods and development tools, will be described in the Development Tool section. However, the flowchart is also a most convenient aid for developing the foundations of structured programming and must be introduced in that capacity here.

A *flowchart* is a directed graph that describes the flow of execution control in the program. The graph is constructed of directed line segments whose orientation, or direction of flow, is indicated by arrows in Figure 4-3. The line segments originate and terminate in *nodes*, as shown in the same figure. A node may represent a data transformation, a decision point, or simply a collection point for the program control paths.

Using this information about the program flowchart, we can define a *well-formed program* as one in which there is precisely *one* input line, and for every node, there exists a path from the program input line through that node to the program output line. This implies that there are no infinite loops and no unreachable code. In addition, a *proper program* contains precisely one output line. (The word *proper* is used in this

---

[30]HIPO diagrams are a method of program documentation outside the scope of this chapter. For details, see *HIPO-A Design. Aid and Documentation Technique, GX20-1851* (White Plains, N.Y.: International Business Machines Corp., October, 1974).

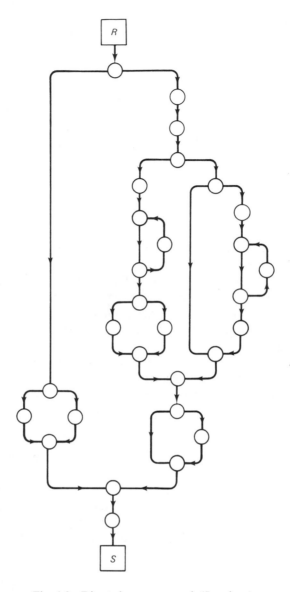

Fig. 4-3 Directed program graph (flowchart)

definition to be consistent with classical structured program definitions. By this definition, well-formed programs with multiple exist paths are improper, but only in terms of the definition.)

The directed graph in Figure 4-3 represents a proper program since (1) there is exactly one input line *R* and one output line *S*, and (2) there exists a path through each node from *R* to *S*. The graph in Figure 4-4 is *improper* and *ill-formed* since there is no path from *R* to *S* through either of nodes 2 and 3, causing the second condition for a well-formed program to be unsatisfied.

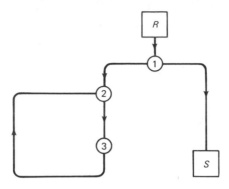

Fig. 4-4 Improper and ill-formed program graph

Two well-formed programs are *equivalent* if they define or perform the same function. It is not necessary that the two programs have identical directed graphs. For example, program X computes the average of two numbers by the procedure $A = (A_1/2 + A_2/2)$; program Y uses the procedure given by $A = (A_1 + A_2)/2$. Programs X and Y are equivalent even though the order of computation is different in each of the two programs and the results may differ due to numerical limitations of the computing system.

If a program contains a data transformation node T where $S = T(R)$, it may be possible to define another program that performs the function specified by node T. We call a program defined in this manner an *expansion* of the original program. A node that cannot be expanded in this manner (e.g., $A = B$) is considered *nonexpansible*.

Consider the proper program shown in Figure 4-5(a). We find that we can amplify the original transformation to the flowchart shown in part (b) of the figure by successive expansions where the proper programs P_{21} and P_{22} are expansions of transformation nodes contained in expansion P_2 and, similarly, where P_1 and P_2 are expansions of nodes contained in proper program P. We might also say that programs P_1 and P_2 are contained in refinements of program P, and that programs P_{21} and P_{22} are contained in refinements of program P_2. Each of the refinements is totally contained in its *abstraction*. Thus, P is an abstraction of P_1 and P_2, etc. *Total containment* implies that the refinements occurring within the individual nodes at any level are independent of each other. This idea is extremely important in the development of the structured programming methodology later in this section.

We define a *proper structured* program as any program *derived by a stepwise refinement process* that is defined by using the three basic control structures: sequence, selection, and iteration, as shown in Figure 4-2. A *well-formed* structured program is a program derived by stepwise refinement that allows the use of the exit control structure (see Sec. 4.3.2) in addition to the three basic control structures. These definitions of proper and well-formed structured programs are justifiable departures from the classical structured program definition that is seen frequently in the software literature. It is important to recognize and understand the differences between our definitions and

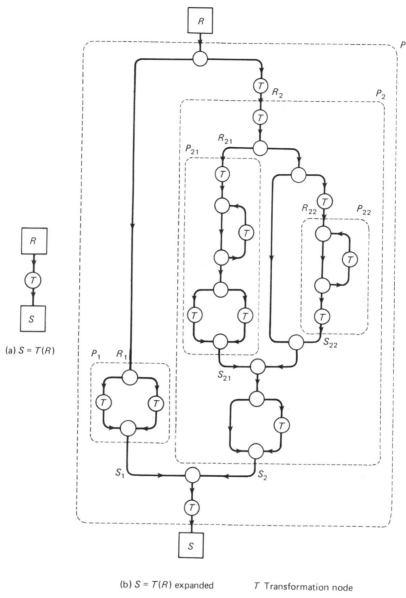

(a) $S = T(R)$

(b) $S = T(R)$ expanded T Transformation node

Fig. 4-5   Program expansions

the classical structured program definition because of the impact of these differences on program structuring.

The classical definitions were originally introduced by Böhm and Jacopini in their 1966 paper. They demonstrated that flowchart programs of any size and complexity can be represented by proper programs built from the small set of simple and regular programs of Figure 4-2. Based on the results of their work, a *structured program* was defined to be any program whose flow of execution control can be described by using only the three basic control structures: sequence, selection, and iteration. Using this definition, it was possible to prove:

> *Structure Theorem:*[31] Any proper program can be transformed into an equivalent "structured program" using the functions and decisions of the original proper program and assignments and tests on one additional variable.

The one additional variable mentioned in the theorem is a flag variable required to provide a means of handling abnormal exit conditions from the three basic control structures. By abnormal exits, we mean exits not allowed for in the three basic structures.

By introducing a fourth basic control structure class that we will refer to as the exit class, we can eliminate the need for the "one additional variable" from the Structure Theorem. Peterson, Kasami, and Tokura[32] demonstrated the value of the exit class of statements on the formation of well-formed structured programs.

The Structure Theorem, as presented by Böhm and Jacopini, states that a structured program can be obtained by performing a series of elementary manipulations or transformations on the logic control structure of a proper, but unstructured, program. These manipulations on the unstructured program, which transform its control structure into a "structured" form, are *not* related to the structured programming process. We can demonstrate this idea simply with the following example.

EXAMPLE 4-1

Consider the proper "spaghetti bowl"[33] program shown in Figure 4-6(a). By duplicating the function performed at node D and eliminating node 1, the program is transformed into the equivalent program shown as the first transformation in Figure 4-6(b), which contains only the three basic control structures specified by the Structure Theorem. A rearrangement of the nodes of the second flowchart (Figure 4-6(b)) results in the final flowchart shown in Figure 4-6(c), which highlights the configuration of the equivalent "structured" program. Since the original proper program (independent of its quality) was completely specified prior to the transformation, it is obvious that no refinement or structuring process was used in creating the equivalent program. Also note that no changes or improvements were made to functions A, B, C, or D while the logic structure was being improved. We now pose the following philosophical question to the reader: "If a program is created by using only the three basic control structures in its flowchart, according to the classical definition of a structured program, but is not developed through the use of stepwise refinement, is the program necessarily structured?" The answer is, obviously, "No!"

The classical structured program definition and the Structure Theorem might lead to the thinking that the way to write structured programs is to write unstructured code

---

[31]A detailed discussion of the Structure Theorem can be found in H. D. Mills, "Mathematical Foundations for Structured Programming," *IBM Technical Report FSC72-6012* (Gaithersburg, Md.: International Business Machines Corp., February, 1972).

[32]W. W. Peterson, T. Kasami, and N. Tokura, "On the Capabilities of While, Repeat, and Exit Statements," *Communications of the ACM*, **16**, 8, August, 1973, 503–12.

[33]A colloquial term used to describe a computer program whose control flow is, at best, nearly incomprehensible.

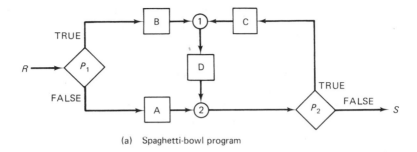

(a) Spaghetti-bowl program

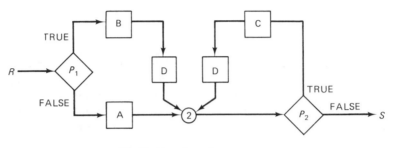

(b) First transformation

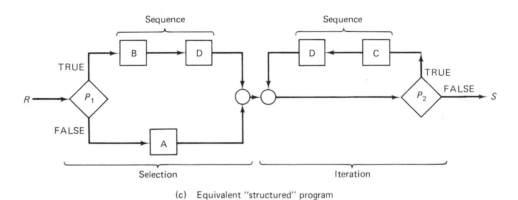

(c) Equivalent "structured" program

Fig. 4-6 Conversion of unstructured to "structured" program

and then convert it to structured form. This is definitely not the case. If a proper program has a logic structure that resembles a "bowl of spaghetti," there is no transformation possible, short of a redesign, that will significantly improve the clarity or maintainability of the program. If the original structure is spaghetti-like, it is reasonable to assume the quality of the remainder of the program is no better. In that case, a proper input program full of "garbage" will have the outward appearance of a structured program, but will result only in properly structured garbage after the transformations.

Our definition of structured programming emphasizes that the program must be obtained through the process of stepwise refinement. Indeed, a proper structured program achieved by the refinement process also contains only the three basic control structures necessary to satisfy the weaker definition of a "structured" program associated with the Structure Theorem and an occasional exit structure. Development of the program logic structure by a stepwise refinement process not only arrives at a valid structure automatically, but it also obviates the need for the Structure Theorem since there is no requirement to ever transform a proper program into an equivalent structured program. Thus, we conclude that the stepwise refinement process is the essential part of the definition of a structured program.

Having equipped ourselves with a basic set of structured programming definitions and concepts, we now proceed to our next objective: a bag of basic control structures to be used in our structured programs.

4.3.2 BASIC CONTROL STRUCTURES

The Böhm and Jacopini paper established that only three basic constructs or logic control structures were sufficient for expressing any program logic. However, their paper proved only that certain types of programs containing unconditional branching statements could be transformed into a "pure" or **go to**-less program, sometimes at the expense of additional variables and computation. Their paper did not claim that the three control structures were the only structures that could be used, nor did it claim that these constructs were the best set of structures for any application.

In this section we describe nine basic control structures that comprise a useful set of tools for the construction of maintainable software. The set is divided into four major structure classes:

1. Sequence—Concatenation
2. Selection —**if - else**
   if - orif - else   often described as   **if - elseif - else**
   case
   posit
3. Iteration —**while**
   until
4. Exit   —**escape**
   cycle

The first three classes contain the elements specified by Böhm and Jacopini and obvious extensions to these elements. The fourth class of structures is considered somewhat controversial because of the inclusion of unconditional branching statements, but the class is important as a solution to the unconstrained and potentially hazardous **go to** statement, and will be justified later in this section.

FUNDAMENTAL ELEMENTS

The nine basic control structures can each be reduced to collections of three atomic components. We use the word *atomic* to characterize the lowest level constituents to which we can reduce the structure of a program. These components, which

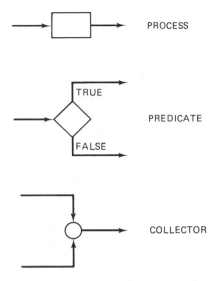

Fig. 4-7 Fundamental structure nodes

we refer to as nodes, are: (1) a process node, (2) a predicate node, and (3) a collector node. The symbols for the components are shown in Figure 4-7.

The *process* node, sometimes alluded to in the literature as a *function* node, is associated with a data transformation in the program flowchart. The process can be as simple as an elementary assignment statement at the machine level, such as A = B, or can, at a higher, more abstract level, contain an entire program segment. For example, the process COMPUTE TARGET RANGE could include arithmetic calculations, several subroutine calls, and a considerable amount of control logic. We define a *proper* process node as a node that contains only a single entry point and a single exit.

Well-formed process nodes contain, by the same reasoning, a single entry point and one or more exit points due to the presence of an abnormal exit from the process. The first condition specified in the definition of a proper program requires that all process nodes internal to a program be proper. Note that a proper node is also well-formed. The well-formed process node shown in Figure 4-8 includes a variation of the predicate node to indicate the logical condition *C*, causing the abnormal exit from the process.

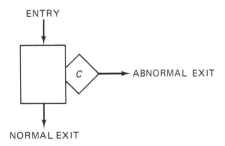

Fig. 4-8 Well-formed process node

The process node, since it is characterized as a function with an input and an output, exhibits some of the properties of the classical engineering "black box."[34] The black box characteristic is extremely important because it allows us to verify the correct performance of the process nodes at each level of abstraction until the entire program can be verified as a process node at the highest abstract level. In this process the immediate lower-level process node is treated as a verified entity or component to reduce the verification complexity to a manageable magnitude. Well-formed, but improper, nodes increase the verification difficulty by introducing alternate paths in the process. If the exit structure is used judiciously, the increase is not of great significance.

The *predicate* node, or decision node, is associated with a predicate function. The predicate function is usually a binary valued logical test that is evaluated each time the program execution enters the predicate node through its input path. The value of the predicate function determines whether the program flow will follow the TRUE output line or the FALSE output line. Program data is not transformed by the predicate node; that is, no operations on data can be performed with this type of node. The predicate node in the simplest sense has two output lines, each related to one of the binary predicate evaluation results, true and false. However, we frequently find programming problems in which more than two results are required from the evaluation at a decision node. In the simple case, the predicate might be "X is equal to Y?" where a true or false evaluation is adequate. In the more complex case, we might ask, "What is the marital status of the subject?" to which the answer would be any one of the group: "Single," "Married," "Divorced," "Widowed," etc. For this case, we devise, by necessity, a special form of a predicate node that is controlled by a mutually exclusive selection of one of several output lines, rather than by a binary-valued logical test. The special selection form of the predicate node is shown in Figure 4-9(a). Each

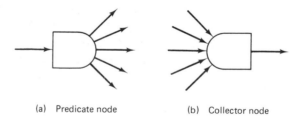

(a)　Predicate node　　　　(b)　Collector node

Fig. 4-9　Special selection form of predicate and collector nodes

output line should be labeled with the condition causing that line to be selected.

The *collector* node combines a set of two or more program control flow lines (input) into a single output line. The number of control lines entering a collector node is two, except for the special cases where the collector node is associated with the special selection form of predicate node or where one or more of the input lines are related to abnormal process node exits. The collector node has the distinctive representation shown in Figure 4-9(b) when its input lines are coupled through a set of

[34]A *black box* is a compact assemblage of equipment (or code) that can be characterized and/or tested as an isolated component of a system.

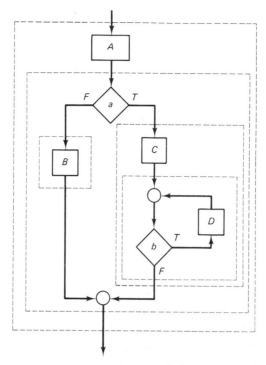

Fig. 4-10 Typical program flowchart

process nodes to the output control lines of the special selection form of a predicate node. In this case, all of the *efferent* paths of a given predicate node will converge at the same collector node. (That is, if the program is structured correctly!)

The three atomic components can be assembled in any configuration to form the program control structure, such as the flowchart shown in Figure 4-10. The program representation in this figure appears to be proper; that is, the program at each level of conceptualization outlined by a dotted line (box) represents a proper process node with a single entry point and a single exit. However, one of the process nodes A, B, C, or D may contain processes with multiple exit paths. For example, when we expand process node B, shown in Figure 4-11(a), we discover that B contains a well-formed, but improper, process node B_1 as shown in Figure 4-11(b). An amplification of process B_1, in Figure 4-11(c), shows that process node B_{12} represents processing required to correctly terminate process B_1 under a discovered exit condition. Thus, process B_{12} appears internal to process B_1, instead of externally as a separate process between predicate node A and collector node α in part (b) of the figure.

Many of the infinite number of possible program structures have the general appearance of a bowl of spaghetti, and are about as hard to digest. By establishing program structure building blocks (akin to molecules made from our three types of atoms) and a structuring methodology, we can scientifically implement structured programs. Since we have already defined the four classes of structures needed to build maintainable software, we can proceed with the definition of the set of nine structures that make up the four classes.

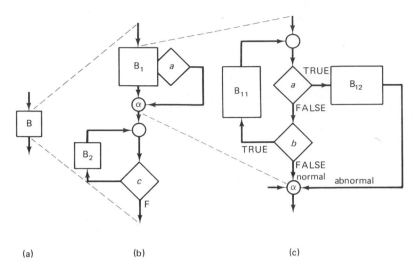

(a)   (b)   (c)

Fig. 4-11   Buried improper program segment

SEQUENCE

The sequence structure is simply the concatenation of two or more process nodes, as shown in Figure 4-12(a). If the process nodes are proper, each with a single entry and a single exit, the linear sequence of nodes can be compressed, or abstracted, into a single process node. In the case that occurs when one or more of the sequence of processes are improper, the sequence compresses into a process node of the type shown in Figure 4-12(b). In the refinement process, a single process node (A) can be replaced by a sequence of two or more process nodes $(A_1, A_2, \ldots, A_n)$, which is an expansion of the single node. This expansion process can be repeated as additional process detail is obtained.

SELECTION

The basic selection structure is the **if-else** binary decision mechanism shown in Figure 4-13. This control structure provides a choice between two alternatives. In the **if-else** structure, process A is executed if the value of predicate p is true; otherwise, process B is executed. The structure is written as

> **if** (p)
>   Process A
> **else**
>   Process B
> **end if**

where process A occurs within the **if** clause of the construct and process B occurs within the **else** clause.

Process B is frequently a *null* process; that is, process A is executed if predicate p is true, and no data transformations are performed if the predicate value is false.

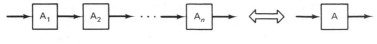

(a)   Proper process nodes

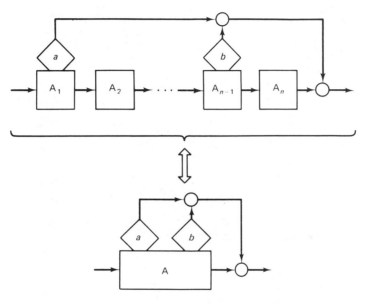

(b)   Improper process nodes

Fig. 4-12   Concatenation of process nodes

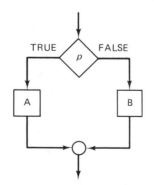

Fig. 4-13   if-else control structure

Under this condition the selection is written

if (*p*)
    Process A
end if

Each of the processes may contain complex logic structures. For example, consider the algorithm for selecting the largest of three values A. B, and C. The flowchart for the algorithm we refer to as MAX3 is shown in Figure 4-14.

The MAX3 algorithm is written as

```
if (a ≥ b)
    if (a ≥ c)
        big = a
    else
        big = c
    end if
else
    if (b ≥ c)
        big = b
    else
        big = c
    end if
end if
```

to correspond to the structure specified in the flowchart.

Here we can recognize for the first time the value of indentation in presenting the program structure in a clear fashion. We could have written the MAX3 algorithm without indentation as

```
if (a ≥ b)
if (a ≥ c)
big = a
else
big = c
end if
else
if (b ≥ c)
big = b
else
big = c
end if
end if
```

and camouflaged the program's structure while reducing the clarity of the pseudocode representation of the algorithm. Indenting the source listing to typographically indicate the depth of nesting of iteration and selection structures is an effective method of emphasizing structure and improving the clarity of the program listing. The rules for indenting the source code are simple:

1. All elements related to a specific level of the control structure are aligned to the same column. Note in the MAX3 listing the alignment of the **if, else,** and **end if** elements for each level of the structure. There is one **if-else** struc-

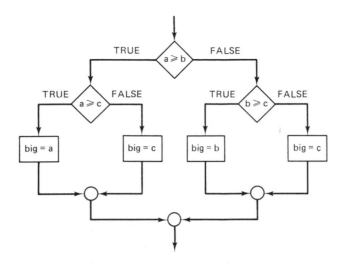

Fig. 4-14 MAX3 algorithm flowchart

ture at level one and two **if-else** structures at level two, as shown in the flowchart.

2. All dependent processes associated with the structure are indented by a fixed amount, usually two to five spaces.[35] The dependent process could also be a control structure. Processes subordinate to the dependent processes are again indented to indicate their relative position in the structure.

There are three special forms of the selection structure that occur frequently in program designs: **if-orif-else**, **case**, and **posit**. Requirements for the first two of these structures are often related to a "transaction center" derived during decomposition of the program into modules, but the requirement can occur due to a multitude of other reasons. A transaction center, as shown in Figure 4-15, transfers control to one, and only one, of a set of mutually exclusive processes (TRANS *n*) in response to the information input to the transaction center. An interactive graphic system, in which user's requests activate special processes, is one application of a transaction center.

The first, or logical, form of the selection structure (**if-orif-else**) is used in applications where the control flow is determined by a series of predicates where each predicate is associated with a specific subordinate process. Positive evaluation of any one of the predicates, which may be a complex logical expression, transfers control to the appropriate process. The second, or numeric, form of the selection structure (**case**) is used in applications where an integer index value is input to the structure to select the appropriate subordinate process. The third special form of the selection structure (**posit**[36]) usually occurs in situations where the execution of a program sequence is

---

[35]The optimum indentation per level for clarity is three spaces. Decreasing or increasing the indentation step size makes the structure more difficult to perceive as a unit.

[36]Posit: To lay down or assume as a fact; affirm; postulate. *Standard Dictionary of the English Language* (New York: Funk and Wagnalls Company, 1960).

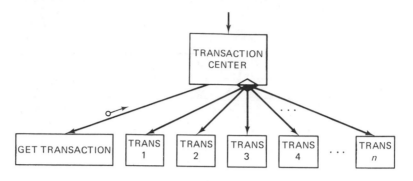

Fig. 4-15 Transaction center structure

initiated on the assumption that the data objects being operated on within the sequence satisfy a specified set of conditions. Upon discovery of a condition that violates the initial assumption, control is passed to an alternate (**else**) code sequence. The three special selections are discussed in detail in the following paragraphs.

The inclusion of the **if-orif-else** structure in the selection structure class can be understood from two different viewpoints. First, the structure, as we will see in examples below, is more representative of the selection function being performed than the equivalent implementation using nested **if-else** structures. Let us consider an application in which we select one of several processes according to an alphanumeric marital status tag read from an input data card. The necessary structure for this selection, when built entirely with the **if-else** construct, is

```
if (status = 'married')
    Process married
else
    if (status = 'single')
        Process single
    else
        if (status = 'divorced')
            Process divorced
        else
            if (status = 'widowed')
                Process widowed
            else
                if (status = 'separated')
                    Process separated
                else
                    Process status error
                end if
            end if
        end if
    end if
end if
```

The flowchart representation of the selection structure based on the **if-else** construct is shown in Figure 4-16.

It is important to note here that the structure implementing the selection process appears to be a nested-**if** structure. In reality, this structure is an either-or type in which the marital status will satisfy only one of the string of conditions.

The selection function can be more clearly written, using the **if-orif-else** structure as

```
if (status = 'married')
    Process married
orif (status = 'single')
    Process single
orif (status = 'divorced')
    Process divorced
orif (status = 'widowed')
    Process widowed
orif (status = 'separated')
    Process separated
else
    Process status error
end if
```

The **if-else** and **if-orif-else** structure implementations for the selection process are logically identical; the **if-orif-else** implementation is, however, more representative of the selection process and possesses much more clarity than the **if-else** representation. We could have added an additional 20 elements to the string of conditions without making the structure appreciably more complex. What could we have done with nested **if**s?

The second justification for the **if-orif-else** structure is based on the human ability of the programmer to interpret the meaning of code that is nested several levels deep, as is the **if-else** version of the marital status selection scheme.

Psychological studies have shown that very few people can grasp as a unit the meaning of a nested logic structure that is more than three levels deep. Beyond that depth the apparent structural complexity increases the difficulty both in creating and maintaining the program. In addition to the comprehension problem, we have to contend with physical limitations of our programming tools. The 80-column computer card, recognized as an input standard for source code, allows only 66 columns for input after we eliminate eight columns for sequence information and another six columns for labeling and continuation information. If we assume an indentation standard of three columns and at some point in our program find a nesting depth of nine levels, we have only 39 columns available for program input. If we manage to create a selection structure involving 25 processes, we will have a situation where the nested **if-else** implementation of the structure will not allow us to punch the source program on a standard input card in indented form.

The flowchart representation of the marital status structure is shown in Figure 4-17. The logical condition selecting each process is written adjacent to the control line

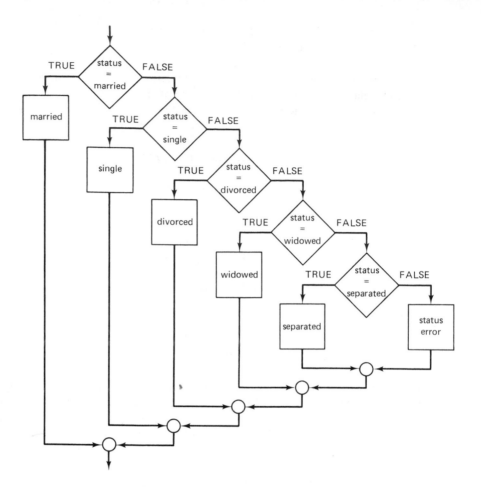

Fig. 4-16 Nested-**if** structure flowchart for marital status selection

linking the predicate node and the associated process. This example used the single transaction variable *status* to select the appropriate subordinate process. One could argue that this transaction could have been implemented nearly as easily with a **case** structure, thereby obviating the need for the **if-orif-else** structure. That is true in this situation, but that is always a problem with simple examples. What if the married process is selected if status equal married or separated for less than 7 months, and the separated process is selected if status equal separated for greater than or equal to 7 months? The more complex selection criteria emphasizes the need for the **if-orif-else** structure in addition to the **case** structure.

The integer form of the special selection structure (**case**) selects one of a set of processes for execution based on the value of an integer index. The arguments justifying the **case** structure are the same as for the **if-orif-else** selection structure. The structure more clearly represents the function it implements than the nested-**if** structure and is easier to interpret. The primary difference between the **if-orif-else** and **case** constructs is the type of data driving the selection process. Let us consider again, for a moment, the problem of selecting a process to be executed based on the marital status of the subject. The **case** structure requires that the process selection be based on an integer index. Thus, the marital status tag must be supplied in numeric form where the code supplied by the input data card (or from a previous process) will represent the process. In this example, let married = 1, single = 2, divorced = 3, widowed = 4, separated = 5. The **case** form of the selection structure is then

```
case of (status)
case (1)
        Process married
case (2)
        Process single
case (3)
        Process divorced
case (4)
        Process widowed
case (5)
        Process separated
else
        Process status error
end case
```

In a "black-box" sense the **case** structure is functionally identical to the nested-**if** structure; that is, the structure could be represented as

```
if   (status = 1)
        Process married
else
    if   (status = 2)
            Process single
    else
        if   (status = 3)
                Process divorced
        else
            if   (status = 4)
                    Process widowed
            else
                if   (status = 5)
                        Process separated
                else
                        Process status error
                end if
            end if
        end if
    end if
end if
```

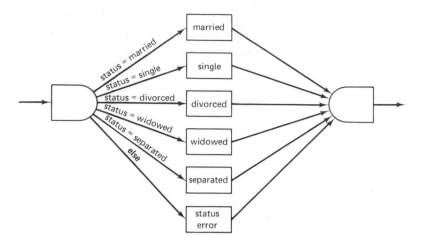

Fig. 4-17   **if-orif-else** logical control structure

This implementation makes the **case** and **if-orif-else** structures logically identical with the constraint that the **case** form of the structure be limited to using simple predicates that test the index value. Since the **case** indices are often tested serially, it is reasonable to arrange the cases in order of most probable occurrence to minimize the testing required to select the desired case.

Some implementations of the **case** structure are similar to the FORTRAN computed-**go to** statement. In this situation a pointer is provided to the beginning of each process in the structure. (At the time the **case** is invoked, the index obtains the correct pointer and transfers control directly to the selected process.) This is obviously the most efficient implementation in terms of execution speed.

The flowchart representation of the marital status structure using the **case** construct is shown in Figure 4-18. The index variable is written adjacent to the input line, and the index number associated with each process is written adjacent to the control line linking the predicate node to the process.

The third special form of the selection structure (**posit**) is also required because of the limitations imposed by the simple **if-else** structure. We have demonstrated the need for the **if-orif-else** and **case** structures on the basis that the structures are more representative of the specific selection process. The nesting in the **if-else** representation of the **if-orif-else** and **case** structures always occurs within the **else** clause of the construct. We must also allow for situations in which the nesting occurs within the **if** clause. Here we have a condition somewhat analogous to a logical inverse of the selection process. Instead of entering the structure and executing only one selected process, we execute all processes, or exit prematurely if a given logical condition within the structure is satisfied.

For example, consider a problem in which we are to execute a sequence of logical processes, P_0, $P_1(f_1)$, $P_2(f_2)$, $P_3(f_3)$ where $f_n = P_{n-1}(f_{n-1})$. If the result of any one of the processes is false, we must execute an error process P_x. If process P_i fails, a specified set of conditions must be restored before executing P_x. The solution can be represented by the nested-**if-else** structure as

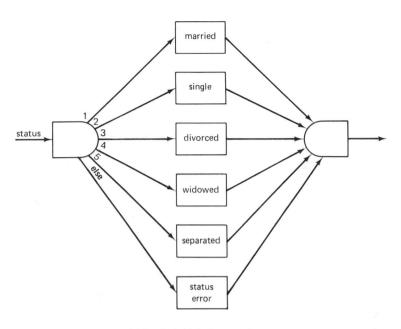

Fig. 4-18 **Case** logical control structure

```
Process P₀
if(f₁)
      Process P₁
      if(f₂)
            Process P₂
            if(f₃)
                  Process P₃
            else
                  Process Pₓ
            end if
      else
            Process Restore
            Process Pₓ
      end if
else
      Process Pₓ
end if
```

The representation of the solution for n = 3 is simple and straightforward. If we extend the problem to include n = 25, we observe that the nesting is out of control. A structure is again required to reduce the nesting problem to a manageable level.

The construct required to satisfy this requirement is the **posit-else** logical structure. The **posit** clause of the structure is executed as long as none of the logical *exit* or error conditions in the clause is satisfied. In other words, before we begin execution of the **posit** clause, we postulate a set of conditions; if any of the postulated conditions are disproved, we immediately abandon the **posit** clause and execute the **else** clause. The construct is written as

```
posit
        Process A
else
        Process B
end posit
```

Looking back at the P_n example, we could describe the solution, using the **posit-else** structure, as

```
posit
        Process P₀
        quit posit if (─┐f₁)
        Process P₁
        if(─┐f₂)
                Process Restore
                quit posit
        end if
        Process P₂
        quit posit if (─┐f₃)
        Process P₃
else
        Process Pₓ
end posit
```

which is considerably easier to read and understand. We have been forced to introduce the concept of an exit[37] (**quit**) mechanism here to complete this special form of the selection structure. In this instance the **quit** provides the limited range branching capability necessary to implement the structure. The branching capability provided by the **quit posit** statement allows control to pass only to the **else** clause of the structure. In addition to improving the format of the code, the **posit-else** structure allows us to include only one copy of process P_x in the source instead of n copies as required by the nested-**if** version.

The **posit-else** structure, which is schematically represented in Figure 4-19, is an important tool in the implementation of the "backtracking"[38] concept in program design. The example involving the sequence of processes P_n we used to introduce the **posit** structure can be construed as an example of the backtracking concept. We initially assumed that the sequence P_n was valid upon entry to the **posit**. At certain points in the sequence, we tested the validity of our assumption and, as long as the assumption was valid, we continued the execution of the sequence; if the assumption was proved incorrect at any point, we "backtracked" to the alternate block (**else**), which

[37]A detailed explanation of exit class of structures and their application is contained in the following section.

[38]M. A. Jackson, *Principles of Program Design* (London: Academic Press, Inc., 1975).

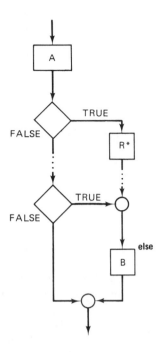

*Process R represents the code required
to restore pre-**posit** conditions prior to
entering **else** clause.

Fig. 4-19 **posit-else** logical control structure

contained the sequence to be executed if the sequence P_n was invalid. In many situations it is necessary to "restore" conditions or variables to a state that existed prior to entry into the **posit**. Those situations require that the conditions be tested in an **if** block and, if the condition for backtracking is satisfied, perform the restoration computations prior to branching to the **else** block of the **posit**. This type of processing is illustrated in the **posit** form of the P_n example in the test of f_2 prior to processing P_2.

ITERATION

Our collection of structured programming tools must contain at least one mechanism to provide a basic looping capability or a controlled repetition of portions of program code. The basic iteration structure can be one of two types, referred to as the **while** and **until** forms. Both forms of the iteration structure are shown in Figure 4-20.

The first, and most widely used, iteration form is the **while** structure. It specifies that process A is to be executed repetitively as long as the controlling predicate p is true. The structure can be represented in source code in several ways. The most obvious way, of course, is

```
while (p)
    Process A
end while
```

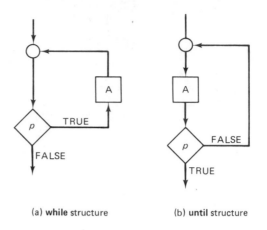

(a) **while** structure   (b) **until** structure

Fig. 4-20   Basic iteration control structures

and is read "*while p is true, execute repetitively process A.*" Other common representations that appear frequently in software literature are

$$\textbf{do while }(p)$$
$$\text{Process A}$$
$$\textbf{end do}$$

and

$$\textbf{iteration }(p)$$
$$\text{Process A}$$
$$\textbf{end iteration}$$

If the predicate is false upon entry to the structure, process A is not executed. Since predicate p is evaluated prior to the execution of process A, it is possible that A may never be executed. If p contains a variable that is initialized before entry into the structure, the variable must be modified as part of the process A. Failure to do this is one way to cause the program to execute an endless loop that violates one of the definitions of a proper program. For example, the sequence

$$\textbf{while } (a > b)$$
$$c = a^2 + b^2$$
$$\textbf{end while}$$

is equivalent to the infinite loop representation

$$\textbf{while } (.\text{TRUE}.)$$
$$\cdot$$
$$\cdot$$
$$\cdot$$
$$\textbf{end while}$$

The **until** form of the basic iteration structure that is shown in Figure 4-20 is written as

until (*p*)

Process A

end until

The representation of the **until** control structure is fundamentally different from the **while** form of the iteration structure in two ways. First, the **until** form tests the predicate *after* each execution of the process rather than before the execution as in the **while** structure. Thus, an **until** loop will always be performed at least once, regardless of the value of the predicate *p*. Second, the **until** iteration terminates when the predicate value is true, whereas the **while** loop terminates when the value is false.

The **until** structure can be interpreted as "Execute process A at least once and repeat *until* condition *p* is true."

The program defined by the code sequence

until (*p*)

Process A

end until

using the **until** structure, is equivalent to the program

Process A

while ($\neg p$)

Process A

end while

utilizing the **while** form of the iteration structure. The flowchart for the **while** representation of the **until** structure is shown in Figure 4-21, which illustrates that the statement

until (*p*)

is not equivalent to the statement

while ($\neg p$)

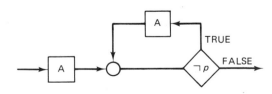

Fig. 4-21   **while** representation of the **until** iteration structure

Another common representation of the **until** structure seen in software literature is

> **repeat**
> > Process A
> **until** (p)

The following example illustrates an application of the **posit** selection structure and the **while** iteration structure.

EXAMPLE 4-2

Let us consider a subroutine required to analyze a character string S, recognizing two substrings S1 and S2, and printing them if and only if both substrings are present. Substring S1 is terminated by the character '@', and S2 is terminated by the character '&'. The string S is less than 100 characters long and terminated by the character '%'. The subroutine call

> CALL SUB (S, P)

passes the location of the string S and a pointer P to the current location in the string. The subroutine is required to print a report containing the two correct substrings as

> STRING 1 = fff. ... ff@
> STRING 2 = ggg ... gg&

when both are present and correct, and otherwise print the complete string starting at the character pointed to by P on entry in the form

> CHARACTER 1 = h
> CHARACTER 2 = i
> > . . .
> CHARACTER n = %

The resulting subroutine was implemented by using the Jackson design methodology. Since we are not interested in the design process here, we will list below only the main portion of the subroutine resulting from the design to illustrate the use of the two structures:

```
SS = P
posit
    blank workstring (WRKSTR)
    PS = 1
    while (S(SS) ≠ '@')
        quit posit if (S(SS) = '%')
        WRKSTR(PS) = S(SS)
        SS = SS + 1
        PS = PS + 1
    end while
    WRKSTR(PS) = S(SS)
    SS = SS + 1
    SAVE = WRKSTR
    blank workstring
    PS = 1
```

```
          while (S(SS) ≠ '&')
              quit posit if (S(SS) = '%')
              WRKSTR(PS) = S(SS)
              SS = SS + 1
              PS = PS + 1
          end while
          WRKSTR(PS) = S(SS)
          print 'STRING 1 = ', SAVE
          print 'STRING 2 = ', WRKSTR
      else
          SS = P
          CHN = 1
          while (S(SS) ≠ '%')
              print 'CHARACTER', CHN, '=', S(SS)
              SS = SS + 1
              CHN = CHN + 1
          end while
          print 'CHARACTER', CHN, '=', S(SS)
      end posit
```

This example also demonstrates the principle of backtracking which we mentioned earlier in the **posit** structure discussion. In this case we assume that substrings S1 and S2 are present and correct. Until we are sure the assumption is true, we do not print either string. If the assumption is false, the **quit posit** statement transfers control to the **else** block of the selection structure to process the invalid string sequence.

EXIT

The fourth class of essential control structures has been cloaked in controversy ever since Dijkstra's famous **go to** letter, which stated the quality of programmers was a decreasing function of the number of **go to** statements used in the programs they produced. At the time the statement was made, we were entering a period of history coinciding with the "software crisis" brought on by the ever-increasing complexity of software requirements and an apparent decrease in the quality of the resulting products. Software development methodologies were incapable of handling the large-scale software products under development.

Dijkstra's proposal is simple. Eliminating the **go to** statement will prevent the creation of unmaintainable programs with control structures that look like a bowl of spaghetti. Many believe that this simple proposal will lead to programs that are simple and elegant, and are easy to read, understand, and modify. The no **go to** rule is simple to understand and definitely improves the source code produced by most programmers. There are too many **go to** statements in most programs, and those programs appear more complex than they are, but this does not justify the elimination of the **go to** from our programming languages. As we mentioned earlier, the absence or rare occurrence of **go to** statements is no more than a symptom of structured programming, as illustrated in Figure 4-22. By losing the perspective given to us by the primary goals

ONLY
50 SOURCE
LINES PER
MODULE

STRUCTURED
PROGRAMMING

USES ONLY WHILE,
IF-ELSE, AND
SIMPLE SEQUENCE
STRUCTURES

NO GOTO
STATEMENTS

Fig. 4-22   Blind man's view of structured programming

of structured programming, we might also find ourselves losing sight of the definition of structured programming.

Before we ban the **go to** statement, we should consider three important points concerning the unconditional branch and its relationship to structured programming. First, the effect of the **go to** statement on program complexity is depicted in Figure 4-23. The figure is obviously a gross simplification, i.e., the scales on the axes are subjective and the surface should be somewhat lumpy, but the elementary principle is still valid and clear. For a simple problem the minimum program complexity does occur with zero **go to** statements. Unfortunately, most examples in technical papers and textbooks like this one fall into a category that supports the incorrect conclusion, often drawn from these examples, that the **go to** statement is unnecessary. As the complexity of the problem to be solved is increased, the attempts to eliminate all **go to** statements artificially increase the program's complexity by adding unnecessary flags to the program and additional logical tests in the predicates in the program control structure. The real world is not a very elegant place, and it is sometimes necessary to use an unsightly **go to** statement to minimize the complexity and enhance the maintainability of the program.

For example, there is a class of *event-driven structures* in which an unconditional branch or error exit is valuable. One such structure is the **posit** construct introduced earlier. Another of these is the SEARCH structure[39] that is shown in Figure 4-24. This structure is a common occurrence in programming. The objective of the SEARCH algorithm is to search a table or file of *n* elements until a specified data element *reference* is located. There must be two ways to terminate the search process: a *normal* exit that occurs when a matching element is located, and an *abnormal* exit when no matching element is located. Associated with each exit from the iteration structure is a process node to perform the necessary computations for the specified exit condi-

[39]D. E. Knuth, "Structured Programming with **go to** Statements," *Computing Surveys*, **6**, 4, December, 1974, 261–301.

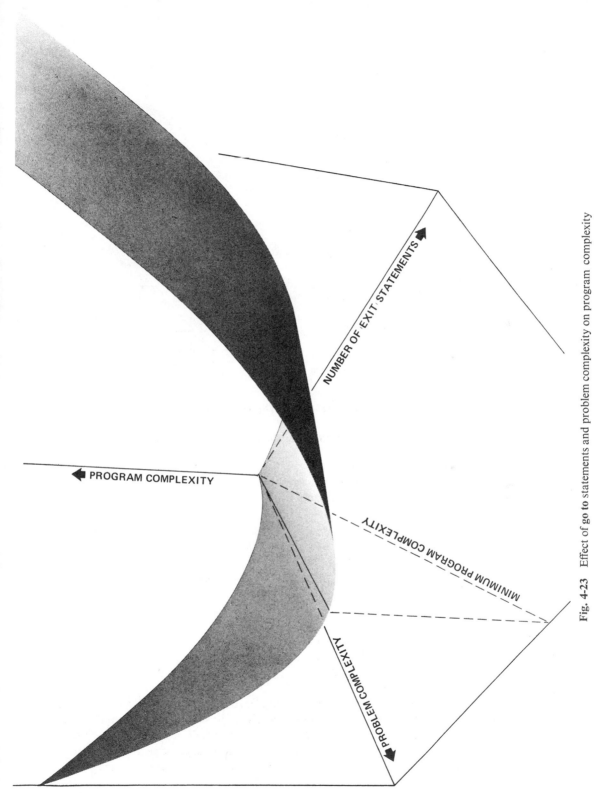

Fig. 4-23 Effect of **go to** statements and problem complexity on program complexity

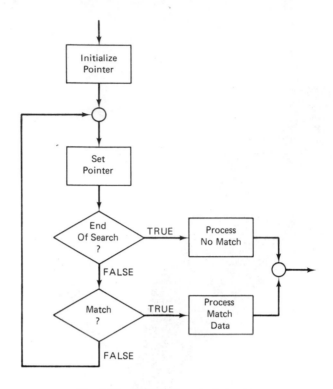

Fig. 4-24 SEARCH control structure

tion. There are many ways to implement the SEARCH algorithm. The code sequence

```
match = false
pointer = initial
until (match)
    if (pointer > n)
        Process no match
        exit until structure
    else
        if (reference = data (pointer))
            match = true
            Process match data
        end if
    end if
    pointer = pointer + 1
end until
```

is a representative implementation of this algorithm. Notice that an unconditional branching statement is used to terminate the iteration under the abnormal exit condition. Alternate implementations can be derived, which do not require the use of the unconditional branch. For example, a flag *endlst* could be set if pointer is greater than maxpointer and tested as part of the statement **until** (*match* | *endlst*). This establishes a single exit path at the expense of the additional variable and test suggested in the Structure Theorem, and at the expense of additional program complexity.

Second, storage space and execution time are frequent program development constraints. It is necessary to provide an unconditional branching capability to implement programs under these constraints.

An investigation by Peterson, Kasami, and Tokura[40] showed that a program could increase in length and execution time if its control logic was limited to the three basic constructs: sequence, **if-else**, and **while**. They also demonstrated that if we allow a program to increase in size while retaining the execution speed of its unstructured equivalent program, the sequence, selection, and iteration structures must be supplemented by a multiple-level exit structure.

Third, the **go to** statement can be used as a primitive to construct missing or more advanced and elegant control structures in a programming language. For example, the **case** control structure is not available in the major high-order programming languages (FORTRAN, COBOL, and most implementations of PL/I). Creative programmers will develop new, powerful control structures, such as the **case**[41] and the **posit**[42] structures, as the need appears. The new structures will be difficult to implement without the **go to** primitive.

The need for an exit class of structures is apparent. Yet, as Dijkstra observed:

> The **go to** statement as it stands is just too primitive; it is too much an invitation to make a mess of one's program. . . .[43]

There are two characteristics about a well-formed structured program that will lay our fears to rest: (1) by using the refinement process to develop the control structure of the program, the unconditional branch statement should rarely occur (some of the program conditions requiring the branch statement are enumerated by Knuth[44] and need not be discussed here) and (2) the first requirement of the well-formed program that we defined in Sec. 4.3.1 limits a program to precisely one input line. The implication of this first requirement is that a sequence of code can be entered only through the path connecting it to the preceding program block, as shown in Figure 4-25(a). Unconditional branches are then limited to paths leading to the end of the program block. Exit paths to any other part of the control structure will create additional input lines to a program block. Note that in our definition of an improper but well-formed process node, the predicate node protruding from the side of the process node to indicate an abnormal exit is actually contained in the process. Thus, the abnormal exit is not reentering the process in Figure 4-25(a), but the exit in Figure 4-25(b) is illegally reentering the previous program block. We must then conclude that any unconditional

[40]W. W. Peterson, T. Kasami, and N. Tokura, "On the Capabilities of While, Repeat, and Exit Statements," *Communications of the ACM*, **16**, 8, August, 1973, 503–12.

[41]N. Wirth and C.A.R. Hoare, "A Contribution to the Development of Algol," *Communications of the ACM*, **9**, 6, June, 1966, 413–31.

[42]M. A. Jackson, *Principles of Program Design* (London: Academic Press, Inc., 1975).

[43]E. W. Dijkstra, "Go To Statement Considered Harmful," *Communications of the ACM*, **11**, 3, March, 1968, 147–48. Reprinted with permission of the Association for Computing Machinery.

[44]D. E. Knuth, "Structured Programming with **go to** Statements," *Computing Surveys*, **6**, 4, December, 1974, 261–301.

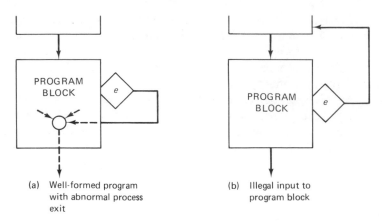

(a) Well-formed program with abnormal process exit

(b) Illegal input to program block

Fig. 4-25 Restricted range of exit

branch or abnormal process exit in a well-formed program must be forward to the end of the associated program block.

We will define two structures in the exit class: **escape** and **cycle**. The **escape** structure is an unconditional branch to the end of the associated structure. If the exit is from an iteration structure, the branch is to the "outside" of the iteration loop, as shown in Figure 4-26(a). Conversely, the **cycle** structure is an unconditional branch to the predicate controlling the next iteration, or to the "inside" of the iteration loop, as shown in Figure 4-26(b). The **escape** structure is defined for all of the selection and iteration structures, but obviously it will be most valuable in the iteration structures for abnormal exits or to mechanize special functions such as the SEARCH control structure. The **cycle** structure is defined only for iteration structures.

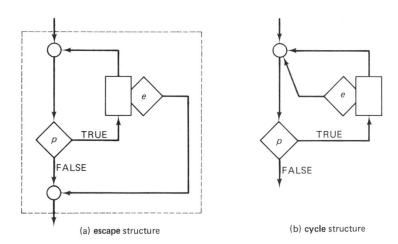

(a) **escape** structure

(b) **cycle** structure

Fig. 4-26 Exit structures

EXAMPLE 4-3

We are to process a stream of text in the following way: we must read and print each character from the input data stream except for three special conditions:

1. If the input character is a period ($\cdot$), an additional space must be inserted in the output string following the period.
2. If the input character is a slash (/), we must advance the output to the next tab-stop position.
3. If two consecutive slashes (//) appear in the input, the output is advanced to the beginning of the next line.

A program that performs this processing is:

```
start: while (true)
           x = next character
           if (x = '/')
               x = next character
               if (x = '/')
                   Execute carriage return
                   cycle start
               else
                   Execute tabulate
               end if
           end if
           escape start if (x = end of string)
           write character (x)
           if (x = '·')
               write character (blank)
           end if
       end while
```

This example is written to illustrate the practical application of a **cycle** statement to branch to the next iteration of the **while** structure labeled *start* and an **escape** to exit the structure under a discovered terminating condition. The **escape** could be eliminated by replacing the **escape** and the code following it with the code

```
           if (x ≠ end of string)
               write character (x)
               if (x = '·')
                   write character (blank)
               end if
           end if
       end while
```

and by replacing the **while** statement with the statement

```
start: while (x ≠ end of string)
```

The modified version without the **escape** has the advantage of placing the terminating condition for the iteration in the **while** statement. Other than that, the clarity of the two versions is about equal. The first version is slightly more efficient because the number of predicate evaluations is decreased. We must point out here that the complexity of the control structure required to eliminate the **escape** increases with the number of nesting levels involved in the exit. It is simple to eliminate single level exits generally, but multiple level exits involving **escape** statements can seldom be replaced by simple **if-else** and iteration structures without paying a high price in program clarity.

The **cycle** statement could have been eliminated by using a flag variable to indicate the occurrence of a double slash in the input stream, but its use would be a pointless increase in complexity in order to eliminate the perfectly understandable **cycle** statement.

4.3.3 PROGRAM DEVELOPMENT TOOLS

There are three basic techniques that can be effectively used to describe a program's logic during the design or refinement process at the module level. These techniques are: (1) flowcharts, (2) pseudocode, and (3) schematic logic. All of these methods are useful, and the superiority of one method over another is primarily a matter of personal choice. We will devote our energy toward the description of pseudocode and schematic logic, while saying little about flowcharts in this section, because the use of flowcharts is generally understood. In the major example at the end of Sec. 4.3.4, Structuring Process, all three design notations will be demonstrated in parallel to simplify the comparison of their major features.

PSEUDOCODE

Pseudocode is a notation that bridges the gap between the programmer's native language and the computer language. The notation is frequently referred to as "structured English" because of the apparent combination of the basic elements of structured programming and the English language. It is a language that allows the programmer to think about the problem to be solved and express the program's logic in a somewhat formalized way without having to be concerned with the syntax of a specific programming language. The notation allows the programmer to deal with the problem at various levels of abstraction without being concerned about program details—much like the flowchart, which can also depict functional properties of a program without complicating the program representation with unnecessary details. Pseudocode resembles a programming language in that explicit operations can be specified such as

> Set initial count = 1
> Print range rate error

It differs from a programming language in two ways:

1. Operations can be specified at any level of complexity. For example:

   > Temporary = (a(i, n+1) − sum)/a(i,i)
   > Compute target rate of closure

2. There are no formal syntactical rules to limit freedom of use. The only conventions governing the use of pseudocode are related to the use of the control structures and the indentation that improves clarity. The pseudocode program descriptions included in the previous examples to illustrate the use of structures are typical of the freedom available.

Pseudocode is also a program design language that is intended for use during the refinement process to describe the program's operation at each level of refinement. This provides a convenient way for a programmer to document the stages of program development for his own use and also allows other programmers to review the function of the program before it is translated into a programming language and facilitates an assessment of the development status at any stage of the refinement process. Since the entire design up to the translation of the pseudocode to a programming language is conducted in English, greater coordination between the members of the development team, management, and the customer is possible.

Since pseudocode allows the designer to work with a language at a level higher than a programming language, it is easier to implement design changes in the program. The changes in program logic are more apparent at the pseudocode level than when the logic is complicated by the details of the language at machine level.

The pseudocode notation also provides a detailed description of the completed source program that can be, or should be, maintained as part of the program documentation as a substitute for flowcharts. As with flowcharts, the pseudocode must be updated to record changes to the program implemented after the design is completed.

Pseudocode has no formal guidelines to direct the user in his application of the tool. The tool should be a natural extension of the thinking process, and should be used in any way that makes sense to the programmer. There are a few general guidelines that will make the use of pseudocode more effective. These include:

Pseudocode is an Extension of the Thinking Process. The statements used should be related to the stepwise refinement process and should result in a structured program. To guide the thinking process and assist in creating an acceptable structure, the use of control structures not allowed on a given project should be discouraged.

Indent Code to Highlight Logic Structure.

Use Self-defining Data Names. The language has no variable length limitations. The name TEMP has several possible meanings. The name TEMPERATURE is more obvious. The name PTR7 may refer to pointer 7, but the name does not provide much information about the intent of the variable. Also the pseudocode statements should be meaningful and self-explanatory.

Keep the Program Logic Simple. The program logic should be kept as simple as possible to reduce the probability of errors and minimize the maintenance effort. Code first for clarity and then modify for efficiency. As Knuth aptly stated:

> "... Programmers waste enormous amounts of time thinking about, or worrying about, the speed of noncritical parts of their programs, and these attempts at efficiency actually have a strong negative impact when debugging and maintenance are considered. We *should* forget about small efficiencies, say about 97% of the time: premature optimization is the root of all evil.
>
> Yet we should not pass up our opportunities in that critical 3%. A good programmer will not be lulled into complacency by that reasoning, he will be wise to look carefully at the critical code; but only *after* that code has been identified. ..."[45]

[45]D. E. Knuth, "Structured Programming with **go to** Statements," *Computing Surveys*, **6**, 4, December, 1974, 268. Reprinted with permission of the Association for Computing Machinery, Copyright 1974.

Use Control Structures in the Form Allowed by the Project. If a specified structure is of the form **if-else-endif**, use the structure in that form. For example,

```
if (malfunction switch = off)
    Calculate mean smog density for 24-hour period
else
    Set mean smog density = 1000 ppm
endif
```

Each statement in a sequence should be written on a separate line. These statements may be expanded in a later step of the refinement process and will cause chaos and confusion if multiple operations are allowed on a single line.

EXAMPLE 4-4

Temperature data in degrees Kelvin is recorded in a file automatically at the rate of one measurement per minute. A subroutine is to be written to provide the average recorded temperature value over a one-hour period. If a zero reading exists in the data file, the mean value for that one-hour period is to be set to 0.0.

A pseudocode solution of the function to be performed by the subroutine is

```
sum = 0
minute = 1
while (minute ≤ 60)
    if (file (minute) ≠ 0)
        sum = sum + file (minute)
    else
        sum = 0.0
        escape while
    end if
    minute = minute + 1
end while
mean = sum/60
```

The pseudocode clearly describes the function to be performed, which can be translated directly into any of the major programming languages. Consider an equivalent program that violates some of the general guidelines suggested for the use of psedudocode. The equivalent program is

$$hrs = 0$$

$$k = 1$$

```
while (k < 61)
if (a(k) ≠ 0) hrs = hrs + a(k)
else hrs = 0.0 ; escape while
end while
avg = hrs/60
```

Hopefully we have violated more of the guidelines than any individual programmer would in order to emphasize the effects of the violations on the code readability. The violations include: (1) no indentation of the code, (2) meaningless variable and data names, (3) multiple operations per line, and (4) an incomplete **if-else-endif** structure. Any one of these violations will significantly reduce the effectiveness of the pseudocode.

SCHEMATIC LOGIC

The third notation for describing a module's logic structure during the design and implementation phases is called schematic logic. The method provides a clear graphical representation of the program structure and a notation that is very amenable to the stepwise refinement process. A predecessor of the notation was introduced by Jackson[46] as a means for describing the structure of the data related to a task and the structure of the resulting program, based on the data structure, which processes that data. A modification of Jackson's original use of the notation provides us with a unique and powerful stepwise refinement design tool.

Schematic logic is a design notation, much like pseudocode, that allows the programmer to think in terms of the problem to be solved in a quasi-formal way without having to deal with the syntax of a programming language. It provides a graphical representation of the various stages of the solution, as does a functional flowchart. However, the schematic logic diagram allows for expansion in the level of representation detail without destroying any of the abstract information describing the program, and without partially or totally reconstructing the program representation. This way, it can present a history of the development through the levels of conceptualization and provide a useful analysis aid in evaluating design trade-offs at any level.

The basic building blocks used with the schematic logic notation are shown in Figure 4-27. The graphic notation depicted in Figure 4-27(a) represents a sequence of operations consisting of processes B, C, D, . . . , n. These operations comprise function A. For example, the function "Process Daily Temperature Data" given in Figure 4-28(a) can be expanded into the sequence shown in Figure 4-28(b). Function A consists of a sequence (reading from left to right) of three processes. The expansion represents the present state of development of Function A, which is certainly not near the machine level of conceptualization. Each of the processes must be expanded further during the development process.

The notation for the selection structures is specified in parts (b), (c), (d), and (e) of Figure 4-27. Each component of this type of structure is marked with a small circle in the upper right-hand corner of the process box. The processes (components) that comprise function A are mutually exclusive, i.e., only one of the processes subordinate to function A will be executed. The logical condition causing the selection of the subordinate process is written adjacent to the process box. For example, if we expand the process "Process marital status" by using the nested-**if** construct depicted in Figure 4.16, we obtain the schematic logic representation shown in Figure 4-29(a) that illus-

---

[46]M. A. Jackson, *Principles of Program Design* (London: Academic Press, Inc., 1975).

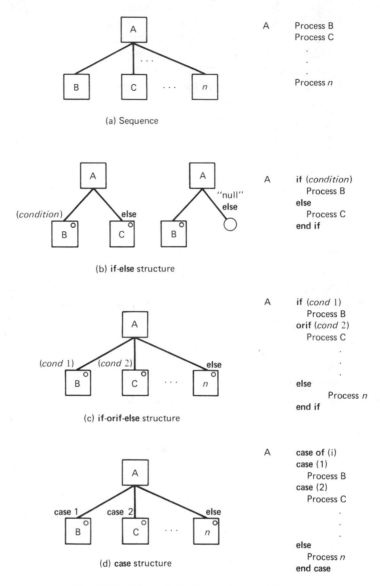

A	Process B Process C . . . Process *n*

(a) Sequence

A	**if** (*condition*)
	  Process B
	else
	  Process C
	end if

(b) **if-else** structure

A	**if** (*cond* 1)
	  Process B
	orif (*cond* 2)
	  Process C
	  .
	  .
	  .
	else
	    Process *n*
	end if

(c) **if-orif-else** structure

A	**case of** (i)
	case (1)
	  Process B
	case (2)
	  Process C
	  .
	  .
	  .
	else
	  Process *n*
	end case

(d) **case** structure

Fig. 4-27 Schematic logic structure notation

trates both the use of the **if-else** notation and an application of structure nesting. The **if-orif-else** and the **case** implementations of the marital status problem are shown in parts (b) and (c) of the same figure. Note that in the selection forms of the notation, as in sequence form, the ordering of the subordinate processes is from left to right.

The iteration structure notation is shown in Figure 4-27(f). This representation defines the function A as an iteration of process B. In the case where the iteration is of the **while** form, process B is iterated *zero* or more times; process B is iterated *one* or more times in the **until** form. The iteration is represented in the schematic logic nota-

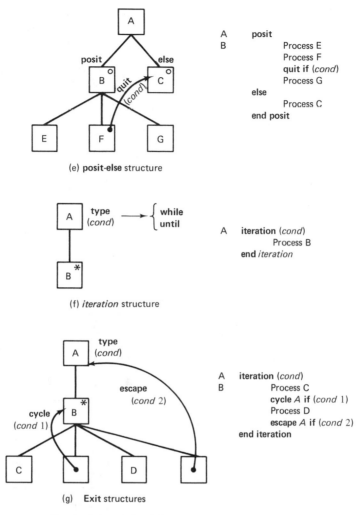

(e) **posit-else** structure

```
A       posit
B               Process E
                Process F
                quit if (cond)
                Process G
        else
                Process C
        end posit
```

(f) *iteration* structure

```
A       iteration (cond)
                Process B
        end iteration
```

(g)   **Exit structures**

```
A       iteration (cond)
B               Process C
                cycle A if (cond 1)
                Process D
                escape A if (cond 2)
        end iteration
```

Fig. 4-27 (*cont'd.*)   Schematic logic structure notation

tion by an asterisk in the upper right-hand corner of the process box. The iteration type and the terminating condition are specified adjacent to the function box.

As an example of the use of the iteration structure notation, consider the "Process Data Covering 24-Hour Period" function introduced in Figure 4-28(b). An expansion of that function presented in Figure 4-30 contains two iteration structures and an **escape** statement necessary to provide an abnormal exit path. The first **while** structure iteratively processes one-hour periods of data until the predicate (hr $\leq$ 24) is satisfied. Note that the terminating condition is not entered adjacent to the primary function until the primary function is expanded.

Subordinate to the process "Process 1-hr Period" is a sequence of four processes.

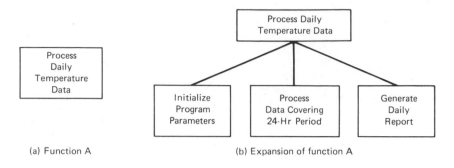

(a) Function A   (b) Expansion of function A

Fig. 4-28 Representation of a sequence of operations in schematic logic

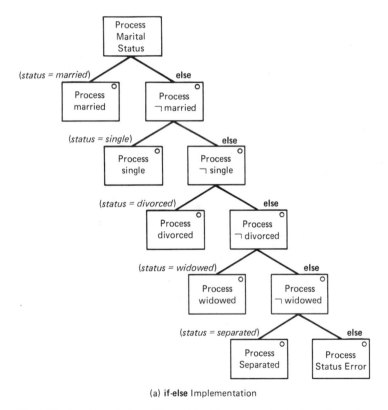

(a) **if-else** Implementation

Fig. 4-29 Implementation of marital status processing using schematic logic

These processes must all be of the same type as specified in the definitions in Figure 4-27; i.e., the group of processes directly subordinate to a function must all be sequence processes, selection processes, or a single iteration process. A mixture of the three process types is invalid. It would not be correct, nor would it make any sense, to combine the "Process Data" box and the "Process 1-min Period" box into a single iteration box. When expanding a function into a sequence of processes, the schematic

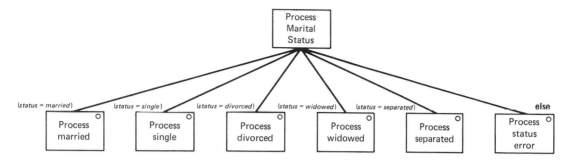

(b) **if-orif-else** Implementation

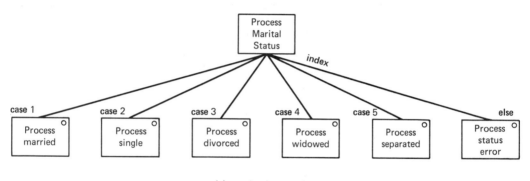

(c) **case** Implementation

Fig. 4-29 (*cont'd.*) Implementation of marital status processing using schematic logic

logic diagram should be self-contained and should not require information subordinate to the sequence. (To test this condition in Figure 4-30, remove the iterative func tion "Process 1-min Period" from the diagram.)

The exit path connecting the process "Accumulate Temperature Data" to "Process Data" is activated under a file error condition. The specific condition and mechanism for the exit are not known at this level of conceptualization and cannot be specified in this expansion. A further expansion of the function "Process Data" shown in Figure 4-31 supplies the details for the exit mechanism and the condition can be entered on the diagram.

The use of the **cycle** statement and other details about the schematic logic notation are illustrated in Figure 4-32. This figure presents a schematic logic version of the text processing example that was used to demonstrate the use of the exit structures. (See Example 4-3.) The most important points demonstrated by the example are: (1) The **escape** statement returns control to the function controlling the iteration. (2) The **cycle** statement passes control to the next iteration. (3) The selection notation requires the specification of an **else** process with an **if** statement even if the **else** process is "*null.*" (A null process can be indicated by a line or the word *null* in the process box as

Sec. 4.3 Theory and Techniques

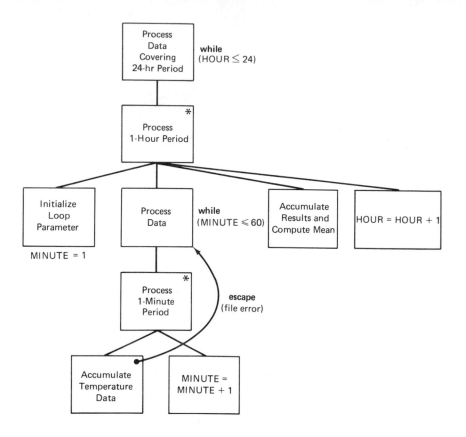

Fig. 4-30 Expansion of a process containing iteration structures

well as the notation shown.) (4) A long sequence of instructions in the program at the machine level cannot reasonably be drawn as a schematic logic sequence with one instruction per box. In this case, a sequence of instructions can be grouped within a box if they are related to an individual process and if they will not be expanded at a later refinement. For example, the process "Initialize Parameters" might include statements like

$$INDEX = 0$$

$$COUNT = 1$$

$$ARRAY = 0$$

The guidelines for the use of schematic logic are almost identical to the guidelines for the application of pseudocode as a design tool. Schematic logic, like pseudocode, is an extension of the thinking process and provides a graphical representation of that process. However, unlike the flowchart and pseudocode representations, the schematic logic diagram retains the history of the development process as an analysis aid for future design trade-off studies. The only major pseudocode guidelines that do not apply to schematic logic are:

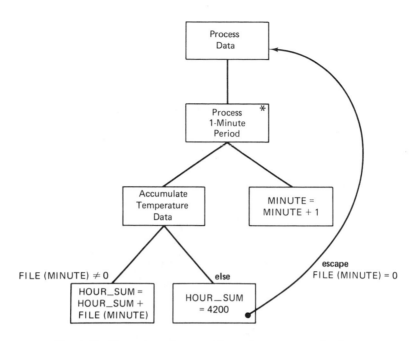

Fig. 4-31   Expansion of process illustrating **escape** mechanism

1. Code must be indented to highlight logic structure. The indentation of the logic control structure is automatic in schematic logic.
2. The pseudocode statements should be meaningful. The box size in the schematic logic diagram limits the information content possible. Descriptive abbreviations are a necessity in this representation.

Effective use of either schematic logic or pseudocode, or both, in a design environment requires that the notation be natural and nonrestrictive so that the programmer's thinking process is not encumbered with the usage guidelines related to the design tools.

4.3.4 STRUCTURING PROCESS

Programming has been considered an art since its emergence as a profession in the 1950s. The reason for the classification can be primarily attributed to the lack of definition or understanding of the design methods used by programmers. Although many excellent programs have been completed during the intervening years, the methods by which they were developed remain a mystery to the observer; the program developer is also frequently at a loss for words when asked to explain his programming methods. Programming still is, to a great extent, an art applied by craftsmen of the trade.

Until recently, very little has been written on the process of designing and implementing program code, and training in the "science" of programming has been almost nonexistent. Consider for a moment the training you received in elementary

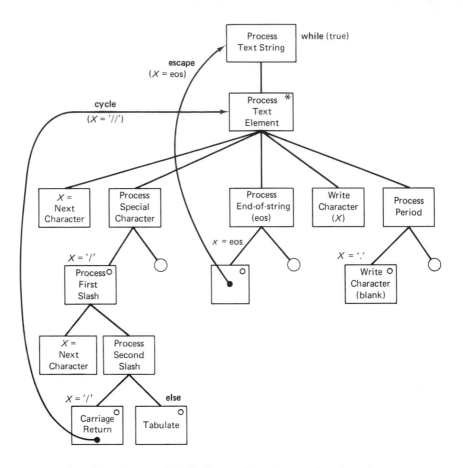

Fig. 4-32 Schematic logic diagram for text processing algorithm

programming. We can assume with relatively high confidence that the training con-sisted of a few brief lectures on the syntax of a specific programming language, sup-ported by either a manufacturer's reference manual or an elementary text covering the language syntax with a few coding examples and homework problems. Upon success-ful(?) completion of the homework assignments and one or more tests on the language syntax, a diploma was awarded, certifying mastery of the "art of programming." (Just like the Scarecrow in the Land of Oz.)

The work of Dijkstra, Wirth, Weinberg, and several others in recent years has contributed much to the realization that the most effective programming methodology is based on the human method of mentally analyzing and solving problems. As Weinberg observed:[47]

> Programming is a mirror of the mind.

[47]G. Weinberg, "Primer on Programming," *THINK*, International Business Machines Corp., October/November, 1974, p. 21.

The mental tool fundamental to effective program development is common to all forms of engineering. This tool for coping with complex problems is *abstraction*. A complex problem cannot be attacked initially in terms of machine instructions, but it can be approached in terms and entities natural to the problem itself. In this process, the abstract program formulated in a suitable language, such as pseudocode, performs operations on abstract data. The operations (e.g., compute mean temperature value) are then considered as program components that are subjected to decomposition to the next *lower* level of abstraction. This process is continued to a level that can finally be understood by the computer.

The process we have briefly outlined is known as *stepwise refinement*. It is a procedure that involves decomposing the function of a module into an expanded set of subfunctions that perform the module function. Each of these subfunctions is independently decomposed further into an expanded, but equivalent, set of subfunctions that are ultimately expanded into operations that can be translated directly into a programming language. Although this refinement technique can be applied to the total decomposition of a program into its elementary program statements, it is most effective as a tool for decomposing each module of a program into the internal logic necessary to perform the module function. Program decomposition techniques, such as those described in Chapter 3, are more effective in establishing the program hierarchy chart and the functional definition of each module.

Note that this method of stepwise refinement permits only the rare occurrence of unconditional branches because the subfunctions have no requirement to communicate with each other. If the requirement does occur during the refinement process, the decomposition is usually in error. The absence of unconditional branches is *not* the goal of the process, but is a *result* of the process. As we will observe in the examples in this section, a branching statement will be used only to improve the clarity and maintainability of the program. We will observe in later sections that programs written in FORTRAN require the use of unconditional branches to emulate the control structures defined in this chapter.

The refinement process requires the use of some type of notation to assist in the mental management of the program development. The pseudocode notation will be used throughout this discussion and in the major example at the end of this section. The flowchart and schematic logic notations will also be used in the major example. Pseudocode has the advantage over the other two methods of being a compact notation, i.e., the space required to describe a program segment is minimal.

Stepwise refinement is an iterative process in which additional details about the module operation are brought out with each pass through the module.

EXAMPLE 4-5

The function

Process Text String

illustrated in Figure 4-32 can be expanded into the sequence of operations

$$
\text{Process Text String} \quad
\begin{cases}
\textbf{while} \ (\text{true}) \\
\quad \text{Process text element} \\
\quad \textbf{escape if} \ (\text{element} = \text{end of string}) \\
\textbf{end while}
\end{cases}
$$

At the next level of decomposition, the operation

Process Text Element

can be expanded into

$$
\text{Process Text Element} \quad
\begin{cases}
x = \text{next character in string} \\
\text{Process end-of-string character} \\
\text{Process special character (/)} \\
\text{Write character (x)} \\
\text{Process period}
\end{cases}
$$

Inserting the expanded function "Process text element" into the function "Process Text String," we observe that the insert does not fit perfectly, i.e., the **escape** statement should not appear at the end of the process, but should be located after the "Process end-of-string" operation. This introduces a second dimension in the iteration process. The first iteration dimension is to progressively lower levels of abstraction. The second dimension is an iteration within the first iteration to resolve any potential conflicts that might occur during the refinement process. As a result of the resolution of the conflict, we have

$$
\text{Process Text String} \quad
\begin{cases}
\textbf{while} \ (\text{true}) \\
\quad x = \text{next character in string} \\
\quad \text{Process end-of-string character} \\
\quad \textbf{escape if} \ (\text{element} = \text{end-of-string}) \\
\quad \text{Process special character (/)} \\
\quad \text{Write character (x)} \\
\quad \text{Process period} \\
\textbf{end while}
\end{cases}
$$

The next level of refinement expands the three processes internal to "Process Text String." The most complex of the decompositions is

$$
\text{Process Special Character} \quad
\begin{cases}
\textbf{if} \ (x = '/') \\
\quad x = \text{next character in string} \\
\quad \textbf{if} \ (x = '/') \\
\quad\quad \text{Execute carriage return} \\
\quad\quad \textbf{cycle while} \ (\text{Process next character}) \\
\quad \textbf{else} \\
\quad\quad \text{Execute tabulate} \\
\quad \textbf{end if} \\
\textbf{end if}
\end{cases}
$$

The expansion requires another second dimension iteration to account for the "x = next character in string" operation. Since x can be an end-of-string character, we can insert a second **escape** statement to process that condition just before the second **end if** statement of the expanded "Process Special Character" function, or we can rearrange the processes so the special character is processed before the end-of-string character. The end-of-string character processing is accomplished by the existing **escape** statement. The resulting program segment is then

```
                          while (true)
                              x = next character in string
                              if (x = '/')
                                  x = next character in string
                                  if (x = '/')
                                      Execute carriage return
                                      cycle while (Process next character)
                                  else
Process Text String                   Execute tabulate
                                  end if
                              end if
                              escape while if (x = end-of-string)
                              Write character (x)
                              if (x = '.')
                                  Write character (blank)
                              end if
                          end while
```

In using stepwise refinement as a programming methodology, each iteration provides a more detailed description of the program control logic. The initial iterations provide very general processes, and the designations of these processes in the development are in language that is very close to the specification. As the refinement process approaches the machine level, the language appears more like a programming language.

One of the disadvantages of pseudocode is apparent in Example 4-5. As each level of detail replaces the previous level, the abstract process descriptions are lost. The major example that follows later in this section demonstrates one method of preventing this occurrence.

There are several important guidelines to keep in mind while developing a program structure by stepwise refinement: we must

Postpone Details. Program details at the abstract design levels are trivia that cloud the thinking process. It is important to consider the major functions of the module early in the refinement without getting confused by details that are not necessary until later refinement steps.

Details should come into focus only when they have a direct impact on the refinement process.

Make Decisions at Each Level of Abstraction Carefully. At each refinement stage, some decisions are obvious and easy to make; other decisions are subtle. We must try to analyze each decision as it is made to thoroughly understand the implications associated with that decision. We must consider all of the alternatives, but not get trapped by the details at far-removed lower levels. This trap is related to the old saying "Can't see the forest for the trees."

Be Flexible. No decision is final. Problems will arise that require earlier decisions to be revoked or modified. We should not be intimidated by the existing structure. Each revision to the program logic due to corrections of discovered errors should improve the overall structure.

Consider the Data. As the refinement process is carried to lower levels of abstraction, data items necessary for the function of the module will be uncovered. As these data items appear (they will also be abstract at first), we need to keep track of them and refine their definitions as greater detail is available. The data items and the logic structure are both functions of decisions made during the decomposition of the module functions. The data required for any program configuration is an important item to consider in the decision process.

The best way to describe the structuring process is by example. We will consider one detailed example here. Our example demonstrates the process and the notations available as design aids in an air pollution data reduction program.

EXAMPLE 4-6

As an example of the stepwise refinement program development methodology, we will implement the design of a simple air pollution data reduction program. The implementation of the design will be described at each refinement step by flowchart, pseudocode listing, and schematic logic diagram to demonstrate and compare the use of the three methods in this type of application.

Program Specification

Air pollution measurements are made at a field monitoring station near the San Diego Freeway in the Los Angeles basin at one-minute intervals for a 24-hour period. The pollution measurements recorded in parts per million (ppm) are stored on magnetic tape. The valid data range is from 0 ppm to 100 ppm of pollutant. The functional requirements for the program are:

1. Compute the average (mean) air pollution value for each of the 24 one-hour periods.
2. Maintain a count of the number of valid data points recorded during each one-hour period. If the data is valid for less than 70% (42 data points) of the total recording period, print an invalid data flag in the output report indicating an equipment malfunction.
3. Write a daily report that contains the hour, the average air pollution level (ppm) for that hour, a count of the valid measurements ($0 \leq$ count ≤ 60) for that hour, and the flag (if

set) that indicates an equipment malfunction during the period. The report should be in the following format:

Hour	Average AP Level (ppm)	Measurements	Malfunction
01	0.012	59	
02	0.053	53	
03	0.076	49	
04	1.069	37	*
05	0.064	48	
06	0.083	57	
07	0.102	59	
.	.	.	
16	24.601	51	
.	.	.	
24	0.021	58	

The most abstract version of the program can be written as a single statement: Reduce air pollution data and generate report for 24-hour period or, in a more abbreviated form, "Reduce Air Pollution Data."

The first refinement step in the development process decomposes the primary program function into a sequence of abstract processes that establish the general operation of the program. The three versions of the first refinement step are shown in Figure 4-33 where the basic data processing steps have been established. The functions of the first and last steps in the program cannot be completely expanded at this time since they depend primarily on the data elements required to execute the processing of the daily data. Many of these elements may not be defined until the final steps of the refinement process. Therefore, we must concentrate our activity on the second abstract function "Process Daily Data."

The first major program decision must be made at this point in our design. Should we save all of the elements, or data, for the output report as it is accumulated in an output area to be written later in one write operation? Or should we write the report one line at a time as the data is available and save the storage space required for a buffer area? In this case, we will risk a sacrifice in speed and generate the daily air pollution report one line at a time. This design decision also requires that a report heading be written in the function "Initialize Program" prior to any other output operations.

The program functional requirements provide a key to the computation necessary in the "Process Daily Data" function. For each hour of the 24-hour period, we must process one hour's stored data. Thus, we conclude that the function that processes the hour's collected data must be executed repetitively 24 times. This is illustrated as the second level of refinement in Figure 4-34. With each pass through the process "Process Hourly Report," we can identify three distinct tasks associated with the hourly report processing: (1) Process a block of data representing a one-hour measurement period, (2) output a line in the daily report corresponding to those measurements, and (3) increment a counter to the next hour. The first two tasks are major and may involve considerable processing. The third task appears minor, but it is an essential element in mechanizing the major program loop that determines the amount of data to be processed. This counter must also be initialized to correctly execute the loop. At this time it is worthwhile to note that the variable HOUR should be set in the

(a) Pseudocode

(b) Flowchart

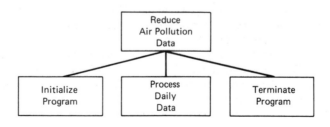

(c) Schematic logic

Fig. 4-33 Stepwise refinement step one

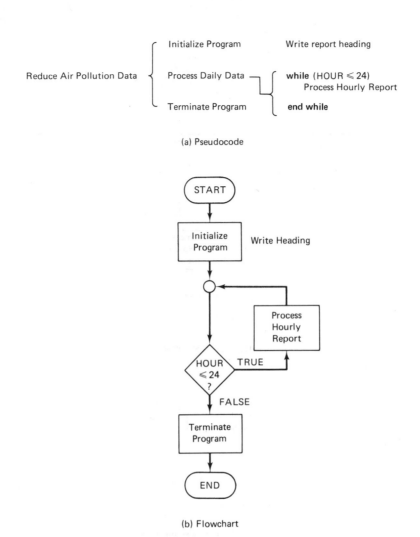

(a) Pseudocode

(b) Flowchart

Fig. 4-34 Stepwise refinement step two

"Initialize Program" process. At each stage in the decomposition, we should study the program in its present level of expansion to evaluate the decisions we have made to arrive at the present program configuration and what consequences might arise from our decisions. We should also evaluate the data implications based on the present design configuration at each step. At the end of the third step shown in Figure 4-35 we have defined the output variables: Average air pollution (AAP), COUNT, malfunction flag (MFG), and HOUR, which also serves as the major loop counter. A list of these data elements must be maintained from this point in the program development. A data list for this design is shown in Table 4-2. As new data items and/or their attributes become known, the necessary information will be added to the list.

The next major step in the refinement process is the expansion of the function "Process 1-Hour Data." We determine from the functional requirements that this function is a sequence

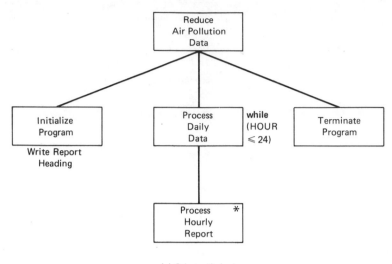

(c) Schematic logic

Fig. 4-34 (*cont'd.*) Stepwise refinement step two

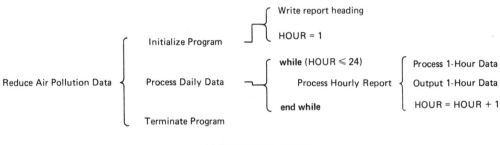

(a) Expanded pseudocode

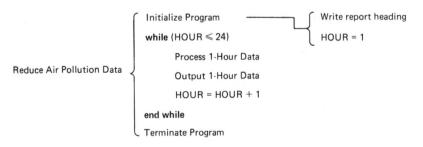

(b) Compressed pseudocode

Fig. 4-35 Stepwise refinement step three

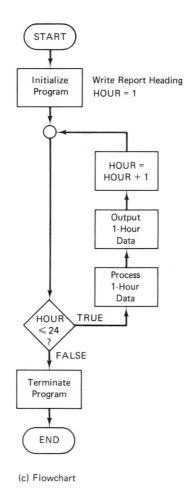

(c) Flowchart

Fig. 4-35 (*cont'd.*)   Stepwise refinement step three

of four steps: (1) Initialize the parameters for processing each data group. (2) Accumulate the valid data within the group for the computation of the average air pollution level. (3) Compute the average (mean) air pollution level. (4) Set the malfunction flag if the percentage of valid data is less than 70% or 42 data items per 60-minute period. This expansion is illustrated in Figure 4-36 as the fourth refinement step.

At this point in the expansion we must make an important decision regarding the processing of the data in the function "Accumulate Data Group." We can read and accumulate each data element individually, which requires a minimum of storage space but requires a separate *read* operation for each of the 60 readings obtained during the one-hour period. An alternative approach is to read the entire hour's air pollution data in one *read* operation and store the data in a temporary array until the data is processed. The alternative requires only one I/O operation and a 60-word array to hold the air pollution data. Here we will select the alternative option that requires the extra storage space in spite of the fact that it is contra-

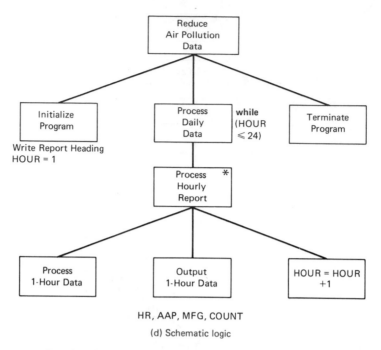

HR, AAP, MFG, COUNT

(d) Schematic logic

Fig. 4-35 (*cont'd.*)   Stepwise refinement step three

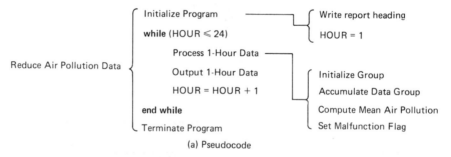

(a) Pseudocode

Fig. 4-36   Stepwise refinement step four

dictory to the earlier decision we made concerning the *write* operation to print data in the daily report. Thus, we must allow for a 60-word **APDATA** array in the data list to store a one-hour data block.

This decision to read the air pollution data in one-hour blocks allows us to decompose the function "Accumulate Data Group" into two processes: (1) read a one-hour block of data (60 elements) into the array **APDATA**, and (2) process data group to obtain the sum of the valid elements of **APDATA**. The resulting abstract program, refinement step five, is illustrated in Figure 4-37.

The next refinement step deals only with the function "Process Data Group." Obviously, the data group contains 60 elements recorded at one-minute intervals. The processing required

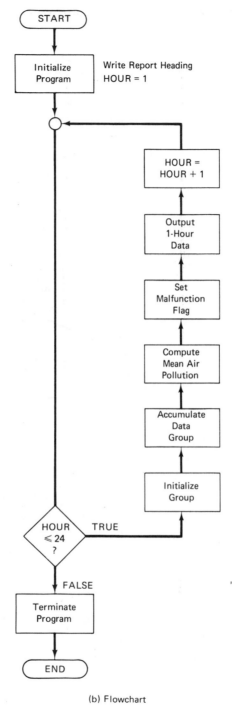

(b) Flowchart

Fig. 4-36 (*cont'd.*) Stepwise refinement step four

Table 4-2 Data List at Refinement Step Three

Data Element	Description	Initial Value	Range
HOUR	Time slot during 24-hour air pollution data collection period	1	1–25
AAP	Average reading of air pollution for each hour (ppm)	—	0–100
MFG	Malfunction flag ƀ = normal * = malfunction encountered	—	ƀ or *
COUNT	Number of valid data readings during 1-hour period		0–60

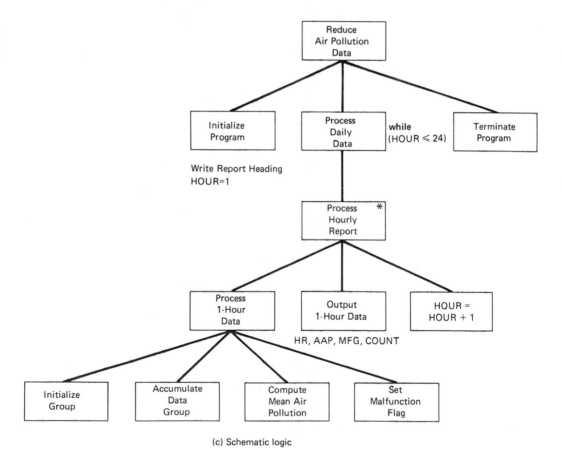

(c) Schematic logic

Fig. 4-36 (*cont'd.*) Stepwise refinement step four

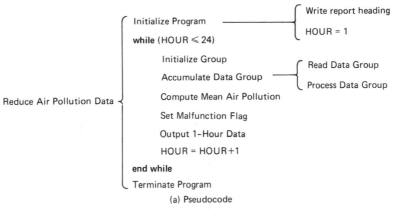

(a) Pseudocode

Fig. 4-37 Stepwise refinement step five

involves summing the valid elements of the group, which are stored in APDATA, to obtain a value for the variable SUM. Thus, the function performed is an iteration of the form **while** (MINUTE ≤ 60). We must introduce two additional variables, SUM and MINUTE, at this decomposition level to store the accumulated SUM of the valid elements of APDATA and to count the number of elements of APDATA that have been processed, respectively. Both of these data elements must be initialized, and the new elements must be added to the data list.

The results of refinement step six are shown in Figure 4-38.

We have already made use of a characteristic of almost all loop operations which is, at least subconsciously, considered in iterations involving counters. For any loop operation, an *initialization* step must precede the operation and an *increment* step must be contained within the operation, as shown in Figure 4-39. The loop is not always incremented at the beginning or the end of the processing within the iteration, but must be incremented within the iteration. (Iterations *not based on a counting mechanism* are not of this form.)

This leads us to the decomposition of the function "Process Element" and the initialization of the loop parameter. The function can be expanded into a primary process "Accumulate Valid Data Element" and a process that increments the iteration parameter MINUTE. We will arbitrarily increment the counter after accumulating the data element that requires the variable MINUTE be preset to one. The results of the seventh stage of refinement are shown in Figure 4-40.

The next process to be expanded is the function "Accumulate Valid Data Element." Our first question is what defines a valid data element? The program specification states the valid data value lies within the range 0 ppm ≤ level ≤ 100 ppm. Next, we ask what processing must be performed to "accumulate" an element? First, if the data is valid, it must be added to the present value of SUM so that the maximum possible value is 60×100 or 6000 ppm. That information is added to the data list. Second, the average air pollution level for a one-hour period, which is computed at the end of the loop, is based on the number of valid data points (COUNT), so the variable count must be incremented at each valid point and also must be initialized to zero prior to entering the function "Accumulate Data Group."

While we are dealing with the problem of valid data, it is worthwhile to pursue the other requirement in the program specification related to valid data; i.e., the equipment malfunction flag. This flag is set if less than a prescribed number (42) of the data points are valid. The "Set Malfunction Flag" process in the program performs this function. We could approach

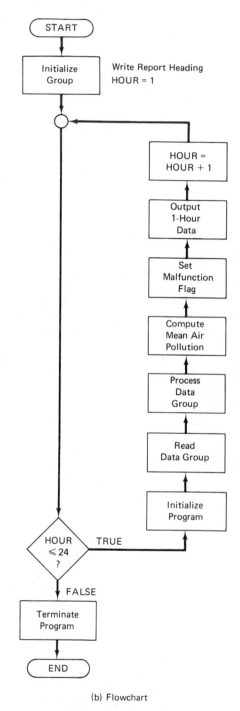

(b) Flowchart

Fig. 4-37 (*cont'd.*)   Stepwise refinement step five

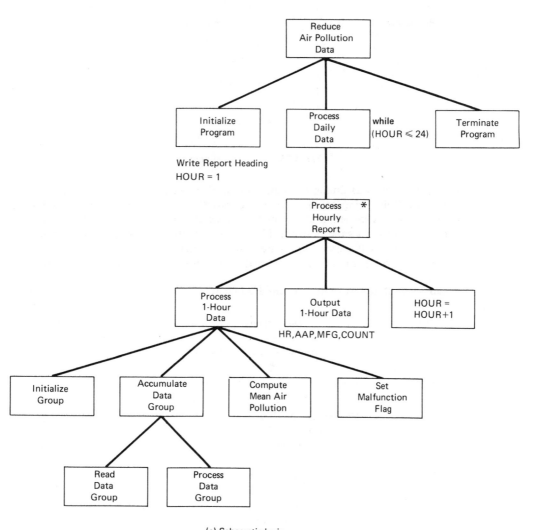

(c) Schematic logic

Fig. 4-37 (*cont'd.*) Stepwise refinement step five

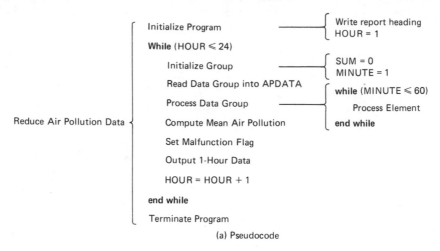

(a) Pseudocode

Fig. 4-38 Stepwise refinement step six

this requirement by assuming the data is valid prior to entering the loop that processes one hour's data (Initializing MFG = ƀ) and setting MFG = '*' only if a malfunction occurs. This is slightly less efficient than the method we select where MFG is set to '*' or 'ƀ', depending on the number of valid points within the data group. The results of the eighth, and last, refinement step are illustrated in Figure 4-41. The final data list is presented in Table 4-3.

We can now write the final version of the air pollution data reduction program in pseudo-

Table 4-3   Data List at Refinement Step Eight

Data Element	Description	Initial Value	Range
HOUR	Time slot during 24-hour air pollution data collection period	1	1–25
AAP	Average reading of air pollution for each hour	—	0–100
MFG	Malfunction flag ƀ = normal * = malfunction encountered	—	ƀ or *
COUNT	Number of valid data readings during one-hour period	0	0–60
APDATA	Sixty-element array to hold one-hour air pollution data block for processing	—	± indeterminate (allows for invalid data)
SUM	Accumulated sum of valid air pollution data elements during one-hour period	0	0–6000
MINUTE	Time slot during one-hour air pollution data collection period	1	1–61

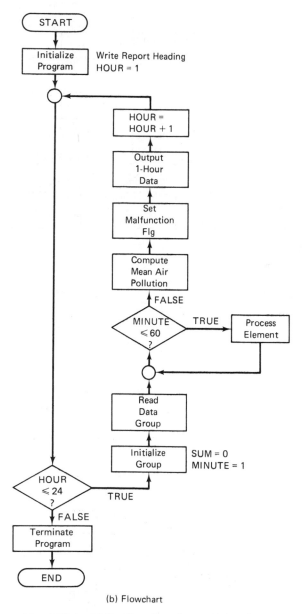

(b) Flowchart

Fig. 4-38 (*cont'd.*)   Stepwise refinement step six

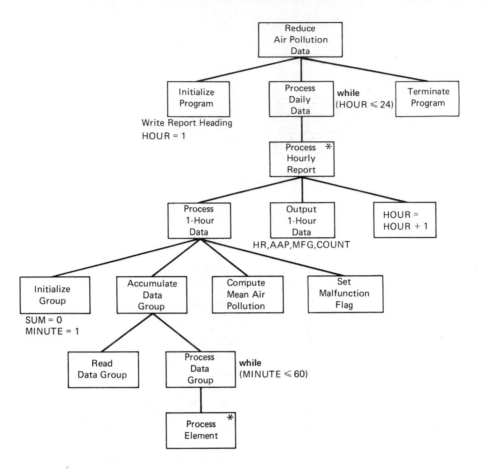

(c) Schematic logic

Fig. 4-38 (*cont'd.*)   Stepwise refinement step six

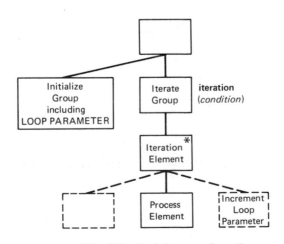

Fig. 4-39   Basic loop configuration

code from any one or all of the three design notations we have used throughout the example as follows:

```
Write report heading
HOUR = 1
while (HOUR ≤ 24)
    SUM = 0
    MINUTE = 1
    COUNT = 0
    Read data group (60 elements) into APDATA
    while (MINUTE ≤ 60)
        if (0 ≤ APDATA (MINUTE) ≤ 100)
            COUNT = COUNT + 1
            SUM = SUM + APDATA (MINUTE)
        end if
        MINUTE = MINUTE + 1
    end while
    APP = SUM/COUNT
    if (COUNT < 42)
        MFG = '*'
    else
        MFG = 'b'
    end if
    Output 1-hour data (HOUR, APP, COUNT, MFG)
    HOUR = HOUR + 1
end while
Terminate Program
```

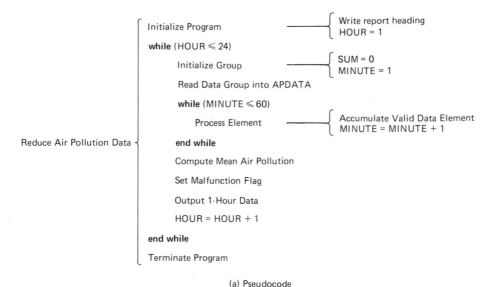

(a) Pseudocode

Fig. 4-40 Stepwise refinement step seven

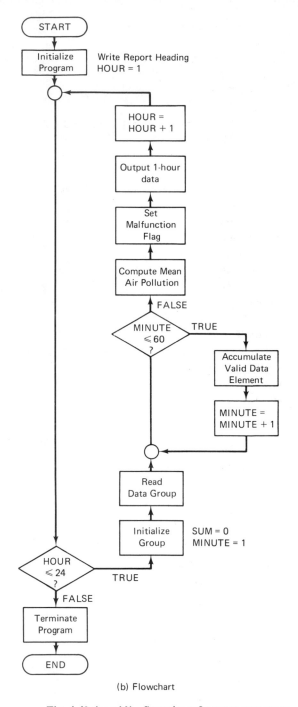

(b) Flowchart

Fig. 4-40 (*cont'd.*)   Stepwise refinement step seven

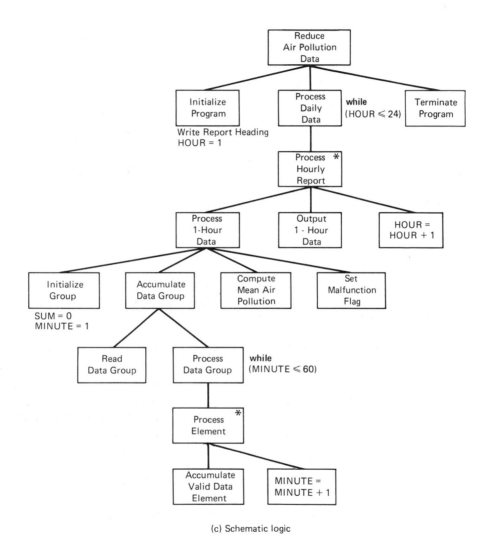

(c) Schematic logic

Fig. 4-40 (*cont'd.*) Stepwise refinement step seven

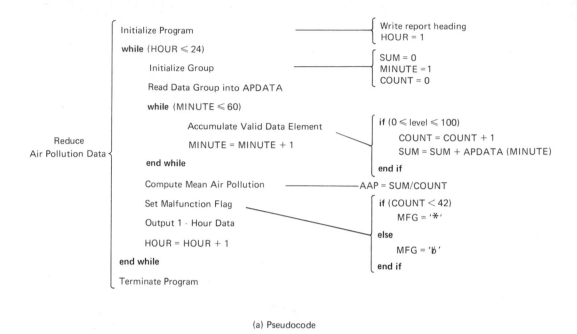

(a) Pseudocode

Fig. 4-41 Stepwise refinement step eight

The pseudocode listing, which looks like a combination of many different languages, is in a form that can readily be used with the data list of Table 4-3 to write a finished version of the program in any major programming language. We assume, of course, that the list of data items has been checked for completeness and that the program has also been checked to verify that the initialization, logic, and processing are all performed correctly.

Stepwise refinement is a technique based on an orderly, human thinking process in which problems are considered at an abstract level as major elements first. The mental process of "chunking" or breaking a problem into subordinate, simpler pieces is then used to decompose the program into successively simpler, smaller, more manageable items until we arrive at a level that can be directly translated into a programming language. Each refinement step is small so that the refinement and any decisions made at that step can be studied carefully. Details that dilute our concentration on the task at hand are postponed until needed.

The technique produces structured programs that satisfy our primary goals:

1. To minimize the number of errors that occur during the development process.
2. To minimize the effort required to correct errors in sections of code found to be deficient and to replace sections when more reliable, functional, or efficient techniques are discovered.
3. To minimize the life-cycle costs of the software.

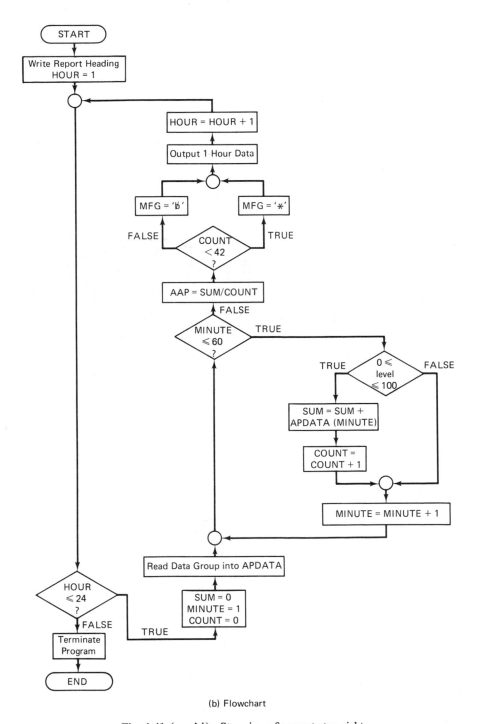

(b) Flowchart

Fig. 4-41 (*cont'd.*) Stepwise refinement step eight

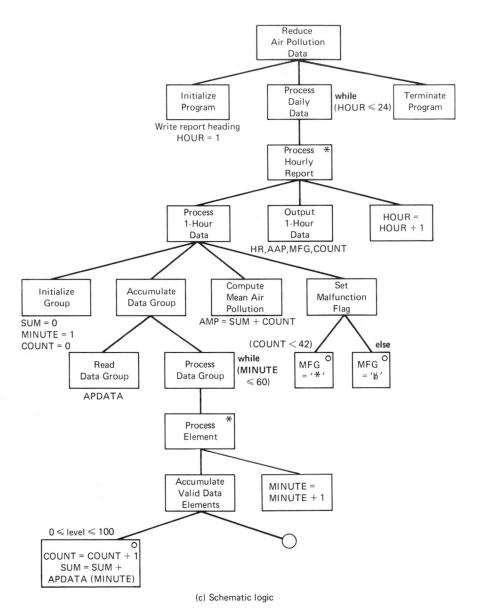

(c) Schematic logic

Fig. 4-41 (*cont'd.*)   Stepwise refinement step eight

4.4

Implementations in High-order Languages

The concepts of structured programming can be implemented in almost all of the current high-order programming languages. Yet, none of the major higher-order languages contains the complete set of essential logical control structures defined in the preceding section. PL/I, PASCAL, and ALGOL are the only major programming languages that provide the basic control structures required to directly implement a structured program. The most widely used programming languages in the United States, COBOL and FORTRAN, are far from ideal as structured programming languages in terms of available control structures. (It is strange that the popularity of a programming language appears to be inversely proportional to the power of its program control statements.) Since ALGOL and PASCAL lack the power of PL/I over a broad range of applications (business/scientific), PL/I appears to be the most acceptable of the major higher-order languages as a structured programming language for the foreseeable future. The PASCAL language and it's variations have also rapidly gained acceptance because of their structuring capabilities and simplicity. A 1976 release of the IBM Optimizing PL/I Compiler[48] has extended structures including **select** (**case** and **if-orif-else**), **until**, and **leave** (**escape**). A summary of the structure capabilities of the three most commonly used programming languages is presented in Table 4-4. ALGOL and PASCAL are not included in this table because, although they are an important languages, they are not widely used in the United States as industrial programming languages.

In reality, all four of the languages mentioned here are used in varying degrees by industry, independent of their proximity to any ideal. Once a language has been adopted, it is difficult and frequently costly for an installation to convert to another language unless the new language is similar in format to the old language, and the old language comprises a subset of the new language. Even if these two conditions are satisfied, an endearing human quality called resistance to change makes adoption of a new language difficult. An example of this quality can be seen in the evolution of American Standard FORTRAN (FORTRAN IV) toward Structured FORTRAN since its inception in 1966. The changes in this direction proposed by the X3J3 FORTRAN committee in 1977 made it clear that alternative methods of implementing a Structured FORTRAN language must be sought.

In this section we will discuss one method of implementing the eight basic logic structures (**if-else**, **if-orif-else**, **case**, **posit**, **while**, **until**, and **escape/cycle**) within the framework of the three high-order languages from Table 4-4. This method provides the basic capabilities necessary to allow structured programming without requiring changes to existing compliers.

We will concentrate our discussion on the implementation of the logic structures in FORTRAN since it is the most difficult of the three languages with which to deal. In that context we will describe the implementation in detail with alternate FORTRAN con-

---

[48] *OS PL/I Checkout and Optimizing Compilers: Language Reference Manual, GC33-0009* (White Plains, N.Y.: International Business Machines Corp., October, 1976).

Table 4-4 Structure Capabilities in Higher-Order Languages

Structure	COBOL	FORTRAN IV	PL/I
if-else	Available	* (Logical **if** limited to single restricted statement) **	Available
if-orif-else	Available as nested-**if**	*	Available as nested-**if** (Implemented as **select** in IBM Optimizing Compiler)
case	*	*	* (Implemented as **select** in IBM Optimizing Compiler)
posit	*	*	*
while	Available as **perform until** with predicate logic inverted	* **	Available as **do while**
until	*	*	* (Implemented in IBM Optimizing Compiler)
escape	*	*	* (Implemented as **leave** for iteration structures in IBM Optimizing Compiler)
cycle	*	*	*

*Requires simulation in programming language.
**Proposed implementation in 1976 FORTRAN standard.

figurations if appropriate. We will then briefly discuss methods of optimizing the resulting code.

The implementation of the structures in the other two major languages follows the same line of reasoning, so the implementations in each language will be reduced to a tabular description that is concise and easy to apply.

4.4.1 FORTRAN IMPLEMENTATION

The original FORTRAN specifications were submitted in November 1954 to allow the IBM 704 computer to process a problem defined in a mathematical notation. Between then and 1957 a group headed by John Backus of IBM completed work on FORTRAN I and presented the first paper on the language at the Western Joint Computer Conference.

Following FORTRAN I, FORTRAN II was released in 1958 as a new version with extended capabilities. It was primarily designed for use with the IBM 704 computer but found much wider acceptance. FORTRAN III was developed by IBM in 1960 and was used internally, but never achieved much acceptance. In 1962, FORTRAN IV was released as the IBM 7000 series computers and with periodic improvements is still the most widely used scientific programming language. The basic control structures in the FORTRAN language changed very little from the version released in 1958. The structures were, and still are, adequate to achieve any program control desired. The control statements available in the language have been attacked by critics of all types. However, we should remember two things: (1) the Fortran standard[49] was developed before structured programming, and before the additional control structures were recognized by the software community, and (2) the "spaghetti bowl" programs developed in FORTRAN by unsophisticated users through the misuse of the **go to** statement must be blamed on the programmer, not the language.

FORTRAN, in spite of the negative light cast upon it by the "purists," does offer advantages as a programming language. It is a fairly low-level language that allows the FORTRAN compiler to generate more efficient object code than higher-level languages like PL/I. FORTRAN is also very widely used. There are few installations that do not possess a compiler for some dialect of the language. Programs written in ANS FORTRAN can be adapted to execute on almost any installation with adequate resources without extensive program modification.

The major disadvantage of FORTRAN is that the language is not block-structured. FORTRAN compilers recognize only simple statements, and the program logic structure must be constructed, using one or more of the allowable forms of the **go to** statement. As we have stated earlier, the **go to** statement by itself is neither good nor bad. Undisciplined use of the **go to**, or any other practice that clouds the function of a program, is to be abhorred. Use of any statement in a way to improve the clarity or maintainability of source code is good and should be encouraged.

Before the implementation of structured programming in FORTRAN can be described, we must emulate each of the basic program constructs by using only the simple statement that is recognized by the FORTRAN compiler.

Structured programming in FORTRAN requires that the basic logic structures be emulated through the use of the simple control statements available in the language. Since FORTRAN is not block-structured, it is necessary for us to emulate in the paragraphs below all eight of the logic structures described in Sec. 4.3.2. The 1977 FORTRAN standard includes the **if-else** and **while** structures. However, since 1977 FORTRAN implementations are not widespread, the discussion will be concentrated on the popular 1966 standard.

IF-ELSE

The **if-else** construct as shown logically in Figure 4-13 can be represented by the FORTRAN code

```
   if (le)            C      IF (le)
                             IF (.NOT. le) GO TO α
        code A                   code A
                                 GO TO β
```

---

[49] *American National Standard FORTRAN (ANS X3.9-1966)* (New York, N.Y.: American National Standards Institute, 1966).

```
        else           C      ELSE
                          α   CONTINUE
            code B                 code B
        end if          C      END IF
                          β   CONTINUE
```

which skips conditional "code A" if the logical condition *le* has the value FALSE or skips "code B" if the logical condition has the value TRUE. Note that comments specifying the structure have been added to clarify the emulating code.

IF-ORIF-ELSE

The **if-orif-else** construct defined in Figure 4-17 can be represented by the FORTRAN statements

```
        if (le₁)        C      IF (le₁)
                               IF (.NOT. le₁) GO TO α
            code A                 code A
                               GO TO γ
        or if (le₂)     C      OR IF (le₂)
                          α   IF (.NOT. le₂) GO TO β
            code B                 code B
                               GO TO γ
        else            C      ELSE
                          β   CONTINUE
            code C                 code C
        end if          C      END IF
                          γ   CONTINUE
```

CASE

The **case** construct, which causes control to be passed to one of a set of functional blocks of code, depending on the value of an integer index variable as shown in Figure 4-18, can be emulated by more than one method. The most common and most practical configuration for simple **case** structures is achieved in FORTRAN, using a computed **go to** statement, **go to** statements at the end of each functional block, and a single collector (CONTINUE statement) at the end of the functional block. The simple structure appears as

```
        case of (index)   C    CASE OF (index)
                               IF (index.LT.1.OR.index.GT.n) GO TO δ
                               GO TO (α, β, . . .), index
        case (1)          C    CASE (1)
                          α   CONTINUE
            code A                 code A
                               GO TO δ
        case (2)          C    CASE (2)
                          β   CONTINUE
```

```
code B                    code B
                          GO TO δ
  .                         .
  .                         .
  .                         .
  .                         .

case else        C        CASE ELSE
                 γ        CONTINUE
  code Z                    code Z
end case         C        END CASE
                 δ        CONTINUE
```

Some FORTRAN compilers allow the value of the index to exceed the number of branches specified in the computed **go to** statement. Usually when this condition occurs, the next statement in sequence is executed. In ANS FORTRAN the computed **go to** statement is undefined if the index is out of range. Therefore, it is necessary to test the value of the index prior to executing the computed **go to** when using this mechanization to ensure that the default code is executed if the index does not satisfy a specified case.

An alternate mechanization of the first form utilizes the feature of the compilers that causes control to pass to the next executable statement when the computed **go to** index is out of range.

```
case of (index)    C       CASE OF (index)
                           GO TO (α, β), index
case else          C       CASE ELSE
    code C                     code C
                           GO TO δ
case (1)           C       CASE (1)
                   α       CONTINUE
    code A                     code A
                           GO TO δ
case (2)           C       CASE (2)
                   β       CONTINUE
    code B                     code B
end case           C       END CASE
                   δ       CONTINUE
```

A more powerful and complex version of the **case** construct allows the case identifiers to possess multiple fixed or undefined values as well as values that are more than a simple integer sequence. For example, consider the situation where "code A" is to be executed for index values 1 and n, "code B" is to be executed for an index value of 4, and "code C" is to be executed for all other possible index values. This obviously will not work in the previous implementation of the **case** control structure. It could be implemented by using an **if-orif-else** structure or the second implementation of the **case** construct as follows:

```
case of (i)        C      CASE OF (i)
case (1, n)        C      CASE (1, n)
                          IF (i.NE.1.AND.i.NE.n) GO TO α
    code A                    code A
                          GO TO δ
case (4)           C      CASE (4)
                   α  IF (i.NE.4) GO TO β
    code B                    code B
                          GO TO δ
case else          C      CASE ELSE
                   β  CONTINUE
    code C                    code C
end case           C      END CASE
                   δ  CONTINUE
```

The form of the **case** construct to be used in a given application is primarily determined by the form of the index. If the case indices comprise a simple integer sequence, the computed **go to** form of the structure is superior. More complex applications require the use of the second form.

POSIT

The **posit** construct introduced in Figure 4-19 can be emulated by the FORTRAN code

```
posit                    C      POSIT
    code A                          code A
    quit posit if (le₁)  C      QUIT POSIT
                                IF (le₁) GO TO α
    code B                          code B
    quit posit if (le₂)  C      QUIT POSIT
                                IF (le₂) GO TO α
    code C                          code C
                                GO TO β
else                     C      ELSE
                         α   CONTINUE
    code D                          code D
end posit                C      END POSIT
                         β   CONTINUE
```

This elementary form of the **posit** construct allows the program control to be transferred to the **else** block only if any of the logical expressions in the **quit** statements are satisfied. A more powerful version of the **posit** construct is represented by

```
posit                    C      POSIT
    code A                          code A
    if (le₁)             C      IF (le₁)
                                IF (.NOT. (le₁)) GO TO α
```

```
        code X                         code X
        quit posit                     GO  TO  β
      end if              C            END  IF
                              α        CONTINUE
           .                              .
           .                              .
           .                              .
        code C                         code C
                                       GO  TO  δ
    else                    C    ELSE
                            β    CONTINUE
        code D                         code D
      end posit             C    END  POSIT
                            δ    CONTINUE
```

The second version of the **posit** construct includes the **quit posit** statement within an **if** block to allow a sequence of code to be executed along with the exit statement. This is useful in applications that require wrap-up processing (code X) in conjunction with the exit from the block.

WHILE

The **while** construct defined in Figure 4-20(a) can be represented by either of two basic implementations in FORTRAN. The first method, based on a positive conditional test, is implemented as follows:

```
    while (le)           C        WHILE  (le)
                                  GO  TO  β
                         α        CONTINUE
        code A                        code A
                         β        IF (le) GO  TO  α
    end while            C        END  WHILE
```

This method allows an iterative execution of functional block "code A" determined by a positive logical evaluation of the predicate *le*, but complicates the FORTRAN code by physically placing the evaluation of the predicate at the end of the functional block.

The second formulation of the **while** construct, based on a negative[50] logical test, physically places the test at the beginning of the functional block. It is mechanized as

```
    while (le)           C        WHILE  (le)
                         α        IF ( .NOT.(le)) GO  TO  β
        code A                        code A
    end while            C        END  WHILE
                                  GO  TO  α
                         β        CONTINUE
```

[50]The negative logical condition is achieved by applying a .NOT. as a prefix to the desired "positive" logical expression.

Both methods are logically correct and each has advantages in writing structured code. Some programmers prefer locating the test controlling the iterative block at the head of the block and tolerate the loss of clarity due to negating the logical condition. The second formulation of the **while** construct is the most popular.

UNTIL

The **until** construct defined in Figure 4-20(b) can also be represented by two FORTRAN implementations. The simplest form of the emulation places the evaluation of the logical experssion at the end of the functional block, like the flowchart of the construct, but bases the iteration on the negative outcome of the predicate. The FORTRAN code for this implementation is

```
until (le)        C     UNTIL (le)
               α  CONTINUE
  code A               code A
                  IF (.NOT.le) TO TO α
end until         C     END UNTIL
```

The second implementation of the **until** construct is slightly more complex than the first form, but has two advantages: (1) the iteration is based on the positive evaluation of the predicate, and (2) the logical expression is physically placed at the beginning of the functional block. The second form is mechanized as

```
until (le)        C     UNTIL (le)
                     GO TO β
               α  IF (le) GO TO δ
               β  CONTINUE
  code A               code A
                     GO TO α
end until         C     END UNTIL
               δ  CONTINUE
```

As with the **while** control structure, the choice of the implementation rests with the programmer.

ESCAPE/CYCLE

The **escape** and **cycle** constructs are implemented as simple **go to** statements in the containing structures. We pointed out that the difference between these structures and the classical **go to** statement is that the **escape** and **cycle** statements only allow branching forward to the end of the block defined by the containing structure. (Remember, the **cycle** statement transferred control to the "inside" of the end of the block. See Exit section.) Since the exit structures are most commonly used within iteration blocks, we will discuss only the emulation of **escape** and **cycle** in those cases.

First, a complete **while** construct containing both an **escape** form and a **cycle** form is emulated as

while (le_1)	C	WHILE (le_1)
	α	IF (.NOT.(le_1)) GO TO δ
code A		code A
if (le_2)	C	IF (le_2)
		IF (.NOT.(le_2)) GO TO β
code B		code B
escape while	C	ESCAPE WHILE
		GO TO δ
end if	C	END IF
	β	CONTINUE
if (le_3)	C	IF (le_3)
		IF (.NOT.(le_3)) GO TO γ
code C		code C
cycle while	C	CYCLE WHILE
		GO TO α
end if	C	END IF
	γ	CONTINUE
code D		code D
end while	C	END WHILE
		GO TO α
	δ	CONTINUE

If an application requires unconditional branches from an inner level of a nested iteration structure to various levels of the nested structure as

```
AB :    while (le₁)
CD :        while (le₂)
                .
                .
                .
            escape AB if (le₃)
                .
                .
                .
            cycle CD if (le₄)
                .
                .
                .
            end while
        end while
```

we represent the structure in FORTRAN without comment statements, as

```
α      IF (.NOT. (le₁)) GO TO δ
β          IF (.NOT. (le₂)) GO TO γ
              .
              .
              .
           IF (le₃) GO TO δ
              .
              .
              .
           IF (le₄) TO TO β
              .
              .
              .
           GO TO β
γ        CONTINUE
       GO TO α
δ      CONTINUE
```

The need for comment statements in the FORTRAN listing to describe the structure of the emulated program becomes more evident as the size and complexity of the program increase. The structure is further enhanced if the FORTRAN listing is indented to correspond to the form of structured program.

A summary of the FORTRAN implementations of the basic logic control structures is presented in Table 4-5.

4.4.2 COBOL AND PL/I IMPLEMENTATIONS

The COBOL and PL/I languages are closer than FORTRAN to directly satisfying the requirements of a structured programming language. The latest 1976 IBM release of a PL/I optimizing compiler with an updated set of logic control structures makes that language very close to acceptable. The only basic structures missing from this new version of PL/I are the **posit** and **cycle** structures which can be emulated simply.

Independent of the language or the version of the compiler, both COBOL and PL/I are adequate vehicles for the implementation of structured programming. The mechanics of emulating the basic structures in the two languages are summarized in Tables 4-6 and 4-7. Programming considerations, including modularity, structures, and coding techniques for improved readability are outside the scope of this chapter, but can be found in several sources such as Hughes and Michtom.[51]

4.4.3 PRECOMPILERS

Many complaints about structured programming are related to the difficulty involved with writing programs directly by using the emulating code shown in the preceding tables. Some of the complaints are well-founded. For example, after having written a perfectly clear program in pseudocode at the machine level, a significant

[51]J. K. Hughes and J. I. Michtom, *A Structured Approach to Programming* (Englewood Cliffs, N.J.: Prentice-Hall, Inc., 1977).

Table 4-5 FORTRAN Implementation of Control Structures

Flowchart	Construct	FORTRAN Equivalent	Comments

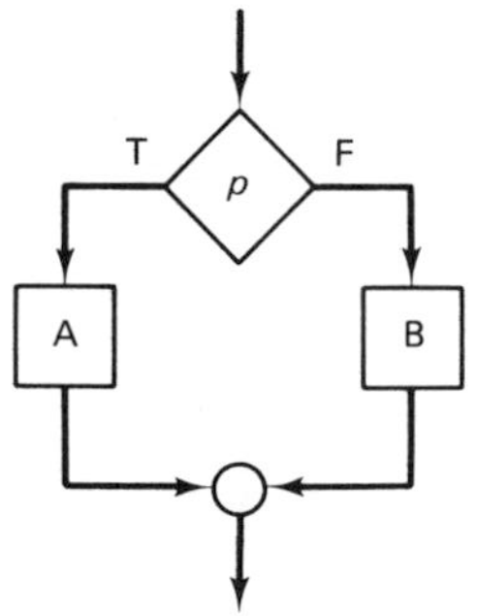

if (p)
  code A

else
  code B
end if

```
   IF (.NOT.(p)) GO TO α
       code A
       GO TO β
α  CONTINUE
       code B
β  CONTINUE
```

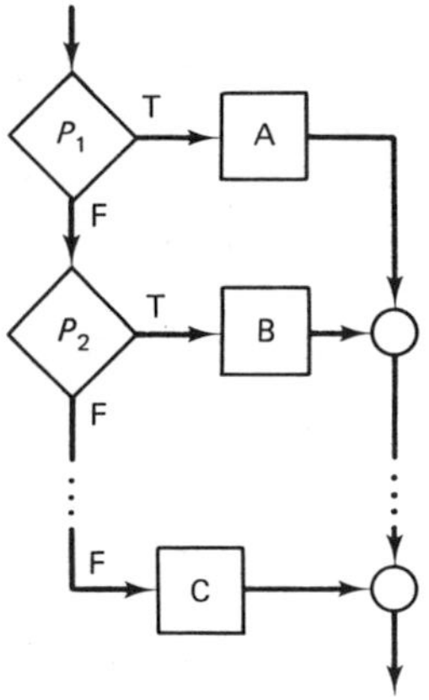

if (p_1)
  code A

or if (p_2)
  code B
  . . .

else
  code C
end if

```
   IF (.NOT.(p₁)) GO TO α
       code A
       GO TO δ
α  IF (.NOT.(p₂)) GO TO β
       code B
       GO TO δ
         . . .
γ  CONTINUE
       code C
δ  CONTINUE
```

1. Alternate flowchart for **if-orif-else** structure shown in Figure 4-17

Table 4-5 FORTRAN Implementation of Control Structures (cont'd.)

Flowchart	Construct	FORTRAN Equivalent	Comments

	case of (i)
	case of (a,b)
	
	  case 1
	
	  case (c)
	  case 2
	
	  case (d)
	  case 3
	  . . .
	
	  case else
	  case n
	  end case
		IF $(i.NE.a.AND.i.NE.b)$
		  *GO TO α
		      case 1
		      GO TO ω
		α IF $(i.NE.c)$ GO TO β
		      case 2
		      GO TO ω
		β IF $(i.NE.d)$ GO TO γ
		      case 3
		      GO TO ω
		      . . .
		δ CONTINUE
		      case n
		ω CONTINUE
			1. Alternate **case** implementation defined in text

	posit
	  code A
	  quit posit if (p_1)
	  . . .
	  code N
	
	  else
	  code X
	  end posit
		code A
		  IF (p_1) GO TO α
		    . . .
		    code N
		    GO TO β
		α CONTINUE
		    code X
		β CONTINUE
			1. Alternate **posit** implementation defined in text

Table 4-5 FORTRAN Implementation of Control Structures (cont'd.)

Flowchart	Construct	FORTRAN Equivalent	Comments

	while (p)
	code A
	
	end while
		α IF (.NOT.(p)) GO TO β
		     code A
		     GO TO α
		β CONTINUE
			1. Alternate **while** implementation defined in text
			2. The logical **if** statement labeled α is a target for any **cycle** statement in code A referencing this block.
			3. The CONTINUE statement labeled β also serves as a target for **escape** statements referencing this block.

	until (p)
	
	code A
	
	end until
		GO TO β
		α IF (p) GO TO γ
		β CONTINUE
		     code A
		     GO TO α
		γ CONTINUE
			1. Alternate **until** implementation defined in text.
			2. The logical **if** statement labeled α is a target for any **cycle** statement in code A referencing this block.
			3. The CONTINUE statement label γ also serves as a target for **escape** statements referencing this block.

Table 4-6 COBOL Implementation of Control Structures

Flowchart	Construct	COBOL Equivalent	Comments

	if (p)
	   code A
	else
	   code B
	end if
		IF p
		   code A
		ELSE
		   code B.
			1. Neither code A nor code B may contain any periods.
			2. Code A cannot contain an **if** that has no corresponding **else.**

	if (p_1)
	   code A
	or if (p_2)
	   code B
	   . . .
	else
	   code C
	end if
		IF p_1
		   code A
		ELSE IF P_2
		   code B
		   . . .
		ELSE
		   code C.
			1. An alternate configuration is
			   IF NOT p_1 GO TO PB.
			      code A
			        GO TO ENDIF.
			   PB. IF NOT p_2 GO TO PC.
			        code B
			          GO TO ENDIF
			     . . .
			   PELSE. code C
			   ENDIF.

Table 4-6 COBOL Implementation of Control Structures (cont'd.)

Flowchart	Construct	COBOL Equivalent	Comments

case of (*i*)
case (*a, b*)
  case 1
  case 2
case (*c*)
  case 3
case (*d*)

    . . .

case else
  case *n*
end case

COBOL Equivalent:

IF *i = a* OR *i = b*
  case 1
  GO TO ENDCASE.
IF *i = c*
  case 2
  GO TO ENDCASE.
IF *i = d*
  case 3
  GO TO ENDCASE.

    . . .

  case *n*
ENDCASE.

1. The **case** structure can also be constructed by using the nested-**if** format or
the GO TO—DEPENDING ON format.
The latter format is the most restrictive.

posit
  code A
quit posit if (p_1)

  . . .

  code N
else
  code X
end posit

COBOL Equivalent:

code A
IF p_1 GO TO ELSEPOS.

  . . .

code N
ELSEPOS.
  code X.

Table 4-6 COBOL Implementation of Control Structures (cont'd.)

Flowchart	Construct	COBOL Equivalent	Comments

	while (p)
	
	    code A
	
	end while
		WHILE.
		    IF NOT p GO TO ENDWHILE.
		    code A
		    GO TO WHILE.
		ENDWHILE.
			1. An alternate implementation uses the construct PERFORM code A UNTIL p. This construct limits the use of the exit structures.
			2. A **cycle** is implemented as GO TO WHILE.
			3. An **escape** is implemented as GO TO ENDWHILE.

	until
	
	    code A
	
	end until
		GO TO LOOP.
		TEST. IF p GO TO ENDLOOP.
		LOOP.
		    code A
		    GO TO TEST.
		ENDLOOP.
			1. An alternate implementation is PERFORM code A. PERFORM code A UNTIL p. which limits the use of the exit structures.
			2. A **cycle** is implemented as GO TO TEST.
			3. An **escape** is implemented as GO TO ENDLOOP.

Table 4-7 PL/I Implementation of Control Structures

Flowchart	Construct	PL/I Equivalent	Comments

	if (p)
	  code A
	else
	  code B
	end if
		IF (p) THEN
		  code A
		ELSE
		  code B
			1. Code A cannot contain an **if** with no corresponding **else** unless the block representing code A is a DO group.

	if (p_1)
	  code A
	or if (p_2)
	  code B
	  . . .
	else
	  code C
	end if
		IF (p_1) THEN
		  code A
		ELSE IF (p_2) THEN
		  code B
		  . . .
		ELSE
		  code C
		END;
			Alternate form available on IBM Optimiging Compiler:
			  SELECT;
			    WHEN (p_1)
			      code A
			    WHEN (p_2)
			      code B
			      . . .
			    OTHERWISE
			      code C

Table 4-7 PL/I Implementation of Control Structures (cont'd.)

Flowchart	Construct	PL/I Equivalent	Comments

case of (*i*)
case (*a,b*)
  case 1
case (*c*)
  case 2
case (*d*)
  case 3
  . . .
case else
  case *n*
end case

SELECT (*i*);
WHEN (*a, b*)
  case 1
WHEN (*c*)
  case 2
WHEN (*d*)
  case 3
  . . .
OTHERWISE
  case *n*
END;

1. The **case** structure can also be constructed by using the nested-**if** format or the computed **go to** format.

posit
  code A
  quit posit if (p_1)
  . . .
  code N
else
  code X
end posit

  code A
IF (p_1) THEN GO TO ELSEPOS;
  . . .
  code N
  GO TO ENDPOS;
ELSEPOS:
  code X
ENDPOS::

Table 4-7 PL/I Implementation of Control Structures (cont'd.)

Flowchart	Construct	PL/I Equivalent	Comments

	while (p)
	  code A
	
	end while
		DO WHILE (p):
		    code A
		CYCLE::
		    END;
		ENDWHILE::
			1. A **cycle** is implemented as GO TO CYCLE;
			2. An **escape** is implemented as GO TO ENDWHILE;. The IBM Optimizing Compiler has a LEAVE structure that passes control to the first executable statement following the iteration structure.

	until (p)
	
	  code A
	
	end until
		GO TO LOOP;
		TEST: IF (p) THEN GO TO ENDLOOP;
		LOOP:
		    code A
		    GO TO TEST;
		ENDLOOP::
			1. IBM Optimizing Compiler allows the format
			    DO UNTIL (p):
			        code A
			CYCLE::
			        END;
			2. A **cycle** is implemented as GO TO TEST;
			3. An **escape** is implemented as GO TO ENDLOOP;. The Optimizing Compiler has a LEAVE structure that passes control to the first executable statement after the iteration loop.

amount of readability is lost when translating the program into a language like FORTRAN, using the emulating equivalent structures.

The most popular solution to the complaints related to the emulating structures is the use of a preprocessor, or precompiler. A precompiler extends the syntax of a specific programming language (like FORTRAN) by allowing the programmer to code the specific control structures such as **if-else**, **case**, **posit**, etc. The direct use of these statements makes it easier to structure programs and harder to create programs that appear to be "bowls of spaghetti." The standard language features of the specific programming language are intact, and statements normally used can be freely inter-mixed with the precompiler statements in a source program. Of course, we recommend that the precompiler statements be used exclusively to express the program control structure instead of statements like the FORTRAN computed **go to**, arithmetic **if**, etc.

The relationship between a typical precompiler and a standard FORTRAN compiler is shown in Figure 4-42 along with the outputs associated with each step in the overall

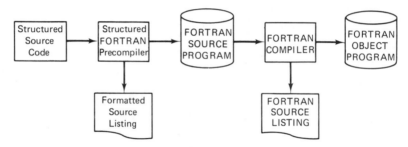

Fig. 4-42 Structured FORTRAN precompiler operation

compilation process. Simply stated, the precompiler scans the input source code for statements it "understands" (keywords), and translates those statements into equiva-lent FORTRAN source code that can be compiled by the FORTRAN compiler. Statements not understood by the precompiler are passed directly to the FORTRAN Source Pro-gram File. Most precompilers do not require the programmer to indent his source program since the indentation function is provided by the precompiler as an option in the preparation of the Formatted Source Listing.

The precompiler must, by necessity, generate statement labels for the emulating FORTRAN source code. The process is usually accomplished by selecting a statement number from a sequence generated by the precompiler, which is initialized by a pro-grammer option. Most precompilers are not "intelligent" and will not verify that the sequence number generated has not previously been used in the source code, so the programmer must be careful in his use of numbers to ensure unique labels in the FORTRAN source code.

Precompilers normally insert the original source statements that have been trans-lated into the FORTRAN source code as comments, which partially corrects the degrada-tion of readability in the FORTRAN source caused by the emulating code.

Most programmers who use a precompiler refer to the FORTRAN listing only as the last resort while debugging their programs. The only times a FORTRAN listing is

```
1    C**     SUBROUTINE HPROC                                                      00000010
             PURPOSE: TO STORE PROCEDURE AND DATA FOR LATER PROCESSING             00000020
     C                                                                             00000030
     C       CALLING                                                               00000040
     C       ROUTINES: TRAN1                                                       00000050
     C                                                                             00000060
     C       CALLS:  ACT1, ENSCAN, HPROR, CTSTM, HEND, KCOMP, KLASS, NSCAN,        00000070
     C               NULAB, BUTIF                                                  00000080
     C                                                                             00000090
     C       INPUT:  COMMON /CARDS/, /CONSTN/, /PROCED/, /STATE/, /MISEOPT/        00000100
     C                                                                             00000110
     C       NOTE:   PROCEDURE PROCESSING AND OUTPUT DONE IN <HEND>, THE           00000120
     C               END AND FORTRAN STATEMENT PROCESSOR                           00000130
     C                                                                             00000140
     C**     PSEUDOCODE REPRESENTATION: PROCESS PROCEDURE STATEMENT                00000150
     C                                                                             00000160
     C       INCREMENT PROCEDURE ARRAY POINTER                                     00000170
     C       IF GREATER THAN 5                                                     00000180
     C         PROCESS AN ERROR - ONLY 5 PROCEDURES PER ROUTINE ALLOWED            00000190
     C         EXIT PROCESSING                                                     00000200
     C       ENDIF                                                                 00000210
     C       INITIALIZE STORAGE AREA AND STORE PROCEDURE NAME AND DATA             00000220
     C       PROCESS STATEMENT ACCOUNTING TO DISK FILE                             00000230
     C       WRITE PROCEDURE CARD IMAGE TO DISK FILE                               00000240
     C       DO UNTIL AN END PROCEDURE CARD IS PROCESSED                           00000250
     C         PRINT IN ONE STATEMENT                                              00000260
     C         PROCESS STATEMENT END LOCATION                                      00000270
     C         PROCESS STATEMENT BEGIN LOCATION                                    00000280
     C         CLASSIFY STATEMENT                                                  00000290
     C         IF END CARD IS ENCOUNTERED                                          00000300
     C           EXIT PROCESSING                                                   00000310
     C         ENDIF                                                               00000320
     C         IF ANOTHER PROCEDURE STATEMENT IS ENCOUNTERED                       00000330
     C           PROCESS AN ERROR                                                  00000340
     C           DUMP ROUTINE THROUGH END CARD                                     00000350
     C           EXIT PROCESSING                                                   00000360
     C         ENDIF                                                               00000370
     C       ENDDO UNTIL                                                           00000380
     C       WRITE CARD IMAGE TO DISK                                              00000390
     C       IF AN END OF FILE OR END CARD OCCURRED                               00000400
     C         PROCESS FORTRAN OR END STATEMENT ... TO POINT OUT PROC FILE         00000410
     C       ENDIF                                                                 00000420
     C**                                                                           00000430
             COMMON/CARDS/LCARD(80),IEOF,NIMCRD                                    00000440
     C                                                                             00000450
     C       THIS IS THE INPUT SPACE COMMON IN USE                                 00000460
     C                                                                             00000470
     C       LCARD = CARD IMAGE ARRAY                                              00000480
     C       IEOF = 1 IF END OF DATA, 0 IF NOT                                     00000490
     C                                                                             00000500
2    CCCCCCCCCCCCCCCCCCCCCCCCCCCCCCCCCCCCCCCCCCCCCCCCCCCCCCCCCCCCCCCCCCCCCCCCC      00000510
             COMMON/CONSTN/ LHK,DUMMY(26)                                          00000520
     C                                                                             00000530
3    C                                                                             00000550
                                                                                   00000560
```

Fig. 4-43 Precompiler-formatted source listing

```
C     THIS IS THE CONSTANT COMMON IS USE                              00000570
C                                                                     00000590
      LPK = HOLLERITH BLANK                                           00000610
C                                                                     00000620
CCCCCCCCCCCCCCCCCCCCCCCCCCCCCCCCCCCCCCCCCCCCCCCCCCCCCCCCCC            00000630
C                                                                     00000650
      COMMON /PROCED/IPROC(40,5),INPROC,KNTPRC,JPROC                  00000660
C                                                                     00000670
C     THIS IS THE PROCEDURE STATEMENT COMMON IN USE                   00000680
C                                                                     00000690
C     IPROC = PROCEDURE STATEMENT ARRAY, WHERE                        00000700
C       WORDS 1-30 = PROCEDURE NAME                                   00000710
C       WORD 31 = LABEL 1                                             00000720
C       WORDS 32-39 = POSSIBLE LABEL 2'S                              00000740
C       WORD 40 = LABEL 2 COUNT                                       00000750
C     INPROC = POINTER TO IPROC ARRAY FOR INPUT                       00000760
C     KNTPRC = THE NUMBER OF PROCEDURES PER ROUTINE                   00000770
C                                                                     00000780
CCCCCCCCCCCCCCCCCCCCCCCCCCCCCCCCCCCCCCCCCCCCCCCCCCCCCCCC              00000790
C                                                                     00000810
      COMMON/STATE/LABEL(4),LIST(1420),ISEQ(8,20),NSTATE              00000820
     1,LINFG,LINEND,LINCHP,MENGTH,LEPINT,LEVFL,ITVPF,LTYPF,INSTK,IRET 00000830
C                                                                     00000840
C     THIS IS THE STATEMENT COMMON IN USE                             00000850
C                                                                     00000860
C     LIST = ARRAY OF STATEMENT TEXT CHARACTERS                       00000870
C     LINBEG = FIRST NON-BLANK CHARACTER IN LIST                      00000880
C     LINEND = LAST NON-BLANK CHARACTER IN LIST                       00000890
C     LPOINT = POINTER TO FIRST TEXT CHARACTER                        00000910
C     MLENGTH = LENGTH OF HIFTRAN COMMENT                             00000920
C     LTYPE = HIFTRAN STATEMENT TYPE                                  00000930
C     ITYPE = PREVIOUS HIFTRAN STATEMENT TYPE                         00000940
C                                                                     00000950
CCCCCCCCCCCCCCCCCCCCCCCCCCCCCCCCCCCCCCCCCCCCCCCCCCCCCCCC              00000960
C                                                                     00000970
      COMMON/USEOPT/LUNIN,LUNOUT,LUNPCH,LINPEG,LIINPEG,LUNPRC,        00000980
     1 INPDM,NINWGT,NPDCM,NLFFTN,LPCLT,INPDP,NDPDM                    00000990
      INTEGER STRING                                                  00001000
C                                                                     00001010
C     THIS IS THE USER OPTIONS COMMON IN USE                          00001030
C                                                                     00001040
      LUNIN = LOGICAL UNIT NUMBER FOR INPUT                           00001050
      LUNPRC = LOGICAL UNIT FOR PROCEDURE STORAGE                     00001060
C                                                                     00001070
CCCCCCCCCCCCCCCCCCCCCCCCCCCCCCCCCCCCCCCCCCCCCCCCCCCCCCCCC.            00001080
C                                                                     00001100
      DATA KPAP /1H/                                                  00001110
      INPROC = INPROC + 1                                             00001120
      IF(INPROC.GT.5)
     . . CALL ERROR(37)
```
```
      ENDIF
      KNTPRC = KNTPRC + 1
      NSTATE = NSTATE - 1
```

Fig. 4-43 (cont'd.) Precompiler formatted source listing

320

```
NO. (...)=NESTING DEPTH     SUBROUTINE HPPRC      HUGHES AIRCRAFT CO. ---- HIFTRAN-2, VERSION 1.0   05/25/77      PAGE NUMBER   3

16 P          C
17 P                    I2 = LPOINT                                          00001130
1 1               DO(I=1,30)                                                 00001140
1 1                 ENDPROC(I,INPRCC) = LRK                                  00001150
 2 2             ENDDO                                                       00001160
 2 2             DO(I=1,30)                                                  00001170
2223              WHILE(K(COMP(LIST(I2),LRK) ,EC, 1)                        00001180
2 2                  I2 = I2 + 1                                            00001190
2 2                  IF(I2.GT.LINENO)                                       00001200
2 4                    ESCAPE DO                                            00001210
2 2                  ENDIF                                                  00001220
2 2               ENDWHILE                                                  00001230
 2 2              IF (LIST(I2) .EQ. KPAR)                                   00001240
 2 4                ESCAPE DO                                               00001250
 2 2              ENDIF                                                     00001260
3 3               ENDDO(I,INPRCC) = LIST(I2)                                00001270
3 3               IF ( I2+1 .EQ. 13Q)                                       00001280
3 3                I2 = I2 + 1                                              00001290
3 4                 WHILE (LIST(I2) .EQ. LRK)                               00001300
3 3                    ENDWHILE                                            00001310
3 3                    I2 = I2 + 1                                          00001320
3 3                    IF (LIST(I2) .NE. KPAR)                              00001330
3 5                     IF (CALL ERROR(-3)                                  00001340
3 3                     ENDIF                                              00001350
3 2                  ENDIF                                                  00001360
3 1               ENDDO                                                     00001370
2 2             ENDPROC(3),INPRCC) = NULAR(X)                               00001380
2 2             IPROC(4,INPRCC) = C                                         00001390
 2              CALL ACTI                                                   00001400

 4              C                                                           00001410
 4              WRITE(LINPRC,100)LRHL,(LIST(I),I=1,66),(ISEQ(K,1),K=1,4)    00001420
 4         100  FORMAT(80A1)                                                00001430

 4              C                                                           00001450
 4                  UNTIL(LTYPE .EC. 29)                                    00001460
 4                    CALL GTSTM(LUNIN,LUNPRC)                              00001470
 4                    IF(LTEOF .EC. 1)                                      00001480
 4                      CALL ERROR(39)                                      00001490
 4                      ESCAPE UNTIL                                        00001500
 4                    ENDIF                                                 00001510
 4                    CALL NSCAN                                            00001520
 4                    CALL RSCAN                                            00001530
 4                    LENGTH=LINENL - LINBEG + 1                            00001540
 4                    IF(LTYPE .EC. -1)                                     00001550
 4                      CALL ERROR(30)                                      00001560
 4                      ESCAPE UNTIL                                        00001570
 4                    ENDIF                                                 00001580
 4                  ENDIF                                                   00001590
 4                  IF(LTYPE .EC. 28)                                       00001600
 4                    CALL ERROR(28)                                       00001610
 4                    LTYPE = 3                                            00001620
 4                  UNTIL(LTYPE .EC.-1)                                    00001630
 4                    CALL GTSTM(LUNIN,LUNPRC)                             00001640
 4                    CALL NSCAN                                           00001650
```

Fig. 4-43 (cont'd.) Precompiler formatted source listing

```
67    0           . . . . .    CALL ESCAN                                               00001660
68    0           . . . . .    LENGTH=LINENO - LINREC + 1                               00001670
69    0           . . . . .    CALL KLASS                                               00001680
70    0           . . . . .    CALL PUTIF                                               00001690
71    0   20      . . . . .    ENDUNTIL                                                 00001700
                  . . . . <--  ESCAPE UNTIL                                             00001710

72  ( 0)  10      . . . <----  ENDIF                                                    00001720
73    0           . .  WRITE (LINREC,100) LABFL,(LIST(I),I=1,66),((ISEC(K,1),K=1,8)     00001740
74  ( 0)  10      . .  ENDUNTIL(LINREC.EQ.1 .OR. LTYPE.EQ.-1)                           00001750
75    0    0      IF (IEOF.EQ.1 .OR. LTYPE.EQ.-1)                                       00001760
76  ( 0)  ( 1)    . CALL MENU                                                           00001770
77    0           . ENDIF                                                               00001780
                  RETURN
                  <------    END
78    0           END
```

NUMBER OF HIFTRAN STATEMENTS IN THIS MODULE IS   35.
```
    IF      STATEMENTS:
    ORIF    STATEMENTS:
    WHILE   STATEMENTS:                 OCCURRENCES: 00000
    DO      STATEMENTS:
    LOOP    STATEMENTS:
    CASE    STATEMENTS:
    UNTIL   STATEMENTS:
    ESCAPE  STATEMENTS:
    CYCLE   STATEMENTS:
    PROCEDURE STATEMENTS:
    PERFORM STATEMENTS:
    QUIT    STATEMENTS:
```

NUMBER OF FORTRAN STATEMENTS IN THIS MODULE IS   44
NUMBER OF COMMENT STATEMENTS IN THIS MODULE IS   95
NUMBER OF ERRORS IN THIS MODULE IS

Fig. 4-43 (*cont'd.*)   Precompiler formatted source listing

322

```
LEVEL 2.1  ( JAN 75 )              OS/360  FORTRAN H EXTENDED              DATE 77.259/11.32.27              PAGE 1

REQUESTED OPTIONS: NODECK,NOLIST,OPT(1),NODUMP,LINECNT=74

OPTIONS IN EFFECT: NAME(MAIN) OPTIMIZE(1) LINECOUNT(74) SIZE(MAX) AUTODBL(NONE)
SOURCE EBCDIC NOLIST NODECK OBJECT MAP NOFORMAT NOGOSTMT XREF NOALC NOANSF TERMINAL FLAG(I)

ISN 0002   C*T   SUBROUTINE RPROC                                                       00000010
           C                                                                           00000040
           C     PURPOSE:  TO STORE PROCEDURE AND DATA FOR LATER PROCESSING            00000060
           C                                                                           00000070
           C     CALLING                                                               00000080
           C     ROUTINES: TRAN1                                                       00000100
           C                                                                           00000110
           C     CALLS:  ACT1, ESCAN, FPROC, GTSTM, HEND, KCOMP, KLASS, NSCAN,         00000120
           C             NULAB, PUTIF                                                  00000140
           C                                                                           00000160
           C     INPUT:    COMMON /CARDS/, /CONSTN/, /PROCED/, /STATE/, /USEOPT/, THE  00000180
           C                                                                           00000190
           C     NOTE:   PROCEDURE PROCESSING AND OUTPUT DONE IN <HEND>, THE           00000200
           C             END AND FORTRAN STATEMENT PROCESSOR                           00000210
           C                                                                           00000220
           C*S   PSEUDOCODE REPRESENTATION: PROCESS PROCEDURE STATEMENT                00000230
           C                                                                           00000240
           C       INCREMENT PROCEDURE ARRAY POINTER                                   00000250
           C       IF GREATER THAN 5                                                   00000260
           C         PROCESS AN ERROR - ONLY 5 PROCEDURES PER ROUTINE ALLOWED          00000270
           C         EXIT PROCESSING                                                   00000280
           C       ENDIF                                                               00000290
           C       INITIALIZE STORAGE AREA AND STORE PROCEDURE NAME AND DATA           00000300
           C       PROCESS STATEMENT ACTION ...                                        00000310
           C       WRITE PROCEDURE CARD IMAGE TO DISK FILE                             00000330
           C       COUNT UNTIL AN END PROCEDURE CARD IS PROCESSED                      00000340
           C         BEGIN IN USE STATEMENT                                            00000350
           C         PROCESS STATEMENT END LOCATION                                    00000360
           C         PROCESS STATEMENT BEGIN LOCATION                                  00000370
           C         CLASSIFY STATEMENT                                                00000380
           C         IF END CARD ENCOUNTERED                                           00000400
           C           EXIT PROCESSING                                                 00000410
           C         ENDIF                                                             00000420
           C         IF ANOTHER PROCEDURE STATEMENT IS ENCOUNTERED                     00000430
           C           PROCESS AN ERROR                                                00000440
           C           DUMP ROUTINE THROUGH END CARD                                   00000450
           C           EXIT PROCESSING                                                 00000470
           C         ENDIF                                                             00000480
           C         WRITE CARD IMAGE TO DISK                                          00000490
           C       ENDDO UNTIL                                                         00000500
           C       IF AN END OF FILE OR END CARD OCCURRED                              00000510
           C         PROCESS FORTRAN OR END STATEMENT ... TO PRINT OUT PROC FILE       00000520
           C       ENDIF                                                               00000530
           CCCCCCCCCCCCCCCCCCCCCCCCCCCCCCCCCCCCCCCCCCCCCCCCCCCCCCCCCCCCCCCCCCCCCC       00000540

ISN 0003         COMMON/CARDS/LCARD(80),IEOF,NUMCRD                                     00000550
           C                                                                           00000560
           C     THIS IS THE INPUT SPACE COMMON IN USE                                 00000570
           C                                                                           00000580
           C       LCARD = CARD IMAGE ARRAY                                            00000600
           C       IEOF = 1 IF END OF DATA, 0 IF NOT                                   00000610

ISN 0004         COMMON/CONSTN/ LBK,DUMMY(26)                                          00000620
           C                                                                           00000630
           C     THIS IS THE CONSTANT COMMON IN USE                                    00000640
           C                                                                           00000650
           C       LBK = HOLLERITH BLANK                                               00000660
           CCCCCCCCCCCCCCCCCCCCCCCCCCCCCCCCCCCCCCCCCCCCCCCCCCCCCCCCCCCCCCCCCCCCCC       00000610

ISN 0005         COMMON /PROCED/IPPROC(40,5),INPPRC,KNTPRC,JPPRC                        00000620
           C                                                                           00000630
           C     THIS IS THE PROCEDURE STATEMENT COMMON IN USE                         00000640
           C                                                                           00000660
           C       IPPROC = PROCEDURE STATEMENT ARRAY, WHERE                           00000680
           C         WORDS 1-30 = PROCEDURE NAME                                       00000690
           C         WORD 31 = LABEL 1
```

Fig. 4-44 FORTRAN compiler source listing from precompiler input

```
C
C                 WORDS 22-29 = POSSIBLE LABEL 2'S
C                 INPROC = POINTER TO POSS ARRAY FOR INPUT
C                 KNTPRC = THE NUMBER OF PRECOMPILES PER ROUTINE
CCCCCCCCCCCCCCCCCCCCCCCCCCCCCCCCCCCCCCCCCCCCCCCCCCCCCCCCCCCCCCCCCC

ISN 0005      COMMON/STATE/LABEL(6),LIST(120),ISEQ(620),NSTATE
             1 ,LINENO,LINFNC,LFNGTH,NFIGTH,LPOINT,LEVEL,ITYPE,LLTYPE,INSTK,IRET
C
C             THIS IS THE STATEMENT COMMON IN USE
C
C             LIST = ARRAY OF STATEMENT TEXT CHARACTERS
C             LINENO = FIRST NON-BLANK CHARACTER IN LIST
C             LINEND = LAST NON-BLANK CHARACTER IN LIST
C             LPOINT = POINTER IN TEXT TEXT CHARACTER
C             LFNGTH = LENGTH OF FORTRAN STATEMENT
C             ITYPE = FORTRAN STATEMENT TYPE
C             LLTYPE = PREVIOUS FORTRAN STATEMENT TYPE
CCCCCCCCCCCCCCCCCCCCCCCCCCCCCCCCCCCCCCCCCCCCCCCCCCCCCCCCCCCCCCCCCC

ISN 0007      COMMON/USER/LIMAIN,LIMNOT,LIMPRC,LIMER,LIMDRC,LIMPRC,
             1         NCMET,KCMETM,KOINC(25),NPROM
ISN 0008      INTEGER STRIK
C
C             THIS IS THE USER OPTIONS COMMON IN USE
C
C             LPMIN = LOGICAL UNIT NUMBER FOR INPUT
C             LIMPRC = LOGICAL UNIT FOR PRECOMPILE STORAGE
CCCCCCCCCCCCCCCCCCCCCCCCCCCCCCCCCCCCCCCCCCCCCCCCCCCCCCCCCCCCCCCCCC

ISN 0013      DATA KPAR /1H)/
ISN 0014      INPROC = INPROC + 1
ISN 0015      IF(INPROC .GT. 6) + 1
ISN 0016      THPROC (INPROC .GT. 6) GO TO 9998
ISN 0017      CALL PFFA(37)
             RETURN
9998 CONTINUE
ISN 0016      KNTPRC = KNTPRC + 1
ISN 0017      NSTATE = NSTATE - 1
C
ISN 0018      I2 = LPOINT
ISN 0019      DO I1=1,20
ISN 0020      I9992=1
ISN 0021      I=99995=20
C            *DO 99994 I=I99992,I99996
ISN 0023      IPROC(I,INPROC) = LRK
ISN 0024      CONTINUE
9994 CONTINUE
ISN 0024      DO(I)=1,20
ISN 0025      I99992=1,20
ISN 0026      I99992=20
ISN 0027      DO 99995 I=I99992,I99996
ISN 0028      WHILE.NOT.(KCOMB(LIST(I2),EQ.1)
ISN 0029      I2 = I2 + 1,KCOMB(LIST(I2),EQ(1) .EQ. 1)) GO TO 99997
C
ISN 0031      IF(I2 .GT. LINEND)
ISN 0032      IF ( .NOT. I2 .GT. LINEND) GO TO 99996
ISN 0033      GO TO 99999
9993 CONTINUE
ISN 0034      ENDIF
C            ENDWHILE
             GO TO 99998
9997 CONTINUE
ISN 0035      IF (LIST(I2) .EQ. KPAR)
ISN 0036      IF (.NOT.(LIST(I2) .EQ. KPAR)) GO TO 99994
C            ESCAPE DO
```

Fig. 4-44 (cont'd.) FORTRAN compiler source listing from precompiler input

```
LEVEL 2.1  ( JAN 75 )         HPROC            OS/360  FORTRAN H EXTENDED                DATE 77.259/11.32.27      PAGE   3
  ISN 0039             GO TO 99969                                                          00001260
                C      ENDIF                                                                00001270
  ISN 0040      99984  CONTINUE                                                             00001270
  ISN 0041             IPROC(I,INPROC) = LIST(I2)                                           00001280
  ISN 0042             I2 = I2 + 1                                                          00001290
                C      IF (I .EQ. 30)                                                       00001300
  ISN 0043             IF (.NOT.(I .EQ. 30)) GO TO 99982                                    00001300
                C      WHILE (LIST(I2) .EQ. LBK)                                            00001310
  ISN 0045      99980  IF (.NOT.(LIST(I2) .EQ. LBK)) GO TO 99979                            00001310
  ISN 0047             I2 = I2 + 1                                                          00001320
                C      ENDWHILE                                                             00001330
  ISN 0048             GO TO 99980                                                          00001330
  ISN 0049      99979  CONTINUE                                                             00001330
                C      IF (LIST(I2) .NE. KPAR)                                              00001340
  ISN 0050             IF (.NOT.(LIST(I2) .NE. KPAR)) GO TO 99978                           00001340
  ISN 0052             CALL ERROR(43)                                                       00001350
                C      ENDIF                                                                00001360
  ISN 0053      99978  CONTINUE                                                             00001360
                C      ENDIF                                                                00001370
  ISN 0054      99982  CONTINUE                                                             00001370
                C      ENDDO                                                                00001380
  ISN 0055      99990  CONTINUE                                                             00001390
  ISN 0056      99989  CONTINUE                                                             00001380
  ISN 0057             IPROC(31,INPROC) = NULAB(Y)                                          00001390
  ISN 0058             IPROC(40,INPROC) =0                                                  00001400
  ISN 0059             CALL ACT1                                                            00001410
                C                                                                           00001420
  ISN 0060             WRITE(LUNPRC,100)LABEL,(LIST(I),I=1,66),(ISEQ(K,1),K=1,8)            00001430
  ISN 0061          100 FORMAT(80A1)                                                        00001440
                C                                                                           00001450
                C      UNTIL(ITYPE .EQ. 29)                                                 00001460
  ISN 0062             GO TO 99974                                                          00001460
  ISN 0063      99976  IF (ITYPE .EQ. 29) GO TO 99975                                       00001460
  ISN 0065      99974  CONTINUE                                                             00001460
  ISN 0066             CALL GTSTM(LUNIN,LUNPRC)                                             00001470
                C      IF(IEOF .EQ. 1)                                                      00001480
  ISN 0067             IF (.NOT.(IEOF .EQ. 1)) GO TO 99973                                  00001480
  ISN 0069             CALL ERROR(38)                                                       00001490
                C      ESCAPE UNTIL                                                         00001500
  ISN 0070             GO TO 99975                                                          00001500
                C      ENDIF                                                                00001510
  ISN 0071      99973  CONTINUE                                                             00001510
  ISN 0072             CALL NSCAN                                                           00001520
  ISN 0073             CALL ESCAN                                                           00001530
  ISN 0074             LENGTH = LINEND - LINREC + 1                                         00001540
  ISN 0075             CALL KLASS                                                           00001550
                C      IF(LTYPE.EQ.-1)                                                      00001560
  ISN 0076             IF (.NOT.(LTYPE.EQ.-1)) GO TO 99971                                  00001560
  ISN 0078             CALL ERROR(38)                                                       00001570
                C      ESCAPE UNTIL                                                         00001580
  ISN 0079             GO TO 99975                                                          00001580
                C      ENDIF                                                                00001590
  ISN 0080      99971  CONTINUE                                                             00001590
                C      IF(ITYPE .EQ. 28)                                                    00001600
  ISN 0081             IF (.NOT.(ITYPE .EQ. 28)) GO TO 99969                                00001600
  ISN 0083             CALL ERROR(39)                                                       00001610
  ISN 0084             LTYPE = 1                                                            00001620
                C      UNTIL(LTYPE .EQ. -1)                                                 00001630
  ISN 0085             GO TO 99965                                                          00001630
  ISN 0086      99967  IF (LTYPE .EQ. -1) GO TO 99966                                       00001630
  ISN 0088      99965  CONTINUE                                                             00001630
  ISN 0089             CALL GTSTM(LUNIN,LUNOUT)                                             00001640
  ISN 0090             CALL NSCAN                                                           00001650
  ISN 0091             CALL BSCAN                                                           00001660
  ISN 0092             LENGTH = LINEND - LINREC + 1                                         00001670
  ISN 0093             CALL KLASS                                                           00001680
  ISN 0094             CALL PUTIF                                                           00001690
                C      ENDUNTIL                                                             00001700
  ISN 0095             GO TO 99967                                                          00001700
  ISN 0096      99966  CONTINUE                                                             00001700
                C      ESCAPE UNTIL                                                         00001710
  ISN 0097             GO TO 99975                                                          00001710
                C      ENDIF                                                                00001720
  ISN 0098      99969  CONTINUE                                                             00001720
```

Fig. 4-44 (*cont'd.*) FORTRAN compiler source listing from precompiler input

```
LEVEL 2.1  ( JAN 75 )           FPPCC          (5/360  FORTRAN H EXTENDED              DATE 77.259/11.32.27          PAGE   4

ISN 0100        C      WRITE(LUNPRC,100) LABEL,(LIST(I),I=1,66),(ISEQ(K,1),K=1,8)                 00001730
ISN 0101        C      ENDUNTIL                                                                    00001740
                       GO TO 99976                                                                 00001740
                99976 CONTINUE                                                                     00001750
ISN 0102        C      IF (IEOF.EQ.1.OR.LTYPE.EQ.-1)                                               00001750
ISN 0104        1      IF (.NOT.(IEOF.EQ.1.OR. LTYPE.EQ.-1)) GO TO 99964                           00001760
                       CALL HEND                                                                   00001760
                       ENDIF                                                                       00001760
ISN 0105        99964 CONTINUE                                                                     00001770
ISN 0106               RETURN                                                                      00001770
ISN 0107               END                                                                         00001780
```

Fig. 4-44 (cont'd.)   FORTRAN compiler source listing from precompiler input

necessary are when: (1) the error must be traced through a program dump, or (2) the error termination indicates the FORTRAN source statement at which the program failed. All other debugging is most effectively performed by using the Formatted (indented) Source Listing.

The Formatted Source Listing for a typical structured subroutine is shown in Figure 4-43, and the resulting Fortran compiler listing is illustrated in Figure 4-44. The HIFTRAN precompiler[52] used in this example is typical of the precompilers widely used to develop structured FORTRAN programs. They are considered the most cost-effective means of reliably implementing complex logical control structures in software.

Bibliography

DAHL, O. J., E. W. DIJKSTRA, and C. A. R. HOARE, *Structured Programming*, New York: Academic Press, 1972.

DIJKSTRA, E. W., "A Constructure Approach to the Problem of Program Correctness," *BIT*, **8**, 3 (August, 1968), 174–186.

———, *A Discipline of Programming*, Englewood Cliffs, N.J.: Prentice-Hall, Inc., 1976.

———, "The Humble Programmer," *Communications of the ACM*, **15**, 10 (October, 1972), 859–66.

HOPKINS, M. E., "A Case for the GOTO," *Proceedings of the ACM Conference* (August, 1972), 787–90.

KERNIGHAN, B. W., and P. J. PLAUGER, *The Elements of Programming Style*, New York: McGraw-Hill Book Co., 1974.

KNUTH, D. E., "Structured Programming with **go to** Statements," *Computing Surveys*, **6**, 4 (December, 1974), 261–301.

MAYNARD, J., *Modular Programming*, Princeton, N.J.: Auerbach Publishers, Inc., 1972.

MCGOWAN, C. L., III, and J. R. KELLEY, *Top-Down Structured Programming Techniques*, New York: Petrocelli/Charter, 1975.

MCKEEMAN, W. M., "On Preventing Programming Languages from Interfering with Programming," *IEEE Transactions on Software Engineering*, **SE-1**, 1 (March, 1975), 19–26.

MILLS, H. D., "Mathematical Foundations for Structured Programming," *IBM Technical Report* **FSC 72-6012**, Gaithersburg, Md., International Business Machines Corp., February, 1972.

MYERS, G. J., *Reliable Software Through Composite Design*, New York: Petrocelli/Charter, 1975.

PETERSON, W. W., T. KASAMI, and N. TOKURA, "On the Capabilities of While, Repeat, and Exit Statements," *Communications of the ACM*, **16**, 8 (August, 1973), 503–12.

STEVENS, W. P., G. J. MYERS, and L. L. CONSTANTINE, "Structured Design," *IBM Systems Journal*, **13**, 2 (May, 1974), 115–39.

[52]*HIFTRAN User's Manual* (El Segundo, Calif.: Hughes Aircraft Company, 1976).

WIRTH, N. "On the Composition of Well-Structured Programs," *Computing Surveys*, **6**, 4 (December, 1974), 247–259.

————, "Program Development by Stepwise Refinement," *Communications of the ACM*, **14**, 4 (April, 1971), 221–27.

————, *Systematic Programming*, Englewood Cliffs, N.J.: Prentice-Hall, Inc., 1973.

WULF, W. A., "A Case Against the GOTO," *Proceedings of the ACM Conference*, August, 1972, pp. 791–97.

YOURDON, E., *Techniques of Program Structure and Design*, Englewood Cliffs, N.J.: Prentice-Hall, Inc., 1975.

————, and L. L. CONSTANTINE, *Structured Design*, New York: Yourdon, Inc., 1975.

5 VERIFICATION AND VALIDATION

MICHAEL S. DEUTSCH

Section Head
Data Processing Laboratories
Hughes Aircraft Company

> *"Who Keeps the Truth from the people stands in the way of God!"*
>
> LEONARD H. ROBBINS
> *The Truth and John Billington.* Stanza 8

The development of software systems involves a series of production activities where the opportunities for interjection of human fallibilities are enormous. Errors may begin to occur at the very inception of the process where the objectives of the software system may be erroneously or imperfectly specified, as well as during the later design and development stages where these objectives are mechanized. The basic quality factor for software is that it performs its functions in the manner that was intended by its architects. In order to achieve this quality, the final product must contain a minimum of mistakes in implementing their intentions as well as being void of misconceptions about the intentions themselves. Because of human inability to perform and communicate with perfection, software development is accompanied by a quality assurance activity.

The Department of Defense, a major procurer of the product under discussion, defines quality assurance as:[1]

> A planned and systematic pattern of all actions necessary to provide adequate confidence that materiel, data, supplies, and services conform to established technical requirements and achieve satisfactory performance.

Verification and validation are major means of providing software quality assurance, and the intent of this chapter is to explore the application of verification and validation techniques toward the achievement of quality assurance goals. Verification and validation are likely to play an increasingly crucial role as data processing continues to

---

[1] *Quality Assurance*, Department of Defense Directive 4155.1 (1972), Enclosure 2.

interact in more and more critical areas, such as health and transportation, where a software failure could have a catastrophic effect on life or property.

Nelson[2] has delineated and described the most prominent software design and implementation errors. These are summarized below:

- Typographical errors where the syntax of a programming language statement has been incorrectly written by a programmer.
- Misinterpretation of language constructions by the programmer.
- Errors in developing the detailed logic to solve the problem.
- Algorithm approximations that may provide insufficient accuracy or erroneous results for certain input variables.
- Singular or critical input values to a formula that may yield an unexpected result not accounted for in the program code.
- Data structure defects either in the data structure design specification or in the implementation of the specification.
- Misinterpretation of specifications.

When it is added to these possible errors the problem that the software requirements may be erroneously, ambiguously, or imprecisely stated, it can be seen that there is a wide spectrum of opportunity for the software development to go awry. Up to this time, the software development community has generally not been particularly effective in containing, unmasking, and rectifying errors before large-scale software systems are delivered for operational use.

The significance of verification and validation efforts, from a budgetary standpoint, may be seen in statistics on the most visible verification and validation activity —program testing. Gruenberger[3] qualitatively addresses the effort required to test a program, once it has been written, by contending that the intellectual effort required for testing approximates that which created it. This qualitative assessment is in concert with community experience on medium- to large-scale software systems where approximately 50% of the software budget is expended on testing and integration. The following quotations on percentage of effort devoted to checkout and testing on these actual spaceborne and command-control projects have been reported:[4]

SAGE	47%
NAVAL TACTICAL DATA SYSTEM	50%
GEMINI	47%
SATURN V	44%

Yourdon[5] furnishes an estimate that on the NASA Apollo project nearly 80% of the

[2]Eldred C. Nelson, "Software Reliability, Verification and Validation," in *Proceedings of the TRW Symposium on Reliable, Cost-Effective, Secure Software* (Redondo Beach, Calif.: TRW, Inc., 1974), pp. 5-12–13.

[3]Fred Gruenberger, "Program Testing: The Historical Perspective," in *Program Test Methods*, ed. William C. Hetzel (Englewood Cliffs, N.J.: Prentice-Hall, Inc., 1973), p. 13.

[4]Barry W. Boehm, *Some Information Processing Implications of Air Force Space Missions: 1970–1980* (Santa Monica, Calif.: The RAND Corp., 1970), Memorandum RM-6213-PR, p. 36.

[5]Edward Yourdon, *Techniques of Program Structure and Design*, ($\bar{C}$) 1975. pp. 254–256. Reprinted by permission of Prentice-Hall, Inc., Englewood Cliffs, New Jersey.

monies expended were devoted to testing. It is predicted that the present 50% figure will increase in the future as the amount of object code generated per line of source code produced by the programmer is amplified.[6] These figures illuminate the significance of one aspect of validation and verification in the software development process.

Software quality is approached by two distinct and complementing methodologies. The first is that of assuring that quality is initially built into the product. This involves emphasis on the early generation of a coherent, complete, unambiguous, and nonconflicting set of software requirements. Experience has shown that the most extensive cause of software delivered with inadequate performance, late, or in a cost overrun condition is an incomplete or inadequate requirements analysis. Implementation may then proceed by using organizational approaches that limit software complexity. Once the software has been initially coded, analysis and testing of the product, the second quality tool, are encountered. Testing is a diagnostic exercise and does not introduce quality into the product per se. It provides only a measure of the existing quality level and may identify the extent and location of the defects. Some explorations have been made into the use of error statistics derived from testing to predict subsequent software performance reliability.

There is a bridge between the two software quality approaches. It concerns the concept that if an initial product can be produced with a high degree of clarity and design simplicity, it is amenable to more effective testing. The emphasis in this chapter is on the analysis and testing facets of the software quality approaches with the organizational aspects being referred to occasionally in order to support and amplify.

Miller[7] refers to the preventive practices of producing a "testable" initial software product under the term "synthesis" techniques. Reifer[8] indicates that the "analysis" approaches include both program testing as well as the theory of formal proofs for program correctness.

The major concentration in this chapter is on pragmatic state-of-the-art technology. As this is a rapidly advancing field, however, there will be a concluding discussion of future tendencies. The section immediately upcoming concentrates on surveying the software community to provide some definitional framework for the terms software reliability, verification, validation, and certification. Attention is next turned to software testing, which is the most visible and most relied upon verification and validation technique in the present state-of-the-art. General software testing principles are initially discussed. Then the topic of automated test tools is addressed. As real-time systems present distinctive testing problems, a section is devoted to this subject. It is more costly to resolve software problems the further into the development cycle they are identified. In appreciation of this, a section summarizes verification and validation considerations, testing and other activities, over the chronology of the

[6]M. R. Paige and E. F. Miller, Jr., *Methodology for Software Validation—A Survey of the Literature* (Santa Barbara, Calif.: General Research Corp., 1972), RM 1549, p. 1.

[7]E. F. Miller, Jr., *Methodology for Comprehensive Software Testing* (Griffiss Air Force Base, N.Y.: Rome Air Development Center, 1975), p. 2.

[8]D. J. Reifer, *Computer Program Verification/Validation/Certification* (Los Angeles, Calif.: The Aerospace Corporation, 1974), Report No. TOR-0074(4112)-5, p. 7.

software life cycle. The last section is dedicated to identifying trends for the future in this field.

5.1
Definition of Terms

The terms software reliability, verification, validation, and certification fill the literature of the software community. They are used with varying expressed or implied definitions. They have already been employed in this chapter without reference to precise definition. This diversification may be traced to the individual author's need to customize a set of terminology that is appropriate and convenient for his specialized area of interest. Often the usage and definition of the terms are simply a matter of interchangeability between authors, i.e., the differences are that of appearance rather than of substance.

The major purpose of the immediately forthcoming pages is to convey a general understanding of this terminology and its application by surveying previous and ongoing usage of the terms.

5.1.1 RELIABILITY

Reliability of the product software is a specific measure of software quality. The achievement of high reliability in the final delivered product is the primary objective of the verification and validation process and the ambition of the total program of software development.

Schneidewind[9] defines software reliability as the probability that a program will operate successfully for at least time "t." A similar but more extensive definition of software reliability is provided by Shooman as retold by Yourdon:[10]

> ... the probability that a given software program operates for some given time period, without software error, on the machine for which it was designed, given that it is used within design limits.

The key issue here is clearly the concept of successful operation over a specific time duration and the ascription of a probability to that success. This is somewhat analogous to the meantime-between-failure (MTBF) metric for hardware.

Errors or defects are uncovered as the software is exercised. The volume, frequency, and severity of errors are the inverse measures of software reliability. Each time an error is detected and successfully rectified, the reliability has improved. Nelson[11] furnishes an algorithmic measure of reliability by first defining the "execution failure probability" as the quotient of the number of inputs for which failures occur and the total number of inputs. He then defines reliability as one minus the execution failure probability.

[9]Norman F. Schneidewind, "An Approach to Software Reliability Prediction and Quality Control," in *Proceedings of Fall Joint Computer Conference, 1972* (Montvale, N.J.: American Federation of Information Processing Societies, Inc., 1972), p. 240.

[10]Yourdon, *Techniques of Program Structure and Design*, p. 245.

[11]Nelson, *TRW Symposium on Reliable, Cost-Effective, Secure Software*, pp. 5-22–23, 5-28–29.

Speaking in a quality control context, Schneidewind[12] advocates as a noble goal the establishment of reliability specifications as quantitative acceptance criteria for software. Here, the software reliability budget would be derived from the total system reliability requirement, and then this budget would be allocated to each software element. A positive reliability value judgment based solely on a very low volume of errors, however, does not consider the impact or potential adverse effect of even a single error. On a very large real-time system, even a specification that permits only a very small error tolerance for an arbitrary number of instructions could cause the system to become incapacitated at a critical moment. Such a contrived, but realistic, situation promulgates two essential points: (1) Software reliability is multi-dimensional. In addition to volume, error severity, as a minimum, needs also to be considered; and (2) The problem of the "single critical error" cannot be persuasively addressed by today's technology within reasonable cost constraints.

There have been substantial investigations into using error statistics collected from software executions in conjunction with a model depicting error depreciation in order to predict future reliability. Schneidewind[13] analyzed error data fron 19 programs of the Naval Tactical Data System and concluded that reliability should be predicted only on an individual program basis because of the large variations in the error depreciation profiles between programs that he encountered. He also suggests that, because of differing impacts on system operations, reliability predictions for several severity levels of errors may be in order. Nelson[14] reports on good agreement between measured reliability and estimated a priori reliability based on program complexity and quality of documentation.

Some interesting tendencies in error statistics have been noted. Collected error data on newly installed versions of the Satellite Control Facility software system revealed that, for each version, the error rate reached a peak approximately one month after installation on the system.[15] Nelson[16] relates that testing uncovers logical errors early while numerical inaccuracies are revealed later.

Except in a very general context, the term "reliability" is awkwardly applied to the software product and is not well understood by software practitioners and theoreticians. This is understandable because the initial application of this terminology to software arose as an analogy to hardware. It later became obvious that there are certain rudimentary differences between hardware and software, particularly with regard to degradation attributes; i.e., software does not "wear out." There has not been a full recovery from this observed dissimilarity and, for the time being, there has not been a reconciled precise and universal definition of software reliability that is pragmatically useful.

The basic goal of verification and validation, the production of reliable software, has now been briefly explored. Next, the definitions and implications of the verification and validation terminology are examined.

[12]Schneidewind, in *Proc. of Fall Joint Computer Conference, 1972,* p. 837.

[13]Ibid, p. 846.

[14]Nelson, *TRW Symposium on Reliable, Cost-Effective, Secure Software,* pp. 5-22-23.

[15]E. F. Miller, Jr., *A Survey of Major Techniques of Program Validation* (Santa Barbara, Calif.: General Research Corp., 1972), RM-1731, pp. 14-15.

[16]Nelson, *TRW Symposium on Reliable, Cost-Effective, Secure Software,* p. 5-17.

5.1.2 VERIFICATION, VALIDATION, CERTIFICATION

There appears to be a reasonable level of agreement among software engineers that the activities of verification, validation, and certification are directed both toward determining that the software performs its intended functions and ensuring reliability of the software. The definitions of these three terms are related to the formalized activites of the overall software development process. A general model of the *system* development cycle is depicted in Figure 5-1 in terms of the products or deliverable items. "System" is emphasized with the realization that data processing may be just one of several segments that comprise the total system and that the data processing system consists not only of software elements, but may also include development of special hardware elements such as displays, logic chips, customized interfaces, etc.

The system development cycle occurs in discrete steps. It may be characterized as, first, a decomposition procedure that defines, in the form of requirements and specifications, the components of the system. This begins at the system/mission level. The definition process then successively branches until specifications for individual elements are produced. From these specifications the software or hardware elements are built. The end item elements are then recomposed in successive stages until an end item system product is assembled, delivered, and accepted by the buyer. The depth of the hierarchy shown in Figure 5-1 for any individual system development may vary, depending on system complexity, governing standards, and ad hoc agreements between seller and buyer. For example, the design specification activity is frequently extended to include a preliminary design specification as well as a detailed design specification; each is normally the major subject of a preliminary and of a critical design review respectively.

Referring again to Figure 5-1, the process may be geometrically viewed as consisting of two symmetrical tree-like structures, one diverging from the system to the element level, and the other converging back to the system level. Each member of the converging tree has a "mirror image" analogous member in the diverging tree. For example, the Data Processing Subsystem #1 End Item (converging tree) was defined by the Data Processing Subsystem #1 Requirements (diverging tree). The requirements and specifications of the diverging tree define and induce the end item products of the converging tree. The verification-validation-certification process seeks to reflect backward and ensure the integrity of the converging tree (the product) with respect to the diverging tree (the definition of the product). Thus, the collective verification-validation-certification activities intend to guarantee that each end item properly reflects its "mirror image" specification/requirements document, that each step is consistent with and implements the intentions of the previous step, and that the data processing segment end item is compatible with the total system. When viewed in the context that is represented diagrammatically by Figure 5-1, an appropriate allocation of the above definition to the individual terms is:

Validation—This activity assures that each end item product functions and contains the features as prescribed by its requirements and specifications at the corresponding level.

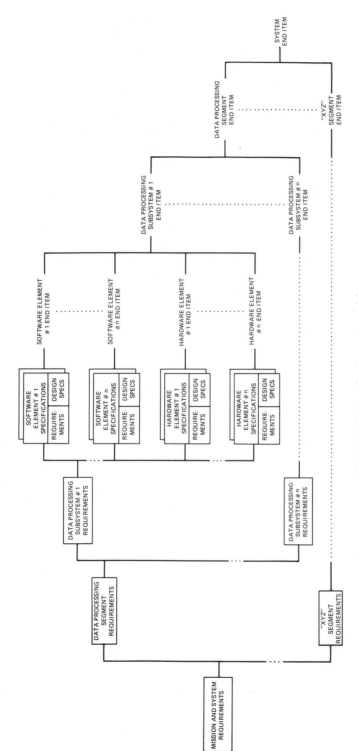

Fig. 5-1 System development model

Verification—This activity assures that each level of requirements or specification correctly echoes the intentions of the immediately superior level of requirements.

Certification—This activity assures that the data processing system (hardware and software) properly interacts within the total system and performs its specified functions within the total system context.

Reifer,[17] after a survey of the software literature, concludes somewhat similar definitions. He does, however, note a cumulative effect in that validation requires the accomplishment of all verification activities. He specifically breaks down the verification activity to consist of these components:

1. Verification that mission requirements have been correctly translated into data processing requirements.
2. Verification that the data processing requirements reflect the computer-applicable portion of the mission requirements.
3. Verification that the computer program design specification represents a true translation of the computer program requirements.
4. Verification that the actual code complies with the computer program design specification.

Reifer[18] also addresses the total system implication of certification:

> Certification extends the process of verification and validation to an operational (real or simulated) environment. Here, the code can be exercised to determine with some confidence whether or not the stated mission requirements are met.

Hetzel[19] contributes a somewhat different definitional framework. Verification is concerned with a program's logical correctness in the test environment. Validation is directed toward a program's logical correctness in a given external environment. He defines certification as connoting an authoritative endorsement implying written testimony that the program is of a certain standard or quality.

Miller[20] relates program validation to the software reliability concept with the following definition:

> *Definition: Program Validation* is the process of assuring that the probability of failure of a given software system on its next invocation is appropriately small, given that:
> 1. There is sufficient quantitative information about the past behavior of the software system (if there is a past), and
> 2. Some means of affirmation of the software system has been (or is being) applied to decrease the probability of a failure.

He refers to certification as a process concluding with some statement of the degree of quality of a software system.

[17]Reifer, *Computer Program Verification/Validation/Certification*, pp. 18–23.
[18]Ibid, p. 25.
[19]William C. Hetzel, in *Program Test Methods*, p. 9.
[20]Miller, *A Survey of Major Techniques of Program Validation*, p. 4.

Definitions of validation, verification, and certification have been advanced by the author based on a geometric argument. Other views, both similar and dissimilar, have been summarized from the literature. It has been contended that complete validation, implying absolute correctness, is presently infeasible with any sizable program.[21] Pragmatic cost effective partial validation is achieved via testing of the software. It has been similarly asserted that certification of large operational programs is not attained with current practices.[22] What is achieved is a validation that the programs have passed certain tests. Despite this recognized limitation, state-of-the-art verification and validation of programs are largely accomplished by exercising the software in a testing process. From the test results, proper functioning of the software and its reliability are inferred.

The next section explores software testing methodologies on a general level; following sections deal with the more specialized subjects of automated testing and testing of real-time systems. A subsequent section addresses verification and validation techniques over the software life cycles, including activities that supplement testing.

5.2
Software Testing Methodologies

5.2.1 INTRODUCTION

It is the purpose of verification and validation to determine that a software product performs according to the intentions of its architects. One community asserts that the ideal manner in which to accomplish this involves viewing the program as a theorem. A formal proof may then be constructed to establish the correctness of the theorem (and program). These techniques are not presently mature enough to be economically viable in practice. There is skepticism that this avenue represents the final answer to the problem regardless of economic considerations. A more practical immediate approach is to develop confidence in a program through accumulated experience of its use on a set of test cases.

Thus, testing is defined as the controlled exercise of the program code in order to expose errors. When, according to pre-established criteria, the number and severity of errors fall below a specified threshold, it is normally concluded that "proper operation" of the software has been demonstrated. The accuracy of this conclusion depends heavily on the framework in which "proper operation" is defined. A complete testing approach would ideally consist of demonstrating successful traversal of all possible paths through a program. Figure 5-2, provided by Boehm,[23] helps explain the futility of such a goal. He points out that there are about 10^{20} different paths through the flow chart, and that, furthermore, several thousand years of computer time would be required to check all paths. An analogous view of comprehensive test-

---

[21]C. V. Ramamoorthy, K. H. Kim, and W. T. Chen, "Optimal Placement of Software Monitors Aiding Systematic Testing," *IEEE Transactions on Software Engineering*, SE-1 (1975), 403.

[22]J. S. Prokop, in *Program Test Methods*, p. 31.

[23]Boehm, *Some Information Processing Implications of Air Force Space Missions*, pp. 23–25.

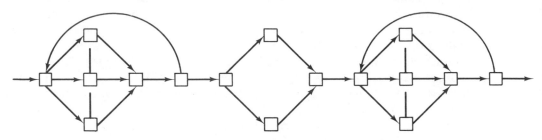

Fig. 5-2 How many different paths through this flowchart?

ing, stated by Huang,[24] is to test a program for all possible input cases to see if the correct outputs are generated. In considering a hypothetical program with two independent integer input variables, he calculated that 50 billion years of computing time would be required to complete the test. Clearly, this is prohibitive, and more pragmatic test goals need to be established. Fortunately, it is almost always the case that a much smaller number of test cases stresses a sufficient, statistically significant number of paths through the program.

Some insight of the objectives of testing can be obtained by delineating the types of errors that testing strives to expose. Such a categorization has been given extensive treatment by Yourdon[25] and is reproduced intact here:

> Logic Errors
>
> Indeed, logic errors *are* normally the most common type of computer bug—and most of our testing efforts are justifiably directed toward these bugs. For the purpose of our discussion, we can consider a logic error to be a solid, repeatable bug. If a given test input exposes the presence of a bug, then the same input, when presented to the program a second time, should expose the same bug the same way.
>
> Documentation Errors
>
> There are some programming applications where a documentation error can be just as serious as a logic error. In most cases, we would be more concerned with errors in the *user* documentation—the documentation that tells a user how to prepare input for the program, how to operate the program, and how to use and interpret the output from the program. There are other situations, though, where errors in the *technical* documentation could be considered critical.
>
> Overload Errors
>
> It is often important to test a program to find out what happens if various internal tables, buffers, queues, or other storage areas are filled up to or even beyond, their capacity. This is an especially critical area of testing in many on-line and real-time systems (e.g., what happens if all the terminal users type an input message simultaneously?), but it can be just as important in many batch-oriented programs.
>
> Timing Errors
>
> This is a category that is usually relevant only to real-time systems. In this case, we are concerned with logic errors that *cannot* be easily repeated; the errors are

[24]J. C. Huang, "An Approach to Program Testing," *ACM Computing Surveys*, **7** (1975), 114.
[25]Yourdon, *Techniques of Program Structure and Design*, pp. 254–56.

usually a function of timing conditions or coincidental combinations of events within the program. In a nonreal-time program, we can usually console ourselves with the knowledge that there are a finite number of cases to be tested (even though the number is so large that we are usually quite unable to perform exhaustive testing). In a real-time system, though, the number of timing possibilities appears (at least at first glance) to be infinite.

Throughput and Capacity Errors

Once again, this is a category that may be relevant only for real-time systems, though it seems that more batch-oriented programs should be tested in this area. We are concerned here about the *performance* of the program; even though it generates the correct output, it may take an unacceptable amount of CPU time to do so, or it may use an exorbitant amount of memory, disk space, etc. This is critical for many on-line systems because the performance of a program is often immediately visible to the user in terms of response time. In a batch program, we might still want to specify (and then test) that the program be able to process one transaction per second, that it take no more than 100,000 bytes of storage, and so forth.

Fallback and Recovery Errors

For a number of programs, the concept of recovery and fallback is quite critical. If there is a hardware failure (or possibly a software failure), an unrecoverable program can cause several hours of lost machine time, or in the case of a real-time, on-line system, great confusion and chaos among the users. Testing in this area should ensure that the programs can be continued from some checkpoint, that files are not damaged, that the entire recovery process can be performed in a reasonable amount of time, and that users, computer operators, and other human beings are not confused by the recovery process.

Hardware Errors and System Software Errors

In most cases, the programmer feels that it is not his responsibility to ensure that the hardware and the vendor's operating system work correctly—and, in most cases, he does not have to. However, if the testing involves an entire *system* and if that system is to be delivered to a noncomputer-oriented user, then someone should have the responsibility of ensuring that the hardware and the vendor's operating system *do* work—for the user will generally not appreciate it when the programmer complains, "But it's not my fault that the on-line order entry system just crashed and lost the entire day's orders—it was a hardware bug!"

Standards Errors

Finally, some people suggest that programs should be tested to ensure that they adhere to various programming standards: that they are modular, well-commented, free of nonstandard programming statements, etc. This is of increasing concern among organizations that are beginning to realize the magnitude of the maintenance effort.

It is well known that the cost of revealing and rectifying errors becomes larger with each successive step in the development cycle. For this reason, a building block approach to testing is usually undertaken, beginning at the element or routine level. Here, it is easier and more economical to detect and isolate errors.[26] Also, at this routine level, it is possible to check more logical paths. After combination into higher

[26]*Software Development and Configuration Management Manual* (Redondo Beach, Calif.: TRW Systems Group, 1973), p. 9–4.

level units, the task becomes less feasible. Ginzberg[27] emphasizes that the amount of difficulty encountered at each testing step is inversely related to the thoroughness of the preceding steps.

There may be some confusion as to the difference between debugging and testing. This distinction is treated by Gruenberger.[28] He asserts that, after the completion of the debugging phase, the mechanical errors of coding have been cleaned up, thus allowing the program to run and produce results.

> . . . when debugging is completed, the program definitely solves some problem. Testing seeks to guarantee that it is the problem that was intended.

The following subsections will explore verification and validation through software testing by addressing, in order, the components of the testing process, the significance of software project size to testing, levels of testing, testing strategies, the use of simulation in testing, and the relationship of systematized design techniques to testing.

One liability in the forthcoming discussion on program testing is worth mentioning. This involves the area of test case design. This subject is treated in connection with structural testing, but it is not precisely addressed in regard to functional testing. (The distinction between structural and functional testing will be highlighted in Sec. 5.2.4.) The design of functional test cases is presently an artistic process that cannot be adequately described in algorithmic terms. Because this type of test case design is so intimately related to the specific applications involved, it is considered not to be within the scope of this text.

5.2.2 COMPONENTS OF THE TESTING PROCESS

The testing process essentially consists of exercising the software and accumulating performance statistics on its operation. The conception, execution, and evaluation of the process are only semi-scientific. Gruenberger[29] partitions testing into scientific and artistic aspects: The prediction of expected program performance prior to testing has a scientific orientation; the determination of what to test for, the design of specific tests, and the management of the test execution are artistic in nature.

The successful engineering of a testing effort usually makes use of a great deal of accumulated software experience on the part of the participants, and, thus, inexperienced beginners are likely not to make a substantial contribution if assigned to this activity. Although partly artistic in nature, testing is not a "black magic" craft, but is a systematic and disciplined activity.

An overall software testing activity would nominally include test planning, test case design, test execution, and evaluation of test results.

The test planning task usually manifests itself in a master planning document.

[27]M. G. Ginzberg, "Notes on Testing Real-Time System Programs," *IBM Systems Journal*, 4 (1965), 68.
[28]Fred Gruenberger, "Program Testing and Validation," *Datamation*, July 1968, p. 39.
[29]Ibid, 39.

This is initially produced early in the development cycle or may have been generated prior to the manufacturing contract during a definition phase. It is updated through progressive stages. This plan specifies the overall test and integration philosophy, strategies, and methodologies to be employed. It traces the testing sequence from unit level tests to final acceptance test and identifies each individual test. This document will either contain or be accompanied by a "requirements-test matrix." This matrix identifies each individual requirement that is being tested and specifies the test or tests in which each requirement is to be verified. Representative forms of a master test flow sequence and requirements/test matrix are depicted in Figures 5-3 and 5-4.

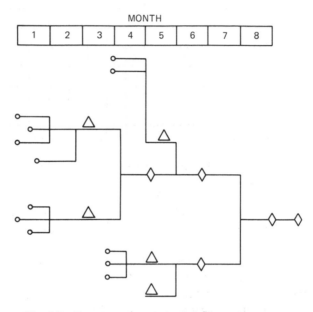

Fig. 5-3 Representative master test flow sequence

Each test indicated in the master test plan is given individual engineering attention, i.e., each test is "designed" and documented in test specifications. For each test a test plan, test procedure, and a test report are produced. These documents are prepared by the developer (or integrator) and may require customer concurrence or approval.

The test plan will contain the test objectives, a test description, a description of the test environment, including required hardware and software, a delineation of the requirements being verified, and an evaluation plan. The evaluation plan will consist of the acceptance criteria and a description of the techniques to be used in analyzing the test data in order to determine compliance with the acceptance criteria.

The test procedure will describe the test sequence, the test input data, the data base, identify the software configuration, and identify the required test personnel and their functions. The test is executed in accordance with the script and environment stated in the individual test specification. The test is typically witnessed by customer and quality assurance personnel. Any observed irregularities are noted and considered

	UNIT TEST #1	UNIT TEST #2	UNIT TEST #3	...	UNIT TEST #n	SUBSYSTEM TEST #1	SUBSYSTEM TEST #2	SUBSYSTEM TEST #n	SYSTEM TEST #1	SYSTEM TEST #2	ACCEPTANCE TEST	ANALYSIS
1.0	X					X				X	X	
1.1						X				X	X	
1.2	X								X	X	X	
2.0		X										
2.1		X										
2.2		X										
2.3									X	X		
2.4												X

Fig. 5-4 Representative requirements/"where verified" matrix

later in the evaluation stage. Output data from the test is captured for subsequent evaluation. A test report is issued, describing the test results in light of the objectives of the test. The results of the analysis of the test data are detailed, and any anomalies are noted.

Observations of the test itself and evaluation of the test output data constitute the basis on which it is determined whether the test objectives have been met, the pertinent requirements verified, and the acceptance criteria satisfied. The evaluation of the output data, if performed manually, is likely to be a tedious and time-consuming process for all but the most elementary of tests. The manual task of error-checking is in itself an error-prone process.[30] This has been one of the major motivations for the development of automatic test tools whose utility and necessity are becoming increasingly paramount. Hetzel[31] notes that automation requires at least a semi-algorithmic process. He attributes possible limitations on the success of automation to the fact that testing is not currently such a process.

Disciplined control of the testing effort is maintained by emphasizing comprehensive and precise definition of test plans, evaluation of test achievement against the test plan at periodic checkpoints, and quantitative measurement and expression of testing extent at checkpoints.[32] Except for very simple programs, utility of automatic

[30]Yourdon, *Techniques of Program Structure and Design*, p. 267.
[31]Hetzel, in *Program Test Methods*, p. 25.
[32]William R. Elmendorf, "Controlling the Functional Testing of an Operating System," *IEEE Transactions on Systems Science and Cybernetics*, SSC-5(1969), 284.

Chap. 5 Verification and Validation

test tools is practically a necessity in order to subcribe to these traits. Automatic test tools will be the subject of a forthcoming section.

5.2.3 SIZE OF SOFTWARE DEVELOPMENT IN REGARD TO TESTING

It is intuitively reasonable to assert that a larger software package will require a more extensive testing effort than would a smaller package (assuming, hypothetically, that all other things are equal). Independent of other factors, the size of the eventual software end product is directly related to the complexity of the development both from a technical and managerial standpoint. This is illuminated by the consideration that a larger program almost invariably produces a larger number of critical logical paths that must be checked and thus requires a larger staff of people. This increased complexity associated with the growing number of contemporary large software projects has been a motivator for the development of automated software testing tools.

The schedule requirements of customers have necessitated the development of large amounts of software over relatively short durations. Such tight schedules compel performing organizations to be more productive per unit of time. This is attained by applying a larger number of people to the problem. As more personnel become involved, the number of transactions between these people increases. The sensitivity to human fallibilities is magnified. There are more opportunities for mismatches of assumptions and logical reasoning to develop and assert a negative influence. The potential for these incompatibities to influence the quality of the product need be considered when planning the testing effort.

Petrovay[33] has used software system size, as measured by source statement count, as one of the determinants for planning an overall software quality assurance program. He first utilizes the estimated statement count in combination with ratings of complexity and criticality to determine a software category. A matrix then matches software category to specific design and development, verification and validation, and management tasks to be performed in each step of the development life cycle. The layout of this process is illustrated in Figures 5-5 and 5-6.

Yourdon[34] has classified software projects into discrete categories, using source statement size. His categorization ranges from simple programs that are less than 1000 source statements to what he describes as "utterly absurd programs" that contain between 1 million and 10 million statements. For each category, he specifies the approximate number of programmers involved, the schedule length, number of software elements, and the number of subsystems. These parameters may be interpreted to identify the escalating extent and complexity of the testing that would be necessary for each category. Software systems in Yourdon's "absurd" category have been built, but these systems, with few exceptions, have not been delivered within originally planned schedules and budgets.

[33]G.O. Petrovay, *Approach to Hughes Software Quality Assurance*, (Culver City, CA.: Hughes Aircraft Co., 1976) HAC Report No. P76-128 pp. 31–36.

[34]Yourdon, *Techniques of Program Structure and Design*, pp. 249–54.

STATEMENT COUNT			COMPLEXITY			CRITICALITY		SOFTWARE
> 100,00	5,000 – 100,000	< 5,000	HIGH	MEDIUM	LOW	CRITICAL	NON– CRITICAL	CATEGORY
x			x			x		CAT. i
x				x		x		CAT. i
x					x	x		CAT. i
x			x				x	CAT. i
x				x			x	CAT. ii
x					x		x	CAT. ii
	x		x			x		CAT. i
	x			x		x		CAT. i
	x				x	x		CAT. i
	x		x				x	CAT. ii
	x			x			x	CAT. ii
	x				x		x	CAT. iii
		x	x			x		CAT. i
		x		x		x		CAT. ii
		x			x	x		CAT. ii
		x	x				x	CAT. iii
		x		x			x	CAT. iii
		x			x		x	CAT. iv

Fig. 5-5 Determination of software category

5.2.4 SOFTWARE TESTING STRATEGIES

A software system is typically organized in a hierarchal structure and is composed of subsystems and lower-level components. The lowest-order component is denoted here as the "unit" (alternately called a "module"). The philosophy of testing at the unit level differs from that of integration testing where the units are interconnected to form higher-level components. Unit-level testing is concerned with the software flow pattern and the exercising of as many paths through the code as are feasible. Integration testing is performed at a level that is concerned with the software execution pattern of higher-level components. The following discussion first addresses unit testing philosophies. Integration testing is then explored by considering integration testing philosophies, techniques for combining software components, and thread testing, which is a technique to demonstrate early operation of certain software functions.

UNIT TESTING PHILOSOPHIES

For all but the most simple software project, it is usual and prudent to approach testing in a progressive hierarchal manner, beginning at the software unit level. This is because the software, when viewed at the system level, can be understood only in

SOFTWARE CATEGORY	DEFINITION	DEVELOPMENT	TEST	EVALUATION	OPERATION
i	TASKS: D & D V & V QA MGMT	TASKS: D & D V & V QA MGMT	TASKS: D & D V & V QA MGMT	TASKS: D & D V & V QA MGMT	TASKS: D & D V & V QA MGMT
ii					
iii					
iv					

- design and development (D&D)
- verification and validation (V&V)
- software quality assurance (QA)

Fig. 5-6 System software quality assurance program

terms of its higher-level components. The intricacies of the actual code cannot be intellectually grasped at that level. Deferring testing until the entire software system can be assembled would be a disastrous experience. Error detection, description, isolation, and rectification would be extremely difficult, if not impossible, and would, at the least, be economically unviable. A large data base of experience has verified that it is less costly to discover and rectify errors early in the development cycle. For these reasons, testing is begun at the unit level. It is at this level that the code can be most easily comprehended and viewed.

It is easier to test software exhaustively in small units. It is here that structurally oriented testing goals, such as number of logical paths traversed, percentage of statements executed, number of possible inputs to be tested, etc., are applied. The expectation is that a very large percentage of errors will be discovered and corrected at this level where the cost of doing so will be minimal. It is less feasible, both technically and economically, to attain these objectives after software units are interconnected. The testing on this level emphasizes the verification of logic, computations, data handling, timing, and sizing.

The goals of logic testing involve the exhaustive exercise of the program code and its component logic structures. The coverage is usually measured according to the amount of source code exercised by the test or by the number of logical paths traversed out of the possible number that exist. Computational testing verifies the quantitative accuracy of the results of operation of the software. Data handling testing ensures that input data is properly ingested, output data is stored in the proper location and format, data convesions have been properly performed, bad data is properly handled, data is not improperly discarded, and timing is within specified limits.[35]

INTEGRATION TESTING PHILOSOPHIES

After successful unit-level testing, the units are connected to determine whether they function together in tandem. This integration will assemble the software into larger components. The assembly process will progress to the integration of the software into subsystems and then finally culminate at the system level where the subsystems are connected together. Integration testing treats the software at the component level rather than at the detailed level of the code that was the subject of unit testing. Thus, the main testing emphasis is on the interaction between software components and their interfaces. As the software is built up into higher-level components, it becomes possible to demonstrate complete processing functions. This, then, allows the validation of performance requirements. Thus, testing assumes a functional theme at this point.

At the system level, subtle errors resulting from the complex interaction between pieces of software never before interconnected will be exposed. The deterrent to "surprises" in this phase of the testing is thorough and comprehensive testing at lower levels. Despite the best efforts of all involved, some errors will still remain undetected until the system level test. A high quality testing effort at earlier levels will, nonetheless, contain the severity and number of these errors.

Up to this point, the testing has likely occurred within the contractor's facility. This has been in a controlled environment, using artificially contrived test case data. On the basis of this testing, it cannot be firmly demonstrated that the software system will perform ably in its actual operating environment. Thus, additional testing is required in the field where the software will eventually operate. At least one and perhaps several additional tests will be necessary at the operational site. It is here that the software system is tested in the actual computers and hardware environment where it is intended to reside. These tests will be run under "live" conditions and in conjunction with other software that may be competing for the resources of the system. It is customary that the actual users eventually operate the system in an operational manner. This testing is usually referred to as acceptance testing or field testing.

METHODS FOR COMBINING SOFTWARE COMPONENTS

The assembly and testing of software organized in a hierarchal structure may be approached in several ways. The options of choice occur in two categories—phased versus incremental and top-down versus bottom-up. In practice, it is often the case that the selection in each category is not monolithic, and hybrid approaches are applied. A reference software component structure is diagrammed in Figure 5-7.

The distinction between phased and incremental integration is best explained by example. The phased approach would typically consist of first testing components

[35]*Software Development and Configuration Management Manual*, pp. 9-9–10.

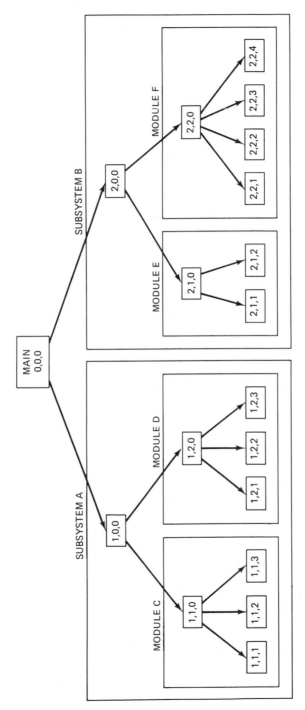

Fig. 5-7 Representative software component structure

(2, 2, 0), (2, 2, 1), (2, 2, 2), (2, 2, 3), and (2, 2, 4) from Figure 5-7 individually. The next step would be to interconnect these four components and test them as the next higher-level component "F" (Figure 5-7). A colorful commentary on the phased approach is provided by Yourdon and Constantine:[36]

> The phased approach to implementation could be described in the following (slightly tongue-in-cheek) manner:
> 1. Design, code, and test each module by itself. (Commonly known as "unit test.")
> 2. Throw all the modules into a large bag.
> 3. Shake the bag very hard. (Commonly known as "system integration and test.")
> 4. Cross your fingers and hope that it all works. (Commonly known as "field test.")

The major liability associated with this approach is that, in simultaneously combining all four components (previous example), the next incident of failure or error cannot be easily associated with the malfunctioning component(s). Thus, fault isolation is difficult.

An analogous description of the incremental approach is offered by Yourdon and Constantine:[37]

> In contrast, some programmers follow an incremental approach to testing. This approach can be paraphrased in the following manner:
> 1. Design, code, and test one module by itself.
> 2. Add another module.
> 3. Test and debug the combination.
> 4. Repeat steps 2 and 3.
> The essential characteristic of this approach, then, is that we are adding only one new (and potentially "buggy") module to the system at a time.

The obvious advantage of the incremental approach over the phased approach is that the process is self-focusing on the source of new errors. Any new malfunction is caused either by a defect in the most recently added component or by some new interaction between the new component and the rest of the system. A regression back to the previous state of the system before the new component was added is easily accomplished. This is a valuable attribute, not present with the phased approach, that facilitates a systematic investigation into the causes and sources of errors.

Any permutation of phased/incremental with top-down/bottom-up is potentially viable, depending on the specific circumstances. An approach in the first category is not married to an approach in the second category; the choice is independent.

For large, complex systems it is most common that integration of the large software components is carried forward in a bottom-up manner. This might typically

---

[36]Edward Yourdon and Larry L. Constantine, *Structured Design.* (Englewood Cliffs, N.J., Prentice-Hall, Inc. 1979) p. 500. Reprinted by permission of Prentice-Hall, Inc.
[37]Ibid, p. 501.

consist of the sequence of module[38] tests, subsystem tests, and the system test. This chronological progression starts at the lower level of the hierarchy (module) and culminates at the highest level (system). In Figure 5-7, Components C, D, E, and F might be viewed as modules. These would be assembled and tested individually. The modules would then be assembled to form Subsystems A and B. These subsystems would then be integrated to construct the entire system.

The top-down approach begins at the top of the structure and then proceeds to test components at progressively lower levels in the hierarchy. For example, referring to Module C in Figure 5-7, Component (1, 1, 0) would be tested first, with testing of Components (1, 1, 1), (1, 1, 2), and (1, 1, 3) to be achieved later.

Bottom-up integration requires "drivers." A driver exercises the software component that is the present testing target by simulating the activity of the next higher-level component. Top-down integration requires "stubs." A stub is a dummy component that simulates the functioning of the next component(s) subordinate to the component that is the present testing target. Yourdon and Constantine[39] may be referenced for detailed information on the attributes of drivers and stubs.

In reality, a combined top-down/bottom-up approach to testing and integration is most frequently the case. In Figure 5-7, Components (0, 0, 0), (1, 0, 0), and (2, 0, 0) are actually modules. Although not shown, such modules probably will have an infrastructure similar to C, D, E, and F. Modules (0, 0, 0), (1, 0, 0), and (2, 0, 0) typically might be developed in parallel with C, D, E, and F. The testing of the elements internal to each module may be accomplished with either approach, depending upon the circumstances. The test configurations for each module are charted in Figure 5-8. Usage of both drivers and stubs is indicated. It can be seen that testing at the module level proceeds from both the bottom and top of the hierarchy. The subsystem test configurations are shown in Figure 5-9. Module (0, 0, 0), if it is available at the time, would be coupled to Subsystems A and B for individual testing of these subsystems. A driver would be substituted for Module (0, 0, 0) if it were not available in time for subsystem testing. The stubs for modules (1, 0, 0) and (2, 0, 0) are incrementally replaced by the actual subsystems. For the system-level test, all drivers and stubs would be replaced by the actual modules.

The structure shown in Figure 5-7 is representative for a system contained in a single computer. In more complicated multiprocessor systems, particularly for real-time applications, the system is contained in several (or more) digital hardware units, both programmable computers and special purpose processors. These systems cannot be represented by a tree-like structure with centralized control at the top. The invocation structure will likely involve data-driven or interrupt-driven interfaces between computers.

[38]"Module," in this context, refers to a distinct functional unit of software that contains a relatively large amount of code. Generally it is the lowest-level component of software identified as a contract end item or configuration item. "Module" has also been used interchangeably with "subroutine" to denote the smallest unit of code in the invocation structure.

[39]Yourdon and Constantine, *Structured Design*, (Englewood Cliffs, N.J., Prentice-Hall, Inc. 1979) pp. 502, 504–5, 511.

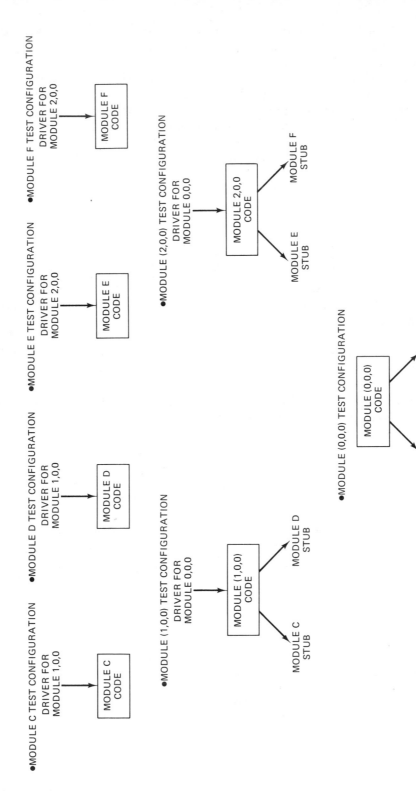

Fig. 5-8 Module test configurations

Fig. 5-9 Subsystem test configurations

Yourdon and Constantine[40] have provided an extensive discussion on the virtues of both the top-down and bottom-up approaches. They first examined each of the supposed benefits of top-down testing. Excerpts from this discussion are:

Top-Down Testing Eliminates System Testing and Integration

This is generally true, but it is a characteristic of incremental testing, not top-down testing per se. . . . top-down testing tends to be done in an incremental fashion, while most bottom-up testing has traditionally been done in a phased manner.

There is nothing to prevent the disciplined programmer from following a bottom-up incremental testing approach. Similarly, there is nothing to prevent the undisciplined programmer from following a phased top-down testing approach!

(IBM's Time Share Option (TSO) for Operating System 360 is an example of a project that combined incremental with bottom-up testing approaches).[41]

Top-Down Testing Tests the Most Important Things First

. . . In some systems, the modules at the bottom of the hierarchy are critically important, and it could be advantageous to test them first.

For example, in a real-time system with stringent processing requirements, the most critical problems may be at the bottom of the hierarchy. . . .

If interface problems . . . are anticipated—and it is reasonable to expect them in any project involving more than one team of programmers—then top-down testing does have some distinct benefits.

. . . The situation of a large, real-time system developed by multiple teams in geographically remote areas of the country: We may anticipate serious problems at both the bottom and the top of the hierarchy. We have no simple answers here: there may in fact be an argument for implementing from the top down and from the bottom up, at the same time.

Top-Down Testing Allows Users to See a Preliminary Version of the System

. . . A skeleton version of a system can be demonstrated to the users to ensure that the programmers are implementing the system that the users requested. . . .

---

[40]Ibid, pp. 512–20.
[41]Allan L. Scherr, in *Program Test Methods*, pp. 155–180.

It is important to realize that if a complete structural design has been accomplished, the programmer can choose to implement any sub-system first; some lower-level sub-systems may be valuable and productive to the user on a "stand-alone" basis.

Top-Down Testing Allows One to Deal with Problems More Gracefully

. . . If the circumstances (which may be beyond our control) are such that the entire system is not finished when the deadline arrives, which parts of the system would we prefer to have finished and demonstrable?

With a *traditional* or phased bottom-up approach, there is a good chance that the programmer will have finished all of the coding and possibly all of the "unit testing." However, there is an equally good chance that the "brown bag" test will have failed— that is, none of the pieces work together because of a bug in one or more modules. From the user's point of view, there is nothing *tangible* that works. . . .

The top-down approach, on the other hand, is more likely to result in a skeleton that will show some tangible evidence of working. . . . Of course, most users will still be displeased: They want the entire system to be delivered on the appointed deadline day. Nonetheless, we must expect that their displeasure will be far greater with a bottom-up approach than with a top-down approach.

Debugging Is Easier with Top-Down Testing

This is not really a characteristic of top-down implementation, but rather of incremental implementation; . . . debugging is considerably easier if we add only one new (and potentially "buggy") module at a time to an existing combination of debugged modules.

Requirements for Machine Time Are Distributed More Evenly Throughout a Top-Down Project

If we analyze the situation closely, though, we find that the phenomenon is caused by incremental testing—not by top-down testing per se. That is, every day we add one new module to the existing system and run through all the test data again—hence we use about the same amount of computer test time each day.

Programmer Morale Is Improved

This point deserves to be emphasized! It is not just the users and the . . . managers who are pleased by the tangible evidence of progress in a typical top-down project— the programmers also derive a great sense of satisfaction from seeing something that actually runs to end-of-job at an early stage in the implementation process.

Top-Down Testing Eliminates Drivers

This statement is true—but the implication that top-down implementation involves less work because of the elimination of drivers is not necessarily true. . . . the top-down approach requires stubs, or dummy modules, instead of drivers—indeed, it requires approximately the same number of stubs as the bottom-up approach requires drivers.

The obvious question is this: Which requires more work, stubs or drivers? Unfortunately, the answer is not so obvious. There are cases where stubs involve more work, and cases where drivers require more work.

In the absence of a complete, prior structural design, coding and testing *must* proceed entirely or essentially in a top-down manner because the bottom-level modules are not known!

Yourdon and Constantine[42] note that the best justification for bottom-up testing concerns the situation where a large portion of system "criticality mass" is located in low-level modules. If the system has only a few critical low-level modules, they add, the project could return to the top-down approach after testing the critical low-level modules.

They also amplify on other considerations that might favor bottom-up implementation: As most systems would typically contain large numbers of modules at the bottom of the structural hierarchy, a favorite management technique has been to assign large numbers of programmers to work on these modules in parallel. Experiences have shown that, with this approach, serious interface problems develop between the low-level modules. However, this seems to be more associated with the ill-advised usage of the phased approach rather than bottom-up. Another problem occasionally encountered is the one where an adequate volume of test case data can be generated only via a driver. In this situation, a bottom-up testing approach is appropriate for these modules.

THREAD TESTING

Thread testing is a technique of functional testing that can demonstrate the operation of key functional capabilities fairly early in the testing activity. A thread is a string of programs which, when executed, accomplishes a distinct processing function. When it is important to demonstrate the operation of certain important functions as early as possible, thread testing can form the basis of the testing approach. Early functional demonstration goals are frequently associated with real-time systems.

A typical thread-testing flow is diagrammed in Figure 5-10. Typically, this type of testing begins by exercising a single thread at any one time. For example, the programs comprising Function A are integrated and tested. Approximately in parallel, the programs comprising Function E are connected. After successful demonstration of Function Thread A, additional programs are added to the string to build Function A.B. The thread is further extended to form Function A.B.C. At this point the testing extends to multiple threads by exercising the A.B.C string in conjunction with the Function E string to form the A.B.C.D.E function thread. Other threads being tested in parallel would eventually be integrated to accomplish final acceptance tests. The testing objectives associated with the functions can be monitored over time by constructing and maintaining a chart like the one shown in Figure 5-11.

The benefits of the thread-testing approach may be summarized as:

- Allows testing and analysis in digestible quantities.
- Provides early demonstration of key functional capabilities.
- Forces the early availability of executable code.
- Requires early compliance with interface and configuration controls.

[42]Yourdon and Constantine, *Structured Design*, p. 520.

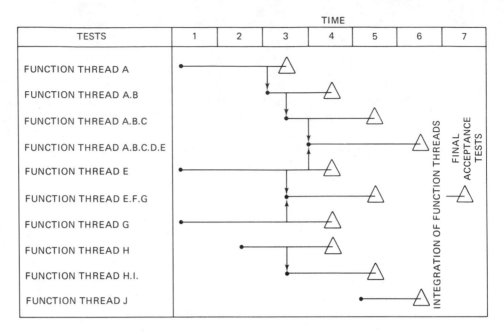

Fig. 5-10 Typical thread testing flow

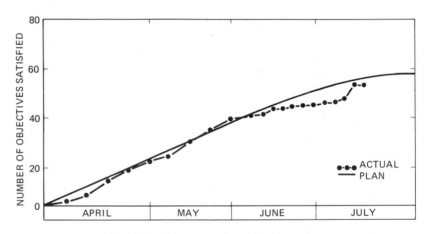

Fig. 5-11 Program testing objectives status

- Provides excellent visibility of status and quality of code.
- Produces early detailed design documentation.

Utilization of thread testing implicitly determines the mix of top-down and bottom-up testing. This is because the definition of the thread also identifies the path through the invocation hierarchy associated with that thread. Also defined as a result of this approach is the order in which software components have to be designed and coded.

Thread testing on a detailed level can form the basis of a very effective project planning and control strategy beginning at the point in the development cycle when the requirements specification is delivered. The scheduling of thread demonstrations provides frequent identifiable milestones against which progress can be measured. This concept is attaining an increased popularity, particularly in connection with large software projects.

This subsection has explored software testing strategies by investigating unit-level testing and then testing involving integration of multiple units. This discussion has assumed that a test environment existed to support this testing. This environment is normally not the actual operating environment of the software, but is usually a simulated environment. Simulation is the subject of the next subsection.

5.2.5 USE OF SIMULATION IN TESTING

Since it is usually not possible to test software under development in its actual operating environment and with real inputs, simulations are employed in the testing environment as a substitute for exercising the software in actual operations. By using simulation, the performance of the software may be observed at an earlier date. Many times, the actual operating environment may not as yet exist; delivery of the software may be one of the requisites for commencing operations; or the users of an existing system may not wish to have current operations disturbed until the new software is ready for a final acceptance test.

Two classes of simulations are used in the test environment:[43]

1. Environmental simulation
2. Interpretive computer simulation

Environmental simulation, as the terminology suggests, feigns the environment in which the software will eventually perform. The environment includes other programs operating in parallel or in series, noncomputer hardware, and external inputs to the program.[44]

Many times the control program and/or operating system may not be available at the time the applications software first becomes available for test. Initial testing then utilizes a simulator for the absent software; this simulator can incorporate many useful debugging features that would probably not be available with the operational versions of the programs.[45]

With the advancing complexity and criticality of software functions, it is often necessary to control test inputs via simulation tools.[46] With particular reference to real-time systems, it has frequently become necessary to use simulation to generate a sufficient volume of test input data to stress the system. For some systems, this has involved simulating the output of various sensing devices such as radars. On interactive

[43]Nelson, *TRW Symposium on Reliable, Cost-Effective, Secure Software*, p. 5–46.

[44]Ibid, pp. 5-48–49.

[45]Robert V. Head, "Testing Real-Time Systems, Part 2: Levels of Testing," *Datamation*, August 1964, p. 54.

[46]Hetzel, in *Program Test Methods*, p. 21.

systems, simulators have been used to prepare scripts of input requests that normally would have been generated by operators at display consoles. Remote terminal simulators have been used to present input messages to the main computer before the terminals are in place. These simulation scripts provide a chronology of inputs that is identical from test run to test run; hence, repeatability of inputs is attained that would not be possible by using real operators, consoles, and terminals.

Interpretive computer simulation is employed to simulate the behavior of the operational computer when that machine is not available for testing the software. Recently, a tendency has been to simulate the instructions of the operational computer by using a microcoded program running in another computer.[47] Prior to implementation, analytical simulations, which model the performance of a computer system parametrically, have been utilized to verify loading, throughput, and capacity.[48] Such simulations have also been used to determine allocation of storage and to determine which programs should be kept in main memory and which should be kept in other storage devices.[49]

5.2.6 TESTING AND SYSTEMATIZED DEVELOPMENT TECHNIQUES

By this time, the concepts have been exposed that strive to organize the software design into a structured hierarchy that contains small, simple software elements which, when fitted together, offer the prospect of containing fewer errors. While it is not the intent here to recount the principles of these concepts, a brief commentary on the relationship to software testing of these systematic or structured approaches to design and programming is relevant. Basically, adherence to a modular organizational pattern during development provides improved reliability and ease of testability of the completed system.[50]

Ideally, the decomposition of a complex processing problem into many small simple components should result in a state where each software component has been produced without errors. However, experiences have shown us that programming has been and will always be an error-prone process. In addition, misunderstandings and differing interpretations of specifications result in interface errors between components. Even with these inevitable fallibilities, these organizational approaches provide a level of "visibility" into the software such that the causes and sources of errors can be more clearly perceived and understood; hence, remedial actions can be more quickly and economically instituted. A modular design with small, simple components assists the preparation of test cases. In code relatively free of complexities, especially branches, the conditions under which control is transferred to a section of code can be more easily identified by inspection, and a test case input is more easily prepared to exercise

[47]Nelson, *TRW Symposium on Reliable, Cost-Effective, Secure Software*, pp. 5-50–51.
[48]Yourdon, *Techniques of Program Structure and Design*, pp. 273–74.
[49]Ginzberg, "Testing Real-Time System Programs," pp. 71–72.
[50]Miller, *A Survey of Major Techniques of Program Validation*, p. 31.

that section of code. When components are logically independent of each other, it is not necessary, when connecting components, to retest by using all permutations of the original test cases.[51] Testing may instead concentrate on interfaces and other higher-level considerations, such as functional requirements.

While program proofs are not yet a practical consideration for large programs, the program that is designed in a structured manner becomes more amenable to proof techniques. Liskov[52] suggests that informal proofs will assist in identifying relevant test cases and that these proofs, combined with exhaustive testing, should be the ultimate strategy for producing reliable software. Indirectly related is the concept of a specification language that can overcome some of the imperfections of written specification methods. The code may be derived directly from the specifications as would the testing objectives; this is because the specification language semantics would represent the conditions to be tested.[53]

This major section, which is now being concluded, has investigated the methodologies of software testing on a general plateau. Contemporary experiences have shown that the manual application of the techniques discussed here to large-scale software systems is beset with limitations. The next section explores how some of these limitations can be overcome. The subject of the section is automatic testing, and the material presented is less generalized and more application oriented.

5.3
Automated Testing

5.3.1 MOTIVATION FOR AUTOMATED TESTING

As software systems have grown to immense proportions in both size and complexity, the effort required to test these systems has grown more than proportionately. The need for a mass application of human resources has arisen. This has been both costly and not particularly effective in terms of the reliability produced. Despite expenditures of up to one-half of software development budgets for testing, significant numbers of errors remain in delivered software and often severely deter normal system operations. This situation has inspired the development of automatic test tools that assist in the production of effective tests and analyze the test results. In essence, much of the time-consuming, mechanical aspects of testing is taken out of human hands.

Automatic test tools provide the following attributes that are not as easily attainable by manual testing approaches:

- Improved organization of testing through automation
- Measurement of testing coverage, and

[51]B. H. Liskov, "A Design Methodology for Reliable Software Systems," in *Proceedings of Fall Joint Computer Conference, 1972* (Montvale, N.J.: American Federation of Information Processing Societies, Inc., 1972), p. 195.
[52]Ibid, p. 191.
[53]Hetzel, in *Program Test Methods*, p. 19.

• Improved reliability

Automatic tools provide machine amplification of human capability and relieve test personnel of routine time-consuming chores.[54] Even though routine, tasks such as manual error checking are preferably removed from human hands. This is because manual error checking itself is an error-prone process performed more reliably through automation. Budget and schedule considerations foreclose on the slow, tedious process of manual testing with the result that volume of testing is often insufficient. Relief is available through utilization of automated tools.

The complex content of large software systems requires the application of many test cases to thoroughly exercise the code. The generation of the test cases and analysis of the paths exercised in order to determine the extent of the resulting testing coverage would quickly exceed human capacity. Testing aids can instrument the code, measure the coverage provided by a test case, and furnish a report that shows the number of times each statement and sequence of statements was executed.

Improved reliability results when potential sources and avenues of errors are more closely investigated; this occurs as more experience in the use of the software is accumulated through carefully directed testing. Automatic tools enable a higher volume of testing than that would be attainable manually for the same cost. Alternately, a testing volume equivalent to that provided by manual techniques can be furnished at a lesser cost. Brown et al.[55] report that the retesting of a very large program aided by automated tools was accomplished with a 30% reduction in computer time and human effort with an increase in test thoroughness.

Hetzel[56] summarizes the arguments for automated tools by noting that: (1) Automation brings more rigor to the testing process. (2) An automatic process is more likely to be accepted for widespread use. (3) Cost and time savings may be accrued by the use of automated tools. Miller[57] suggests that with automated tools a less expensive category of technical personnel can be applied to the testing effort.

Two qualifications on the use of automated tools are worth denoting. First, program measurement tools will introduce side effects in the form of increased execution time and storage utilization. Thus, there may be limitations on their appliance to testing of real-time systems. Second, the utilization of automated tools is not always cost effective. They are useful when working with fairly large volumes of test cases.[58] For simple programs with small volumes of test cases the cost can outweigh the benefits—especially when modifications to the test tools are required.

The following subsections describe automatic test tools in terms of their generic elements, explore test goals and measures, and discuss test case generation. Finally, an example application of a test tool to a sample program is illustrated with the test tool outputs highlighted and described.

[54]E. F. Miller, Jr., and W. R. Wisehart, *Automated Tools to Support Software Quality Assurance* (Santa Barbara, Calif.: General Research Corp., 1974), p. 4.

[55]J. R. Brown, A. J. DeSalvio, D. E. Heine, and J. G. Purdy, in *Program Test Methods*, pp. 201–2.

[56]Hetzel, in *Program Test Methods*, p. 27.

[57]Miller, *Methodology for Comprehensive Software Testing*, p. 112.

[58]Yourdon, *Techniques of Program Structure and Design*, p. 270.

5.3.2 GENERIC ELEMENTS OF AUTOMATED TEST TOOLS

Practically the entire software development process can be assisted by some form of automated tool. An example breakdown of automated tools according to functional classification is provided by Ramamoorthy and Ho:[59]

I. System Design Analysis
   A. *Automated design tools* which provide a rigorous methodology for stating design requirements.
   B. *Automated simulation tools* which model the system hardware/software to study its characteristics.
II. Source Program Static Analysis
   A. *Tools for code analysis* which perform syntax analysis on the source code and look for error-prone constructions.
   B. *Tools for program structure checks* which generate graphs and look for structural flaws.
   C. *Tools for proper module interface checks* which detect inconsistencies in the declaration of data structures and improper linkages among modules.
   D. *Tools for event-sequence checking* which compare event sequences in the program with conventions of event sequences (e.g., I/0 sequences).
III. Source Program Dynamic Analysis
   A. *Tools for monitoring program run-time behavior* which collect program execution statistics.
   B. *Tools for automated test case generation* which aid testers to construct test cases which will comprehensively exercise the code.
   C. *Tools for checking assertions* which detect violations of assertions embedded into the code by testers.
   D. *Tools for inserting software defenses* which provide security measures to protect a program against unexpected or unauthorized modifications.
IV. Maintenance
   A. *Tools for documentation generation* which record information extracted during code analysis and program structure analysis for documentation.
   B. *Tools for validating modifications* which aim at predicting the effect of proposed changes.
V. Performance
   A. *Tools for program restructuring* which assist in reorganizing programs for optimization.
   B. *Tools to extract and validate parallel operations* which identify parallel tasks to aid parallel processing scheduling.
VI. Software Quality Validation Tools which strive to assign a figure-of-merit to a program on the basis of comparison to desirable characteristic attributes.

[59]C. V. Ramamoorthy and Siu-Bun F. Ho, "Testing Large Software with Automated Software Evaluation Systems," *IEEE Transactions on Software Engr.*, SE-1 (1975), 50–54.

The above categorization is specified only to illuminate the spectrum of applications for which automated tools have been constructed. The interest in this discussion focuses on a restricted subset: those tools which assist in the preparation of test cases and provide facilities for measuring the performance of the software and effectiveness of test cases. Such tools derive their information from the source text of the program that is being analyzed and tested and may be called Source Analyzer Systems (SAS). SASs would contain functions classified above under the headings Source Program Dynamic Analysis, Source Program Static Analysis, and Maintenance.

There are five basic functions performed by the SAS:

1. Analysis of source code and creation of a data base
2. Generation of reports based on static analysis of the source code that reveal existing or potential problems in the code and identify the software control and data structures
3. Insertion of software probes into the source code that permit data collection on code segments executed and values computed and set in storage
4. Analysis of test results and generation of reports
5. Generation of test assistance reports to aid in organizing the testing and deriving input sets for particular tests

The elements of a typical SAS while performing these functions are diagrammed in Figure 5-12.

The static analysis module analyzes the static structure of the code without actually executing the program. Typically, such a module partitions each routine into sequences of statements between branching nodes (statements to or from which program control is transferred). The thoroughness of testing is often judged by measuring the number of these sequences exercised by test cases. This partition provides a data base (SAS function 1) that supports a later evaluation of test thoroughness by the analyzer module. The static analysis module also analyzes the static invocation structure of the program; the routines invoking and invoked by a particular routine are characterized in a tree structure. This information is captured in a data base file and also formatted for output as a printed report (SAS function 2).

The instrumentation module acts as a preprocessor by inserting additional statements within the original source code. During execution, these additional statements or "probes" intercept the flow of execution at key points and record program performance statistics and signals in an intermediate file (SAS function 3). Typically, the instrumentation permits tallies to be kept on which statements are executed and how many times, which statement sequences are traversed and how many times, and which subroutines are called from each routine. The probes facilitate recording of minimum/maximum data ranges and intermediate values of specified variables. The instrumentation module might also provide the capability to inject assertions into the source code. Assertions are statements made by the test investigator regarding the expected ranges of variables or the instantaneous relationship between several variables. If an assertion is violated during execution, it is flagged and recorded.

After compilation into object code, the instrumented module is "fit" into a test harness for execution. This test harness can take several forms. The test harness might

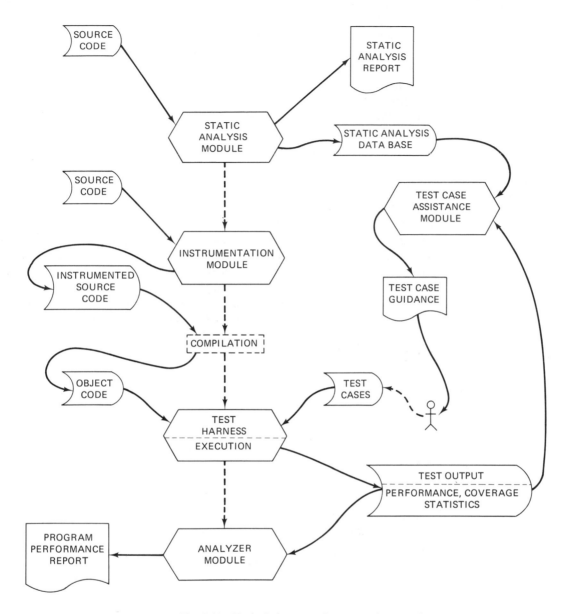

Fig. 5-12 Typical elements of automated test tool

be a special test-bed software device that acts as a main program and controls the transfer of test input data to the program being tested.[60] Another possible form of the test harness might be that of a physically separate test computer and software that control the flow of test data to the software being tested that is located in an interconnected machine. This test computer could be the residence of a program simulating

[60]Yourdon, *Techniques of Program Structure and Design*, p. 270.

the real-time output of a sensing device, industrial process, or remote terminal consoles.

The analyzer module functions as a postprocessor after the program execution. It formats and edits data recorded in an intermediate file during program execution and provides a printed report (SAS function 4). The report furnishes information on testing coverage, including:

- Statements executed and frequency; percentage of statements executed
- Statement sequences traversed; percentage of sequences traversed; listing of sequences not traversed
- Data ranges of variables
- Assertion violations

The analyzer module may also compare anticipated test-case output augmented by any user-supplied evaluation criteria (prestored in a file) with actual output and list resulting discrepancies. This module may be located in a separate test computer wherever immediate evaluation of test data is necessary.

The test case assistance module aids testing personnel in the selection of test inputs that will economically attain comprehensive testing goals (SAS function 5). The module uses the static analysis data base and the coverage data recorded during executions to guide the testers in the preparation of additional test cases. These then exercise paths in the program not executed by previous test cases. An algorithm detects statements and branches not exercised and indicates conditions necessary to traverse that path.

5.3.3 TEST GOALS/MEASURES AND TEST CASE GENERATION

The end objective of all verification and validation activities is to ensure that the delivered software product satisfies all specified functional and performance requirements and the identified design objectives.[61] If test cases are selected strictly with these high-level objectives in mind, then the set of test cases is not necessarily representative of the anticipated operational usage,[62] in which case reliability of the software is not necessarily demonstrated nor guaranteed. It is a frequent occurrence to find software errors, during operational use, that were not discovered during testing because no test case ever exercised certain sections of code.

Subordinate test goals that are oriented toward an examination of the structure of the software source code is a necessary ingredient for producing reliability. In this connection, Miller[63] suggests consideration of these questions when establishing testing goals:

1. Is the program logic flow correct?
2. Are program interfaces properly designed and implemented?

[61]D. W. Kelliher, *Software Quality Assurance and Production Control Practices in the Acquisition of Large Systems* (McLean, Va.: MITRE, 1975), Technical Report MTR-6906, p. I-6.

[62]J. R. Brown and M. Lipow, "Testing for Software Reliability," in *Proceedings International Conference on Reliable Software 1975*, IEEE Cat. No. 75CH0940-7CSR, p. 518.

[63]Miller, *Methodology for Comprehensive Software Testing*, p. 21.

3. Are the program performance measures (execution time and program text size) within acceptable bounds?
4. Is the software sufficiently error-tolerant?
5. Is the software adequately error-resistant?

Adequate attention to these questions necessitates a testing activity that thoroughly exercises every routine and function of every program in the system. This will involve the construction, execution, and evaluation of a huge number of test cases that, in all likelihood, will be economically beyond human capacity. Thus, automated tools are relied on to evaluate test results, to measure the extent of the software exercised, and to assist in generating test cases that will exercise those portions of the software not previously covered.

Krause et al.[64] note that in NASA's *Space Shuttle Request for Proposal*, a capability is called for to

> generate a thorough program test plan which will exercise all routes through the program code and which will explore the entire expected range of variables.

This is typical of the customers' contemporary awareness to the software reliability problem. However, the impracticality of testing all possible logical paths was illustrated earlier. More practical test goals are mandatory.

Miller[65] advocates a testing goal that deals with segments of statements denoted by the terminology "Decision-to-Decision Paths (DD-paths)." A DD-path is essentially the sequence of statements between program nodes or decision elements. Based on this element, he defines, to the first order, a measurable and attainable test objective as:

> Provide usefully small sets of test cases for single modules which, in aggregate, exercise each DD-path at least once.

A program submitted to this level will attain this state:[66]

1. Each statement in the program text will have been executed at least once.
2. Each decision in the program text will have been brought to each of its possible outcomes at least once, although not necessarily in every combination.

Miller further notes that, in reaching this state, the testing will have detected a high proportion of program mistakes. Also, such a strategy is automatable, measurable, and indicative of general software quality. However, this does not guarantee that errors derived from interactions between DD-paths will not result.

Test case selection should be approached in a rigorous manner since testing costs have a direct proportional relationship with the number of test cases required. A

---

[64]K. W. Krause, R. W. Smith, and M. A. Goodwin, "Optimal Software Test Planning Through Automated Network Analysis," in *Proceedings of 1973 IEEE Symposium on Computer Software Reliability*, p. 18.

[65]Miller, *Methodology for Comprehensive Software Testing*, pp. 36–37.

[66]Ibid, p. 38.

testing activity should strive for selection of the minimum number of test cases that satisfy test goals and objectives.

In order to devise test case data sets, the program is partitioned into its component modules that are, in turn, decomposed into smaller logical blocks or DD-paths.[67] The basic testing coverage measure is the percentage of DD-paths exercised. The strategy for attaining a target coverage percentage varies slightly from single module testing to multiple module testing.

Four phases of single module testing can be defined:[68]

1. Beginning phase
2. Continuing phase
3. Concluding phase
4. Retesting phase

In the beginning phase, "natural" or functionally oriented test cases are devised and executed. The specific motivation for these initial test cases will vary according to the mission of the system. A coverage report is produced for each series of test cases, noting the percentage of DD-paths traversed, the specific DD-paths exercised, and the specific DD-paths not exercised.[69] At this point, the start of the continuing phase, untested regions are identified from the coverage report. Specific DD-paths are selected as the next testing targets. The execution of a particular DD-path is induced by devising test case inputs that force the desired flow to occur.[70] This process has been described as the most difficult problem in testing.[71] The test input variables are determined by "backtracking" through the program flow from the target DD-path. Miller[72] asserts that this heuristic process is only semi-automatable with state-of-the art techniques.

The next coverage report is examined, a DD-path target is selected, and a test case is devised. This procedure is repeated into the concluding phase where the DD-path coverage is brought to 100% or above the coverage percentage testing goal. It has been observed in practice that a substantial amount of collateral testing is achieved, i.e., other untested segments of a program are incidentally exercised although they have not yet become explicit testing targets.[73] Hence, the number of test cases will be much lower than the number of DD-paths.

The retesting phase occurs when the existing version of a module is modified. An automated tool can help identify those modules that invoke the changed module and those modules that the changed module invoke in order to determine if any other modules may be affected by the change. The original set of test cases can be re-

[67]Miller and Wisehart, *Automated Tools to Support Software Quality Assurance*, p. 7.

[68]Miller, *Methodology for Comprehensive Software Testing*, pp. 41–42.

[69]Miller and Wisehart, *Automated Tools to Support Software Quality Assurance*, p. 12.

[70]E. F. Miller, Jr., and R. A. Melton, "Automated Generation of Testcase Datasets," in *Proceedings International Conference on Reliable Software*, IEEE Cat. No. 75CH0940-7CSR, 1975, p. 53.

[71]Miller, *Methodology for Comprehensive Software Testing*, p. 14.

[72]Ibid, p. 10.

[73]Ibid, p. 79.

executed with the changed software.[74] Untested DD-paths become targets for additional testing.

A strategy for multi-module testing can be prescribed similarly to that for single module testing.[75] The testing is continually directed toward the module that is least tested as measured by percentage of DD-paths executed. For the bottom-up testing approach, this involves selecting the least tested module that is farthest down in the invocation hierarchy. For top-down testing, the target becomes the least tested module residing at the level in the invocation hierarchy at which testing is currently proceeding.

The next subsection shows an illustrative example of the application of an SAS to a testing problem.

5.3.4 TYPICAL APPLICATION OF AN AUTOMATED TEST TOOL

The sequence of events in the software testing procedure with the aid of an SAS is shown in Figure 5-13 as exemplified by the capabilities of the RXVP System.[76] The individual boxes define complete steps in the operation, each producing outputs that feed subsequent operations either directly or through updates to the central data base.

The complete operation shown in Figure 5-13 covers the five SAS functions outlined in the subsection on Generic Elements of Automated Test Tools. In the discussion, each step identified with a circled number will be described in terms of outputs generated and the purpose of those outputs in the testing process.[77]

STEP 1: BUILDING THE DATA BASE The system reads source code as its input, in the form that it is supplied to the compiler (or preprocessor in the case of a FORTRAN augmentation such as IFTRAN or HIFTRAN). Simple commands are also supplied as a separate input file to direct the operations.

The system first derives its data base from the source code. Line numbers are assigned to each line of text; the full text is stored as a token string; the control structure and symbols are identified; and a directed graph model of the control structure is built.[78] The resulting information is stored in the data base that becomes the controlled copy of module text as well as the source of all outputs generated in later steps. At this point a summary of the analyses is produced; this serves as the directory for the data base.

Figure 5-14 shows the library summary for a library data base after the comple-

---

[74]Ibid, pp. 75–79.

[75]Ibid, pp. 72–91.

[76]RXVP is a FORTRAN/IFTRAN Source Text Analysis System built and marketed by General Research Corporation of Santa Barbara, Calif.

[77]In describing these operations, the subroutine SOLVE, used as an example elsewhere in the book, and the subroutine VALID8 will be the subjects of analysis. The source texts of the subroutines are shown in IFTRAN from which HIFTRAN is derived. The syntax is identical, except that IFTRAN does not contain an ESCAPE construction that has been simulated by the FORTRAN GO TO.

[78]The control structure of a module is defined in terms of the sequence of statements lying between the outcome of a decision up to and including the next decision. This sequence is immediately executable, once the initial decision outcome has been evaluated, and is the basic logical segment of the control structure. The sequence is called a Decision-to-Decision Path (DD-Path).

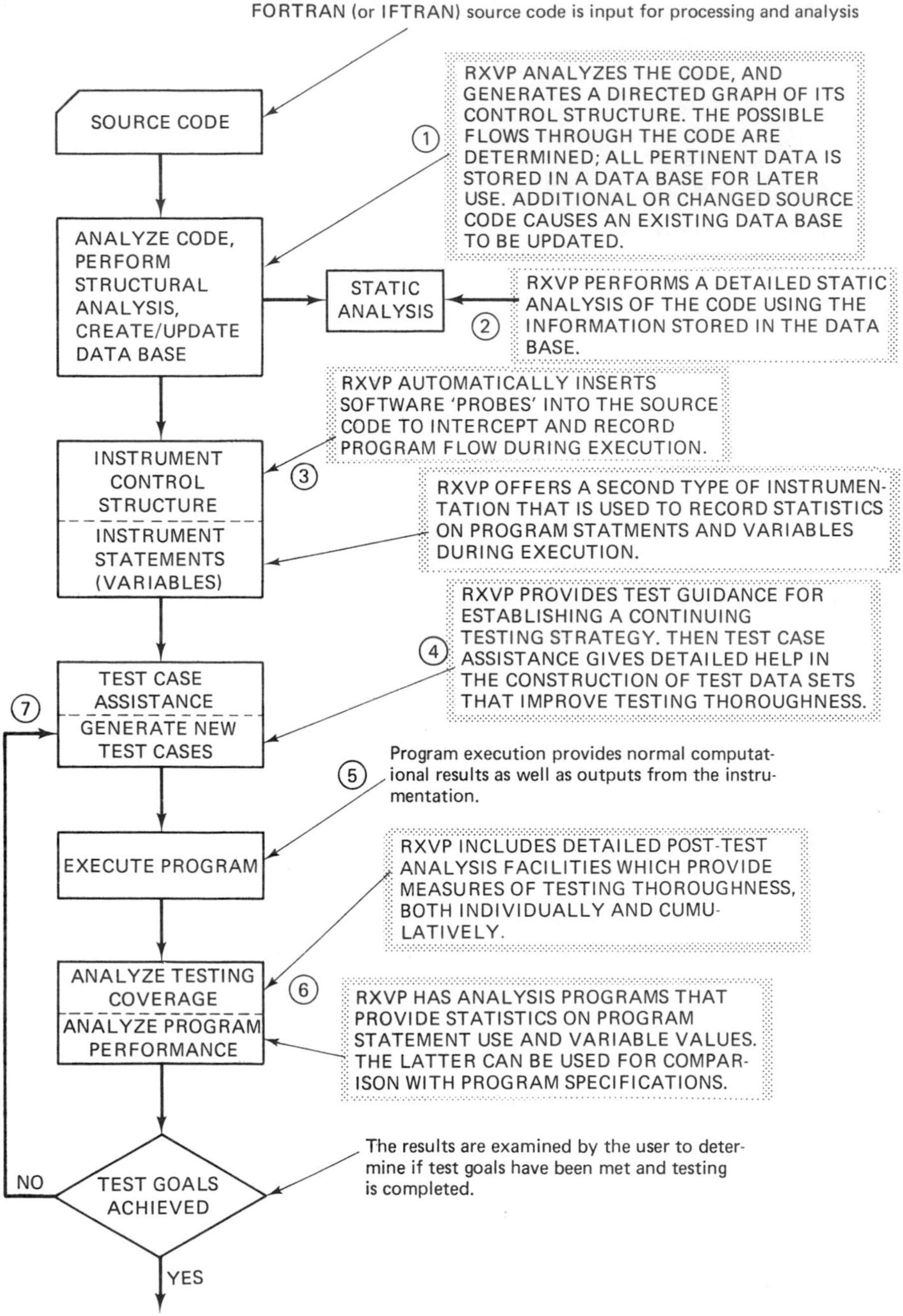

FORTRAN (or IFTRAN) source code is input for processing and analysis

SOURCE CODE

(1) RXVP ANALYZES THE CODE, AND GENERATES A DIRECTED GRAPH OF ITS CONTROL STRUCTURE. THE POSSIBLE FLOWS THROUGH THE CODE ARE DETERMINED; ALL PERTINENT DATA IS STORED IN A DATA BASE FOR LATER USE. ADDITIONAL OR CHANGED SOURCE CODE CAUSES AN EXISTING DATA BASE TO BE UPDATED.

ANALYZE CODE, PERFORM STRUCTURAL ANALYSIS, CREATE/UPDATE DATA BASE

STATIC ANALYSIS

(2) RXVP PERFORMS A DETAILED STATIC ANALYSIS OF THE CODE USING THE INFORMATION STORED IN THE DATA BASE.

(3) RXVP AUTOMATICALLY INSERTS SOFTWARE 'PROBES' INTO THE SOURCE CODE TO INTERCEPT AND RECORD PROGRAM FLOW DURING EXECUTION.

INSTRUMENT CONTROL STRUCTURE

INSTRUMENT STATEMENTS (VARIABLES)

RXVP OFFERS A SECOND TYPE OF INSTRUMEN-TATION THAT IS USED TO RECORD STATISTICS ON PROGRAM STATMENTS AND VARIABLES DURING EXECUTION.

(4) RXVP PROVIDES TEST GUIDANCE FOR ESTABLISHING A CONTINUING TESTING STRATEGY. THEN TEST CASE ASSISTANCE GIVES DETAILED HELP IN THE CONSTRUCTION OF TEST DATA SETS THAT IMPROVE TESTING THOROUGHNESS.

TEST CASE ASSISTANCE

(7)

GENERATE NEW TEST CASES

(5) Program execution provides normal computat-ional results as well as outputs from the instru-mentation.

EXECUTE PROGRAM

RXVP INCLUDES DETAILED POST-TEST ANALYSIS FACILITIES WHICH PROVIDE MEASURES OF TESTING THOROUGHNESS, BOTH INDIVIDUALLY AND CUMU-LATIVELY.

ANALYZE TESTING COVERAGE

ANALYZE PROGRAM PERFORMANCE

(6) RXVP HAS ANALYSIS PROGRAMS THAT PROVIDE STATISTICS ON PROGRAM STATEMENT USE AND VARIABLE VALUES. THE LATTER CAN BE USED FOR COMPAR-ISON WITH PROGRAM SPECIFICATIONS.

The results are examined by the user to deter-mine if test goals have been met and testing is completed.

TEST GOALS ACHIEVED

NO

YES

Fig. 5-13 Application of RXVP in software testing

SYSTEM WRAPUP...

MODULE DESCRIPTOR BLOCKS AS THEY ARE CURRENTLY KNOWN..

NO. NAME	TYPE	MODE	LANGUAGE DIALECT	STMTS	EXEC STMTS	1ST EXEC	ARGS	ENTRS	SYMS	DDPS	INVOKES	LONG NAME
1 LINEAR	PROGRAM	TYPELESS	IFTRAN	55	13	30	0	1	23	3	5	
2 GETSYS	SUBROUTINE	TYPELESS	IFTRAN	40	13	20	4	1	12	7	2	
3 FORM	SUBROUTINE	TYPELESS	IFTRAN	71	27	22	4	1	24	15	1	
4 VALID8	SUBROUTINE	TYPELESS	IFTRAN	54	23	19	3	1	18	13	2	
5 SOLVE	SUBROUTINE	TYPELESS	IFTRAN	83	39	27	6	1	31	21	3	
6 OUTPUT	SUBROUTINE	TYPELESS	IFTRAN	52	17	20	4	1	18	7	0	

LIBRARY HEADER ---

MODE OF ACCESS	NEW
LIBRARY SIZE	36500
NUMBER OF MODULES	6
NUMBER OF ENTRIES	6

Fig. 5-14 Library summary

tion of Step 1. The column headings are:

NO.	Module number assigned in this data base
NAME	Program, subroutine, or function name as known to the compiler
TYPE	Program/subroutine/function
MODE	FORTRAN mode of functions (REAL/INTEGER/LOGIGAL)—TYPELESS for subroutines and programs
LANGUAGE	FORTRAN
DIALECT	IFTRAN
STMTS	Total number of statements in the module including comments, data declarations, and format statements
EXEC STMTS	Total number of executable statements
1ST EXEC	Statement number of first executable statement
ARGS	Number of arguments of a subroutine or function
ENTRS	Number of entry points in the module
SYMS	Total number of symbols mentioned in the module
DDPS	Number of Decision-to-Decision paths
INVOKES	Number of external calls made by the module

The LIBRARY HEADER summarizes the physical makeup of the library as of the run date given. The entries that are not self-explanatory are described:

MODE OF ACCESS	NEW (first written)
	R/W (being updated)
LIBRARY SIZE	Total number of words used by data base

This report is produced at the end of every run that accesses or updates the data base and is the summary of present status of the library. The reports would be kept on file by the program librarian. The current status is always stored in the library. The module names are the key to accessing data on a specific module from the data base for all other reports.

STEP 2: PRODUCING DOCUMENTATION REPORTS   After the data base is created, the documentation reports are generated. These reports provide information that will be used to document the code and to aid the test group in understanding code organization. Documentation reports (Figures 5-15 through 5-18) are described in the following paragraphs.

Module Text (Figure 5-15). The text of a module as stored on the data base is the source of this report. The left-most column is the statement number, and adjacent to that in parentheses is a nesting level number that identifies nesting depth for the structured languages. The statement is printed, indented consistent with nesting level, and then, for each statement that starts a DD-path, the path number is printed. This module text printout is the basic module description report that gives the statement numbers, which are referred to in other reports, identifies all of the DD-paths, and lists the full module text.

Invocation Matrix (Figure 5-16). This report provides the overall view of the module interconnections in the form of a square matrix. All the module names are

```
STATEMENT LISTING             SUBROUTINE SOLVE ( ARRAY, SOLUTN, ORDER, EPS, ITER, CONVRG )                    PAGE    27

 NO. LEVEL   LABEL  STATEMENT TEXT...                                                                          DDPATHS
-----------------------------------------------------------------------------------------------------------------------
  1                 SUBROUTINE SOLVE ( ARRAY, SOLUTN, ORDER, EPS, ITER, CONVRG )                              (  1)
  2            C    ------------------------------------------------------------
  3            C    ROUTINE TO COMPUTE SOLUTION TO A SYSTEM OF SIMULTANEOUS
  4            C    EQUATIONS BY THE GAUSS-SEIDEL METHOD
  5            C
  6            C    DESCRIPTION OF VARIABLES
  7            C    ARRAY   -   COEFFICIENT ARRAY FOR SYSTEM (INCLUDES R.H.SIDE)
  8            C    SOLUTN - SOLUTION VECTOR
  9            C    ORDER - ORDER OF SYSTEM
 10            C    EPS - CONVERGENCE TOLERANCE
 11            C    ITER  - MAXIMUM NUMBER OF ITERATIONS
 12            C    CONVRG - CONVERGENCE FLAG
 13            C    COUNT - ITERATION COUNTER
 14            C    RESID - SOLUTION ERROR
 15            C    DEBUG   - DEBUG OUTPUT FLAG
 16            C    LUNIN   - LOGICAL INPUT UNIT
 17            C    LUNOUT  - LOGICAL OUTPUT UNIT
 18            C
 19            C    ------------------------------------------------------------
 20                 COMMON / MISC / DEBUG
 21                 COMMON / UNITS / LUNIN, LUNOUT
 22                 DIMENSION ARRAY ( 80, 81 )
 23                 DIMENSION SOLUTN ( 80 )
 24                 INTEGER ORDER, COUNT
 25                 LOGICAL CONVRG, DEBUG
 26                 INITIAL ( .ALL. I .IN. ( 1, ORDER ) ( SOLUTN ( I ) .EQ. 0.0 ) )
 27                 IF ( DEBUG )                                                                               (  2-  3)
 28 ( 1)            .  WRITE ( LUNOUT, 910 ) ITER
 29                 ENDIF
 30                 CONVRG = .TRUE.
 31            C    ------------------------------------------------------------
 32            C    SET RESIDUAL TO VERY LARGE NUMBER
 33            C    ------------------------------------------------------------
 34                 RESID = 1.E20
 35            C    ------------------------------------------------------------
 36            C    CALCULATE SYSTEM SOLUTION
 37            C    ------------------------------------------------------------
 38                 DO ( COUNT = 1, ITER )
 39 ( 1)            .  IF ( RESID .GT. EPS )                                                                   (  4-  5)
 40 ( 2)            .  .  RESID = 0.0
 41 ( 2)            .  .  DO ( I = 1, ORDER )
 42 ( 3)            .  .  .  SUM = 0.0
 43 ( 3)            .  .  .  DO ( J = 1, ORDER )
 44 ( 4)            .  .  .  .  IF ( I .NE. J )                                                                (  6-  7)
 45 ( 5)            .  .  .  .  .  SUM = SUM + ARRAY ( I, J ) * SOLUTN ( J )
 46 ( 4)            .  .  .  .  ENDIF
 47 ( 3)            .  .  .  ENDDO                                                                             (  8-  9)
 48 ( 3)            .  .  .  TEMP = ( ARRAY ( I, ORDER + 1 ) - SUM ) / ARRAY ( I, I )
-----------------------------------------------------------------------------------------------------------------------
```

Fig. 5-15 Module text

```
NO. LEVEL   LABEL   STATEMENT TEXT...                                                DDPATHS

49 ( 3)             . . TEMPX = ABS ( SOLUTN ( I ) - TEMP )
50 ( 3)             . . RESID = AMAX1 ( RESID, TEMPX )
51 ( 3)             . . SOLUTN ( I ) = TEMP
52 ( 2)             . ENDDO
53 ( 2)             . IF ( DEBUG )                                                   ( 10- 11)
54 ( 3)             . . IF ( MOD ( COUNT, 10 ) .EQ. 0 )                              ( 12- 13)
55 ( 4)             . . . WRITE ( LUNOUT, 900 ) COUNT, ( SOLUTN ( I ), I = 1, ORDER )( 14- 15)
56 ( 3)             . . ENDIF
57 ( 2)             . ENDIF
58 ( 1)             ELSE
59 ( 2)     C       . **** GRC CHANGE -- ELIMINATE ESCAPE 20
60 ( 2)             . GOTO 20
61 ( 1)             . ENDIF
62                  ENDDO
63            20    CONTINUE
64                  ASSERT ( RESID .LE. EPS )                                        ( 16- 17)
65          C       TEST ITERATION COUNT FOR CONVERGENCE
66          C
67          C
68 ( 1)             IF ( COUNT .GE. ITER )                                           ( 18- 19)
69 ( 1)     C       . SET NONCONVERGENCE SWITCH
70 ( 1)     C
71 ( 1)     C
72 ( 1)             . CONVRG = .FALSE.
73                  ENDIF
74 ( 1)             IF ( DEBUG )
75 ( 1)             . WRITE ( LUNOUT, 920 ) COUNT                                    ( 20- 21)
76                  ENDIF
77                  FINAL ( .SOME. I .IN. ( 1, ORDER ) ( SOLUTN ( I ) .NE. 0.0 ) )
78                  RETURN
79          C
80           900    FORMAT (5X,I4,8E15.3)
81           910    FORMAT (5X,20HENTER SOLVE. ITER = ,I4)
82           920    FORMAT (5X,20HEXIT SOLVE. COUNT = ,I4)
83                  END
```

Fig. 5-15 (cont'd.) Module text

```
LIBRARY DEPENDENCE TABLE

*************************
** INVOKEE *      *      *
*  *         *FGLOSV*AAMX*
*   *        *OEIUOA*BMOM*
*    *       *RTNTLL*SADI*
*     *      *MSFPVI* X T*
*      *     * YAUED* 1 *
*       *    * SRT 8*    *
*        * * *      *    *
*         * *       *    *
* INVOKER **        *    *
*************************
* FORM     **      *X   *
* GETSYS   *X*  X*      *
* LINEAR   * X*XX *    X*
* OUTPUT   *  *  *     *
* SOLVE    *  * *XXX  *
* VALID8   *    **X   *
*************************


THE FOLLOWING MODULES ARE NOT INVOKED BY ANY MODULE ON THE LIBRARY

      FORM

THE FOLLOWING MODULES DO NOT INVOKE ANY MODULE ON THE LIBRARY

      LINEAR      OUTPUT      SOLVE      VALID8
```

Fig. 5-16 Invocation matrix

listed with the rows named for invoking modules, and the columns are named for invoked modules. An X at the intersection means that the module named for the row invokes the module named for the column.

Invocation Bands (Figure 5-17). The invocation matrix describes a single level of invocation for the entire library; the bands report shows all levels of invocation (upward and downward) for a single module. The accessed module is listed at level 0; its invocation chains downward are listed under positive levels, and invocation chains that lead to the module from higher levels are listed under negative levels. This report completely describes the module's position in the invocation hierarchy and shows the other modules in the system that will need to be retested if the referenced module is changed.

Invocation Space (Figure 5-18). This is the most detailed report of module invocations for a single module. First it lists all first-level invocations *from* the module, giving invoked module names in alphabetical order, each one followed by a list of the numbered statements that contain that invocation. Then the report shows an alphabetical list of all modules with invocations to the referenced module that give statement number and text of the invocation. This report enables the tester to easily identify the actual arguments used in all invocations to and from the module.

STEP 3: MODULE INSTRUMENTATION Collection of program flow statistics is facilitated by the instrumentation of the program control structure. The system examines the code and automatically inserts a call to a data collection routine that is invoked each time a control branch is taken. When the instrumented code is executed, the collection routine notes the module and code section executed and builds up a data file from which the test analyzer generates its reports. Typical controls for this step allow selection of modules and define the level of instrumentation. RXVP has

```
INVOCATION BANDS              SUBROUTINE SOLVE ( ARRAY, SOLUTN, ORDER, EPS, ITER, CONVRG )              PAGE    34

TO LEVEL 2

LEVEL      -5        -4        -3        -2        -1         0         1         2         3         4         5
-------------------------------------------------------------------------------------------------------------------
                                                              SOLVE
                                                   LINEAR               ABS
                                                                        AMAX1
                                                                        MOD
-------------------------------------------------------------------------------------------------------------------
```

Fig. 5-17 Invocation bands

INVOCATION SPACE   SUBROUTINE SOLVE (ARRAY, SOLUTN, ORDER, EPS, ITER, CONVRG)

INVOCATIONS FROM WITHIN THIS MODULE

MODULE ABS
STMT =   49   ABS (SOLUTN (I) - TEMP)

MODULE AMAX1
STMT =   50   AMAX1 (RFSID , TEMPX)

MODULE MOD
STMT =   54   MOD (COUNT , 10)

INVOCATIONS TO THIS MODULE FROM WITHIN LIBRARY

MODULE LINEAR
STMT =   46   CALL SOLVE (ARRAY , X , ORDER , EPS , ITER , CONVRG)

Fig. 5-18 Invocation space

the option of instrumenting either at the module entries only or at each control branch point, including module entry.

If more detailed performance statistics are desired, the next level of instrumentation provides data collection calls for each assignment statement, permitting a complete record of the values stored during execution. This level of instrumentation would normally only be applied to selected modules where the more detailed information is needed to ensure that testing covers a proper range of computational results.

STEP 4: TEST ASSISTANCE   Testing is now ready for a set of test cases. It is assumed that some form of prior testing has produced a set of working test cases. At the first cycle of testing these existing cases are executed with the instrumented code. After these initial tests are analyzed and the reports examined, this step will entail generation of new or modified test cases as needed to achieve testing goals. Before discussing the extension of test cases (Step 7), the reports generated by analying the initial test case will be examined.

STEP 5: TEST EXECUTION   While the instrumented code is running, it produces its normal outputs and also invokes the data collection routine. In its simplest form the data collection routine merely writes a trace file that records the sequence of DD-paths executed or the sequence of variable values assigned. More extensive data collection routines can perform some analysis and summarizing during execution to reduce the amount of data collected. RXVP has three options, (1) variable trace, (2) DD-path trace, and (3) DD-path summary by counting executions and recording only the counters on the trace file.

STEP 6: TEST ANALYSIS   The function of the post-test analyzer is to supply the reports that can be evaluated against testing goals. DD-path coverage analysis reports execution counts by module and DD-path as well as summary data on testing progress. The variable trace analyzer reports the maximum, minimum, first, last, and average value of all variables traced.

Coverage Summary (Figure 5-19). The top-level view of testing progress is shown by this report. For each test case and for the cumulative of all tests, the table lists:

TEST CASE	Sequential test number
MODULE NAME	Name of all instrumented and invoked modules in the test
NUMBER OF DD-PATHS	Total number of DD-paths in the module

Under SUMMARY—THIS TEST

NUMBER OF INVOCATIONS	Total times module was invoked in the single test
DD-PATHS TRAVERSED	Number of distinct DD-paths executed by this test case
PERCENT COVERAGE	Distinct DD-paths executed by this test case as a percent of the total DD-paths in the module

			SUMMARY -- THIS TEST			CUMULATIVE SUMMARY			
TEST CASE	MODULE NAME	NUMBER OF D-D PATHS	NUMBER OF INVOCATIONS	D-D PATHS TRAVERSED	PER CENT COVERAGE	NUMBER OF TESTS	INVOCATIONS	TRAVERSED	COVERAGE
1									
	LINEAR	3	1	2	66.67	1	1	2	66.67
	GETSYS	7	1	4	57.14	1	1	4	57.14
	FORM	15	1	11	73.33	1	1	11	73.33
	VALID8	13	1	10	76.92	1	1	10	76.92
	SOLVE	21	1	15	71.43	1	1	15	71.43
	OUTPUT	7	1	4	57.14	1	1	4	57.14
	$$ALL$$	66		46	69.70	1		46	69.70

Fig. 5-19 Coverage summary for one test case

Under CUMULATIVE SUMMARY[79]

NUMBER OF TESTS	Total number of test cases accumulated
INVOCATIONS	Cumulative number of module invocations over all tests
TRAVERSED	Cumulative number of distinct DD-paths executed over all tests
COVERAGE	Cumulative distinct DD-paths executed over all tests as a percent of the total DD-paths in the module

DD-Paths Not Hit (Figure 5-20). This report tells the tester which DD-paths were not executed by each test case, and which remain untested after all tests are accumulated. The report also displays single test and cumulative test information.

DD-Path Execution Counts (Figure 5-21). This report gives the finest detail on DD-path execution for each test case. For each DD-path an entry is made under NOT EXECUTED where execution count is zero. For execution counts greater than zero, the bar represents the count as a percent of the maximum number of executions for a single path. The exact number of path executions is entered under NUMBER OF EXECUTIONS. This report shows where the most execution time is being spent in a module in addition to the module summary line at the bottom. The report also shows more graphically than the list of numbers where there are large segments of code that are not being tested.

Performance Test Analysis (Figure 5-22). The more detailed variable trace analyzer produces the report shown in part in Figure 5-22, which is keyed directly to the source statements. Three types of reports are given. If the statement has no value computed (e.g., a CONTINUE, WRITE, READ, CALL, or assignment of a constant), then only the execution count is printed. Statements that test logical expressions report times true, times false, and final value of the logical expression. Statements that compute a numeric value (e.g., assignment, arithmetic IF, or DO) report initial, final, maximum, and minimum values.

Referring to Figure 5-13, the decision point has been reached where it is determined whether to continue testing or terminate. If the test goal is simple, such as full coverage of all DD-paths, then the standard analyzer report will immediately disclose the testing status (see Figure 5-19).

When the decision is made to continue testing, a return is made to test assistance in order to generate new test cases. The following paragraphs describe the process of generating test cases for DD-path coverage and show the test analysis reports as a result of executing all test cases.

STEP 7: TEST ASSISTANCE   Figure 5-19 shows that of a total of 66 DD-paths, the first test case has executed only 46. The objective of continued testing is to generate test cases that will include at least one execution of the untested DD-paths. This testing goal should be considered a minimum level of testing in which all statements are executed at least once and each decision is exercised through all possible outcomes. Although this is far from a complete test that exercises all logical

---

[79]At this point only one test case has been run; thus the cumulative has no additional information. See Figure 5-27 for cumulative results of two test cases for module SOLVE.

```
=============================================================================
                                      LIST OF DECISION TO DECISION PATHS NOT EXECUTED
=============================================================================
MODULE  I TEST   I PATHS   I
NAME    I NUMBER I NOT HIT I
=============================================================================
<LINEAR > I   1   I    1    I    1   3
          I CUMUL I    1    I    1   3
-----------------------------------------------------------------------------
<GETSYS > I   1   I    3    I    3   5   7
          I CUMUL I    3    I    3   5   7
-----------------------------------------------------------------------------
<FORM   > I   1   I    4    I    3   5   8   15
          I CUMUL I    4    I    3   5   8   15
-----------------------------------------------------------------------------
<VALIO8 > I   1   I    3    I    3   8   13
          I CUMUL I    3    I    3   8   13
-----------------------------------------------------------------------------
<SOLVE  > I   1   I    6    I    3   13   14   16   18   21
          I CUMUL I    6    I    3   13   14   16   18   21
-----------------------------------------------------------------------------
<OUTPUT > I   1   I    3    I    3   5   7
          I CUMUL I    3    I    3   5   7
-----------------------------------------------------------------------------
```

Fig. 5-20 DD paths not hit (1 test case)

```
RECORD OF DECISION TO DECISION (DD PATH) EXECUTION

MODULE  $SOLVE  $        TEST CASE NO.        1

                                                                        I  I NUMBER OF
DD PATH I  NO. NOT EXECUTED  I  NUMBER OF EXECUTIONS -- NORMALIZED TO MAXIMUM  I  I EXECUTIONS
NUMBER  I                    I.----20.----40.----60.----80.----100.           I  I
        I                    I                                                 I  I
   1    I                    I                                                 I  I  1  1
   2    I                    I                                                 I  I  2  1
   3    I     00000          I  XXXX                                           I  I  4  5
   4    I                    I  XXXXXXXXXXXXXXXXXXXXXXXXXXXXXXXXXXXXXXXXXXXX    I  I  5  1
   5    I                    I  XXXXXXXXXXXXXXX                                 I  I  6  60
   6    I                    I  XXXXXXXXXXXXXXX                                 I  I  7  20
   7    I                    I  XXXXXXXXXXXXXXXXXXXXXXXXXXXXXXXXXXXXXXXXXXXXXX  I  I  8  20
   8    I                    I  XXXX                                           I  I  9  60
   9    I                    I                                                 I  I 10  5
  10    I                    I  XXXXXXXXXXXXX                                   I  I 11  15
  11    I                    I  XXXX                                           I  I 12  5
  12    I                    I                                                 I  I
  13    I     00000          I                                                 I  I
  14    I     00000          I                                                 I  I
  15    I                    I  XXXX                                           I  I 15  5
  16    I     00000          I                                                 I  I
  17    I                    I  XXXX                                           I  I 17  5
  18    I     00000          I                                                 I  I
  19    I                    I                                                 I  I 19  1
  20    I                    I                                                 I  I 20  1
  21    I     00000          I                                                 I  I


  TOTAL OF   6   NOT EXECUTED    EXECUTED  15/ 21        TOTAL NUMBER OF DD PATH EXECUTIONS =   205

                                                        PERCENT EXECUTED =    71.43
```

Fig. 5-21 DD path execution counts

```
                                                                      EXECUTION
NO.   LABEL   SOURCE TEXT                                               COUNT
-----------------------------------------------------------------------------------

45            DO 19996 COUNT = 1 , ITER                                   4
                                             INIT =  1          FINAL =  6
                                             MIN  =  1          MAX   =  6

46   C        IF (RESID.GT.EPS)                                           0
47            IF ( RESID .GT. EPS )                                       6
                                             TRUE               FINAL IF FALSE
                                             FINAL IF FALSE     5                1

48            GOTO 19993                                                  5
49            GOTO 19994                                                  1
50   19993    CONTINUE                                                    5
51            RESID = 0.0                                                 5
52   C        DO ( I = 1,ORDER)                                           0
53            DO 19992 I = 1 , ORDER                                     20
                                             INIT =  1          FINAL =  4
                                             MIN  =  1          MAX   =  4

54            SUM = 0.0                                                  20
55   C        DO (J = 1,ORDER)                                            0
56            DO 19991 J = 1 , ORDER                                     80
                                             INIT =  1          FINAL =  4
                                             MIN  =  1          MAX   =  4

57   C        IF (I.NE.J)                                                 0
58            IF ( I .NE. J )                                            80
                                             TRUE               FINAL IF FALSE   60
                                             FINAL IF FALSE     60      FALSE     20

59            GOTO 19988                                                 60
60            GOTO 19989                                                 20
61   19988    CONTINUE                                                   60
62            SUM = SUM + ARRAY ( I , J ) * SOLUTN ( J )                 60
                                             INIT = 0.          FINAL =  3.497842
                                             MIN  = -15.03687   MAX   =  5.054457

63   C        ENDIF
64   19989    CONTINUE                                                   60
65   19990    CONTINUE                                                   20
66   C        ENDDO
67   19991    CONTINUE                                                   80
68            TEMP = ( ARRAY ( I , ORDER + 1 ) - SUM ) / ARRAY ( I , I ) 20
                                             INIT = .2497720    FINAL = -3.799568
                                             MIN  = -4.11U891   MAX   =  3.002674

69            TEMPX = ABS ( SOLUTN ( I ) - TEMP )                        20
                                             INIT = .2497720    FINAL = .8800409E-03
                                             MIN  = .78075764E-03  MAX   = 4.11U891

70            RESID = AMAX1 ( RESID , TEMPX )                            20
                                             INIT = .2497720    FINAL = .4550057E-02
                                             MIN  = .3109755E-02   MAX   = 4.11U891

71            SOLUTN ( I ) = TEMP                                        20
                                             INIT = .2497720    FINAL = -3.799568
                                             MIN  = -4.11U891   MAX   =  3.002674

72   C        ENDDO                                                       0
73   19992    CONTINUE                                                   20
74   C        IF (DEBUG)                                                  0
75            IF ( DEBUG )                                                5
                                             TRUE               FINAL IF TRUE     5
                                             FINAL IF TRUE      5       FALSE     0

76            GOTO 19985                                                  5
77            GOTO 19986                                                  5
78   19985    CONTINUE                                                    5
-----------------------------------------------------------------------------------
```

Fig. 5-22 Performance test analysis

paths (all DD-path sequences) through the program, it is more comprehensive than is generally achieved by tests that sample only selected values in the input space. Furthermore, the process of generating new test cases focuses attention on the source code of the program and frequently reveals errors that would go undetected when looking only at execution results.

Testing Strategy. There are two basic strategies that can be followed in completing the testing for coverage of DD-paths. A "bottom-up" approach would examine untested paths in the modules lowest in the program's invocation hierarchy to determine what changes of input data are needed to reach these paths. A "top-down" approach examines the untested paths in the highest module of the invocation hierarchy, which in turn will probably lead to added coverage at the lower levels. Both strategies have their advantages and disadvantages, and generally some mixture of the two is employed. In this discussion we again select the module SOLVE and present what is basically bottom-up testing since SOLVE is at the lowest level of the invocation hierarchy.

Testing Assistance. The first step of test assistance draws on the PREDICATE ANALYSIS. A predicate is a decision element statement. This lists the decision statements for the untested DD-paths and gives information about the variables that appear in the predicates (see Figure 5-23a). From this report we see that three of the paths are controlled by the variable DEBUG which is read in as an input in the module LINEAR (see Figure 5-23b). Therefore, any test case can be simply changed to make DEBUG false.

We also see from this report that the other three missed paths are controlled by the variables COUNT and ITER. COUNT is a local variable in a module that is the loop variable of the DO loop. Thus, Path 16 will be reached if the DO LOOP exit is reached (as will Path 18). These conditions are achieved by a failure to converge within the allowable limits of ITER. To reach these paths, either a nonconvergent case must be supplied or the value of ITER reduced. ITER is also read in the module LINEAR and can be reduced to a small number by a simple data input change. The final path can be reached only if COUNT is a multiple of 10 and not yet converged. This is an example of a predicate that is dependent on the behavior of the algorithm that is implemented in such a way that precludes derivation of a test case by looking at the source code.

Reaching Set Assistance. The previous discussion described test assistance in terms of predicate variables that are easily mapped into the input space of the program. From experience with sample testing problems, it appears that approximately 50–70% of the test cases for untested DD-paths can be found by such an approach. The problem of finding a test set that involves the internal logic of the program will now be discussed. The report that responds to this situation is called the reaching set report. A reaching set comprises the union of all DD-path sequences that lead from one DD-path up to and including another path.

Two forms of the reaching set are derived. The noniterative reaching set shows the union of only forward flow paths from the initial path to the final path. The iterative reaching set includes feedback paths. We will show an example for the module VALID8. The three untested paths in VALID8 are 3, 8, and 13 (from Figure 5-20). The predicate analysis for VALID8 (Figure 5-24) shows that 3 and 13 are reached by

PREDICATE ANALYSIS   SUBROUTINE SOLVE (ARRAY, SOLUTN, ORDER, EPS, ITER, CONVRG)

PREDICATES CONTROLLING DD-PATHS...
PATH LIST... 3,13,14,16,18,21

DD-PATH   3   STMT 27   IF (DEBUG)   ** DDPATH   3 IS FALSE BRANCH

DD-PATH 13   STMT 53   IF (DEBUG)   ** DDPATH 13 IS FALSE BRANCH

DD-PATH 14   STMT 54   IF (MOD (COUNT, 10) .EQ. 0)   ** DDPATH 14 IS TRUE BRANCH

DD-PATH 16   STMT 62   ENDDO (DO (COUNT = 1, ITER))   ** DDPATH 16 IS LOOP ESCAPE

DD-PATH 18   STMT 68   IF (COUNT .GE. ITER)   ** DDPATH 18 IS TRUE BRANCH

DD-PATH 21   STMT 74   IF (DEBUG)   ** DDPATH 21 IS FALSE BRANCH

Fig. 5-23   (a) Predicate analysis for SOLVE

VARIABLE TRACE REPORT -

MODULES INCLUDED --
    FORM
    GETSYS
    LINEAR
    OUTPUT
    SOLVE
    VALID8

SYMBOL	MODULE	STMT NO.	STATEMENT TEXT
DEBUG	FORM	17D	COMMON / MISC / DEBUG
		21D	LOGICAL VALID, CONVRG, DEBUG
	GETSYS	16D	COMMON / MISC / DEBUG
		19D	LOGICAL VALID, CONVRG, DEBUG
	LINEAR	23D	COMMON / MISC / DEBUG
		27D	LOGICAL VALID, CONVRG, DEBUG
		36*	READ (LUNIN, 900) DEBUG, ORDER, ITER, EPS, BIG
		53F	900 FORMAT (L1,I4,I5,E20.5,E20.5)
	OUTPUT	16D	COMMON / MISC / DEBUG
		20D	LOGICAL VALID, CONVRG, DEBUG
	SOLVE	20D	COMMON / MISC / DEBUG
		25D	LOGICAL VALID, CONVRG, DEBUG
	VALID8	14D	COMMON / MISC / DEBUG
		17D	LOGICAL VALID, CONVRG, DEBUG
COUNT	SOLVE	24D	INTEGER ORDER, COUNT
		38*	DO (COUNT = 1, ITER)
ITER	LINEAR	36*	READ (LUNIN, 900) DEBUG, ORDER, ITER, EPS, BIG
		53F	900 FORMAT (L1,I4,I5,E20.5,E20.5)
	OUTPUT	1*	SUBROUTINE OUTPUT (X, ORDER, ITER, CONVRG)
	SOLVE	1*	SUBROUTINE SOLVE (ARRAY, SOLUTN, ORDER, EPS, ITER, CONVRG)

Fig. 5-23 (b) Variable trace for untested predicates of SOLVE

```
PREDICATE ANALYSIS              SUBROUTINE VALID8 ( ARRAY, ORDER, VALID )                        PAGE    3
---------------------------------------------------------------------------------------------------------

PREDICATES CONTROLLING DD-PATHS...
PATH LIST... 3,8,13

---------------------------------------------------------------------------------------------------------

DD-PATH   3   STMT 19    IF ( DEBUG )                                      **  DDPATH    3 IS FALSE BRANCH

DD PATH   8   STMT 35    IF ( ABS ( ARRAY ( I, I ) ) .LT. SUM )           **  DDPATH    8 IS TRUE BRANCH

DD-PATH  13   STMT 46    IF ( DEBUG )                                      **  DDPATH   13 IS FALSE BRANCH

---------------------------------------------------------------------------------------------------------
```

Fig. 5-24 Predicate analysis for VALID8

setting DEBUG to False. Path 8 is controlled by the predicate (ABS(ARRAY(I, I)) .LT. SUM), and to find a noniterative reaching set from the entrance of the module to path 8 is the goal. This collection of code is shown in Figure 5-25. It can be seen that this predicate will be reached regardless of the decision branches taken from prior predicates. After seeing all of the code that affects the decision process, it can be concluded that the desired test will be achieved by having a row in ARRAY with off-diagonal elements whose sum is less than the diagonal element. Now, the input data controlling the outcome of this predicate can be traced by using the variable trace report for untested predicates of VALID8 (Figure 5-26). It shows that the value of ARRAY is assigned by the value of the symbol ELEMNT. The source of the input data for ELEMNT, from Figure 5-26, can be tracked back to a read statement in the module FORM. Noting from the last line on Figure 5-26 that SUM will always be positive or zero, an input value for ELEMNT can be selected to assure the exercise of DD-path 8.

A new test case was generated to handle this case. Figures 5-27 and 5-28 show the summary and NOTHIT reports as a result of adding the new test cases for modules SOLVE and VALID8 to our test set. Additional test cases may be contrived by using the methodology just described until the testing goals are attained.

Automated test tools are currently gaining widespread use and acceptance. They are attaining recognition as cost effective devices that provide the ability to exhaustively test software to a level that would otherwise be cost prohibitive when using manual means. This section has strived to provide the reader with an understanding of the fundamental advantages of these tools as well as an insight into the details of an example application of an automated tool.

5.4

Testing Real-time Systems

Since real-time systems possess additional attributes that must be accorded special consideration in the testing process, special mention is provided here.

"Real time" can be defined as:[80]

> Pertaining to the performance of computation during the actual time that the related physical process, event, or phenomenon transpires. . . . Thus, for computations to be considered as taking place in real time, they must proceed fast enough so as to permit the results to influence the related process that is underway.

The ever-increasing volume and complexity of problems presented to industry and government (including the military) have led to more extensive application of data processing technology. Responding to this motivation, the development of technology has kept pace to some extent and has made itself more cost effective hardwarewise. Thus, more and more critical functions that require quick responses to developing situations have been entrusted to data processing—such as air traffic con-

[80]Martin H. Weik, *Standard Dictionary of Computers and Information Processing* (New York, N.Y.: Hayden Book Company, Inc. 1969), p. 295.

REACHING SET ANALYSIS   SUBROUTINE VALID8 (ARRAY, ORDER, VALID)

NON-ITERATIVE REACHING SET FROM STATEMENT 19 TO STATEMENT 46

DDPATHS IN REACHING SET
2   3   4   5   6   8   9   10

SOURCE CODE IN REACHING SET

```
19          IF ( DEBUG )
20 ( 1)     . WRITE ( LUNOUT, 910 ) VALID
21          ENDIF

25          DO ( I = 1, ORDER )

29 ( 1)     . . SUM = 0.0
30 ( 1)     . . DO ( J = 1, ORDER )
31 ( 2)     . . . IF ( I .NE. J )
32 ( 3)     . . . . SUM = SUM + ABS ( ARRAY ( I, J ) )
33 ( 2)     . . . ENDIF
34 ( 1)     . . ENDDO
35 ( 1)     . . IF ( ABS ( ARRAY ( I, I ) ) .LT. SUM )

39 ( 2)     . . . VALID = .FALSE.
40 ( 2)     . . . WRITE ( LUNOUT, 900 ) I

42 ( 2)     . . . GOTO 20
43 ( 1)     . . ENDIF
44          . . ENDDO
45    20    CONTINUE
46          IF ( DEBUG )
```

Fig. 5-25 Non-iterative reaching set

MODULES INCLUDED --
FORM
GETSYS
LINEAR
OUTPUT
SOLVE
VALID8

SYMBOL	MODULE	STMT NO.	STATEMENT TEXT
ARRAY	FORM	1*	SUBROUTINE FORM (ARRAY, ORDER, BIG, VALID)
		190	DIMENSION ARRAY (80, 81)
		45*	ARRAY (I, J) = ELEMNT
	GETSYS	1*	SUBROUTINE GETSYS (ARRAY, ORDER, BIG, VALID)
		180	DIMENSION ARRAY (80, 81)
		26	CALL FORM (ARRAY, ORDER, BIS, VALID)
		30	CALL VALID8 (ARRAY, ORDER, VALID)
	LINEAR	250	DIMENSION ARRAY (80, 81)
		29*	DATA ARRAY (6480 * 0.0/, X / 80 * 0.0 /
		40	CALL GETSYS (ARRAY, ORDER, BIG, VALID)
		45	CALL SOLVE (ARRAY, X, ORDER, EPS, ITER, CONVRG)
	SOLVE	1*	SUBROUTINE SOLVE (ARRAY, SOLUTN, ORDER, EPS, ITER, CONVRG)
		220	DIMENSION ARRAY (80, 81)
	VALID8	1*	SUBROUTINE VALID8 (ARRAY, ORDER, VALID)
		160	DIMENSION ARRAY (80, 81)
DEBUG	FORM	170	COMMON / MISC / DEBUG
		210	LOGICAL VALID, CONVRG, DEBUG
	GETSYS	160	COMMON / MISC / DEBUG
		190	LOGICAL VALID, CONVRG, DEBUG
	LINEAR	230	COMMON / MISC / DEBUG
		270	LOGICAL VALID, CONVRG, DEBUG
		36*	READ (LUNIN, 900) DEBUG, ORDER, ITER, EPS, BIG
		53F	900 FORMAT (L1,I*,I5,E20.5,E20.5)
	OUTPUT	160	COMMON / MISC / DEBUG
		200	LOGICAL VALID, CONVRG, DEBUG
	SOLVE	200	COMMON / MISC / DEBUG
		250	LOGICAL VALID, CONVRG, DEBUG
	VALID8	140	COMMON / MISC / DEBUG
		170	LOGICAL VALID, CONVRG, DEBUG
ELEMNT	FORM	31*	READ (LUNIN, 910) I, J, ELEMNT
		66F	910 FORMAT (I5,I5,E20.5)
		370	ASSERT (I .GE. 1 .AND. I .LE. ORDER .AND. J .GE. 1 .AND. J .LE. (ORDER + 1) .AND.
			ELEMNT .LE. BIG)
SUM	VALID8	29*	SUM = 0.0
		32*	SUM = SUM + ABS (ARRAY (I, J))

Fig. 5-26 Variable trace for untested predicates of VALID8

TEST CASE	MODULE NAME	NUMBER OF D-D PATHS	SUMMARY -- THIS TEST			CUMULATIVE SUMMARY			
			NUMBER OF INVOCATIONS	D-D PATHS TRAVERSED	PER CENT COVERAGE	NUMBER OF TESTS	INVOCATIONS	TRAVERSED	COVERAGE
1	LINEAR	3	1	2	66.67	1	1	2	66.67
	GETSYS	7	1	4	57.14	1	1	4	57.14
	FORM	15	1	11	73.33	1	1	11	73.33
	VALID8	13	1	10	76.92	1	1	10	76.92
	SOLVE	21	1	15	71.43	1	1	15	71.43
	OUTPUT	7	1	4	57.14	1	1	4	57.14
	$$ALL$$	66		46	69.70	1		46	69.70
2	LINEAR	3	1	2	66.67	2	2	2	66.67
	GETSYS	7	1	4	57.14	2	2	6	85.71
	FORM	15	1	11	73.33	2	2	13	86.67
	VALID8	13	1	10	76.92	2	2	12	92.31
	SOLVE	21	1	14	66.67	2	2	20	95.24
	OUTPUT	7	1	4	57.14	2	2	7	100.00
	$$ALL$$	66		45	68.18	2		60	90.91
3	LINEAR	3	1	2	66.67	3	3	3	100.00
	GETSYS	7	1	4	57.14	3	3	6	85.71
	FORM	15	1	11	73.33	3	3	13	86.67
	VALID8	13	1	8	61.54	3	3	13	100.00
	SOLVE	21	0	0	0.00	3	2	20	95.24
	OUTPUT	7	0	0	0.00	2	2	7	100.00
	$$ALL$$	66		25	37.88	3		62	93.94

Fig. 5-27 Summary after three test cases

```
=============================================================================================
MODULE  I TEST   I PATHS   I                LIST OF DECISION TO DECISION PATHS NOT EXECUTED
NAME    I NUMBER I NOT HIT I
=============================================================================================
<LINEAR >  I 3     I 1    I 2
           I CUMUL I 0    I
---------------------------------------------------------------------------------------------
<GETSYS >  I 3     I 3    I 3  5  7
           I CUMUL I 1    I 5
---------------------------------------------------------------------------------------------
<FORM   >  I 3     I 4    I 3  5  8  15
           I CUMUL I 2    I 5  8
---------------------------------------------------------------------------------------------
<VALID8 >  I 3     I 5    I 3  9  10  11  13
           I CUMUL I 0    I
---------------------------------------------------------------------------------------------
<SOLVE  >  I 3     I 21   I 1   2   3   4   5   6   7   8   9   10  11  12  13  14  15  16  17  18  19  20
           I CUMUL I 1    I 21
                          I 14
---------------------------------------------------------------------------------------------
<OUTPUT >  I 3     I 7    I 1  2  3  4  5  6  7
           I CUMUL I 0    I
---------------------------------------------------------------------------------------------
```

Fig. 5-28 Not-hit report after three test cases

trol, control of industrial manufacturing processes, and control and guidance of satellites. In concert with the more prolific application of real-time data processing to critical functions are the potentially disastrous consequences that could result from software errors that cause malfunction or disablement of a system. The launch failure of the Mariner I spacecraft and the destruction of a French meteorological satellite occurred as a result of software errors.[81] Thus, the nature of real-time functions and the associated complex time-dependent interactions present additional problems not encountered by batch-oriented systems.

The criticality of the functions, more stringent timing and storage constraints, and the more competitive environment demand higher testing standards. Head[82] describes the testing problem in real-time systems as two-fold:

1. More intensive testing is needed to achieve a reliable operational status.
2. It is more difficult to satisfy the higher testing standards.

Head[83] further identifies the attributes of real-time systems that complicate the testing effort. These are paraphrased as:

1. Magnitude of programming effort—Many real-time systems have a very large number of programs that have to be interconnected and tested.
2. Repeatability—Because of slight differences in timing, the same sequence of test case inputs, phased slightly differently each time, may result in different outputs. This will be particularly evident on interactive systems that involve operator inputs from display consoles or remote terminals.
3. Equipment interaction: Multiprocessing—Many real-time systems involve multiple processors that must exchange information. Development of software typically is performed by machine-oriented groups of personnel who work in semi-isolation to produce their machine-peculiar subsystem. As two or more subsystems are tested and integrated, the impact of the lack of communication is felt.
4. Program interaction: Multi-programming—Several programs will typically share the computer at the same time. Without strict control of interfaces, significant errors will result because of unplanned or erroneous program interaction.
5. Inherent logical complexity—Real-time systems will usually contain many more decision points or branches than batch-oriented, scientific computation problems.
6. Random access storage—Real-time systems typically access storage much more often in a random manner than sequentially. As a consequence, it is more difficult to discover and isolate problems.

Another consideration in the testing of real-time systems involves the credibility

[81]H. Hecht, "Fault-Tolerant Software for Real-Time Applications," *ACM Computing Surveys*, **8** (1976), 392.

[82]Robert V. Head, "Testing Real-Time Systems, Part 1: Development and Management," *Datamation*, July 1964, p. 42.

[83]Ibid, pp. 42–48.

of testing in an environment other than the one in which the system will eventually operate. Testing is normally first performed at the manufacturer's facility before moving on to the operational site. An extra effort is necessary to simulate with reasonable exactness the operating environment and live inputs. Such an effort improves the confidence of the customer or user that the system will operate properly in the operational environment.

Yourdon and Constantine,[84] in their discussion of top-down versus bottom-up testing strategies, note that real-time systems may have attributes that need special consideration. The most critical problems may be in the software elements at the bottom of the structural hierarchy. It is in several of these elements that much of the execution mass, and, hence, the time consumption, is often situated Because of stringent timing requirements on the system, it may well be that the overall success of the development pivots on an early secureness of these few key software elements. Therefore, a bottom-up testing approach is advocated if these time-critical conditions are present. After these elements are tested, the testing can return, if desired, to the top-down philosophy.

Most real-time systems involve communication exchanges that are initiated or driven by the availability of data that requires processing. This availability may be signalled by an "interrupt" sent from one processing element to another. These exchanges may be between programs operating in the same computer, between programs operating in separate computers, or between a program and an external digital hardware device. Included in this latter category might be a radar signal processor that provides position and range information, or a digitizer from a temperature sensor associated with a chemical manufacturing process. These communication exchanges may also be regarded as critical aspects of the system. Since data exchanges and interrupt handling will exercise the control or executive program, it can reasonably be argued that testing of these functions should proceed from the top down. The previous paragraph advocated beginning from the bottom up on time-critical elements; here the top-down approach is favored for critical communication interfaces. The above examples provide a substantial argument for testing from the top down and bottom up at the same time.

Desmonde[85] has outlined a seven-phase testing procedure for a typical real-time system (which appears to be an interactive reservations system). The approach is oriented around the validation of "threads." To reiterate, a thread is a string of programs that accomplishes a single processing function. In this system a thread is initiated by an entry from a remote terminal console. The testing begins with the exercise of single threads and then progresses to testing of multi-threads. The testing phases are paraphrased here:

(a) Phase I—This consists of testing individual elements, testing of threads one at a time, and tracking of paths through each thread by using different inputs. A simulated control program is used in this phase. This provides the flexibility

---

[84]Yourdon and Constantine, *Structured Design*, p. 520.

[85]William H. Desmonde, *Real-Time Data Processing Systems: Introductory Concepts* (Englewood Cliffs, N.J.: Prentice-Hall, Inc., 1964), pp. 153–56.

to use debugging aids, such as tracers and memory prints, that would most likely not be available with the actual control program.

(b) Phase II—This again tests threads one at a time and traces paths through the threads. However, in this phase the actual control program is utilized. Testing occurs by using only one entry at a time per thread.

(c) Phase III—The procedures from Phase II are repeated here while using more than one entry at a time for the same thread.

(d) Phase IV—This is the first time the entire configuration is tested. Simulated inputs are used to test more than one thread at a time in order to detect interference among threads. A major objective in this phase is to stress the system and determine its throughput capacity. This is accomplished by loading the queues to capacity and observing whether the system takes the proper emergency measures. Also, invalid messages are input in order to observe if they are appropriately rejected.

(e) Phase V—In this phase the on-line terminals are incrementally connected. The testing begins with a single terminal, one thread test and builds into a multi-terminal test.

(f) Phase VI—The transition from artificial to real entries is made in this phase. Again, the number of terminals participating in the testing is gradually increased.

(g) Phase VII—This phase consists of a trial operation period. The period concludes when the incidence of bugs is reduced to an acceptable level, and the system performs smoothly.

A word of caution needs to be introduced here on the use of program measurement tools that instrument the code. The instrumentation introduces side effects. Significant changes in time and space (storage) may be incurred. As time and storage are key factors in real-time systems, automated test tools should be utilized with great caution.

The amount of difficulty encountered at each level of testing depends inversely on the thoroughness of testing at the previous level. This is applicable to all types of systems, but its importance is magnified with real-time systems. After a real-time system is operational, it becomes especially difficult to isolate and correct errors; thus, the importance of adequate pre-installation testing is amplified.[86]

The problems encountered in the development of conventional data processing systems are magnified by the added complexity of real-time systems. It is, therefore, important that the system concept be validated before the start of implementation. This is often accomplished by modeling the system in an analytical simulation to verify timing, capacity, and throughput. Such simulations have also been used to determine allocation of storage and to determine which programs should be kept in other storage devices.[87]

During the design of the real-time system, equal attention must be directed toward the preparation of program test facilities. These include all the utility programs, test

[86]Ginzberg, "Testing Real-Time System Programs," p. 58.
[87]Ibid, pp. 71–72.

evaluation programs, and simulations necessary to execute the testing effort. The development of these programs must be planned in concert with the master project schedule so as to be available to support development and testing of the operational programs. In one large real-time installation more than twice as much labor was expended to develop test tools as was used to develop the operational programs.[88]

This last section concludes the treatment of testing as a verification and validation technique. The next section places this material in perspective by reviewing verification and validation over the software life cycle. This includes other verification and validation activities in addition to testing.

5.5

Verification and Validation Over the Software Life Cycle

5.5.1 INTRODUCTION

The finished software product is the result of a series of production activities represented by a software life cycle. The production of the software has performed the transformation:

REQUIREMENTS AND FUNCTIONAL SPECIFICATIONS $\longrightarrow$ SOFTWARE

Verification and validation seek to reverse this process by providing the effect of the transformation:

SOFTWARE $\longrightarrow$ REQUIREMENTS AND FUNCTIONAL SPECIFICATIONS[89]

With contemporary practices, verification and validation efforts are applied largely to the software itself in the form of testing; more advanced tendencies, indicating an awareness that verification and validation cannot be cost effectively ignored until testing and integration, show a direction toward more formal validation of requirements and specifications. In this section, the chronology of verification and validation activities that extend over the software life cycle is discussed with the emphasis on classical practices.

It is important to recognize that a data processing system consists of both software and hardware, commercial programmable computers, and possibly special-purpose hardware. In addition, the data processing system may be just one component of a larger system. For example, an airborne fire-control system would consist of the air-to-air missiles, the radar, avionics, fire-control computer and software, and the aircraft itself. The software development, and the verification and validation activities in particular, must be synergistically combined with the development of computing hardware and the other system components.

It is the intention of this section to "walk through" the verification and validation considerations over the chronology of the software life cycle. Much of the material presented here will be a recapitulation of information provided in earlier sections of this chapter. This redundancy is purposely perpetrated in this life-cycle context with

---

[88]Desmonde, *Real-Time Data Processing Systems*, p. 151.
[89]Miller, *Methodology for Comprehensive Software Testing*, p. 24.

the hoped-for result that the reader's degree of understanding of verification and validation concepts will be enhanced.

5.5.2 SYSTEM LIFE CYCLE/SOFTWARE LIFE CYCLE: DESCRIPTIONS

The software production process must include consideration of two life cycles: the software development life cycle and the system (overall system) acquisition life cycle. The composition of the production activities in the software development life cycle is influenced by the phase of the system acquisition life cycle in which the software procurement occurs. Petrovay[90] fuses representative descriptions of both cycles from various Department of Defense (DOD) directives and analyzes the correlation between the two cycles. The following descriptions draw heavily from this work.

SYSTEM ACQUISITION LIFE CYCLE   This life cycle, applicable to the procurement of the overall system, consists of the conceptual, validation, full-scale development, production, and deployment phases. The purpose of this sequence is to allow the customer visibility into progress and provide decision points before committing to full-scale development of the system. The software life cycle occurs at least once within the system life cycle, as do life cycles for other components of the system.

Figure 2-5[91] delineates the system acquisition life cycle paralleled by the software development life cycle; this situation presumes that the software life cycle will be traversed only once throughout the system life cycle. Special software developments during the system life cycle may occur before the full-scale development phase in order to assist studies, experimental developments, and design validation exercises. This special type of software is associated with its own software development life cycle even though the phases in this life cycle are likely to be less rigorous and more informal than those associated with the development of the operational software; this is likely to be particularly true of the verification and validation activities, so there may be several software life cycles within the system acquisition life cycle.

Traditionally, it has been a planning direction by customers to be able to use this software developed early in the system life cycle in subsequent phases all the way to the full-scale development phase from which a prototype system results. Despite these intentions, the reality of the situation is almost always that the early software was developed for very specialized and limited applications. The cost of modifying, interfacing, and *validating* this early software for operational use exceeds the cost of developing new software from a revised and current set of requirements. Such goals are thwarted by a combination of: new and evolving requirements, differing design and programming standards, differing configuration control and management practices, more stringent documentation requirements, and more intensive verification and validation requirements that are applied to the operational software development as the system progresses toward finalization. These forces conspire against the attainment of this long-term amortization objective, however noble it may be.

If long-term usage of the software is seriously contemplated, management con-

---

[90]Petrovay, *Approach to Hughes Software Quality Assurance*, pp. 23–30.
[91]This figure appears in Chapter 2, this volume.

trols, engineering practices, and validation standards appropriate to the full-scale development phase should be applied initially. This, of course, will magnify costs and schedule duration. In the past such additional expenditures have seldom been approved with the usually good foresight that such software is highly likely to be discarded for the reasons cited in the previous paragraph.

SOFTWARE DEVELOPMENT LIFE CYCLE   The software development life cycle can be subdivided into seven phases (based on DOD directives): definition, analysis, design, development, testing, evaluation, and operational maintenance.[92] One or more of these software life cycle phases may be emphasized, de-emphasized, or bypassed, depending on the critical nature of the software development and the system life-cycle phase in which the software development occurs. A brief representative allocation of tasks to phases follows; the partitioning of the development cycle for any single project is subject to variance.

- Definition Phase—This is essentially a requirements definition phase. The products of this phase are a set of system level functional requirements and a set of detailed functional requirements for each Computer Program Configuration Item (CPCI). These requirements are documented in a System Specification and a development specification for each CPCI. They are scrutinized at the System Design Review (SDR).
- Analysis and Design Phases—These two phases collectively identify an intended design approach. Algorithms are selected; data structures are identified; software is broken down into units of work, and an initial program functional design is constructed. The central output is a preliminary design specification for each CPCI. These are reviewed at Preliminary Design Review (PDR) meetings. Detailed designs of each CPCI are documented in computer program product design documents and reviewed during Critical Design Review (CDR) meetings.
- Development, Test, and Evaluation Phases—These phases consist of coding and debug, software integration and test, hardware/software integration and test, initial operational test and evaluation, acceptance testing, and operational test and evaluation.
- Operations and Maintenance Phase—This phase embraces all the activities that are required to continue operational use of the software. This includes rectification of errors that are discovered while the software is operational and software upgrades up to some "modest" level. For major or significant upgrades to operational software, the formality of the software development cycle is again employed either in total or in part.

5.5.3 V&V PLANNING PRIOR TO FULL-SCALE DEVELOPMENT

An overall software production approach is normally established by the contractor before he enters into the full-scale development phase of the system life cycle. The vehicle for establishing such an approach may be the contractor's proposal or, in the case of more complex systems, special contract definition studies performed prior to

[92]Petrovay, *Approach to Hughes Software Quality Assurance*, pp. 27–30.

full-scale development. The factors addressed in defining the production approach include software design objectives, software test approach, software performance measures and standards, deliverable software requirements, and software documentation requirements.[93] Each of these factors will have verification and validation implications.

The early specification of software design objectives increases the overall effectiveness and efficiency of the programming function in relation to the available manpower and hardware resources.[94] It is here that design standards that produce an easily testable system should be specified, e.g., the utilization of modular or structured design and programming practices. Requirements on the applications software should be identified to provide the necessary interfacing with automatic testing aids to be utilized that are available or are expected to be available for the development. Objectives and standards involving error detection, fault isolation, and data recovery that aid the testing of the software should be stated. Also, specific modes of system operation that will be used to support testing should be defined.

A software test approach should be outlined, addressing the following specific factors and goals:[95]

- Identification of multiple levels of contractor testing
- Creation of test requirements and specifications
- Preparation of test scripts and procedures oriented toward compliance with test objectives and requirements
- Demonstrations of system integrity, serviceability, and performance in stressed situations
- Use of a test and integration group autonomous from the developers
- Testing of the overall system at both production and operational sites
- Verification of documentation
- Training of user personnel with operation and maintenance of the system as part of the testing effort
- Handling of software change proposals emanating from testing activities

A testing philosophy is recommended. The trade-offs of top-down versus bottom-up testing and phased versus incremental integration should be evaluated on a preliminary basis within the context of the prospective system under consideration.

The responsibilities for the various levels of testing should be established. These will include informal testing conducted by the development contractor for which no formal customer consent is required, formal testing conducted by the development contractor at the contractor's plant for which customer witness and sign-off is required, formal testing conducted by the integration and test contractor at the development contractor's plant for which customer witness and sign-off is required, and formal testing conducted by the integration and test contractor at the operational site.

Software performance measures and standards should be specified so as to initiate a foundation for assessing the quality of the software.[96] An early comprehensive effort

[93]Kelliher, *Quality Assurance and Control Practices in the Acquisition of Large Systems*, pp. xi–xii.
[94]Ibid, p. I-3.
[95]Ibid, p. I-6.
[96]Ibid, p. I-11.

directed toward defining these measures and standards will be a major contributor toward providing a direction to the verification and validation effort. As a minimum, an inclusive list of major performance metric parameters should be delineated before full-scale development goes into effect. Preferably, acceptance standards for many of the measures should also be developed; of course, some of the performance standards cannot be reasonably identified until the manufacturer is well into the full-scale development effort, despite the magnitude of the investigation at an early time. Some examples of performance measures are:[97] computing capacity utilization, storage utilization, response times, period between successive operations of periodic functions, and startup/startover times.

The deliverable software requirements are represented by a list of Computer Program Configuration Items (CPCIs) that are to be delivered with the system to the customer. This list contains operational software items and support software items. The support software includes programs that are used as aids for developing new operational programs, for entering new data into the system, for test and analysis, and for software and hardware maintenance.[98] Not all support programs will necessarily be deliverable items (such as test tools), and these may be developed with some leniency in documentation, configuration control, and testing requirements. However, in the case of Defense systems, as indicated in DOD directives,[99] all unique support items required to develop and maintain the delivered computer resources over the system's life cycle are now specified as deliverable, in which case they should be developed under the same standards as other deliverable items. All major support programs, particularly automated testing tools, should be identified early in order to correctly scope the magnitude of the entire software development. Experiences with large software projects indicate that support software is a major source of underestimation whenever cost overruns occur.

The software documentation requirements are represented by a list of documents required to be delivered over the duration of the software development contract. Included on this list are test specifications and reports. The contents and formats of these documents should be defined before the full-scale development begins. For example, the specification document for each individual test might typically contain a statement of prerequisite conditions, test equipment, inputs, outputs, support resources, error messages, completion codes, personnel requirements, interfaces, data bases, measurement and analysis methods, tolerances, time estimates, storage and recording requirements, and clear pass/fail criteria.[100]

5.5.4 VERIFICATION AND VALIDATION PRIOR TO TESTING

A significant number of errors are introduced into the software by programmer mistakes during the coding process. These may result from actual coding errors or by programmer misinterpretation of the design specification. However, a sizable

[97]Ibid, pp. I-11–13.

[98]Ibid, p. I-15.

[99]*Management of Computer Resources in Major Defense Systems*, Department of Defense Directive 5000.29 (1976), p. 3.

[100]Kelliher, *Quality Assurance and Control Practices in the Acquisition of Large* Systems, p. I-8.

number of errors also emanate from the earlier requirements definition and design processes. Rubey[101] reveals error statistics from a dozen aerospace software projects where 246 errors out of a total of 646 significant errors originated in the software specifications. He also quotes statistics from another study where two-thirds of the errors originated in the software specifications. Out of the 246 errors from the dozen aerospace projects, 145 were detected by review of the specifications while 101 remained undetected until testing of the code.

The notion is again reiterated that errors become more costly to rectify the further into the development they are detected. Large numbers of errors left undiscovered until testing and integration of the software may, therefore, impinge significant cost penalties on the project. Press[102] has accumulated statistics from several companies prominent in the development of large-scale software systems that depict the escalating relative costs to correct errors as later stages of the development cycle are traversed. This profile significantly reveals that it is 10 to 100 times more costly to correct an error after the software is operational than it would have been if detected during the preliminary design period. It appears, then, that it would be a cost-effective endeavor to avoid and discover specification errors before testing commences.

The basic structure of software testing, beginning with unit testing and advancing upward to system testing, is such that the most significant errors are not detected until late in the testing activity.[103] Acceptance or system testing, sometimes the only place where complete functions are tested, may be the first opportunity to uncover errors that were made very early when the software functions were defined. The use of the thread testing technique, described previously in this chapter, strongly mitigates this phenomenon.

Press[104] lists inspection, specification languages, specification standards, and simulation among the verification and validation techniques that should be applied in order to catch software design errors early. These techniques represent a more sophisticated approach to the problem with a broad base of applications. A more classical ad hoc approach to design verification is the paper "walk through." This is essentially an informal design review. This technique has been previously explored in Sec. 3.5.1.

The most obvious approach for ensuring that specification and requirements errors do not go undetected until testing is to produce documents that are complete, thorough, consistent, and unambiguous initially. Tools directed toward this end include specification languages, consistency checkers, and structured analysis techniques. Structured analysis, as an example, is both an aid in writing requirements and reviewing existing requirements documents not developed by using structural analysis; it is a method for modeling complex systems in a top-down hierarchal form and involves an activity model and a data model.[105] It is not the intention here to provide

[101]Raymond Rubey, "Verification of Requirements and Design Through Structured Analysis Techniques," in *Presentations at the Invitational DOD/Industry Conference on Software Verification and Validation*, 1976, p. 96.

[102]Barry Press, in *Presentations at the Invitational DOD/Industry Conference on Software Verification and Validation*, 1976, p. 29.

[103]Rubey, in *Conference on Software Verification and Validation*, p. 96.

[104]Press, in *Conference on Software Verification and Validation*, p. 31.

[105]Rubey, in *Conference on Software Verification and Validation*, p. 97.

a survey or overview of these tools, but only to mention that they exist. Specifics of their capabilities and applications are provided in Chapter 3.

Whatever tools are available to assist the requirements definition process, human skills must still be relied on to correctly prescribe the actual functional requirements. The functional requirements represent the intentions of the specification writer as to what he believes the functions of the software should be. No verification technique can ensure that the functional requirements faithfully represent the intentions of the writer since the reference to "truth" resides in the writer's mental processes.

5.5.5 DESIGN REVIEWS AND AUDITS

At periodic points in the software development, design reviews are conducted in order to permit customers, users, and management to assess progress. These design reviews are a vehicle to force design information into the public domain for scrutinization, and, hence, serve as a basic verification and validation method. The chronology of the design reviews may span several phases of the system acquisition life cycle. The specific number, format, and content of the reviews will depend on the customer, nature of the system, and contractual obligations. The following discussion centers on the design reviews and audits prescribed by DOD.[106] Since these are oriented toward stringent design review and control standards required for critical defense systems, they are not necessarily of universal application. However, this design review schedule can be utilized as an initial model that may be tailored for specific application according to the nature of the individual system. The actual allocation of subjects and documents for each review is established in a systems engineering management plan negotiated between customer and manufacturer on each individual project. A brief description of each design review follows in chronological order and includes annotations of test preparation and planning considerations. The material is derived largely from DOD directives.[107]

System Requirements Review (SRR)—The SRR is conducted to determine initial progress and direction of concept definition studies and convergence on an optimum and complete system configuration. Items to be reviewed include in-process results of preliminary requirements allocation and integrated test planning.

System Design Review (SDR)—The SDR evaluates the optimization, traceability, correlation, completeness, and risk of the allocated functional requirements, including the corresponding test requirements for the Data Processing Segment of the system. The review is conducted when the definition effort has proceeded to the point that requirements and design approach have achieved a precise level of definition. This normally occurs at the end of the validation phase or early in the full-scale development phase of the system life cycle. The principal items reviewed are the Data Processing Segment Requirements Specification and the Development Specification (requirements) for each CPCI. Preliminary test plans are reviewed to determine com-

---

[106]*MILITARY STANDARD: Technical Reviews and Audits for Systems, Equipment, and Computer Programs* (Washington, D.C.: Department of Defense, 1976), MIL-STD-1521A.

[107]Ibid, pp. 12–67.

patibility with the test requirements of the Segment and with the CPCI Development Specifications. All computer programs required for testing support are to be carefully identified in the specifications.

Preliminary Design Review (*PDR*)—The PDR is a formal technical review of the basic design approach for a CPCI. There would normally be one successful PDR for each CPCI. A collective PDR for a functionally related group of CPCIs, treating each CPCI individually, may be held when such an approach is advantageous. The PDR is held after authentication of the CPCI Development Specification and the accomplishment of preliminary design efforts, but prior to the start of the detail design. The principal items reviewed are the updated CPCI Development Specification, informal preliminary design documentation, and drafts of test plans/procedures. All development and test tools that are planned for use during program development, but are not deliverable under terms of the contract, are to be identified. Changes to the CPCI Development Specification are inspected to determine whether the test requirements in that document adequately reflect the changes.

Critical Design Review (*CDR*)—The CDR is a formal, technical review of the CPCI detailed design conducted prior to the start of coding. The CDR is intended to ensure that the detailed design solutions, as reflected in the draft CPCI Product Specification, satisfy performance requirements established by the CPCI Development Specification. The CDR is also accomplished for the purpose of establishing integrity of computer program design at the level of flow charts or computer program logical design prior to coding and testing. The principal items reviewed are the complete draft of the CPCI Product Specification and drafts of test plans/procedures. All changes to the CPCI Development Specification and available test documentation are examined to determine compatibility with the test requirements of the Development Specification. While the CDR is normally accomplished prior to releasing the CPCI for coding, this will not preclude releasing-for-coding portions of complex CPCIs that are necessary to maintain schedule.

Functional Configuration Audit (*FCA*)—The FCA verifies that the CPCI's actual performance complies with the requirements of the Development Specification. Data from test of the CPCI is perused to verify that the item has performed as required. FCAs may be conducted on an incremental basis. The FCA for a complex CPCI may be conducted on a progressive basis with completion of the FCA occurring after completion of the level of integrated testing that may be required to validate the CPCI. The principal items provided to the customer for the FCA are the CPCI test plans, procedures, and report, plus the updated Development Specification and draft Product Specification. The CPCI test procedures and results are reviewed for compliance with the Development Specification requirements. Requirements of the Development Specification not validated by the CPCI test are identified, and a solution for subsequent validation is proffered (such as validation in the subsystem or system tests). An audit of the test plans/procedures is made and compared against the official test data, including checks for completeness and accuracy. Deficiencies are documented, and completion dates for all discrepancies are established and recorded. An audit of the test report is performed to validate that it accurately and completely describes the CPCI test.

Physical Configuration Audit (*PCA*)—The PCA is a formal examination of the

CPCI end-item (the code). The CPCI is matched against its technical documentation and configuration management records in order to establish the baseline version of the CPCI. The PCA is conducted after delivery to the customer of the final draft of the CPCI Product Specification. The PCA includes an audit of the Product Specification and an inspection of the format and completeness of the user's manual and any other manuals or handbooks due for acceptance at this time. Other specific review tasks also include: examine Product Specifications for format and completeness, and scrutinize FCA minutes for discrepancies that require action.

Formal Qualification Review (FQR)—The FQR verifies that the actual performance of a CPCI, as determined through testing, complies with its Development Specification and identifies the test reports/data that document the results of tests of the CPCI. When feasible, the FQR is combined with the FCA at the end of CPCI testing prior to PCA, if sufficient test results are available at the FCA, to ensure that the CPCI will perform in its system environment. Otherwise, the FQR may be considered an extension of the FCA and may be conducted at the subsystem/system/segment levels.

Design reviews and audits should not be relied on as crutches to redirect errant technical approaches. More often than not, reviews result in what is mainly a scrutinization for inconsistencies in the design. The technical approach to the design is frequently not challenged.[108] Hence, responsibility for the integrity of the design and product remains largely in the hands of the manufacturer.

5.5.6 DEVELOPMENT TESTING AND INTEGRATION TESTING

Software is developed, tested, and integrated by using building blocks of software elements that are assembled in progressive phases into higher-level units, thus forming a distinct hierarchy. The testing of the software begins by the organization responsible for the program coding and debugging of the individual software elements. This engineering organization is responsible for testing and assembling the software elements into a Computer Program Configuration Item (CPCI), normally the lowest level item formally deliverable to the customer and maintained under formal configuration control. The CPCI is alternately known as a module. The responsible engineering organization that develops and tests the CPCI and its components also delivers the final CPCI to the integrator upon successful testing. Hence, testing up to this level is very often known as "development testing." After validation at the CPCI level, multiple CPCIs are assembled into subsystems, and the several subsystems are then integrated into the data processing system segment. An integration group independent of the development organization conducts this higher-level testing that is called "integration testing." The foregoing process is charted in Figure 5-29. The next lower-level component of the CPCI is shown designated as a Computer Program Component (CPC) or submodule. A CPC is composed of routines.

Development testing concludes with a formal test of the assembled CPCI. The testing is planned and executed in accordance with formal test plan and test procedure

---

[108]Donald J. Reifer, in *Presentations at the Invitational DOD/Industry Conference on Software Verification and Validation*, 1976, p. 52.

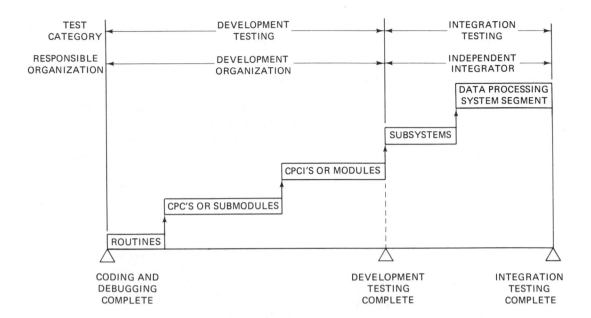

Fig. 5-29 Development and integration testing

documents. Previously, CPCs and routines have been tested on an informal basis, i.e., the tests are conducted without customer witness or sign-off under the guidance of the manufacturer's management. Although informal, these tests should be conducted in a rigorous manner and written test plans and procedures should be produced prior to their execution.

The basic objective of development testing is to exhaustively exercise the software so as to discover and correct as many errors as possible while the software is still in the hands of the developers. The cost of rectifying errors will be increased after the software is turned over to the integration organization. The emphasis during development testing is focused initially on checking internal logic on a routine-by-routine basis. Goals for testing the internal structure may be expressed in such terms as: exercising every instruction, exercising a certain number of logical paths, or exercising every decision element. Such goals are assisted by automated testing tools and may not be achievable without them. As testing progresses to the CPC and CPCI levels, the emphasis shifts to verifying interfaces, computational accuracies, timing, and sizing. The formal CPCI test may be partially directed toward verification of some system level performance requirements that can be addressed at the CPCI level. The thread testing approach described in thread testing earlier in this chapter is a vehicle for directing the testing toward a performance orientation at an early date.

Integration testing occurs in several progressive phases prior to the delivery of the software to the customer. This formal testing requires customer approval of test plans, procedures, and test results; he normally witnesses the execution of the actual tests. Emphasis during integration testing concentrates on verifying performance requirements and interfaces. Integration testing intends to demonstrate that observed performance of the software is in concert with required performance while operating in as near an operational environment as possible.[109]

5.5.7 ERROR TRENDS THROUGHOUT TESTING

Examination of error report statistics gathered from the testing associated with a large-scale, complex, real-time development reveals some significant and interesting trends over the testing duration and the initial period of operations. Figure 5-30 exhibits the profile over time of the rate of errors reported for each successive phase of testing.

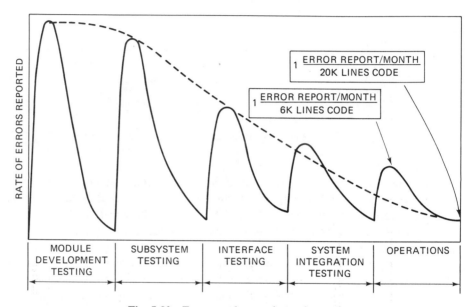

Fig. 5-30   Error trends over the testing cycle

Within each testing category, the error report rate rises sharply (as the test team intensifies its efforts), reaches a peak, and then declines as the causes of the errors are isolated and then corrected. The error report rate again escalates as the testing progresses to the next phase. The peak rate of errors does show a steady decline with each progressive stage of testing. The explanation for the repetition of the error-rate ascent/descent profile appears to be twofold: (1) Each test is conducted by a different test team; the complacent disposition unconsciously developed by a test team concluding their testing effort is replaced by a fresh, unbiased outlook of a new test team initiating the next phase of testing; the fresh approach directly yields new sources of errors; (2) Each successive phase of testing will exercise more extensive and complex interactions between software elements that were not previously tested, thus discovering more errors. Nelson[110] documents a very similar error trend from statistics

[109]*Software Development and Configuration Management Manual*, p. 9–14.
[110]Nelson, *TRW Symposium on Reliable, Cost-Effective, Secure Software*, pp. 5-16–17.

reported from the Site Defense Program; he notes that logical errors tend to be discovered early in the testing while numerical inaccuracies are detected later.

Some residual errors are usually accepted at the end of each phase, provided that they are not critical in nature. The testing phase is concluded as a practical matter, and the liens are carried into the next test phase. There is a tendency at the higher levels of integration to reach closure of the test phase with a higher rate of residual errors. This situation exists because the more complex processing interactions not previously tested produce deficiencies that require more time to rectify than might be available within the scheduled duration of the test. This practice of early closure is not necessarily advocated on a technical basis as it may, if not cautiously handled, produce an unstable baseline for the next phase. What is evident is the exercise of management's perogative (both buyer and seller collectively) to show compliance with intermediate schedule milestones.

At the onset of operations, Figure 5-30 shows the incidence of errors declining from 1 error report per month for each 6000 lines of code to 1 error report per month for each 20,000 lines of code at a steady-state level. This error profile might be predicted to recur each time a new software version is introduced to the system. Two possible explanations have been advanced for the constant steady-state error detection rate after software is operational:[111] (1) Correction of an error may produce the "ripple effect" by implanting other errors into the system; (2) Since in most software systems a small portion of the code is exercised most of the time, large sections of the code are minimally exercised with the result that errors in those sections are not discovered until much later. Figure 5-31 shows the incidence of the steady-state error by severity category. The collection of these statistics can aid in planning the level of effort required to maintain the software. However, such figures should be employed with some caution since the experiences on one project are not necessarily transferable to other projects.

5.5.8 TESTING DURING MAINTENANCE PHASE

Continuous modification of software after initial delivery occurs as a result of accrued experience with the use of the software and changing requirements. Changes required during maintenance may be due to:

- Errors not discovered during original testing
- Failures outside the data processing system, which can be corrected by software changes
- Changing requirements for use of system
- Modifications to make people in system more efficient
- Modifications to make hardware and software more efficient
- Modifications to algorithms to take account of experience with real data

Some commerical users of software have been known to spend approximately 50% of their data processing budgets on maintaining existing programs.[112] On some

---

[111]Ramamoorthy and Ho, "Testing Large Software with Automated Software Evaluation Systems," pp. 48–49.

[112]Yourdon, *Techniques of Program Structure and Design*, p. 248.

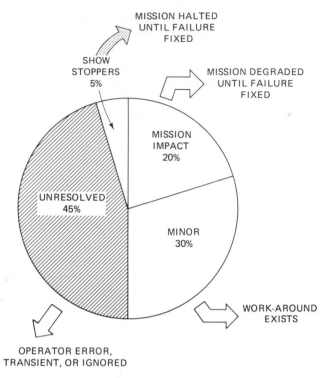

MISSION HALTED
UNTIL FAILURE
FIXED

SHOW
STOPPERS
5%

MISSION DEGRADED
UNTIL FAILURE
FIXED

MISSION
IMPACT
20%

UNRESOLVED
45%

MINOR
30%

WORK-AROUND
EXISTS

OPERATOR ERROR,
TRANSIENT, OR IGNORED

Fig. 5-31 Operational error reports by severity category

defense systems, 80% of the total software life cycle costs have been expended on maintenance. These high proportion is partially the result of the difficulty that is encountered in making software changes. Other figures show that the probability of correctly modifying a program on the first attempt is less than 50%.[113] Hence, if only for economic reasons, these statistics should suggest that the entire process of software modification, including verification and validation, should be treated very carefully.

Miller[114] specifies two fundamental questions in maintaining software:

1. If a particular module has been changed, what other modules have to be retested?
2. If a series of changes has been made throughout a software system, which modules will have to be retested to restore the system's testedness level?

The answers to these questions essentially define the test plan for the subject software changes. This information is most easily acquired by applying an automated tool with capabilities equivalent to the one exemplified in the section on automated testing. By means of static analysis, this tool can easily identify the set of modules that invoke the changed module and the set of modules that the changed module invokes. The dynamic analysis capabilities, through instrumentation, can identify the decision-to-decision paths and single modules that remain untested on re-execution of the old

[113]Ibid, p. 271.
[114]Miller, *Methodology for Comprehensive Software Testing*, p. 13.

test case set with the changed software.[115] These untested DD-paths and modules then become the targets for additional retesting.

Elmendorf[116] has outlined the philosophy of regression testing in order to assure that software changes do not inadvertently propagate errors into other previously operable functions: During development, the testing program normally starts with small, simple test cases and then builds up to large, complex ones. With regression testing as applied to maintenance changes, the chronology is reversed. The complex test cases are run first. If these are unsuccessful, the simpler, localized cases are run to isolate the problem.

The use of a system may progress to a position that was not originally envisioned when the system was developed. If it is to play a more critical or crucial role, the customer may wish to revalidate the system with higher standards in mind. As part of such an effort, portions of the software may be upgraded to make it more fault-tolerant so that the system would continue to perform at some minimum level when faced with unexpected demands. In this situation a retesting program would be undertaken during maintenance. The objective of the revalidation effort is to obtain a more reliable system. This would occur as a result of (1) the fault-tolerance software upgrades, and (2) the retesting that forecloses on more of the opportunities for errors to occur. This sequence has occurred when a system that was originally developed as a backup to another system now assumes the primary mission.

This last major section has recounted and summarized the role of verification and validation over the software life cycle. The discussion has been oriented toward contemporary practices. The next section extends this viewpoint into the future by briefly examining current directions.

5.6

Future Trends

This chapter began with an examination of definitions for verification and validation. Subsequent sections surveyed in detail the use of software testing as a verification and validation technique. The last section placed testing into perspective with other aspects of verification and validation that are applied over the software life cycle. The investigations into these subject areas have suggested some trends for the future in verification and validation.

Future directions and advances appear to be concentrated in these categories:

1. More extensive use of automated tools to achieve more complete system validation
2. More testing during development period
3. Use of constructive and static approaches to achieve verification and validation

[115]Ibid, p. 109.
[116]Elmendorf, "Controlling the Functional Testing of an Operating System," p. 288.

These future trend areas are not mutually exclusive nor discrete; their development is intertwined both in a parallel sense and in a serial sense. The first two categories seem to be a direct extension of present-day technology while the linkage to the third category is a bit more vague.

The software development process is more accurately viewed when the technical engineering problem is considered in conjunction with the human engineering aspect of the process. The application of talented personnel should, theoretically, be a sufficient requisite on which to forecast success. However, basic human fallibilities open loopholes for errors to occur. Engineering, scientific, and management practices are frequently corrupted by human errors of consistency and omission. Computer automated tools have been and will continue to be developed to implement functions that are most prone to consistency and omission errors if performed manually.

Although more detailed classifications are possible, automated tools may be partitioned into two basic groups: (1) those tools that assist in the definition and design of the software, and (2) those tools that help evaluate the software, once it is built. The first group of tools performs clerical functions of checking for completeness, consistency, and omission errors during requirements definition and design activities. The usefulness of such tools depends on the ability to express requirements and software design in machine-readable form. Thus, the future utility of these tools is, to a large degree, directly keyed to progress in the development and widespread use of specification languages, program design languages, and automated documentation systems.

The RXVP source text analysis system, explained in a previous section, is typical of the evaluation tools. This technology is already in a highly developed state although much necessary research continues to be directed toward the automatic generation of an optimal set of test cases. Widespread use and acceptance of these tools are presently hampered by (1) reluctance by management to forsake traditional manual methods that have been previously successful on small software projects, and (2) availability of tools only to companies that have been able to finance their development. Each of these restraints is expected to be slowly eroded in the next several years. The first problem will be overcome through an educational process, particularly with regard to cost benefits of the automated tools and the prospect of being denied contracts for large software projects if the tools are not used. The second difficulty is more acute. More companies may be willing to invest the necessary funds for automatic tool development in order to protect future business. The purchase rights to some already-existing tools are presently being marketed by their developers. A further possibility is that, for projects where a government agency is the procurer, automatic test tools may be available as government-furnished equipment.

As the more prolific usage of automated tools is expected over the software life cycle from requirements definition through testing, a more complete verification and validation of the system results. It is also expected that errors would be detected earlier in the development cycle with such approaches leading to cost containment.

There has been an increasing awareness that errors are less costly to resolve when discovered and isolated at the earliest possible date. This has motivated an amplified emphasis on more thorough testing of the software by the development organization before handover to an independent integrator. This accentuated testing has mainly taken the form of preparing test cases that will approach exhaustive exercise of the code. In most cases, automated testing aids are necessary to accomplish comprehensive testing coverage. These more stringent testing objectives are likely to be adopted on a more widespread basis in the near future as automated test tools become more extensively available and are more widely used.

It is the forward-looking concept of some that nearly error-free programs can be constructed by applying certain organizational techniques and that the correctness of these programs can be certified in a static manner (without actual execution) by using mathematical proofs. The constructive approach to the development of programs is with us today in the form of "structured" design and programming. The static approach concerns "program proofs," a popular subject of current research. Practical application of program proof techniques to programs of significant size may be at least a decade away.[117]

The proof concept employs the program source statements to prove mathematical theorems about program behavior.[118] The expected program behavior is characterized by a set of assertions. The intentions of the designers are reflected in these assertions about values of variables at end or intermediate points of the programs; then, the program can be converted into a theorem and the assertions proved.[119] Program proofs are intended to place verification and validation on a more sound theoretical foundation. The ad hoc process of testing certifies only that a program has passed certain test cases. Paige and Miller[120] assert the intuitive notion that proof techniques, if they can be automated, would seem to provide a better check than monitoring the performance of software to a set of sample data. One of the difficulties of the correctness proof approach is developing the assertions that are to be proved.[121]

A major obstacle limiting wider use of these techniques is the length of the necessary computations, which can be longer than the program itself. Economic feasibility requires further development of automatic theorem proving tools.[122]

Structuring of programs into small modular units will make them more amenable to proof techniques.[123] In particular, application of structured programming to reduce the complexity of the software will enable assertions to be produced more easily.

It should be recognized that mathematical proofs do not form an infallible technique. Like other processes, they may be subject to invalid conclusions. The situation has been documented where a published and accepted proof survived 12 years before it was discovered to be faulty.[124] The performing of testing as well as proving could achieve highest confidence in the results since these two methodologies

[117]Miller, *Methodology for Comprehensive Software Testing*, p. 17.

[118]Ibid, p. 17.

[119]Paige and Miller, *Methodology for Software Validation*, p. 37.

[120]Ibid, p. 38.

[121]Miller, *A Survey of Major Techniques of Program Validation*, p. 29.

[122]Ibid, p. 58.

[123]Liskov, in *Proc. of Fall Joint Computer Conference*, 1972, p. 193.

[124]Carl Engelman, *Presentations at the Invitational DOD/Industry Conference on Software Verification and Validation*, pp. 5–6.

have compensating strengths and weaknesses.[125] This approach might be exemplified by the case of real-time programs. Program proving, as a static analysis tool not involving actual program execution, would verify only mathematical correctness. It could not verify totally proper operation because real-time programs may have complex timing dependencies with other elements in the processing environment. Successful operation of the real-time software in its environment would be demonstrated by testing.

Miller[126] projects that, after a period of maturation for proof techniques, it may be only a straight-forward adaptation of automatic testing tools that is required to develop automatic proving tools. This is consistent with the observation of a common attribute associated with the acceptance and widespread use of advanced verification and validation concepts: automation. The effectiveness of these concepts is greatly enhanced when computer resources can replace human resources. Widespread availability of tools to perform the clerical functions of definition and design and to assist testing is foreseeably imminent. Automation of program proving for practical use must wait an extended period. Program proofs, however, will always encounter grave difficulties in addressing errors associated with overload conditions, timing, throughput, capacity, fallback, and recovery. The most powerful application of proofs is likely to be in a joint arrangement with testing.

There are other advanced techniques, such as symbolic execution or automatic analysis of specifications to derive test cases, that are the subjects of current research. These techniques, in the view of this author, are not likely to attain pragmetic significance relative to complex real-world large-scale software projects any time in the near future.

[125]Susan L. Gerhart and Lawrence Yelowitz, "Observations of Fallibility in Applications of Modern Programming Methodologies," *IEEE Transactions on Software Engineering*, SE-2 (1976), 204–6.

[126]Miller, *Methodology for Comprehensive Software Testing*, p. 18.

6 SECURITY AND PRIVACY

PATRICK A. HASCALL

Data Processing Software Development Laboratory
Hughes Aircraft Company

> *Better put a strong fence*
> *'round the top of the cliff,*
> *Than an ambulance down in*
> *the valley*
>
> JOSEPH MALINS
> *A Fence or an Ambulance*
> Stanza 7

This chapter pertains to the generation of secure computer software and the protection of the privacy of individuals whose personal information is stored in computer systems. The terms *security* and *privacy* are not synonymous; *security* is the technological problem of providing protection for information, whereas *privacy* is the sociological problem of deciding how much information may be divulged.

Computers are being utilized in many applications that range from inventory and factory process controls to communication systems and data banks, with new applications devised continually. The value and quantities of the data being processed in this wide range of systems provide an inviting target for industrial spying, fraud, or sabotage. Because computers process large amounts of data rapidly, the seriousness of each violation can quite possibly be increased. For example, in a recent study of bank losses, the average loss without the fraudulent aid of computers was $19,000; with computer aid the average loss rose to $450,000.[1] To illustrate further the fact that computer manipulation is varied and widespread, these examples are given:

- Six persons were charged for altering the credit records in a credit bureau by adding favorable information to and deleting unfavorable information from the records of as many as 100 people.[2]

[1] *Computerworld* (Boston), March 8, 1976, 13.
[2] Ibid. Sept. 13, 1976, 1, 4.

- A former employee of a company used a remote terminal to obtain a considerable portion of an expensive proprietary program.[3]
- A health insurance company lost $128,000 over a two-year span because an employee filed false medical claims for his relatives. The fraud was discovered only because one form was filled out incorrectly; even then, the insurance company had to call the doctor listed in the claim to discover that the operation had not been performed.[4]
- Certain insurance investigators were taught in normal training sessions how to obtain data from IRS and FBI data banks. Penetration techniques included having an insurance agent pose as an officer from a neighboring police department in order to gain access to the data banks.[5]
- During an 18-month period, employees of a furniture firm that had a computerized inventory system stole $200,000 worth of furniture. Whenever a piece of furniture was stolen, the thieves would employ a computer terminal to alter the inventory file and mark the stolen piece as misplaced. If an order for the stolen piece arrived at the warehouse, the thieves would locate an identical piece, say that the stolen piece had been found, and then ship the identical furniture (which was then listed as misplaced). The scheme was detected only because the wife of an employee observed suspicious activity around one of the loading docks.[6]
- And finally, the traditional story was told of the programmer of a bank accounting system who was caught depositing the fractions of a cent interest to his own account.

These are just a few of the computer fraud schemes that have been discovered. There is a good possibility that many more sophisticated schemes are devised and may never be detected.

In order to discuss security in a computer system, the stage must be set and the players of the game defined. The information to be protected is contained in a computer system, the stage (including the Central Processing Unit (CPU), short and long term storage, terminals, any required communications lines, and the operating system or supervisor), and is stored in objects. The following italicized items represent the players. An *object* can be a data file, a magnetic tape file, the code for a program, a message queue, or any other set of information that can be treated as a basic unit by the operating system. A *process* consists of the routines and data files (essentially a set of objects) required to perform a particular task and information about the current state of the task; thus, a process is a dynamic representation of the execution of a program. Since a process must be protected by the operating system, the process is also considered an object. A *processor* is the hardware (i.e., CPU) and software (i.e., operating system) that actually performs the task, using the instructions and data contained in the process. *Users* of a system are those who initiate and are responsible for a process in the system. *Penetrators* are the individuals who attempt to violate the

[3]Ibid. June 28, 1976, 1, 2.
[4]Ibid. May 31, 1976, 1, 2.
[5]Ibid. Nov. 1, 1976, 1, 4.
[6]Ibid. March 1, 1976, 1, 4.

security of a particular system and who are sometimes legitimate users of the system with devious intentions.

The entities that must be protected are processes and objects, so protection must be given when the information is being used and while it is being stored. Computer security can be generally defined as protecting objects and processes from penetrators while allowing legitimate users access to the objects and processes in a controlled manner.

An attempt to penetrate the security of a computer system takes one of three forms:

1. Obtaining information from the computer.
2. Depriving others of the use of the computer system.
3. Modifying the information in the system for fraudulent purposes or sabotage.

Of the three forms, the first is the hardest to prevent or detect. Stealing information from the computer can be compared to a thief's sneaking into an office, opening the safe by using the combination, and microfilming the contents. However, by contrast, the penetrator into many computer systems has access to more information, can copy the information faster, and has a smaller chance of being caught.

In the second penetration form, a legitimate user can be prevented from using the system, or portions of the system, by an illegal infiltrator in several ways. For example, a penetrator can write a program that has an infinite loop, thereby monopolizing the central processor and degrading the level of services made available to other users, or write a program that monopolizes all of the tape drives in the system and blocks the execution of any other job that requires tape drives. Another technique would be to tap a communication line and add spurious messages, either causing the link synchronization to be broken or requiring the system to sort out and discard the extra messages, thereby reducing the efficiency of the communication system.

The third form of breaching computer security, modification of the contents of the information in the system, can be used for either sabotage or fraud. As an example of sabotage, an invader may be able to alter a portion of the operating system and cause the system to fail. Sabotage also invalidates the results of a program if the infiltrator inserts errors into the input data or a computational error into the program. However, all sabotage is not by design; many forms of sabotage occur unintentionally, brought about by programmer or procedural errors; the unintentional mistakes, unfortunately, can be as costly as the intentional ones. Fraud, on the other hand, is the manipulation of the inputs or contents of a system in order to obtain specific erroneous results, which generally net economic benefits to the penetrator.

Now that it has been illustrated that computers are often misused for illegal purposes, the stage and players are set, and the three major classes of computer penetration have been discussed, it may be noted that the use of security techniques in the design and implementation of program systems helps to reduce this white-collar thievery. However, the generation of secure software serves as only *part* of the solution; procedural techniques, administrative controls, recovery techniques, and the legal and social environments must also be considered by the software engineer. Unfortunately, these factors are often beyond one's control. For a comprehensive discussion of these ideas, see *Security, Accuracy, and Privacy in Computer Systems* by Martin[7] as they will not be detailed in this chapter.

The introduction to the concepts regarding security and privacy that are presented in this chapter begin with the basic levels of protection that may be required by a software engineer in order to provide security and/or privacy, and include a brief overview of the tools and techniques available to the software engineer for the generation of secure software. This introduction is followed by a detailed description of each of the tools and techniques. The discussion concludes with privacy considerations and ways to measure the level of security in a system.

6.1

Levels of Protection

To reiterate, the basic purpose of security in a computer system is to protect the information within the system. However, in most multi-programmed computer systems, the information must be shared between many users. Thus, any security system must allow the sharing of information while at the same time preventing any information access that does not conform to the security scheme. In fact, protection in a computer system and sharing of information go hand-in-hand. In general, complex sharing schemes require complex protection mechanisms.

The following analysis discusses the six levels in which a computer user may want to share information with other programmers and gives examples of how each level aids (or does not aid) the software engineer in the quest for security.

1. The lowest level of protection is that of no protection at all; in such a system a penetrator can force access to any piece of information in the system no matter what sharing scheme exists.

At first glance it would appear that many programs, and perhaps some files, do not really require protection, and in those cases an unprotected system seems to be adequate. However, even if the owner of a program does not care if everyone can read or use that program, unauthorized modifications to this program still are a concern. One example is the case of the lowly library routine that performs the sine function. It appears to fall in the category of not requiring protection; after all, everyone has free access to the routine, so there is no need to steal it. In fact, the source code for the routine is probably available in some system manual. The main concern is that someone may alter the routine so that it no longer gives the correct result. The modification may be simply a prank or it may be industrial sabotage.

2. An isolation system is desirable for the user who does not want to share files or programs with anyone else.

[7]James Martin, *Security, Accuracy, and Privacy in Computer Systems* (Englewood Cliffs, N.J.: Prentice-Hall, Inc., 1973).

One way to provide isolation is to physically isolate a set of programs and files by dedicating one computer to one specific set of programs and files. For example, in military operations, classified jobs must be completely isolated from unclassified jobs; the switch between classified and unclassified jobs entails zeroing core, removing disk packs or turning off disk drives, and may require re-initializing the operating system.

The second way to provide isolation is to create a virtual computer by making a computer system act as though a set of programs and files is the only set of objects in the system even though several such sets may be present. The concept of virtual machines will be treated in more detail later. As seen from the above examples, isolation gives a very high level of protection, but it allows no sharing.

3. The lowest level of protection that allows sharing is an all-or-nothing system. This means that if a user has access to any file or routine, any operation on the file or routine can be performed.

The owner of a set of files cannot specify how the files are to be manipulated by another user—only that the other user has permission to access the files. It is not possible to prevent accidental or intentional modification of a shared file by an authorized user. This situation is still better than the case of no protection at all because the user can at least limit the number of people who can sabotage the programs or files. This system behaves like an isolation system if a user gives no one access to his files and routines.

4. Controlled sharing, which consists of both allowing the use of an object and placing restrictions on the type of use allowed, maintains a high level of protection because the user of an object is granted only the minimum access rights needed to perform a particular task. The access rights specified are usually a small set of common access modes, such as read, read-write, and read-execute. With this form of sharing, a secure library of programs can be generated.

To illustrate, as long as no one is given write access to the routines in the library, the users of the library are protected from sabotage. A data base system with read-only access can be employed with the assurance that no user will accidently, or perhaps not so accidently, alter any of the values in the data base.

Some fairly advanced sharing schemes can be implemented by using controlled sharing. One example is the case of two researchers, Jim and Joan, who decide to pool resources and create a common data bank to store information about students in a particular college. Jim is studying drug abuse while Joan is doing statistical studies for the university. In order to obtain any valid information from the students, Jim must guarantee complete privacy, particularly in connection with the school administration. Therefore, Jim does not want Joan to be able to access any of the records about drug abuse by any particular student. The university is interested in some of the general statistics about drug abuse and so allows Jim the use of the data compiled by Joan in return for the statistics. Thus, the information about the students is divided into two parts: general background data used by both Jim and Joan, and drug abuse data used by Jim alone.

This structure can be successfully effected through controlled sharing by creating two files. One file contains the drug-related information while the other holds background data, and some mechanism ties together related records in both files. Jim would possess read-write access to the drug information file and read-only access to the background data file, while Joan would have read-write access only to the background data file. Any attempt by Joan to obtain drug abuse data is blocked, even though she may know the exact location where data for a particular student is stored. Jim can use information from the background data file, but cannot modify the file.

This system can be generalized by adding another file for each type of data about the students who are to be protected. The system created may not be the most efficient, but is workable.

5. The fifth level of protection allows users to specify access controls or the ways in which objects can be used.

In the controlled sharing concept, the types of sharing are limited to those provided by the sharing scheme, but it is impossible to implement all of the access modes that any user may ever want. By allowing the user to specify access modes, a richer sharing environment is created, and the user tailors the degree of protection to his own needs. The user-specified access restrictions can be divided into three forms: user dependent, context dependent, and data dependent.

With *user-dependent* access controls, the restrictions on the manipulation of an object, such as a file or routine, depend on who is attempting to use the object. One example of such a system is an inventory file, in which some users can only read the file, others can modify specific parts of the file, and only a select few can modify the entire file.

With *context-dependent* access controls, the environment in which a user of an object is operating affects the access to the object. A user may be denied access to a file or set of files if he is working with a terminal that is outside a physically secure area. Operating with a file may be restricted to a time period from 9:00 AM to 5:00 PM, with perhaps a limited use allowed from 7:00 AM to 9:00 AM and 5:00 PM to 9:00 PM. An inventory system may be set up so that only terminals in the receiving department add to the inventory counts, only terminals in the purchasing department interrogate the files to determine which items need to be reordered, and only the shipping department reduces the inventory counts to account for materials that have been shipped.

The third form of user-specifiable access control is *data-dependent* control. The user may be allowed or denied access to a record, depending on the contents of the record. If the inventory file for the company contains sensitive information about a product under development, most of the users of the inventory file may be blocked from using the information. Personnel who access an employee information system may be prevented from reading the records of an employee whose salary exceeds $20,000. In the drug abuse file example, all the information about the student could be placed in one file, and Joan would not be given the capability to access other than the general background data about each student.

6. So far, the sharing and protection schemes have involved preventing or restricting access to information; however, the user may want to limit the way the information is manipulated after access has been permitted, i.e., the protection mechanisms may allow a routine to utilize personal information in a statistical analysis, but may not allow a direct printout of the information.

A concept closely related to the limited-use problem is keeping track of information that is being shared. In some cases, it may be necessary to know the location of all copies of shared information. A point in case is that anyone may ask to see his credit record, and if he finds an error in the record, it may be necessary to find all of the copies of the erroneous data and correct them. If the credit records are maintained in a computer system, limiting the use of the records reduces the problem of tracking down all of the incorrect records because the search is limited to only those users who are allowed to both access the record and retain a copy of the record.

As can be seen from the above analysis, the software engineer may have a choice of the level of protection he wishes to utilize to provide security for information he places in a computer system. His only problem is to actually provide the level of protection he desires.

6.2

Chapter Overview

The software engineer employs several tools to carry out any of the sharing schemes described in the previous section. In this context, *tools* are anything available for use by the software engineer to help supply security. These tools can be either techniques that the software engineer utilizes during the implementation of a program, or the existing software or hardware.

The first and most basic tool is the operating system that, for this discussion, includes the memory-addressing hardware. The operating system determines if a process is allowed to access an object, protects (or should protect) the object from illegal manipulations by other processes, and controls legitimate accesses to the object. Thus, the operating system sets the tone for the protection schemes that can be carried out within the system.

A second tool that serves the software engineer is an authentication system, which insures that a user of a system is who he claims to be.

While cryptography, the third tool, has a long history of use in protecting the contents of military, business, and political messages, it also provides protection in computer systems. Cryptography prevents the compromise of information that is "physically accessible" to a penetrator. In this sense, the term "physically accessible" includes information susceptible to electronic surveillance techniques, such as wiretapping, and information stored in objects inadequately protected by the operating system.

The software engineer can imbed other tools besides authentication and cryptography into a program. Specifically, audit trails, threat detection mechanisms, and internal consistency checks can provide security for a program. Audit trails and threat detection mechanisms serve as deterrents to penetrators; if a penetrator knows that his use of a program will be recorded in an audit trail or that a threat detection mechanism will detect and, perhaps, record his attempt to penetrate a program's security, he may decide to leave that program alone. Internal consistency checks are devised to help prevent fraudulent or incorrect use of a program, since data values outside of the range anticipated by the program designer can be detected.

Finally, confinement, the last tool discussed here, comes into play if the software engineer wishes to use a routine that is suspected of releasing information to unauthorized personnel. Confinement assures that no data path exists to enable a suspect routine to release information to a routine or user outside of the confined region.

Although the above tools are discussed as separate entities, they are usually used jointly. A hypothetical example of how a software engineer may have to combine the use of these tools is the case of an on-line file update system where each user may possess different file access capabilities. A good authentication mechanism often stops one user from obtaining extra access rights by masquerading as another user. The operating system hinders a user from circumventing the authorization mechanism, prevents unauthorized access to the files by a different file system, and helps enforce the modes of access allowed to each user. A file update system, a set of programs that in itself uses several of the tools, provides the data and context-dependent access restrictions, checks the validity of each operation, and records some form of audit trail as a deterrent to a user who finds a way to bypass the security provisions. Cryptography guards data transmissions and, as a second level of security, protects the files in the system.

The above example is extremely simple, incomplete, and, unfortunately, unrealistic. There are many security considerations that are omitted from the example, resulting in its incompleteness, but a complete definition of such a system would fill this chapter. The example is unrealistic because it assumes the existence of an operating system that would provide the types of security mentioned. Virtually all commercially available operating systems provide little or no protection from a determined penetrator.

Provision of security in a program system requires resources and thus competes with other capabilities in a program; so the software engineer is faced with the traditional trade-off situation. For example, the data-dependent access restrictions and validation of each and every access may require too much computational overhead to be acceptable in a real-time system. Management sometimes decides to risk occasional disclosure of information in the files, or downtime caused by unintentional errors or sabotage, rather than degrade the performance of the system. The organization of the files and random access to the files may preclude the use of any strong cryptographic system. An audit trail recording every file update and access often gives rise to an overwhelming amount of data and may be unwieldy in use. Security must be more thoroughly integrated with the program design than most program capabilities; it is difficult, costly, and probably impossible to add security to a program after it has been designed and implemented.

The tools that a software engineer utilizes include: (1) the operating system; (2) authentication mechanisms; (3) cryptography; (4) confinement; (5) audit trails, threat detection, and internal consistency checks. The discussion will continue with a detailed description of the first tool, the operating system.

6.3

Operating Systems

The operating system forms the base upon which every program must be built. Any program generated on a particular operating system can be only as secure as the operating system. As with all types of security systems, including physical security, anyone trying to break the security will attempt to find the weakest point and attack the system there. Therefore, the software engineer must be aware of the capabilities and flaws in the operating system that is to be used before a secure program system can be designed and put into effect, if indeed a secure program system can be generated at all.

Writing a program that designates user-specifiable access controls to be run under an operating system that does not even provide isolation is like storing gold in a vault with a four-foot thick steel ceiling and walls, and a sand floor. Like the thief who would not bother trying to cut through the steel walls, the penetrator would seek out any flaws in the operating system and use them to obtain the contents of the files protected by the programs rather than attempt to penetrate the programs directly.

The discussion of the operating system can be broken into four basic areas. First to be described are methods by which various protection schemes can be implemented by an operating system. The second area shows how the operating system decides which users are authorized to use which files or routines; this discussion presents the two contrasting views of authorization specification (access controls lists vs. capabilities). The third area describes the manner in which an operating system supplies support for user-specified access controls. And, finally, the fourth area consists of examples of operating systems and presents both the potentials and flaws in the systems.

6.3.1. PROTECTION MECHANISMS IN OPERATING SYSTEMS

The operating system can provide the protection schemes of isolation, unrestricted sharing, and controlled sharing, but is limited only to giving support for user-specification of access controls. This section discusses briefly the mechanics of supplying the first three protection schemes by describing initially how relocation registers can provide a very low level of security, and then how the form of the register can be expanded in steps until it provides a high level of security and allows controlled sharing. The fourth protection scheme, which is user specification of access controls, is introduced in this section and discussed in more detail after the next section.

In the discussion of protection mechanisms in operating systems, no precise definition of the implementation of any particular mechanism will be presented. The intent is to convey the basic concepts involved, so that the reader recognizes the various techniques, and to provide a base for discussion about a generalized authorization scheme. A reader who is interested in the mechanics and problems involved in implementing the various sharing schemes involving registers is invited to read "Capability-Based Addressing" by Fabry,[8] or *Timesharing System Design Concepts* by Watson.[9]

PROGRAM ISOLATION

Isolation in a computer system is established by either dedicating the entire computer to a single user, or, in a multi-programming environment, by requiring the operating system to place barriers between programs that are in the system concurrently. However, even a computer that is dedicated to a single user really has two programs that must be protected from each other: the user's program and the operating system (another program, admittedly larger than most, but still written by fallible humans). In general, the mechanisms that place the barrier between the operating system and a single user protect the operating system from the user; the user can only hope that the operating system will not erroneously access his program.

In the single-user environment, protection is provided by a relocation (or base) register that separates the user's program and the operating system. The relocation register is added to any address formed by the user's program before the hardware performs the actual memory access. Addresses constructed by the operating system are not added to a relocation register, so the operating system resides in low core. If the addresses generated by the user's process (before the relocation register is added) are not allowed to be negative, the memory containing the operating system is protected from the user's process. On the other hand, the operating system can generate any address and thereby can access any portion of memory allocated to the user's program. Thus, relocation registers create the minimal level of protection required in a single-user environment.

When several users are allowed to share the computer simultaneously, simple relocation registers become inadequate because the register provides only a lower bound for any address used by a process. Figure 6-1 illustrates the impossibility of protecting two distinct programs by using relocation registers. User 1 is protected because the relocation register contained in User 2's process allows User 2 to use only the memory contained from the beginning of his program to the end of storage. However, the corresponding storage area accessible by User 1 includes User 2's program. It can be determined from the above discussion that the relocation register is effective only in the single-user environment. Therefore, in order to provide effective isolation and thus protection in a multiprogram environment, the relocation register must be expanded to include a base address and length.

[8]R. S. Fabry, "Capability-Based Addressing," *Communications of the ACM,* **17,** 7 (July 1974), 403–12.

[9]Richard W. Watson, *Timesharing System Design Concepts* (New York: McGraw-Hill, Inc., 1970).

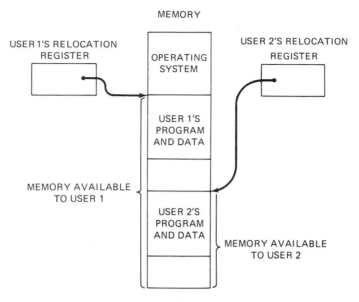

Fig. 6-1 Multiple users in a relocation register environment

A register containing a base address and length is called a descriptor register. When a process forms an address by using a particular descriptor, hardware checks assure that the physical memory address is found in the partition defined by the descriptor. The program has complete access to anything in the partition by virtue of possession of the descriptor register, but it is prevented from accessing anything beyond the end of the partition. For example, if in Figure 6-1 User 1 had a descriptor rather than a relocation register, he would not be able to access User 2's partition. Long-term storage, such as disk storage, can be partitioned and protected by the same technique; however, the implementation is usually in software rather than in hardware.

In an addressing scheme based on descriptor registers, each process can be issued partitions in both core memory and long-term storage areas. The descriptor registers, which are consulted whenever the process accesses any partition, prevent a process from accessing any partition belonging to another process. Descriptor registers provide the basis for a virtual computer; that is, the computer simulates several computers. Each user works with one of the simulated computers rather than with the entire machine. The processor is dedicated to one user for a relatively short period of time, then switches to another process, and so on. The processor also maps the user's virtual storage to real storage; each user might believe he has a considerable amount of memory for the storage of information, but the operating system will store most of the information on disk and put only a small portion of the information in memory at one time.

Descriptor registers are managed by the processor in a virtual computer environment in order to prevent one process from obtaining a descriptor for another process's segment. This management of descriptors in the virtual computer environment requires instructions to change descriptor registers, a mechanism to block the user's execution of the instructions that modify the descriptor registers, and a safe place to store the descriptor registers when the processor is servicing other processes.[10]

Loading a new descriptor register changes the partition of memory accessible to the user. This operation must be restricted, or any user can load his descriptor register with any value—a poor situation for an attempt to provide isolation because he could increase the size of the segment described by the descriptor to include another user's memory. Thus, the operating system must retain exclusive use of the operation that loads the descriptor register. An indicator, called the "privileged state bit," determines if the user or the operating system is currently in control and, therefore, if the descriptor register can be loaded. The indicator turns on only when control is passed to the operating system and turns off when control returns to the user. Long-term storage is protected by restricting the use of the instructions accessing the long-term storage. These instructions also can be executed only when the supervisor maintains control; in some cases, execution of one of the instructions causes an automatic transfer to the operating system.

In order to let several users share the computer, there must be storage space for the representation of the descriptor registers that are not in use. In some machines, there are a number of descriptor registers present; an index register determines which one is currently acting as the control on memory accesses. In other cases, the descriptor register values not currently being used are stored in some area protected from the user. If a user could access the descriptor register representations, he could increase the length of his partition to access the storage of other users or to sabotage other users by modifying or destroying their descriptors. Therefore, the entire set of descriptors is generally protected by storing the representations in the partition allocated to the supervisor.

In the descriptor-based multi-programmed system just discussed the processor, memory, and peripheral devices are shared among the users of the system, providing a virtual machine for each user. The use of descriptor registers prohibits any interaction between users, except for the competition for time on the real processor and communication lines to the peripheral devices. In principle, this mechanism appears simple and easy to implement, and when implemented correctly, the descriptor-based system can achieve isolation between users. The programs are then completely protected from one another. However, implementation errors or design flaws in most current operating systems allow a determined user to break the barrier between processes either to steal information or to perform sabotage.

UNRESTRICTED SHARING OF INFORMATION

The key point in the protection mechanism of the virtual system just described is the complete isolation of the users except for the competition for the system resources. Any file, data base, or library routines created by one user are inaccessible to other users within the system. In many cases, this is not desirable. For example, two users working on the same set of programs (and so requiring access to the same

---

[10] Jerome H. Saltzer and Michael D. Schroeder, "The Protection of Information in Computer Systems," *Proceedings of the IEEE*, **63**, 9 (Sept. 1975), 1285.

long-term storage) cannot run concurrently. In many systems, a common data base must be updated from several locations. If a user group introduces a common library of utility routines to be drawn on by all members in the group, an expansion of the descriptor-based isolation system to allow some form of sharing becomes necessary.

Unrestricted sharing is the second form of protection that can be implemented through the operating system. It is implemented not by expanding the definition or function of the descriptor registers, but by making available multiple descriptor registers, in a descriptor table, for each process. This has the effect of breaking the memory available to a process into areas called segments with a descriptor that addresses each segment. The user then breaks this process into distinct logical units, placing each unit into a segment. Segments can reside either in core or in long-term storage.

Figure 6-2 depicts a single user who has broken the process into a main program,

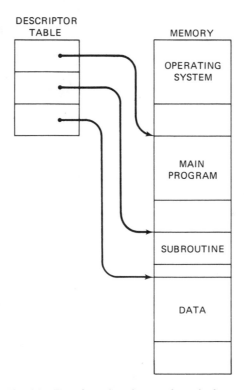

Fig. 6-2 Descriptor-based protection: single user

a block of data, and a subroutine, all in core. The descriptors give the user access to only these three areas of memory; the other areas, including the operating system, are protected from the user. Figure 6-3 shows the same system with the first user sharing the subroutine with a second user. The second user has a descriptor to the subroutine, and will be able to use the subroutine but will not be able to access the first user's main program or data. Of course, only one of the users would be executing and

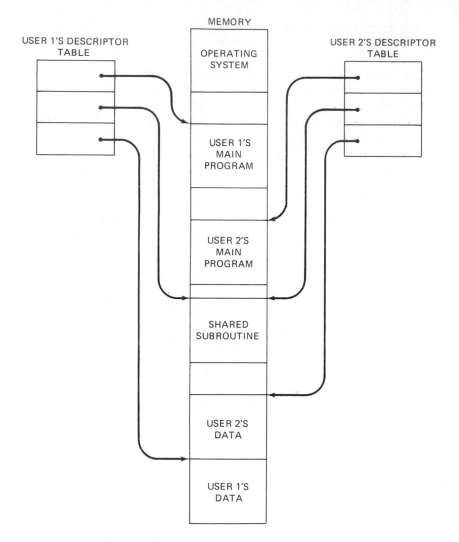

Fig. 6-3 Descriptor-based protection: multiple users

actually using his descriptors at any one time; the other user's descriptors would be stored by the operating system. This method can be expanded to arrange sharing of several routines by a number of users by increasing the number of descriptors available to each person and the number of copies of the descriptors for each routine. Under unrestricted sharing the processes are protected from one another, but the processes are still allowed to share segments.

CONTROLLED SHARING OF INFORMATION

The operating system's use of the multiple-descriptor method just described denotes that when a process gains access to a segment (either a routine or data), any operation can be performed on the segment. In order to control the access to a segment, a bit field (called the access control field) is created for each segment and the access rights to the access modes for the segment are placed within the bit field. The access modes that can be specified are generally limited to read, write, and execute; thus, the access control field can be three bits long, with each bit representing one mode of access. The segment can be written only if the bit associated with write access is on; the other modes work correspondingly.

The access control field can be stored with the segment or with the descriptors that are used to access the segment. In general, associating the access control field with the segment rather than with the descriptor is too restrictive because every user possesses the same rights to the segment; it is impossible to permit one user to write data into a data base and permit another user to only read data from the data base. Therefore, this section deals primarily with provision of controlled sharing by associating an access control field for an object with the descriptor for the object.

An access control field is added to the descriptor by expanding the definition of the descriptor register to include the access control field for the segment as well as the base address and length of the segment. Figure 6-4 shows a possible format for the expanded descriptor register that has the access specifications set so that the segment can be read and written, but not executed. Figure 6-5 depicts a data segment being shared by its owner and another user. The owner has read-write access while the user can only read the segment.

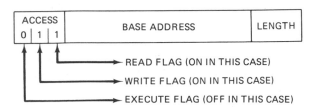

Fig. 6-4   Descriptor register with an access field

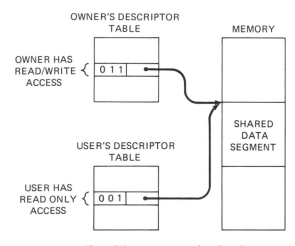

Fig. 6-5   Shared data segment using descriptors

Controlled sharing allows a limitation of the access rights to a segment, helping to provide a higher level of security than that supplied in unrestricted sharing. For example, in Figure 6-5 the user is prohibited from writing into the data base and cannot sabotage the data base even though the data base can read. Thus, even if a user is authorized to access a segment by a particular set of access rights, the segment cannot be utilized in any way other than originally authorized.

It can be seen that the three protection mechanisms (isolation, unrestricted sharing, and controlled sharing) that can be provided by an operating system are all implemented by employing various forms of relocation or descriptor registers. The user, via the operating system, must apply these protection mechanisms to the segment as a whole and is restricted to working with the modes of access explicitly provided by the computer system. In contrast, the fourth protection scheme (user specification of access controls) can only be supported by an operating system because the user must be free to implement an arbitrary protection mechanism that may be applied to selected portions of a segment rather than the entire segment as a single unit, and to make provision for any combination of user, data, or context-dependent access restrictions.

USER-SPECIFIED ACCESS CONTROLS

This discussion takes the usual approach to user-specified access controls; that is, the operating system will provide a base for protected subsystems.[11] A protected subsystem consists of a set of routines that may be written by a user, can be called only at specific entry points, and is otherwise inaccessible to users. This causes the information within the subsystem to be protected from processes outside of the subsystem. Any information stored in a protected subsystem can be obtained by a user only by his calling the subsystem at one of its entry points and asking for the information. The protected subsystem then performs any necessary authorization checks before returning the information to the user who called the system. If the protected subsystem obtains reliable information about who the caller is and where he is calling from, the subsystem can perform user and context-dependent access restriction checks. Obviously, data-dependent access restrictions are relatively easy to implement as the subsystem must simply scan the data for restricted information before it is given to the caller. Protected subsystems will be discussed in greater detail after the concept of a domain is presented under the heading of Access Specifications.

Before leaving the discussion of protection mechanisms in operating systems, the reader should be aware that while the segment has been used as the primary example of the objects that are to be protected, there are other types of objects such as magnetic tapes and disk files that must be handled in a different manner by the operating system. The differences in handling segments and other objects are primarily the instructions used to manipulate the objects and the operations that can be performed on the object. The implication to the user is that the access modes may be different for each type of object. For example, it is not possible to directly execute a disk file that contains an executable program; the file must be loaded into memory before the program can be executed. The basic concept of a protection mechanism—that is,

[11] *Ibid.* p. 1281.

separating the objects into distinct units through the use of descriptor registers and restricting the operations that can be performed on the objects—remains the same; only the modes of access and details of how the operating system perform the operation are changed for each object type.

The first major portion of the presentation about operating systems has concentrated on the four main protection mechanisms only and has been concerned with how the operating system and its supporting hardware can protect information currently being utilized by one or more users. The second major security-relevant portion of the operating system determines which information a user is allowed to access (in other words, how the operating system decides which processes receive which descriptors) by presenting how the access specifications are stored, used, and manipulated.

6.3.2 ACCESS SPECIFICATIONS

Access specifications, the representations of which users are allowed to access which objects, are required by the operating system in order to enforce a particular sharing scheme desired by a software engineer. If Users 1 and 2 want to share a routine, the system must be apprised of that fact and must know what mode of access is to be allowed to each. Even if only a single user is to access a routine, the system must know that only one user has access to the routine and who the user is.

The access specifications do not, in and of themselves, provide security—that is up to the operating system with the help of the protection mechanisms previously described. The discussion here centers on a description of the access specifications that must be stored (by describing an access matrix), and then turns to two contrasting ways in which the specifications are stored: capabilities and access control lists. These two storage forms will be compared with respect to modification of the access specifications and accountability (the determination of who may use a particular piece of information in the system).

ACCESS MATRICES

The access matrix, which is a very generalized method for storing access specifications, will be used as a framework for the description of access specifications. Using Lampson's[12] terminology, the access specifications consist of what forms of access to objects (the items such as files or routines that are protected by the system) are allowed within a particular domain. A domain is a collection of entities (users, processes, or procedures) that has access to a set of objects. Each domain has the potential for a unique set of objects and access rights to the objects. Every entity in a particular domain has exactly the same access rights to the collection of objects, but each entity may belong to more than one domain. One example of a domain is a user who has a set of files and routines; in this case the user is the entire domain because no one else has access to these files and routines. If the user creates a new routine and wishes to test the routine without risking damage to other files and routines,

[12]B. W. Lampson, "Protection," in Proc. Fifth Princeton Symposium on Information Sciences and Systems, Princeton University, March 1971, pp. 437–43, reprinted in *Operating Systems Review*, **8**, 1 (January 1974), 18–24.

s/he can place the routine to be tested in a new domain and allow the domain access only to the additional files and routines required for execution of the new routine. The remainder of the routines and files will be completely protected from the routine being tested.

Domains themselves are treated as objects that must be protected by the system because access rights to a domain are stored by the system. Accessibility to a domain allows various manipulations of the access rights that the domain has to other objects.

In order to interpret the access matrix, the row corresponding to a domain is selected. The individual elements along this row indicate the type of access the domain is allowed to the object heading the column containing the element. For example, in Figure 6-6, Element (Domain 2, Process 1) indicates that Domain 2 has both execute

OBJECTS

	Domain 1	Domain 2	Domain 3	Process 1	Process 2	File 1	File 2	Queue 1
Domain 1	Owner* Control			Execute* Owner Read*		Owner* Read* Write*		Owner* Add* Delete*
Domain 2		Owner Control	Owner Control	Execute Read	Execute* Owner Read	Owner Read*	Owner* Read* Write*	Add Delete
Domain 3				Execute Read			Read	

*COPY flag is set

Fig. 6-6 Access specifications stored in an access matrix

and read access to Process 1. Element (Domain 2, Domain 3) shows that Domain 2 has owner and control access to Domain 3. As shown n Figure 6-6, the domains are represented by rows in the access matrix, the objects (process, file, queue, and domain) by columns, and the access rights (read, write, and execute) by entries in the access matrix. The owner and control access signifies that Domain 2 can add access rights to the entry and modify or delete access rights currently in the entry. The copy flag associated with every access right in the matrix indicates that the domain having that particular access right can pass the right on to another domain. In contrast, an access right with no copy flag cannot be passed to another domain.

The system does not necessarily interpret the meaning of the access rights contained in the matrix. The system does, however, give a meaning to the access rights that it must enforce, such as owner and control. The meaning of the remaining rights is left to the routines that manipulate the objects. For example, Domain 1 has the right to add or delete from Queue 1. To add an item to the queue, the domain actually calls a queue manipulation routine, which checks to insure that the domain possesses the access rights required for the operation. The system simply provides a bit pattern to the routine; the routine interprets the contents of the field. In fact, the system does not have to distinguish between object types in this context; that can be left to the routines that manipulate the objects.

The system obviously does not keep a copy of the access matrix stored internally because the matrix is sparse and storage would be wasted. The matrix can be stored as three-field entries in a table. The fields are domain, object, and access rights. Even this wastes space because only a small percentage of the domains are being used at any given time, and only the corresponding portion of the table is required to define the access specifications for those domains. The alternative is to store the protection information with the domain (store the matrix row by row as capabilities) or with the object (store the matrix column by column in access-control lists).

CAPABILITIES

Storing the protection information with the domain signifies that each domain has a list of the objects that it can access and the rights it has to each object. In some systems, simply knowing the name or physical location of an object allows a domain to access the object; the access modes to the object are not restricted. Since these systems do not provide an adequate level of security, the discussion here will center on the more protection-directed concept of a capability.

A capability[13] contains the access rights to an object and a reference to the object, and is similar in structure to a descriptor. The difference between a capability and a descriptor is that the descriptor references an object by the physical location of the object, whereas a capability references an object by name. In a capability system, the operating system maintains a map of object names to physical location; since the capabilities reference the objects by name, the operating system is free to move the objects' physical locations so long as the map is properly maintained.

In order to permit a user to use an object, he receives a capability to the object. He stores the capability wherever he wishes (subject to restrictions discussed later) and simply presents the capability to the operating system along with a request for access to the object. The system checks the access rights to be sure the request for access is allowed by the capability, and then uses the object name to obtain the physical address of the object from the memory map.

The capabilities must be protected, just as the descriptors, so users cannot illegally modify the access specifications represented by the capabilities. This protection can be provided by hardware (using tagged architecture) or by software (the operating system refuses a user direct access to the storage containing the capabilities).

In tagged architecture[14] an extra bit is appended to each word in memory, but the bit is not accessible to a user. If the bit associated with a particular word is off, that word is taken to be an ordinary instruction or data word. However, if the bit is on, the word is taken to contain a capability and cannot be manipulated by a process using normal instructions. When the process desires to access a segment, it calls the supervisor and passes the address of the capability for the segment along with the address within the segment and the type of access requested. The supervisor first checks to see if the bit is on and the word is indeed a capability, and then uses the contents of the capability to access the segment. When the system places capabilities into user's memory, the operation automatically sets the bit to indicate that the word contains a capability. To complete the scheme, the user must be prevented from manipulating the capability. This can be done either by halting execution of a process if a capability-

[13]Fabry, "Capability-Based Addressing," p. 404.
[14]*Ibid.*, p. 408.

tagged word is accessed incorrectly, or by turning the tag bit off whenever other store instructions write into the word. Thus, the instructions that access capabilities cannot be employed for normal data or instruction words, and instructions that are utilized on data or instruction words cannot be used on capability words.

A second method of protecting capabilities is breaking each segment into two parts—one for data and/or instructions and the other for capabilities. Any reference to a capability then uses the capability part of the segment, and references to data or instructions use the other part of the segment. Whether the capabilities are protected by a tagged architecture or by being in a protected part of a segment, the user maintains control over the location of the capability even though he cannot specify the contents of the capability.

Figure 6-7 depicts a simple capability system. Suppose User 1 contacts the system,

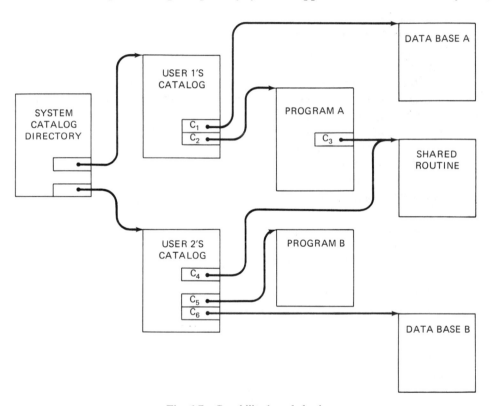

Fig. 6-7 Capability based sharing

perhaps from a terminal, and is authenticated. The system locates the directory (a segment containing a list of capabilities) belonging to User 1 by using a capability obtained from the system directory during authentication and thus has a list of the segments available to User 1. He then requests that the system execute Program A. At this point, the processor has capabilities for both Program A and User 1's directory. Program A utilizes capability C_1 in the directory to access Data Base A. He can employ the capability C_3 that resides in Program A to access the shared routine. When User 2 is executing and has control of the processor, she executes Program B and can also use the shared routine. User 2 decides to place the capability for the shared routine in her directory rather than in Program B, illustrating that the location of the capability depends on the user's preference.

ACCESS CONTROL LISTS

In a system based on access control lists,[15] the protection information is stored with the object itself. Basically, a list of the authorized users and the rights of each user is associated with each object. Whenever an access to the object is made, the list is checked by the system to be sure that the user is authorized to use the object and that he possesses the rights necessary to perform the requested operation.

The users need only have the name or some other form of pointer to the object in order to attempt an access. Since the security is enforced by the system (using the access-control list), these pointers can be manipulated freely by the users. Even if a user does manufacture the pointer to an object for which he is not allowed access, the system will prevent the access from taking place.

To facilitate the modification of access control lists, the list is usually placed in a segment by itself along with a descriptor for the object it protects. The names with which the users access the object actually direct the operating system to the segment containing the access control list; then the descriptor contained in this segment is used to access the object. Therefore, the access control list is used as an indirect reference to the object.

One additional piece of information must be protected for access control lists to work: the user's identification. When a user enters the system and is authenticated, his identification must be accurately stored with the process and checked against an access-control list when access to an object is attempted. Obviously, if a user can alter the identifier after authentication, the system will not be able to apply the access specifications properly. Thus, the user's identifier must be stored in an area inaccessible to him.

Figure 6-8 depicts the same user-and-object organization as does Figure 6-7, the difference being in the use of access control lists rather than capabilities. As an example of how access control lists are employed, in Figure 6-8 User 1 is executing Program A and is attempting to read from Data Base A. The pointer for the access control list for Data Base A contained in User 1's directory is presented to the system along with the request to read from the data base. The system uses the pointer to locate the access control list for the data base and obtains User 1's access rights from the list. After checking to be sure that the access rights are adequate for the operation, the system consults the descriptor to the object contained in the list to complete the request to read the data base. In a sharing scheme, the access-control list for the shared routine must contain the identifiers for every person who executes the shared routine. The implications of this will be discussed later.

---

[15] Jerome H. Saltzer, "Protection and the Control of Information Sharing in Multics," *Communications of the ACM,* **17,** 7 (July 1974), 389–90.

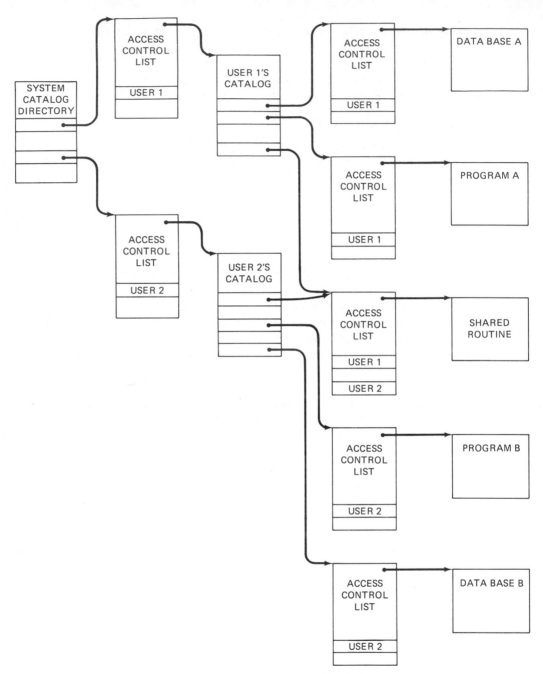

Fig. 6-8 Access-control list sharing

It is obvious that if the access-control lists are implemented exactly as described, the overhead will be very high because of the search through the list for every access to an object. One way to reduce the overhead is by checking the access-control list only on the first access to the segment. If access is permitted, some form of temporary pointer is given to the process. This temporary pointer directly accesses the object without checking the access-control list, but the process is not allowed to keep the pointer between invocations. The temporary pointer could be the descriptor in the access-control list or a capability; a simple pointer would be inadequate because the access rights must be retained and checked for each access. The result of utilizing the temporary pointer is a hybrid system with the power of access-control lists and the speed of capabilities. Some disk file systems are examples of this technique. The access-control list is checked when the disk file is opened, but not for subsequent operations on the file. The mode of access is retained and checked for each operation; for example, if a file is opened for read-only access, an attempt to write on the file will result in an error message from the file system.

As another expansion to access-control list systems, it is helpful to place a number of users into a group and provide equal access rights to each member of the group. In this case, an instructor may want to allow all of the students in his class use of a data file. The teacher does not want to place the entire class in the access-control list only to have to change the list for the next quarter. Users can be grouped by adding one or more identifiers onto the user-identification field, both in the access-control list and the user identifier that is associated with each process. When checking the access-control list, the system looks for either a user identifier match or a group identifier match. During the authentication sequence, the system must associate the user with a particular group, perhaps through a form of access-control list.

To summarize the differences between capabilities and access-control lists, employing capabilities is analogous to passing out keys for a door and everyone with a key may enter, whereas using access-control lists is analogous to having a guard stand at the door with a list of all those he will allow to pass through the door.[16]

MODIFICATION OF ACCESS SPECIFICATIONS

The descriptions so far have been of static authorization specifications. However, in most cases the access matrix of a system is dynamic with entries being added, modified, and deleted. Therefore, the representations of the matrix (forms of either capabilities or access-control lists) must be modifiable. While capabilities are more efficient during execution, access-control lists win out when the authorization specifications must be changed.

The discussions of modification of access specifications will cover three topics:

1. How sharing authorization can be granted.
2. Who can modify sharing authorization.
3. How sharing authorization can be revoked.

Under each topic, both access-control lists and capabilities will be discussed and compared with respect to ease of use.

As an example of how sharing authorization can be granted, User A may wish to let User B execute a routine owned by User A. In a system that uses access-control

---

[16]Jerome H. Saltzer and Michael D. Schroeder, "The Protection of Information in Computer Systems," p. 1287.

lists, User A simply tells the system to add User B to the access-control list for the routine and restrict the access mode to read-execute only. Of course, User A must obtain User B's identifier, and User B must obtain the name of the object.

The problem of granting access is much more complex in a capability-based system. If User A can write the capability into User B's directory, User A can also overwrite any capability in the directory. Conversely, if User B can read the capability from User A's directory, User B can also read the remaining capabilities in the directory. A "mailbox" type of operation can be arranged to protect both users involved in the transaction.[17] This operation consists of three basic steps:

1. User A and User B exchange identifiers by some path that is outside the system.
2. User A gives User B's identifier to a job running with User A's identifier and has the job transmit the capability to User B by placing it in the mailbox that is designated for User B.
3. User B gives User A's identifier to a job that then looks in the mailbox to find a capability that is labeled as coming from User A.

Two users arrange to make a mailbox by sharing a segment solely for the purpose of transmitting messages and capabilities. With a large number of users, this becomes impractical because of the large numbers of segments required, so the system can perform the mailbox service rather than individuals. A segment is set up for each user, and messages for the user are placed in the mailbox. The system adds the sender's identifier to each message so the receiver can verify that a capability obtained from the mailbox segment comes from the correct user.

The question now arises as to who is authorized to (or capable of) granting access or modifying the current access rights to an object. Anyone who has a capability for an object can give the capability to another user. A possible exception is if the ability to pass the capability to another user is a right (the copy right) that is contained in the capability. If an owner of a routine gives out capabilities without the copy flag set, he knows that the capability will not be passed on to an unauthorized user. If the system does not support a copy flag, whenever the owner of a routines gives a capability for the routine to another user, the owner essentially loses control over the access to the routine.

In a system using access-control lists, both self control and hierarchial control of access-control lists are possible. Granting access or modifying the current access rights to an object is performed by modifying the access-control lists; the right to perform the modification must be stored in some access-control list. If this right is stored in the access-control list itself, a self-control system is formed. A user creates an object, with the associated access-control list, and can grant himself the only ability to modify the list. In a hierarchical control system, the right to change an access-control list is stored in a different access-control list. In one form of hierarchical control, the access-control list for an object is stored in a user's directory (also an object), and the ability to modify the directory designates the ability to modify the

[17]Ibid. p. 1294.

access-control list. The result is a tree structure of directories. (This scheme is illustrated further during the description of the Multics operating system.)

Dynamic modification of access specifications also indicates the ability to revoke access to an object. With an access-control list, anyone who can modify the list simply removes the identifier of a user from the list, blocking further access. Revoking access in a capability system is a much trickier situation. A user does not have access to a capability given away and may not even know how many copies of the capability have been made. Thus, in general, capability-based schemes do not allow revocation of access.

Revocation of access in a capability-based system can be performed if indirect capabilities[18] are allowed. In this situation, a user does not give a capability to the object to other users; instead, a capability to the capability for the object is given. The system must be designed to allow the indirect reference required for operation. Now the original user retains control over the only capability to the object and can revoke all access to the object by destroying this capability. Of course, he would first make a copy of the capability so the object would not be lost. This scheme can be generalized so that the user essentially holds an access list of capabilities, resulting in a hybrid system that leans toward capabilities. To illustrate this idea, a user can create an object and five capabilities to that object. One capability is retained for exclusive use while the other four are used as targets for the indirect capabilities passed to other users. The user must retain a mapping of capabilities to users; for example, he must know that the second capability in the list is used by John Doe and that the third capability is used by a computer science class. Thus, the user can selectively revoke access by destroying the corresponding capabilities in the list. The degree of selectivity depends on the number of users who have indirect access through each capability.

INFORMATION USE ACCOUNTABILITY

To reiterate, accountability is the determination of who may use a particular piece of information in the system. Accountability is required in order to review a list of users accessing a particular object, bill those who are using an object, or determine that no one can access the object; and thus the object can be deleted from the system.

In an access-control-list system, a list of the users who currently have access to a segment is readily available, but there is also another group of users who merit consideration. If the access lists form a hierarchical tree (rather than a form of self-control), any user whose directory is higher up in the tree, but still on the same branch, can force access to the segment. A search of the tree (going backward from the access-control list for the segment) is required to enumerate these users.

Accountability is a difficult problem in a capability-based system because a user can copy a capability many times and scatter the copies throughout memory. Accountability requires the ability to detect all of these copies. The only method of detection of all instances of a capability for a particular segment would be to search all of

[18]D. Redell, "Naming and Protection in Extendible Operating Systems," Ph.D. Thesis, U. of Calif. at Berkeley, 1974. (Available as M.I.T. Project MAC Technical Report TR-140.)

memory, a serious breach of privacy for the users of the system. Even if all of the copies of the capability are located, the problem is not yet solved. A user may have a capability to read a segment that contains one of the copies and therefore may be able to use the copy. There may be an extremely large number of users who can reach one of the copies by a long path. The search for all users who can access an object is extremely costly. Thus, accountability is very high in access-control-list-based systems, due to the simple listing procedures, and low in a capability-based system because of the cost and potential security breach involved in the search for all of the capabilities for an object.

One can detect from the above comparison of access-control lists and capabilities that the conceptual view of sharing and authorization mechanisms provides two basic contrasting views. Capabilities display more efficiency during execution, but are much harder to control. Access-control lists work more slowly, but revocability, accountability, and ease of use are improved. Hybrid systems, such as access control lists with an underlying capability or descriptor system, or indirect capabilities can combine the benefits of both systems. The discussion will now return to user specifications of access controls through the use of protected subsystems.

6.3.3 PROTECTED SUBSYSTEMS

In some cases, the sharing and protection schemes provided by the operating system may not be suitable, and a user would like to be able to create a more complex protection scheme. Consider the case of a data-base system where access to particular records in the data, or even to particular fields in a record, may be restricted. One approach is the creation of a program that accepts and interprets user requests, validates the request based on some protection specification, reads the data base, and returns only the requested information. The routine and data base together form what is called a protected subsystem. This implies that the data base is only accessible to the program and that the program itself is protected. With either an access-control list or the capability techniques discussed so far, it is impossible to be able to access a program, but not the files that the program requires. For example, in an access-control list system, the user must be given explicit access to the data base in the access-control list for the data base; otherwise, no access is allowed. In a capability-based system, the user cannot have a capability for the data base, so the capability would be placed in the routine that reads the data base. Even this does not protect the capability adequately because a user must have read-execute access to the routine before even the routine itself could use the capability. However, if the user has read-execute access, the capability can be obtained and the data base read directly.

In order to provide a useful protected subsystem, the system must provide some expansion of powers when the subsystem is called. In other words, the domain must be changed. One example of this is the supervisor of most systems. Whenever a user calls the supervisor, the system goes into supervisor mode, and additional instructions and memory are made available to the processor. This suggests one way to provide protected subsystems is to expand the user/supervisor mode bits into several discrete states rather than two. This has, in fact, been implemented on the Multics system where eight levels are provided. For more detailed information about the problems and mechanics involved in the generation of protected subsystems, the reader is referred to the article by Saltzer and Schroder (footnote 10). These problems involve not only the construction of the protected subsystem but methods of transferring control to and returning from the subsystem.

6.3.4 COMMON OPERATING SYSTEMS

This section presents examples of operating systems for two reasons. The first reason is to illustrate the methodologies of protection and sharing just presented. The second reason is to analyze the operating system by presenting the definitions of several systems and then discussing some of the security implications in each. These implications pertain to the presence of penetration routes and forms of sharing that cannot be securely implemented in the system. The software engineer must perform this type of analysis on any operating system he uses in order to utilize the protection mechanisms of the operating system adequately.

Three operating systems will be discussed: IBM OS/360, Multics, and HYDRA— each illustrating a different aspect of operating systems. OS/360 serves solely as an example of an operating system that provides a low level of security; Multics exemplifies a system that utilizes access-control lists, and HYDRA is a capability-based system. Both Multics and HYDRA provide a significant increase in security over OS/360.

IBM OS/360

The IBM OS/360 is a common system that typifies many commercial systems, not necessarily in implementation but rather in the level of security provided since several of the services provided and security flaws are characteristic of many other systems.

Briefly, the OS/360 system is defined as follows: the memory system is divided into blocks; a four-bit lock pattern is associated with each block. The program status word (PSW) contains a corresponding four-bit key; a write to memory is allowed only if the key in the PSW matches the lock associated with the memory block being accessed, or if the key is zero. In later 360 hardware, a bit has been added to the lock to allow read protection as well as write protection; this has the effect of partitioning memory into discrete areas. The system has a user/supervisor bit; the instruction set available to the user is limited and does not include either I/O instructions or the instructions that change either the user/supervisor bit or the memory locks and keys. Although the OS/360 system contains sufficient mechanisms to provide an isolation form of protection, unfortunately both design flaws and implementation errors have resulted in the creation of an insecure system. Rather than discuss the forms of protection that OS/360 could provide if it were securely implemented, the discussion will center around some of the flaws that make the system insecure.

One major flaw appears in file and routine naming and access conventions.[19] First of all, if a user guesses the name of a file, he may possibly access the file. A

[19]G. Scott Graham and Peter J. Denning, "Protection—Principles and Practice," *AFIPS Conference Proceedings*, **40** (SJCC 1972), p. 426.

second and more subtle problem is the manner in which the system searches for a routine that has been referenced. There are some cases when the system expects a particular routine to be loaded and used; however, if the user creates a routine with the same name as the system routine, the user's routine will be called rather than the system routine. Since the routine is called by the operating system, the user's routine will have control of the processor and will assume supervisor mode. A variation of this attack resulted in successful penetration of the Multics system as well as the IBM OS/360.

A second major design flaw in the IBM OS/360 concerns the supervisor's storing security-relevant information in memory available to the user. A programmer can take advantage of this fact in several ways to compromise the system. In one penetration route,[20] the user initiates a direct memory access immediately preceding a supervisor call to open a file. The supervisor first checks to see if the user may open the file and then applies information stored in user space to perform the open. If the timing is correct, the direct memory access can be made to write over the information after the security check has occurred but before the system accesses the information to perform the open. The file open originally requests a file normally available to the user while the direct memory access substitutes a request for a file that is supposedly protected from the user. In a second penetration route,[21] an address for a system routine is stored in user space. The user loads his own address over the system routine address and will eventually be called by the supervisor in supervisor mode. This route was blocked by an appropriate system modification, but a slightly different technique again penetrated the system. A second modification was then made to block the use of the second route; again a slight modification provided a new penetration route. At this point, the systems programmer gave up. This illustrates that it sometimes may be impossible to patch security into a system not originally designed for security.

MULTICS

The Multics[22,23,24] system, built by the Massachusetts Institute of Technology and Honeywell with security in mind, serves as a prime candidate for study by those interested in security. This section is not intended to be a complete discussion of Multics; instead, the basic system will be presented—first by a brief overview and then by a more detailed analysis. The detailed analysis will include the software protections such as storing, using, and controlling access specifications; authentication of users; details on the hardware protection mechanisms; and some of the weaknesses of Multics.

[20]Gerald Popek, "Privacy and Security in Computer Systems," Engineering 226Z Section 3, U. of Calif. at Los Angeles (Winter 1975).

[21]Richard Bisbey, "Privacy and Security in Computer Systems," Engineering 226Z Section 3, U. of Calif. at Los Angeles (Winter 1975).

[22]A. Bensoussan, C. T. Clingen, and R. C. Daley, "The Multics Virtual Memory: Concepts and Design," *Communications of the ACM*, **15**, 5 (May 1972), 308–18.

[23]F. J. Corobato and J. H. Saltzer, "Multics—The First Seven Years," *AFIPS Conference Proceedings*, **40** (SJCC 1972), pp. 571–83.

[24]Jerome H. Saltzer, "Protection in Multics," pp. 388–402.

In brief, Multics provides object sharing and security through access-control lists at the user's interface. Passwords authenticate the users of the system. Control over the access-control lists is hierarchical, mimicking the structure of most business organizations. Users are supplied with a segmented virtual memory while paging techniques map the segments into the users' virtual memory during execution. The security specifications designated by the access-control list are carried out during execution by a descriptor structure.

The detailed discussion of Multics will begin with how the access specifications are represented and used during the execution of a program.

ACCESS SPECIFICATIONS IN MULTICS.   In Multics, the access specifications are stored in access-control lists. These access-control lists are stored in directories; the directories are also objects that are protected by the system. In this discussion, the emphasis is placed only on the protection of segments and directories, even though Multics supports other objects as well. The other types of objects gain protection by the same basic mechanisms as segments and directories, the main difference being that the actions that can be performed on the objects may not be the same.

Every object must be listed in a directory; the directory entry consists of the name of the object and its access-control list. Since each directory must be listed in some other directory, a hierarchical structure of access specifications is formed. A simple example of such a system is given in Figure 6-9. From this example it appears that

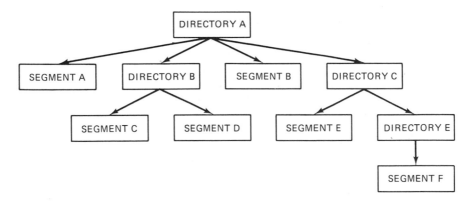

Fig. 6-9   Hierarchical directory structure in Multics

the branches of the tree are isolated; but in actuality, the sharing of files is controlled by the access-control lists, not the hierarchical access specification structure. For example, the access-control list (contained in Directory C) for Segment E can contain an entry allowing anyone allowed in the Multics' system use of Segment E.

In order to utilize the access-control lists properly, Multics associates some identifier with each process. A user responsible for a process is called a principal, and the process is given an unforgeable name denoted a principal identifier. (The authentication method that assures that the correct identifier is associated with a user will be presented later.)

The principal identifier actually includes three parts; each part corresponds to a different division of the users of the system. The first part names the individual, the second specifies the name of the project, and the third determines the name of the compartment. The first identifier separates the users into individuals. The project identifier allows for sets of users who are working on the same task. The compartment identifier furnishes a third form of a named group that is useful for such purposes as protecting files from undebugged or suspect programs.

The access-control lists act much the same as in previous descriptions, with two differences. First, if the identifier of the process attempting to access a segment is contained in the access-control list for the segment, the segment is mapped into the virtual memory of the process. The second difference is the use of the three-part identifier.

As an illustration of the use of the three-part identifier, a user named "Smith" working on a project named "Accounting" and using the compartment named "Z" would be given the principal identifier

SMITH·ACCOUNTING·Z

It is the three-part identifier that is compared to the elements in the access-control list to determine if the process will be allowed to use the segment.

The access-control lists also contain similar three-part identifiers, but to grant more generalized forms of sharing, any of the three-parts in a particular identifier can contain a "don't care" indicator. If the access-control list contained

SMITH·ACCOUNTING·Z

the process of the same name would be given access to the segment. An access-control list entry of

·ACCOUNTING·

would give access to anyone working on the accounting project, no matter which compartment they were in. If Smith created a segment that she wanted to access from several compartments and/or projects, she would use

SMITH·*·*

as the access-control list entry. The use of the "don't care" indicator takes advantage of the groupings provided by the three-part identifier. For example, if the individual and compartment identifiers are marked as "don't care," but the project is specified in an entry in an access-control list, any member of that project can use the object protected by the list.

Associated with each identifier in the access list is the mode of access allowed to the user. For a segment, the possible modes of access are read, write, and execute. The access mode combinations that are allowed for a segment are none, read only for data, read-execute for a pure procedure (pure meaning that the procedure does not modify itself), read-write for writable data, and read-execute-write for an impure procedure. Directories can be listed, can have an existing entry modified or deleted, or can have new entries added.

The manner in which the access-control lists are searched exists as a way to grant an individual member of a project or compartment different access rights than the rest of the project or compartment, since a search through an access list is terminated when the first identifier match is made. If the entries in the access-control list for the individual are placed before the entry for a project, the access rights will be taken from the individual's access-control list entry rather than from the project's entry. For example, Smith and Brown may be the only members of the "Payroll" project allowed to change the "Salary" file, while the remainder of the users in the project must be allowed to read the file. The required access list is:

> SMITH·PAYROLL·*read-write
> BROWN·PAYROLL·*read-write
> *·PAYROLL·*read

If Smith and Brown are outcasts rather than privileged users in the "Payroll" project, their access mode can be "none," completely denying Smith and Brown access to the "Salary" file. The access lists are initially sorted on the first field so that the "don't care" indicators are at the bottom of the list. Then each subgroup is sorted in the same manner on the second field and so on. The result is that the more specific elements in the access list are at the top of the list and are checked first when access is attempted.

The modification of the access-control lists is protected by the same mechanism that protects the other objects in the system. Since the access-control lists are stored in directories, the ability to add, delete, or modify entries in a directory allows the modification of the access specifications contained in the access-control lists found in the directory. The right to alter a directory is contained in the access-control list for the directory. Referring to Figure 6-9, the ability to modify (or even use) Directory C is controlled by an access-control list in Directory A; this relationship creates the hierarchical directory structure.

Whoever has the ability to modify the directory at the top of the hierarchy has considerable powers. First, access can be gained to any object in the system. Again referring to Figure 6-9, if someone can modify Directory A, he or she can also modify access-countrol lists for Directories B and C and can gain the right to modify either Directory B or C. Thus the access-control lists contained in Directories B and C can be modified, and access rights to Segments C, D, and E, and Directory E gained. Second, either s/he or other users (usually system administrators) who can modify the directory at the top of the hierarchy can create the directories at the next lower level and dictate the access rights of those who will use the directory. This, coupled with the fact that each directory can contain an initial access-control list automatically given to any object when it is first entered in the directory, allows the system administrator to place very rigid controls on the users of the system. For example, the administrator can originate a directory and give the intended user of the directory permission to add entries to the directory. The initial access-control list in the directory is only used for all of the new entries with the user having no control over who may use the objects he adds to the directory. Thus, the administrator controls the access lists for any object in the system, assuring, for example, that no member of a project will share information with someone outside of that project. Because of the hierarchical nature of the directories, anyone who has complete access to a directory can create a structure below the directory and will have the same powers over that structure that the system administrator has over the entire system.

For the Multics system to be able to utilize the access-control lists properly, it is essential that every user be supplied with the correct principal identifier when he attempts to log on. Otherwise, a user can pretend to be the system administrator (or for the less ambitious, any other user) and access objects for which he has no authorization. The method by which Multics authenticates users is presented next.

USER AUTHENTICATION IN MULTICS. Multics utilizes a password scheme to authenticate the identity of each user. Every user in a Multics system is registered with a unique name, usually consisting of the last name plus a few initials. Whenever the user attempts to enter the system, the password is requested. If a correct password cannot be supplied, s/he is not allowed to use the system. If the correct password is given, authorization to initiate a job is given.

Every job, whether batch or interactive, may be initiated only by an authenticated user. Batch jobs, once read by the card reader, are held by the system until execution is requested by an authenticated process. Any batch job so initiated then becomes an authenticated job and may also initiate jobs. Chains of jobs can be formed, but the chain must be started by a user who has been authenticated by the system. To make the operation of batch jobs easier, a user can request the execution of a job before the card deck which represents the job is read in, and the system will hold the request until the cards are read.

The passwords used in Multics are protected both when used and stored by the system. When a user logs in, he is asked for his password. Before he types his password on the terminal, the terminal is either turned off, or the area on which he will type his password is blacked out by typing several characters over each space. This action helps prevent accidental disclosure of the password. Once a user is authenticated, he can change his password as often as he wants. One available program generates eight-character passwords with English language characteristics. These passwords, easy to remember and pronounce, lessen the chance that they will be written down and compromised. The passwords are encrypted by using a one-way encryption scheme before they are stored in the system. Thus, even the system administrator cannot discover a user's password.

Multics also provides several methods for detecting and preventing attempted penetration by the guessing of a password. Whenever a log-in with an incorrect password is attempted, an entry is placed in a threat-monitoring log. The user is allowed to attempt to log-in up to 10 times, then the communication line is broken by the system; this helps to prevent automated penetration attempts.

When a user logs in, the location and time of his last use of the system are printed, so the user may be able to detect the penetration if anyone has previously logged into the system with his password without authorization.

The Multics system has been designed to allow an additional authentication procedure (beyond the password authentication provided by the system) to be applied to users in a particular project. The project administrator sets up a procedure that is executed whenever a user signs on under the project name. This procedure demands additional authentication and starts log-out if the authentication is not completed properly. For example, the procedure can simply check a list of users who are on the project and reject users not on the list. The project administrator can also allow unauthenticated users to log-in under his project name. This allows "anonymous" users, providing for use of the system by individuals not registered in the system. A teacher can have a project that is to be used for a particular class. Rather than require each member of the class to be registered with the system administrator, the teacher can authorize the students to log-in "anonymously." Since part of the student's identifier is the project name, they will be able to access only the objects available to members of the project.

While the access specifications are stored in access-control lists, they are carried out during execution by a descriptor mechanism.

EXECUTION TIME ENFORCEMENT OF SECURITY SPECIFICATIONS.   During execution, protection is provided by:

- a descriptor mechanism
- an expansion of the user/supervisor bit used in OS/360
- limitations on the supervisor's access powers
- asynchronous Input and Output buffering
- protection of storage residues (data left in a segment after the user returns the segment to the system)

During execution, each process in Multics is given a descriptor segment containing an array of descriptors that serves to enforce the access specifications of the system. A process is given a descriptor for a segment only if the access-control list for the segment contains the principal identifier of the process. The protection information contained in the access-control list is used in the generation of the descriptor. A set of pointers assures that changes to an access-control list will be reflected immediately in all the descriptors for that segment. Each access to a segment in the process converts to a segment number (used as an index into the descriptor segment) and a word number within that segment. Therefore, every access to memory must make use of the hardware-enforced descriptor protection mechanism. Since a process has its own descriptor segment and address space, it can access only the segments for which it has been given permission. If a segment is being shared by two or more processes, each process will have its own descriptor for the segment and may have different access privileges.

The supervisor is sheltered from users by a ring structure, an expansion of the user/supervisor bit in OS/360, which provides several levels of privilege. In Multics the indicator of the level of privilege for a segment is contained in the descriptors for the segment. There are eight rings (number 0–7), with the lowest numbered ring having the highest privileges. The hardware in Multics allows a process to use only the descriptors that have a ring number greater than or equal to the ring that is indicated by the descriptor used to access the procedure currently being used by the process. The supervisor executes in the lowest rings; only the higher rings are available to users. The user's processes have descriptors that enable him to call the supervisor, but only at specified entry points called gates. These gates assure that control goes to the supervisor correctly and provide the only means by which a process can access the supervisor.

The ring structure designed for the supervisor is also available to the user's process. For example, if Rings 5, 6, and 7 are available to the user, he can set up his main program in Ring 5 and execute subroutines that he mistrusts in Rings 6 or 7.

His main program will be protected from the subroutines in the same manner the supervisor is protected from his entire process. Thus, the user can create protected subsystems.

The ring structure found in Multics closes a penetration route that makes the IBM OS/360 vulnerable. Rather than use a bit in memory to determine whether the supervisor or a user is executing (as in OS/360), in Multics the privileges available to the current operation depend on the ring number contained in the descriptor that was used to obtain the last instruction. The supervisor's indicator cannot be left on since whenever control passes to a user's segment, the ring number is automatically changed because a different descriptor must be consulted to obtain instructions from the user's segment. The implementation of descriptors with base address and length in Multics prevents a user from passing to the supervisor an argument that would cause it (as in OS/360) to jump to an address beyond the end of its segment and, thus, into another user's segment with the system still thinking it had remained in the supervisor's segment.

The supervisor does not have any more power than is necessary for functionality of the system. Although the supervisor maintains the means to access all of a user's segments, since they will be in a higher ring, the ring still possesses only the access rights given in the descriptor for the segment. Thus, data bases can be rendered nonexecutable, and pure procedures can be made nonwritable. This protects the user from his own mistakes in programming, since a call to the supervisor to execute a data base segment will result in a protection violation.

The input and output (I/O) are handled so as to avoid conflicts between an executing process and direct-access channel programs that could be used by a penetrator. All I/O operations are performed in a buffer in the supervisor area. When input is complete, the supervisor gives the data to the user's process. Likewise, the supervisor does not accept data from the user for output until the buffer is filled. Asynchronous I/O, when implemented in this manner, cannot be used to penetrate the system.

Finally, the information stored in a segment that is returned to the system, called storage residue, must be protected. In Multics, all memory access is through the virtual memory system. Therefore, no one can access any storage that is not part of his own virtual memory. The only way a user can access a storage residue is to request a new segment and then attempt to read the information left in the segment by its previous owner in hopes he could obtain important data. Multics prevents this action by returning zeroes for reads of virtual storage that has not been initialized. Even though storage residues may be present, they remain inaccessible.

Weaknesses in Multics.   The weaknesses in Multics stem from its hierarchical nature (in both directory structure and the ring structure that provides protected subsystems), its complexity (in both size of operating system code and user interface), and its unprotected communications lines. The discussion of the weaknesses proceeds in that order.

In Multics, the execution-time protection capabilities are hierarchical in nature. Whenever a routine is executing, it may use any segments residing in a ring with the same or higher number, assuming that the principal identifier of the process that contains the routine exists in the access-control list of the segments. The type of access can be restricted, but the restriction applies to all of the routines in the process. Routine A can be protected from routine B by placing routine A in a ring with a lower number, but this puts routine B at the mercy of routine A. If the two routines are executed in the same ring, neither is protected. If a user wants to protect the segments available to a process from a borrowed (or rented) proprietary program, he has to run the proprietary program in a ring with a higher number than the remainder of the process. This may not be acceptable to the owner of the proprietary program, who would prefer that the routine be protected from the process that is utilizing it. Thus, certain types of sharing, such as the mutually suspicious subsystems just described, are precluded, limiting the forms of protection that can be provided by Multics. The hierarchical nature of the directory structure also creates security difficulties. Suppose a user has two directories with the access-control list for the second contained in the first. If he has given John Doe the capability to modify the second directory, he cannot place the access-control list for a new segment in the directory and expect to protect the segment from Doe, because Doe could place his own name in the access-control list for the segment. If Doe has modify-access to the first directory, he cannot be stopped from using the segment no matter into which directory the user places it. In fact, there is no list in the Multics system that enumerates all the users who are able to force access to a segment because of the ability to modify a directory, even though this information is important to the user.

One weakness that is not readily observable to the user is the complexity of the supervisor. Multics is composed of around 2000 program modules, of which 300 run in the most protected area. Each of these modules has the ability to create descriptors and so has the ability to compromise security. At an average of 200 lines per module, that is 60,000 lines of code. This leaves quite a bit of room for errors or misimplementation.[25]

The user's interface is quite complex. When he creates a segment, he must decide whom to put in the access-control list. He is aided in this operation by the default initial access-control list, but there are several additional items that must be considered. For example, the access capabilities for a procedure segment and a data segment will probably be different. He also must decide if the segment is to be protected by requiring that it be executed or used in a low-numbered ring. The user must be very careful when deleting a name from an access-control list because a user whose name is eliminated may then be given wider powers by a different element in the access-control list. For example, if the directory is

```
SMITH·ACCOUNTING·*read
   *·ACCOUNTING·*read-write
```

deleting the first entry will not prevent the use of the segment by Smith. Instead, he will have both read and write access. This may or may not be what was intended. The complexities in the user's interface may cause users to make errors in security-relevant decisions or to use shortcuts to make implementation of the system easier. If a user placed an entry in the access-control list granting the use of the segment to

[25]Ibid. pp. 398–99.

anyone, he would not have to worry about the complexities of the system, but neither would he have any protection for the segment. In either case, the system complexities could indirectly cause security flaws.

The communications lines in Multics are not protected. A penetrator could tap the phone line, obtain a user's password, and enter the system while posing as a legitimate user. This type of penetration may be detected either by examining billing logs or by the user detecting on his next run that the time or location of the last use of his password is abnormal. However, this type of detection merely alerts the user and may come after the damage has been done.

CONCLUSIONS. The Multics system is reasonably well designed and implemented. A fairly wide range of sharing capabilities has been provided. The cost of using the system is not prohibitive; hardware implementation of protection mechanisms has kept the security overhead down. Many of the routes used to penetrate the IBM 360 operating system have been eliminated. In general, Multics performs as advertised. However, some users may require more complex sharing schemes, such as cooperation between two mutually suspicious subsystems in the same process, and therefore cannot use Multics. Unfortunately, no other commercially available operating system will support mutually suspicious subsystems.

HYDRA

The goal of the HYDRA system is not to provide a complete operating system but to furnish a base on which operating systems can be built and studied.[26] As such, it supplies a set of primitive operations (called a Kernel) upon which the operating systems rely to give services and security to users. Rather than study an operating system that could be implemented on HYDRA, the basic HYDRA system itself will be studied in this analysis. An intelligent penetrator (and most are) would utilize any security flaws in the HYDRA base to penetrate an operating system (structured from the HYDRA base) that otherwise has no security flaws.

The HYDRA system was implemented on the Carnegie-Mellon Multi-Mini-Processor (C.mmp). As the name suggests, it was constructed at Carnegie-Mellon University and is a system of mini-computers rather than a single large-scale computer. The system consists of up to 16 Digital Equipment Corporation PDP-11 mini-computers, with 32 million bytes of common primary memory. A clock provides a common time base, and the mini-computers are able to interrupt each other. Each mini-computer has its own primary and secondary storage and I/O devices.

Basically, protection and sharing in HYDRA operate through the employment of capabilities. The capabilities are implemented in software; the storage structure and access mechanisms prevent the system's users from manipulating or forging capabilities. The more detailed discussion of HYDRA will start with the physical representation of the objects, proceed to the structure of the protection mechanism, describe the operation of the protection mechanism, and then present the difficulties in providing protection in HYDRA.

[26]W. Wulf and others, "HYDRA: The Kernel of a Multiprocessor Operating System," *Communications of the ACM*, **17**, 6 (June 1974), 337–45.

OBJECT REPRESENTATION IN HYDRA.   As in Multics, the basic units manipulated and protected by HYDRA are called objects, which are used to represent the resources available in the system. Every object has a name, a type, an access count, and a representation. The representation can be broken down further into data and a capability list. All objects follow the same general form, but for any particular object some of the basic parts may be null.

The name of an object is a unique 64-bit value that is generated by the central clock of the system, making it impossible for the system to confuse two objects.

The type field of an object places the object into a group of similar objects. HYDRA does not interpret the type field; the field is used only to group the objects. The contents of this field are actually the name of a particular object that represents the entire group.

An access count for each object is maintained to determine when the object is to be deleted from the system. The access count records the number of capabilities that contain references to the object. When this count reaches zero, the object is automatically deleted.

The representation of an object is in two parts. First is a capability list that supplies the references to other objects. The capability list of an object cannot be altered in any manner by another object, no matter how liberal the access rights to the object; the capability list can be manipulated only by the HYDRA system itself. The second part of the object representation is the data part that maintains descriptive information about the object. To illustrate, the data part for a procedure provides storage for the code and internal data required to execute the procedure.

The objects are one of the three parts of the protection mechanism structure.

PROTECTION MECHANISM STRUCTURE IN HYDRA.   The HYDRA protection mechanism uses three basic objects: procedures, local name spaces (LNSs), and objects. An understanding of the relationships between these objects is essential to the understanding of HYDRA operation.

A procedure is essentially equivalent to a subroutine in that it performs a function or set of related functions. The procedure, along with the parameter list, also specifies the relationships between the procedure and the remainder of the objects in the system. The procedure's capability list, which may be augmented by capabilities in the parameter list, defines what other objects in the system the procedure can use and the type of use that is allowed. Except for the WALK right, an access mode which will be explained later, the procedure can access objects only by using the capabilities in the list. The data part for a procedure houses the code and the local data for the procedure.

A LNS contains all of the capabilities that may be used by a procedure during a particular invocation. The LNSs are generated by the HYDRA system by combining the capabilities in the procedure capability list (called caller-independent capabilities) with the capabilities in the argument list (called caller-dependent capabilities). (The generation of LNSs will be discussed in more detail in the next section.) The caller-independent capabilities correspond to objects the procedure may reference no matter who the caller is, whereas the caller-dependent capabilities correspond to objects that may vary, depending on who calls the procedure. For example, in a file system, a caller-independent capability would be for an I/O routine while a caller-dependent capability would reference the specific file to be manipulated. Once a LNS is created, it becomes an independent object that is used by the procedure and exists until the procedure returns to the caller. A process can have more than one LNS associated with it, supporting the possibility of recursive code (that is, a procedure that can call itself) or sharing pure procedures.

A process is a dynamic collection of LNSs. The collection represents the current state of a sequential group of procedure calls. The procedure in control of the processor always uses the LNS that is at the top of the stack to address the objects that the procedure accesses. As a procedure is called, its LNS is added to the process stack, and as the procedure terminates, its LNS is deleted from the top of the stack.

A more precise definition of LNS generation, along with other operations of the protection mechanism, is the next topic for discussion.

PROTECTION MECHANISM OPERATION IN HYDRA. The discussion of the operation of the protection mechanism in HYDRA centers around two actions performed by the system: generating a new LNS and expanding the number of capabilities available to a process through the WALK right. Obviously, there are many more functions provided by the system; however, these two are the most important to the protection mechanisms in HYDRA.

The most important operation of the protection mechanism is that of changing protection domains by generating a new LNS. In HYDRA, the system provides a CALL and a RETURN to initiate the change. During a CALL to a procedure, HYDRA generates a new LNS for that procedure and places the LNS on the process stack. During a RETURN from the procedure, the LNS is deleted from the stack. Since a procedure utilizes only the top LNS in the process stack, the CALL and RETURN actions in effect change the protection domains.

The generation of the new LNS for a procedure involves the combination of the caller-independent capabilities in the called procedure's capability list and the caller-dependent capabilities passed as arguments to the procedure. The caller-independent capabilities transfer directly to the LNS; the caller-dependent capabilities are checked and transformed before they are placed in the LNS. The capability list for the called procedure contains a template for each caller-dependent capability. The template specifies the checks to be made on the parameter capability and partially defines the form of the capability that will be placed in the LNS. The template contains a type field that specifies the type of object the parameter capability must represent. It is also possible to have a template that accepts any object type. The template also contains a check-rights field, specifying the minimum rights to the object that must be contained in the parameter capability. If either the type or the check-rights field test yields an error, an error code is returned, and the called procedure is not invoked. If the tests do not result in an error, a new capability for the object is generated and placed in the new LNS. The access rights in the new capability are derived from the access-rights field of the template, not from the check-rights field of the template or the access rights of the parameter capability. The called procedure can thus have greater access rights to an object than the procedure that passed the capability to the object as a parameter.

A procedure can access capabilities from another object's capability list by using the WALK right. The WALK right, as are all other rights, is indicated in the access rights field in the capability for an object. Given the WALK right to an object and an integer number, it is possible to use the capability in the object's capability list indicated by the integer. Because of the WALK right, an object can access objects that are not listed in its LNS; it can access any object available through the use or repeated use of the WALK right. For example, consider a set of four objects: A, B, C, and D, where A has a capability for B, which has the capability for C, which has the capability for D. The capabilities involved include the WALK right. Thus, A can access B directly, or A can use the WALK right through B to access C, or A can "WALK" through both B and C to access D.

WEAKNESSES IN HYDRA. The previous section described how a process in HYDRA increases its access powers by augmenting the access rights field when the capability for an object is passed to the procedure and by using the WALK right on capabilities possessed by the procedure. While this provides a generalized sharing environment, the wide powers available to a procedure create security difficulties as the caller of any procedure must assume that the expansion of rights to an object does not give the procedure excessive access to the object, that the capabilities are passed on only to other authorized procedures, and that the WALK right is not used to gain unauthorized access to an object.

The above security difficulties are illustrated in the case of a company using a proprietary program to gather statistics from a data base. The owners of the proprietary program do not want the company to read or alter the program, so they give the company only the capability to execute the program. Conversely, the company does not want the proprietary program to alter any of the values in the data base, so it wants the proprietary program to have only read access to the data base. This is an example of mutually suspicious subsystems. The company has two problems. First, it must be sure that the proprietary program, when receiving the capability for the data base in a procedure call, does not expand the access rights beyond the required read access. The company must also be sure that the capability is not passed to another procedure within the proprietary program package in such a manner that the access rights are expanded. In other words, the company must verify at least part of the proprietary program before the security of the data base can be assured. This practice is not feasible if only the object code of the proprietary program is available to the company and, in any case, may be objectionable to the owners of the program. The owners of the proprietary program has a more difficult problem. They do not want the company to alter the billing section in the program so that revenue will be reduced. They originally give a capability that authorizes only execution of the program, believing the system will protect the program. However, once a capability is given, no control over the use of that capability is retained. The company can pass the capability for the proprietary program to a procedure written by the company. During the call, access rights to the proprietary program can be expanded to include the right to modify the program, then the company procedure can alter the billing code at will. Therefore, the only protection that the proprietary program has is the honesty of the company and the secrecy of the billing procedures, neither of which provide adequate security.

The WALK right creates another penetration route by allowing a procedure to use the capabilities in the capability list of another procedure. Such a use requires the WALK right to the procedure, but, again, the WALK right can be obtained by a penetrator by passing the capability for the procedure to another procedure that he has written, and expanding the access rights to include the WALK right. Thus, whenever a capability for a procedure is given away, not only the procedure itself becomes vulnerable, but also any capabilities found in the procedure's capability list will be accessible.

The HYDRA system was not designed to support the ownership of any object. Once a user gives away a capability to an object, the user loses ownership control over that object. This is normal in any capability-based system. However, in HYDRA an object is deleted only when the access count to the object reaches zero. The creator of an object cannot delete an object even if he discovers that it is being misused. Of course the object's usefulness could be essentially destroyed by performing an operation on the object that alters its essential properties; for a procedure, such an operation is writing zeroes over the object code for the procedure. Again, because of the ability to expand the access rights to an object during a procedure call, the creator of an object cannot share an object and still retain any special rights to the object.

CONCLUSIONS. HYDRA provides a powerful and effective sharing scheme, but only in a nonthreatening environment. The expansion of access rights can be used to pass capabilities through procedures while at the same time preventing an untested program from using the capabilities erroneously. However, the expansion of access rights prevents the protection of a shared object in a hostile environment by allowing a penetrator to give himself any access rights he desires.

The primitive operations of the HYDRA system do provide for a wide range of sharing and protection schemes by allowing for the construction of many different operating systems. For example, an access-control list security system such as Multics could be constructed. The security of such a system would depend on the operating system's ability to restrict the use of the expansion of access rights during a procedure call and to provide a reliable naming scheme. Obviously, an operating system based on capabilities would be very easy to implement. It is the versatility of the system that creates difficulties in the implementation of a particular protection scheme. The implementor must restrict the use of a procedure call, at least with respect to the expansion of access rights, in order to provide adequate security. HYDRA provides flexibility, but does not aid the implementor in limiting the power available to the user.

6.4

Authentication

Authentication, or ensuring that users are who they say they are, is the second tool available for the generation of a secure computer program. If users are not properly authenticated, a penetrator can pretend to be a system administrator (or any other user in the system) to gain wider access rights. Authentication is generally performed by the operating system; however, as in the case of a project leader in a Multics system who writes a routine to authenticate users of the project identifier, the software engineer may have to provide some form of authentication in the program.

The discussion of authentication begins with some of the ways a system authenticates users, moves to how the user can authenticate the system (and why this must be done), and, finally, describes methods by which an authentication mechanism can deter penetration attempts.

6.4.1 AUTHENTICATION OF THE USER BY THE SYSTEM

A computer system can authenticate a user by three basic methods: by the location of the user, by something the user has, or by something the user knows.[27]

AUTHENTICATION BY LOCATION

In the simplest form of authentication, user location, the computer assumes that if the user is operating a particular terminal, he is a certain authorized individual or a member of a privileged group of individuals allowed access to the machine. A computer operator's console is one example of such an authentication scheme. To prevent a penetrator's access to the console, it is physically secured; the computer does not provide any security. Unauthorized entry to the console may be prevented by guards and/or locked doors. In other cases, the terminal itself may be locked.

The use of the physical location of the user to provide authentication has two major weaknesses. First, the physical security of the entire transmission line from the terminal to the computer must be ensured. Otherwise, the penetrator could tap the line either to record the transmissions or to simulate the actual terminal. The second weakness is that while physical security can provide a strong deterrent for penetrations, it seldom completely protects an object. A lock on a terminal can be broken, or if the penetrator is more subtle, the lock may be picked, or a duplicate key made.

AUTHENTICATION BY CHARACTERISTICS

A user may possess some object or characteristic that is examined to provide authentication. Objects include keys and cards with magnetic stripes that are interpreted by some input device. Physical characteristics such as fingerprints, voice prints, signatures, hand shapes, and retina prints can also be used to authenticate the identity of a user. Texas Instruments has a voice verification system in which four words are selected at random from a 16-word set.[28] The average time to complete verification is 5.6 seconds. The Identimat 2000 (an authentication device) measures the length of a person's fingers in order to provide authentication.[29] Any science fiction reader can attest to the usefulness of retina prints in the identification of an individual.

In order to apply the authentication technique involving user or object characteristics, one chances transmitting the characteristics over insecure lines. The lines can be tapped, the information recorded, and the recording played back by the penetrator

[27]Martin, *Security, Accuracy, and Privacy in Computer Systems*, p. 133.

[28]*Computerworld* (Boston), August 23, 1976, p. 7.

[29]D. R. Cone, "Personnel Identification by Hand Geometry Parameters," Stanford Research Institute (1969). Available from Identimat Corporation, Northvale, N.J.

to simulate the original user. The loss of a key or card means that anyone who finds the card or key has the potential to penetrate the system although the potential can be lowered through the use of additional authentication mechanism such as the password scheme to be discussed next.

AUTHENTICATION BY KNOWLEDGE

The final method of authentication involves a piece of information the user knows. In general, some form of password is invented although more complex schemes are possible. When a user contacts the system, s/he gives a name and is, in turn, asked for a password. If the name and password match those contained in the computer system, authentication is complete. In order to protect the password, it is usually not printed on the terminal, or the terminal provides a blocked out area where the password is to be typed. As an example of one of the more complex password schemes, the user can be asked further questions, such as his aunt's middle name, from a list stored in the computer. The authentication scheme can be strengthened by asking several such questions at random from the list.

The implementation of authentication by passwords shows several grave defects. First, the choice of a password is, in general, very poor as the user wants a password that is easy to remember and so selects something that has a personal significance. It would be interesting to know what percentage of passwords currently in use are either the name of a relative, a friend, a birth date, the name of a character in a favorite novel, or a word relevant to the hobby of the user of the password. Users also tend to use the same password on more than one system. All of this reduces the number of passwords through which a penetrator must search, assuming that a brute force technique is being used. Some systems aid the user by providing a routine that generates random passwords. If the passwords generated by the routine are too difficult to remember (such as LBTXHP), users will sometimes write the password down rather than risk forgetting it. The existence of a written copy increases the chances of compromise; some of the routines generate random passwords that mimic English words in that they are easy to pronounce and remember, so a written copy is not required.

The fact that the password is used outside of the computer system is another defect that provides several chances for compromise. A penetrator can look over the shoulder of the user as the password is typed into a terminal or can remove the ribbon from a terminal in order to obtain the password. The penetrator can also place a tap on the line from the terminal to the computer and record the password.

A password system is vulnerable because of the list of passwords that must be stored in the computer. If this file is not adequately protected, it will be an obvious target for any infiltrator. Even a protected file is vulnerable to illegal access through the proper channel. For example, if a system administrator has access to the password file, bribery or blackmail can be used to procure the contents of the file. However, it is not really necessary for anyone to have access to the password file; in fact, the file does not even need to contain the password. When a password is first placed in the system, it can be transformed by using a function that is hard or impossible to invert and the transformation stored rather than the original password. Whenever a user enters the password at a terminal, the same transformation is used, and the result is compared to the transformation stored in the password file. Since the function is hard to invert, the contents of the password file cannot be passed through any simple function to obtain the original password. A penetrator can simulate the function on a computer and try all possible passwords until he finds one that generates a match to the transformed result that is stored in the password file, but judicious choice of password length and function complexity can block such action by making the average time to a solution as long as desired. For example, an eight-character password (using letters only) and a function that can be performed in one millisecond would require an average of 3.3 years to determine a password, given its transform.

The remaining problem is the user who forgets the password. There must be a mechanism by which the user can obtain a new password. One possible method is to allow the user to go to a system administrator, present some form of identification, and then be allowed to enter a new password into the system. The administrator still will not be able to observe the new password. A user's password can be changed by an administrator without the user's permission, but at least the user would be notified of the change by not being allowed to use the system on his next log-on attempt.

The security provided by passwords can be extended by rules regarding the use of the passwords. In a very hostile environment, a list of passwords can be maintained by both the user and the computer system. Each password is used once (or a limited number of times), deleted from the list, then the next password is utilized. Even if a user has a single password, the length of time or number of times that it can be used may be limited. When the limit is reached, the user is forced either to change the password or to discontinue use of the system. A penetrator who obtains a password is then limited in his use of the password.

6.4.2 AUTHENTICATION OF THE SYSTEM BY THE USER

The forms of authentication discussed so far are the authentication of the user to the computer system; the user has no assurance that he is communicating to the correct computer system. If a penetrator has access to the transmission line, a mini-computer can be interposed so that the user is talking to the mini-computer rather than to the desired computer system. The mini-computer is programmed to mimic the actions of the computer system with which the user believes he is in communication and thus can record all of the information that the user provides for authentication. At that point, the mini-computer terminates the log-on, and the penetrator can use the recorded authentication information to enter the system. If a common error message is sent to the user, he may never know what the penetrator has accomplished. In a system where passwords are used only once, the same technique is possible. The user is made to believe that the log-on was successful (thus removing the current password from the user's list); then he is notified, by the mini-computer, that the system is going down and will be out of service for a specified time period. The penetrator now has a password and a time period for which the password is usable since it can be assumed that the user will not attempt to access the system during this period. When the penetrator uses the password, it will be crossed off of the valid systems password list, so the next time the user attempts to log-on, his password list and the systems list will still be synchronized.

In order to prevent circumvention of the authentication mechanism by mimicry, an elaborate handshake sequence can be generated. In this method, the user provides partial identification, the system in return provides partial identification, and so on until both the system and user are satisfied. At least part of this sequence should be unique for each user; that is, the system should provide a unique piece of information to each user. However, unless the handshake is very carefully designed, with perhaps a one-time password provided by both sides, a penetrator can still use the mini-computer in the transmission line to infiltrate the system. In this case, both the user and the system must be mimicked. First, the penetrator mimics the system to obtain the user's password as previously described. Then the penetrator contacts the system and acts like the user by giving the user's password in order to obtain the system's response. The penetrator creates some sort of line error, such as simulating a broken connection, and the system terminates the log-on. The penetrator can mimic the system at some later time when the user attempts to log-on, this time to obtain the user's second response in the handshake sequence. This process is continued until the entire handshake sequence is obtained.

Crytography as an authentication mechanism has one advantage over other methods of authentication in that the user is authenticated to the system at the same time the system is authenticated to the user. The use of cryptography as an authentication mechanism will be discussed in a later section.

6.4.3 THREAT DETECTION AND RECORDING AS DETERRENTS

Up to this point in the discussion, authentication mechanisms have attempted to allow only legitimate users to log-on to the system, and have merely rejected any endeavor to the contrary. However, if a penetrator realizes that trial and error attempts will be monitored and perhaps recorded, s/he may decide to attempt a penetration in another manner. Threat detection and compromise recording, two methods that serve as deterrents to penetrators, will be discussed in the section on program and file security.

The weakness common to all three forms of authentication is the use of insecure communication lines. The next tool to be discussed, cryptography, can be utilized to alleviate this weakness, provide security and other additional benefits to communications systems in general, and furnish another layer of protection within the computer system.

6.5

Cryptography

Cryptography, the third tool in the arsenal of the software engineer, can be used to protect information even though it falls into unauthorized hands. Many computer systems transmit data over telephone lines, microwave relays, or other insecure paths that can be easily tapped by a penetrator. Through the magic of electronics, the penetrator can have a complete record of both sides of an interaction between a computer and a user on a terminal or of all the information passing through a data link. Because of this possibility, cryptography has found its way into computer communications.

The need to protect messages from prying eyes has been recognized for quite some time. One of the simpler ciphers has been attributed to Caesar, who supposedly used it in his correspondence. Cryptography has traditionally been used by the military to protect the transmission of sensitive information, has also been used in business and political communications, and has protected the privacy (and physical well being) of lovers.

This discussion of cryptography first presents the basic cryptographic techniques, including a set of evaluation criteria and a brief description of how analysts break cryptograms (cryptanalysis). Second to be discussed is how computer cryptographic techniques differ from traditional cryptography and how cryptography can be used in a computer system. Next is a discussion of the discipline required in a cryptographic system, followed by some cryptographic design principles. Finally, hardware cryptography and cryptographic routines are presented.

6.5.1 CRYPTOGRAPHIC TECHNIQUES

Briefly, cryptography is transforming a message so that even if a penetrator sees the message, he cannot understand it. The original message is called the *clear*. The transformation process is called *enciphering* and usually utilizes a specific *key* that determines which of the many possible transformations of the message is actually produced. The transformed message is the *cryptogram*, which must be *deciphered* (by using the same key) in order to recover the original message. The penetrator (or *enemy*) attempts to *decrypt* the cryptogram to obtain the original message without the knowledge of the key or the specific technique.

The schematic of a generalized cryptography system is shown in Figure 6-10.

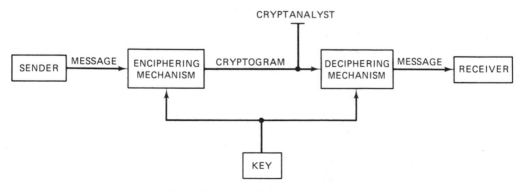

Fig. 6-10 Generalized cryptography system

First, the key is generated and sent in a secure manner to both the sender and the receiver. The sender generates a message in the clear. It is enciphered and then transmitted to the receiver. The receiver deciphers the cryptogram by using the key, and recovers the original text. It is assumed that any disclosure of information would occur only between the enciphering mechanism and deciphering mechanism. The clear message at both ends has to be protected by other security measures.

The cryptographic techniques (or *ciphers*) can be broken into two classes: simple and compound. The simple ciphers are the building blocks from which the compound ciphers are composed.

SIMPLE CIPHERS

There are three basic forms of a simple cipher: substitution, transposition, and Vigenére; each will be discussed separately. A closely related concept, a *code*, will also be presented. Except for certain cases of the Vigenére cipher, the simple ciphers generally provide little security.

SUBSTITUTION CIPHERS.   In this class of ciphers, characters or groups of characters are replaced by substitute characters or groups of characters.

The simplest of the methods is to replace each single letter with a fixed substitute. If the text and substitutes are letters, the key is some permutation of the alphabet. The first letter in the key is substituted for A, the second for B, and so forth. Examples of a key, clear text, and a cryptogram follow:

alphabet:	ABCDEFGHIJKLMNOPQRSTUVWXYZ
key:	NMIUAZCRWFSODVTKBYJHGPELQX
clear text:	WETHEPEOPLE
cryptogram:	EAHRAKATKOA

In simpler forms of cryptography, blanks are often eliminated.

Two examples of a simple substitution cipher may be familiar to the reader. First is the cipher used in *The Gold Bug*, by Edgar Allan Poe, which was used to describe the location of a pirate's treasure. A second example is the Captain Midnight Secret Decoder Badge, where numbers are substituted for letters. Captain Midnight would, on his television show, read a series of numbers that could be deciphered into a clue about the next week's show.

More complex systems substitute for digrams (two-character groups), trigrams (three-character groups), or larger groups of letters rather than single characters. The keys for such substitutions grow rapidly as the size of the group of letters increases. For example, if groups of five letters were used in the substitution, the key would be 26^5 elements. Each element would have to be a unique sequence of 5 letters.

Arithmetic operations can be utilized to implement n-gram substitution. For example, successive n-grams can be multiplied by a matrix that has an inverse. Each letter or character is assigned a unique number, ranging from 0 to one less than the size of the character set. The matrix used in the multiplication is the key, and its inverse is used to decipher the cryptogram.

Another variation of substitution is called multiple mixed alphabet substitution. This is simply a set of n simple substitutions that are used in order on successive letters in the message. The key is comprised of the keys for the individual substitutions and the order in which the substitutions are to be used. For example, a key could consist of the following simple substitution keys:

1—GOAIDMREWLXTZQKFSBNVYPUJCH
2—LPFNDKMIRSNAXUZGBEOCQTJVHY
3—PLHOFBSJVYRNDMAECQTWZXKIUG

and the order of 123. With this key, a clear text of AAABBB becomes GLPOPL. If the order is 213, AAABBB becomes LGPPOL.

TRANSPOSITION CIPHERS. For this type of cipher, the message is divided into groups of n characters; then each group is permuted in the same manner. The *period* of the transposition is the size of the group. The key is the actual permutation used and can conveniently be represented as a permutation of the first n digits. For example, if n is four, one possible key would be 3412. The message 1234 becomes 3412, and the message WETHEPEOPLEOFTHE becomes THWEEOEPEOPLHEFT.

Transpositions can be applied sequentially, creating a compound transposition. The result is a transposition whose period is the least common multiple of the periods of the transpositions used.

VIGENÉRE CIPHERS (AND VARIATIONS). The simplest example of this type of cipher is the Caesar cipher. Each letter in the message is advanced in the alphabet by a fixed number of letters. The amount of advancement is the key, which ranges from 0 to 25. For a key of 1, A becomes B, B becomes C, and so on. Z becomes A, completing the chain. For other than alphabetic messages, the character set is ordered, and each character in the message is advanced in this ordering by the key amount. For a character set of size n, the Caesar cipher is simply addition, modulo n, of the position of the message letter in the character set to the key, giving the location in the character set of the cryptogram letter. (In modulo n addition, the answer is constrained to be less than n; if a result greater than n is obtained, n is repeatedly subtracted from the answer until the answer is less than n. For example, using modulo 3 addition, $1 \oplus 0 = 1, 1 \oplus 1 = 2, 1 \oplus 2 = 0, 2 \oplus 0 = 2, 2 \oplus 1 = 0, 2 \oplus 2 = 1$.) In the more general Vigenére system, the key consists of a series of letters; the period of the cipher is the number of letters in the key. Each successive letter of the message is encrypted, using the location in the character set of the matching key character as the key. For this discussion the character set will be numbered from 0 to $N - 1$. For example, with the key ABMQ we obtain

message: WETHEPEOPLE.......
key: ABMQABMQABM........
cryptogram: WFFXEQQEPMQ.......

In variations to this technique, the message is subtracted modulo 26 from the key, or the key is subtracted modulo 26 from the message.

Two or more Vigenéres may be applied in sequence. As in a compound transposition, the period of the result is the least common multiple of the periods of the individual Vigenéres.

A special case of the Vigenére occurs when the key is infinite (or appears to be infinite). This is called the Vernam system. This is a simple cipher that can provide complete security if the key consists of random letters. A key consisting of meaningful text produces a *running key* cipher.

An interesting variation of the Vigenére-type cipher, called the Autokey cipher, uses either the message itself or the resulting cryptogram as the key. A starting key (of *n* characters) is used to encipher the first *n* characters of the message and the encipherment is continued, using the message or cryptogram (displaced *n* characters) as the key. For example, if the key is ABMQ, we have

        message: WETHEPEOPLE.......
        key: ABMQWFFXAUJ.......
        cryptogram: WFFXAUJLPFN.......

when the cryptogram is used as the key.

If the message is used as the key, we have

        message: WETHEPEOPLE........
        key: ABMQWETHEPE.......
        cryptogram: WFFXATXVTAI.......

CODES.   Codes have long been used in computer systems, but usually to save space rather than to provide security. In a code system, a symbol or group of symbols is used to specify a particular message. For example, eye color could be coded as 1 for green, 2 for grey, 3 for blue, and so on. Codes are essentially a form of substitution on a semantic level with the key serving as the mapping between the coded symbols and the meanings for the coded symbols.

The form of the key for a code system illustrates the major difference between cryptography and codes. A cryptographic system is designed so that any message may be enciphered, but a code system can be used only to send messages that use the semantics available in the key.

COMPOUND CIPHERS

The simple cryptographic techniques can be combined in two ways to form compound ciphers. The first way is to provide a dynamic selection of which simple cipher to use. In such a system, several of the simpler cryptographic techniques are possible, and the key for a particular message contains an identification of the particular technique used as well as the key for that technique. In a more complex system, a scheme like that in multiple mixed alphabet substitution can be utilized. The key then contains the order in which several techniques will be used as well as the key for each technique.

A second way of combining two or more techniques is to apply them successively to the same message. This forms a system that is the product of the two techniques. One example of such a system is a fractional cipher where each letter is replaced by two digits; the resulting number stream is transposed, and then letters substituted for the two-digit groups.

The choice of a simple cipher or group of simple ciphers that form a compound cipher depends on the desired characteristics of the cipher to be used. These characteristics are contrasted in the next section.

CRYPTOGRAPHY SYSTEM EVALUATION

Claude E. Shannon, in an excellent paper on cryptography,[30] listed the following five criteria for the evaluation of a cryptographic system:

1. *Level of Secrecy.* The amount of security required of a cryptographic system depends on the particular problem being solved. In some systems, the level of secrecy is perfect. In these systems, the cryptogram can be deciphered only with the use of the key. In other systems, several solutions to a cryptogram may be possible. Among the systems that can be solved uniquely, there is a wide range in the effort required for the solution.

2. *Key Size.* The key must be generated and transmitted to both the sending and receiving locations. The method of transmission must be completely secure. The key must also be stored or perhaps memorized by the users of the system. Although disk and magnetic tape storage have reduced the problems of storage, it still may be desirable to have a small key that is easy to change and store.

3. *Ease of Use.* When enciphering or deciphering is performed manually, the need for a simple operation is obvious. In a computer system, complex operations can be performed by software or hardware. The main concern is the speed of the operation (so computations or transmissions are not excessively delayed) and computer storage required.

4. *Error Propagation.* In some types of cryptography systems, an error in one letter in the cryptogram will create multiple errors when the cryptogram is deciphered. In general, this trait is undesirable; however, there are cases in which high error propagation can be utilized to discover transmission errors and penetration attempts.

5. *Message Expansion.* Some secrecy systems increase the size of the cryptogram relative to the size of the message. One example of this would be the use of null messages or characters to confuse enemy analysts by altering the statistics of the language.

As Shannon pointed out, these criteria are incompatible when dealing with natural languages. (Natural languages are those such as English or FORTRAN. This is in contrast to artificial languages that can be created to reduce the possibility of cryptanalysis.) Some compromise must be made, depending on the nature of the particular application. Examples of compromises of each of the five criteria follow:

1. If the amount of secrecy required is not high (as in a system where only accidental disclosure is to be prevented), any of the simple methods that have been presented can be used.

2. If an infinite key (or, more practically, a very large key) is available, the Vernam system with a completely random key will provide absolute secrecy.

3. If there is no limitation on the complexity of operation (no limit on time and core), an extremely complicated cipher can be used.

[30]C. E. Shannon., "Communication Theory of Secrecy Systems," *Bell Systems Technical Journal,* **28,** (October 1949), 14–15.

4. If propagation of errors is allowed, there are several good "mixing" transformations (to be discussed later) that can be used.
5. If the message is allowed to expand, random letters can be added to the cryptogram at specific locations and meaningless messages can be sent to confuse the enemy analyst.

The discussion of which of the criteria are less important in computer cryptography will be presented after cryptographic techniques in a computer are described.

BREAKING CRYPTOGRAMS

With an ideal secrecy system, the only information that any enemy cryptanalyst (who attempts to determine the clear text of a cryptogram or the key without initially knowing the key) will be able to determine from a cryptogram is that a message was sent. For example, the Vernam system with an infinite random key is a perfect system. Each letter in the message is masked by one letter in the key; for a given message all cryptograms of the same length are possible. Suppose a cryptanalyst has a four-letter cryptogram that was enciphered by using the Vernam system. The only way to decrypt the cryptogram is to generate all keys of four letters and decipher the cryptogram by using these keys. The result will be all words of four letters, each with the same probability of being correct; the cryptanalyst is no better off with this than with the cryptogram.

In less than ideal systems, with sufficient time and a large enough sample of enciphered material, a cryptanalyst can reduce the possible messages to a small set or to a unique solution. Since ideal systems are not practical for all cases, the less than ideal systems must also be utilized. One very important measure of a nonideal system is the work factor. A cryptanalyst may be able to discover a unique solution to a cryptogram, but if the average time required to discover this solution is on the order of 50 years, the result will probably not be very useful. This is considerably better than a cryptogram that does not yield a unique solution, but does yield five solutions with a few days' effort.

A cryptanalyst depends on the statistical properties of a language in his quest for the solution to a cryptogram. These statistical properties are caused by the redundancies in the language. In English, the prime example of this redundancy is in the letter pair "qu." The "u" is redundant because in normal English words, a "q" is always followed by a "u." One of the more basic set of statistics about a language is the frequency counts of single letters, digrams, and trigrams.

If the cryptanalyst has a cryptogram of sufficient length, he can run several statistical tests on the cryptogram, which may limit the amount of work he must perform to determine the original message or the key to the message. For example, a simple substitution cipher can be easily solved (if it is long enough) by counting the frequencies of the letters in the cryptogram. The letter with the highest frequency is probably the substitute for "e" because "e" is used more often in English than any other letter. Similarly, the frequency of the remaining letters in the cryptogram help the cryptanalyst determine the remainder of the key. It is easily seen that the use of a statistical analysis to solve a simple substitution cipher is much faster than an attempt to try all possible keys to solve the cryptogram.

There are two methods to remove the tool of statistical analysis from the cryptanalyst if an ideal cryptographic system is not used. The first method is to remove the redundancy of the language; this is only possible if codes can be used. In a computer system, some of the fields within a record can be coded, eliminating the redundancy within those fields. For example, a "yes" or "no" answer on a questionnaire can be coded in one bit, rather than in a field three characters long. In this case, the interdependence between several bits has been completely eliminated. Unfortunately, there are fields in a record, such as name and address fields, that cannot be coded; and a record in a computer system generally has a relatively rigid structure, generating a new group of statistics for the arsenal of the cryptanalyst. For example, the records are generally blank filled, of fixed length, and the records in a file are often sorted on the first field.

A second method of disarming the statistical analysis of a cryptogram is to disrupt the relationships that the cryptanalyst utilizes. Shannon[31] calls this disruption either confusion or diffusion, depending on which relationships are involved. The technique that accomplishes the disruption causes each letter in the cryptogram to depend on many letters in the message rather than on a few or simply one. This has the unfortunate result of creating a secrecy system with a high propagation of error, but if this characteristic can be tolerated, a very secure system can be devised. The idea is to apply a simple cipher, followed by a good mixing cipher, followed by another simple cipher (resulting in a SMS cipher). In general, the mixing ciphers are block ciphers; that is, a fixed length block of characters is enciphered in one operation. For example, with a block size of 48 characters, a mixing cipher could consist of the following steps:

1. Perform substitution on the 16 three-letter groups in the block.
2. Perform a transposition on the 12 four-letter groups.
3. Add the first 24 letters to the second 24 letters, using modulo arithmetic.
4. Repeat steps 1, 2, and 3 six times.

Due to the complex nature of the operations required for the mixing ciphers, implementation of a mixing cipher is easier (and less prone to errors) if computer hardware or software is utilized.

COMPUTER VS. MANUAL CRYPTOGRAPHY

The characteristics of a computer cause cryptography when implemented in a computer to be different from traditional cryptography in three areas: complexity of operation, simplification of the alphabet, and enhancement of key use. The first of these, complexity of operation, takes advantage of the accuracy and speed of computers; cryptographic methods that would be unwieldy for manual operation can be

[31]Ibid. pp. 53–55.

used on computers. For example, a single error in the enciphering or deciphering of a cryptogram that utilizes a mixing cipher could create an incoherent jumble of an entire block of the message. Because of the complexity of the cipher, such a mistake is likely unless extreme care is taken in the manual cryptographic process.

For computer use, the substitution and Vigenére cryptographic techniques can be simplified, primarily because of the reduced size of the computer alphabet as compared to the larger letter alphabets, since all data stored in a computer system consist of the digits 0 and 1. This simplifies simple substitution into two cases, either substituting 0 for 1 and 1 for 0, or substituting 0 for 0 and 1 for 1. The key can be represented as a binary digit with a 1 representing the reversal of the digits and a 0 representing the second case. Table 6-1 illustrates the relationship between the clear text, key, and cryptogram. Note that in this case the effect of substitution can be achieved by addition modulo 2 of the key to the message and thus is identical to a Vigenére with a period of 1.

With a multiple mixed alphabet substitution, the key consists of a string of bits. Each bit represents the selection of one of the two possible substitution tables. To implement this system, the key (repeated as often as necessary) is added, modulo 2, to the message. This looks suspiciously like a Vigenére cipher with a key of the same length. Table 6-1 also illustrates that simple substitution or Vigenére can be imple-

Table 6-1 Simple Substitution with a Binary Alphabet

Clear	Key	Cryptogram
0	0	0
1	0	1
0	1	1
1	1	0

mented by using an "exclusive or." One major advantage of using the modulo 2 addition (or the "exclusive or") for cryptography is that the operation is essentially its own reciprocal. For example:

$$
\begin{array}{rl}
\text{clear text:} & 1100 \\
\text{key:} & \oplus 1010 \\
\hline
\text{cryptogram:} & 0110 \\
\text{cryptogram:} & 0110 \\
\text{key:} & \oplus 1010 \\
\hline
\text{clear text:} & 1100
\end{array}
$$

This allows the use of a single routine for both encryption and decryption when the Vigenére cipher is used.

Computational techniques can be used to enhance the secrecy provided by a key. A key of 32 bits in length, used in a Vigenére cipher, will not be resistant to analysis. However, if this key is used as a seed to a pseudo-random number generator, and the resulting pseudo-random bit string is used as a key, a large quantity of information can be enciphered without repetition of the key. The resulting system will not be as strong as one using a completely random key because the pseudo-random string will have statistical properties that could be exploited by an analyst, but it will be a significant improvement over the original 32-bit key.

The cryptographic techniques most suited to computer cryptography techniques are the Vigenére system and the simple cipher—mixing cipher—simple cipher (SMS) combination. Possible methods of key distribution and use are:

- use of a single key
- synchronized use of a list of keys
- synchronized generation of a key from a key base or by a pseudo-random number generator
- use of a single key that is modified by the contents of each message block.

Referring back to Shannon's five criteria, the SMS cipher is a relaxation of the ease of use and error propagation requirements, whereas the Vigenére cipher is a relaxation of the key size requirement. As each of the two ciphers has its own peculiarities, the selection of the cipher (and method of key use) depends on the characteristics of the particular application.

The simple cipher-mixing cipher-simple cipher system (SMS) can use all four methods of key generation and use. Because of the work factor involved in breaking the cipher, even a single key can be utilized. However, it is safer to use one of the other three key-generation methods even though more work is involved. Since the key does not have to be generated on a bit-for-bit basis with the message to be enciphered, the amount of work required to generate the key is not as high as with the Vigenére system. The SMS system has a high propagation of error. Therefore, an error in a single bit of the cryptogram will create multiple errors in the decrypted message. Error detection is enhanced at the cost of a garbled message if the message cannot be retransmitted. The SMS system requires more computer time than the Vigenére because of the complexity of the enciphering process. In systems with a high data rate, this can be a severe disadvantage.

With the Vigenére cipher, the large volume of traffic usually present in a computer system precludes the use of a single key or a short list of keys because a key should be used only once (or at worst, repeated at infrequent intervals). The remaining two key generation methods are well suited to the Vigenére system; they both can provide an infinite key that appears to be random. The major problem with this system is in the area of error detection. A single-bit error during transmission remains a single-bit error after decryption, which reduces the chances for error detection. The Vigenére system is very fast and provides perfect security if the key is completely random.

With either the Vigenére or SMS enciphering method, the synchronized use of a key (whether pregenerated and stored or continuously generated) can create problems if the key synchronization is lost. The consequences of the loss of synchronization depend on the ability of the sender and receiver to detect and recover from the loss. If the key is being modified by the contents of each message block and an undetected single-bit error occurs, the receiver will not be able to generate the next key in the series, and the communications link will effectively be broken.

The discussion now turns from how cryptography is performed to where in a computer system it can be used. Further implications are noted of the choice of cipher method, key generation, and key use as related to specific applications.

6.5.2 CRYPTOGRAPHY APPLICATIONS IN COMPUTER SYSTEMS

Cryptography can be applied to three major areas in computer systems: authentication, protection in communications, and protection of information in files. Each of the areas has its own unique characteristics that affect the exact technique that will provide the required level of security effectively. The discussion of each of these areas will include some of the characteristics associated with the choice of cryptographic technique.

AUTHENTICATION BY CRYPTOGRAPHY

Authentication by the use of cryptography is a simple operation because exactly the same key must be utilized in both the enciphering and deciphering operations. A typical authentication sequence of a user at a terminal (assuming the terminal is capable of encryption) is:

- The user sends the ID (in the clear) to the computer.
- The computer obtains a key associated with the user ID and uses the key to decipher any subsequent transmissions.
- The user loads the key into the terminal and proceeds with normal communication with the computer.

If a penetrator attempts to masquerade as a user, chances are that an incorrect key will be loaded into the terminal, and the computer (utilizing the correct key) will decipher the messages into gibberish, thus detecting the penetration attempt. The major advantages to this method of authentication are the information required for authentication (the key) need not be transmitted over insecure lines, and authentication can be applied to any device (terminals or other computers) that communicates with a computer.

Any of the ciphers or methods of key use can be employed to provide authentication; however, the use of a single, relatively short key or key base will simplify the operation for a terminal user. A relatively secure cryptographic method should be used because an infiltrator may attempt to cryptanalyze the communications between the terminal and the computer in order to discover a user's key and thus obtain the means to penetrate the computer.

CRYPTOGRAPHY IN COMPUTER COMMUNICATIONS

A considerable amount of computer information is transmitted over telephone lines, either as communication between two computers or a computer and a terminal. This information can be tapped relatively easily. Other forms of electromagnetic communication, such as microwave, can also be easily tapped. Cryptography can provide effective security when insecure means of communication are utilized.

An enemy, to use the traditional name, who is eavesdropping in a communications network has several methods to compromise the network. The information can be recorded for later use, message blocks (a fixed size portion of the message enciphered as a single unit) intercepted, false message blocks added, or existing blocks altered. Encrypting the message prevents the information from being of use to the enemy, but in and of itself does not protect the message from sabotage created by the disruption of communications. This disruption can be prevented by detecting any message blocks that arrive out of sequence, and by performing special processing to either reject spurious blocks or request retransmission of blocks that have been intercepted or altered.

In order to facilitate the detection of sabotage attempts, a portion of each message block should contain "housekeeping" data.[32] An important part of this information is a sequence number or some other bit pattern that only one message block would be expected to contain. If a saboteur is able to place a forged message block into the stream, the housekeeping bit pattern will probably not match. The probability of a successful forgery depends on the number of bits dedicated to the authentication of each block. For example, if 10 bits are allocated for block authentication, a forged block will be accepted one time out of 1024 for a probability of less than 10^{-3}. If 20 bits are used, the probability is less than 10^{-6} that a forged block would be accepted.

The housekeeping data can easily be generated by producing a longer key than is required (assuming that the key is being continuously generated) and by using the extra bits as the message block identifier. If this technique is used, the housekeeping data need not be enciphered, and error detection can occur before deciphering the message block. This method does not aid in the detection of blocks that have been tampered with unless the tampering affects the housekeeping data. To increase the chances of detecting altered blocks, the housekeeping data can be enciphered as part of the message block. The use of a cipher with a high propagation of error assures, in most cases, that the alteration of any part of a cryptogram will cause errors in the housekeeping information when the message is decrypted. Thus, the use of message block identification and a high propagation of error cipher can be used to detect message blocks that have been altered or are out of order with a probability determined by the number of housekeeping data bits used.

The ease with which a message block can be retransmitted depends on the method of key use. If a key list or pseudo-random number stream is used, the retransmission can use the next key in sequence. However, if the key is modified by the contents of the message, the receiver will not be able to update his key properly in order to obtain any further messages. In this case one of the four following methods must be used by the sender:

1. the key must not be updated until there is no chance that a retransmission will be required.
2. each key must be saved until there is no chance that it will be required in a retransmission.
3. a key transformation that is reversable must be used.
4. a buffering technique must be used so blocks need not be reenciphered.

[32]Paul Baran, "On Distributed Communications: IX. Security, Secrecy, and Tamper-Free Con-Considerations," Doc. RM-3765-PR, RAND Corp., Santa Monica, Calif. (August 1964), pp. 22–23.

Each of these methods increases the storage and computational complexity of the enciphering process.

CRYPTOGRAPHY TO PROTECT FILES

The storage of data in a file for later retrieval is analogous to communications over a line with a time delay. Writing data in a file can be compared to sending a message, whereas reading data from a file is similar to receiving a message. The information in the file can be read any time after it has been placed in the file, but information in a communication system is usually received immediately after transmission. As most computer systems used for file manipulations are not considered secure (just as communication lines are not secure), cryptography can be used to protect the information in the files. The delay between writing and reading information from a file causes several characteristics and problems not encountered in a traditional communication system. These differences, which influence the choice of cryptographic technique and key-generation method, are the topic of this section.

One major difference between a file system and a communication system is the amount of data available to the cryptanalyst. In a communication system, a wiretapper has only one chance to intercept any message block. In a computer file system, he may be able to copy the entire file. Since it must be assumed that the penetrator will have the entire file at his disposal for analysis (comparable to a long sequence of message blocks), the method of key-generation and use is affected. For example, in a communication system, changing the key at frequent intervals means that the cryptanalyst will have a limited number of message blocks enciphered by using a particular key. In a computer file system, changing the key requires reenciphering the entire file with the new key, giving the cryptanalyst much more material with which to work since he will have the entire file rather than a few message blocks. The cryptanalyst's job is also easier if more than one copy of the same material enciphered with a different key can be obtained. Thus, a frequent key change loses some of the security advantages it enjoyed in a communication system.

In both computer file systems and communications systems, the Vigenére cipher with a large key does provide complete security for a file if the enemy does not know the key. In a file system the use of a pregenerated, completely random key requires a key file as long as the file that is to be enciphered. This is not only undesirable because of space required, but this key file must also be protected. If it is assumed that the penetrator can gain access to the data file, it must also be assumed that he can gain access to the key file. Thus, either a pseudo-random number string key or a key modified by the contents of each record must be used.

When sequential access to a file is used, the system is very close in form to a communication system with the exception of the time delay. When random access is required, the problem is much more difficult because many of the methods of key generation and use are unacceptable. For example, using a pseudo-random string as a key would require the generation of the string up to and including the portion used to encipher the requested record. Using a key modified by the contents of the file would require deciphering the file up to the requested record. For a random access enciphered file system to be practical, the key for an area of the file must be generated by using the address of the area. For a Vigenére cipher, it is convenient to use a record in the file as the basic unit and use the record number to generate the key for the record. For a SMS block cipher, the block number can be used to generate the key. The method by which a block or record number is used to generate the key is very sensitive because the numbers follow a rigid pattern. Unless the key generation is sufficiently complex, an analyst will be able to reproduce the key for each block. One possible key generation technique is to have a basic key for the file, use a SMS-type cipher to encrypt the record number using the file key, and use the result either as the record key or as an input to some key-generating mechanism. The SMS cipher is used because of its complexity and high work factor.

The fact that the file system acts as a time delay line creates difficulties for a file that has been enciphered by using a SMS cipher. The time delay between "sending" and "receiving" the data negates the possibility of retransmission of a block if an error is detected. Since the SMS cipher has a high propagation of error, a single-bit error in a record can turn the entire record into garbage. Unless adequate steps are taken, the data in the record will be irrecoverable. First, a backup of the data, perhaps on tape, can be stored in an area that is physically secured. This method is not acceptable for a file that is heavily used; rather, a scheme for error detection and correction is used. The high propagation of error in the SMS cipher aids in error detection, and a suitable error-correction code allows the original record to be recovered if the number of bits in error is not too high.

Random access files that are constantly being updated present another problem. Since the key for each record must be calculated from the record number, a cryptanalyst can monitor a record as it changes and obtain several copies of the same record that have been encrypted by using the same key. This is a very dangerous situation. To minimize this problem, the file can be reencrypted at suitable intervals with a new key.

The choice of cryptographic method is only part of the problem facing a software engineer attempting to use ciphers. Some of the other considerations of cryptography will now be presented.

6.5.3 DISCIPLINE

The utilization of any cryptographic system must be accompanied by tight discipline in the design, implementation, and usage of that system. As previously discussed, the design must account for not only the normal noise on a transmission line, but also for deliberate sabotage attempts. This includes detection of intercepted, forged, or tampered message blocks and the ability to recover from these conditions. The enciphering process should not be meshed into the design of the system; rather, it should be a relatively independent section. The proper control of a cryptographic process is difficult enough without adding the complexity of a high degree of interaction with other portions of the system.

An undisciplined system that uses cryptography can rapidly lead to chaos. The key for each file must be carefully recorded and stored; if the key is lost, the user is no better off than the person from whom he is trying to protect the file. If the keys for a file are changed frequently, an audit trail must be maintained so that the file can be reconstructed. Above all, the use of the keys must be regulated and the keys protected. An extremely complex cryptographic program will be of little value if an enemy analyst can walk into an office and obtain a copy of the key from the top of a desk or from an unlocked file cabinet. As in all other forms of security, a penetrator will find and exploit the weakest link in a cryptographic system.

6.5.4 CRYPTOGRAPHIC DESIGN PRINCIPLES

This section presents some basic principles for the software engineer to follow in designing and using a cryptographic system. The importance of each principle depends on both the cryptographic technique selected and the type of system in which it is implemented. The intent here is to provide an idea of some of the major considerations for computer cryptography; a reader attempting to design a cryptographic system is referred to the references on cryptography for a more detailed analysis.

The first assumption that a software engineer must make is that the cryptanalyst will be able to discover which cryptographic technique will be used; he may be able to steal the program or to bribe to obtain knowledge of the exact method used. Therefore, any fixed algorithm (one without a variable key) should not be used. The programs should be written so that they can be easily altered if security is compromised. For example, the period of transposition that is part of a SMS cipher can be in a data statement so that it is easily modified, or the pseudo-random number generator can be altered, or the seed values in the key-generation routine can be changed. Even if easy modification of the program is provided, the security of the system must not depend on the secrecy of the program.

The system should be designed so that the key can be easily changed. If the process of changing a key is too difficult, users will tend to use the same key for too long. This would give a cryptanalyst a longer period of time to discover and employ the key to decipher subsequent cryptograms. The key should be changed at a frequency that will, on the average, not give the analyst enough time to be able to discover the key even though he will probably know the cryptographic technique used and will have high-speed computers at his disposal. In order to increase the useful life of a key, it should be complex enough so that it cannot be discovered with trial and error methods by using fast computers. The key should be carefully chosen, as letter or number combinations such as a person's name or birth date can be guessed easily. To be safe, one should select the keys that are generated by some random process or a good pseudo-random process.

Whenever possible, each individual in the system should be given only the minimum requirements necessary to perform his duties. For example, a user can be given the key, but it should be difficult for him to obtain copies of the encryption-decryption routines. This will prevent the user from executing these routines outside the normal system security. Conversely, a programmer who has access to the routines should not be given the key for any files. The system security should not depend on the separation of access to the keys and cryptographic routines, but the cost of obtaining both a key and a deciphering routine can be raised.

A cryptanalyst should be given as little material as possible with which to work. The software engineer should not use the system random-number generator in the cryptographic system. If an unusual generator is used, the analyst will have a much harder time characterizing the results of the generator. As many of the English language statistics should be deleted as possible. This removal can be accomplished by using codes in place of English words, substituting random characters in place of blank fields, or using a good mixing cipher. Avoidance of enciphering and transmitting messages is necessary when the cryptanalyst can guess the meaning of the message unless the information is of little value, and the key is subsequently discarded. Transmittal or storage of nonessential data or characters, such as record numbers, end of record, or end of transmission characters in the clear, is also a safeguard against a penetrator. If the information to be enciphered has a long, profitable life span, a complex enciphering technique and once-only key should be used and, as an additional protective measure, the file should then be locked in a safe.

A cryptanalyst should not be able to obtain a portion of a message in both enciphered and clear form; since the analyst will know the method used to encipher the message and will be aided by computers, the work factor of the cryptographic system will be reduced. A file that has been enciphered should never be made available in the clear, even in part. Likewise, a file that may have been partially compromised must never be encrypted. If an analyst can obtain samples of text in both enciphered and clear form, the system should be designed so that the key cannot be discovered in time to apply that knowledge.

Any cryptographic system must be designed to account for active wiretappers. The system must be able to detect falsified messages or messages with which someone has tampered, and must be able to recover from such sabotage. The cryptographic technique and retransmission methodology must be resistant to line errors introduced by a cryptanalyst for the purpose of observing specific messages or repeated messages.

Last, but not least, anyone designing a cryptographic system must be aware of the methods used by cryptanalysts. Many algorithms might appear to be secure to the uninitiated when in reality they can be broken easily by a cryptanalyst. The reader may refer to Kahn[33] and Wolfe[34] regarding the basics of cryptanalysis. Shannon[35] also presents some ideas on making a cryptographic system theoretically secure, regardless of the methods used by a cryptanalyst. The software engineer may also take advantage of hardware and software cryptographic methods devised by those experienced in cryptography; these methods are the topics of the next sections.

6.5.5 HARDWARE CRYPTOGRAPHY

The most effective method of implementing cryptography in a communications line would be with a hardware cryptographic device. Hardware is much faster for complex cryptographic methods and cannot be tampered with by systems program-

[33]David Kahn, *The Codebreakers* (New York: The Macmillan Company, 1967).
[34]J. M. Wolfe, *A First Course in Cryptanalysis*, 3 vols. (Brooklyn, N.Y.: Brooklyn College Press, 1943).
[35]C. E. Shannon, "Communication Theory of Secrecy Systems," pp. 656–715.

mers. One example of hardware cryptography is the IBM Lucifer system.[36] Although Lucifer works only for terminal-to-computer communication, it illustrates some of the possibilities of a hardware crytpography system.

The key in the Lucifer system is a 128-bit string that is input into the hardware by either a magnetic stripe card or a 16-byte read-only memory device that is plugged into the Lucifer hardware. In the first case, user identification precedes any enciphered data transmission so that the computer can select the proper key from its files. Lucifer has the capability of sending both clear text and enciphered text so the initial identification exchange is possible. In the second case, using a read-only memory device, the terminal always uses the same key, so the computer inspects the terminal identification to select the corresponding key.

The Lucifer system takes advantage of hardware speed to facilitate the use of a complex cipher of the SMS type. The message is split into 128-bit blocks and processed one block at a time. The enciphering process consists of 16 rounds, with an interchange of the two halves of the block between each round. The first step in each round is the performance of one of two nonlinear transmformations on each of the 8 bytes in the top half of the block. Eight of the key bits (one for each byte) determine which of the transformations is chosen. The top half of the block is then added, modulo 2, to an equivalent length of the key and the result scrambled. The two halves of the message are then added, again modulo 2. Each round takes different portions of the key. The number of rounds in the encryption adds to the strength of the system.

Although the Lucifer system employs a single key for what could be a long period of time, it is still considered to be a very secure system. An SMS cipher raises the work factor to a very high level, making it impractical to attempt to discover the key even if samples of clear and encoded material are available. A single key eliminates the difficulties encountered in systems where a synchronized key list exists.

6.5.6 CRYPTOGRAPHY PROGRAMS

Cryptography routines can give a high level of security to computer files and communications, but only if they are used properly. This is not to say they will provide complete security, but then neither does a bank vault. If the cryptography routine is carefully chosen and adequate procedural techniques are followed as discussed under Cryptographic Design Procedures, a penetrator will find it impractical to cryptanalyze the protected files rather than steal the enciphering routine and key.

Figure 6-11 is an example of a FORTRAN routine enciphered by using a simple substitution and an alphabet of only the characters that are allowed in FORTRAN. There is sufficient material so that the reader should be able to solve the cryptogram easily, especially given the rigid syntax of FORTRAN routines. Figure 6-12 shows the same routine, again enciphered with simple substitution, but this time using the full EBCDIC character set. Even though the second cryptogram cannot be solved precisely because of the nonprintable characters, it still is not secure because a penetrator can obtain a dump of the enciphered routine and use two-digit hexadecimal numbers as characters. Simple substitution simply will not provide adequate protection in a hostile environment.

[36]*IBM Research Reports,* **7,** 4 (1971). Published by IBM Research, Yorktown Heights, N.Y.

```
000000C+*UN+8Z-  0*CNU806JT-3000000000000000000000000000000000000000000000000
Y0UJJJJ0JJJ00JJJ0JJJ0JJJJJ0JJJJJJJJJ0JJJ000JJJ00JJJJ0JJJJJJJJJ0J0JJJ00JJJJJJJ00J
Y0U000UL000U000000008FZCOUN+8Z-  04ZVV0CNU808F 07ZUC80-0 V M -8C0N7000000000000
Y0CJ000U00U0UUUUU00JU*Q07Z-wZ-.08F 0MZ-ZM+M0 V M -80N70J0C+*D Y8N0000000000J0J0J
Y0JJJJJJJ000J00 JJUJJJ670NMJZ08N0-3T0UVJYZ-.08F 0MZ-ZM+M0 V M M80Z-08F 0000000000
Y0U000UL0UU0U0000000Z8FU V M -80N70JT08F -0U U J8Z-.08F 0UUNY CC04Z8F000000000000
Y0000UCUUU0U000000008F 0C+*D Y8N0J70NMJZ21J8NJ-0+-8ZV08F 0 -8ZU 0J00JQ0JJ0JJ000JJ
Y0U000U0000U0UUUU00UZCUCNC8 wH08F 0JUUJQ04ZVV08F -0* 0U0Z-8 WH0000000000000000000
Y0UUJCCUUU0U0U00U00U00U000U0000U000U0000U00000000000000000000000000000000000000
0J0000wZM -C2N-0J6-300JJ0J0JJ0JJJ0JJ0JJJ0000JJJJJJJJ0JJ00JJJ0000000000000000000
Y0UUU000U000U0U0000UC8JU6UVNNUON-0C+*D Y8NUC000000000000000J0JJJ0000JJJ00000JJJJ
Y0JJJJJJJ000UU0U00000000000000000000000000000000000000000000000000000J00JJJJJJJJ
000UU0--0KU-0S010000000000000000000000000000000000000000000000000000000000000000
00000JwN0J$$0Z0KJ1T-- JJJJJJJJ0000000000000000000000000000000000000000JJ00JJJJ00J
Y0UUU0000U0U0U0U0U00000000000000000000000000000000000000000000000000000000000000
Y0UU000000U0UUU0U00UZ-Z8ZJVZ, 0MZ-00JV+ 0UNZ-8 0U8N07Z0C80 V M -80000000000000000
Y0JJJ0JJJJ00JJ00JJJJZ-0C+*D Y8NU0000JJ00JJJ00JJJ0000000000000000000000000000000000
Y0C000000U00000U0U0U0000000000000000000000000JJJJJJJJJJ0JJ0J00JJJJ0JJJJJJJJJJJJJ0
00U0J00UMZ-0KUZ00000U000U0000000000000000000000JJJJ0JJ0JJ0J00JJ00JJ0JJJJJ0J0J0J0J
Y0UU000000000U0U000000000000000000000000000000000000000000000000000000000000000
Y 00U0J000J03U000000VNNU06N07Z-w0CMJVV C80UJV+ 0Z-0C+*D Y8N0000000000000000000000
Y0JJJ0JJJ0JJ0JJJ0000JJJJ00JJJJJJJJJJJJJJJJ0 JJJ00JJJ00JJJJJJJJJJJJJJJJ0JJJJJJJJJJ0
00000000JZZ0K0Z02010000000000000000000000000000000000000000000000000000000000000
00U0JJ00UwN0A$UM0K0ZZT-U0000000000000000000000000000000000000000000000000000000
0JJJJJJJJ00JZ70UJ6MZ-3H.8HJ6M330MZ-0K JM0J0U000000000000000000000000000000000000000
0U0A$0YN-8Z-+  U0U0C00000000000U0U00000000J0JJJ0JJJJ0JJJ0JJJJJJJ0JJ00JJ0JJJJJJJJ0
Y0UUC00U0U0U0UU0JU0U+80CMJVV CU0 V M -80Z-07Z0C80 V M -80N708F 0C+*D Y8N0000000000
Y0U0000000U000000000000000000000000000000000000000000000000000000000000000000000
0J0JJJ0008 MU0KJJ6Z3JJ000J0J0JJJ0000 JJJJJJJJJJJJJJ0JJJJ0J0JJJ0JJJ0JJJ0JJJJJJJ0000
000000000J6Z30UK0J6MZ-3000000000000000000000000000000000000000000000000000000000
00U0U000J6MZ-30K08 MU0000000000000000000000000000U00000000000000000000000U00000J
00J1$$0YN-8Z-+ J00J00JJ0JJJJJJ0000000000000000000000000000000000000000000000000
Y0UU0J0000U000000000000000000000000000000000000000000000000000000000000000000000
Y0U0J0000U00000000UUZ-8U8F 0CNU8 WUJ00JQT07ZD U V M -8C0U 0JVZ- 000JJJJJJ0J0J0J00
Y0U000000U0U0U000U00000000000000000000000000000000000000000000000000000000000000
C0000040Z8 06/T1A$306J6Z3TZK1T-30000000000000000000000000000000000000000000000000
00J1A$J7N0MJ806 1F0TA )$H1$3J0000JJJ00JJJ0J0J0J0JJJJJ00000JJJJ0J0J0J00J0000000000
00000U0 8+0-00000000000000000000000000000000000000000000000000000000000000000000
000000 -w0000000000000000000000000000000000000000000000000000000000JJJ0J00J0J00J
```

Fig. 6-11   FORTRAN program enciphered using simple substitution

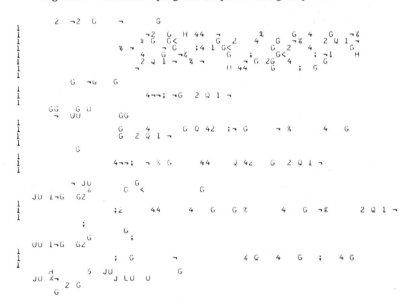

Fig. 6-12   **FORTRAN** program enciphered using simple substitution with unprintable characters

Figure 6-13 presents the enciphering and deciphering routines given by Martin.[37] These routines are adequate for many commercial purposes—provided the key and seed values are changed frequently.

---

[37]James Martin, *Security, Accuracy, and Privacy in Computer Systems,* © 1973, pp. 458–459. Reprinted by permission of Prentice-Hall, Inc., Englewood Cliffs, New Jersey.

```
(NOFIXEDOVERFLOW):LPC:PROC OPTIONS(MAIN);
ON ENDFILE (SYSIN) GO TO FIN;
DCL (S1,S2,S3) FIXED BINARY(31,0);
DCL (R) BINARY FLOAT (21);
DCL (TEXT,MESS,ALPH,KEY) CHAR(48);
DCL (ENCODE,DECODE)(48,48) CHAR(2);
DCL L(2);
DCL N(48,48);
DCL X(48,48,2) FIXED BINARY;
/** SET UP ENCIPHERING TABLES *************************************/
S1=23518967;
S2=50173031;
S3=72735419;
KEY=
'NY+BTGV FCED18WS:)X564AQZ,.-OLOPIKJM=U97322"(;HR';
ALPH=
'ABCDEFGHIJKLMNOPQRSTUVWXY71234567840-.,)(:;"=+ ?';
DO I=1 TO 48;
    N(I,*)=INDEX(KEY,SUBSTR(ALPH,I,1));
    DO J=1 TO 48;
        X(I,J,1)=I;
        X(I,J,2)=MOD((I+J),48)+1;
    END;
END;
DO K=1 TO 48;
    DO I=1 TO 48;
        R=MOD(S1,66103)/66103;
        S1=S1+312754**(R+1);
        J=CEIL(R*48);
        N1=N(J,K);
        N(J,K)=N(I,K);
        N(I,K)=N1;
        J=CEIL(MOD(S2,73937)/1541.1);
        S2=S2+J*121767;
        L=X(J,K,*);
        X(J,K,*)=X(I,K,*);
        X(I,K,*)=L;
    END;
END;
DO K=1 TO 48;
    DO I=1 TO 48;
        J=CEIL(MOD(S3,38692)/806.1);
        S3=S3+J*512778;
        L=X(K,J,*);
        X(K,J,*)=X(K,I,*);
        X(K,I,*)=L;
    END;
END;
DO I=1 TO 48;
    DO J=1 TO 48;
        ENCODE(I,J)=SUBSTR(KEY,X(I,J,1),1)||SUBSTR(KEY,X(I,J,2),1);
        DECODE(X(I,J,1),X(I,J,2))=SUBSTR(ALPH,I,1)||SUBSTR(ALPH,J,1);
    END;
END;
/** DECIPHERING ROUTINE *********************************************/
A1:DO M=1 TO 48;
    GET EDIT (MESS)(A(48));
    DO K=1 TO 48 BY 2;
        I=INDEX(KEY,SUBSTR(MESS,K,1));
        J=INDEX(KEY,SUBSTR(MESS,K+1,1));
        SUBSTR(TEXT,N(K  ,M),1)=SUBSTR(DECODE(I,J),1,1);
        SUBSTR(TEXT,N(K+1,M),1)=SUBSTR(DECODE(I,J),2,1);
    END;
    PUT SKIP EDIT (TEXT)(A(48));
END;
GO TO A1;
FIN:END LPC;
```

Fig. 6-13 Relatively secure enciphering and deciphering routines.[37] The enciphering routine performs bigram substitution on non-adjacent characters. The seed values for the random number generators, or the random number generators themselves, can be modified in addition to changing the key.

The National Bureau of Standards has proposed a standard encryption and decryption method for federal use, which is similar to the LUCIFER method. The major differences are a 64-bit block size and the exact encryption methods used within the 15 iterations on each block. The algorithm is designed so that the key is adequate for a considerable period of time or for an entire file.[38]

Several interesting and beneficial side effects occur from the application of cryptography in a computer systems. In a computer communications network, it protects the data that is transmitted; in addition, it can provide for a method of sabotage and error detection. In an interactive computer system, cryptography can furnish a method

[38] *Computerworld* (Boston), June 7, 1976, pp. 6–9.

```
(NOFIXEDOVERFLOW):LPC:PROC OPTIONS(MAIN);
ON ENDFILE (SYSIN) GO TO FIN;
DCL (S1,S2,S3) FIXED BINARY(31,0);
DCL (R) BINARY FLOAT (21);
DCL (TEXT,MESS,ALPH,KEY) CHAR(48);
DCL (ENCODE,DECODE)(48,48) CHAR(2);
DCL L(2);
DCL N(48,48);
DCL X(48,48,2) FIXED BINARY;
/** SET UP ENCIPHERING TABLES ************************************/
  S1=23518967;
  S2=50173031;
  S3=72735419;
KEY=
'NY+BTGV FCED18WS:)X564AQZ,.-OLOPIKJM=U97322?"(;HR';
ALPH=
'ABCDEFGHIJKLMNOPQRSTUVWXYZ1234567890-.,)(:;"=+ ?';
  DO I=1 TO 48;
    N(I,*)=INDEX(KEY,SUBSTR(ALPH,I,1));
    DO J=1 TO 48;
      X(I,J,1)=I;
      X(I,J,2)=MOD((I+J),48)+1;
    END;
  END;
  DO K=1 TO 48;
    DO I=1 TO 48;
      R=MOD(S1,66103)/66103;
      S1=S1+312754**(R+1);
      J=CEIL(R*48);
      N1=N(J,K);
      N(J,K)=N(I,K);
      N(I,K)=N1;
      J=CEIL(MOD(S2,73937)/1541.1);
      S2=S2+J*121767;
      L=X(J,K,*);
      X(J,K,*)=X(I,K,*);
      X(I,K,*)=L;
    END;
  END;
  DO K=1 TO 48;
    DO I=1 TO 48;
      J=CEIL(MOD(S3,38692)/806.1);
      S3=S3+J*512778;
      L=X(K,J,*);
      X(K,J,*)=X(K,I,*);
      X(K,I,*)=L;
    END;
  END;
  DO I=1 TO 48;
    DO J=1 TO 48;
      ENCODE(I,J)=SUBSTR(KEY,X(I,J,1),1)||SUBSTR(KEY,X(I,J,2),1);
      DECODE(X(I,J,1),X(I,J,2))=SUBSTR(ALPH,I,1)||SUBSTR(ALPH,J,1);
    END;
  END;
/** ENCIPHERING ROUTINE *****************************************/
A1:DO M=1 TO 48;
    GET EDIT (TEXT)(A(48));
    DO K=1 TO 48 BY 2;
      I=INDEX(ALPH,SUBSTR(TEXT,N(K,M),1));
      J=INDEX(ALPH,SUBSTR(TEXT,N(K+1,M),1));
      SUBSTR(MESS,K,2)=ENCODE(I,J);
    END;
    PUT EDIT (MESS)(SKIP,A(48));
  END;
  GO TO A1;
FIN:END LPC;
```

Fig. 6-13 (*cont'd.*) Relatively secure enciphering and deciphering routines.[37] The enciphering routine performs bigram substitution on non-adjacent characters. The seed values for the random number generators, or the random number generators themselves, can be modified addition to changing the key.

of user authentication that does not require the transmission of sensitive data, such as a password, over insecure data lines. It can also supply a mechanism to prevent the accidental disclosure of any information that is stored in the computer. Cryptography may also be more traditionally used to protect tapes, disk packs, or even card decks when they are sent by messenger or mail.

Cryptographic techniques lend themselves well to computer applications. The highly repetitive operations and rigid rules required are generally easy to implement. In fact, the use of computers to encrypt data allows the implementation of cryptographic systems that are too complex or too bulky to work with by hand. Unfortunately, these same computer capabilities are available to persons attempting to decrypt the cryptogram without the advantage of having the key.

Cryptography protects files and communications that may be intercepted by unauthorized personnel. Similarly, confinement, the next topic for discussion, is a technique to prevent disclosures that can be applied to routines which are suspected of leaking information.

6.6
Confinement

The prevention of unauthorized information disclosure or leakage from an untrusted routine is called confinement.[39] Virtually every software engineer will eventually be faced with the problem of using a routine (written by someone else) that may be considered untrustworthy. If the program simply operates incorrectly, the software engineer can accummulate evidence of the error through adequate testing. This section is concerned with techniques for confining the routine to prevent the routine from leaking information to a penetrator by blocking the information paths out of the routine.

6.6.1 DATA LEAKAGE PATHS

A routine can leak in several ways through the storage facilities of the computer system. The most obvious leak is placing the information in a permanent file that is owned by the penetrator. The penetrator can read the file to obtain the data whenever convenient. If the routine places the data in a temporary file, the penetrator must work a little harder to obtain the information. One must test to see if the temporary file is present and, if it is, read the data before the temporary file is deleted. Tests for the presence of the file must be performed at a frequency that will ensure detection of the file even though its lifespan may be very short. Finally, the routine can store data internally and return the data to the penetrator when the routine is called.

The routine can leak information to a penetrator through the normal communication channels. The leakage can be overt, as when the routine sends an unauthorized message to the penetrator, or covert, as when the routine hides information in an authorized message. A prime example of a covert data path is in the bill for services rendered by a proprietary routine. The algorithm that computes the bill will reside within the proprietary routine and can examine any data available to the routine. In the case of a proprietary routine that performs accounting, the billing algorithm may have access to sensitive information about the financial status of the company using the routine, and will have the capability of determining whether the penetrator should purchase or sell the company's stock. The decision made by the billing algorithm can be passed to the penetrator by a minor change in the bill format (i.e., by either abbreviating or spelling out a word in the bill). Sensitive information can also be encoded

---

[39]Butler W. Lampson, "A Note on the Confinement Problem," *Communications of the ACM*, **16**, 10 (October 1973), 613.

into the least significant digits in the bill by replacing the last two digits in each entry of an itemized bill with special codes containing the message.

The final form of leakage occurs through paths not normally used for information transfer. These paths can be very subtle and ingenuous, and are difficult to characterize. For example, if the penetrator is in a position that allows him to see the tape drives, he can have the routine encode the data into tape accesses. The routine requests two tapes, designating one as a timing device and the other to send the data. A write on the timing tape indicates a bit is about to be sent. If the bit is a one, the second tape is written; otherwise it is not written. Then the timing tape is written again, signifying another bit is about to be sent. It is obvious that this data path will be slow and prone to errors, but it is a data path. However, the intelligent penetrator who has devised this scheme will immediately look for a way to automate the procedure. The file system in most computer systems provides a base for such an automation, as described by Lampson.[40] Usually the file system will not allow concurrent access to a file if one user is writing the file, and the other users of the system have the ability to test the status of a file to see if it is currently available for use. Thus, two routines who have access to the same file share a Boolean-type variable that can be used to transmit a bit stream. Actually, three files are required—one to signify that the bit has been sent, one to represent the data, and one to signify that the bit has been received. The following sequence of operations describes how a routine can covertly send information to a penetrator:

1. The routine either opens the data bit file to signify a 1 or closes the data bit file to signify 0. Then the sent bit file is opened to signal the penetrator that a bit has been sent.
2. The penetrator must wait until an attempt to open the sent bit file fails, then he attempts to open the data bit file. If he can open the file, the data bit is interpreted as a 0; if he cannot open the file, the data bit is a 1. After he interprets the data bit file, he opens the received bit file.
3. The routine waits until an attempt to open the received bit file fails, signifying that the penetrator has recorded the value of the data bit. He then closes the sent bit file.
4. The penetrator waits for the sent bit file to be closed and then closes the received bit file.
5. The routine waits for the received bit file to be closed and then initiates transmission of the next bit.

This example appears somewhat contrived. Since the routine and the penetrator share files, it would be easier for the routine to write the information into one of the files and let the penetrator read data from that file. However, the user of the routine that is sending the information may be suspicious of the routine and check its activities. In that case it would be dangerous to have the routine write any sensitive information into a shared file because the user of the routine may detect the presence of the sensitive information in the file. The penetrator may prefer a slow but steady flow

[40]Ibid. p. 614.

of information rather than chance being detected. This technique also works for data base files that are not normally written. The user of the routine may periodically compare the data file used by the routine with a copy, to ensure that no data is being written into the file. The user would eventually detect the use of the file to transfer data, but the user would not detect the opening of a file for a write if the write is never performed. Thus, the sharing of files, even though no data is written in the files, can be used to transfer information between the routine and a penetrator with little chance of detection.

In general, the use of paths not normally used for data transmission is implemented by having the receiver observe the impact on the system made by the sending routine's requests for service. Some of the data channels will be very noisy, such as varying the paging rate of the routine as suggested by Lampson,[41] but error detection and correction codes can be used to improve the accuracy of the communication channel. The main point is that the routine sending the information demands a service from the system, and the owner of the routine can detect the impact of a request.

6.6.2 CONFINEMENT RULES

The main security idea behind confinement is to enumerate the number and extent of the data paths and then block the paths that the software engineer believes the penetrator will exploit. The confinement of only the suspect routine may not be adequate as the routine may call other routines that may leak information. All of the routines that are called by the suspect routine must be classified as secure or untrustworthy, and all untrustworthy routines must be confined. The supervisor should be included in this process, even though it is not possible to confine the supervisor. Once the set of routines that must be confined is determined, the software engineer can proceed to confine the set by blocking the data paths.

First, a confined routine must not share any file with any routine that is not also confined. This will block both direct transfer of information through the file and use of the fact that the file is open or closed to transfer information. Therefore, the routine must be able to utilize only the files designated by the user, and the system must be able to adequately protect these files. The writer of the routine may object to the use of files specified by the user because the information placed in the files by the routine may be of a proprietary nature. The user of the routine and the writer of the routine must together determine a scheme that is satisfactory to the protection requirements of both.

The problem of the routine that stores information internally can be solved in two ways. The easiest is for the user to demand an exclusive copy of the routine. This copy can be protected so that the writer cannot execute it. Then even if the routine does store information, it is inaccessible to the writer of the routine. A solution that is more difficult to enforce is requiring that the routine have no place to store the information so that it will not be destroyed when the routine is exited. Many proprietary routines are delivered without an associated program listing, and it is difficult to determine if the storage is present.

Normal communications channels, such as interprocess communications, are

[41]Ibid. p. 614.

generally harder to detect and block. One notable exception to this is the subroutine call mechanism. The disclosure of information through a subroutine call is precluded because the software engineer will confine all untrustworthy routines that may be called. Other channels, however, are not so simple. The software engineer can prohibit the use of any interprocess communication if the routine will still function under such conditions. Again, it may be difficult to determine if the routine will use the interprocess communication capabilities, depending on the operating system design. An alternative would be to periodically monitor the messages sent by the routine.

Messages hidden in legitimate communications between the routine and its writer may be very difficult to discover without the aid of an expert in cryptography. The format, content, and frequency of such messages should be limited. For example, the bill for the services of a routine should follow a single format. The contents of the bill should be summarized whenever possible; a single total would be better than an itemized list. The bill could be stored by a trusted intermediary, and only the monthly totals given to the two involved parties. The routine may still be able to pass data to its writer through the bill, but the transmission rate will be much lower.

Information transfer through channels not normally employed for data transfer (covert channels) usually involves the impact of a routine on the system and, thus, involves the supervisor. According to the strict rules of confinement, since the routine to be confined utilizes the supervisor, the supervisor should be either confined or trusted. Since confinement of the supervisor is not possible, it must be trusted. In this, as in other security considerations involving the supervisor, the software engineer is usually given little choice; he is limited to the capabilities of whatever supervisors are available.

If the supervisor is properly designed, it can block the covert channels or at least severely limit the data transfer rate. For example, data transfer that uses tape drives as a semaphore can be blocked if the supervisor does not always perform the physical write when the request is made. The supervisor can save physical blocks independently for each tape drive and then perform the write when a random number of blocks have been saved. The supervisor is effectively adding enough noise to the transmission line to completely block it. Using disk files as semaphores can be prevented if the supervisor makes a copy of the file for the confined program whenever a routine outside of the confined system attempts to write on the file. The supervisor either adds noise to the transmission or provides an environment in which a routine outside of the confined system cannot detect changes brought about by routines inside of the confined system. Completely blocking all channels, even if they could be enumerated, would probably be prohibitively expensive; but the data rate of many of the channels may be low enough to ignore.

When trying to confine a routine, the software engineer must worry about storage, legitimate data channels, channels not intended for data transfer, and other routines that might be called by the suspect routine. It appears to be possible to completely confine a routine, but this is costly, and not all routines can operate properly when completely confined. With suitable restrictions to the operations of a confined routine and some help from the supervisor, many routines may be suitably confined even though not all data paths are blocked. The discussion now turns to how a software engineer can raise the security of routines that he writes.

6.7

User Programmable Security Techniques

The software engineer is faced with two major security problems: the protection of the representations of his files and programs, and the generation of secure programs. This section is concerned only with the latter problem; the file and program representations can be protected only by the operating system (or by cryptography). There are two facets to the generation of a secure program: frustration of penetration attempts and enforcement of access restrictions not supported by the operating system.

6.7.1 PREVENTION OF PENETRATION ATTEMPTS

Penetration can be prevented either by blocking the penetration routes or by using a scheme that deters a possible penetrator's exploitation of an existing penetration route. The methods to be discussed in this section are applications of authentication, threat detection and recording, and auditing.

A routine may have to perform its own authentication either if the operating system does not perform authentication or if the authentication performed by the system is inadequate for the security requirements of the routine. If the routine must completely authenticate a user, the authentication schemes previously described (e.g., password authentication) can be employed. The routine's augmentation to the system's authentication can include checking such information as the user's location or the time of day in order to enforce user-context access restrictions. In general, the routine must depend on the system to provide this additional information; if the system is not reliable in this respect, user context access restrictions cannot be enforced.

One simple form of password protection that may prevent unauthorized use of an otherwise unprotected routine is the placing of a single password in the routine in a data statement, using unprintable characters so a program listing will not give the password away. In a routine that uses card input, the field, which should contain the password, can be hidden among other fields on one of the first data cards. A further complication is to name the password in the routine BLANK. Then the comparison of the input password and the stored password appears to be an input consistency check, especially because of the unprintable characters used in the initialization of BLANK. This simple scheme will block a casual browser, but a determined penetrator would probably not be stopped for long; the major flaw is that the scheme depends on the secrecy of the scheme itself, not on the secrecy of the password.

Threat detection and recording is an important tool for preventing unauthorized use of a routine. In this technique, the routine makes a record of any suspicious activity or terminates execution if such activity is detected. For example, if a user repeatedly fails authentication attempts, he may be a penetrator trying random passwords. A second form of threat detection is to perform consistency checks to assure that input data and/or internal variables are within appropriate ranges. An adequate set of threat detection checks severely limits the ability of a penetrator to use a routine fraudulently. If the threat detection capabilities of a system are kept relatively secret, a penetrator may not be as careful and may blunder into one of the detection mechanisms. Conversely, if it is widely known that the system is capable of detecting threats, the penetrator may possibly decide that the risks outweigh the benefits and leave the system alone.

The presence of adequate auditing procedures also serves as a deterrent to penetrators because the information stored for an audit trail may, at a later date, pinpoint the user responsible for fraudulent activity. A penetrator will be much less likely to use trial and error methods to obtain information from or modify a data base if he knows that an erroneous transaction will probably be recorded.

The software engineer should work closely with an auditor during the design of any program that is part of a system that must be audited. To help prevent computer fraud, the program should be designed to output data for normal auditing procedures and for any special audits that may be requested by the management of the firm using the program.

6.7.2 ACCESS RESTRICTION ENFORCEMENT

The software engineer must enforce access restrictions that are not performed by the operating system. In general, the operating system restricts access to files or routines; the routine itself must restrict access to records within the file or fields within the record. A routine that retrieves data from a data bank can be procedural (a special procedure is written to satisfy a particular request) or nonprocedural (the user is given a list of operations implemented by the routine and can request any of the operations). Again, an adequate authentication mechanism is required in order to apply the access restrictions properly.

The easiest way to implement access to a data bank, at least for security purposes, is to use nonprocedural techniques; the user gives a checklist of operations he wants performed to the routine. The data bank routine interprets this checklist and returns the results to the user if there are no security violations. The difference between data-dependent and data-independent access restrictions can be seen easily in this system. The data-independent restrictions can be implemented when the routine initially scans the checklist. A user either has access to a particular field or he does not; therefore, any request can be rejected immediately if access rights are violated. A data-dependent access restriction is performed as the request is processed. Although the nonprocedural technique restricts the user to a limited number of operations, such a system can support very complex requests if properly designed. For example, one of the operations on the checklist could be LIST. The data bank can then ask for amplifying information and discover that the user wants to list all of the records in the inventory file with a particular set of characteristics.

A nonprocedural data retrieval system is inadequate for some forms of access. There may be a particular request that does not match the checklist because the user is not provided with a large enough vocabulary. There may be a particular request that is made at a high frequency, and the overhead of the nonprocedural system may be too high. It may be necessary to perform processing on each record as it is retrieved from the data base, and there may be no convenient interface between the data retrieval system and the routine to do the processing. For these purposes, a procedural data retrieval system provides the needed capabilities as well as additional security difficulties. Basically, a new routine is written or an older routine is modified to fulfill a request.

The most secure form of procedural access to a data base is to have the custodian of the data base write each routine. Since he is responsible for the security of the data base, and is in fact part of the secured system, the security of the system is more likely to be maintained. If the system is very busy, this may put an unreasonable burden on the custodian, or the data retrieval system may become cluttered with routines, some with only slight differences.

In order to reduce the burden on the custodian and the retrieval system, it may be necessary to allow users to write their own retrieval routines. This situation is very unhealthy for security unless very rigid rules can be imposed. One way to provide security and still allow users to access the data base directly is to control the access paths to the data and give each user the rights to use only certain access paths. For example, the information about the patients of a doctor can be organized as shown in Figure 6-14. The names of the patients go into one file; the data about the patients

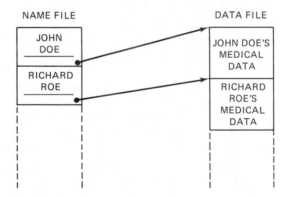

Fig. 6-14 Protection through access path control

goes into the second file. The doctor can access the name file that has links to the data file, and thus has the complete record for each patient. A researcher has access to the data group and can perform statistical analysis, but cannot correlate the data to a name because he does not have access rights to the name file. This application of the control of access paths provides a special form of protection—that of an individual's privacy. The privacy question will now be discussed in more detail.

6.8

Privacy

The question of privacy arises in any computer system that stores personal information about individuals; the software engineer must be aware of the legal responsibilities to the individuals who have information stored in a data bank. The legal responsibilities describe the lowest level of security permissible in any data retrieval system; sociological pressures may make a higher level of security desirable. The software engineer does not decide the legal and sociological questions; he must create a program that correctly implements the decisions that are made. This section discusses repositories of information about individuals (data banks), how individual privacy can be compromised, and how the compromise can be prevented.

6.8.1 DATA BANKS

There are two basic forms of data banks: a dossier data bank and a statistical data bank. A dossier data bank can return information that includes an individual's identification; it is very possible that the individual's privacy may be violated. In a dossier data bank, questions often concern characteristics about specific individuals, such as a request for the grades of a student. A statistical data bank returns only numbers and summaries; no identification of any individual is made. A researcher attempting to correlate aspects of a student's environment with achievement in school might ask: "What is the scholastic average of students in the data bank who:

- have divorced parents?
- live in an urban area?
- have at least 2 siblings?"

In a data bank security system, the software engineer must consider the worth of the information to the individual as well as the value of the information to the owner of the information (the owner of the data bank) and to the penetrator.[42] For example, an individual would be less likely to answer a questionnaire about drug abuse correctly, or at all, if he believes there is a chance that the authorities may eventually obtain the information. A lawsuit may result if an individual discovers that sensitive personal information placed in the data bank in strict confidence has been made public. Each of these is an additional cost factor that must be considered when the data bank is designed.

6.8.2 STATISTICAL ACCESS AND INFERENCE

At first glance, a statistical data bank appears to provide privacy as no individual's identification is provided in answer to any request. In reality, it is possible to obtain a dossier on an individual if the user knows enough background information about the individual by inferring facts from the results of several questions.[43] For example, suppose the user of a statistical data bank knows this about John Doe:

Sex: Male

Age: 25

[42]Rein Turn and Norman Z. Shapiro, "Privacy and Security in Databank Systems—Measures of Effectiveness, Costs, and Protector-Intruder Interactions," *AFIPS Conference Proceedings* (FJCC 1972), pp. 439–40.

[43]Lance J. Hoffman and W. F. Miller, "Getting a Personal Dossier From a Statistical Data Bank," *Datamation*, **16**, 5 (May 1970), 74.

$$
\begin{aligned}
\text{Marital Status:} &\quad \text{Single} \\
\text{Profession:} &\quad \text{Engineer} \\
\text{Degree:} &\quad \text{Master of Science} \\
\text{Residence:} &\quad \text{Newport Beach, CA}
\end{aligned}
$$

If a query to the data bank about the number of people with these characteristics returns the answer: "None," the user knows that there is no John Doe information in the data bank. If the answer is 57 (and the user knows beforehand that there is information about John Doe in the data bank), further information about Doe can be derived from the data bank. The user can ask for the number of individuals who have the characteristics of John Doe and add a single extra characteristic to each question. The additional characteristic may be, "and has not been convicted of a felony." If the answer is again 57, the user can conclude that John Doe has not been convicted of a felony. It is not possible to determine that he has been convicted of a felony unless all members of the data bank with his known characteristics have been convicted of a felony. If the answer to the initial question about John Doe's known characteristics is one (direct disclosure), the user has hit the jackpot; he can now check for the presence or absence of any characteristic about Doe listed in the data base. The user can ask for the number of individuals with Doe's characteristics, and then add a salary range. As soon as the user obtains an answer of 1 to this type of query, he has a basic range for Doe's salary and can perform a binary search to determine Doe's exact salary.

6.8.3 PRIVACY COMPROMISE PREVENTION

Prevention of privacy compromise in a statistical data bank can take two forms. In the first form, the data bank records all queries and then analyzes each new query to ascertain that the answer to the new query, when combined with all previous answers, does not constitute a privacy compromise. While this method eliminates the possibility of a compromise, it also reduces the utility of the data bank. For example, one user can be refused the answer to a query because of a series of queries asked by another user in another town six months before.

The second form of prevention of privacy compromise in a statistical data bank is simply a set of heuristic rules, each of which reduces the possibility of compromise. These rules are:

- One should not answer any query when fewer than three individuals are in the category specified by the query to avoid direct disclosure.
- One could add uncertainty to the data as it is placed in the data bank. For example, a random number (with known statistical properties) can be added to each individual's salary. Any statistical query about salaries will be correct if the sample size is large enough, but as the number of individuals in the query category decreases, the uncertainty of the response to the query will increase.
- One could add uncertainty into the answers from the data bank. For example, the answer to a query about the number of individuals with a particular characteristic can be rounded to the nearest ten, or the answer to a query about

the average salary of a group can be given as a range (say, $5,000 to $10,000) rather than as a single value.

Which of these rules will be used and how stringently they will be applied depends on the level of privacy required in the system and how the information in the data bank is to be used.

A dossier data bank may have an additional privacy problem; if information in the bank is extremely sensitive (such as drug abuse data), the individual may not want to have his name in the bank, creating difficulties if more information about the individual is to be added to the data bank periodically. This problem can be solved by giving each individual a code name or number as an identifier in the data bank. The individual can memorize his own code name and perhaps telephone in information; even the researcher may never know the name of any individual. Another alternative is to separate any identifying information into a new file, assign a unique number to each individual, and place this number with the information about the individual in both files. In extreme cases, a third file can be used to link the identified information to the data, and a third party used to ensure privacy. When a researcher wishes to add information to the data bank, he looks up the individual's identifier in his file and obtains a unique code for the individual. The researcher sends the code and the data to the third party, who looks up a number corresponding to the code in his link file, and sends the number and the data to the data bank. The data bank then files the data, using the number from the third party as an identifier.

The question of how much information about an individual can be released before privacy is breached must be decided by society; the software engineer enforces this decision. However, he or she may have to provide more stringent security to increase confidence in the data bank and ensure the individual's cooperation.

Thus it appears possible, given adequate operating system support, to create sophisticated protection schemes—ranging from the isolation of a process in a computer to the protection of individual privacy. The next section describes how the level of security of a protection scheme (or operating system) can be determined.

6.9

Security Measurement

Rating the level of security (certification) of any program or operating system is a subjective problem. It is not possible to give a system a rating on a scale from one to ten, as the level of security depends on the intended use of the system and the environment in which it will be placed. Thus, anyone rating the security of a system should have a set of security requirements in mind. Three methods for determining the level of security of a system are: knowledge of the design and coding methods used in construction of the program, use of penetration teams, and program proofs.

An indication of the level of security can be obtained by observing the quality of the code in the system. For example, a program should be modular and have all security-relevant code isolated. Any defaults in the system should be to the least level of privilege, and the security provisions should be designed so that they will be easy to use. This method will give only a rough idea about the security level, but it can be used as a starting point for a more serious search for flaws.

Penetration teams can be set up to determine an approximate cost for penetration of a system. One byproduct of this effort is that system errors are discovered and may be patched; however, the error may not be correctable without rewriting major portions of the system. It is also possible for a penetration team to isolate forms of errors and generate an automated search for other instances of these types of errors.[44]

The strongest form of certification is to prove formally that the software performs exactly as specified and that the forms of security claimed by the system are actually carried out. This is difficult for even small programs, and is generally impractical for a set of programs as large as an operating system. One approach to this problem is to generate a security kernel, such as the Virtual Machine Monitor (VMM) at the University of California at Los Angeles, and prove that the relatively small kernel is correct.[45] One of the difficulties occurs because the proof simply indicates that the system adheres to a particular set of security rules; there is no assurance that the set of rules is adequate.

Security in a computer system is a weak-link phenomenon; a penetrator will attempt penetration at the weak points in the system. In order to show that a system is secure, it must be proven that no weak links in the security exist, a difficult task. However, each system can be rated on its ability to block access paths—perhaps leaving access paths with low transmission rates open for penetration. Such a system would be adequate for protection of relatively low value information.

6.10
Summary

A software engineer can provide security by blocking unauthorized access to information completely or by raising the cost of such access so as to raise the price of penetration higher than the value of the information obtained thereby. The tools available to provide security include:

- The operating system, which determines how users can access objects in the system and provides the base for security provisions programmed by the software engineer.
- Authentication, which prevents a penetrator's masquerading as a legitimate user by ascertaining that a user is who he says he is.
- Cryptography, which protects information even though it may be accessible to a penetrator and can provide authentication.
- Confinement, a method that may allow the use of a potentially hostile routine by blocking data paths out of the routine.
- Mechanisms programmed by the software engineer, such as threat detection

---

[44]Bisbey, "Privacy and Security," Engineering 226Z, U. of Calif. at Los Angeles (Winter 1975).
[45]Popek, "Privacy and Security," Engineering 226Z, U. of Calif. at Los Angeles (Winter 1975).

and compromise recording that serve as deterrents to penetration attempts and to restrict a penetrator's ability to misuse a system without discovery.

Each of these tools blocks penetration attempts in a different manner. The operating system and authentication mechanism place barriers around information to prevent the penetrator's gaining access to the information. Cryptography prevents the penetrator from understanding the information even if he can obtain it. Confinement prevents a routine from leaking information to the penetrator when the routine is executing with the software engineer's permission. Finally, threat detection and compromise recording make penetration attempts unappealing to an infiltrator by raising the risks of apprehension.

The reader should be aware that the intent of the chapter is to present the security difficulties—and some of the solutions—not to supply a definitive explanation of security. A reader attempting to generate a system that must withstand determined penetration attempts is advised to study the problem of security in more detail. The references in the bibliography provide a starting point for further study.

Bibliography

General

MARTIN, JAMES, *Security, Accuracy, and Privacy in Computer Systems*, Englewood Cliffs, N.J., Prentice-Hall, Inc., 1973.

SALTZER, JEROME H., and MICHAEL D. SCHROEDER, "The Protection of Information in Computer Systems," *Proceedings of the IEEE*, **16**, 9 (September 1975), 1278–1308.

VAN TASSEL, DENNIS, *Computer Security Management*, Englewood Cliffs, N.J., Prentice-Hall, Inc., 1972.

Operating System Security

FABRY, R. S., "Capability-Based Addressing," *Communications of the ACM*, **17**, 7 (July 1974), 403–12.

——, "Dynamic Verification of Operating System Decisions," *Communications of the ACM*, **16**, 11 (November 1973), 659–68.

GRAHAM, G. SCOTT, and PETER J. DENNING, "Protection—Principles and Practice," *AFIPS Conference Proceedings*, **40** (1972 SJCC), 417–29.

GRAHAM, ROBERT M., "Protection in an Information Processing Utility," *Communications of the ACM*, **11**, 5 (May 1968), 365–69.

LAMPSON, B. W., "Protection," in Proc. Fifth Princeton Symposium on Information Sciences and Systems, Princeton University, March 1971, pp. 437–43, reprinted in *Operating Systems Review*, **8**, 1 (January 1974), 18–24.

WATSON, RICHARD W., *Timesharing System Design Concepts*, New York, McGraw-Hill, Inc., 1970.

Authentication

EVANS, ARTHUR, and WILLIAM KANTROWITZ, "A User Authentication Scheme Not Requiring

Secrecy in the Computer," *Communications of the ACM*, **17**, 8, (August 1974), 437–42.

PURDY, GEORGE B., "A High Security Log-in Procedure," *Communications of the ACM*, **17**, 8 (August 1974), 442–45.

Cryptography

BARAN, PAUL, "On Distributed Communications: IX. Security, Secrecy, and Tamper-Free Considerations," Doc. RM-3765-PR, RAND Corp., Santa Monica, Calif., August 1974.

CHESSON, FREDRICK W., "Computers and Cryptology," *Datamation*, **19**, 1 (January 1973), 62–64, 77–81.

FEISTEL, HORST, "Cryptography and Computer Privacy," *Scientific American*, **228**, 5 (May 1973), 15–23.

FRIEDMAN, THEODORE D., and LANCE J. HOFFMAN, "Execution Time Requirements for Encipherment Programs," *Communications of the ACM*, **17**, 8 (August 1974), 445–49.

KAHN, DAVID, *The Codebreakers*, New York, The MacMillian Company, 1967.

SHANNON, C. E., "Communication Theory of Secrecy Systems," *Bell Systems Technical Journal*, **28** (October 1949), 656–716.

WOLFE, J. M., *A First Course in Cryptanalysis*, 3 vols., Brooklyn, N.Y., Brooklyn College Press, 1943.

Confinement

LAMPSON, BUTLER W., "A Note on the Confinement Problem," *Communications of the ACM*, **16**, 10 (October 1973), 613–15.

Privacy

HAQ, M. I., "Insuring Individuals Privacy From Statistical Data Base Users," *AFIPS Conference Proceedings*, **44** (SJCC 1975), 941–46.

HOFFMAN, LANCE J., and W. F. MILLER, "Getting a Personal Dossier From a Statistical Data Bank," *Datamation*, **16**, 5 (May 1970), 74–75.

MINSKY, NAFTALY, "Intentional Resolution of Privacy Protection in Database Systems," *Communications of the ACM*, **19**, 3 (March 1976), 148–59.

TURN, REIN, and NORMAN Z. SHAPIRO, "Privacy and Security in Databank Systems—Measures of Effectiveness, Costs, and Protector-Intruder Interactions," *AFIPS Conference Proceedings* (FJCC 1972), 435–44.

7 LEGAL ASPECTS OF SOFTWARE DEVELOPMENT

C. H. REDDIEN

Data Processing Systems Laboratory
Hughes Aircraft Company
Member of California Bar Association

*A moment's insight is
sometimes worth a life's
experience.*

OLIVER WENDELL HOLMES
"The Professor at the
Breakfast Table"

7.1
Introduction

The earlier chapters deal with the management and programming techniques applicable to software development. By adapting these techniques to a particular software environment, the reader generally presumes to be in full control and able to enter the software business world. In fact, many technically oriented individuals are often quite content to limit their inquiries to the technical aspects only. This phenomenon persists until the novice software developer is "outfoxed" by a competitor or is "burned" by the improper performance of his creation.

This chapter provides the basic legal considerations of which a software developer should be aware in order to survive in business and to protect the product of all of those hard labors. By no means should the reader be misled into believing that the material presented here will replace the need for professional legal counsel; on the contrary, this chapter is intended to help the software developer astutely determine at which point an attorney is needed and how to interact effectively with that attorney.

This chapter is designed for sectional reference as well as for end-to-end reading. The individual sections are self-contained. Thus, if one's interest lies only in copyrights, for example, he can turn immediately to Sec. 7.3 and find the information necessary to generally understand that aspect of the law. On the other hand, he may also read the entire chapter, which by the very nature of law is divided into mutually exclusive categories, for a general treatment of the varied legal aspects of software.

Subjects are organized to provide the legal foundation for a software developer to enter and compete in the business community with his idea or his product. Section 7.2 considers the types of business forms a software developer can choose or implement (choose 1) to best develop and market his software. Section 7.3 is an introduction to the basic legal principles required for one to function in the business community, including proprietary rights in software. Section 7.4 discusses possibly the greatest concern of the software developer—the potential liabilities associated with defective software he developed. Section 7.5 introduces other areas of the law that affect the day-to-day workings of a business utilizing software.

Most of the subjects contained here are rooted in historical concepts of law, such as contracts, torts, and agency; but in this discussion modern interpretations are applied to these concepts in order to keep pace with our increasing technology. The law reflects society, and the interpretations of laws indicate the sociological trends of the society. The courts interpret regulations as they apply to particular facts arising from one disputed situation. In general, these interpretations follow guidelines that have been established by the intent of the respective Supreme, State and/or Federal Courts, and legislatures as described in Congressional reports. Thus, the courts' decisions are somewhat predictable.

The American legal structure has two principal systems: the Federal and the State. Depending on the nature of the subject matter, one system or the other, or in certain cases both systems, will assume jurisdiction over a legal matter. Both Federal and State systems have a complex maze of bureaus for legal administrative regulations (the executive branches of government) and a multi-level court system for legal adjudication (the judicial branch). The executive branches of Federal and State governments hold the responsibility of enforcing all Federal or State laws and regulations, respectively. All disputes arising under the U.S. or State Constitutions or the laws thereunder are reviewed, interpreted, and resolved in the respective judical branches.

In the Federal system, the principal forums of interest in this discussion are the Court of Customs and Patent Appeals, the administrative agencies, the Federal district courts, the Federal Court of Appeals, and the United States Supreme Court. Figure 7-1 shows the overall organization of the Federal judicial system.

As this figure shows, cases heard in lower courts may be reviewed by a higher court upon request (appeal). The Federal judicial system, as pointed out earlier, has authority to decide only controversies in matters set forth in the United States Constitution or its amendments and in the Federal Statutes.

The various state judicial systems generally parallel the Federal judicial system with the obvious exception of the Court of Customs and Patent Appeals.[1] A discussion of the exact structure of each state's system is not appropriate here; however, as one example, the California state judicial structure is shown in Figure 7-2.

Through these States and Federal court systems flow two basic types of legal matters—criminal and civil. Criminal matters deal with deciding whether or not an individual or a group of individuals is guilty of violating one or more of the laws that

---

[1]Each state's judicial system differs slightly from that of the other states.

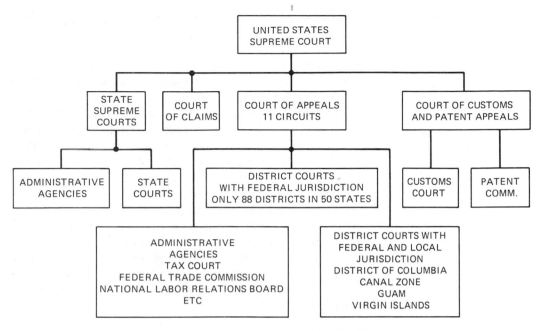

Fig. 7-1   Organization of the federal judicial system

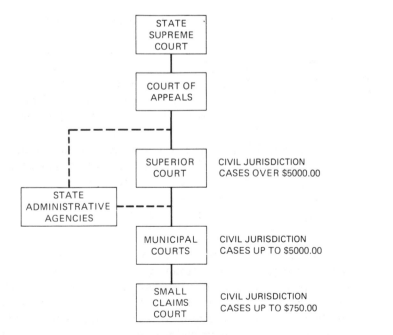

Fig. 7-2

are considered as act(s) against society. The government, representing society, is always the prosecutor in these cases. These criminal laws carry a punishment of a fine and/or imprisonment. Civil law deals with disputes arising between members of society where the conduct of one or both parties has resulted in some sort of property damages to a party. Generally, such damages are based on a compensation or restitution theory, e.g., breach of contract or negligence.

Civil law also includes a segment of the law known as *equity*. Equity finds its roots in old English law that allowed the peasants with special disputes, not adequately covered by the laws, to have an audience with the king in order to seek a just resolution. The best example of current equity application is that of injunction, i.e., a court order that enjoins or restrains a certain conduct of one or more of the parties to an action to avoid irreparable damage to the other party.

This chapter addresses the civil segment of the law primarily, though portions of the laws discussed obviously have criminal applications, e.g., misrepresentation and fraud. In general, though, failure to perform in the situations described will result only in monetary or personal losses, not incarceration. Hopefully, with the insight provided by this chapter and appropriate consultation with professionals at various stages of the business development, the reader will minimize the need to appear in any of the court systems.

7.2

Considerations of Selecting a Business Form

The principal forms in which a software developer may start a business are:

The Sole Proprietorship—a business owned and operated by an individual.

A Partnership (general and limited)—an association of two or more persons who serve as co-owners of a business for profit.

A Corporation—a *legal entity* consisting of one or more natural persons, established by law, usually for a specific purpose, continued by a succession of members.

Each of these business forms has advantages and disadvantages that must be considered before deciding on the particular form best suited for a software supplier's needs. The particulars will be discussed specifically in the following subsections; but before addressing the nature of each type of business, it is appropriate to discuss the principal factors involved in deciding on the form best suited for the developer's particular circumstances.

NATURE OF THE BUSINESS. The type of business and nature of conducting the business are important in determining which of the three types of businesses is to be chosen. Specifically, one must ask: is the business speculative in nature or does it have inherent risks that are adequately protected through insurance; is the business large financially; is it interstate; does the business lend itself to multiple entities? The corporate form that provides stability and limited liability (depending on the conduct of the parties) is generally best suited for the high risk and/or larger businesses.

FLEXIBILITY OF THE BUSINESS OWNERSHIP. The flexibility of the business ownership is a critical item, i.e., transfer of ownership due to disagreement or death; joint ownership of other businesses; separation of ownership and management of the business. The various forms of business have particular characteristics relative to these considerations. For example, a partnership must dissolve upon the death of a partner, whereas a corporation does not when an executive or a major stockholder dies; or in a partnership, all general partners own and conduct the business, whereas in a corporation the shareholders may only vote for directors who, along with selected officers, conduct the business.

SPECIAL CONSIDERATIONS OF BUSINESS MANAGEMENT. The key consideration here is the developer's decision to delegate or retain knowledge of a program or responsibility for the program and the question of the businesses operating more efficiently (including administratively and employee relations) under one form of business or another. In this context, it should be noted that corporations have more "red tape" than the other business forms, but corporations also allow for inducement of key employees through stock option plans.

INVESTMENT REQUIREMENTS OF THE BUSINESS. The ability to raise capital to initiate and conduct the business is important in the formation and growth of the specific business one chooses. Large capital investments are best generated in a corporate form, but the issuance of corporate stocks and promissory notes requires a permit from the State Commissioner of Corporations. Additionally, interstate issues must satisfy Security and Exchange Commissions (SEC) requirements. Long-term lenders generally prefer the continuity of a corporation, but, depending on the circumstances, may still require the personal surety of corporate backers.

TAX CONSIDERATIONS. The tax factors are quite complex and deal primarily with the distribution of income and ability to use certain deductions. In essence, the differences are based on the fact that income to a sole proprietorship or a partnership is income to the individual, whereas income to a corporation is income to the corporate entity. What this income tax interpretation means is that profit derived from a sole proprietorship or partnership is taxed as income to the individual, i.e., with a maximum rate of 70%, and losses are considered as losses to the individual and can offset other sources of income. However, profit gained from income to a corporation is taxed as corporate income (22% of the first $25,000 net profit and 48% of the balance of the corporate net income less exemptions), and losses are losses only to the corporation, not to the individuals. Distribution of the corporate profits to shareholders is taxed a second time when paid to owners as dividends. The dividends are income to individuals and are taxed accordingly. There is an advantage allowed to corporations through full tax benefit of pension plans which is not available to the other two business forms.

Clearly, a complete review of these five factors with professional legal and financial counsel should be undertaken prior to initiation of a business. It is not unusual for a business to have a small beginning as a sole proprietorship, later expand into a partnership, and ultimately be incorporated.

7.2.1 SOLE PROPRIETORSHIP

The sole proprietorship is the basic form of business. It thrives today, as it always has, for several practical and economic reasons:

- It is not subject to as many regulations, reporting requirements, and "red tape" as either the partnership or corporate forms.
- Start-up costs are smaller.
- The owner is able to make immediate decisions without further coordination and approval.
- Business losses can be used to offset other personal income for income tax purposes.
- Management of the business and business operations is less formal than either the corporate or partnership form.

Thus, the sole proprietorship is the simplest and least expensive business to get started. As far as conforming to Federal, State, and local ordinances, e.g., zoning or labor laws, there is little difference between the forms of business.

The principal disadvantages to the sole proprietorship and the reasons why growing businesses tend to transform eventually from the sole proprietorship form to another type business are:

- The owner is personally liable for all business liabilities and indebtedness. Thus, all the owner's personal assets are security for the business debts or liabilities.
- It is difficult to raise investment capital. All investments generally must be provided by the owner or secured by the owner's personal property.
- The business generally comes to a standstill when the owner dies or is incapacitated.
- All net business profits are taxable as ordinary income to the owner.

The key disadvantage is, of course, that of liability. The software developer should review Sec. 7.4 of this chapter in light of the nature of the software being developed (along with future software development expectations) to properly assess the potential risks. Clearly, professional guidance should be sought in these evaluations. If the risks are too great and insurance is not available or is too costly to limit the risks, then another form of business, i.e., incorporation, is in order.

7.2.2 PARTNERSHIPS

A partnership, as distinguished from the sole proprietorship, is an association of two or more persons for the purpose of carrying on a business as co-owners for profit. Thus, in principle, a partnership has the same advantages and disadvantages as the sole proprietorship. But the entity characteristics of a partnership do make its operation different. Some of the differences are delineated below.

The partnership, as opposed to a corporation, is not a legal entity in common law; therefore, the debts of a partnership are the debts of the individual partners, and any one partner may be held liable for the partnership's entire indebtedness. Nevertheless, a partnership is a business entity in the following respects:

1. For accounting and bookkeeping purposes, the assets, liabilities, and business transactions of a partnership are treated separately and distinctly from the individual assets, liabilities, and nonpartnership transactions of the partners. In this context, even though the partnership is not required to pay Federal income tax, it must file an information return each year. The individual partners are also required to report and pay any tax due therefrom. The profits from the partnership are taxable income to the partners.

2. In the generation of investment capital, the assets and liabilities of the partnership and the individual partners are considered separate and distinct. Thus, the creditors of a partnership, who do not have personal surety, have prior rights over the personal creditors to the partnership assets, whereas the creditors of the individual partners have prior rights over partnership creditors to the personal assets.

3. A partnership as established by state statute (e.g., California, and in Federal courts) may sue and be sued in the partnership name.

4. Generally, any title to real estate may be acquired in the partnership's name. Title so acquired can be conveyed only in the partnership name as provided in Section 7(c) of the Uniform Partnership Act or Section 15006 of the California Corporations Code.

5. A partnership can be adjudicated a bankrupt. This can be established separately, or with one or more, or all of the general partners. Further, such bankruptcy proceedings may involve the partnership without involving the individual separate assets of the members of the firm.

The important features of a partnership are that each partner has a right to take part in the management of the business, to handle the partnership assets for partnership purposes, and to act as an agent of the partnership. Clearly, the choice of partners must focus on desirable personal traits. A partner holds a position of trust that, through negligence or misconduct, can ruin the partnership and the co-partners.

The partnership relationship is usually established by a contract that sets out the conduct of the partners, but it may come into existence through the mere conduct of the parties without benefit of contract. The importance of this relationship is that, if a partnership exists, the personal assets of the involved parties are liable for partnership liabilities. Co-ownership, i.e., joint tenancy, tenancy in common, tenancy by the entireties, joint property, or part ownership, does not establish a partnership whether such co-owners do or do not share any profits made through use of the property. Sharing gross returns does not establish a partnership, whether or not the persons sharing them have an interest in any property from which the returns are derived. For an entity to exist as a partnership, the source of profits must be from a business in which the parties sharing the profits have an ownership interest in the business. Under the Uniform Partnership Act, receipt by a person of a share of the profits of a business is *prima facia* evidence (i.e., he would have to prove otherwise) that he is a partner in the business, except where the profits were received in payment of

1. a debt by installments or otherwise,

2. wages of an employee or rent to a landlord,
3. an annuity to a widow or representative of a deceased partner, and
4. interest on a loan, though the amount of payment would vary with the profits of the business.

Note that a partnership may be established by a representation of a partnership by a nonpartner as if he were a partner, a treatment as such by the partnership, and reliance on the existence of such a partnership by a third party. This concept is called *Partnership by Estoppel*. It means that the partnership, because of the misrepresentation and third party reliance, cannot defend the partnership assets against the third party's claim on the grounds that the nonpartner did not have partner status.

There are various types of partners:

A Real Partner, a partner who is recognized as having all legal rights and liabilities of a full partner.

A General Partner, a real partner who is usually active in the partnership business.

A Silent Partner, a real partner who has no voice and takes no part in the partnership business.

A Secret Partner, a real partner whose membership is not disclosed to the public.

A Limited Partner, also known as a special partner, one who as a member of a limited partnership, in which the partnership business is run by one or more general partners, is liable for partnership indebtedness only to the extent of the capital that he has contributed or agreed to contribute.

An Ostensible Partner, not a real partner, but one who represents himself as a real partner.

The advantages of a partnership are:

- The partners can expand the partnership more easily through individual contributions of ideas and capital.
- Responsibility for decisions and losses is shared.
- Partnership losses can be used to offset taxable income from other income sources of the individual partners.
- A partnership is better able to raise capital investment than is a sole proprietorship business.
- Management is more efficient since it is easier to share responsibilities and supervision of business affairs.

The principal disadvantages are:

- Each real partner is personally liable for the partnership liabilities.
- Each real partner is an agent of the partnership and may obligate the partnership and the other partners.
- Greater possibility of conflict between partners may result in dissertion or dissolution of the partnership.
- The partnership terminates on the death or incapacity of a partner.
- Profits are shared and are added to the taxable income of the partners.

The balance of risk of personal liability versus the advantages of a partnership is even more critical than in the sole proprietorship for the software developer. The principal reason is that the other partners are agents of the partnership, and their representations as to the software are binding on the partnership. Thus, any liabilities arising from those representations may be satisfied from any one or all of the partners' personal assets. This liability may be minimized through the use of a limited partnership. A limited partnership is constrained, though, by the limited partners not having any management or control of the business, which may obviate the reason for the partnership altogether.

Checklist for partnership agreement:

1. Effective date of partnership.
2. Name of partnership.
3. Address of the principal location of the partnership.
4. Names and addresses of all partners.
5. Description of the purpose of the partnership.
6. Term of the existence of the partnership.
7. How interest, if any, is to be paid on invested capital.
8. Distribution of profits and losses among partners—silence implies equal distribution.
9. Income and expense provisions for partners.
10. Duties of each partner in support of partnership business, e.g., amount of time each partner is to be committed to the business.
11. The powers of each partner.
12. Description of how the partnership shall be managed and controlled.
13. Provisions for bookkeeping.
14. Provisions for loss of partners/dissolution of partnership, e.g., retirement, death, withdrawal, incapacity.
15. Provisions for closure and distribution of partnership assets, including name and good will upon dissolution of the partnership.
16. Provisions for arbitration in case of dispute between the partners.

7.2.3 CORPORATIONS

The corporation is a legal entity that is separate and apart from the stockholders. It can be sued and can enter into contracts. It consists of one or more natural persons; is established by law, usually for a specific purpose; and is continued by a succession of members, stockholders.

Table 7-1 shows a simplified comparison of these various forms of doing business. As shown, the fundamental difference between the corporation and other forms of business is that the corporation is an entity unto itself, shielding the ultimate owners, the shareholders, from liability. The price paid for this shield is a formality of doing business that is established by statute and a double income tax situation. Further, as will be discussed later, this shield may be pierced in certain circumstances, making the personal assets of the shareholders available to satisfy corporate liability.

Table 7-1 Comparison of Business Forms

	Sole Proprietorship	*Partnership*	*Corporation*
Creation	Personal preference	By agreement of partners	By statutory authorization (formalities of paper work set by statute)
Entity	Not legal entity	Not legal entity	A legal entity
Reporting/ bookkeeping	Personal business accounting. No special tax report	Partnership bookkeeping separate from partners. Must file information tax report	Corporate accounting and annual reports set by statute. Corporation files own tax forms separate from shareholders
Duration	Up to individual	Dissolution by agreement, withdrawal of partner, incapacity or death of partner or bankruptcy	May be perpetual
Liability of principals	Unlimited personal liability	Real partners have unlimited liability	Shareholders are not liable (unless corporate veil can be pierced)
Title of property	In owner's name	Held in partnership name or partners' names	Held in corporation's name
Transferability of interest	Total transferable	Interest of a partner is not transferable without the consent of all other partners	Shares of stock are freely transferable subject to securities laws.
Management and control	Individual owner's control	Each partner has equal rights in management and control	Corporation business is managed by board of directors and selected officers; the board is elected by shareholders. Statutory formalities of meetings of shareholders and directors
Agency	Agency only on agreement of owner	Partners are all individually principals and agents of the partnership and co-partners	Shareholder is neither a principal nor an agent of the corporation
Suits by and against	All suits are against and by owner	In suits by partnership, all partners are parties plaintiff; suits against the partnership, all partners are parties defendant	May be sued and sue in corporation name only (sue shareholders in action to pierce corporate veil)
Taxes on income	All business income is taxable income to owner (max. 70%)	Each partner's share is taxable income to partner (max. 70%)	Double tax: Corporation must pay corporation tax on profit (22% on first $25,000 and 48% of income over $25,000). Dividends, if distributed, are taxable income to shareholders
Losses—taxes	Can offset owner's income from other sources	Each partner's share of loss can offset income from other sources	Loss can be carried only by corporation, not shareholders

Figure 7-3 shows generally the process required to form a corporation. A sample set of articles of incorporation is included at the end of this subsection. These articles are based on the General Corporation law of the State of California and they vary from state to state. Generally, the articles require the names and addresses of three directors of the corporation or "incorporators." Some states require further that the incorporators be natural persons, i.e., not corporations, and that the purpose of the corporation be stated more specifically.

There are also special rules of incorporation for "Close" Corporation—a corporation with not more than 10 holders of shares (this must be specified in the Articles). This type of corporation functions much like a partnership, but in a corporate structure, i.e., the formalities are less stringent in the Close Corporation. This has many advantages for the smaller operation, which must be more flexible than larger companies.

Costs for forming a corporation vary from state to state, depending on statutory requirements and the needs of the corporation. Generally, for a small corporation the basic filing fees range from $50 to $500. The expenses rise according to the complexity of the stock and financial structure of the corporation. Professional services are also additive, as are the "corporation kits" (meeting minute book, stock book, corporation seal, and stock certificate).

In several areas caution is required in the formation of the corporation:

• Subscribers of the stock, persons subscribing to buy shares of stock in the new corporation, must furnish consideration for the stock. The sufficiency and nature of that consideration are generally set forth in the corporation statutes. Some states will not allow the corporation to commence business unless some minimum amount of consideration to be given for the subscription has been paid.

• Promoters' contracts that are entered into in anticipation of the creation of the corporation, if not ratified by the corporation, are not a liability of the corporation upon formation, i.e., the promoter is personally liable for the contracts, leases, purchase orders, and the like.

• Promoters must disclose to other shareholders any personal profit gained from promoting the corporation.

• Each state and Federal government law that regulates the issuance and transfer of shares in a corporation under its respective jurisdiction should be carefully reviewed to prevent possible violations that could subject the directors and promoters to civil or criminal liabilities.

• The corporate entity will be disregarded whenever it is used to defeat public convenience, justify wrong, protect fraud, promote crime, or circumvent the law. This is known as *piercing the corporate veil*. One rule used in this regard is the oneness of ownership and management of the corporation. Within this context, the shield of limited liability of the shareholders is eliminated, and shareholders become *personally* liable.

Once a corporation is formed, the formalities of corporate operation begin. The directors generally are required to meet on a regular basis, subject to the needs of the corporation, sufficient to manage and control the corporation. The directors are entrusted with general management, subject to limitations of the corporation law and

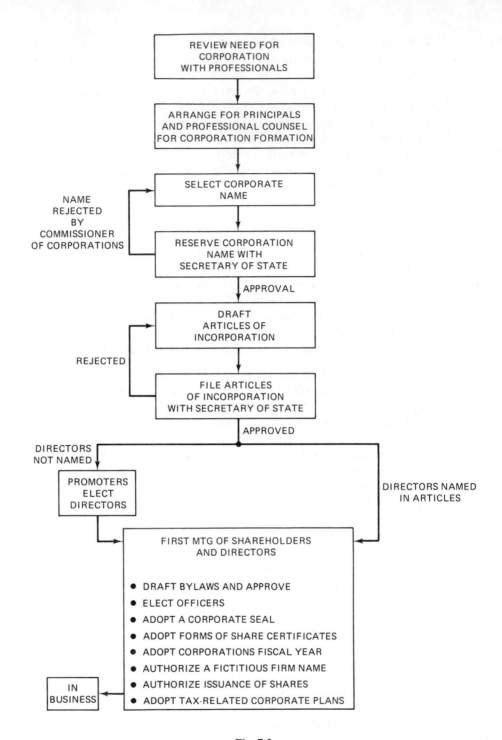

Fig. 7-3

the Articles of Incorporation or bylaws of the corporation, and in this capacity must exercise authority in good faith and in a manner in the best interest of the corporation. The directors' standard of care in the exercise of duties includes reasonable inquiry into corporate affairs with the general yardsticks being "an ordinarily prudent person under similar circumstances." Further, the directors have a fiduciary (trusted) relationship with the corporation that requires full disclosure of any conflict of interest the directors may have in any of the corporate dealings. In this regard the directors' failure to perform up to the standard of care of fiduciary status could result in removal and possibly personal liability for any ill-gotten gains and losses to the corporation.

The shareholders are required generally to have at least one shareholders' meeting every year. This meeting is to be held at a specified time and place (some states require the notice of subjects to be discussed), and all shareholders of record must be given adequate notice. There must be a quorum (a majority of shareholders either in person or by proxy) present in order for the directors to conduct a valid meeting. At these meetings shareholders can deal with all topics of the corporation including, but not limited to

Subject	Vote Required
Removal of directors	Set by bylaws
Change in bylaws	Set by bylaws
Election of directors	Set by bylaws
Reorganization (merger)[2]	2/3 of each class of shares
Change in articles	2/3 directors and majority of outstanding shares
Change Lose Corporation status	2/3 of each outstanding class of shares
Sale of substantial assets	2/3 of each outstanding class of shares

The shareholders further have certain rights that are generally protected under state statutes or common law, which include:

1. Right to certificates—shares of stock.
2. Right to vote his share of stock—subject to restrictions and limitations set out in the Articles of Incorporation.
3. Right to examine corporate books and records.
4. Right to dividends.
5. Right to a pro-rata share of the proceeds after payment to creditors of the dissolved corporation.
6. Right to minority shareholder protections to prevent arbitrary abuse of power by majority stockholders or directors.

[2]The types of reorganization (merger, mortgage of assets, stock for stock exchange, stock of assets exchange) have varying requirements, and particular state statutes should be reviewed.

The advantages of a corporation are:

- Limited liability of shareholders.
- Lower income tax on corporate income.
- The ability of a corporate entity to survive.

The principal disadvantages of a corporation are:

- More "red tape."
- More structured form of business.
- Profits are taxed twice if distributed to shareholders as dividends.
- Losses are losses only to the corporation and cannot be used to affect other income of shareholders.
- Formation is more complex and costly than other forms of business.

Example of Articles of Incorporation

ARTICLES OF INCORPORATION OF X.M.P.L. CORPORATION

The Undersigned Incorporator hereby executes, acknowledges, and files the following ARTICLES OF INCORPORATION for the purpose of forming a corporation under the General Corporation Law of the State of California:

ARTICLE ONE: The name of the corporation shall be X.M.P.L. CORPORATION.

ARTICLE TWO: The purpose of the corporation is to engage in any lawful act or activity for which a corporation may be organized under the General Corporation Law of California other than the banking business, the trust company business, or the practice of a profession permitted to be incorporated by the California Corporations Code.

ARTICLE THREE: The name and address in this state of the corporation's initial agent for service of process in accordance with subdivision (b) of Section 1502 of the General Corporation Law are:

> Phil N. Blanks
> 1 At a Time
> Somewhere City, California 00000

ARTICLE FOUR: For this article there are two alternatives (only one should be used).

Alternate 1: The Corporation is authorized to issue only one class of shares and the total number of shares with the Corporation is authorized to issue is _____ (_____).

Alternate 2: The Corporation is authorized to issue (number) classes of shares, designated "common shares" and "preferred shares." The total number of common shares which the Corporation is authorized to issue is _____ (_____), . . . , and the total number of preferred shares which the Corporation is authorized to issue is _____ (_____). The preferred shares may be issued in two or more series, and the Board of Directors of the Corporation is authorized to determine the designation and to fix the number of shares of any such series.

INSERT ANY RIGHTS REFERENCES, PRIVILEGES and restrictions granted to, or imposed upon, the respective classes or series of shares of the holders thereof, or that the board, within any limits and restrictions stated, may determine or alter the rights, preferences, privileges, and restrictions granted to, or imposed upon, any wholly unissued class of shares or any wholly unissued series of any class of shares.

OPTIONAL ENTRIES

IN WITNESS WHEREOF, the Undersigned Incorporator has executed the foregoing Articles of Incorporation on _____, 19__.

_____
Phil N. Blanks, Incorporator

The Undersigned declares that he is the person who executed the foregoing Articles of Incorporation and that such instrument is the act and deed of the Undersigned.

_____
Phil N. Blanks

Additional Provisions Permissible Under the General California Corporation Code:

§204. *Permissible Provisions of the Articles*

The articles of incorporation may set forth:
(a) Any or all of the following provisions, which shall not be effective unless expressly provided in the articles:
  (1) Granting, with or without limitations, the power to levy assessments upon the shares or any class of shares;
  (2) Granting the shareholders preemptive rights to subscribe to any or all issues of shares or securities;
  (3) Special qualifications of persons who may be shareholders;
  (4) A provision limiting the duration of the corporation's existence to a specified date;
  (5) A provision requiring, for any or all corporate-actions (except as provided in Section 303, subdivision (c) of Section 708 and Section 1900) the vote of a larger proportion or of all of the shares of any class or series, or of a larger proportion or of all of the directors, than is otherwise required by this division;
  (6) A provision limiting or restricting the business in which the corporation may engage or the powers which the corporation may exercise or both;
  (7) A provision conferring upon the holders of any evidences of indebtedness, issued or to be issued by the corporation, the right to vote in the election of directors and on any other matters on which shareholders may vote;
  (8) A provision conferring upon shareholders the right to determine the consideration for which shares shall be issued.
Notwithstanding this subdivision (a), in the case of a Close Corporation any of the provisions referred to above may be validly included in a shareholders' agreement. Nothing contained in this subdivision (a) shall affect the enforceability, as between the parties thereto, of any lawful agreement not otherwise contrary to public policy.
(b) Reasonable restrictions upon the right to transfer or hypothecate shares of any class or classes, but no restriction shall be binding with respect to shares issued prior to the adoption of the restriction unless the holders of such shares voted in favor of the restriction.

(c) The names and addresses of the persons appointed to act as initial directors.

(d) Any other provision, not in conflict with law, for the management of the business and for the conduct of the affairs of the corporation, including any provision which is required or permitted by this division to be stated in the bylaws.

7.3

Legal Considerations of Setting Up a Software Business

Regardless of the form of business the software developer selects for his operational needs, several areas of the law should be reviewed before embarking into day-to-day business dealings. This section summarizes the legal considerations associated with obtaining protection of the software developed, contracting with users, being aware of how software is taxed, and utilizing agents or employees to develop and/or market the software. All of these subjects are, of course, integrated in varying degrees into business decisions, depending on the particular circumstances. It is not the purpose of this discussion to attempt to provide such circumstances, but to provide the background necessary to recognize that these areas do impact business conduct.

7.3.1 PROTECTION OF SOFTWARE PROGRAMS

The issue of the legal protections to be afforded software programs has been the source of controversy for many years in this country and others.[3] Congress possesses the authority to grant protection for the promotion of progress in sciences and useful arts under Article 1, §8 of the United States Constitution. The choices of protection are patents, copyrights, or a trade secret. The characteristics of each of these protections are summarized in Table 7-2. Each has advantages and disadvantages as well as limitations that must be carefully weighed when deciding on the manner of protection.

PATENT—AS LEGAL PROTECTION OF SOFTWARE

The choice of a patent to protect the software is, of course, the most desirable choice of the three protections in that it gives the owner a monopoly on the program for 17 years, with strict procedures against patent violators. The disadvantages are the disclosure of the ideas to others, the expense of enforcement, and the risk of rejection.

The availability of patent protection for software programs has been a controversial subject throughout the "western world," including the United States. The issue of the patentability of software was adjudicated by the United States Supreme Court in Gottschalk *v*. Benson 409 U.S. 63 (1972) rev'g In re Benson 441 F. 2d 682 (C.C.P.A. 1971) (referred to as Benson hereafter). Before discussing this landmark case and the trends since Benson, it is best to review the applicable sections of Title 35 that are controlling in the determination of software patentability.

---

[3]Stanislaw J. Soltysinsk, "Computer Programs and Patent Law a Comparative Study," *Rutgers Journal of Computers and the Law*—1972–1973, pp. 1–82.

Table 7-2 Summary of Software Protection Alternatives

Type of Protection	Term of Protection	Qualification for Protection	Right Under Protection	Comments
Patent	17 years	Invention must have • Novel (unobviousness) • Utility	What covered: • Item itself • An underlying concept. Rights—exclusive right to make, use, and sell the invention or discovery throughout United States and its territories	Patent rights are effectively precluded to software under Supreme Court decision in Gottschalk v. Benson (409 U.S. 63, 1972)
Copyright*	Author's life plus 50 years	Useful works of art that are: • Authored (result of some degree of intellectual labor • In writing (in perceptible or tangible form)	Sole right to print, copy, publish, or sell material copyrighted	• Requires disclosure of software program, but does afford protection • For protection must show access and unjustified appropriation
Trade secret	Not limited	The secret must be: • A formula, pattern, device, or compilation of information used in a business that provides an advantage over competitors • Substantially a secret (difficult for others to acquire)	Sole use	Has the advantage of secrecy with protection against usage. Note: must show that other party obtained secret improperly

*The Copyright Revision Act of 1976, effective January 1, 1978, provides that new copyrights (after January 1, 1978) shall have a term equal to the life of the author plus 50 years; or in the case of joint authorship, the life of the surviving author plus 50 years. Prior to January 1, 1978 the duration of a coypright was 28 years, with one renewal permitted. At present the application to software is not totally resolved.

Title 35 of the United States Codes embodies the laws applicable to patents. The key sections are:

Section 101 states what may be patented:

§101. *Inventions Patentable*

Whoever invents or discovers any new and useful process, machine, manufacture, or composition of matter, or any new and useful improvement thereof, may obtain a patent therefor, subject to the conditions and requirements of this title. July 19, 1952, c. 950, § 1, 66 Stat. 797.

Sections 102 and 103 establish the condition for patentability and the nonobvious subject matter restriction:

§102. *Condition for Patentability: Novelty and Loss of Right to Patent*

A person shall be entitled to a patent unless—

(a) the invention was known or used by others in this country, or patented or described in a printed publication in this or a foreign country, before the invention thereof by the application for patent, or

(b) the invention was patented or described in a printed publication in this or a foreign country or in public use or on sale in this country, more than one year prior to the date of the application for patent in the United States, or

(c) he has abandoned the invention, or

(d) the invention was first patented or caused to be patented, or was the subject of an inventor's certificate, by the applicant or his legal representatives or assigns in a foreign country prior to the date of the application for patent in this country on an application for patent or inventor's certificate filed more than twelve months before the filing of the application in the United States, or (as amended July 28, 1972, Pub. L. 92-358, § 2, 86 Stat. 502.)

(e) the invention was described in a patent granted on an application for patent by another filed in the United States before the invention thereof by the applicant for patent, or

(f) he did not himself invent the subject matter sought to be patented, or

(g) before the applicant's invention thereof the invention was made in this country by another who had not abandoned, suppressed, or concealed it. In determining priority of invention there shall be considered not only the respective dates of conception and reduction to practice of the invention, but also the reasonable diligence of one who was first to conceive and last to reduce to practice, from a time prior to concept by the other. July 19, 1952, c. 950, § 1, 66 Stat. 797.

§103. Conditions for Patentability; Nonobvious Subject Matter

A patent may not be obtained though the invention is not identically disclosed or described as set forth in Section 102 of this title, if the differences between the subject matter sought to be patented and the prior art are such that the subject matter as a whole would have been obvious at the time the invention was made to a person having ordinary skill in the art to which said subject matter pertains. Patentability shall not be negated by the manner in which the invention was made. July 19, 1952, c. 950, § 1, 66 Stat. 798.

The critical question involving software is whether or not it is patentable subject matter within the meaning of Section 101. Software has generally been regarded as mathematical in nature and thus falls in a category of a mental or intellectual operation. This would put it in a class with teaching techniques, scientific principles, and other abstract solutions, all of which are denied patent protection.

Prior to Benson, there were a series of cases decided by the Court of Customs and Patent Appeals, which "fired" the controversy of the patentability of software. The initial patent doctrine advanced in patentability of software controversy was in the matter of In Re Abrams[4] where the court proposed the so-called "mental steps" doctrine. In Re Abrams basically stated that if the novelty of the process did not reside in the positive and physical steps with the so-called mental steps being incidental to the process, then the claim was not patentable. Thus, software that was incidental to the patentable process could be protected. The "mental steps" doctrine was

[4]In Re Abrams; 188 F. 2d. 165 (C.C.P.A. 1951); cf. In Re Yuan; 188 F. 2d. 377 (C.C.P.A. 1951).

expanded in In Re Prater[5] and In Re Bernhart[6] to allow processes which could be performed by physical means (hardware) and the human mind (software) to be patented. Finally, in 1970 in In Re Musgrave[7] the Court of Customs and Patent Appeals virtually eliminated the "mental steps" doctrine by allowing any process in

consonance with the Constitutional purpose to promote the progress of useful arts

to be patented. The stage was set as the result of these cases for clear guidelines to be established in Benson.

In Re Benson involved a software process for changing binary coded decimals to binary numbers for use with a switch network. The Supreme Court adjudged the process not patentable subject matter as defined within the meaning of Section 101. In doing so, unfortunately, the court failed to establish the firm guidelines expected. The Court left open such questions as to how the Court would view hardware claims that involve computer program, or claims that involve software and read-only memory machine to implement processes. The Court's opinion did not definitely reject any of the prior theories expounded by the Court of Customs and Patent. Justice Douglas, speaking for the Supreme Court, stated:

> We do not hold that no process patent could ever qualify if it did not meet the requirements of our prior precedents. It is said that the decision precludes a patent for any program servicing a computer. We do not so hold. It is said that we have before us a program for a digital computer but extend our holding to programs for analog computers. We have, however, made clear from the start that we deal with a program only for digital computers. It is said we freeze process patents to old technologies, leaving no room for the revelations of the new, onrushing technology. Such is not our purpose. What we come down to in a nutshell is the following.
>
> It is conceded that one may not patent an idea. But in practical effort that would be the result if the formula for converting binary code to pure binary were patented in this case. The mathematical formula involved here has no substantial practical application except in connection with a digital computer, which means that if the judgment below is affirmed, the patent would wholly pre-empt the mathematical formula and in practical effect be a patent on the algorithm itself.[8]

Since the Benson case, several cases have left open the question of patentability of software and have suggested that in incidents in which the software and specific hardware are interrelated to enable the performance of a function, then the claim may be patentable.[9] In In Re Johnston[10] the Court of Customs and Patents Appeals employed the statements of Justice Douglas in Benson to adjudge an automatic finan-

---

[5]In Re Prater; 415 F. 2d. 1393 (C.C.P.A. 1968) aff'g and *rev'g in part on rehearing*, 415 F. 2d 1378 (C.C.P.A. 1968).

[6]In Re Bernhart; 417 F. 2d. 1395 (C.C.P.A. 1969).

[7]In Re Musgrave; 431 F. 2d. 882 (C.C.P.A. 1970).

[8]In Re Benson; 409 U.S. at 72.

[9]In Re Knowlton; 481 F. 2d. 1375 (C.C.P.A. 1973); In Re Comstock; 481 F. 2d. 905 (C.C.P.A. 1973).

[10]In Re Johnston; 502 F. 2d. 765 (C.C.P.A. 1974).

cial record-keeping system utilizing an IBM 1400 series computer patentable. Thus, the door to software patents is not closed.

If the software developer attempts to obtain a patent for a software program, Table 7-3 gives an indication of his probability of success. The following steps should be a guide to pursuing a patent:

Table 7-3   Patentability of Software Summary

Claim	Hardware/ Software	S/W Program in Algorithm or Idea	Specification of Computer	Patentability
Apparatus	Yes	Yes	Yes	No (Benson)
"	Yes	No	Yes	Yes
"	Yes	No	No	Yes

Claim	Machine Implemented Process	S/W Program in Algorithm or Idea	Mental Process	Patentability
Method	No	Yes	—	No
"	Yes	No	No	?
"	No	No	Yes	No

1. records must be kept, dated, and initialed (witness preferred);
2. the invention must be explained as soon as possible—date, initial, and witness;
3. the invention must be novel, useful, and unobvious, i.e., not prior art;
4. qualified legal counsel must be sought (patent attorney);
5. patent application must be made as soon as possible.

It should be remembered that the expense of enforcing the patent may be excessive, and the risk of losing very high.

COPYRIGHT—AS LEGAL PROTECTION OF SOFTWARE

The copyright protection outlined under Title 17, Section 1, of the United States Code[11] grants the author-recipient the exclusive right to print, publish, copy, vend, translate, deliver, and perform the copyrighted work for a period of the author's life plus 50 years.[12] The unauthorized exercise of the rights is copyright infringement

[11]Public Law No. 94–533, 90 Stat. 2541; 17 U.S.C. §§ 101 et seq. effective January 1, 1978, commonly known as the Copyright Revision Act of 1976 amends in its entirety the United States copyright law, but continues to embrace the details set out in this chapter. Note, however, that the formalities are less stringent under the new act and the protection much broader.

[12]Under the Copyright Revision Act of 1976, effective January 1, 1978, works created after January 1, 1978 will be protected from the moment of creation to the life of the author (or surviving author in the case of joint authors) plus 50 years (17 U.S.C. §§ 302). Works made for hire will be protected for 75 years from the date of first publication or 100 years from the date of creation, whichever expires first. Renewals for copyrights accrued prior to January 1, 1978, which have not been renewed, can be renewed in the last year of their initial term (28th) for a second term of 47 years (17 U.S.C. §§ 304(a)). Copyrights in their renewal term at any time between December 31, 1976, and December 31, 1977, inclusive, are automatically extended without a need for further filings. Copyrights whose

providing the recipient with the remedies from injunction and damages to impounding and destruction of the infringing material [17 U.S. U.S.C. §101 (1970)]. Unfortunately, there is no clear definition as to what conduct constitutes infringement.

Copyright protection was made expressly available to software in May 1964 when the Copyright Office decided that computer programs could be registered if they met its requirements. *The office disclosed that arguably a program is not a writing of an author, and a reproduction of the program in machine language might not be a copy acceptable for copyright registration.* Regardless of the argumentative nature of software programs, the Office

> in accordance with its policy of resolving doubtful issues in favor of registration whenever possible[13]

began accepting computer programs. *The action of the Copyright Office only raises the presumption that computer programs are copyrightable,*[14] but the trend is to provide copyright as a protection for software.

The requirements that a software program must meet for registration consist of the following as defined in Copyright Office Circular 61:

1) The elements of assembling, selection, arranging, editing, and literary expression that went into the compilation of the program are sufficient to constitute original authorship.

2) The program has been published with the required copyright notice; that is, "copies" (i.e., reproductions of the program in a form perceptible or capable of being made perceptible to the human eye) bearing the notice have been distributed or made available to the public.

3) The copies deposited for registration consist of two complete copies of the program in the form as first published. If the first publication was in a form (such as machine-readable tape) that cannot be perceived visually or read by humans, a visually perceptible reproduction or description (such as printout of the program) must also be deposited.

4) An application for registration is submitted on Form A. Detailed instructions for registration are given on the application form.

5) The applicant also submits a brief explanation of the way in which the program was first made available to the public and the form in which the copies were published. This explanation is not essential in every case, but it will generally facilitate examination of the claim.

The procedure that the developer should follow to obtain a copyright is:

1. Obtain application forms and affidavit from Copyright Office, Library of Congress, Washington, D.C.

---

initial term ends, and were eligible for renewal during 1977, are handled in a special manner; if renewal registration was made prior to January 1, 1978, the copyright duration is extended 75 years; if renewal registration is made after January 1, 1978, but before December 31, 1978, the copyright duration is extended only 47 years.

[13]Copyright Office, Cir. 31D Jan. 1965, 3,000.

[14]Wihtol vs. Wells, 231 F. 2d. 550 (7th Cir. 1956).

2. *Print the program with the COPYRIGHT notice on it* and make the printed program available to the public. The printing can be in the perceptible form of transfer (e.g., tape, printout). The notice may consist of the letter C enclosed in a circle, thus ©, accompanied by the initials, monograms, or symbol of the owner, provided his name appears on some accessible part of the copies.
3. Send two copies of the work to the Register of Copyrights, Library of Congress, Washington, D.C. (If initial form of work is not perceivable by human eye (e.g., a tape), transform the work into a printout or detailed description and include with initial form, along with a completed application for registration and an affidavit that indicates how the program was made (authorship) and the form in which the copies were published (writing)).

Note that this procedure applies to books as well. This is important because books, such as operating manuals, are an integral part of a sales package generally.

The protection afforded a copyrighted program extends only to the particular expression that the program takes—not to the idea or algorithm (unlike patents) on which it is based. Thus, the copyright protection will fail without an actual infringement (e.g., unauthorized duplication). Note that in the instance in which a software program is closely interrelated with hardware, a copyright may be as effective as a patent. That is, it would be virtually impossible not to duplicate the program in order to perform the same function. This may be true in many cases where optimal interfacing with hardware peripherals is accomplished through operating system or applications software routines or in specific iteration techniques. Therefore, careful consideration should be given to the use of the copyright protection where the software is closely related to specific hardware.

The determination of infringement is still an open question since no court has adjudicated what conduct constitutes infringement. Obviously, the water will be very muddy in situations involving complex programs and involving concepts used in the literary field that are inadequate to handle the technical nature of computer programs. Key elements that should be considered in developing the criteria for infringement of software copyrights are:

- Commonality of purpose of the programs
- Similarity of instruction sequences or patterns of instructions, i.e., repetition of instruction sequences
- Significance of dissimilar material, i.e., value of extraneous code
- Common errors (this will be an obvious clue)

The exact nature of the criteria to be established is speculative. But the increased numbers of software registrations per year indicate a high confidence in the courts to eventually define an effective protection against software privacy.

TRADE SECRET—AS LEGAL PROTECTION OF SOFTWARE

Trade secret protection is a tort (civil) remedy established to protect businessmen from the unlawful or unethical acquisition of business secrets by competitors (e.g., industrial espionage or competition by an ex-employee). This protection is afforded to any device, pattern, formula, or compilation of information (e.g., mailing lists) used in business to gain an edge over competitors. Clearly the software program falls under the umbrella of trade secrets.

In order to exercise the tort remedy, the owner of the trade secret must prove:

1. the existence of the trade secret,
2. the value of the trade secret to the business,
3. the owner's right to use the trade secret, and
4. acquisition of the secret by the defendant by unlawful or unethical means.

The last element, 4, may be shown in one of four ways, according to the Restatement of Torts §757:

1. Discovery by improper means
2. Breach of fiduciary (position of trust) relationship
3. Knowledge of secrecy and that disclosure by the third party was breach of fiduciary relationship or based on improper acquisition
4. Knowledge of secrecy and the disclosure was a mistake

The advantages of trade secret protection are:

- No need to disclose software program as in copyright or patent procedures
- Not limited to written claim (as in patent)
- No cost to maintain
- Courts tend to protect business integrity

The principal disadvantage is that of proving that the defendant obtained the trade secret unlawfully or unethically. If the program is obtained by legitimate means, no protection is provided.

7.3.2 CONTRACTS

Once a software businessman has determined how to protect his product, he must consider the details of the document, the contract that will bind him to the buyer of his software. The law of contracts forms the basis for all business transactions. The contract embodies the intent and expectations of the parties and all of the details of the rights and duties of the parties thereto. In a software development context, this ranges from a procurement specification to a lease agreement for either computer time or use of a particular program. An important factor that the software businessman should remember is that very likely those expectations of a party which are not written into the contract cannot be enforced. Therefore, a basic understanding of law of contracts and the essentials of a software contract, including a checklist, are provided here.

FORMATION OF A CONTRACT

There are four classical elements essential to the formation of a contract:

1. Manifestation of Mutual Assent
2. Consideration

3. Legality of Object
4. Capacity of the Parties

The last two elements will be considered first since they are most likely to be fulfilled in a normal software business environment.

LEGALITY OF OBJECT.   The legality of the object of the contract simply refers to the court's refusal to enforce bargains that violate established law. An example of this might be a contract to develop a software program that, when doing the accounting for stock transactions, systematically places fractional parts of a cent in a personal account of an officer of a company. Thus, if a transaction requires a sale of 7 shares in a market that buys only in blocks of four at $2.50 a block, the seller's account would be credited with $4.37, and the officer's account would be credited with $.005. It is surprising how fast the illegal fraction adds up in an active brokerage.

The object of the above contract is the taking of moneys due to clients of the brokerage firm for the purpose of personal gain of the officer. This is theft—a crime by statute. The courts would not enforce such a contract, i.e., force performance by either party.

CAPACITIES OF THE PARTIES.   The subject of capacity to contract, the fourth element in forming a contract, is important because the courts deem it necessary to protect certain individuals who are easily duped in the formation of an agreement and who are generally considered unable to comprehend the nature and effect of the transaction. The principal classes of individuals who are afforded legal protection in contract formation are:

Class	Protection
Minors	Minor has the option to void the contract / adult cannot; exception is contract for necessities of life.
Insane persons	Insane person has the option to void the contract / other party cannot; exception is contract for necessities of life.
Intoxicated persons	Contract is voidable at intoxicated person's option.
Aliens	Illegal aliens cannot enforce their contracts in this country.
Private corporations	Powers to contract limited by state statutes: i.e., no recovery against the private corporation that has exceeded its powers to contract
Public corporations	Powers to contract limited to those powers granted by their parent authority: i.e., no recovery against the public corporation that has exceeded its power to contract

As indicated earlier, it is unlikely that a protected individual, as shown above, will be involved in a software development or utilization contract, but it is possible as in the case of a corporation's exceeding its power to contract under the corporation's articles of incorporation.

MANIFESTATION OF MUTUAL ASSENT.   The manifestation of mutual assent is that an agreement reached by the parties is so basic that the resultant contract is referred to as the agreement between the parties. The concept of an agreement, of course, is much broader than an enforceable contract. The latter is limited to a promise exchanged for a promise or a promise exchanged for an act or forebearance to act that is manifested by what is communicated between the parties.

The manner in which parties manifest mutual assent is by an offer and an acceptance of that offer. The determination of what constitutes a valid offer and valid acceptance has been the source of extensive litigation over the years. It is important to distinguish an offer from an invitation for an offer. For example, a quotation of prices that contains no promise to perform and leaves many terms unexpressed and a proposal in jest (e.g., "I'll take a dollar for my house.") are not offers. A reasonable man would not believe that an offer has been made in these circumstances.

The terms of the offer that become the terms of the contract when accepted must be definite and certain. The court must be able to understand the terms that are to be enforced and the extent to which the terms have been performed.

This definiteness of the offer is always a question. Some material terms required to be set forth in the agreement are the parties to the agreement, the time of performance, the place of performance, the description of subject matter, the price, the quantity, or a reference to some standard by which these essentials can be made definite or certain. Under the Uniform Commercial Code (U.C.C.) that governs the sale of goods, an indefiniteness in an agreement can be cured by the application of commercial standards that supply terms left open in the contract. Of course, there are not many commercial standards that could be used in a software contract. With the advent of more universal use of software standards and practices, some of which are set out in earlier chapters of this book, the current burden placed on the definiteness aspect of software development contracts will be lessened.

The offer must be communicated to the offeree (the person receiving the offer) by the offeror (the person making the offer). No communication of an offer, except by an authorized agent of the offeror or the offeror himself, is considered valid. Thus, an acceptance made to an offer that was communicated by a third party not acting as an agent of the offeror would not constitute formation of a contract.

It can be noted though, that an offer made by the offeror, which is erroneously transmitted, may result in an enforceable contract. The contract will be enforced if the offeree accepts the offer and did not know nor could reasonably be expected to know of the transmission error. Cases on this point have established that an erroneously transmitted offer does constitute a valid contract when accepted. In such cases the transmitter has been held liable for damages that resulted from the error. This is an important *caveat* for software developers whose software could be used as part of the transmission system.

The offer, once communicated, may be terminated other than by acceptance in the following manners:

Expiration of the time specified on the offer or the expiration of a reasonable time if no time is specified.

Revocation—the communication by the offeror that he is revoking the offer. This must be done prior to acceptance.

Rejection—the offeree rejects the offer by either a counteroffer (change in a term of the offer) or total rejection.

Death or insanity of the offeror—the offeror no longer has the capacity to enter into a contract.

Insanity of offeree—the offeree no longer has the capacity to accept.

Destruction of the subject matter—the contract or one of the parties can no longer perform; therefore, the law provides for the immediate termination of the offer to avoid contractual litigation.

Legislation subsequent to the offer that makes illegal the contract contemplated by the offer.

Acceptance of the offer, the other half of the manifestation of mutual assent, must be unequivocal; it must embrace every and all terms of the offer without adding, deleting, or changing any of the offer terms and must be communicated by the offeree to the offeror. At common law, and by statute in many states, anything short of unqualified acceptance is considered a rejection or a rejection accompanied by a counteroffer. The Uniform Commercial Code, which has been enacted in many states, departs from the common law in that to the extent the acceptance agrees with the offer there is a contract. Changes in the offer are considered proposals for change, addition, or deletion to that contract. The code departs even further from common law when the offeror and offeree are merchants. In this instance, the new terms become part of the contract unless the offer expressly limits acceptance to the terms of the offer, the additional terms materially alter the offer, or the offeror promptly rejects the new terms (UCC Section 2-207).

Communication of acceptance as in the offer is critical to the formation of the contract. Generally, an acceptance is not effective until it is communicated. There are two well-established exceptions to this rule:

1. If the offeree uses the method of transmission used by the offeror, e.g., mail, telegram, messenger, etc., then the acceptance is effective upon dispatch. This rule has been expanded to include methods of transmission other than that used by offeror, which might reasonably be expected to be used in view of the position of the parties' business usages and surrounding circumstances.
2. If the offeree is silent, his inaction will be construed as an acceptance *only* in situations: (a) where the offeree with an opportunity to reject goods or services uses (takes the benefit of) them; (b) where the offer allows for silence as proper acceptance and offeree intends by his silence to accept; or (c) where in previous dealings between the parties the offeree has given the offeror reason to understand that silence is intended by the offeree to be an acceptance.

Assuming that a proper offer and acceptance have been communicated, there are still a few considerations to assure that there is an agreement. Certainly, in any circumstance where one of the parties has misrepresented the subject matter or facts material to the agreement or has used undue influence in obtaining the other parties' consent, the contract is voidable. Thus, the innocent party can avoid liability under the contract and may have other causes of action for the improper conduct of the other party. The more common pitfall is that of a mistake in the terms of the agreement other than those mistakes due to the transmission of the offer. As a general rule, if the mistake is mutual and is material (a substantial influence on the decision of the patries) to the agreement, there is no contract. This rarely occurs in sophisticated contracting, but if the parties resort to ambiguous terminology, it can happen; for example, "FORTRAN LANGUAGE TO BE USED"—ONE PARTY ASSUMES FORTRAN II—THE OTHER FORTRAN IV LEVEL G OR H.

The more common mistakes are unilateral in nature and occur because of computational errors made by the offeror in generating a bid. In these instances, as in all unilateral mistakes, material or otherwise to the contract, the courts will enforce the contract except where the offeree knew of the error or reasonably should have known of the error and attempted to take advantage of the mistaken party.

Once the agreement is established and the terms defined, the contract is generally required by statute to be reduced to writing. The reason has its origin in old English law where it became obvious that if the contract were not in writing, the terms of the contracts, as well as the contracts, had the problems of all undocumented history. The terms were only as good as the memories of those who could attest to their content, and, of course, there were many who had moments of convenient forgetfulness. Thus, out of the old English law originated the Statute of Frauds, the essentials of which have been adopted by almost every state in this country. The statute states that any contract for the sale of land, guaranty contracts, contracts with terms that cannot be performed within one year, or contracts for the sale of goods valued at $500 or more must be in writing.

In conjunction with the Statute of Frauds, the Parol Evidence Rule was instituted. This rule prohibits the use of verbal statements to modify, add to, or delete any of the terms of a written contract. The implication is clear that if the term is not written into the contract, the term is simply not part of the contract and, therefore, not enforceable. The software seller or buyer must ensure that all terms and understandings are in the contract if he is to have a valid agreement with the purchaser of his products.

CONSIDERATION. The previous topic discussed the fact that enforceable contracts are those agreements that are limited to a bargain for exchange of a promise for a promise or of a promise for an act or a forebearance to act. Consideration, the last of the four elements of a contract to be defined, is essentially whatever is given in exchange for something else, i.e., the promise, the act, or the forebearance to act. The central idea is that the parties have bargained with each other. It is not enough that consideration exists. The consideration must be legally sufficient.

Legal sufficiency means the promise must be either a legal detriment to the promisee (the doing or undertaking to do that which the promisee was under no prior legal obligation to do, or the refraining from doing or undertaking to refrain from doing that which he was previously under no obligation to refrain from doing) or a legal benefit to the promisor (the obtaining by the promisor of that which he had no prior legal right to obtain). The following is a tabulation of some of the types of consideration and whether or not they are legally sufficient:

Consideration	Legal Sufficiency	Reason
Past consideration	Not sufficient	A promise made for something the promisee has already done is unenforceable (under the UCC 2-209(1) a modification to a contract may be valid without consideration).
Pre-existing duty	Not sufficient	A promise to do something the promisor is already under a duty to do is no greater obligation to promisor (no legal detriment).
Illusory promise	Not sufficient	Where one party in a bilateral contract (an agreement for promise in exchange for a promise) is not bound, there is no detriment (note requirements contracts are not necessarily illusory).
Settlement of a disputed claim	Sufficient	If there is a valid dispute, then there is detriment and benefit in the settlement of the price.
Payment manner different from obligation	Sufficient	If there is a legal detriment by paying differently from the obligation, then there is sufficient consideration.
Promise to pay a debt barred by statute of limitation	Sufficient	Where a debt is no longer enforceable because of statutes that limit the time of enforcement, the new promise to pay is viewed as valid consideration.
Promise to pay debt discharged by bankruptcy	Not required	Construed as valid without consideration.

There are certain instances under the UCC that do not require consideration to be enforced—any claim arising out of a breach of contract, a written and signed offer by a merchant, an agreement modifying a contract for the sale of goods, and the establishment of a letter of credit or modification of its terms.

It is important to note that sufficiency does not mean the adequacy or value of the consideration. The courts treat the parties as having freely agreed to the exchange and are not concerned with whether the bargain was good or bad. The only situations where adequacy is considered are from a question of duress, undue influence, or fraud. Thus, the reader should beware of bad bargains (i.e., caveat emptor).

Another caveat in dealing with consideration is that if the consideration would normally be found not sufficient (e.g., a gratuitous promise) but the promisee changes his position in reliance on that promise, the courts out of justice will enforce the contract. A possible example might be if a software contractor gratuitously promises to include an accounting routine in the software he delivers, so the buyer reduces his accounting staff while relying on the expected time-savings support the program. A court of equity may enforce the software contractor's promise under a concept called promissory estoppel. Note that under the UCC such a promise may be valid as a modification of a contract.

NEGOTIATIONS

The negotiation of a contract is a field unto itself. It requires technical, legal, and financial expertise to understand and bargain for the best contract position. There are complete books on the psychology and approaches required for negotiating any contract. Probably the most important point to remember is: understand what is being signed, including the risks that are associated with performance of any terms of the contract.

Generally, the negotiating team consists of one or more individuals from each of the disciplines indicated in the previous paragraph, with appropriate management supervision. In such cases the strategy of establishing an initial position on the terms (which terms are negotiable) for the negotiation is determined in advance along with a designated spokesman for the group. If a negotiator does not have the luxury of all the expertise, then he may find himself at a disadvantage. The best way to avoid this is to understand the job required (size and complexity) and the financial aspects of doing that job (costs, cost savings, etc.) as best he can. By doing this the potential risks will be minimized. Further, the checklist in the next subsection will provide an understanding of the terms that should be included or at least considered.

Most negotiators have been "outfoxed" and have been very lucky on one occasion or another. Remember that no terms are freely given in negotiations; therefore, the software contractor must be prepared for hard bargaining. If he is ill-equipped for the job, he should hire a professional negotiator as his representative. Further, he should not sign anything until he has benefit of legal counsel—as has been illustrated, lack of understanding, short of misrepresentation, is no excuse for making an undesirable bargain under the law.

WRITING SOFTWARE CONTRACTS

The writing of a software contract is tailored to the job to be done—either the licensed use of a software program or the development of a software program(s). Generally, a contract should be very specific because of broad judicial interpretations under the UCC [Computer Service Centers, Inc., v. Beacon Manufacturing Co., 328 F. Supp. 653 (DSC 1970); Clements Auto Co. v. Service Bureau Corp., 298 F. Supp. 115 (D. Minn. 1969) aff'd as modified, 444 F. 2d. 169 (8th Cir. 1971)]. As the use of software contracts increases, the uncertainty of legal interpretation will disappear.

The following software contract checklist serves as a guide to the points that should be covered in any contract, development, or licensing of software programs. This list is general in nature and not intended to be all inclusive. The importance of the checklist is not for writing the contract, since the legal counsels of the parties are well able to write the contract and may use their own forms, but in pinpointing the important issues that should be addressed in the contract. Prior knowledge of the really important issues helps to avoid any ambiguous clauses that might result in disputed interpretations.

Standard Clauses
- Names and Addresses of Parties

- Effective Date of Contract
- Duration of Contract
- Governing State or National Law Clause
- Arbitration Clause for Resolution of Disputes
- Survival Clause (Severability Clause)
- General Notice Clause
- Definition of Terms Used in Contract
- *Force Majeure* (Acts of God, Strikes, etc.)

Special Clauses
- Specification/Description of Software
    Size
    Timing
    Software/Hardware Interfaces
    Program Language
    Machine Compatibility
    Accuracy
    Input Requirements
        Form
        Format
        Rates
    Output Requirements
        Form (printout display)
        Formats
        Human Factors Restrictions
        Rates
    Diagnostic Capabilities
        Printout
        Stop Points
        Step Capability
    Support Software Required
- Documentation
    Number of Documents
    Level of Detail
    Types of Documents
        Operations Manuals
        Design Documentation
        Program Listings
        Program Descriptions
- Maintenance
    Who Performs/Restrictions on Personnel
    Computer Availability (time, hands-on operations, and the like)
    Performed at What Site
    Response Time (limitations on time to correct or respond to notification of error)
    Special Work Conditions

Special clauses can be more particularly described by incorporating other documents attached as appendices.

Special Maintenance Considerations (free for 90 days, and the like)
- Provisions for Updates
    Buyer's Rights to Improved Programs
    Conditions for Delivery and Installation
- Development Computer Requirements
    If at Buyer's Site
        Definition of Computer Usage (e.g., wall clock time, CPU time, and the like)
        Amount of Time
        Restrictions on Usage (e.g., at night, 5 min, out of hour, batch executions, hands-on operation)
        Limitations Due to Interruptions Caused by Software "Hangs"
    If a Seller's Site
        Excuse of Performance Due to Computer Loss
        Requirements for Commercial Computer Time Availability
        Compensation for Premium Computer Time Costs
- Ownership/Usage Rights
    If Developing Software
        Who Owns Software Developed
        Who Gets Copyrights
    If Buyer Owns Software
        Does Seller Get Usage Rights
        Limitations of Seller's Usage
            Making Copies
            Usage in Company
    If Seller Owns Software (Licensing of Software)
        Buyer Has Exclusive or Nonexclusive Use
        Limitations of Buyer's Usage
            Buyer's Rights to Make Copies/Software and/or Documentation
            Frequency of Use
            Duration of Use
        Restrictions on Modifications
        Who Owns Buyer's Modifications
- Training Requirements (buyer's operative personnel)
    How Much Training (to what level)
        Hours/Day
        Personnel
        Training Restrictions to be Performed
        Pre-Installation
        During Installation
        Post-Installation
    Where is Training to be Performed
        Pre-Installation
        During Installation
        Post-Installation

How Long is Training to Last

Availability of Computer Time

- Testing/Trouble Shooting

    Level of Acceptance Testing

        Buyer Imposed Testing Requirements

        Seller Test Requirements

    Where are Tests to be Performed

    Availability of Computer Time (defined)

    Restrictions on Test Periods

    Restrictions on Computer Usage (hands-on operation)

- Installation Support

    Availability of Support

    Type of Support

    Time for Installation

- Definition of Acceptance (Delivery)

    When Conditions Met (e.g., criteria for acceptance testing)

    Form of Software [cards, tape (source held in escrow)]

    Documentation

    Repair Period

- Compensation

    Price

    Manner of Payment

    Special Pay-as-You-Go Clauses

    Options to Buy

    Options to Renew License

    Security Provisions for Payment

    Inspection of Records (important in licensing)

    Default Provisions

        Delivery of Software

            Penalties for Being Late

            Rewards for Early Delivery

        Failure to Make Payments to Provide Inspection of Records

            Penalty Provisions

            Reversion of Rights

- Warranties

    Warranty of Ownership

        Who Defends

        Who Assumes Responsibility for Damage

    Warranty of Performance

        Who Assumes Responsibility for Damage to Third Party

        Responsibilities/Warranties of Use to User

- Protection of Confidential Information

    Definition of Information to Be Protected

    Security Procedures for Protection of Information Transmitted between Buyer and Seller

Security Procedures for Protection of Software and Documentation
- Assignment Provisions
    - Restrictions on Buyers
        - Limitations on Assiging Usage
        - Limitations on Assignment of Rights to Options
    - Restrictions on Sellers
        - Restrictions on Subcontracting Performance
        - Restriction of Assignment of Usage Rights

7.3.3 TAX CONSIDERATIONS

Not only must the software seller consider the legal aspects of choosing a business form, determining how to protect his software program, and entering into a valid, safe contract, he must also be well aware of the tax considerations involved in forming his own enterprise. Taxes, both Federal and State, have become one of the prime considerations of the business community. Through taxation, the government has the ability to stimulate or depress the business activities of our society. Needless to say, the government has not forgotten about software. This subsection is primarily concerned with the taxation of software development and/or purchase and lease. For tax considerations associated with the forms of a business, see Sec. 7.2.

FEDERAL TAX TREATMENT

The Internal Revenue Code is, of course, the primary tax consideration in the United States. The treatment of software has been a little confusing principally because software programs tend to be a "mystery" to most who are unfamiliar with them and because software programs are not simply identifiable with the IRS's categories. But the IRS has prevailed and Table 7-4 summarizes the categories and the tax treatment of the various software expenditures. There are some obvious ambiguities. The correlation of software development costs and research and experimental expenditures is not that unreasonable and, in fact, shows some insight by the IRS into software development. A key point for the reader to note is that the developer must be consistent, once the choice of business expense or capitalization is made. The choice is complex and closely aligned with the financial planning of the company. Therefore, tax decisions should be made carefully with proper tax counselling. Table 7-5 reflects a comparison of the amortization versus expense approaches, using a normal trapezoid spending curve. For this discussion, it is adequate to point out that the capitalization method defers the deduction for expenses into the future when income from the developed software is expected.

The major ambiguity in the categories is the different treatment afforded software that is purchased as part of a computer (not separately stated from hardware) and that which is purchased separately. They are considered tangible and intangible assets, respectively. The tax ramifications are significant. Table 7-6 reflects the various amounts deductible under the various tax methods, assuming the following example: cost of the software, $100,000, a useful life of 5 years, and no salvage value. As one can see, the various methodologies distribute the deductions quite differently. Both

Table 7-4 Summary of Federal Tax Treatment of Software

Deductible Item	IRS Category	Tax Treatment	Problems/Comment
Software development expenses	Same as a research and experimental expenditure	(a) Can deduct as an ordinary business expense OR (b) Can capitalize development costs and amortize them over a period of 5 years (shorter if useful life is shown to be less than 5 years) from the date of completion	Must be consistent as to choice When capitalization is used, it is very difficult to show shorter useful life.
Software lease expenses	Rental expense	Normal business deduction	
Software purchase expenses			
• Bought as part of computer hardware package	Tangible asset (same as hardware capitalization)	Capitalized as a tangible asset • Can take advantage of depreciation • Can use straight-line of declining balance, or years-digits method, or another consistent method of depreciation	Clearly there is an edge to computer manufacturers who sell software as part of hardware since the depreciation method of software alone is constrained to the straight-line method computation.
• Bought separately from computer hardware	Intangible assets	Amortized over a 5-year period or a shorter period where it can be established as appropriate	

Table 7-5 Tax Deduction Comparison for Software Development Costs

Year	Cost Project 1	Cost Project 2	Cost Project 3	Business Expense Deduction 1	2	3	Total	Amortization Deductions 1	2	3	Total
1	100,000			100,000			100,000				
2	200,000	50,000		200,000	50,000		250,000				
3	100,000	100,000	100,000	100,000	100,000	100,000	300,000				
4		50,000	200,000		50,000	200,000	250,000	80,000			80,000
5			100,000			100,000	100,000	80,000	40,000		120,000
6								80,000	40,000	80,000	200,000
7								80,000	40,000	80,000	200,000
8								80,000	40,000	80,000	200,000
9									40,000	80,000	120,000
10										80,000	80,000

the declining balance and sum of the years' digits allow large early deductions. This may be advantageous from overall financial perspectus of the company, i.e., early recovery of tax dollars. In considering a corporation, for every $100 deductible, $48 of taxes do not have to be paid. In other words, the corporation obtains a 48%

Table 7-6 Tax Deduction Comparisons for Purchased Software

Year	Software as Intangible Amortization	Software as Tangible (Not Separable from Hardware)					
		Straight-Line Method		Declining Balance		Sum of the Years Digits	
1	20,000	(1/5)	20,000	(2 × R^*/5)	40,000	(5/15)	33,333
2	20,000	(1/5)	20,000	(2 × R_1/5)	30,000	(4/15)	26,667
3	20,000	(1/5)	20,000	(2 × R_2/5)	12,000	(3/15)	20,000
4	20,000	(1/5)	20,000	(2 × R_3/5)	7,200	(2/15)	13,333
5	20,000	(1/5)	20,000	(2 × R_4/5)	4,320	(1/15)	6,667
Total deduction:	$100,000		100,000		93,520**		100,000

*R means the remaining balance, i.e., previous balance − prior year's deduction.

**The remaining $5,460, not written off, could have been written off as a loss for the fifth and last year of the assets useful life, if it is abandoned then. As an alternative, the taxpayer could change to a straight line and recover the remaining cost or adjusted basis.

discount on the purchase. For a sole proprietor, the effective discount may be as high as 70%.

STATE TAX TREATMENT

Each state is grappling with the project of taxing software. The state income taxes, where they exist, mostly parallel the Federal tax treatment; state and local property taxes are another matter. Generally, the tax assessors have been eager to raise funds for the local governments at the expense of software that they assess for property value and, of course, on which they collect taxes. California, hoping to settle the dispute between software developers and users and the tax collectors, approved the following software property tax valuation as documented in the California Revenue and Taxation Code Section 995:

> Storage media for computer programs shall be valued on the 1972 lien date and there-after as if there were no computer programs on such media except basic operational programs. . . .

The act went on in Section 995.2 to define basic operational programs as:

> The term "basic operational program" as used in Section 995 . . . means a computer program which is fundamental and necessary to the functioning of a computer. A basic operational program is that part of an operating system including supervisors, monitors, executives and control or master programs which consist of the control program elements of the system. . . .
>
> Excluded from the term "basic operational program" are processing programs which consist of language translators, including but not limited to, assemblers and compilers, service programs, including but not limited to, data set utilities, sort/merge utilities, and emulators, data management systems, also known as generalized file

processing software, and application programs including but not limited to payroll, inventory control and production control. Also exluded . . . are programs or parts of programs developed for or by user if they are developed solely for the solution of an individual operational problem of the user. . . .

The act, of course, has been applauded by developers and users alike.

Most other states have not pinned down the status of software as finely as California. Therefore, the local laws should be reviewed, either to support a change in software status or to define it as best suits the needs of the local community.

7.3.4 AGENCY

Since the software developer may not be the type of person or have the resources to properly market his product or his expertise, or may not be able to accomplish the task himself, he must be aware of the laws of agency that control his relationship with people he may require to support him. Agency is a relationship between two persons whereby one of them is authorized to act for and/or on behalf of the other. The person authorized to act is the agent while the person giving the authorization is the principal. The agent, within the scope of the agency's authority, may bind the principal, creating rights and duties on the part of the principal to third parties. Further, the principal is responsible for certain of the agent's acts that occur in the course of performing his duties.

CREATION OF AGENCY

There are four ways in which an agency can be created, assuming the capacity of the principal, i.e., the principal can authorize the agent only to perform acts for which he has capacity (see discussion of capacity in contracts section above):

1. By contract—an agreement between the parties as to the scope of the agency and authority of the agent
2. By operation of law—agency established by statute
3. By estoppel—where one party presents another as if he were an agent and induces reasonable reliance of a third party to deal with that party as an agent
4. By ratification—the adoption or confirmation by one person of an act that has been performed on behalf by another without his authority.

Under these four definitions, there are two types of agents—actual and ostensible. The actual agent is one authorized to represent the principal. The ostensible agent is one to whom the principal has given no authority, but by the principal's conduct has induced others to reasonably believe that he has authority to act.

The actual agent may fall into two classes, a general agent or special agent. The differences lie in the scope of authority. Special agents, like brokers, are authorized to act for the principal only in specific transactions. The actual agent, when authorized by the principal, may also employ a subagent to assist in the transaction. The subagent, like the actual agent, has the authority to bind the principal.

RELATIONSHIP BETWEEN AGENT AND PRINCIPAL

Under the Restatement of the Law of Agency 2d, the duties owed by the agent to the principal are:

1. Duty of care and skill—Agent must act with care and skill equal to the standard in the locality for similar kind of work (Section 379).
2. Duty of good conduct—Agent must not act with impropriety (Section 380).
3. Duty to give information—Agent must use reasonable efforts to give his principal relevent information (Section 381).
4. Duty to keep and render accounts—Unless otherwise agreed, the agent must give an accounting of all transactions on behalf of principal (Section 382).
5. Duty to act only as authorized—Agent must act within the scope of conduct authorized by principal (Section 383).
6. Duty not to attempt the impossible or impractical—Agent is under a duty to terminate services that subject the principal to risk of expense if such services appear impossible or impractical (Section 384).
7. Duty to obey—Unless otherwise agreed, the agent must obey all reasonable directions of the principal in the scope of the agency (Section 385).
8. Duties after termination of authority—Agent must no longer act as an agent after termination of authority (Section 386).

It should be remembered that an agency relationship is a fiduciary relationship (a position of trust or confidence), which means the agent must act with loyalty and good faith. The agent must, therefore, act solely in the interest of the principal, not in his own interest or in the interest of another (i.e., must not allow a conflict of interests).

The duties owed the agent by the principal are in two categories, contract and tort. The contractual duties are set forth in the Restatement of the Law of Agency 2d as follows:

1. Duty to furnish opportunity for work—The principal after contracting an agent must not interfere with the opportunity to work (Section 433).
2. Duty not to interfere with agent's work—The principal must refrain from unreasonable interfering with the agent's work (Section 434).
3. Duty to give agent information—The principal must provide the agent with all information he has reason to know regarding risk of harm or loss by the agent and any information required by the agreement (Section 435).
4. Duty to keep and render accounts—Unless otherwise agreed, the principal must keep accounts of amounts due agent (Section 436).
5. Duty of good conduct—Unless otherwise agreed, the principal must conduct himself so as not to harm the agent's reputation or ability to work (Section 437).
6. Duty of indemnity exists—Unless otherwise agreed, principal is under a duty to indemnify an agent for certain circumstances arising out of performance of authorized acts (Section 439):
   a) Authorized payments for principal

b) Payments where agent is authorized to make himself liable for the benefit of principal

c) Payments of damages to third parties required because the authorized performance of an act constitutes a tort or breach of contract.

d) Expense of defending against third parties

e) Payments resulting in benefit to principal

7. Duty to pay compensation—Unless otherwise agreed or by circumstances, the principal has a duty to compensate the agent for services performed (Section 441); amount of compensation is either amount agreed to or fair value (Section 443).

8. Duty not to terminate employment—The principal has a duty not to terminate the employment in violation of the employment agreement (Section 450).

9. Liability of principal to subagent—The principal is not contractually liable to subagents, but is liable for tort liability and indemnification (Section 458).

Tort duties arise from an employment relationship. In this context, the principal owes the duties of

1. providing reasonably safe conditions of employment,
2. disclosing any unreasonable risks,
3. compensating employees for tortuous conduct of other employees not co-employees (not fellow servants).

The first duty to an employee is of particular importance since it extends to maintenance, inspection and repair of the premises, tools and instruments under the control of the principal.

At common law, the principal could defend against these tort liabilities by using several theories: lack of negligence of the employer; contributory negligence of the employee; fellow servant rule; and assumption of risk. Generally the theories were quite effective in limiting employers' liabilities and usually resulted in long, tedious litigation. In order to ensure more rapid and certain relief, most states have enacted Workmen's Compensation Statutes. Under these statutes, the common law defenses are not applicable; and the awards are made by commissions or boards, not the courts. Courts usually have only review jurisdiction.

LIABILITY OF PRINCIPAL AND AGENT TO THIRD PARTIES

The liability of principals to third parties for the acts or omissions of his agents is based on two theories, contract and tort. The contractual theory is based on the authorization of the agent to contract with third parties when acting within the scope of his actual or apparent authority. Table 7-7 summarizes the types of authority and whether third party liability lies with the principal. Note that these liabilities are only if the agent is acting within the scope of his authority. Further, from an evidencing standpoint, statements or admissions made by an agent within the scope of his authority are admissible against the principal.

Table 7-7 Summary of Principal's Liability to Third Parties
for Acts of Agents Within Authority

Types of Authority	Definition	Liability of Principal to Third Parties
Express Authority	Express authority as defined in words or writing by principal	Yes
Apparent authority	Ostensible authority manifested by principal to third party	Yes
Implied authority	A real authority based on consent of principal inferred from words or conduct of the principal and inherently required to accomplish the principal's directions	Yes
Delegation of authority	Authorized by principal Unauthorized by principal	Yes No
Authority by necessity	Under emergency situations or situations of necessity the law confers authority	Yes

The tort liability of a principal to third parties falls in two categories:

1. Principal authorized his agent to commit the tortuous act
2. Tort committed by agent in the course of his employment (the Doctrine of *Respondeat Superior*)

In the first case, the principal is liable per se. In the second, the principal may be liable if he cannot show that the agent was acting outside the scope of his employment, e.g., agent had an accident when on a joy ride in the company car—principal may be liable unless he can prove the agent was in no way acting within scope of his employment. Since an independent contractor is not an agent, the doctrine of Respondeat Superior does not apply, though other duties may still apply.

The agent may subject himself to liabilities to third parties when performing on behalf of the principal. The agent is always liable for the wrongful acts or negligence that cause damage to third parties regardless of whether such acts were authorized or unauthorized by the principal. But the agent may or may not be liable for contractual delegations, depending on the circumstances. Table 7-8 summaries the agent's exposure to third party liability.

TERMINATION OF AGENCY

The agent's authority may be terminated in the following circumstances (note that these may not terminate the agent's power):

- Mutual agreement of agent and principal
- Fulfillment of purpose of the agency
- Revocation by the principal by notice to agent

Table 7-8 Summary of Agent's Liabilities to Third Parties

Status of Principal	Definition	Rights of Principal Against Third Party	Rights of Agent	Rights of Third Party Against Agent
Undisclosed	Agent appears to be acting on own behalf	Full rights except where agent specifies acting for self or contract real or where agent is party to negotiable instrument	Full rights	Agent personally liable unless third party elects to hold principal liable after identify known
Partially disclosed	Third party knows of principal but not identity	Full rights	Full rights	Same as above
Disclosed	Actual agency	Full rights	None	None
Partially incompetent	Principal is an infant or insane	Full rights as described under contract law	None	Agent does not warrant capacity, therefore not liable
Nonexistent	Person professes to act for nonexistent principal			Agent personally liable

- Renunciation by the agent by notice to principal
- Bankruptcy of the principal or agent
- Death of the principal or agent
- Insanity of the principal or agent
- Change in business circumstances
- Loss or destruction of the subject matter
- Loss of qualification of principal or agent
- Disloyalty of agent (conflict of interest)
- Change in law whereby the exercise of authority is illegal
- Outbreak of war where principal and agent are citizens of different countries.

The distinction between the termination of authority and power of an agent is important. Unless all third parties are given notice of the termination of authority, the ability of the agent to bind the principal continues.

7.4

Liabilities for Software Performance

To this point in the discussion the thrust has been to establish the basic legal awareness necessary to establish and operate a software development business. Now we must address the legal realities of producing a software package that either does not perform according to expectations or that injures someone by improper operation.

This section addresses three major segments of the law that have a significant role in establishing liability for the performance of software: Contract Remedies, Tort Remedies (e.g., Negligence), and Privacy Law Remedies. Each area is independent, but the same software defect or failure could result in the liability of the software developer under any one or all of these segments.

Careful consideration should be given to the circumstances under which liability applies since through an understanding of these circumstances, the software developer can, at least to some degree, assess the risks to his business. Each software application should be evaluated in light of the design specifications, the risks assumed by the buyer, the use the software is to be put to, the possibility of third party injuries, and, of course, the funding and development schedule. The bottom line is if we are going to stay in business, we had best evaluate the risk of liability and take all reasonable steps to minimize those risks.

7.4.1 CONTRACT REMEDIES

Generally, the relationship between the software program supplier and the user is a contractual one such as a sales agreement, lease, or development contract. In this context, breach of the terms of the agreement gives rise to recovery under general contract theories. As pointed out in the prior section, the inclusion in the contract of all the understandings that constituted the agreement as well as a clear description of all the specifics of the software and software performance is critical in determining whether or not the action of either party constitutes a breach of contract. Even a contract written with clarity presents great difficulty in determining whether or not the software program is defective.

The first step in making an assessment as to breach of contract involves deciding the nature of the provisions of the contract to be enforced. The provisions can be either promises or conditions or both. A promise is a duty to perform. A condition is an event or nonevent whose occurrence gives rise to a duty to perform or extinguishes the contract. There are basically three types of conditions:

1. Express conditions—an act or occurrence that must either occur or be excused before giving rise to the duty of counterperformance.
2. Implied in fact condition—a condition necessary to performance by either party that the parties would have agreed on had they thought to express themselves.
3. Implied in law condition—an implied condition by the courts where it is fair, just, and equitable to act in a certain manner and to assure performance of the bargain that was made.

If the condition is established, then the legal effect of the occurrence (performance) or nonoccurrence of the condition is summarized in Table 7-9. As reflected in the table, the courts are anxious to protect each party's expectations.

The problem in software contracts is determining at which point there has been a breach of the terms of the contract. Clearly, the perspective of the user, who has a problem to be solved, and the supplier, who has software to sell or lease, is quite different. Thus, determining whether there has been a breach is a difficult matter.

Table 7-9 Summary of the Legal Effects of Performance of Conditions

Performance of Conditions	Legal Effect of Conduct	Comment
CONDITIONS PERFORMED		
Condition precedent to counterperformance	Occurrence of a condition precedent is performance and makes the other party's duty of counterperformance arise.	Typical of a condition precedent is an express condition precedent to perform to another's or a third party's satisfaction. Under the majority of states, the condition is not satisfied if the other party is honestly dissatisfied. In a minority of states, the condition is satisfied if an average reasonable person would have been satisfied.

Conditions concurrent with counterperformance	Occurrence of a condition concurrent is performance and makes the other party's duty of performance absolute.	Generally, conditions concurrent are not expressed but implied by law when
		Performances are capable of simultaneous performance *and*
		   The same time is set for performance *or*
		   Time is set for one performance and not the other *or*
		   No time is set for either performance *or*
		   The same period of time is set for both performances

Conditions subsequent to counterperformance	Occurrence of a condition subsequent extinguishes a duty to perform that has already arisen.	Conditions subsequent are always expressed. They are analogous to the statute of limitations.
CONDITIONS NOT PERFORMED		
Conditions excused: by tender	If a condition precedent exists that can be performed, a rejected tender of performance excuses the duty of performance. If a condition concurrent exists, a rejection of a tender makes the other party's duty to perform absolute and excuses the performance of tendering party.	If time is of the essence, rejection of the tender gives rise to suit for total damages. If time is not of the essence, then there is only a minor breach that can be cured. Time can be made of the essence by giving notice that the other party is to perform within a reasonable time. Failure to perform constitutes a major breach.
by failure of prior condition	No duty to perform	If D is to develop a software program as a condition precedent to U's duty to pay and U fails to supply the computer or actively interferes with D's performance, there is a failure of an implied in fact condition of cooperation excusing D's condition precedent to develop the software. U's duty to pay becomes absolute, giving D a cause of action for breach of contract.
by anticipatory breach	In a bilateral contract a party whose duty to perform is based on a condition precedent, such party's unequi-	A better rule applied in some states allows the repudiator to withdraw his repudiation unless the repudiatee has acted on it to his detriment.

Table 7-9 Summary of the Legal Effects of Performance of Conditions (cont'd.)

Performance of Conditions	Legal Effect of Conduct	Comment
	vocal repudiation of his promise prior to performance has the following effects in a majority of states:	
CONDITIONS NOT PERFORMED		
by anticipatory breach (continued)	Excusing repudiatee's condition Gives rise to immediate cause of action	
by prospective inability to perform	If, by his conduct, a party indicates that he will be unable to perform, then there is a split of authority: Only excuses duty of counterperformance *or* Acts like anticipatory breach	See local law for which rule applies—California applies the anticipatory breach concept.
by severability	May recover on contract even though not fully performed if contract is severable.	Sales contracts are generally severable, but development contracts generally are not.
by waiver or estoppel	If a party does not perform in reliance on the representation of the other, the party is excused.	
by substantial performance	Doctrine used to avoid hardship in cases involving the following factors: Extent to which injured party will obtain the substantial benefit that he reasonably anticipated.	
Conditions excused by substantial performance (continued)	Extent to which injured party can be compensated by damages. Extent to which performance has already been rendered. Amount of hardship in denying recovery. Whether nonperformance is willful, negligent or innocent. Greater or lesser uncertainty that party will finish performance.	

Table 7-9 Summary of the Legal Effects of Performance of Conditions (cont'd.)

Performance of Conditions	Legal Effect of Conduct	Comment
by impossibility	Nonperformance will be excused if performance was objectively impossible.	
Conditions not excused condition precedent	Duty of counterperformance does not arise.	
condition concurrent	Same as condition precedent if neither party has performed or excused.	
condition subsequent	Duty of performance that has already arisen will not be extinguished.	
if became absolute promise (condition)	Legal effect depends on nature of breach:	
	Minor breach—gives rise to actual damages and suspends duty of counterperformance.	
	Major breach—gives rise to cause of action on entire contract and keeps duty of counterperformance from arising.	

There are only a limited number of cases that have been tried in this area of law, but their results are significant:

Carl Beasley Ford Inc. v. Burroughs Corporation 361 F. Supp. 325 (E. D. Pa 1973).

In a case that involved the sale of an electronic accounting system, an electronic accounting machine, and an oral agreement to deliver thirteen (13) programs. [Only twelve (12) programs were delivered and the system did not perform adequately.] The court held the following:
   a) The burden of proof is on the defendant supplier to show it did not cause the software failure.
   b) The contract is a contract for a certain result (buyer's perception) and not for certain services.

Clements Auto Company v. Service Bureau Corporation 444 F. 2d. 169 (8th Cir. 1971) aff'g modified 298 F. Supp. 115 (D. Minn. 1969).

This case involved the sale of an inventory and reporting data processing services for improved business that did not help the business. The court held that:
   The clause limiting liability was effective to deny the plaintiff (the complaining party) full recovery in an action on contract.

The importance of these two cases lies in the fact that if the contract tends toward ambiguity, the courts first tend to favor the less knowledgeable user, but will usually limit liability to that specified in the contract (such limiting contract clauses are called disclaimer clauses). Thus, both the supplier and the user should be specific in detailing the expectations and specifications of the software programs. This accuracy will assist the courts in determining whether or not there has been adequate performance of the provisions of the contract.

7.4.2 TORT REMEDIES

Tort law is based on the concept of compensation (making whole). Within this concept the courts through decisions and the legislatures through statutes have established certain guidelines of what property rights are, in fact, compensable and what duty is owed by members of society to conduct themselves in a manner so as to protect that property.

The compensable conduct generally falls short of conduct that gives rise to criminal prosecution, although clearly criminal conduct may also give rise to civil tort liability, e.g., an auto accident involving a drunk driver may give rise to criminal prosecution for driving under the influence as well as giving rise to a tort action for negligence resulting in damage to some vehicle or other property.

The tort action is distinguished not only from criminal action, but also from contract action in which the injury usually originates from a breach of the agreement rather than a breach of duty of conduct imposed by law. Again, the same act that results in the breach of a contract may result in a breach of duty in a tort.

The principal areas of interest in the tort field are intentional torts, negligence, products liability, misrepresentation, and implied warranty, which is both a part of tort and of contract law. These are the critical areas that will most affect the liability of the software developer for the software product. Other areas of tort law that apply to the conduct of the software business are discussed in Sec. 7.5, Other Legal Considerations.

INTENTIONAL TORTS

An intentional tort is an act or omission intended to bring about the harm that results thereby (without the consent of the injured party or a privilege to act recognized by the law). In these cases the following must be proved in order to recover damages:

1. The act by defendant
2. Invasion of an interest
3. Defendant's intent
4. Causal relationship
5. Lack of consent or privilege

The intent here does not have to be as specific as in criminal law (e.g., premeditated); it merely has to be that the invasion was intended by the act. Damages need not be shown in order to recover compensation; in fact, punitive damages are generally awarded. Punitive damages exist to deter such intentional conduct.

NEGLIGENCE AS A TORT

> Negligence is any conduct, except reckless disregard of an interest of others, that falls below the standard established by law for the protection of others against unreasonable risk of harm. (Restatement of Torts 282)

Elements that must be proven in order to recover in an action for negligence are:

- An act that the actor as a reasonable person should realize as involving an unreasonable risk of causing an invasion of an interest of another. (An omission is actionable if the actor is under a duty to act.)
- Duty of care in the defendant owed to the plaintiff to exercise a certain degree of care (standard of care).
- Breach of that duty by defendant.
- The breach of duty was the *cause in fact* of plaintiff's injury.
- The breach of duty was the *proximate cause* of the injury.
- The damages that resulted.

The major hurdles in applying the negligence concept to software occur principally in two areas—duty of care and proximate cause. The act of providing the software is easily established, but the standard of care used in programming the software is virtually nonexistent. The established standard of care utilized in fields of specialty is that standard of the prudent person with the skill and experience claimed by the defendant. In answer to the question, "What is the standard of care for a software engineer?" almost every major company developing software has attempted to establish a "good programming practices" document to act as guides in developing software. Thus far, no industry-wide standard has been adopted; for as many ways as there are to solve a problem, there are ways to program. Who is to set the standard? As software becomes more and more a part of every facet of government, industry, and our lives, clearly the pressure for standardization will increase to a point where certain programming practices will become universally adopted. Until that time, the task of establishing the standard of care to be exercised by a software engineer and the breach of that standard will be a difficult one.

The fact that a program failed is easily established from the output as are the resultant injuries. The proximate cause element is not quite as easily ascertained. In a complex program it may be difficult to determine exactly what event caused the injury. And in other cases in which the program is being executed concurrently with other programs in a large computer, or in which there is a failure in the computer that causes the program to fail, the reconstruction of the failure may be impossible.

An alternate negligence concept, *Res Ipsa Loquitur* (the thing speaks for itself), has been suggested to establish the inference of negligence. In this concept the plaintiff need prove only the following:

- The injury that occurred would not have happened normally without someone being negligent.
- The instrument was in the exclusive control of the defendant.
- The plaintiff was free from fault.
- Damages.

Though this approach has not been used yet in software litigation, it is consistent with the trend to protect the consumer.

The final hurdle the plaintiff must jump in proving negligence against the software seller is the defenses. In tort law the conduct of the plaintiff in the disputed act may also be scrutinized by the defendant. Certain types of conduct give rise to the following defenses:

Assumption of Risk—Plaintiff voluntarily and with knowledge assumes the risk of injury (expressly assumed through an agreement between the parties or impliedly assumed through usage with knowledge of greater than reasonable risk).

Contributory Negligence—The plaintiff contributes through his negligent conduct to his own injury. This defense at one time was generally considered a complete bar from recovery and still is in some states. California and some other states have adopted a new, more realistic concept of comparative negligence. In those states, where the defense of contributory negligence is still a complete bar to recovery of damages, most courts have adopted the Last Clear Chance rule to help the plaintiff. Under this rule, if the plaintiff shows that the defendant knew of the plaintiff's peril (even though a result of plaintiff's negligence) and the defendant had the last clear chance to avoid the injury, defendant is liable.

Comparative Negligence—The parties are apportioned damages according to their relative contribution to the total damages.

The question of liability for software errors to third parties (other than the supplier and user) also is an important one. The grounds for such third party liability are either strict liability or negligence. In both cases the third party must prove the same elements that the user would have to prove. In the landmark case of MacPherson *v.* Buick Motor Co. [217 N.Y. 382, 111N.E. 2d 1050 (1916)] the courts eliminated the traditional requirement that third party be in privity (have a contractual relationship) with supplier. Thus, the software engineer is held accountable for being able to foresee an injury to a third party through the use of the software as the result of a defect in the software engineer's program—especially if he knows the application of the program. The software engineer is under a duty to properly test and validate the software. The extent of testing, which is generally costly, must be traded off against the risk of harm to the user or a third party. Other factors, such as good will of the business, also enter into the quality of testing that precedes delivery of the software program. If the user presses for early delivery or abbreviated testing, there may be an assumption of risk by the user. The software supplier is advised to get any verbal understanding concerning either delivery or testing in writing and restrain software delivery until he is *reasonably* assured of its performance.

PRODUCTS LIABILITY AS A TORT

Products liability exists as a strict liability concept applied to products. When a producer places a product on the market with knowledge that it will be used without inspection, and an injury to a person, property or possibly business occurs due to a defect in the product, the law holds the producer strictly liable for the damages. The theory applies to anyone in the products distributive chain and does not require privity between the injured party and the producer.

The application of products liability in the software field has been slow in implementation, but the potential for application is increasing. More and more computer software houses are producing and marketing standard software packages for such functions as inventory control, accounting, reporting, or billing. These software packages are used by many businesses to prepare and control the flow of products, the dealings with customers, and the maintenance of employee records and payrolls. Thus, the probability of injury by an unsuspecting user of the software increases as does the risk of liability of the software producer/distributor.

MISREPRESENTATION AS A TORT

Misrepresentation is a tort of deceit and is defined as follows by the Restatement of Torts Second Section 525:

> One who fraudulently makes a misrepresentation of fact, opinion, intention or law for the purpose of inducing another to act or refrain from an action in reliance thereon in a business transaction is liable to the other for the harm caused to him by his justifiable reliance upon the misrepresentation.

The elements required to prove liability for misrepresentation include:

- Misrepresentation by defendant—generally this is restricted to fact, not opinion, but in a case that the defendant is relied on to have special information or superior knowledge concerning the subject of the statement, an action may exist for damages. In some cases involving a duty to speak, e.g., fiduciary relationship, nondisclosure also may give rise to an action in misrepresentation.
- Knowledge of falsity by defendant.
- Intention by defendant to induce reliance (substantial certainty of reliance shows intention).
- Justifiable reliance by plaintiff.
- Damage to plaintiff—out of pocket expenses or benefit of the bargain, depending on jurisdiction.

It is important to note that in some jurisdictions a cause of action may exist where the statement is an innocent or negligent misrepresentation, thus eliminating the need to show knowledge of the falsity of the representation.

The importance of misrepresentation as a cause of action for damages is illustrated in Clements Auto Supply v. Service Bureau Corporation. (See Contract Remedies.) In that case the court found that no liability could be demonstrated for breach of contract because of contract disclaimers and because the source of the defects were associated with the inaccuracy of plaintiff's own operators. The court did, however, find liability for misrepresentation. The defendant software service corporation represented to Clements

> that there were controls built into the system which were adequate to prevent any but a minimal number of errors.[15]

[15]Clements Auto Company v. Service Bureau Corporation, 298 F. Supp. 119, (D. Minn. 1969).

The plaintiff showed that the system lacked the capability to verify the operator's work. The plaintiff went on to prove that other misrepresentations along with the self–protect capability induced the plaintiff to purchase the software system.

Obviously, careful representation of the capabilities of the software and results of the use of that software help avoid any problems in misrepresentation, but agents and salesmen sometimes get overly zealous in their efforts to close their deals. The software supplier should instruct salesmen in the potential damages that may result from an erroneous representation. Further, there is some basis to believe that if all of the capabilities and characteristics of the software are adequately and clearly disclosed in the sales literature given to users, that liability may be avoided.[16] Again, the specific requirements for establishing misrepresentation vary from jurisdiction to jurisdiction. Therefore, a contract giving rise to liability in one state may not establish liability in another.

IMPLIED WARRANTY

Implied warranty also finds its origins in the Tort of Deceit; however, it is a blend of both tort and contract law. In the absence of negligence, a producer or other seller may be strictly liable for a breach of an implied warranty of fitness or merchantability of his product.

The California law, which is a reflection of the uniform code, defines implied warranty as follows:

California Commercial Code §2314: Implied Warranty: Merchantability; Usage of Trade

(1) Unless excluded or modified (Section 2316), a warranty that the goods shall be merchantable is implied in a contract for their sale, if the seller is a merchant with respect to goods of that kind . . .

(2) Goods to be merchantable must be at least such as
   (a) Pass without objection in the trade under the contract description; and
   . . .
   (c) Are fit for the ordinary purposes for which such goods are used; and
   (d) Run, within the variations permitted by the agreement, of even kind, quality and quantity within each unit and among all units involved; and
   (e) Are adequately contained, packaged, and labeled as the agreement may require; and
   (f) Conform to the promises or affirmations of fact made on the containers or label if any.

(3) Unless excluded or modified (Section 2316) other implied warranties may arise from course of dealing or usage of trade.

Commercial Code §2315: Implied Warranty: Fitness for Particular Purpose:

Where the seller at the time of contracting has reason to know any particular purpose for which the goods are required and that the buyer is relying on the seller's skill or

---

[16]Fruit Industries Research Foundation *v.* National Cash Register Company, 406 F. 2d. 546 (9th Cir. 1969), where a representation that the computer hardware peripherals could handle throughput requirements was refuted by sales literature. No liability was found for misrepresentation.

judgment to select or furnish suitable goods, there is unless excluded or modified under the next section an implied warranty that the goods shall be fit for such purposes.

Commercial code §2316: Exclusion or Modification of Warranties:

. . .

(2) Subject to subdivision (3), to exclude or modify the implied warranty of merchantability or any part of it, the language must mention merchantability and in case of a writing must be conspicuous and to exclude or modify any implied warranty of fitness the exclusion must be by a writing and conspicuous. Language to exclude all implied warranties of fitness is sufficient if it states, for example, that "there are no warranties which are extended beyond the description on the face hereof."

. . .

(4) Remedies for breach of warranty can be limited in accordance with the provisions of this division on liquidation or limitation of damages and on contractual modification of remedy . . .

Thus, under implied warranty, purchasers or users who buy directly from the defendant, and/or in some jurisdictions remote purchasers, may collect damages from the defendant by proving the following:

- The sale of goods by defendant.
- Reliance by plaintiff on the skill and judgment of the defendant.
- The defendant's having knowledge of the intent or purpose of the goods.
- The goods not being merchantable or not being fit for a particular purpose.
- The plaintiff's damage.

There are two critical problems with this cause of action, the first being the question of software programs qualifying as goods, and the second being the limitations due to contractual disclaimers.

California Commercial Code Sections 2314 and 2315 and the Uniform Commercial Code both require that in order to have the Uniform Commercial Code apply, the product must adhere completely to the definition of goods. The UCC Section 2-105 defines goods as follows:

(1) "Goods" means all things (including especially manufactured goods) which are movable at the time of identification to the contract for sale . . .

(2) Goods must be both existing and identified before any interest in them can pass . . .

As pointed out in earlier discussions, software programs in their tangible form, i.e., stored on magnetic tapes, punched cards, or printouts, may qualify as goods, as would software program output reports, even though the services of software engineer would not. Not all courts have been convinced of the applicability of the UCC to software,[17] but the general trends indicate that the UCC will spread its umbrella to cover software programs.

[17]Computer Service Centers, Inc., *v.* Beacon Manufacturing Co., 328 F. Supp. 653 (D.S.C. 1970).

Assuming the courts should find that the software contract does qualify under the UCC, the plaintiff must overcome any disclaimers (limitations on seller's liability) in the contract. California Commercial Code Section 2316, above, indicates how the software supplier can, by properly drafting his contract, avoid liability for breach of the implied warranties. The purchaser must show the disclaimer is not conspicuous or that it is unconscionable. Generally, larger companies that sell software spend considerable effort in preparing contracts that include these disclaimer clauses. The "bottom line" is to make sure that the contract reflects the understandings of the parties as regards warranties and/or limitations on liabilities for breach of warranties.

7.4.3 PRIVACY

The last major liability a software businessman may incur concerns privacy. The right of privacy is generally defined as a cause of action in damages for an unwarranted invasion of the plaintiff's interest in being left alone or to live a life of seclusion. A defendant's conduct that intrudes wrongfully into plaintiff's private affairs; exposes publicly embarrassing private facts about plaintiff; appropriates plaintiff's name or likeness for the benefit or advantage of defendant; or places plaintiff in a false light in the public eye, is considered actionable. The importance of this field of law to the software developer/user is the trend toward greater protection of the individual's right to privacy as it regards computer data systems.

The concept of right to privacy, though recognized in ancient common law, was not given a remedy. Liability for invasion of that right is a development of modern common law. Some jurisdictions originally denied such a right except to the extent that it was conferred by statute. The developments of the law in the area of right to privacy over the last few years, though, is phenomenal. Pressure for the new development is based on the fear of being a statistic in a George Orwell "1984" society and the proliferation of computer technology, which has provided a cost-effective way to store and retrieve vast amounts of data rapidly.

Modern common law of right to privacy, where it is applied, provides four distinct invasions of privacy:

1. Intrusion into plaintiff's private affairs—the intrusion may involve physical entry, viewing, or eavesdropping, but it must be an intrusion that offends ordinary sensitivities.
2. Public disclosures of embarrassing private facts about plaintiff—the disclosure must be public; the facts disclosed must be private, and the publicity must offend a reasonable person of ordinary sensitivities.
3. Appropriation of plaintiff's name or likeness for the benefit of defendant—the unauthorized exploitation of plaintiff's name or picture.
4. Giving a false public image of plaintiff—there must be the publication of false or misleading statements about plaintiff that would cause a reasonable person to suffer mental distress.

These rights are deferred by the defenses of consent or privilege, i.e., public figures or newsworthy facts. Nonetheless, this concept provides the foundation for the protection of an individual's right to privacy.

The right to privacy concept was ill-equipped to provide protection against the invasion of the computer age, however. The use of computers to store and retrieve records of all types of information has mushroomed during recent years with both governmental agencies and private agencies able to accumulate, store, and recover personal information on individuals for any number of reasons. As the numbers of computer services expanded and the numbers of cases of erroneous records and proliferation of those records increased, the pressure to control the collection, use, and dissemination of personal data mounted. Virtually every governmental agency collected data on individuals for one reason or another and made such data available to the public. The Federal government enacted in the Privacy Act of 1974[18] the first piece of legislation aimed at stemming the flow of personal data brought on by advanced technology.

The Privacy Act of 1974, signed into law January 1, 1975, was directed only at the accumulation, storage, and dissemination of individual data by federal agencies, excepting law enforcement agencies. In this act Congress set safeguards for an individual against invasion of privacy by permitting the individual to:

- determine what records pertaining to him are being collected and disseminated.
- review and copy all or any part of the information collected pertaining to him.
- correct or amend such records through an established procedure that required designation of such disputed facts on all records.
- prevent records pertaining to him obtained by an agency for a particular purpose from being used or made available for another purpose without his consent.

The agencies that collect information on individuals are limited to the collection of relevant data required to perform that agency's duties. The agency further must maintain an accounting of that date, nature, and purpose of each disclosure and the name and address of the person or agency to whom the disclosure was made. Such accounting must be maintained for five years. Disclosures are limited to:

- Officers and employees of the agency with a need to know the data
- As required under Section 552 (this section provides for disclosures to law enforcement agencies)
- For routine use (the purpose for which it was intended)
- To the Bureau of Census for purposes of planning or carrying out a census or survey or related activity.
- To a recipient who proves in writing the data will be used only for statistical research (identification must be deleted in these cases)
- To the National Archives as a record of historical value
- To another agency or instrumentality of the United States for civil or criminal law enforcement (disclosure requires a written request by the head of the agency or instrumentality and must be limited to a particular portion specified in the request)

[18]Privacy Act of 1974, Public Law 93-579/93rd Congress S. 3418/December 31, 1974, Section 2(b).

- To a person showing compelling circumstances affecting health or safety of the individual (notification must be sent to the individual at last known address)
- To either house of Congress or committees thereof, assuming a matter within its jurisdiction
- To the Comptroller General or his agent for the purpose of performing the duties of the General Accounting Officer
- Pursuant to an order of a court of competent jurisdiction

The act goes on to provide civil remedies and criminal penalties for failure to conform to the conduct outlined in the act. An individual may bring a civil act against an agency for intentional or willful failure to conform to the extent actually damaged (not less than $1,000). The court may award attorney's fees and court costs on such cases in addition to the damages. Any employee or officer of an agency who willfully discloses information for which disclosure is prohibited, or gains such information under false pretenses or maintains such records but fails to comply with notice requirement, shall be guilty of a misdemeanor. The misdemeanor carries with it a fine of not more than $5,000.

The final segments of the Privacy Act create a Privacy Protection Study Commission consisting of seven members. Duties designated to this commission include the studying of data books, data processing programs, and information systems of governmental, regional, and private organizations to determine the standards and procedures in force for the protection of personal information. The commission recommends to the President and Congress those requirements and principles necessary to protect the privacy of individuals and the legitimate interests of the government and society.

In an attempt to safeguard the rights of their citizens the states have also begun efforts to control data processing information. In 1973 California created a California Information Systems Implementation Committee.[19] The purpose of that committee was to (1) review electronic data processing policies and recommend additions and deletions, and to (2) develop electronic data processing procedure for implementing the policies of protecting the privacy and confidentiality of records. The thrust of this committee's efforts, as well as the laws that have resulted, has been directed at governmental activities. For example,

STATE UNIVERSITIES AND COLLEGES. Employee records Chapter 1299. Senate Bill No. 1588, approved September 28, 1976, added Section 24317 to the California Education Code, establishing the right of employees to review, copy, and request correction of facts in their employee file and the procedures by which the universities or colleges are to handle such requests.

CALIFORNIA RIGHT TO FINANCIAL PRIVACY ACT. Chapter 1320, Assembly Bill No. 3387, approved September 28, 1976. The act provides that no officer, employee, or agency of a state or local agency or department thereof may request or obtain from a financial institution, copies of financial records or information from such records on any customer except in specified circumstances and by specific procedures. The act limits the use of financial records authorized to be received also.

[19] Article 2, California Information Systems Implementation Committee, Stats 1973, C 259, p. 654 urgency, eff. July 12, 1973.

A knowing violation of the act results in a misdemeanor carrying a punishment of up to one (1) year in prison or a fine of not more than $5,000. The courts are also authorized to award attorney's fees and costs for individuals who successfully enforce liability for a violation.

Minnesota is another state that in 1974 enacted privacy legislation that parallels the Federal Privacy Act.

Generally, all of the new legislation affects the public sector as opposed to the private sector, but the trend is clear. The Federal government and the State governments recognize the potential dangers of the enormous information capacities of data processing systems. They understand that they must enact legislation that defines the delicate balances of society's interest in the free flow of information and of the individual's right to privacy. The course of such future legislation on computer data systems will be influenced greatly by the abuses made of such systems and the protections afforded under other areas of the law, e.g., torts. The software developer is in a key role in the evolution of constructive legislation. A conscientious effort must be made to structure and validate software to avoid improper or inaccurate disclosures, to include protective measures to avoid improper manipulation of software to provide such disclosures (see Chapter 6), and to caution data systems buyers to use protective mechanisms on the software and protective procedures that will minimize the possibility of improper or inaccurate disclosure of personal data. These efforts, along with active participation in the legislative process and in providing public awareness of the system's safeguards, may ensure the development of privacy legislation and public acceptance that best reflects the potentials of data systems and the rights of individuals.

7.5
Other Legal Considerations

The number of secondary legal implications (as contrasted to those legal areas previously discussed) that affect any business operation are far too numerous to address fully here. These legal considerations merit some discussion, however:

- The expanding field of labor law, which will affect the software developer's employment practices.
- Business competition laws (antitrust laws) that have become a guide to proper business practices.
- The miscellaneous business torts that may inflict liability on the developer for improper business practices.
- Developments in the use of computer outputs as evidence in court proceedings.

Again these areas are independent, but each has some significant legal effect on the software developer's business operations.

7.5.1 LABOR LAW

Earlier in this chapter we discussed the Law of Agency, which illustrated that certain basic rights and duties of employees and employers exist. As the manufacturer of software programs will probably hire employees, he should have some exposure to the idea of labor law. Agency does not reflect all of the law applicable to the relation between employee and employer. Labor relations alone is a specialty in the legal field. The legal problems are generally complex, but, oddly enough, they probably represent only one-fifth of the total labor relations problems. The remaining four-fifths are problems of human relations. This section will outline only the basic principles of law applicable in this field. It is not intended to provide a complete understanding of labor relations.

Labor law is characterized by change. Since the turn of the century, the awareness and protection of employee rights have been focal points of much legislation. Major legislation in this area includes:

- 1890—*The Sherman Anti-trust Act* prohibited combinations and conspiracies in restraint of trade and was held to apply to some union activities.
- 1914—*The Clayton Act*, an amendment of the Sherman Act, provided that no restraining order or injunction could be granted in cases between employer and employee involving a dispute concerning terms or conditions of employment, unless necessary to prevent irreparable injury to property or to a property right of the applicant for which there is no adequate remedy at law. The Labor section of the Clayton Act were adjudged unconstitutional in 1921.
- 1932—*Norris-LaGuardia Act* severely limited injunctive power of federal courts in labor disputes. (This was ineffective.)
- 1935—*National Labor Relations Act* granted employees the right to organize free of employer interference and to bargain collectively.
- 1938—*The Fair Labor Standards Act* sometimes known as the Wage and Hour Act. The act establishes minimum wages; requires payment at one and one-half times the employee's "regular rate" of pay for all work in excess of 40 hours in any work week; and regulates the employment of minors. The Wage and Hour Administrator publishes rules and regulations and interpretive bulletins and many individual interpretations.
- 1947—*Labor-Management Relations Act*, better known as the Taft-Hartley Act, as amended [61 Stat. 136-162; 29 US (§§ 141-188)] regulates labor relations in business involved in interstate commerce. The National Labor Relations Board (NLRB) Act was amended to condemn certain union practices as unfair labor practices. The Norris-LaGuardia Act was amended to permit injunction upon application by the NLRB and upon application of the Attorney General of the United States to enjoin for a period of 80 days a threat or strike or lockout in a major industry that would affect national health and safety.
- 1959—*Labor Management Reporting and Disclosure Act* (29 USCA 401 et seq.) that seeks to strengthen internal union democracy and also deals with certain conduct of union officials and employers.

Most states have enacted legislation that provides for control of the relations between labor and management. California, for example, utilizes a Labor Code that governs employment relationships. The code includes provisions regulating payment of wages, assignment of wages, hours and wages of women and minors, employment agencies, and Workman's Compensation rules.

The United States Supreme Court declared invalid most of the states statutory and common law rules for employees engaged in interstate commerce that applied to collective bargaining situations in Garner v. Teamsters, AFL (1953) 346 U.S. 485. It also withdrew from the states' courts the jurisdiction to give relief in collective bargaining. The doctrine established in Garner is "the doctrine of federal pre-emption" which in effect states that any employer engaged in interstate commerce (defined as affecting commerce) must observe only the provisions of the Taft-Hartley Act and the remedies provided by that act. The Court has established only two exceptions where state courts retained jurisdiction—cases based on coercive conduct[20] and common cases based on tort law for violence.[21] The Court also has upheld state statutes preventing mass picketing, threatening employers, obstructing streets and picketing homes.[22]

In light of the doctrine of pre-emption, a review of some of the substantive elements of the Taft-Hartley Act is in order. This summary is by no means all inclusive.

Section 7 provides that employees may choose either to form and join unions, or refrain from forming a union.

Section 8(a) provides that it is an unfair labor practice for an employer to discriminate against any employee for joining or not joining a union, or for engaging or not engaging in union activities. Further, it stipulates that, if the employees desire, the employer must bargain with the employees collectively, and prohibits strikes to coerce the employer into refusing to do business with another or use another's products or recognize one union when another is certified.

Section 8(d) details the duty to bargain collectively.

Section 9 provides for the board to determine when a union is an appropriate unit for collective bargaining with an employer. It further provides that the board can decide which of two contending unions will represent the employees. Secret elections are also provided for in this section.

Section 10 establishes the legal procedures to be followed in unfair labor practice cases.

Sections 201–204 set up the Federal Mediation and Conciliation Service.

Sections 206–210 detail the procedures to be followed in national emergency strikes.

Section 301 provides for legal actions in Federal district courts arising from violations of the collective bargaining agreements.

Section 302 restricts payments to employee representatives, defines what negotiated employee benefit plans are legal, and requires that certain pro'sions be inserted on instruments establishing the employee benefit plans.

Section 303 has given rise to legal actions by employers against unions for violations of Section 8(b).

The National Labor Relations Board is the principal body that sets the rules and

---

[20]Garner v. Teamsters, AFL 346 U.S. 485 (1953).
[21]United Construction Workers v. Laburnum Construction Corp. 347 U.S. 266 (1956).
[22]United Auto Workers v. Wisconsin Employment Relations Board, 351 U.S. 266 (1956).

regulations under the act and decides most of the cases that arise under the act. As established in Section 9 of the Taft-Hartley Act, the NLRB determines whether or not a particular union can represent the employees in collective bargaining. In these cases the filing party submits a petition (on a form provided by the board). The petition is investigated and a determination is made as to whether the facts justify an attempt to get the parties to agree to an election. If an election is justified, one of two forms of the agreement is available: Agreement for Consent Election, which provides for an election and notification of the results, and Stipulation for Certification upon Consent Election, which provides for any party to complain about the conduct of the election directly to the board. If the parties do not agree on a consent election, a hearing is held by the hearing officer. When the hearing is complete the transcript is forwarded to the board, which issues an order directing the election or refusing it. If the board agrees to election, a secret ballot election is usually held by a field examiner. Notices of time and place of election are posted on the employer's premises.

The NLRB also establishes, as per the act, the duties for collective bargaining, which include but are not limited to:

- the duty for the union and employer to meet if either desires;
- the duty to deal with the representatives;
- the duty of the parties to negotiate in good faith;
- the duty to sign the negotiated agreement when either party requests it.

The types of issues that are subject to bargaining are wages, hours, vacation, holidays, sick leave, merit increases, union security, pensions, group health and accident insurance, seniority, job classifications, apprentices, promotions, descipline, discharge, homework, subcontracting, grievance machinery, no-strike clauses, no-lockout clauses, duration of contract, and renewal. All issues permissible in collective bargaining must be negotiated.

The NLRB enforces the act by preventing unfair labor practices. The board cannot initiate a proceeding; it can commence action only after a charge is filed. This is done on a standard NLRB form filed with an appropriate regional office. The matter is referred to the field examiner for investigation. If an amicable solution is not available, the regional director issues a complaint. The respondent must file an answer. If the matter is not then settled, a formal public hearing takes place. The Taft-Hartley Act lists which activities of unions constitute unfair labor practices in Section 8(b).

Other employee problems that the software seller may face include:

PAYMENT OF WAGES.   There is no applicable Federal law, but state laws generally govern. The California Labor Code, Division 2, Part 1, defines stringent provisions for the payment and collection of wages.

Section 201 shows that if an employer discharges or lays off an employee, all wages earned are due and payable immediately.

Section 202 provides that an employee who resigns must be paid all wages earned within 72 hours thereafter.

Section 203 gives the penalty for nonconformance with 201 and 202. The penalty is the continuance of employee's wages at the same rate until full wages are rendered; such wages shall not continue more than thirty (30) days.

Section 204 provides, except as otherwise stated, that wages must be paid at least twice per month.

Section 206 designates the immediate payment of the conceded portion of any disputed wage.

Section 207 provides for posting of notice of regular pay days and Section 208 defines the place for payment.

Sections 210 and 211 determine remedies for violation of payment of wage sections.

Section 226 requires that employers give itemized statements of wages and deduction to employees.

Chapter 2 of Division 2, Part 1, of the California Labor Code establishes stringent requirements regulating assignment of wages. In general, the assignment must be specific; the spouse (if any) must join in the assignment, and it must be acknowledged before a notary public.

HOURS OF WORK. The only federal law applicable is that defined in the Taft-Hartley Act, Section 6: i.e., for all work in excess of 40 hours in one week, the employee must be paid at one and one-half (1-1/2) times his regular pay rate. This applies only to nonexempt employees. In 1972 the Department of Labor issued a decision that affects the exempt status of programmers (29 CFR, Part 541):

> The employer representatives contended that computer programmers and systems analysts should be considered professional employees. Some supporters of this position would include the position of junior programmer in this category. The testimony brought out, however, that a college degree is not a requirement for entry into the data processing field, that only a few colleges offer any course in a field designated as computer science, and that there are presently no licensing, certification, or registration provided as a condition for employment in these occupations. . . .
>
> On the other hand, employee representatives were opposed to expansion of the regulations to allow the professional exemption for data processing employees. They were in agreement that a prolonged academic background is not essential in this field. They also brought out that this relatively new occupation area is in a state of flux and that job titles and duties are not regularized and overlap and intermix in a confusing manner. They also felt that to expand the exemption was an invitation for employers to work such employees longer hours with no additional compensation.
>
> . . . at the present time the computer sciences are not generally recognized by colleges and universities as a bona fide academic discipline with standardized licensing, certification, or registration procedures. There is too much variation in standards and academic achievement to conclude logically that data processing employees are a part of a true profession of the type contemplated by the regulations. (29 CFR, Part 541.)

Further in that decision, the Labor Department recognized that if a programmer could exercise discretion and independent judgment in his job, such as analysts, then the individual may qualify as exempt.

California Labor law is definitive in this area. Part 2 of Division 2 of the California Labor Code establishes a working day to be eight (8) hours and requires one day of rest in seven days. Section 1350.5 of California Labor Code provides that employers may employ females a maximum of 10 hours during any one day of 24 hours or up to 58 hours in one week. Sections 1290 through 1311 define stringent requirements on employment of minors, including penalties for violation. Section 1290 sets out specific limitations on the type of work allowed for minors under the age of 16 years old.

STRIKES, PICKETING AND LOCKOUTS. The right to strike by unions is acknowledged by the Taft-Hartley Act, Section 13 (29 U.S.C. § 163). The act does, however, impose some limitations on strikes. Section 206 (29 U.S.C. § 176) provides for an eighty (80) day "cooling off period" in industries where a strike would affect the nation's health or safety. Section 8(d) (29 U.S.C. § 158) specifies that where a collective bargaining agreement is in effect, there must be a 60-day notice to the other party and 30-day notice to the Federal Mediation and Conciliation Service and State Conciliation Service (where applicable).

The right to picket has been held to be an exercise of the right of free speech when peacefully implemented. Generally, local laws govern picketing. Most require that pickets must not physically obstruct access to the employer's establishment and that the banners the pickets may carry and the statements they make should be orderly and truthful. Under § 301 of the Taft-Hartley Act (29 U.S.C. § 195), the union may sue for a strike in violation of a contract. Further picketing, when accompanied by violence, by threats of violence or loss of jobs, or by intimidation and mass picketing are unfair labor practices under the Taft-Hartley Act. The Norris-LaGuardia Act provides for injunctions in such cases, but there are constitutional problems that cloud the enforcement of such injunctions.

The right to lock out employees is not as clearly established as the right to strike or picket. It is the natural counterpart to a strike and in that context is probably a lawful act. It can be presumed, though there is little case law on the matter, that the same restrictions that apply to strikes will in general apply to lockouts.

7.5.2 LAW AND BUSINESS COMPETITION

In the late nineteenth century the United States began to establish by statute certain competitive practices. At that time the American marketplace was coping with realization of the immense power and control of the emerging monopolies. The result was a series of Federal and state laws aimed at preventing combinations or conspiracies in restraint of trade and unfair competition. This legislation now forms the basis of the enforcement of competitive business practices. Software developers, as all other businessmen, must understand and comply with these standards.

The Federal Trade Commission and the Attorney General enforce good business practices at the Federal level. The foundation of their authority stems from three major pieces of legislation:

1890—*The Sherman Act* (15 U.S.C.A. 1-7), which provided:

> Every contract, combination in the form of trust or otherwise, or conspiracy, in restraint of trade or commerce among the several States or with foreign nations, is hereby declared to be illegal

(Section 1), and

> every person who shall monopolize, or attempt to monopolize, or combine or conspire with any other person or persons, to monopolize any part of the trade or commerce among the several States; or with foreign nations, shall be deemed guilty of a misdemeanor. (Section 2)

1914—The Clayton Act provided a broader competitive practices definition than the Sherman Act. The act has five substantive sections; three of which greatly affect competitive practices, two of which have had little effective importance:

Antitrust Sections of the Clayton Act

Section 7, as amended in 1959, illustrated that

> no corporation engaged in commerce shall acquire, directly or indirectly, the whole or any part of the stock . . . and no corporation . . . shall acquire the whole or any part of the assets of another corporation . . . where in any line of commerce in any section of the country, the effect of such acquisition may be substantially to lessen competition, or to tend to create a monopoly.

(15 U.S.C. Paragraph 18)

Section 8, which shows that

> no person at the same time shall be a director of any two or more corporations, any one of which has capital, surplus, and undivided profits aggregating more than $1,000,000, . . . if such corporations are or shall have been theretofore, . . . competitors, so that the elimination of competition by agreement between them would constitute a violation of any of the anti-trust laws.

This section has been relatively unenforced because of evasion tactics by corporations.

Sections 10 prohibits dealings between common carriers and any other firms where there are interlocking directors, officers, substantial interests or combinations of these.

Price Discrimination Section of the Clayton Act

Section 2, as modified by the Robinson-Putman Act, makes discrimination in price unlawful

> where the effect of such discrimination may be substantially to lessen competition . . . or prevents competition with any person who either grants or knowingly receives the benefit of such discrimination.

Exclusive Dealings Section of the Clayton Act:

Section 3 notes that tying agreements or exclusive dealings agreements are unlawful where the effect

> may be to substantially lessen competition or tend to create a monopoly in any line of commerce.

1914—Federal Trade Commission Act (15 U.S.C.A. 41 et seq.). This act defined that unfair methods of competition in commerce, and unfair or deceptive acts or practices in commerce are unlawful. These acts also provide civil remedies and criminal penalties for violations.

The states have also addressed the issues of restraint in trade and trade practices. For example, Division 7, Part 2, of the California Business and Professions Codes sets forth the preservation and regulation of business competition in California. The intent of the California legislature and the scope of the legislation are reflected in these several sections:

Section 16600:

> Except as provided in this chapter, every contract by which anyone is restrained from engaging in a lawful profession, trade, or business of any kind is to that extent void.

Section 17000 (Chapter 3 of Division 7, Part 2):

> The legislative declares that the purpose of this chapter is to safeguard the public against the creation or perpetuation on monopolies and to foster and encourage competition by prohibiting unfair, dishonest, deceptive, destructive, fraudulent and discriminatory practices by which fair and honest competition is destroyed.

Within the context of Chapter 3 (Sections 17040 et seq.) California prohibits such practices as:

- Locality discrimination
- Sales under cost; gifts (§ 17043)
- Loss leaders[23] (§ 17044)
- Secret rebates or refunds (§ 17045)
- Threats, intimidation, or boycotts (§ 17046)

Sections 17070 through 17094 set forth the civil liabilities (including injunctions). Sections 17095 and 19796 set forth liabilities of agents, and Sections 17100 and 17101 provide penal provision for violators of Part 2, Chapter 3.

The situations in which the competitive practices statutes apply are too numerous to identify in this text. It is enough to point out to the software manufacturer that any dealings that tend to lessen competition, and on their surface reflect a deceptive business practice, may be a violation punishable under these statutes.

7.5.3 MISCELLANEOUS BUSINESS TORTS

The software developer or supplier has other areas of tort law to consider in doing business. These areas are defamation, disparagement, and interference with business relationships. The importance of these areas of tort law are independent of

---

[23]Loss Leader is defined in California Business and Profession Code, Section 17030 as:

> "Loss leader" means any article or product sold at less than cost:
> (a) Where the purpose is to induce, promote, or encourage the purchase of other merchandise; or
> (b) Where the effect is a tendency or capacity to mislead or deceive purchasers or prospective purchasers; or
> (c) Where the effect is to divert trade from or otherwise injure competitors.

Sec. 7.5 Other Legal Considerations

the performance of the software and are associated mainly with liabilities arising from business conduct.

DEFAMATION

Defamation is an invasion of the plaintiff's interest or reputation by defendant's communications to third parties. Defamation takes two forms: (1) Libel—defamation in written form, and (2) Slander—defamation in verbal form. The importance of this tort lies mainly in the potential dangers of statements against the personalities of competitors or employees. An over-zealous statement may result in a law suit. This tort requires proof of:

1. Defamatory statements:
   (a) Libel must show defamatory written statement. At common law plaintiff did not have to prove special damages [loss of reputation that has resulted in pecuniary (monetary) harm]. California requires proof of special damages unless the defamatory statement is "libel per se" (defamatory on its face without explanation). Innuendos require proof of special damages.[24]
   (b) Slander must show defamatory statement. Both common law and California divide slander into two classes for purposes of proof of special damages. "Slander per se" does not require proof of special damages. Examples of such statements are statements that make an accusation of crime; impute a present loathsome disease; tend to directly injure in office, profession, trade or business; or impute impotence or want of chastity.[25] Innuendo requires proof of why it could be understood to be defamatory.
2. Publication—Communication to someone other than plaintiff who understands the statement to be defamatory. An example might be dictation of a letter by "A" to a secretary, calling agent "B" a "liar and a thief." "B" has been defamed by "A," and the defamation was published by the dictation.

The principal defense in a defamation action is the proof of the truth of the statement. Another defense is related to privileges of community either absolute (certain governmental proceedings have immunities) or conditions (statements made about public officials and public figures, statements made in protection of private interests or fair comment in interest of community). Conditional privileges can be lost if the statement is false and intentionally misstated, or is made without reasonable basis for belief of its truth.

DISPARAGEMENT

Disparagement is an injurious falsehood diminishing "saleability." There are two principal parts of this tort: (1) a slander of title, and (2) a trade libel. The former is unlikely to be encountered, but is possible. It involves publication (either verbal or written), without privilege, of untrue matters disparaging another's title to any type of property. The plaintiff-owner must be caused pecuniary damage. Trade libel involves the disparagement of the quality of property. Like slander of title, it can be

[24]California Civil Code Section 45a.
[25]Ibid Section 46.

either written or verbal. The comments of an overactive sales representative about a competitor's product may result in liability for a software supplier.

Unlike defamation actions, all disparaging actions require proof of special damages. The defenses available to defamation apply in disparagement.

INTERFERENCE WITH ECONOMIC RELATIONSHIPS

This tort is aimed at protecting economic relationships that have been established by contract protecting future economic relationship. This is accomplished by providing a cause of action by an injured party for:

Interference with an Existing Contact. This generally requires an intentional inducement of a contracting party to either terminate a contract terminable at will, make performance of a contract more difficult, or breach the contract. It has been suggested that this cause of action should be extended to negligent inducement, but as yet no state has acted in this direction.

Interference with Future Relationships. This action is based on the same actions as the interference with contract except that it is aimed at future relationships. Generally, unfair competition practices, such as "kickbacks," duress, or misrepresentation, are involved.

The defenses of privilege generally do not apply here since the acts are intentional, but possibly a motive of serving a proper personal or social end may still confer a privilege. The privilege would apply in a case where an opinion is requested, and an honest opinion is provided.

7.5.4 USE OF COMPUTER OUTPUTS AS EVIDENCE

Along with the increased technology of computers and the expanded use of them by business comes the question of admissibility into evidence of the only intelligible statement of information possessed by the software engineer—the computer printout. The problem emanates from principles of evidence that rely heavily on testimony of witnesses who have personal knowledge of the facts. Generally, a document cannot be entered into evidence if the maker is not available to testify to the truthfulness of the assertions contained in the document.[26] Only with much hesitancy is the common law allowed in court testimony of witnesses to be supplemented by documentary material.[27] The courts and statutes have evolved certain rules that allow some variance in the rigid restrictions against use of unsupported documents. The principal vehicle has been the development of exceptions to the hearsay rule.[28]

The exceptions to the hearsay rule generally evolved as a practical necessity. The

---

[26]McCormick, *Handbook of the Law of Evidence*, § 250 (Cleary 2d. ed., 1972).

[27]Ibid §§ 218–243, §§ 299–303, and §§ 304–314 (Cleary, 2d. ed. 1972).

[28]The hearsay rule, as defined in the California Evidence Code, Section 1200, is:

> (a) Hearsay evidence is evidence of a statement that was made other than by the witness while testifying at the hearing and that is offered to prove the truth of the matter stated. . . .

exceptions were allowed on a rationale that statements made under certain specific circumstances have a high degree of trustworthiness in their truthfulness. The particular exception that most affects the software and computer industry is the business records exception that is defined in the California Evidence Code, Section 1271, as:

> Evidence of a writing made as a record of an act, condition, or event is not made inadmissible by the hearsay rule when offered to prove the act, condition, or event if:
> (a) The writing was made in the regular course of a business;
> (b) The writing was made at or near the time of the act, condition, or event;
> (c) The custodian or other qualified witness testifies to its identity and the mode of its preparation; and
> (d) The sources of information and method and time of preparation were such as to indicate its trustworthiness.

The basis for the trustworthiness is that the maker of the record will properly perform his duties and that records on which businessmen rely in the regular course of business are very likely to be accurate and credible.

The use of computers and software accounting methods has changed the traditional manner of record keeping. Man is less and less a participant in the record-keeping process and more and more a monitor. Accounting information is transformed to a computer-compatible input and input into the computer. From that point on, the system has few of the old characteristics; for example:

Data storage, search, and printout are automatic.

Inputs are stored in data bases that are not generally cumulative as in traditional account entries.

The evidence of the account (the ledger sheets) have become magnetic tapes, punched cards, paper tapes, or stored on disks. Printouts may not be made on a regular basis as in ledgers.

Computer systems also have areas of potential errors:

> Translation of input data into machine-compatible inputs
> The software program
> The computer
> Erroneous input data

The last error is common to both traditional and computer methods.

The mystery of computers, the fact that the printouts can be reproduced regularly, and that it is difficult to have a "maker" of the record who is close enough to the process to attest to its identity and mode of preparation, has made the courts reluctant to utilize computer data. Several attempts have been made to broaden the language of the business records exception to eliminate the need for subpoena of every individual associated with preparing the record: e.g., keypunch operator, computer operator, software supplier, computer supplier, etc.

A suggested approach to statutory relief of this problem is seen in the South Australian Evidence Act, Amendment Act 1972, §§ 59a to §§ 59c. The act first defines a computer in Section 59a as a device that is by electronic, electro-mechanical, or other means capable of recording and processing data according to mathematical and logical rules and of reproducing that data or mathematical or logical consequences thereof.

The section then defines the computer output as a

statement or representation (whether in written, pictorial, graphical, or other form) purporting to be a statement or representation of fact . . . (a) produced by a computer; or (b) accurately translated from a statement or representation so produced.

The act does not require personal knowledge in the maker, but does allow the court to control the admissibility by requiring the output to be based on information normally accepted in court as evidence.

The same effect as the South Australian Act can be accomplished through common law interpretation of the business records exception. The courts would probably require as support, in lieu of testimony of a maker, showing that:

1. The printout was made during a period when the computer was used regularly to store and process information for the purpose of business record keeping.
2. During the period of use, the inputs were regularly translated and input to the computer.
3. The computer was operating properly during this period.
4. The output was derived from information supplied in the normal course of business (may require originals or copies of all pertinent inputs).

Possibly the courts will also require the presenting party to show that the software has functioned properly during these periods.

To what extent the State and Federal governments will accept and utilize the computer printout has yet to be totally resolved. Until the situation is resolved, accurate records of inputs to computers and activity of accounts must be kept in order to protect the business user properly.

Table of Cases

Carl Beasley Ford, Inc. *v.* Burroughs Corporation, 361 F. Supp. 325 (E.D. Pa 1973).

Clements Auto Co. *v.* Service Bureau Corp., 298 F. Supp. 115 (D. Minn.—1969) aff'd as modified, 444 F. 2d. 169 (8th Cir. 1971).

Computer Service Centers, Inc. *v.* Beacon Manufacturing Co., 328 F. Supp. 653 (DSC 1970).

Fruit Industries Research Foundation *v.* National Cash Register Company, 406 F. 2d. 546 (9th Cir. 1969).

Garner *v.* Teamsters, AFL (1953) 346 U.S. 485.

Gottschalk *v.* Benson, 490 U.S. 63 (1972) rev'g. In Re Benson, 441 F. 2d. 682 (C.C.P.A. 1971).

In Re Abrams, 188 F.2d. 165 (C.C.P.A.) 1951.

In Re Berhart, 417 F.2d. 1395 (C.C.P.A. 1969).

In Re Comstock, 481 F.2d. 905 (C.C.P.A. 1973).

In Re Johnston, 502 F.2d. 765 (C.C.P.A. 1974).

In Re Knowlton, 481 F.2d. 1375 (C.C.P.A. 1973).

In Re Musgrave, 431 F.2d. 882 (C.C.P.A. 1970).

In Re Prater, 415 F.2d. 1393 (C.C.P.A. 1968) aff'g and rev'g in part on rehearing 415 F.2d. 1378 (C.C.P.A. 1968).

In Re Yuan, 188 F.2d. 377 (C.C.P.A. 1951).

MacPherson *v.* Buick Motor Co. (217 N.Y. 382, 111 N.E. 2d. 1050 (1916)).

United Auto Workers *v.* Wisconsin Employment Relations Board, 351 U.S. 266 (1956).

United Construction Workers *v.* Laburnum Construction Corp., 347 U.S. 266 (1956).

Wihtol *v.* Wells, 231 F.2d. 550 (7th Cir. 1956).

Bibliography

Article 2, California Information Systems Implementation Committee, Stats. 1973, C259, p. 654 urgency, eff. July 12, 1973.

California Business and Professions Code, Section 1660 et seq.

California Business and Professions Code, Sections 17000–17101.

California Civil Code, Section 45 et. seq.

California Commercial Code, Section 2314, 2315, 2316.

California Corporations Code, Sections 200 et seq.

California Corporations Code, Section 1502.

California Corporations Code, Section 15006.

California Education Code, Section 24317.

California Evidence Code, Sections 1200 et seq.

California Labor Code, Division 2, Part 1 and Part 2.

California Revenue and Taxation Code, Sections 995 et al.

California Right of Financial Privacy Act, Chapter 1320, Assembly Bill No. 3387, Approved September 28, 1976.

Clayton Act, 15 U.S.C.A. 12 et seq.

Copyright Office Circular, 31D Jan. 1965, 3,000.

Federal Trade Commission Acts, 15 U.S.C.A. 41 et seq.

Labor Management Relations Act (Taft-Hartley Act), 29 U.S.C.A. Sections 141–199.

Labor Management Reporting and Disclosure Act, 29 U.S.C.A. 401 et seq.

McCormick, *Handbook of the Law of Evidence*, Sections 200–315, Cleary, 2d ed., 1972.

Privacy Act of 1974, Public Law 93-579/93rd Congress S. 3418/December 31, 1974, Section 2(b).

Restatement of Agency, 2d. Sections 379–386.

Restatement of Agency, 2d. Sections 433–458.

Restatement of Torts, 2d. Sections 282, 525.

Restatement of Torts, 2d. Section 757.

Sherman Act, 15 U.S.C.A. 1–7.

Soltysinsk, Stanislaw J., "Computer Programs and Patent Law: A Comparative Study," *Rutgers Journal of Computers* (1972–1973), pp. 1–82.

Southern Australian Evidence Act, Amendment Act 1972, Sections 59a to 59c.

Uniform Commercial Code, Chapter 2.

Uniform Partnership Act.

United States Codes, Title 17, Sections 100 et seq.

United States Codes, Title 35, Sections 100 et seq.

United States Labor Department Reports, (29 CFR, Part 541).

at last,

THE DAWN

APPENDIX
SOFTWARE ENGINEERING EDUCATION: A CONSTRUCTIVE CRITICISM

RANDALL W. JENSEN
Senior Scientist

CHARLES C. TONIES
Laboratory Manager
Data Processing Systems Laboratory
Hughes Aircraft Company

Abstract

Computer science and engineering (CSE) departments in the nation's colleges and universities are currently targets of much criticism by professional software people. A common complaint is that the curricula are of a patchwork nature and do not relate directly to many of the most important problems that software engineers face in the commercial or industrial environment.

If we define software engineering as the establishment and application of sound engineering principles to obtain economical software that is reliable and works efficiently on real computers, it is mandatory that we recognize software engineering as more than simply converting a given set of program specifications to executable code. We must deal with the entire software life cycle that spans the time from the conception of the product, through the development phase, and finally to the end of its operational life. Software projects usually involve a myriad of managers, engineers, programmers, and customers, which leads to the need for effective management and communications to ensure the best possible product.

Therefore, software engineering education must be more than a simple combination of courses selected from existing computer science and engineering curricula. The software engineering curriculum must include, in addition to the classical offerings, principles of management and communication sciences and software-related engineering design methodologies not included in existing courses.

Our academic and industrial experience leads us to advocate the following basic areas of software engineering education: management science, computer science, engineering fundamentals and physical sciences, communication skills, and problem solving.

Disparities between academic attitudes and profit-making realities are described and fundamental elements of an effective curriculum are proposed in this paper. Teaching techniques are also suggested that bring the student closer to the condi-

Abstract

tions s/he will encounter on the job, and an outlook for software engineering as a profession is presented.

Introduction

Software development in industry is big business and getting bigger. The investment in software-development projects last year by the Department of Defense alone exceeded $3 billion in direct costs. The number of people engaged in work requiring direct participation in software development or maintenance activities is increasing exponentially. The opportunities for trained software engineers are there and they are expanding.

The business is also expanding in another sense. The products—the systems being developed—are growing larger and more complex. We are speaking now of applications-oriented systems, e.g., the real-time aircraft or spacecraft monitoring operations, process control programs, hardware test monitoring setups; even the friendly banker's time sharing system or the local department stores' inventory control programs are of significant size and complexity.

To bring these software systems into existence is not a one- or two-person task. Though some programmers and system architects will refer to their creation as "our baby," the fact is that today's systems result from the efforts of groups of individuals carrying out a carefully planned and controlled series of activities. The days when software could be produced like an offspring, in a private and personal way, are essentially gone. Enlightened managers and buyers now recognize the importance and the risks associated with software development, and few projects of any substantial size are successfully accomplished without explicit planning, control, and a high degree of visibility.

Unfortunately, software projects that meet schedule, cost, and performance objectives are still the exception in the industry, not the rule. Some of the most common complaints are:

- Software deliveries are always far behind schedule, at higher costs than expected, and inadequate in performance.
- Software is constructed so poorly that it is almost impossible to maintain, and the software structure prevents improvement at tolerable costs.
- Software is unreliable and requires constant maintenance to correct errors discovered during operation.

The explanation of the industry's poor record does not lie in the fundamental difficulty of the work; technological breakthroughs are required on few, if any, software projects; in fact, in an aggregate sense, all necessary engineering and managerial talents exist in quantity in this country. So where does the problem lie? The actual difficulty has been in matching the appropriate resources to the problem. This in turn derives from two factors:

1. Inability to identify and appreciate all aspects of the problem.
2. Poor packaging of the resources, i.e., the required talents are distributed over

a large group of individuals rather than being combined in the relatively few which a project can support.

Software engineering education can serve to alleviate the first of these factors by exposing students to the full scope of the software development environment, and the second by preparing each software engineer with a better cross section of abilities with which to operate in that environment.

Fundamental Software Engineering Curriculum Elements

Before we can discuss the software engineering curriculum, we must establish a working definition for software engineering. The most reasonable of many definitions that have been proposed was suggested in 1972 by F.L. Bauer [1] of the Technical University, Munich, Germany. He defined software engineering as:

> the establishment and use of sound engineering principles in order to obtain economically software that is reliable and works efficiently on real machines.

The most important attribute implied by the term "engineer" is that of a problem solver. The software engineer must be able to determine the actual needs of a user; select a general approach to the system development; analyze requirements to determine and resolve conflicts: establish a design to achieve the desired performance within constraints imposed by cost, schedule, and operating environment; develop new technical solutions; and, finally, manage a group of individuals with a wide range of personalities, disciplines, and goals.

Freeman, Wasserman, and Fairley [2] present another attribute of the software engineer by comparing the software engineer to the family doctor. Both are generalists who have skills that cover a wide range of areas. Even though the family doctor is knowledgeable of and applies much of medical science, he also must be knowledgeable in many other areas outside of medical science, such as psychology and sociology. Similarly, the software engineer must be knowledgeable in many areas of computer science, particularly those related to the development of software, including an understanding of hardware and firmware principles. He must also be familiar with areas outside his "specialty," including management and psychology among others.

Furthermore, as medical science is taking steps to establish specific training programs for the family practitioner, steps must also be taken to establish a specific program for the training of software engineers.

Under Bauer's definition of software engineering, it becomes apparent that the present approaches to constructing a software engineering curriculum fail in three ways: (1) The emphasis of the curricula is oriented toward science instead of engineering. This is illustrated by the phrase "The scientist analyzes; the engineer synthesizes.", (2) the wide range of topics that must be included in the training cannot be fitted into a Bachelor or Master of Science program as either now exists, and, (3) some of the necessary courses do not presently exist. The approach to constructing a software engineering curriculum demonstrated by the IEEE Computer Society Model Curricula Subcommittee [3] is typical of the "bottom-up" method of curriculum development in which software engineering is defined by combining elements of computer science with a dash of engineering and stirring gently. The result of the bottom-up method is a better-trained computer scientist, but not a software engineer. There is no honest way we can convince ourselves that the complaints heard every day about the quality of software will change or diminish simply by adding a few engineering courses to the computer science curriculum.

Rather than adhering to the bottom-up approach, perhaps a better way to design the curriculum is through abstraction, an important tool for dealing with complex problems. The first step in the abstraction process is to ask ourselves, "What is a software engineer?" From our definitions, we conclude that he is part generalist in the computer science field and part manager. We also conclude that the majority of his fundamental knowledge must come from the computer science and management science fields. Another very important skill area, which is ignored in most science and engineering curricula, is based on the engineer's need to communicate with a wide range of people and machines.

Thus, at the first level of abstraction, we observe that the software engineering curriculum is made up from five primary areas as shown in Figure A-1. The sixth area,

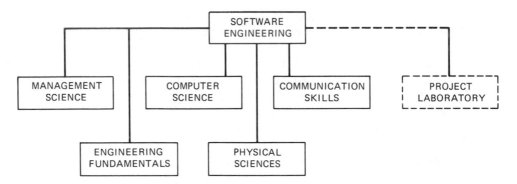

Fig. A-1 Software engineering

project laboratory, provides a means to apply the knowledge and experience gained from the first five areas in a single activity to improve the engineer's problem-solving abilities in a "real-world" environment. We will concentrate our discussion on the management science, computer science, communication skills, and project laboratory areas, since the remaining two areas are fundamental elements of all engineering curricula.

MANAGEMENT SCIENCE

Let us describe the software development process in a manner that brings out its management related demands, and identify some of the problems we are having in meeting them in industry today. We will then relate these to some software engineering curriculum topics.

We can think of the process as a series of interactions in which human beings operate on the subject matter of the problem while utilizing a physical environment that includes computers, offices, air conditioning, etc. The physical environment represents an important set of considerations, but we will not treat them here. The interactive process is depicted in Figure A-2 where it has been somewhat arbitrarily decomposed into six phases. The process begins with a conceptual phase, proceeds to a definition phase, and only then does a statement of requirements appear. Traditionally, these first two phases are ignored in the academic environment and are usually neglected in the industrial world, yet they are as important as any other phase.

The arrows entering from above represent the players bringing their influence to bear on the subject matter of the particular phase. The subject matter of a given phase is the output of the previous phase. It is the objective of the operatives (the players) to transform the output of the previous phase into appropriate input for the following phase, and to do so with maximum efficiency. In theory the process is a pure feed-forward operation. In practice, of course, it is not.

Each phase potentially causes some feedback; that is, the necessity to revert to some earlier phase to correct an error, to further refine the work of the earlier phase, or to accommodate a new input from one of the players. Each phase also produces entropy (wasted energy) because communications are not perfect, cooperation among the players is not perfect, honest mistakes—sometimes even deliberate mistakes—are made, facilities are not optimized, and because many other factors exist, all of which mitigate against perfect efficiency. The costs of feedback and entropy are high, and although they cannot be eliminated, they can be controlled. The most successful software development projects have recognized these effects and have taken deliberate action to minimize them. The techniques used fall in the area of management science.

Some of the specific management science topics that would produce the highest payoff for the graduate software engineer are shown in Figure A-3. Beginning at the left edge of Figure A-3, the *Project Definition* area is addressed to the problems of establishing a complete set of requirements (from which designs can be drawn) and the identification and quantification of the resources that will be required to carry out the project. Techniques and tools have been developed for both of these activities, but none seem to be addressed in existing CSE curricula. As we pointed out above, most projects get off on the wrong foot because the problem definition and project planning functions are not treated with sufficient attention and competence. These projects invariably suffer setbacks and overruns as a result.

In considering the *Cost Analysis* area, we can determine that it is closely allied with project planning because the cost of the resources to be applied to the project is an important tradeoff parameter. There exists a traditional attitude that cost matters should be left to senior managers and accountants. In practice, they are not. The manager must rely on the data processing expert for judgments on such matters as vendors' products, feasible software productivity rates, projected software maintenance requirements, and many others. Cost considerations permeate every aspect of the work in a business environment. The software engineer who has a working knowledge of corporate cost estimation and accounting practices, and who can use effective estimation techniques, will have a multiple-year head start toward positions of higher responsibility.

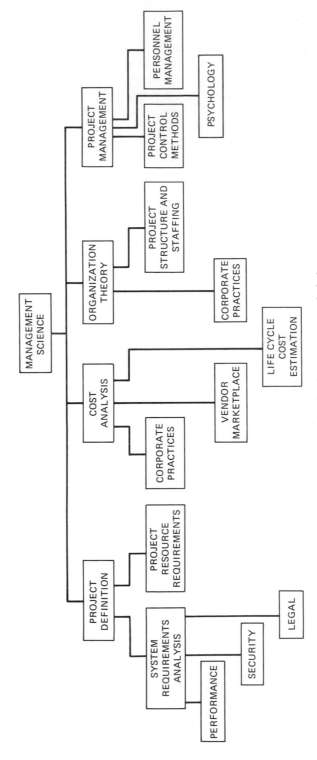

Fig. A-2 Software development process in industry

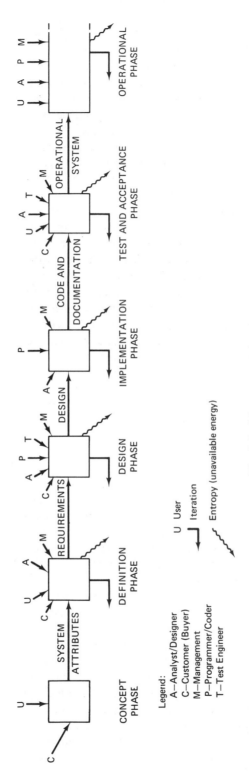

Legend:

A—Analyst/Designer
C—Customer (Buyer)
M—Management
P—Programmer/Coder
T—Test Engineer

U   User

⌐   Iteration

⌁   Entropy (unavailable energy)

Fig. A-3   Management science

We are in somewhat better shape in the *Organization Theory* area. Liberal arts requirements in most schools provide exposure to sociological and psychological concepts, and most people have had direct experience in organizing people in the course of their educational and private lives. But more exposure is needed. Industrial relations course material should appear in the curriculum, and specific methods of organizing for software development should be taught—for example, the pros and cons of the chief programmer team approach.

In the *Project Management* area we include control methods and personnel management. Numerous project control techniques and tools exist (PERT and C-SPEC, for example), and the software engineer will have to live with some of them. As he or she advances, it will be necessary to manage them. Some type of survey of the field should be provided in the curriculum to at least stimulate interest in this aspect of the "real world" operation and to convey the importance of explicit project control. With respect to personnel management, there are two major points to be made. First, another look at Figure A-2 reminds us that the world of the software engineer is filled with personnel interactions. With or without direct supervisory responsibilities, he or she will be involved in managing relationships in one way or another. It is also true that subordinates are more comfortable and perform better if they understand the reasons for their management's actions. The second point is that managing creative people is different than managing others, and managing software-oriented people is somewhat different than managing other creative people. The profession has its own advantages and disadvantages; it has its unique opportunities and pitfalls, and it attracts people with particular characteristics. An awareness of these considerations will give the software engineer a significant start toward a career in management, should he or she so choose.

COMPUTER SCIENCE

Experience is one of the best tools we can use to our advantage in establishing a software engineering curriculum. We observe that the primary technical skills required by a software engineer are based in computer science in much the same way other branches of engineering are derived from their counterparts in the physical universe. For example, electrical engineering relies on a foundation in electromagnetic physics and is often referred to as "applied" physics. Similarly, chemistry forms the theoretical basis for chemical engineering.

This analogy between the various branches of engineering and their physical science counterparts can be carried into the curriculum content. Electrical engineers apply principles of semiconductor physics as part of their normal design activities, yet their training seldom includes the semiconductor physics course as taught in the physics curriculum. In general, the engineering courses covering this subject are less comprehensive than the physics courses and present the subject only at the depth required to prepare the engineer for this circuit design function. If additional semiconductor knowledge is desired, an upper division or graduate course on the subject is made available as an elective course. The Physics Department's class offering often satisfies the requirements for the more comprehensive course. The relationship between software engineering ("applied" computer science) and computer science is very similar. The depth of knowledge necessary for any given subject is determined by the need for that knowledge in the engineer's activities. For example, consider the compiler course as taught in a typical computer science curriculum. The software engineer needs to understand compilers much the same way the electrical engineer needs to understand solid state physics. He must learn the compiler functions and limitations to accomplish his normal tasks but, like the electrical engineer and the transistor, seldom needs to design one. Thus, the traditional computer science compiler course becomes an upper division elective intended for those who want to specialize or gain more depth in the subject.

A parallel evaluation can be made of many traditional courses. As a matter of fact, it wasn't very many years ago that the electrical engineering curriculum was suffering growing pains similar to those now being felt by the software engineering field, as the engineering curriculum separated itself from classical physics and was established as an independent course of study.

It is time to recognize the inevitable metamorphosis from computer scientist to software engineer and work toward a more reasonable, independent curriculum that prepares the student for his role in software engineering.

The technology area of software engineering training can be divided into six major areas, as shown in Figure A-4. Each of the major areas is further divided into items that can be considered as topics included in the training program. The topics defined here may not be equivalent to existing computer science courses because of the depth of knowledge required in any subject. Other topics may be the same as existing courses in name only. We will attempt to point out these discrepancies in the following paragraphs.

The *Programming* area contains three topics. The first topic, Introduction to Program Design, replaces the traditional introductory programming course with a heavier stress on program formulation and less emphasis on any specific language syntax. The second topic, Design Methodologies, builds upon the element methodologies mastered in the first topic to provide alternate and more powerful approaches to program design. Programming Languages is a comparative languages course that provides the engineer with a knowledge of the available major computing languages and an appreciation for the advantages and disadvantages of each language in a given class of applications. The traditional languages course covering the theory and implementation of programming languages becomes an elective subject.

The *Computer Structure* area provides the fundamental firmware and hardware background. A knowledge of both hardware and firmware is essential since these subjects provide basic constraints on the development of any piece of software. Because a software engineer is frequently involved in the specification of hardware and firmware to perform a task, training in this area must be sufficient to support this type of activity.

The *Software Systems* area includes topics related to software systems which furnish fundamental software constraints on the development of a new product much like the hardware and firmware constraints described in the Computer Structure area. The software engineer must understand the interrelationships among the operating system and compilers available as resources and the software he is developing to make the most effective use of the total data processing system. As in the specification

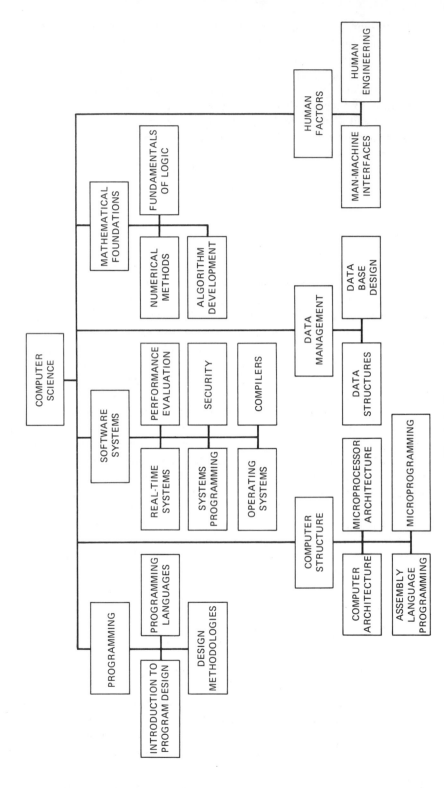

Fig. A-4 Computer science

of hardware and firmware, the definition of the operating system and compiler resources may be part of the engineer's task. Thus, his depth of understanding must be adequate to perform this task. Operating System and Compiler Design are specialized topics beyond the scope of software engineering and should be available as electives.

Real-time System Design is a topic requiring a deeper or more thorough understanding than other topics in this area because a significant portion of all software being developed now and in the foreseeable future will be operated in a real-time environment. Software design methodologies are also affected by the presence of real time processing, which influences the depth of understanding required.

Security is a topic that should appear in many of the major areas but is included here because it is most important in the Software Systems area. We must consider the security of software (i.e., proprietary software) in the programming area and the contribution made to system security by the hardware in the Computer Structure area in addition to the major contribution made by the operating system. We must also consider the security and privacy of data in the Data Management area.

The *Data Management* area gives an essential background in data structures, data base design, and data base management systems. In the past, the use of data structures and data management techniques were considered to be primarily tools of business data processing. As the size and power of computing systems have increased, so has the use of data bases in both business and scientific processing. Data structures and data management tools are now major elements in the design of any large software system and an important part of a software engineering curriculum.

The *Mathematical Foundations* area is as fundamental to software engineering as it is to any other field of engineering. Each branch of engineering has its own special mathematics requirements; software engineering's special requirements include Numerical Methods and Fundamentals of Digital Logic. The numerical methods requirements, which implies a host of prerequisite mathematics, is necessary because the software engineer must be familiar with various numerical algorithms and the trade-offs involved in using them and must understand the errors associated with numerical processes. The third topic, Algorithm Development, is also important because the software engineer must be familiar with various data processing algorithms and the methodologies involved in their derivation. It will also be necessary for him to apply his knowledge to modify existing algorithms or create new numerical or processing algorithms.

The most ignored, yet one of the most important areas of software development, is the *Human Factors* or *Human Engineering* area. The software engineer designs products to be used and maintained by people. From the first encounters with the user to determine the user's needs, to the end of the life cycle of the software s/he must consider human factors related to the product. This is especially true with the rapid growth of interactive systems in which the human has become an integral part of the closed system.

COMMUNICATION SKILLS

The third area of basic skills essential to the software engineer deals with communications. In any engineering project, only a small part of the total activity is involved in the actual detailed design and production of the final product. The remainder of the project time is involved in some type of communication, either written or oral. For example, the engineer participates in the preparation of the proposal, definition of user requirements, design proposals and documentation, status reports, user and system documentation, maintenance reports, and a myriad of other forms of both oral and written communications. Communications among all members of the design team, as well as communications among the software engineer and his management and the customer, must at all times be lucid and accurate; communication failures are expensive.

The topics within the *Communication Skills* area are shown in Figure A-5. They

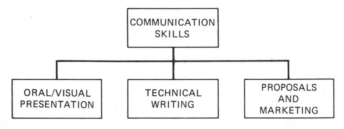

Fig. A-5 Communication skills

include all normal forms of communication, both oral and written (technical writing). Communication is so important that we feel all software engineers must be thoroughly competent in each of the skills. They should be able to communicate both effectively and clearly if they are to take advantage of their other technical skills. One of the major shortcomings of the educational system in this country is its failure to stress these skills in all academic programs.

PROJECT LABORATORY

Most of the topics covered in the software engineering curriculum will be presented as problem-solving techniques, each technique presented within the scope of the related subject matter. However, there is no place within the program that permits the unified application of these techniques in a realistic, or at least as realistic as possible, software development project. The project laboratory will allow the engineering student to participate in all of the stages of the project from the formulation of the concept to the delivery of a documented and validated system that is impossible to achieve in the short time period allowed by normal academic courses. Projects that are simple enough to complete in one quarter are generally too simple to allow the student to gain much experience in the application of the problem-solving techniques learned during his regular classwork.

This fourth major component of the software engineering curriculum allows the student to participate both as an individual and as a member of a development team throughout a complete software project. Obviously, the project laboratory will involve a significant portion of the student's time in an academic year and will place a burden on the instructor, but is an essential part of his education. Similar project laboratory courses are currently standard elements in other engineering curricula and have been demonstrated to be extremely valuable.

Teaching Problems

There are two easily recognizable problems associated with the software engineering curriculum. The first, and probably most severe, problem is attributable to the infancy of the new profession. The second problem is related to the differences between the academic and industrial settings. It is important that we understand these problems so that attempts can be made to overcome them as further advances are made into software engineering education.

THE NEW PROFESSION

The most serious problems facing any new academic subject are shortages of teaching material and qualified personnel to teach the subjects required by the field. Since the term "software engineer" has existed less than 10 years, and a reasonable definition for fewer years than that, it is understandable that only a handful of textbooks are even marginally acceptable for a curriculum of this type. These textbooks must, of course, be supplemented by technical papers from various sources. At this time, there are few proven software design methodologies, and the published technical information is contradictory. Also, the literature on important topics, such as design methodologies and problem-solving techniques as they apply to software engineering, is minimal. Compounding the teaching material shortage problem is the rapidity of change and growth in the software development field. It is frequently mentioned in electrical engineering that a textbook is out of date by the time the book is published. The problem is at least equally as severe in the software field. It is difficult to write a book in this area because it is usually out of date before the ink is dry on the manuscript.

It is also difficult to find adequately trained faculty members to teach software engineering courses. Many topics are modifications of existing computer science courses, but a significant portion of the most important topics are new and deal with a rapidly evolving technology.

ACADEMIC VERSUS INDUSTRIAL ENVIRONMENT

When comparing any academic engineering environment to its industrial equivalent, the most common observation is "artificial." This condition is not unique to software engineering, but it is probably more severe here than in any other engineering field. There are three primary areas in which the gap between industry and academia is most critical.

First, the industrial and student software development groups have, by necessity, vastly different goals and characteristics. The industrial team is a broad group of individuals of many special skills. The leader of the team is a highly skilled professional (software engineer) who is capable of supervising the entire software development as well as contributing significantly to the system definition and design. The team also includes several less skilled professionals and nontechnical support people. The team is motivated to develop a reliable, useful product with the maximum efficiency allowed within schedule and cost constraints. In the educational environment, the teams are ideally composed of several students of nearly equal abilities to prevent domination of the group by a student of superior ability. The educational goal is to encourage each of the team members to maximally develop his own capabilities. The student's goal is to deliver the product and get the grade. No concern is shown for maintainability or future improvements. The basic motivational differences prevent the academic group from mirroring the industrial counterpart.

Second, the general industrial environment is difficult to simulate in terms of the resources involved in software system development and operation. The practicing engineer must be able to estimate the cost of a software development project accurately, including cost parameters for staffing and the indirect costs of an organization as well as the system necessary to support the development and the operating software. Since the academic course work must concentrate only on the development of software systems, it is difficult for the student to develop an appreciation for the cost of building and maintaining a software system. Maintenance costs can exceed development costs by orders of magnitude, over the operating life of the product. While many of these resource considerations can be taught, the appreciation for their importance usually comes only after many years of experience.

Third, there is a time lag between the development of new design methodologies or tools and their introduction into the academic environment. The lag is difficult to overcome because of the time required to organize the new ideas into a teachable form, prepare new course materials, gain acceptance for the ideas, and integrate them into an existing curriculum. Each of the steps in establishing a new idea into the course work involves a considerable amount of valuable time. The university is at a disadvantage, not only because of the time lag with respect to the improving software development practices in industry, but also because of confusion in the entire software community, both academic and industrial, due to the lack of agreement on effective methods for software development. For example, the structured or hierarchical approach to development has always been basic to any engineering discipline and a universal organizing principle in all of the physical sciences. Yet, there is a great deal of contradictory and misleading material describing "structured programming" and structured implementation techniques which has served to negate years of progress in the field of software development.

Summary and Outlook

Software engineering is emerging as a legitimate academic discipline primarily because of problems related to the increasing magnitude and complexity of the software products presently being produced or envisioned in the near future. These problems, coupled with the rapid growth in software development technology, have made it apparent that curricula based on traditional computer science and engineering courses are inadequate to produce an individual possessing the broad background necessary to be called "software engineer." It will be difficult to establish a software engineering curriculum at the present time for several reasons. The most important of these reasons are:

- Curriculum must be explicitly defined and approved by the university. The first step, of course, is a detailed definition of the engineer's skills and the depth of understanding needed in each topic area.
- Very little experience in teaching software engineering and an acute shortage of teaching material. The texts and papers available are marginally appropriate for the course, at best.

If the development of a coherent curriculum is based upon the concepts suggested in this paper, we are confident that the best needs of the students, industry, and the university will be well served.

We see the area of software engineering education developing rapidly into a unique, independent field of study, just as other branches of engineering came into existence. Increasing pressure from industry will positively influence the growth rate of the field and provide a continuous demand for well-trained software engineering graduates.

References

1. BAUER, F. L., "Software Engineering," *Information Processing 71*, Amsterdam, North Holland Publishing Co., 1972, p. 530.

2. FREEMAN, P., A. I. WASSERMAN, and R. E. FAIRLEY, "Essential Elements of Software Engineering Education," *Proceedings of 2nd International Conference on Software Engineering*, October 1976, pp. 116–122.

3. MULDER, M. C., "Model Curricula for Four-Year Computer Science and Engineering Programs: Bridging the Tar Pit," *Computer*, December 1975, pp. 28–33.

INDEX